Aga Khan III

VOLUME I
1902–1927

O mankind, We have created
you male and female, and
appointed you races and tribes,
that you may know one another

The Quran

Indeed, all the problems that fall to the League [of Nations]
may ultimately be reduced to one – that of man, and the
dignity of man . . .
The tribulations of one people are the tribulations of all.
That which weakens one weakens all. That which is a gain
to one is surely a gain to all.

Aga Khan III in a speech to the League of Nations,
Geneva, 6 October 1937.

Aga Khan III

SELECTED SPEECHES AND WRITINGS OF SIR SULTAN MUHAMMAD SHAH

Edited, Annotated and Introduced
by
K. K. AZIZ

VOLUME I
1902–1927

KEGAN PAUL INTERNATIONAL
London and New York

First published in two volumes in 1998 by
Kegan Paul International

UK: P.O. Box 256, London WC1B 3SW, England
Tel: (0171) 580 5511 Fax: (0171) 436 0899

E-mail: books@keganpau.demon.co.uk
Internet: http://www.demon.co.uk/keganpaul/

USA: 562 West 113th Street, New York, NY 10025, USA
Tel: (212) 666 1000 Fax: (212) 316 3100

Distributed by
John Wiley & Sons Ltd
Southern Cross Trading Estate
1 Oldlands Way, Bognor Regis
West Sussex, PO22 9SA, England
Tel: (01243) 779 777 Fax: (01243) 820 250

Columbia University Press
562 West 113th Street
New York, NY 10025, USA
Tel: (212) 666 1000 Fax: (212) 316 3100

© Kegan Paul International, 1998

Phototypeset in Baskerville
by Intype London Ltd
Printed and bound in Great Britain by MPG Books Ltd, Bodmin, Cornwall

British Library Cataloguing in Publication Data
Aga Khan *III 1877–1957*
The collected works of Aga Khan III.
1. India. Islam. Role of politics
I. Title
297.19770954

ISBN 0–7103–0427–7

Library of Congress Cataloging-in-Publication Data
Aga Khan III. 1877–1957.
[Works. 1991)
Aga Khan III: selected speeches and writings of Sir Sultan Muhammad Shah /
edited annotated and introduced by K.K. Aziz.
p. cm.
ISBN 0–7103–0427–7
1. Ismailites. 2. Islam—20th century. 3. Muslims—India. 4. India—Politics
and government—20th century. I. Aziz. Khursheed Kamal. II. Title.
BP195.I8A5 1991
297'.822—dc20   91–12693
CIP

To the Memory of

Api Bilquis (Mrs M. B. K. Malik)
Zubair Hamid
Nasim (Mrs Sarwar Khan)

My very dear cousins
who left me too soon and on whose passing
away the lids of sorrow fell over the eyes of gladness

AGA KHAN III

Aga Khan III (1877–1957) was the 48th Imam of the Shia Ismaili Muslims. Through his intimate knowledge of Eastern as well as Western cultures, he was uniquely placed to play a significant role in the international affairs of his time, and his long public career had many dimensions. He was a member of the Indian Imperial Legislative Council (1902–1904), President of the All India Muslim League (1906–13), and founder of the All India Muslim Conference (1928–29). He successfully campaigned for separate electorates for all Muslims of India, leading a delegation in 1906 to the Viceroy for this purpose. He was the leader of the Muslim, and the entire Indian, delegation to the Round Table Conference in London (1930–32), which discussed India's constitutional future. In 1934 he was appointed a member of the British Privy Council. He served as India's representative at the Conference for the Reduction of Armaments in Geneva in 1932, and as the chief delegate of India at the League of Nations in the 1930s. In 1937 he was unanimously elected President of the League.

Aga Khan III was a social reformer whose concerns included the alleviation of rural poverty and the uplift of women in society. An advocate of modern education, he became an ardent supporter of male and female educational advancement in India and East Africa, and played a key role in the development of the Muslim University of Aligarh. A keen connoisseur of culture, he advocated a truly multicultural education blending the best and highest of Western and Eastern literary classics. He was a champion of amity between nations and peoples. In India he consistently supported the ideal of Hindu-Muslim unity, reminding both that India was their common parent. On the international scene he strove consistently for world peace.

Coming from diverse and often unobtainable sources, this

monumental work covering the years from 1902 to 1955, represents the first ever systematic publication of the speeches and writings of a major Muslim figure on the world stage in the first half of the twentieth century. Among the topics covered are constitutional progress in India, education, rural development, Hindu-Muslim unity, Indians in Africa, the renaissance of Islamic culture, the importance of science and technology, the status of women, Islam in the modern age and Pan-Islamism.

The Editor
Professor K. K. Aziz (born 1927), the only surviving son of the late Shaikh Abdul Aziz (the distinguished Mughal historian and the first editor of the text of the Punjabi epic, the *Hir* of Waris Shah), was educated in Batala, Lahore and Manchester. He has served on the academic staff of the Government College, Lahore, and the Universities of the Punjab, London, Khartoum and Heidelberg. He has been an occasional lecturer on historical, political and Islamic themes at the Universities of Karachi, Peshawar, Dacca, Islamabad, Hull, Newcastle-upon-Tyne, Geneva, Oxford, Cambridge, Durham and Bergen. In Pakistan he has held such appointments as Deputy to the Official Historian, Chairman of the National Commission on Historical and Cultural Research, and Special Policy Adviser to the Prime Minister. He is currently the (British) Old Ravians Research Fellow at Cambridge.

Professor Aziz is a Punjabi, happily married, knows eight languages, and has just completed an extensive study of symbolism in Islamic art.

Other books by K. K. Aziz

Britain and Muslim India
Some Problems of Research in Modern History
The Making of Pakistan
Ameer Ali: His Life and Work
The Historical Background of Pakistan
The All India Muslim Conference
The Indian Khilafat Movement
Britain and Pakistan
Party Politics in Pakistan
The British in India
Complete Works of Rahmat Ali (2 vols.)
Muslims under Congress Rule (2 vols.)
A History of the Idea of Pakistan (4 vols.)
Rahmat Ali: A Biography
Prelude to Pakistan (2 vols.)
Public Life in Muslim India
The Pakistani Historian
The Murder of History
An Historical Handbook of Muslim India 1700–1947
(2 vols.)
A Chronology of Muslim India, 1700–1947

CONTENTS

VOLUME I 1902–1927

LIST OF ABBREVIATIONS   xxi
ACKNOWLEDGEMENTS   xxiv
PREFACE   xxv
INTRODUCTION   1

1   IN THE DAYS OF MY YOUTH   199
A Chapter of Autobiography
15 August 1902
Naoroji M. Dumasia, *A Brief History of the Aga Khan with an Account of His Predecessors, the Ismailian Princes or Benefatimite Caliphs of Egypt*, the Author, Bombay, 1903, Appendix III, pp. 168–76.

2   MUSLIM EDUCATION IN INDIA   204
Presidential Address to the All India Muhammadan Educational Conference
Delhi: 1902
Naoroji M. Dumasia, *A Brief History of the Aga Khan with an Account of His Predecessors, the Ismailian Princes or Benefatimite Caliphs of Egypt*, the Author, Bombay, 1903, Appendix V, pp. 184–202.

3   THE FINANCES OF INDIA – I   216
Budget Speech in the Council of the Governor General
Calcutta: 25 March 1903
Abstract of the Proceedings of the Council of the Governor General of India Assembled for the Purpose of Making Laws and Regulations, Vol. 42, Calcutta, 1903, pp. 91–7.

4   THE FINANCES OF INDIA – II   223
Budget Speech in the Council of the Governor General
Calcutta: 30 March 1904
Abstract of the Proceedings of the Council of the Governor-General of

India Assembled for the Purpose of Making Laws and Regulations, Vol. 43, Calcutta, 1904, pp. 491–9.

5   THE TRUE PURPOSE OF EDUCATION   233
Speech at the Muslim Educational Conference
Bombay: 1904
Naoroji M. Dumasia, *The Aga Khan and His Ancestors*, The Times of India Press, Bombay, 1939, pp. 184–8.

6   THE DEFENCE OF INDIA   238
An Article
London: September 1905
The Nineteenth Century and After, London, September 1905, pp. 367–75.

7   A BILL OF MUSLIM RIGHTS   249
The Memorial Presented by a Muslim Deputation to the Viceroy of India
Simla: 1 October 1906.
Nawab Imad-ul-Mulk Bahadur (Syed Hossain Bilgrami, C.S.I.), *Speeches, Addresses and Poems*, Government Central Press, Hyderabad Deccan, 1925, pp. 139–44.

8   SOME THOUGHTS ON INDIAN DISCONTENT   261
An Article
London: February 1907
National Review, London, February 1907, pp. 951–72.

9   ADVICE TO THE MUSLIM LEAGUE   284
Inaugural Address to the Deccan Muslim League Meeting
Poona: 12 August 1908
The Civil and Military Gazette, Lahore, 18 August 1908.

10   THE PROBLEM OF THE MINORITIES
IN INDIA   288
Interview with *The Times*
London: 14 February 1909
The Times, London, 15 February 1909, and *The Civil and Military Gazette*, Lahore, 14 March 1909.

11   RECENT DEVELOPMENTS IN INDIAN
POLITICS   294
Letter to the London Muslim League
London: 23 February 1909
The Civil and Military Gazette, Lahore, 19 March 1909.

12   THE MUSLIM PROBLEM IN INDIA   298
Speech at the First Annual General Meeting of the London
Muslim League
London: 24 June 1909
The Times, London, 25 June 1909.

13   ACCEPTANCE OF THE MORLEY-MINTO REFORMS 302
Telegram to *The Times*
London: 15 November 1909
The Times, London, 16 November 1909.

14   MUSLIMS AND THE MORLEY-MINTO REFORMS   303
Letter to *The Times*
London: 16 November 1909
The Times, London, 18 November 1909.

15   SOME ASPECTS OF INDIAN REFORMS   307
An Article
London: December 1909
National Review, London, December 1909, pp. 577–89.

16   DUTIES OF MUSLIM LEADERSHIP
IN INDIA   320
Speech at a Reception Given by the Muslim Citizens of Bombay
Bombay: 10 January 1910
Naoroji M. Dumasia, *The Aga Khan and His Ancestors*, The Times
of India Press, Bombay, 1939, pp. 174–7.

17   THE OBJECTIVES OF THE ALIGARH
COLLEGE   325
Reply to the Address from the Trustees of the MAO College
Aligarh: 26 January 1910
The Times of India, Bombay, 27 January 1910.

18   THE AWAKENING OF MUSLIM INDIA   328
Inaugural Address to the All India Muslim League Third Annual
Session
Delhi: 29 January 1910
Syed Sharifuddin Pirzada (ed.), *Foundations of Pakistan: All India
Muslim League Documents, 1906–1947*, National Publishing House,
Karachi, n.d. (?1969), Vol 1 (1906–24), pp. 94–103.

19   BRITISH MONARCHY AND THE EMPIRE   341
Interview with the Reuters Agency

London: May 1910
The Civil and Military Gazette, Lahore, 3 June 1910.

20   AN AGENDA FOR THE INDIAN MUSLIMS   343
Interview with *The Times of India*
Bombay: 23(?) December 1910.
The Civil and Military Gazette, Lahore, 25 December 1910

21   LORD MINTO'S VICEROYALTY   346
An Article
London: January 1911
National Review, London, January 1911, pp. 852–60.

22   THE MUSLIMS OF THE BRITISH EMPIRE   355
A Lecture
London: 3 July 1911
The Times of India, Bombay, 22 July 1911.

23   INDIA'S EDUCATION AND HER FUTURE
POSITION IN THE EMPIRE   364
An Article
London: July 1911
National Review, London, July 1911, pp. 779–92.

24   EDUCATIONAL NEEDS OF MUSLIM INDIA   377
Inaugural Speech at the All India Muhammadan Educational
Conference
Delhi: 4 December 1911.
The Times of India, Bombay, 5 December 1911

25   TRANSFER OF THE CAPITAL TO DELHI   384
A Statement on the Repeal of the Partition of Bengal
Delhi: 17 December 1911
The Times, London, 18 December 1911.

26   THE REPEAL OF THE PARTITION OF
BENGAL   386
Statement on the Annulment of the Partition of Bengal
10 February 1912
Comrade, 10 February 1912.

27   EDUCATION FOR NATIONAL
REGENERATION   393
Speech at the Madrasah-i-Anjuman-i-Islam, Bombay

Bombay: 4 March 1912
The Times of India, Bombay, 5 March 1912.

28   THE NEED FOR A MUSLIM UNIVERSITY   396
Interview with *The Times of India*
Bombay: 8 March 1912
The Times of India, Bombay, 9 March 1912.

29   AN APPEAL TO THE INDIAN MUSLIMS TO HELP THE
REFUGEES OF THE BALKAN WAR   401
A Cablegram to the Raja of Mahmudabad
London (?): December 1912
The Times of India, Bombay, 9 December 1912.

30   INDIA AND THE BALKAN WAR: POSITION OF
MUSLIMS   403
An Article
Bombay: 13 February 1913
The Times of India, Bombay, 14 February 1913.

31   ON THE NECESSITY OF HAVING HINDU
UNIVERSITIES IN INDIA   410
Speech at a Function in Honour of the Deputation of the Hindu
University
Bombay: 23 February 1913
The Times of India, Bombay, 24 February 1913.

32   PUBLIC SERVICES IN INDIA   416
Evidence Given Before the Royal Commission on the Public
Services in India
Bombay: 3 March 1913
Royal Commission on the Public Services in India, *Appendix to
the Report of the Commissioners, Volume 6: Minutes of Evidence Relating
to the Indian and Provincial Civil Services Taken at Bombay from the
1st. to the 12th. March 1913, with Appendices*, His Majesty's
Stationery Office, London, 1914, Cd. 7579, pp. 54–69.

33   THE IDEALS OF MUSLIM INDIA   458
Speech at the Fifth Annual General Meeting of the London
Muslim League
London: 14 July 1913
The Times of India, Bombay, 2 August 1913.

34 RESIGNATION FROM THE ALL INDIA MUSLIM
LEAGUE PRESIDENTSHIP   463
Letter to Sayyid Ameer Ali
Paris: 2 November 1913
The Times, London, 8 November 1913.

35 INDIANS IN SOUTH AFRICA AND THE EMPIRE   468
Speech at a Meeting Held to Protest Against the Treatment of
Indians in South Africa
Bombay: 10 December 1913
The Times of India, Bombay, 17 December 1913.

36 THE INDIAN MUSLIM OUTLOOK   480
An Article
London: January 1914
The Edinburgh Review, Edinburgh, January 1914, pp. 1–13.

37 THE STATE OF MUSLIM POLITICS IN INDIA   493
Reply to the Address of Welcome by the Muslim Community of
Burma
Rangoon: 6 February 1914
The Rangoon Gazette, Rangoon, 9 February 1914.

38 ADVICE TO THE INDIAN RESIDENTS IN BURMA   500
Reply to the Address of Welcome Presented by the Indian and
Other Communities of Burma
Rangoon: 13 February 1914
The Rangoon Gazette, Rangoon, 16 February 1914.

39 VOLUNTARY WORK AND THE WAR EFFORT   505
Speech at a Meeting of the Indian Volunteers Committee
London: 1 October 1914
The Times of India, Bombay, 26 October 1914.

40 TURKEY, THE WAR AND MUSLIM INDIA   510
Message to the Indian Muslims on Turkish Entry into the War
London: 2 November 1914
The Times, London, 4 November 1914.

41 THE EXAMPLE OF SIR PHEROZESHAH MEHTA   512
Speech at a Meeting Held in Memory of Sir Pherozeshah Mehta
London: 8 December 1915
The Times of India, Bombay, 8 January 1916.

42   THE QUATRAINS OF UMAR KHAYYAM   519
Foreword to John Pollen's Translation of Umar Khayyam
London: 1915
John Pollen, *Omar Khayyam, Faithfully and Literally Translated (From
the Original Persian)*, East and West, London, 1915, pp. vii-viii.

43   IN DEFENCE OF LORD HARDINGE   522
Letter to *The Times*
London(?): 17 July 1917
The Times, London, 23 July 1917.

44   GOKHALE'S LAST POLITICAL TESTAMENT   525
Letter to *The Times*
London: 12 August 1917
The Times, London, 15 August 1917.

45   INDIA IN TRANSITION: A STUDY IN POLITICAL
EVOLUTION   530
Extracts from a Book
London and Bombay: June 1918
The Aga Khan, *India in Transition*, Philip Lee Warner, London,
1918.

46   TRIBUTE TO E. S. MONTAGU AND LORD SINHA   612
Speech at a Banquet Hosted in Honour of Lord Sinha
London: 7 March 1919
*The Insistent Claims of Indian Reforms: Speeches at a Banquet in
London on 7 March 1919*, Philip Lee Warner, London, 1919,
pp. 34–7.

47   THE POST-WAR FUTURE OF TURKEY   633
Letter (with Sayyid Ameer Ali) to *The Times*
London: 3 June 1919
The Times, London, 6 June 1919.

48   INDIAN MUSLIM SENTIMENT AND TURKEY   643
Letter (with Sayyid Ameer Ali) to *The Times*
London: 2 August 1919
The Times, London, 2 August 1919.

49   SUFFRAGE FOR THE INDIAN WOMEN   645
Letter to *The Times*
London: 8 August 1919
The Times, London, 11 August 1919.

50   THE MAKING OF THE 1919 REFORMS   648
Evidence Before the Joint Select Committee on the Government
of India Bill
London: 10 October 1919
*Joint Select Committee on the Government of India Bill, Vol. 2: Minutes
of Evidence,* His Majesty's Stationery Office, London, 1919,
pp. 487–96.

51   THE DIMENSIONS OF THE TURKISH PROBLEM   681
A Memorial to the Prime Minister of England on Behalf of His
Majesty's Muslim Subjects
London: 12 December 1919
The Indian Annual Register 1921, Calcutta, n.d., Part 1, pp. 145–8.

52   THE FUTURE OF INDIA   687
Speech at a Dinner in Honour of E. S. Montagu
London: 19 December 1919
The Times, London, 20 December 1919.

53   BRITISH POLICY IN THE EAST – I   691
An Article
London: 5 November 1920
The Times, London, 5 November 1920.

54   BRITISH POLICY IN THE EAST – II   698
An Article
London: 6 November 1920
The Times, London, 6 November 1920.

55   INDIA'S CONNECTION WITH BRITAIN   704
Interview with the Press
Bombay: 22 January 1921
The Civil and Military Gazette, Lahore, 25 January 1921.

56   INDIA DESIRES   706
Speech at the Farewell Luncheon to Lord and Lady Reading
London: 13 March 1921.
The Times, London, 14 March 1921.

57   INDIAN MUSLIM CONCERN FOR TURKEY   710
Telegram to Lord Reading
London: 8 July 1921
The Morning Post, London, 9 July 1921

58   PEACE WITH TURKEY   711
Letter to *The Times*
Paris: 8 November 1921
The Times, London, 12 November 1921.

59   REMEMBERING SIR PHEROZESHAH MEHTA   716
Foreword to H. P. Mody's Biography of Sir Pherozeshah Mehta
Bombay: 1921
H. P. Mody, *Sir Pherozeshah Mehta: A Political Biography*, The Times
of India Press, Bombay, 1921, pp. vii-ix.

60   ISSUES IN INDIAN POLITICS   720
Interview with *The Bombay Chronicle*
Bombay: 3 February 1922
The Bombay Chronicle, Bombay, 4 February 1922.

61   CANCER MORTALITY   724
Letter to *The Times*
London(?): 7 June 1922
The Times, London, 8 June 1922.

62   A ROYAL VICEROY   726
An Article
London: 21 June 1922
The Times, London, 21 June 1922.

63   BONAR LAW AND THE TURKISH QUESTION   731
Letter to *The Times*
London: 9 October 1922
The Times, London, 10 October 1922.

64   POSSIBILITY OF A TURKISH SETTLEMENT   734
Interview with *The Times of India*
Bombay: 15 December 1922
The Times of India, Bombay, 16 December 1922.

65   COUNSEL TO THE MUSLIMS OF INDIA   737
Speech at the Anjuman-i-Islamia High School, Bombay
Bombay: 15 January 1923
The Times of India, Bombay, 16 January 1923.

66   THE INDIAN QUESTION IN KENYA   744
Letter to *The Times of India*
Bombay: 23(?) January 1923
The Times of India, Bombay, 26 January 1923.

67 REFORMS IN INDIA AND KENYA   748
Interview with the Associated Press of India
Bombay: 14 March 1923
The Civil and Military Gazette, Lahore, 17 March 1923.

68 HOPES OF TURKISH PEACE   750
Reply to the Address of Welcome Presented by the Muslims of
Madras
Madras: 15 March 1923
The Times of India, Bombay, 17 March 1923.

69 THE POLITICAL SITUATION IN INDIA   753
Interview with *The Times of India*
Bombay: 7 April 1923
The Times of India, Bombay, 7 April 1923.

70 ON THE LAUSANNE TREATY WITH TURKEY   757
Message to the Muslims
Lausanne: 27 July 1923
The Times, London, 28 July 1923.

71 THE NEW MUSLIM WORLD   761
An Article
London: October 1923
The Edinburgh Review, Edinburgh, October 1923, pp. 230–6.

72 APPEAL TO TURKEY TO RETAIN THE KHILAFAT   768
Letter (with Sayyid Ameer Ali) to the Turkish Prime Minister
London: 24 November 1923
The Times, London, 14 December 1923.

73 REASONS FOR THE APPEAL TO TURKEY   772
Letter to *The Times*
London: 16 December 1923
The Times, London, 17 December 1923.

74 DANGERS OF A FRESH WAR   775
Interview with the Press
Bombay: 13 January 1924
The Times of India, Bombay, 14 January 1924.

75 OPTIMISM AND GOOD WILL   776
An Article
London: 13 April 1924
The Sunday Express, London, 13 April 1924.

76   INDIA'S STEEL INDUSTRY   780
Letter to *The Times*
London: 28 April 1924
The Times, London, 29 April 1924.

77   THE MOROCCAN WAR SUFFERERS   782
Letter (with Lord Lamington and Sayyid Ameer Ali) to *The Times*
London: 17 October 1924
The Times, London, 18 October 1924.

78   LORD MILNER'S "CREDO"   783
Letter to *The Times*
Aix les Bains: 3 August 1925
The Times, London, 5 August 1925.

79   HOW TO LIVE LONG   786
An Article
London: 8 December 1925
The Evening Standard, London, 8 December 1925.

80   FELICITATIONS TO THE SHAH OF PERSIA   790
A Message
London(?): 21 December 1925
The Times, London, 22 December 1925.

81   THE FUTURE OF INDIAN INDUSTRY   792
Interview with *The Times of India*
Bombay: 8 January 1926
The Times of India, Bombay, 9 January 1926.

82   THE TREATMENT OF THE INDIANS
IN SOUTH AFRICA   794
Speech at a Public Meeting Held to Protest Against the Treatment
of Indians in South Africa
Bombay: 15 January 1926
The Times of India, Bombay, 16 January 1926.

83   APPEAL ON BEHALF OF A MOSQUE   800
Speech at the Stone-laying Ceremony of a Mosque
Nairobi: 24 March 1926
The East African Standard, Nairobi, weekly edition, 27 March
1926.

84 PATRIOTISM AND SOCIAL REFORM AMONG KENYA'S
INDIANS 802
Summary of Two Addresses Given Before the Ismaili Community
Mombasa: 1–7 April 1926
The Mombasa Times, Mombasa, 15 April 1926, and *The East African
Standard*, Nairobi, 17 April 1926.

85 ON INDIAN UNITY 803
Statement to the Press
Bombay: 9 December 1927
The Times, London, 10 December 1927.

86 AN APPEAL FOR A PERMANENT MUSLIM
ORGANIZATION IN INDIA 805
A Manifesto
Bombay: 29 December 1927
The Times, London, 30 December 1927.

LIST OF ABBREVIATIONS

ADC	aide-de-camp
AFC	Air Force Cross
Bart.	Baronet
BCL	Bachelor of Civil Law
BT	Bachelor of Teaching
CB	Companion of the Order of the Bath
CBE	Commander of the Order of the British Empire
Cd.	Command (Paper)
CH	Companion of Honour
CID	Criminal Investigation Department; Committee for Imperial Defence
CIE	Companion of the Order of the Indian Empire
Cmd.	Command (Paper)
CMG	Companion of the Order of St. Michael and St. George
CP	Central Provinces
CSI	Companion of the Order of the Star of India
CVO	Commander of the Royal Victorian Order
DCL	Doctor of Civil Law
DFC	Distinguished Flying Cross
DSO	Distinguished Service Order
FBA	Fellow of the British Academy
FRS	Fellow of the Royal Society
GBE	Knight Grand Cross of the Order of the British Empire
GCB	Knight Grand Cross of the Order of the Bath
GCIE	Knight Grand Commander of the Order of the Indian Empire
GCMG	Knight Grand Cross of the Order of St. Michael and St. George

GCSI	Knight Commander of the Order of the Star of India
GCVO	Knight Grand Cross of the Royal Victorian Order
GOC	General Officer Commanding

HC	House of Commons; High Court
HE	His Excellency
HH	His Highness
HL	House of Lords
HRH	His Royal Highness

ICS	Indian Civil Service
IMS	Indian Medical Service
ISO	Imperial Service Order

JP	Justice of the Peace
JPC	Joint Parliamentary Committee

KC	King's Counsel
KCB	Knight Commander of the Order of the Bath
KCIE	Knight Commander of the Order of the Indian Empire
KCMG	Knight Commander of the Order of St. Michael and St. George
KCSI	Knight Commander of the Order of the Star of India
KCVO	Knight Commander of the Royal Victorian Order
KG	Knight of the Order of the Garter
Kt.	Knight

LRCP	Licentiate of the Royal College of Physicians

MAO	Muhammadan Anglo-Oriental
MBE	Member of the Order of the British Empire
MC	Military Cross
MLA	Member of the Legislative Assembly
MLC	Member of the Legislative Council
MRCP	Member Royal College of Physicians
MRCS	Member of the Royal College of Surgeons

NATO	North Atlantic Treaty Organization
N-C-O	Non-Co-operation Movement
n.d.	not dated
n.p.	no publisher mentioned
n.p.p.	no place of publication mentioned
NWF	North-Western Provinces (of Agra and Oudh)

OBE	Order of the British Empire
OM	Order of Merit

PC	Privy Councillor; member of the Privy Council

q.v.   quod vide (which see)

RAF   Royal Air Force
Ret.   Retired
Rs.   Rupees
RTC   Round Table Conference(s)
Rt. Hon.Right Honourable

Shs.   Shillings

UNO   United Nations Organization
UP   United Provinces

VC   Victoria Cross

ACKNOWLEDGEMENTS

The Publishers gratefully acknowledge the permission of the estate of the late Sir Sultan Muhammad Shah, **Aga Khan III**, to reproduce excerpts from His Highness's books **India in Transition** and **Memoirs of the Aga Khan**, together with numerous other speeches and writings.

The Publishers wish to mention with gratitude the contributions made by journals of record during the period 1902 to 1955 by publishing articles, interviews and letters by the late Aga Khan. They are primarily *The National Review* (London), *The Civil and Military Gazette* (Lahore), *The Times* (London), *The Times of India* (Bombay), *Reuters News Agency, His Majesty's Stationery Office* (London), *The Edinburgh Review* (Edinburgh), *The Rangoon Gazette* (Rangoon), *The Indian Annual Register* (Calcutta), *The Morning Post* (London), *The Bombay Chronicle* (Bombay), *The Sunday Express* (London), *The Daily Herald* (London), *The Daily Sketch* (London), *The Listener* (London), *League of Nations Official Journal* (Geneva), *The Star of India* (Calcutta), *The Asiatic Review* (London), *The Ismaili* (Bombay), *The Muslim Times* (London), *The Iran Society* (London), *The East African Standard* (Nairobi), *The Tanganyika Standard* (Dar-es-Salaam), *The Platinum Jubilee Review* (Karachi), *The Sunday Post* (Nairobi), *Pakistan Horizon* (Karachi), *The Zanzibar Times* (Zanzibar), *The Pakistan Observer* (Dacca), *Dawn* (Karachi).

The publishers would also like to acknowledge permission to reproduce the illustrations in these volumes from the Library of the Secretariat de Son Altesse l'Aga Khan, Mr. I. Gulgee; and The League of Nations Library.

PREFACE

Sir Sultan Muhammad Shah Aga Khan III (1877–1957) has many
claims on the historian's attention. He was the Imam of the
Ismailis, and as such for over 50 years the spiritual leader of an
important, devoted and energetic community of Islam. In India,
he guided and directed the Muslim nationalist movement for a
far longer period than any other political figure: leading the
Simla Deputation, nursing the All India Muslim League into a
strong and united organization, inspiring the foundation of the
All India Muslim Conference, acting as the spokesman of India
and also of her Muslims at the Round Table Conference and
other bodies and committees entrusted with the task of framing
the reforms of 1935, and playing an important role in the evolution of the idea of Pakistan. Not content with being a mere
politician, of however high a stature, he threw himself into the
work of social reform and educational advance with his characteristic insight, deep commitment, and enthusiasm.

In East and South Africa, he encouraged and worked for the
uplift of society, especially in the fields of education, economy,
communal amity, and race relations. In Europe, he fought for
the rights of Muslim India through the London Muslim League
and the Pan-Islamic Society, for an accelerated constitutional
advance of India at the British-Indian parleys in 1918–19 and
1930–34, for the continuation of the Turkish *khilafat* as a centre
and rallying point of the world of Islam, for international co-
operation and concord and world security at the League of
Nations, and for a European understanding and knowledge
of Oriental, particularly Persian, literature both for the sake of
intellectual pleasure and inter-civilizational rapport and understanding.

To his Muslim followers and fellow-believers he showed the
path to a liberal and rational interpretation of Islam, the accept-

ance and practical interpretation of which would bring them into the mainstream of modern life without in the least betraying the fundamental tenets and injunctions of their religion. By issuing this call to re-examine and reconstruct the original message of the Quran without departing from its spirit, he put himself firmly in the company of Sir Sayyid Ahmad Khan, Sayyid Ameer Ali and Sir Muhammad Iqbal in India, Shaikh Muhammad Abduh in Egypt, Khiruddin Pasha in Tunisia, and the "Young Ottomans" (Ibrahim Shanasi, Namik Kamal and Zia Gökalp) in Turkey. The Aga Khan and Ameer Ali, both Shia by faith, occupy a unique place in this distinguished line of Sunni reformers of Islam.

It is a sad reflection on modern Muslim historiography that the professional chronicler as much as the general educated reader needs a reminder about the contribution of such a man to his own modern history. Even in Pakistan, in whose nationalist movement he played a leading role, his achievements have received little acknowledgement: a cursory and fragmentary mention in history books, the naming of one or two roads after him (old roads which people continue to call by their old names), and the issuing of a postage stamp bearing his picture. That is about all. Even those few who remember him know of him as a celebrated horse breeder, a magnate with the Midas touch, a spiritual potentate, and an Imam who was weighed in gold or diamonds on his jubilees. His real accomplishments are as little known to them as to those who teach and write history.

In this work I have tried to redress the balance, and to remove the general ignorance about, and create an interest in, a great man who did so much to shape our recent past. The Aga Khan invited my first attention in the early 1960s when, after the usual apprenticeship spent in earning a doctorate at a British university, I began to study and write on the history of modern Muslim India. In 1965 the idea occurred to me of collecting his writings and speeches with two objects in view: first, to compile, edit, annotate and publish them so that a complete record of his words was preserved; and then to attempt a study of his ideas and public life.

It has taken me nearly 30 years to realize the first part of my ambition. During this period I experienced many frustrations: indifference from quarters from where I had expected ready co-operation, silence in response to my letters of inquiry and the reminders which followed them, denials of requests for help in tracing the scarce material, and so on. But I persisted (I cannot explain why even to myself), and the result is contained in these two volumes. Now that much of the original material has been put together, I hope I can turn to the next item on the agenda, a political study of the Aga Khan, with greater confidence, fewer setbacks, and less discouragement. The intention and the will are there; the final execution is in the hands of my Maker.

In the present compilation I have cast my net as widely as I could. The search has been long, but in the end rewarding. I have looked for and finally located and procured what I believe to be everything that the Aga Khan spoke or wrote about in his long public career: speeches, addresses, interviews, articles, testimony given before commissions and committees of inquiry, political memoranda, letters to newspapers, messages, etc., etc. I have tried to make the collection as comprehensive as possible. Yet no work done by human hands is perfect or complete. It is quite possible that a few items have escaped my search. I shall be grateful if any such desiderata are pointed out to me by my readers, so that they can be included in the next edition of the book.

I hope this collection will be of use to the historian and to the practitioner of related disciplines. But my expectations go further. I also feel that there is much in the message and the wise words of the Aga Khan III which is relevant to the world of today. He was not only a statesman but also a thinker. Many of the philosophical questions he posed and tried to answer still tease the reflective mind. The problems relating to the revival of Islam, the resurrection of spiritual values, the application of the Quranic injunctions to the present-day world, the nature and contents of the civilization and culture of Islam, the strains which are inevitable in the struggle between rigidity and compromise, the debate on conservatism *versus* liberalism, the argument between religion and science, the prerequisites and implications of the creation of a *modern* Islamic state, the role of the intellectual in a nation's public life, the fissiparous tendencies implicit in a multi-language society or state — all these points were touched upon by the Aga Khan in his day, which is a tribute to his vision; and all of them are still agitating the minds and hearts of Muslims all over the world, which imparts an urgent pertinence to what he said.

For the non-Islamic world, too, there is much of value in this collection. The Aga Khan, in spite of being one of the founding fathers of Pakistan, was an ardent advocate of Hindu–Muslim harmony in the Indian subcontinent. Both in India and Africa, he put his shoulder to the wheel of progress in the fields of race relations, urging the British government and the white settlers in Africa to treat the local black population with respect and the

Indian migrants to make friends with their African fellow-citizens. He used the Security Conferences and the League of Nations as platforms from where to plead the case for international disarmament, peace and mutual understanding at a time when the world was riven by jealousies, rivalries and ominous ambitions.

I think it is fair to myself and to my publisher to record the fact that I am neither an Ismaili nor a Shia (nor, for that matter, a Sunni), but a plain Muslim. I have discovered the Aga Khan as a statesman of rare qualities and a great servant of Islam, and have, therefore, considered it worth my while to spend so much time and energy on preparing this book.

Now a few points about the contents and arrangement of this book.

Where I have compiled the text from more than one source, all the sources are mentioned at the end of the text. The text retains the original spellings of the proper names as used by the Aga Khan or the contemporary press which was reporting him; but in my notes and the quotations contained in them I have employed the modern, current orthography. At a few places I have deleted some words or omitted a few sentences from the original text with a view to avoiding obvious repetition, removing certain rhetorical phrases which are liable to creep into public speeches and addresses, and avoiding hurt to any susceptibilities; without, however, changing in any way the words used by the Aga Khan or to the slightest degree altering or amending the sense of what he wanted to convey. All such omissions are indicated by points of suspension.

In annotating the text I have tried to furnish the reader with as much background information as would be needed in order to grasp the meaning and context of what the Aga Khan said or wrote, and with all available details about the occasion and place of the utterance. If at times my notes appear to be too long or extensive beyond need, my labours should be taken as a measure of my anxiety to facilitate the use of this compilation. It must be kept in mind that the present generation of students and general readers is separated from the period covered by the material presented here by a half century.

The bibliographies contained in the notes are, with some exceptions, confined to contemporary accounts and works based on original sources.

Even this far-ranging and documented annotation did not satisfy me. It explained and supplied the context in which the Aga Khan made a speech or wrote an article; but it did not depict the historical continuity of his thoughts and deeds. To fill this gap I have written an introduction of some length, which gives an account of his origins and family, a biographical sketch of his private life and public career, a summary of his ideas and opinions, an assessment of his major contributions to modern history, and some reference to the legacy he has left behind him.

The appendices supply some general information relevant to the Aga Khan's public life. In the longest among them I have brought together biographical details about every person to whom the Aga Khan refers in his works. A bibliography on the Aga Khan completes the annotation.

I am aware of the fact that it is not a normal practice to edit a statesman's works with an apparatus criticus which almost matches in length the original text. I have three arguments to offer in justification of my decision. First, the Aga Khan's place in modern history and the long span of time during which he exercised unprecedented influence on public events and policies entitle him to such treatment. Secondly, and this is an embarrassing admission to make, his life and achievements are not as well known to the present generation as they should be. He is a name on the page of history books, but only a name. Even the professional historians of India or of Islam do not go beyond a passing reference to him. In part, this indifference is due to an ignorance of what he said and did. His two books, *India in Transition* (1918) and *The Memoirs of Aga Khan* (1954), have been out of print for many years. His speeches and addresses are buried in a large number of generally inaccessible or scarce newspapers, journals, pamphlets and proceedings of the organizations and parties with which he was associated. The scholar, the student and the general reader ought to have his works available to them in order to appreciate his achievements. And these works must be accompanied by an ample background spelling out their origin, context, time-frame and occasion, so that the reader understands their relevance and significance.

Thirdly, there is little chance that anyone else will repeat this exercise, at least in the foreseeable future. Hence my desire to make this edition as definitive as my labour and private resources permit. The reader will be the judge of the extent of my success.

For the preparation of this book I am beholden to my wife, Zarina, much more than ever before. She has been of great help in my work on the 27 books which I have written or edited in the last 40 years. But on this one she surpassed herself. For nearly one year when we lived in Cambridge, and I was putting this large manuscript together for the publisher, she acted as a full-time secretary, adding to the normal duties of that office her keen personal interest in the Aga Khan's career and therefore in the book and the loving care with which she took my life into her solicitous charge, turning drudgery into cheer and hard labour into unflagging zest. In whatever words I try to say my thanks to her the expression falls short of the intention. I hope she accepts this confession of failure as a measure of my gratitude.

To Dr Karim Janmohamed, formerly Senior Lecturer in History, University of Nairobi, I owe a very special debt. In the last five years of my work on this book he collaborated with me in searching for the items to be included, hunting out some African sources of whose existence I was not even aware, extending his investigations and inquiries to Canada and India through correspondence which resulted in many happy discoveries, and spending long hours with me in the Cambridge University Library in comparing and collating what was available there with what was already in our hands. It was his bright idea to put before each document a faithful précis of it; he went further and took upon himself the onerous but extremely useful task of drafting these abstracts. He made several valuable suggestions when I was writing the Introduction, and I had no hesitation in accepting them. He has added to what is already due to him by a voluntary offer to read the proofs of this voluminous collection, thus saving my weak eyes from unbearable strain. The goodness of this deed I alone can judge.

Throughout this partnership I found Dr Karim Janmohamed a colleague who had been trained well in the technique of historical research. But he is also much else. I admire and respect his spirit of dedication, his habit of looking after the small details which one is apt to ignore, his capacity for hard work, his smiling acceptance of stern criticism, the arrows of which I sometimes directed towards him, his anxiety to learn from sources and facts, his sense of responsibility, and his ability to distinguish the relevant from the irrelevant. I thank him for the assistance he provided, for the pleasure I experienced in working with him, and for the friendship he offered and I grasped with both hands, because it is a very precious commodity in today's world of selfishness and hypocrisy. Perhaps he will not find this book unworthy of the effort he has put into it.

A book which has taken so many years in the making has attracted the attention and sympathy of a large number of people in several countries. It may be invidious to select a few names from amongst them, but I must put on record my thanks to those who went out of their way in encouraging me, supplying me with copies of what I required, and in other ways facilitating my research and writing: Secretary, Anjuman-i-Islam (Bombay), Mrs Valerie Bloomfield (London), Dr Dietmar Dilthy (Berlin), the late Professor Abdul Hamid (Government College, Lahore), Miss Efti Heracleous (London), the late Mr Ashiqueali H. Hussain (Karachi), M le Docteur François Jonquille (Paris), the late Mr Aminullah Khan (Karachi), Professor W. J. M. Mackenzie, CBE, FBA (Manchester and Glasgow), Mrs Naznin Hirji (London), Mr Sherali Allidina (Karachi), Mr Zulfikar S. Mawani (Vancouver), Professor Sir Kenneth Robinson (London), Mr Kutub Kassam (London), and Mr Mumtaz A. M. Sadruddin (Vancouver).

I am grateful to Mr Peter Hopkins, my publisher, for his consistent and unfaltering interest in the publication of this work, and to my editors, for conjuring up a fair and decent book out of a very imperfect manuscript.

I completed the body of this work in 1990. Therefore, all bibliographical sources do not go beyond this point.

Finally, I appreciate greatly and acknowledge gratefully the courtesy and help received from the librarians and staff of the following institutions where I worked during the preparation of this book: Institute of Commonwealth Studies, London; Senate House Library, University of London; British Library and Reading Room, London; University of Cambridge Library; Centre of South Asian Studies, University of Cambridge; Südasien Institut, Heidelberg; University of Heidelberg Library; India Office Library and Records, London; University of Khartoum Library; School of Oriental and African Studies, University of London; Royal Commonwealth Society, London; Institute of Ismaili Studies, London; John Rylands University Library, Manchester; British Museum Newspaper Depository, Colindale; Bibliothèque Nationale, Paris; Stadtbibliothek, Berlin; Institute of Commonwealth Studies, Oxford; Trinity College, Cambridge; Pakistan Institute of International Affairs, Karachi; Royal Institute of International Affairs (Chatham House), London; London School of Economics and Political Science, London; and Institute of Social Anthropology, University of Bergen, Norway.

10 April 1997   K. K. Aziz
Cambridge

INTRODUCTION

In the history of modern Muslim India the Aga Khan occupies a place which, without employing any hyperbole, may be called unique. This uniqueness springs from a happy concatenation of a variety of factors and circumstances, some inherited through the courtesy of nature, some forced upon him by the tide of events, some created by himself through sheer ability and hard work, and some thrust upon him by the exigencies of time. The positions he held in public life, the parties and organizations he led or patronized, the long innings he played on the stage of history, the variegated conditions in which he was called upon to act, the range of problems he had to face and solve, the wide compass of commitments and engagements which drew him into a strenuous life, the heavy responsibilities which he carried and discharged on the whole with success, the diversity of causes he upheld and fought for, and the supremely active and interesting life that he lived till the very end – all this makes him a giant among his contemporaries; and these contemporaries were not men of small stature. Competing with the greatest in the public life of the subcontinent, he yet imprinted his personality on an era.

Two other factors contributed to his inimitable standing. One was the unprecedentedly long sweep of years of his public career. There is no other leader in Indian political annals, of any religion or sect or party, who looms so large in history across so many years. For half a century he strode the scene like a colossus. The other factor was his entry into public life when he was already standing on the topmost rung of leadership. He did not work his way up the ladder of preferment or pass through a period of probation. He began his career in 1902 with the ensigns of supreme power flying high, and ended it with his death in 1957. Throughout the intervening years his courage was not chilled by age nor his vision dimmed by exhaustion.

He was a man of many dimensions and facets. In the realm of

1

religion, he was the hereditary *Imam* of the Ismailis, combining in his person the ultimate spiritual and mundane authority which only a pontiff may command. In national politics he headed the All India Muslim League (permanent president for several years), the All India Muslim Conference (founder and president), the London Muslim League (patron), the momentous Muslim deputation to the Viceroy of India at Simla in 1906, and the Indian delegation to the three Round Table Conferences in London. In educational leadership he was twice president of the All India Muhammadan Educational Conference and one of the principal makers of the Aligarh Muslim University. On the international scene three matters engaged his affections. The unity and welfare of the Islamic world were dear to his heart and his exertions on its behalf kept him busy all his life. For several years he was anxiously concerned for the future of the *khilafat* and the territorial integrity of Turkey, though for his pains he had to face many risks, including, ironically, the wrath of the new rulers of Turkey herself. He had an abiding interest in world peace, and struggled hard for its achievement, privately in remonstrances with his friends in high places, publicly in speeches and negotiations at the Disarmament Conference and the League of Nations.

Blessed with rare political vision, he was probably the first Indian to realize that federalism was the only workable and lasting solution to the Indian constitutional problem. He was also among those who wished for and suggested a united India of free states and later, when political developments denied the consummation of this ideal, he argued forcefully and logically in favour of the two-nation theory whose practical application was to create Pakistan.

Morally and intellectually he left his mark on many places. In religious matters, the cargo of his thought was heavy, and his views, imbued with modern liberalism, refuted both scholastic obscurantism and reactionary traditionalism. Socially, he attempted to improve society through discerning and sage advice and comprehensive and wide-ranging steps which were refreshing in content and radical in scope. He was one of the richest men in the world, and yet spoke on behalf of the oppressed and the poor of the land, suggesting radical remedies.

A man of exceptional perseverance and deep convictions, once an idea took hold of him he pursued it relentlessly, repeating it on platform, from the pulpit, in print – doing everything in his power for its successful realization. In the process, he himself produced plenty of ideas, stirred many passions, and compelled thought. In possession of a mind of high perspicacity, he had an instinctive sense of proportion, always knowing what was a big issue and what a small one, and focusing his energies to concentrate on the big issues with verve, wisdom and foresight.

No historian can neglect the life and work of such a statesman: the Aga Khan has a high claim on our attention on grounds both of personal impact and of long-term influence.

Family

Over the centuries the ancestors of the Aga Khan moved from land to land with the changes and circumstances of Islamic history. Their first origins lay in Arabia where their names mark the earliest development of Islam as a faith and as a culture. From there they moved to Iraq, which was the centre of their power for some time. The next stop was Egypt where, as the Fatimids, they ruled over an important part of the Muslim empire, adding to its political glory and inspiring its intellectual and artistic achievements. The growth of the city of Cairo and the founding of al-Azhar university are two examples of their legacy.

Their next home was in Iran where they spent several centuries first as lords and rulers of Alamut and the surrounding territories and finally settling down in Anjudan near Qumm. From this point onwards the historian is on firmer ground and can identify individual figures and narrate their movements with greater confidence.

The earliest such figure was Abul Hasan Shah who was appointed Governor of Kirman by Karim Khan Zand, and for some time the office inhered in the family. One of Abul Hasan's predecessors, Hasan Ali, is said to have accompanied Nadir Shah to India as one of the commanders in his army. From the end of the eighteenth century, the family's fortunes were intertwined with the internal, domestic and dynastic politics of the imperial Qajars. One of his descendants made Mahallat his permanent place of residence, and from this decision resulted the hereditary title of the family: Mahallati or Lord of Mahallat.

Abul Hasan's son, Khalilullah (1792–1817)[1], was befriended by the second Qajar emperor, Fath Ali Shah. He had a reputation for piety and enjoyed a popular following. In the concluding years of his life he lived in Yezd, where he was assassinated at the

---

[1] This and the following dates define the *imamate*, not the span of life.

3

instigation of a fanatical *mulla*. The emperor was outraged and drastic action followed. The *mulla* was dragged to the court, ordered to be cast naked into a freezing pond and then beaten with thorny sticks; the chief assailants were also punished. To make further amends, the monarch invited Khalilullah's son, Hasan Ali Shah (1817–81) to his presence, recognized and acknowledged him as the successor *Imam* to his father, made him governor of Qumm and Mahallat, and honoured him in other ways. Greater favours followed. The young man was virtually adopted by the emperor, brought up at the court, and later married to the ruler's daughter. On his appointment as governor of Mahallat he was popularly known at the court as Aga Khan Mahallati, which subsequently became an hereditary title confirmed by the ruler. He was the Aga Khan I, grandfather of Sultan Muhammad Shah Aga Khan III.

In 1834 Shah Fath Ali died and, as has happened so often in the East, the event was a signal for a war of succession. In the ensuing conflict the Aga Khan sided with Muhammad, grandson of the dead ruler, who won the contest and ascended the throne. The Aga Khan was made the governor of Kirman, and in that capacity he liberated Kirman (which had been captured by the rival claimant), rendered other valuable services and generally acted with courage and wit.

Four years later, however, an ill wind blew his way, bringing in its train humiliation, defeat and exile: at the prime minister's connivance, an officer of lowly origin demanded the hand of the Aga Khan's daughter (who was also Emperor Fath Ali's granddaughter) in marriage for his son, and the insult cut the *Imam* to the quick. At the same time, the prime minister refused to pay the expenses incurred by the Aga Khan in the Kirman campaign. The infuriated governor decided to avenge the wounding personal insult and to extract the money due to him in one blow. He revolted and proclaimed his sovereignty in Kirman. The triumph was short-lived. He was intercepted, taken prisoner, brought to Tehran, and put in jail. But before he could be sentenced, his wife sent her younger son to the court, where the boy recited before the emperor some poems in praise of the virtues of forgiveness. The monarch was duly impressed and pleased, and the Aga Khan was set free. But the disappointed prime minister persevered in his inimical designs: he provoked the Aga Khan into another rebellion and involved him in another armed conflict with the ruling power. One more unfortunate skirmish, one more narrow escape, and the harrowed prince fled to Afghanistan.

By good fortune Afghanistan was at war with Britain, or rather with British India, at this time. Detecting an auspicious coincidence of his own plan for safety with the British need of allies, the fleeing prince offered his services to the British, who naturally expressed their gratitude and accepted his help, and equally naturally pledged their support to him in regaining his position and estates in Iran. The prince provided assistance in two important ways: his soldiers fought well, quelled a mutiny among the Indian troops, defended Herat successfully, and later helped the British in Sind; and he exercised his diplomatic skill, learnt in the arduous Iranian school, in pacifying the Afghans and serving as a bridge with the Sindhis. The British acknowledged his role as a supporter and ally and granted him a pension worth Rs. 40,000 a year.

But all his gallantry, devotion and sacrifices in the cause of British expansion brought him no nearer to recovering his Iranian rights and properties. It was his misfortune that fresh political developments drove Iran and Britain to a mutual understanding and an unwritten but fast alliance. The Iranians were now quick to remind their new ally that an agreement of 1814 stipulated the extradition of Iranian subjects hostile to their government. Iran was now hunting for the Aga Khan in the field of diplomacy and international law. Apparently the British no longer cared much for what happened to the Aga Khan who had, so recently, risked his future and his life for their sake, but his petitions and remonstrances earned him some respite. The British and the Iranians agreed, for the time being, to deny him easy access to Iran. As Sind lay next to Baluchistan and Baluchistan to Iran, he was asked to settle in Calcutta, which lay the whole width of India away from Iran and was the capital of the British Indian Empire. He agreed under protest, but felt frustrated. The death of Muhammad Shah, the Iranian ruler, in 1848 brought a ray of hope. Lord Palmerstone tried to secure the Aga Khan's admission into Iran, but failed in his efforts. To save his face, and as a recompense, he agreed to the Aga Khan's transfer from Calcutta to Bombay.

At last the family had a new home. Feeling happier, the Aga Khan built himself a palatial residence on the Malabar Hill overlooking the sea and a number of residences around his seat for his close relatives. The Ismaili community established an imposing centre, the Aga Hall. A complex of like amplitude sprung up in Poona, where the family and its personal retinue spent their summers. A slightly smaller centre was set up in Bangalore in south India. The Aga Khan's eldest son, Ali Shah, made several long visits to Baghdad and Karbala, trying to bring about some kind of *rapprochement* between the family and the Iranian ruling house. But these efforts came to naught.

The Aga Khan's last years were spent in peace and quiet. He had found a place to settle down, created for himself a highly respected position in public and official quarters, reorganized the Ismaili community and established an efficiently run head-quarters for it. Thus it came to pass that history paved the way for the emergence, in the next century, of one of the major leaders of Muslim India.

After an adventurous and hectic life Shah Hasan Ali Shah Aga Khan I passed away in April 1881, and was buried in a specially erected mausoleum called "Hasanabad" at Mazagaon in Bombay. He was succeeded by the Aga Khan II, Agha Ali Shah (1881–5), who had received varied and useful training under his prede-cessor. During his father's second revolt Ali Shah had gone to Karbala with his mother (the Iranian princess royal), and lived there and in Baghdad, spending his time in the company of Zill-us-Sultan who had sat on the Iranian throne for forty days before being replaced and exiled by Muhammad Ali Shah.

Ali Shah had married in Iraq and two sons were born of this marriage. Soon after his return to Bombay his wife died, and he married the daughter of a Shirazi family settled in Bombay. She too was lost to him soon, and he then married a grand-daughter of Emperor Fath Ali Shah who was a niece of Shah Muhammad Ali Qajar and a daughter of a nobleman Nizam-ud-Daulah (Nizam-ud-Daulah had helped the Aga Khan I at the court of Iran before his own voluntary retirement from public duties and withdrawal to a life of prayer and contemplation; his remarkable daughter, whom we will meet more intimately in the following pages, was responsible for the training and education of the Aga Khan III, and for managing and improving the fortune of the Aga family). After this marriage the Aga Khan II and his wife lived in Baghdad for some time and then in Karachi where their only son, the Aga Khan III, was born. It was on the death of his father that he moved from Karachi to Bombay with his wife and son.

The Aga Khan II had received a sound education in religious and secular studies. Learned men had been sent for from Iran and Arabia to teach him Arabic, Persian, philosophy, literature and Shia theology. It is reported that he was particularly fond of ethics and metaphysics, and also oriental literature. His primary concern lay in the improvement of the education of his community's children, and he opened the first school for the *Khoja*[1] children in Bombay. In co-operation with Rahmatullah M. Sayani, a distinguished public figure and one of the earliest Muslim politicians of the subcontinent, he established several educational and philanthropic institutions for the welfare of the Muslims of Bombay. He was president of the National Muhammadan Association till his death, and for some time, during Sir James Fergusson's governorship, an additional member of the Bombay Legislative Council. In 1874 he had served as a member of a commission appointed by the government to study and report on proposals for the amendment of laws relating to the Ismaili community. He was an ardent sportsman, a lover of horses, and a superb marksman.

The *imamate* of the Aga Khan II was short lived. The unexpected deaths of both his elder sons (from his first wife), Shahabuddin Shah and Nur Shah, shook him and darkened his later years. A chill caught outdoors deteriorated into pneumonia from which he did not recover. He died in August 1885 in Poona, and his body was embalmed and taken to Najaf on the west bank of the Euphrates in Iraq where he was buried near the grave of Caliph Ali.[2]

Life

Sultan Muhammad Shah the Aga Khan III, who succeeded his father as *Imam* in 1885, was the only surviving son of the Aga Khan II and the only son born of his third wife, the Iranian princess. He was born in Karachi on 2 November 1877, and not destined to know his father for long, losing him before his eighth birthday and becoming the 48th *Imam* of the Ismailis at a tender age. In late 1896 he was married to his cousin Shahzadi, the daughter of Agha Jangi Shah.

Before giving a brief account of the long and eventful career of the Aga Khan, the reader ought to be introduced to his mother who proved to be the greatest influence in his life. Mothers often play a decisive role in the character-building of great men, and the life and opinions of this mother made an indelible impress

---

[1] *Khoja*, a distortion of *Khwaja*, is the name given to Ismailis of Indian origin.
[2] Three different places of his burial are mentioned. N. M. Dumasia (*The Aga Khan and his Ancestors*, Bombay, 1939) gives it as Karbala, Willi Frischauer (*The Aga Khans*, London, 1970) as Kufa, and the Aga Khan III (*Memoirs*, London, 1954) as Najaf. I presume the son knows better.

on the young child's personality, on his character as a grown-up man, and on his affections and feelings when middle-aged.

Lady Ali Shah, as she was called by everyone, was a masterful royal princess and a woman of uncommon attainments, possessing a rare ability to supervise the callow years of her son, and commanding a natural gift for organizing, overseeing and managing the affairs of the *Imam*'s community. In physical appearance she was remarkable. The most striking features were her big lustrous eyes, large face and thick black hair. She always wore long baggy trousers (*shalwar*) which were gathered tight at the ankles. When she appeared in public she was draped in resplendent *saris* of rich brocade. Her hospitality was legendary, and she regularly hosted exclusive parties for the élite women of Bombay.

She cultivated happy and friendly relations with all the British governors of Bombay and with some Viceroys of India. During the First World War she placed her organizing ability, vast influence and considerable resources at the service of the government. The women of the community, along with those of the Parsi religion (the only emancipated females in the India of those years), tended the wounded soldiers arriving from Mesopotamia and other theatres of war. Large funds were collected and essential supplies were procured.

Edwin Samuel Montagu, the Secretary of State for India, called upon her during his Indian visit and presents a charming vignette of her. Lady Willingdon, the wife of the Governor of Bombay, accompanied him to the Aga Khan Palace, and Montagu noted in his diary, "I am the first male that she had seen socially except Lord Willingdon. She sat very nervously holding Lady Willingdon by both hands, but she is a dear old lady, and she and Lady Willingdon seem to be the greatest friends, visiting one another at intervals.... of course she is a great figure in Mesopotamia, and related to the ruling people in Persia. Her courage is extraordinary, she was really most delightful to me; presented me with a large basket of flowers and one of those decorative necklaces of tinsel – all the old courtesies, and I enjoyed my twenty minutes there very much."

She supplemented her native shrewdness with wide travelling which took her to Europe, Iran, Arabia, Syria, Iraq and the various holy places of Islam. These journeys widened the horizon of her experience and understanding, and brought her in touch with the Ismailis living outside India. She made good use of her worldly wisdom in that she bought new estates and made profitable investments. This financial flair was inherited by her son and great grandson.

This augmentation of the Aga Khan estate certainly helped her young son. But a far greater boon he received from her was his excellent education and grooming. It was she who selected his tutors, picked the subjects to be taught and determined the order in which they were to be taken up; it was she who introduced him to the beauty and mystic profundity of Persian poetry, and chose the five languages other than the native Persian which he had to learn and master. Her loving but strict and watchful hand produced a well-read and highly educated son who could understand the world, judge men, and converse intelligently and learnedly on most subjects with experts and scholars.

The mother's influence on the son's intellectual make-up and development was decisive. But of even greater significance was her spiritual training of the young boy. "Every night in those years," he wrote later in his *Memoirs*, "I would go to her apartment and join with her in prayer – that prayer for unity, for companion-ship on high, which is the core of Muslim faith. This shared experience gave us both, I think, the strength to bear our load of fatigue and anxiety, mental and spiritual, which was by no means light during these difficult years."

She also passed on to him some of her own interest in and enjoyment of mysticism. Her son recalled that "my mother was herself a genuine mystic in the Muslim tradition (as were most of her closest companions); and she habitually spent a great deal of time in prayer for spiritual enlightenment and for union with God. In such a spirit there was no room for bigotry. Like many other mystics my mother had a profound poetic under-standing. I have in something near ecstasy heard her read perhaps some verse by Roumi or Hafiz with their exquisite anal-ogies between man's beatific vision of the Divine and the temporal beauty and colour of flowers, the music and the magic of the night, and the transient splendours of the Persian dawn. . . . she was deeply versed in Persian and Arabic literature, as were several of her ladies-in-waiting and closest women friends. My mother knew a great deal of poetry by heart and she had a flair for the appropriate classical quotation – a flair which, I may say, she never lost throughout her long life. Even when she was nearly ninety she was never at a loss for the right and apt quo-tation, not merely from one of the great poets such as Hafiz and Firdausi or Roumi, but from many a minor or little-known writer. One little anecdote may illustrate this. Shortly before she died a

9

cousin of mine quoted one night at dinner a verse of Persian poetry which is rarely heard. In order not to bother my mother or worry her, I attributed it to Hafiz. Not at all, said my mother, that is not by Hafiz, and she gave the name of the line and the name of the rather obscure poet who wrote it. A consequence of this characteristic was that at mealtimes at my mother's table there were no occasions of idle gossip or tittle-tattle. Our conversation was of literature, of poetry; or perhaps one of the elderly ladies, who travelled from and to Tehran a great deal, would talk about her experiences at the Court of the Shah."

Thus Lady Ali Shah gathered in herself the affection and duties of a loving mother, a strict teacher, a hawk-eyed tutor, a wise guide, an exemplar of culture and literary taste, an initiator in esoteric understanding, a spiritual guide, and a disciplined character-builder. Rarely has a son been brought up with greater care and even more rarely has he owed so much to his mother.

Now I return to the life and activities of the young prince. As soon as he had come of age (in 1898) he set out to see the world,[1] and for the next three years he was absent from home except for a couple of short hurried visits. As far as is known, the first country he visited was England, where he was received by the Prime Minister, Lord Salisbury, the Secretary of State for India, Lord George Hamilton, the Duke of Connaught and some other men in high places. On a royal invitation he stayed with Queen Victoria at Windsor Castle, when she decorated him with his first British title, the Order of the Knight Cross of the Indian Empire (KCIE). He used his time well by meeting several influential public figures and making some life-long friends. From England he proceeded to a round of journeys visiting East Africa, Egypt, France, Germany, Russia and Japan, not necessarily in that order.

The pleasure of seeing new places went hand in hand with the discharge of political and religious obligations. In Berlin he was able to persuade the Emperor, Kaiser Wilhelm, to concede an important demand of the Indian (mainly Ismaili) settlers in German East Africa to be permitted to grow rice along the fertile banks of the Rufiji River. The Kaiser also agreed to raise their

---

[1] Starting from the very beginning, his wayfaring became so frequent that it is difficult to keep a complete and correct record of it. In his *Memoirs* he neither mentions all his travels nor dates those of which he provides an account. We are also handicapped by the absence of a comprehensive and documented biography of the man.

status and remove some petty annoyances. From Berlin the Aga Khan had to return to London to attend the funeral of Queen Victoria. After this dismal duty he went to Paris, where he met his kinsman, the Shah of Iran, and the two men repaired to Ostend to talk over some serious matters, including the forced conversion of the Zoroastrians in Iran which was bringing a bad name to Islam and creating resentment among the Parsis of India (the Parsis being the descendants of Iranian Zoroastrians who had migrated to India to escape persecution). He managed to prevail upon the monarch to put an end to the practice. This was the first of many times when he interceded on behalf of or expressed sympathy for the non-Muslim peoples of India and other lands, thus earning a reputation for religious tolerance and broadmindedness. In Constantinople he was the guest of the Ottoman Sultan, and in East Africa he was decorated with the Brilliant Star of Zanzibar, first class.

After a brief stay in India he was back in London to attend the coronation of King Edward VII, where he was awarded the honour and title of the Order of the Grand Cross of the Indian Empire (GCIE). He paid a second visit to Germany to receive from the Kaiser's hands the distinction and insignia of the Royal Prussian Order of the Crown, first class (which he returned in 1914 on the outbreak of the war).

On his return to India in 1902, he was nominated a member of the Imperial Legislative Council for a term of two years. His speeches in the chamber were not mere tributes to the sagacity and benevolence of British rule but cogent and sometimes lengthy arguments in favour of certain basic reforms in the educational system and in the structural organization (including Indianization) of the Indian Army. At the end of his tenure in 1904, the Viceroy, Lord Curzon, offered him a second term which he declined.

It was in about 1896 and again in 1897 that the Aga Khan had been in Aligarh and met the aged Sir Sayyid Ahmad Khan and made friends with Nawab Muhsin-ul-Mulk. The Muhammadan Anglo-Oriental (MAO) College aroused his interest and sympathy. It was these contacts made in the late 1890s, and his own deep concern with Muslim education, which in 1902 brought him an invitation to preside over that year's annual session of the All India Muhammadan Educational Conference in Delhi.

This was his first appearance on the national platform. It is of some historical significance to recall that his last appearance in 1936 was also on the rostrum of this Conference in Rampur. The two events draw the boundaries of a 34-year Indian public career of unique standing and contribution; they also demonstrate his special interest in Muslim education in India. His presidential address of 1902 was an eloquent appeal in favour of liberal, modernistic tendencies in religious thinking and renewed efforts to improve the standards and facilities of education. The speech established his leadership of Muslim India at the astonishing age of twenty-five, and marked the first step in his long campaign to pull the Muslims into the modern world, with their faith renewed and strengthened and their ability to face new circumstances raised and refined. In 1904 he delivered the inaugural address at the Muslim Educational Conference session in Bombay. In the following year he paid another visit to East Africa.

By 1906 the 28-year-old Aga Khan had become a national leader of such stature that he was called upon to lead a deputation of distinguished Muslim spokesmen from all over the subcontinent to the Viceroy, Lord Minto. He was on his way to Europe when his selection was decided upon and he had to cancel his journey and return to India from Aden. On 1 October he led the deputation to Lord Minto in Simla, and a new chapter began in the constitutional history of India and the political fortunes of its Muslim population.

During his stay in Simla the Aga Khan suggested to Nawab Muhsin-ul-Mulk that a political party was necessary in order to organize and awaken the Muslims if the Simla demands were to be pursued to their final consummation and their benefits to be put to proper use; some other leaders in Bengal, the United Provinces and the Punjab had been making similar plans since 1902. The result was that in the December of the same year (1906), the All India Muslim League was established at the annual session of the All India Muhammadan Educational Conference held in Dacca. The new party elected the Aga Khan as its permanent president (each annual session chose its own president), an office which he continued to occupy until 1913.

What the Aga Khan achieved in 1907–9 was even more important than what he had done in Simla or inspired in Dacca. In these two years he fought a running battle with the British Government and especially with John Morley, the Secretary of State for India, which was at times open warfare and at times guerilla action. With the close support of Sayyid Ameer Ali, he nursed British public opinion by writing letters to *The Times*, using his contacts and friendships to influence men who were making decisions, organizing and using the platform of the

London Muslim League to publicize his point of view, goading the All India Muslim League to persist in putting pressure on the Viceroy and the Government of India, writing articles in British journals, and employing all ways and means within his reach to finally make the British Government and Parliament concede separate electorates to the Muslims of India. Had the attempt failed later Indian history would probably have been different: some historians are prepared to argue that this was the first step which led, by stages, to the creation of Pakistan thirty-eight years later.

During these hectic years he found time to travel to Singapore, Malaya, China and Japan in 1907. In 1908 he married Teresa Magliano, a talented Italian sculptress; the wedding took place in Egypt (he had divorced Shahzadi some years earlier). In the same year Teresa bore him his first son, who was named Muhammad Mehdi.

The year 1910 was a very busy one for the Aga Khan. In January he gave the inaugural address at the annual session of the All India Muslim League in Delhi, which even today makes profitable reading. Later he spent several months in an exhausting tour of the subcontinent, taking the case for the creation of a Muslim university at Aligarh to the common man and collecting a very large sum of money for the purpose. The campaign was arduous, long and far-stretching; even Sir Sayyid Ahmad Khan had not travelled so extensively in his day on behalf of the MAO College. For the first time the issue of Muslim education was brought to the doorstep of virtually every middle-class home. But the year was also one of personal tragedy for him. His first-born, Mehdi, died when he was only two years old.

On 13 June of the next year (1911) his wife presented him with another son, Aly (who was destined to lead a colourful life, to be the father of the 49th *Imam*, and to die in a car accident in Paris on 12 May 1960). In July the University of Cambridge awarded him the honorary degree of Doctor of Laws. In December he gave the inaugural address at the annual session of the All India Muhammadan Educational Conference in Delhi. It was also in this year that he was advanced in his Indian decorations to the Order of the Grand Cross of the Star of India (GCSI).

In 1912 he visited Russia. In March 1913 he appeared as a witness in Bombay before the Royal Commission on the Public Services in India. His evidence, spread over many pages in the official records of the inquiry, shows a deep understanding of the problems involved in administering the country, a fresh approach which produced many useful and some novel suggestions, and an interest in reforming the bureaucratic machinery. In the autumn of this year he clashed with Muhammad Ali[1] over the policy to be pursued by the Muslim League and the status of the London Muslim League, and as a result resigned from the office of the permanent president of the All India Muslim League.

In 1914 he toured Burma, East Africa and Egypt. In 1916 the British Government granted him an eleven-gun salute and the rank of a first class ruling chief for life. He spent the winter of 1917–18 in writing his only full-length political testament, *India in Transition*, which appeared in June 1918 from Bombay. It was a carefully thought out and persuasive appeal for constitutional reform, recasting of the provinces, improving education and agriculture, emancipating women, and putting Anglo-Indian social relations on a sound footing. In continuation of his views contained in the book, in October 1919 he appeared before the Joint Select Committee of the Houses of Parliament on the Government of India Bill, and expounded his views on reform.

The next four years were devoted to the twin problems of the future of Turkey and the *khilafat*. This was a repeat performance of what he had faced and achieved in 1907–9. His love of Islam was the connecting link. The future of Muslim India was at stake when the Morley-Minto reforms were being enacted into law. Now, after the war, it was the fortunes of Turkey which caused him untold anxiety and compelled him to fight another battle with the British Government. Once again with the support of Sayyid Ameer Ali, he mounted a two-pronged campaign. First, maximum pressure was put on Whitehall to treat Turkey justly in the post-war peace settlement and not to dismember its territories. All arguments from history, ethics, expediency and politics were marshalled. By turns he beseeched, warned and threatened the British Government. He used his friendship with Lord Beaverbrook and Lord Rothermere to turn the powerful voices (which soon grew into growls) of *The Times*, the *Evening Standard* and other newspapers against the official policy on Turkey. Ultimately the victory was won through a three-sided assault: in London the

---

[1] Then a young Congressman and Muslim Leaguer engaged in conspiring against the London Muslim League, Ameer Ali and the Aga Khan, as is fully documented in M. Y. Abbasi, *London Muslim League, 1908–1928: An Historical Study*, Islamabad, 1988. Later a prominent leader in the Khilafat Movement; still later a delegate to the Round Table Conference.

Aga Khan and Ameer Ali fought the Prime Minister and the Foreign Secretary to a standstill, in India the vehement and self-sacrificing Khilafat agitation made the life of the Government unbearable, and in Turkey the armies of Mustafa Kamal Pasha beat the Greeks (who were being instigated and abetted by the British Government) out of Turkey. The humiliating and cruel Treaty of Sèvres was annulled and replaced by the Treaty of Lausanne. The Aga Khan went to Lausanne in person in July 1923 to witness this triumph.

The second prong of the Aga Khan's campaign aimed at persuading the Turks to retain the historical institution of *khilafat*. In spite of the fact that both he and Ameer Ali were Shia by faith and therefore unable to acknowledge the religious status of the *khilafat*, the two statesmen, in an act of unmatched courage and rare foresight, wrote a long letter to the Turkish Prime Minister, Ismet Pasha (later Inünü), begging him in the name of the entire Muslim world, Shia and Sunni, and for the sake of the future of Islam, to keep the *khilafat* intact and thus allow Turkey to continue to command the spiritual esteem and allegiance of the world of Islam, and give every Muslim a centre to which he could look with confidence and affection. The leaders of the Indian Khilafat Movement were saying the same thing. But the appeal failed, and the Grand National Assembly of Angora abolished the *khilafat* and sent the last holder of the supreme office into exile. It must have been a bitter blow to the Aga Khan who had made a compromise with his own faith to stand up and fight for an institution which his followers, like other Shias, did not recognize.

In 1923 the Aga Khan was awarded the decoration of the Order of the Grand Cross of the Victorian Order (GCVO). In the next two or three years he attended to the racial problems of East Africa and did some valuable work for the British Red Crescent Society. In 1924 the Government appointed a committee to study the racial question in Kenya and offered its chairmanship to the Aga Khan. He refused the appointment but consented to act as a member; John Hope Simpson (later Sir John) presided over the committee. In April 1926 he was in East Africa on a visit. Towards the end of this year his wife, Teresa, died in Paris, and was buried in Monte Carlo.

For some time the Aga Khan had been asking the Muslim members of the central and provincial legislatures of India to form a party to safeguard the interests of their constituents. In 1928 some members of the central legislature and the Bombay assembly took the initiative under his instructions, but as the plan unfolded, the scope and membership of the proposed party expanded so much that it included nearly every school of thought or existing political group. It was named the All India Muslim Conference, and its first session was held in Delhi on 31 December 1928 and 1 January 1929. The Aga Khan was elected president and delivered his address on 31 December. A comprehensive resolution was passed on 1 January summarizing Muslim demands. The importance of the Conference lies in two things: it was the most representative Muslim organization ever, and its decisions became the Magna Carta of the Muslim delegates to the Round Table Conference.

In December 1929 the Aga Khan married Andrée Carron in Aix-les-Bains. Beginning a year later, between November 1930 and December 1932, the Indian Round Table Conference met in three sessions in London. The Aga Khan spoke in the full session only twice: the real work was done in the committees. But even more important than these conclaves were the private meetings and negotiations in which the principal issues were meticulously debated. The crucial talks took place between the Aga Khan (aided by Sir Muhammad Shafi, M. Jinnah, Zafrullah Khan and Dr Shafa'at Ahmad Khan) and M. K. Gandhi (accompanied by Mrs Sarojini Naidu) in the Aga Khan's suite in the Ritz Hotel. Nothing came out of them. In the first session of the conference the Congress was absent and the Hindu Mahasabha dominated the Hindu liberals. In the second, Gandhi was present as the sole spokesman of the Congress and was in no mood to listen to the Muslims. Rejecting every other delegate's credentials as false, claiming for the Congress (and therefore for himself) the status of the only spokesman of the whole of India, and actually afraid of (and under pressure from) the Hindu Mahasabha, Gandhi made no compromises and promised no concessions – not even when all the minorities of the subcontinent clubbed together and presented a joint list of agreed demands. The conference ended without much enthusiasm, but at least a new constitutional measure was on the anvil. For the Aga Khan it was a matter of deep satisfaction that his 1918 suggestion of a federal India was now to serve as the foundation of the new constitution. But the British and Congress view of a federation was that of a "close" type, and ultimately it split India.

These were the busiest years of the Aga Khan's life. The Round Table Conferences were not yet finished when, in January 1932, he was asked to represent India at the Conference for the

Reduction and Limitation of Armaments which met at Geneva. At the same time he was sent to the League of Nations as India's chief delegate. He continued to represent India at the League of Nations from 1932 to 1938 (except for 1934). The year 1933 opened on a happy note: on 7 January his second son, Sadruddin,[1] was born. In July the Aga Khan helped in the preparation of the memorandum submitted jointly by the All India Muslim Conference and the All India Muslim League to the Joint Committee on Indian Constitutional Reform; it was submitted on 1 August. In October and November he assisted others in drafting the joint memorandum of the British Indian Delegation to the same Committee. Early next year he again called for a merger of the two Muslim organizations, the League and the Conference, and was also sworn to the Privy Council, the first Indian to be thus honoured other than members of the Judicial Committee. He also visited Burma during this year.

In February 1936 he delivered the presidential address at the annual session of the All India Muhammadan Educational Conference in Rampur. On 13 December he was blessed with a grandson: a son was born to Prince Aly Khan and was named Karim – he was to succeed the old man as the 49th *Imam* of the Ismailis. In September 1937 the Aga Khan was elected president of the League of Nations.[2] The League, and through it the international community, had done him a great honour, but, as luck would have it, the first half of his presidentship at the Palace of Nations in Geneva was to coincide with the greatest personal grief of his life.

One day in November 1937 Lady Ali Shah suffered a stroke while stepping out of the Turkish bath in her palace in Bombay. The Aga Khan was in Antibes when the news reached him. He flew to Bombay and found her with seriously impaired faculties. She could only recognize him during brief spells of consciousness.

Many years earlier she had expressed a wish to be buried in a Muslim country, and though it was difficult to move her in this state of health he arranged for her to travel to Baghdad where she was taken to a relative's house. He returned to Europe and spent the Christmas holidays with his grandsons, Karim and

---

[1] In recent years Prince Sadruddin has rendered distinguished service to the United Nations as High Commissioner for Refugees and the Special Co-ordinator of humanitarian and economic assistance programmes relating to the people of Afghanistan as well as Iraq and Kuwait.

[2] Out of 50 votes, he received 49 (one ballot was spoilt).

Amyn, in Gstaad in Switzerland. Then he paid short visits to Syria and India. He was in Cairo in the first days of February when he was told of the deteriorating condition of his mother. He cancelled his tour, reached Baghdad on 5 February and was at his mother's bedside at 3 p.m. She briefly opened her eyes, regained consciousness, and saw her son: two hours later she died with her head resting in his lap. She was buried in Najaf, near her husband's last resting place. She was in her eighty-eighth year when, in the Aga Khan's words, she went "on the safe and quiet journey from the midst of the living to achieve the peace and happiness for which all Muslims yearn". She had been a very special kind of mother to him, and only the passage of time could assuage the pain.

He visited India in the winter of 1939–40, not knowing that he would be unable to be there again in the next four years to witness the momentous events which would be changing her history. He was in France when the country fell to the Germans and he moved to Switzerland. His health had been troubling him for some years and Swiss medical facilities were very good. The neutrality of Switzerland assured him a quiet and peaceful life. But the price he had to pay was political silence. He was allowed to make his home there on the express condition that he made no political statements and took no part in active politics, Swiss or foreign.

In 1943 he divorced Andrée Carron (the obituary notice in *The Times* gives the year 1942), and in 1944 married Yvette Labrousse.

The end of the war enabled him to resume a normal life. In June 1945 he went to East Africa to preside over the first session of the East African Muslim Conference. In August we see him in South Africa. In the summer of 1946 he went to India and East Africa to attend the ceremonies connected with the Diamond Jubilee of his *imamate*. He took this opportunity to preside over the second session of the East African Muslim Conference.

Until now the Aga Khan had only one citizenship, that of British India. It is reported that in 1947 he was offered and accepted Pakistani citizenship. In 1949 he also accepted Iranian citizenship.

He visited Pakistan, the home of his dreams, in February 1950. In January 1951 he visited Burma and later he went to East Pakistan (now Bangladesh) to receive an honorary degree from the University of Dacca. From there he came to Karachi were he created a political storm by suggesting that the country should drop Urdu and adopt Arabic as her national and official language. The Urdu-speaking migrants from India who were concentrated in Karachi resented the advice and interpreted it as an attack on their culture. Some other Pakistanis enamoured of Urdu sided with them. In this emotional disturbance nobody debated the pros and cons of what he had said and the logic behind it. From Karachi he went to Iran and also visited Syria. He returned to Pakistan in February 1952 and gave a lecture at the national Institute of International Affairs. In 1954 he was again in Pakistan and then visited other countries in connection with the Platinum Jubilee[1] of his *imamate*. In the same year his *Memoirs* were published in London by Cassell. In 1955 he visited Egypt, and in the same year received from the British Government the very high decoration of the Knight Grand Cross of Saint Michael and Saint George (GCMG).

In 1955 or 1956, due to the Aga Khan's failing health, a permanent home was made for him in Switzerland where he availed himself of the good climate and good doctors. Begum Aga Khan selected a beautiful villa, "La Rivière", in Versoix by Lake Geneva. The property was purchased and renamed "La Barakat" ("the blessing" or "good fortune"). He still spent much time in "Villa Yakimour" near Cannes in France, often in the company of his grandson and successor, Prince Karim. In the spring of 1957 he came to Chantilly, but his condition soon worsened and, on the Begum's instructions, he was flown in a chartered Viscount to Geneva, from where an ambulance took him to his villa. Karim was summoned from Harvard University, and Aly Khan and his daughter, Yasmin, so dear to the old man, soon arrived. In the early hours of 11 July the Aga Khan's heart began to sink. The Begum and Karim kept up vigil. Aly and Sadruddin were around. At 1.40 p.m. he breathed his last and joined his Maker.

On 12 July the will he had made in London on 25 May 1955, was read out by a solicitor with the whole family present; it contained the following statement: "I appoint my grandson Karim, the son of my son Aly Salomone Khan, to succeed to the title of Aga Khan and to be the Imam and Pir of all my Shia Ismailian followers." With the death of the 48th Imam Prince Karim had assumed, in fact and in law, the status and duties of the 49th *Imam* of the Ismailis.

The Aga Khan had expressed a wish to be buried in Aswan in Egypt, and orders were immediately issued for the preparation

[1] These jubilees had no religious significance and were primarily ceremonial in character.

19

of a temporary resting place in the grounds of the house which he had built there. The heavy oak coffin was carried by a hearse from Versoix to the Geneva airport. The body was then flown in a chartered D.C. 6 to Cairo, and thence to Aswan; the Begum, Prince Karim and Aly Khan travelled with the mortal remains. At the villa, after the customary prayers, Aly, Sadruddin, Karim and Amyn carried the coffin on their shoulders to the vault. With this burial on the banks of the ancient Nile, an era came to an end.

The Aga Khan's supreme hereditary position as the *Imam* of the Ismaili community calls for a brief reference to the history of Islam, and it seems appropriate to recount the origins and evolution of the office in his own words: "The Prophet died without appointing a Caliph or successor. The Shia school of thought maintains that while direct Divine inspiration ceased at the Prophet's death, the need of Divine guidance continued and this could not be left merely to millions of mortal men, subject to the whims and gusts of passion and material necessity, capable of being momentarily but tragically misled by greed, by oratory, or by the sudden desire for material advantage. These dangers were manifest in the period immediately following our Holy Prophet's death. Mohammed had been, as I have shown, both a temporal and a spiritual sovereign. The Caliph or successor of the Prophet was to succeed him in both these capacities; he was to be both *Emir-al-Momenin* or 'commander of the true believers' and *Imam-al-Muslimin* or 'spiritual chief of the devout'. Perhaps an analogy from the Latin Western world will make this clearer: he would be 'Supreme Pontiff "as well as" Imperator or temporal ruler'.

"Ali, the Prophet's cousin and son-in-law, the husband of his beloved and only surviving child, Fatima, his first convert, his bold champion in many a war, whom the Prophet in his lifetime said would be to him as Aaron was to Moses, his brother and right-hand man, in the veins of whose descendants the Prophet's own blood would flow, appeared destined to be that true successor; and such had been the general expectation of Islam. The Shias have therefore always held that after the Prophet's death, Divine power, guidance, and leadership manifested themselves in Hazrat Ali as the first Imam or spiritual chief of the devout. The Sunnis, however, consider him the fourth in the succession of Caliphs to temporal power.

"The Imam is thus the successor of the Prophet in his religious

20

capacity; he is the man who must be obeyed and who dwells among those from whom he commands spiritual obedience. The Sunnis have always held that this authority is temporal merely and secular, and is exerted only in the political sphere; they believe therefore that it appertains to any lawfully constituted political head of a State, to a Governor or to the President of a republic. The Shias say that this authority is all-pervading and is concerned with spiritual matters also, that it is transferred by inherited rights to the Prophet's successors of his blood."[1]

The Shia unanimity of allegiance lasted only till Imam Ja'far al-Sadiq. On his death in AD 765 a group of Shias accepted as the next *Imam* his younger son, Musa al-Kazim, and followed his line of descent until the twelfth *Imam* who, according to their belief, had disappeared or "withdrawn" for a time but is still alive and would appear again before the end of the world as the *mahdi* or guide. This group is called the *athna 'ashari* Shias or the Twelvers, and the overwhelming majority of Shias belong to it. The Ismailis gave their allegiance to Imam Ja'far al-Sadiq's elder son Ismail, from whom they derived their name. Throughout their history, the Ismailis have been led by a hereditary *Imam* who, according to their beliefs, has descended from Prophet Muhammad through Hazrat Ali and Hazrat Fatima, the Prophet's daughter.

The exact date and precise circumstances of the introduction of Ismailism to the Indian subcontinent are hard to come by. Apparently Ismaili activity on certain levels continued in Sind in the centuries following its conquest by the Muslims; and in the years 1200–1250 there are traces of such activity in Delhi. One Pir Shamsuddin came to Sind from Iran and founded his dynasty of *pirs* there; this may have been sometime between 1300 and 1350. It was in the fifteenth century that the great *da'i* (preacher) Pir Sadruddin came to India and converted several thousand Hindus to his faith. He founded and organized the community of these converts into the *Khojas* or "honourable converts". He is buried near Uchch. Many Ismailis in India and Pakistan are descendants of this *Khoja* community. They live chiefly in Sind, Kach and Gujerat. Significant Ismaili settlements also exist in Chitral, Hunza, Gilgit and Bangladesh.

Outside the subcontinent of India the historical centres of Ismailism have existed for a long time in Syria, southern Egypt,

[1] *Memoirs*, London, 1954, pp. 178–9.

the Yemen, Iraq, Iran, Afghanistan and Central Asia.[1] There are fairly sizeable diasporas in East Africa, South Africa and Burma; more recently some Ismaili communities have grown up in the United States, Canada, Spain, Portugal, France and Great Britain.

Historical Background

Every great man is partly the child of his age and partly its father. The age makes him what he is; in turn, he shapes the age to his own liking. The Aga Khan acted and reacted in a certain milieu. To help the reader understand his ideas and actions I give here a rapid survey of the political developments in India, and where necessary elsewhere, during the years of his public life and the period immediately preceding it.

It was only after the failure of the mutiny of 1857 that the Muslims awoke to the realization of their true position in India. The establishment of British rule not only signalled their downfall but also marked an end to their existence as a separate and dominant group in Indian political life. The British believed that the Muslims had instigated the 1857 uprising and their attitude was one of vengefulness. Nor were the Muslims very friendly with the Hindus, whom they considered their old subjects, new rivals,

---

[1] For the long and complex history of the Ismaili community see Hamid Algar, "The Revolt of Agha Khan Mahallati and the Transference of the Ismaili Imamate to India", *Studia Islamica*, Vol. 29 (1969); Hamid Algar, "Aqa Khan", *Encyclopaedia Iranica*, Vol. 2; Farhat Dachraoui, *Le Califat Fatimide au Maghreb, 296–365 H./909–975 Jc.*, Tunis, 1981; Farhad Daftary, *The Ismailis: Their History and Doctrines*, Cambridge, 1990; Habib Feki, *Les idées religieuse et philosophiques de l'Ismaélisme Fatimide*, Tunis, 1978; Asaf A. A. Fyzee, "The Ismailis", in A. J. Arberry (ed.), *Religion in the Middle East*, Cambridge, 1969, Vol. 2; A. al-Hammad, *Qiyam al-dawla al-Fatimiyya bi-bilad al-Maghrib*, Cairo, 1980; Abbas Hamdani, *The Beginning of the Ismaili Da'wa in Northern India*, Cairo, 1956; W. Ivanow, *Studies in Early Persian Ismailism*, Leiden, 1948; W. Ivanow, *Brief Survey of the Evolution of Ismailism*, Leiden, 1952; Bernard Lewis, *The Origins of Ismailism: A Study of the Historical Background of the Fatimid Caliphate*, Cambridge, 1940; Wilferd Madelung, "Ismailiyya", *Encyclopaedia of Islam*, 2nd edn, Vol. 4; Wilferd Madelung, "Shiism: Ismailiyah", *Encyclopaedia of Religion*, Vol. 13; Azim Nanji, *The Nizari Ismaili Tradition in the Indo-Pakistan Subcontinent*, Delmar, N.Y., 1978; S. Hossein Nasr (ed.), *Ismaili Contributions to Islamic Culture*, Tehran, 1977; M. G. S. Hodgson, *The Order of the Assassins*, The Hague, 1955; H. Halm, *The Empire of the Mahdi: The Rise of the Fatimids*, Leiden, 1996; F. Daftary (ed.), *Mediaeval Ismaili History and Thought*, Cambridge, 1996; Samuel M. Stern, *Studies in Early Ismailism*, Jerusalem-Leiden, 1983. Two bibliographies are: I. K. Poonawala, *Bibliography of Ismaili Literature*, Malibu, 1977 and N. Tajdin, *A Bibliography of Ismailism*, Delmar, N.Y., 1985.

and in any case beneath equal privilege. For the first time the Muslims felt the ill wind of fear, insecurity and prostration.

To a great extent the man who saved them from self-pity and hopelessness was Sir Sayyid Ahmad Khan (1817–98). He gave his community three directions: loyalty to the British, exertion in education and aloofness from politics. The loyalty was justified on three grounds. First, British rule was not going to end in the foreseeable future, and being a minority it was common-sense to be on good terms with the masters. Second, Hindus and Muslims were two unequal "nations", and the latter would always remain a minority. Every advance towards democracy would mean the suppression of the Muslims under the rule of the Hindu majority. If democracy was a foretaste of independence under an unalterable Hindu government, he wanted neither the one nor the other. Hence his opposition to the introduction of parliamentary institutions and to any increase in the recruitment of Indians to public service by open competition. Third, he was convinced of the unarguable superiority of the British (and European) way of life to the Indian (or Oriental). It was only from and through the British that Muslims could learn to improve their status and to stand on their feet.

His second call was for education and more education: the Muslims' imperial sway was over; now they had to compete with the Hindus and others for jobs and other openings. The key to all progress was good education. This thought was an obsession with him: for over thirty years he devoted himself to convincing his people to obtain schooling and to make more schools available. In 1875 he established the Muhammadan Anglo-Oriental College in Aligarh which was to become the first Muslim university in India.

Finally, he considered politics an unnecessary and undesirable encumbrance: the British were suspicious, the Hindus were far superior intellectually and materially, and the Muslims were poorly equipped for political adventure. They must keep themselves aloof from all political activity and devote their energies and resources to educational uplift.

In religion the Sayyid was a liberal modernist and more: the revealed truth, he said, could only be understood through reason. Physical and natural sciences, far from being in conflict with the faith, were proofs of God's existence and a confirmation of His message. There could be no contradiction between the word of God (His revelation) and the world of God (the phenomena of nature). He suggested some radical reforms in the Islamic legal concepts, rituals and ceremonials. He also brought out the close affinity between Islam and Christianity in his commentary on the Bible. In social life he stood for simplicity, honesty, straight dealings, cultured deportment and other homely virtues.

The work of Sayyid Ahmad Khan was carried forward by his colleagues and junior partners at Aligarh. Their combined efforts produced what came to be known as the Aligarh Movement, which was fundamentally a cultural movement aiming at a regeneration of liberal values in literature, social life, education and religion.

A parallel tendency appeared in Bengal where the large, compact but poor Muslim population was shown the way to better things by Sayyid Ameer Ali, Nawab Abdul Latif Khan, Karamat Ali Jaunpuri and others. Independently of the Aligarh influence, they also preached the message of liberalism, enlightenment, progress, modern values and social uplift. In one respect the Bengali renaissance went beyond the Aligarh gospel. Muslim politics was born in Bengal. Ameer Ali founded the National Muhammadan Association at a time when Sayyid Ahmad was begging his people to avoid politics like the plague – and there had been one or two predecessors even to the Association. Ameer Ali's own books inspired fresh thought. The *Spirit of Islam* was a new interpretation of the faith and its history written with erudition and enthusiasm. He wielded great influence on the new generation, and his advocacy of such matters as female emancipation and the reform of Islamic law affected the thinking of the community's eκlite.

The combined effect of Aligarh and Bengal reformism was revolutionary. The Muslims developed a confidence in themselves and in their traditions, and hope for their future; they came to respect themselves. Muslims were catching up in education and they had begun to take an interest in commerce and industry.

In the meantime the constitutional development had gone apace. In 1858 the control of India passed from the hands of the East India Company to the British Crown. The Government of India Act of 1858 provided for the appointment of a Secretary of State for India, who replaced the Court of Directors and the Board of Control. A council of sixteen members advised the Secretary of State and was responsible for conducting the business that had to be transacted in Britain regarding the governance of India. All the armies of the Company were merged into the military forces of the Crown.

The Indian Councils Act of 1861 created a Council of the Governor General of India, consisting of the Commander-in-Chief, five ordinary members, and between six and twelve additional members appointed for the purpose of making laws and regulations. Provincial administrative and legislative institutions and procedures were prescribed, but the Governor General could veto provincial laws. The Presidencies were to be headed by Governors and the other Provinces by Lieutenant Governors.

This enactment was amended by the Indian Councils Act of 1892. The Governor General's Council was expanded. Expenditure proposals for the annual financial statement were to have the sanction of the Governor General prior to being laid before the Council. The provincial councils were enlarged and authorized to discuss the budget and raise administrative questions, but not to vote on them. The Governor General's Council was also denied this power. The non-official (additional) members of the Council were to be appointed in two different ways: a minority of them by simple nomination by the Governor General, the majority by "recommendations" of local bodies, religious communities, municipalities, universities, chambers of commerce and the like. The Government of India admitted in its dispatch of 1892 that India was "essentially a congeries of widely separated classes, races and communities with divergencies of interests and hereditary sentiments which could be properly represented only by those who knew and shared their sectional opinions".

By the turn of the century Muslim India was pulsating with new ideas. A new generation, fresh to the opportunities of life, better educated, aware of its solidarity and hopeful of its future, looked upon the Aligarh injunction against politics with disfavour. The Hindus had organized themselves in a congress and gained by the decision. Seeds of representative institutions sown by the Indian Councils Act of 1892 might soon sprout into more far-reaching reforms. The age of political activism was dawning, and it was only through politics that the Muslims could convey to the British their desires and aspirations. But traditions die hard, and men bred in the Aligarh stable hesitated to take the plunge. The decision was taken out of their hands by two developments.

In October 1905 the Government of India announced and implemented a partition of the Presidency of Bengal with the dividing line between the Hindu West and the Muslim East. The

25

new Muslim province was given the official title of Eastern Bengal and Assam, and contained a population of 31 million, of whom 18 million were Muslims and 12 million Hindus. The Hindus of West Bengal resented the action and charged the government with favouring the Muslims, "vivisecting" the Bengali homeland, disrupting the Bengali "nationality", and injuring the "nationalist" and "patriotic" movement and spirit of the people of India. In fact, the opposition was based on other considerations. The high caste Hindus feared loss of their social superiority and political monopoly, the educated Hindus feared competition with the Muslims for jobs, and the generality of Hindus disliked the idea of sharing power with the Muslims. In short, they objected to the creation of a Muslim-majority province. Soon the Hindus of other provinces and the Indian National Congress gave them full support, and an all-India agitation against the partition was begun.

The agitation carried a message loud and clear to the Muslims and disquieting tidings. The agitation was as much anti-Muslim as it was anti-British. The Hindus were not prepared to countenance the creation of a Muslim-majority province. This exposed the hollowness of the Congress claim that it stood for Hindu-Muslim unity and that it did not distinguish between a Hindu Indian and a Muslim Indian. Muslim interests were not safe in Congress hands. The community would never be treated fairly and justly by the Indian "nationalists". Any broad-based Indian nationalism was bound to be Hindu (or at least *not* Muslim) in character. The lesson was learnt: the era of politics had set in and it was no longer possible to shut one's eyes to political changes. This realization led straight to the idea of the establishment of a Muslim political organization.

This resolve was fortified by another factor. The principle of representation, in however crude a form, had been conceded to the provinces by the Indian Councils Act of 1892. Now rumour ran that this principle was to be extended to a wider field. Muslim interest demanded that their claim to legislative seats ought to be pressed upon the British. This task could only be performed by a political party which spoke for them and in which the Muslims of the subcontinent had trust and confidence.

Even more important than organizing a party was the devising of a system of representation which did not leave the Muslims dependent on the Hindu majority vote in an election. So the leaders drew up a plan of separate electorates for their community and presented it to the Viceroy, Lord Minto, at Simla on

1 October 1906. The deputation which saw Minto consisted of representatives of all shades of Muslim opinion and was led by the Aga Khan. It made two distinct demands. First, in all local and provincial elections, Muslims must be separately represented and their representatives must be separately elected by purely Muslim electors. Second, Muslims must be given weightage in all elected bodies, i.e., they should have more seats than their ratio of population warranted.

The first demand was made on two grounds: that in the then existing state of communal tension no Muslim elected through a joint electorate would genuinely reflect the will of the community, and that in the absence of separate electorates every contested election would lead to communal riots. The demand for weightage was supported by two more arguments: that Muslims still owned much of the landed property in India, and that they formed a very large proportion of the Indian Army. The Viceroy, in his prepared reply to the address presented by the deputation, accepted both the demands contained in the memorial.

Between 1902 and 1905 Muslim leaders had made some attempts to negotiate with the non-Muslim politicians. The Aga Khan had remonstrated with Sir Pherozeshah Mehta about the necessity of persuading the Congress to gain Muslim confidence. When these efforts failed, it was felt that the only hope lay in the establishment of a Muslim political body to secure, in the Aga Khan's words, "independent political recognition from the British Government as a nation within a nation."

In pursuance of this objective Muslim leaders from all over India who had gathered in Dacca in December 1906 to attend the annual session of the All India Muhammadan Educational Conference decided to establish a political party of their own. The Aga Khan, who was not present, had already spoken to Nawab Muhsin-ul-Mulk about this, and the Nawab had spread the word. Now Nawab Salimullah Khan of Dacca moved a resolution for the creation of a Muslim party to be called the All India Muslim League. The objectives of the League were fixed as: "(a) To promote among the Musalmans of India feelings of loyalty to the British Government and to remove any misconceptions that may arise as to the intentions of Government with regard to any of its measures; (b) To protect and advance the political rights and interests of Musalmans of India and respectfully to represent their needs and aspirations to Government; (c) To prevent the rise among Musalmans of India of any feelings of hostility towards other communities without prejudice to other objects of the League." The Aga Khan was elected permanent president of the League.

The Muslims had won a relatively easy victory in India where Lord Minto's sympathy for their cause had been of great advantage. To persuade the British Government in London to concede separate representation to them was a much harder task and tested the mettle of the Aga Khan (and Ameer Ali) to the full.

During the last months of 1906 John Morley, the Liberal Secretary of State for India, had been developing his ideas about Indian reforms and keeping Minto informed of his thoughts. At the other end, Minto was doing the solid work by appointing a committee to thrash out the complicated changes. The committee finished its labours in early 1907 and a dispatch on reforms was sent to London on 19 March. It contained a recommendation for enacting into law the Muslim demand for separate representation. Discussion, and consequent amendment of the dispatch, continued for the next year and a half. But towards the end of 1908 Morley changed his mind on the question of Muslim representation and replaced the earlier provision of separate electorates with a new proposal for an electoral college by which Muslims and non-Muslims would together elect a number of Muslims and these in turn would elect the representatives.

The Muslim League sent a deputation from India to see Morley on 27 January 1909, but it failed to convince him of the injustice of his scheme. Morley refused to budge because, as he confessed to Minto in a letter, he did not want to annoy the Hindus. On 25 August 1909 the reform regulations were passed by the Secretary of State's Council, but only with the help of Morley's casting vote. But when the rules and regulations were published in November they were found to contain a scheme for separate Muslim representation in the shape in which it had been requested by the Simla deputation. Between August and November 1909 Morley had changed his mind once more and finally abandoned his electoral college scheme. The heroic efforts of the Aga Khan, Ameer Ali, the London Muslim League in Britain and of some of the League leaders in India had proved fruitful.

Under the new Act of 1909 the provincial councils were enlarged to a maximum of 50 members in the larger provinces and 30 in the smaller. The method of election was partly direct and partly indirect. Small non-official majorities were provided in the provincial councils but an official majority was retained at the centre. Besides the Viceroy and his Executive Councillors, nearly sixty members were added to the Imperial Legislative Council. Members could raise questions relating to administration and policy, but the government had a built-in majority in the house. The new councils were not invested with any powers to control the government. Interpellation was permitted, but questions could be disallowed without giving any reason. Resolutions could be moved, but they had no binding force. The system, in the words of Sir Reginald Coupland, was representative but not responsible.

Harder days were ahead. In August 1911 the Viceroy, Lord Hardinge, suggested to the Secretary of State for India, Lord Crewe, a "modification" of the partition of Bengal. His scheme was to reunite the five Bengali-speaking divisions into a presidency administered by a Governor in Council; to create a Lieutenant Governorship in the Council of Bihar, Chota Nagpur and Orissa; and to restore the Chief Commissionership of Assam. Simultaneously, the capital of India was to be shifted from Calcutta to Delhi. The Marquess of Crewe was delighted. It was decided that these "boons" would be announced by King George V in person at the Coronation Durbar at Delhi on 12 December. Everything happened as arranged. The partition was annulled. The Hindus and the Congress were pleased, but the Muslims were bitterly disappointed and estranged from the British.

A marked change came over Muslim politics. The Muslim League, at its annual session held from December 1912 to January 1913, changed its aim from "loyalty" to a demand for a "form of self-government suitable to India". Until about 1922 the League worked in co-operation with the Congress. The breach with the British had brought the two parties closer.

The new friendship produced quick results. The League and the Congress met in a joint session in 1916 in Lucknow and formulated common reform proposals to be put before the government for immediate implementation. This was the famous – or infamous – Lucknow Pact. It was the first Hindu-Muslim pact. It was also the first and the last occasion when the Hindus conceded separate electorates to the Muslims. The price that the Muslims had to pay was not then counted by anyone except a few leaders in Bengal and the Punjab. In agreeing on the quantum of Muslim representation in the provincial councils, the Congress had insisted on smaller representation than the population in Bengal and the Punjab and a generous representation in provinces where the Muslims were a small majority. The full horror of this provision dawned upon the League leaders only in 1937 when they discovered that even if the party won every Muslim seat in Bengal and the Punjab it could not form a stable government, because in 1916 it had sold its right to rule the two biggest Muslim provinces in exchange for a heavy Muslim weightage or advantage in overwhelmingly Hindu provinces.

The Congress-League scheme of reforms was, however, not only far ahead of the times but in fact did not aim at realizing responsible government. It contented itself with leaving an irremovable executive at the mercy of a legislature which could paralyse it without directing it. The official reply to the Lucknow agreement came from the new Secretary of State for India, Edwin Samuel Montagu, on 20 August 1917 in the shape of an announcement in the House of Commons. It defined the policy of the government as "increasing association of Indians in every branch of the administration, and the gradual development of self-governing institutions, with a view to the progressive realization of responsible government".

Montagu followed up his word with deed. He visited India from November 1917 to April 1918 and, in co-operation with the Viceroy, Lord Chelmsford, held discussions with Indian leaders of all opinions. The result of the conversations and the Viceroy—Secretary of State deliberations was the Montagu-Chelmsford Report which was published on 8 July 1918 (one month after the Aga Khan's *India in Transition* had appeared).

The report disapproved of separate electorates in principle, but retained them in practice because Muslims regarded them "as their only adequate safeguard". Separate representation was extended to the Sikhs, but refused to other minorities. A new device said to have been thought up by Lionel Curtis was applied to India – dyarchy. Certain subjects in each province were to be "transferred" to the control of ministers chosen from, and responsible to, the majority in the legislative council. The other subjects were to be "reserved" to remain under the control of the Governor and his Executive Council, whose members would be officials responsible not to the provincial legislative council, but to the Secretary of State. The Governor was empowered to enact any bill, including a money bill, over the head of the legislative council if he "certified" that it was essential.

In the centre the legislative council was to be replaced by a bicameral parliament: the Council of State (upper house) and the Indian Legislative Assembly (lower house). A great majority of members in both houses were to be elected members. Finally, at the end of 10 years a commission would be appointed to examine the working of the system and to advise as to whether the time had come for complete responsible government in any province or provinces or whether some "reserved" subjects could be "transferred".

Both the League and the Congress found these recommendations so different from their own that they did not even attempt to negotiate with the government with a view to a compromise. They contented themselves with sharp criticism. The proposals of the report were incorporated in a Bill which, after full consideration by a joint committee of both houses of Parliament (before whom the Aga Khan appeared), was adopted by Parliament and received the Royal Assent on 23 December 1919.

Accordingly, the provincial legislatures were enlarged, with the elected portion not less than 70 per cent in any case. Franchise was extended, mainly by lowering the property qualifications. Contrary to the report's recommendation, separate electorates were conceded to all minorities. Devolution of authority from the centre to the provinces was for the first time made definite, precise and binding. In the provinces, law and order and land revenue were "reserved" subjects, while others were "transferred" to ministers. The report's plea for a mainly nominated upper house in the centre was rejected, and the Council of State was made partly elective and partly nominated. Both houses were to be directly elected. The Governor General's Executive Council was to continue to be responsible only to the Secretary of State for India. The Governor General could "certify" and thus enact any law over the head of the legislature.

I must break the chronological order here and go back a little to take notice of another very important issue, that of Turkey and the *khilafat*.

It was towards the close of the nineteenth century that Turkey began to attract the attention of Muslim India and to play a part in her politics. The Muslims of India had a strong feeling of identity with the world community of Islam. They had helplessly seen the conquest of one Muslim land after another by European powers. The Anglo-Russian Convention of 1908 had reduced their next-door neighbour Iran to a mere dependency. Afghanistan had been humiliated and invaded several times. The Ottoman Empire was the only Muslim power which had maintained a semblance of authority. The Indian Muslims looked to it as a bastion of Islam.

The establishment of European rule in Muslim North Africa

had produced a sharp reaction among the Indian Muslims. The gallant fight put up by Tripoli evoked great sympathy and admiration. Then came the Balkan wars, and Turkey was reduced in Europe to Eastern Thrace, Constantinople and the Straits. The Turkish Sultans were also Caliphs of the Muslim world. When Turkey chose to fight on the side of Germany their sympathies were with the Turks, though they could not express their sentiments openly. The British had hoped to neutralize Muslim hostility by promising to respect the status of the Caliph and the right of the Turks to their homeland when the war ended and a peace settlement was made. At the end of the hostilities British statesmen and ministers made noises which contradicted their war-time promises, given openly and solemnly. The Indian Muslims organized what is known as the Khilafat Movement to put pressure on the Government of India and the British Government to respect their word and act justly with Turkey.

During the war, of course, the Allied powers had entered into a number of secret agreements aimed at breaking up the Ottoman Empire and distributing it among themselves. Under the Sykes-Picot Agreement of 16 May 1916, Mesopotamia was to go to Britain, and Syria and Cilicia to France. Under the Treaty of London of 26 April 1915 and the St Jean de Maurienne Agreement of 17 April 1917, a large area extending inland from the Aegean and Mediterranean coasts, including Adalia and Smyrna, was earmarked for Italy. The Constantinople Agreement of 18 March 1915 had promised the possession of the Straits and Constantinople to Russia; but the Soviet Government denounced it. After the armistice of Mudros with Turkey on 30 October 1918, Allied forces took control of Constantinople. Turkey lay prostrate at the mercy of Britain, France and Italy, all of whom coveted her lands.

Turkey was saved by its own magnificent valour (under the hardest possible conditions), by the agitation of the Indian Muslims in favour of the *khilafat*, and by the campaign mounted in London in her favour by the Aga Khan and Ameer Ali.

The Allies imposed the Treaty of Sèvres on Turkey on 10 August 1920, according to which Eastern Thrace, Gallipoli and the Aegean islands were ceded to Greece; Smyrna was to be administered by Greece for five years and then to decide its future by a plebiscite; and the Straits and the Dardanelles were to be demilitarized and placed under international supervision.

But by this time the Sultan of Turkey, with whom the Allies had signed the treaty, had been replaced by a national government at

Angora, and Mustafa Kamal had begun liberating his country. He attacked the French forces in Cilicia and Italian forces in Konia. Italy withdrew and gave up her claims to any part of Asia Minor. In June the Turkish forces threatened British troops stationed on the Asiatic side of the Straits; in response, the Allies called upon Greece to launch a major offensive against Mustafa Kamal. With Lloyd George's encouragement the Greeks had occupied Smyrna in May 1919, though it had previously been allotted to Italy. Now Greek forces advanced into Anatolia, and another Greek army landed in Eastern Thrace and occupied Adrianople.

At the end of 1920, Venizelos, the Greek Prime Minister, fell from office and King Constantine returned to power. France became suspicious of British motives. Only Lloyd George stuck resolutely to his pro-Greek and anti-Turkish policy, and therefore, in 1921, when the Greeks could have extricated themselves from Asia Minor, they did not do so, trusting to Lloyd George's support. In the summer they began a new offensive aimed at Ankara. In October, France and Turkey signed a treaty at Ankara, ending the war between the two countries and providing for French evacuation of Cilicia and surrender of territory in northern Syria.

Events moved fast in 1922. In March the Viceroy of India published a memorandum giving sympathetic support to Turkish aspirations. As it ran counter to British policy, Montagu, who had sanctioned its publication, was forced to resign. In August the Turkish forces broke the Greek position in Afium Karahissar. In September the Turks entered Smyrna, and continued to advance towards Chanak, a point on the southern shores of the Dard-anelles held by British troops. Poincaré ordered French troops at Chanak to withdraw. Abandoned by their allies and even by the Dominion Governments, Britain at last realized the necessity of making peace. On 11 October a convention was signed.

This obliged Britain to make a new settlement with Turkey and it was signed at Lausanne in July 1923. Turkey retained Eastern Thrace, including Adrianople; demilitarized zones were estab-lished on both sides of the Dardanelles (including Gallipoli and the Chanak area) and on both sides of the Bosphorus; navigation of the Straits was granted to the ships of commerce of all nations in time of peace and of neutrals in time of war involving Turkey, and to warships of all nations in time of peace or Turkish neu-trality.

The Indian Khilafat Movement put intense pressure on the

Government of India for a just settlement with Turkey. In this demand there was near perfect unity in the subcontinent. Though the Shias could not, in accordance with their doctrine, recognize the Sultan of Turkey as the Caliph, driven by a common desire to save Islamic political power from extinction, they joined hands with other Muslims in the movement to save the *khilafat*. In 1920 a deputation of the Khilafat Movement leaders headed by Muhammad Ali came to England to put its case before the government. Lloyd George was not pleased to receive it and gave it a cool reception. Ultimately the Indian agitation and the sympathetic attitude of Lord Reading, the Viceroy, and Edwin Montagu, the Secretary of State for India, weighed with the British Government. In London itself, Muslim pressure – exerted by the Aga Khan and Ameer Ali (helped in this cause by many British friends) – was building up on Whitehall. Some leading newspapers and journals, particularly *The Times*, the *Manchester Guardian* and *New Statesman*, castigated the official foreign policy for their own reasons.

The abolition of the *khilafat* by Turkey in 1924 was a great blow to the Muslims of India, who had campaigned so devotedly and suffered so many hardships to safeguard the Caliph's position and powers. Gradually the enthusiasm of the people died down, the leaders of the Khilafat Movement developed new interests, and Turkey disappeared from the political horizon of Muslim India.

The Khilafat Movement had brought the Hindus and Muslims very close. The Congress, seeing its opportunity, gave its full support to the movement, partly to bring the Muslims into the mainstream of Indian nationalism and partly, as Gandhi said, to save the cow from the Muslim knife. But solidarity born of expediency cannot last. With the end of the agitation, Hindu–Muslim riots and hardened attitudes reappeared. This unfortunate state of affairs was to continue till Independence, and even after that.

To return to constitutional developments, towards the end of 1927 the British Government, as required by the Government of India Act of 1919, appointed a statutory commission to inquire into the working and future of the Indian constitution. Sir John (later Lord) Simon was the chairman, and all members were British. In a speech in the House of Lords, Lord Birkenhead, the Secretary of State for India, had defended the all-British composition with the argument that a body with any Indians on it could not present an agreed report. This stung the Congress leaders. The All-Parties Conference, which had been convened by the Congress to protest against the personnel and terms of reference of the Simon Commission, was now asked by the Congress leaders to prepare a constitution for India to confound the British. The Conference appointed a committee to do the job. Led by Pandit Motilal Nehru (Jawaharlal's father), it consisted of M. S. Aney, M. R. Jayakar, S. R. Pradhan, Tej Bahadur Sapru, N. N. Joshi, Sardar Mangal Singh, Sayyid Ali Imam and Shoib Qureshi. The two Muslims were unrepresentative of their community and had long been repudiated by the great majority of Muslims. The Sikh member was disowned by the Sikh League shortly afterwards.The Indian Christian Conference also dissociated itself from the principles adopted by the Committee in the protection of minorities.

The main recommendations of the Nehru Report may be summarized thus: (a) India to have the same constitutional status in the British Empire as the self-governing Dominions and to be styled the Commonwealth of India; (b) legislative powers to be vested in a parliament of two houses – a senate of 200 members elected by provincial councils on a popular basis and a house of representatives of 500 elected directly by universal adult franchise; (c) executive power to be vested in a governor-general acting on the advice of a council of ministers responsible to the legislature; (d) joint mixed electorates for all elections, and immediate abolition of separate Muslim representation. It also rejected federalism as a possible solution to the communal problem.

Now the Muslims realized fully where they stood in the Congress scheme. The immediate result of the publication of the report was that all shades of opinion united in opposition to it. The two wings into which the Muslim League had been split since 1924 came closer. Jinnah did his best to persuade the All Parties Convention which was meeting in Calcutta in 1929 to accept some of the Muslim demands, but failed. The Congress, on the other hand, hastened to accept all the recommendations of the report, and congratulated the members of the Committee on "their patriotism and their farsightedness". It then passed a resolution declaring that if the British Government did not accept this report in its entirety by the end of 1929 the Congress would start a non-co-operation movement.

In 1928 the Muslim League was in disarray. The Muslims were split into several groups, without a central organization or a firm leadership. In response the Aga Khan urged the community's legislative representatives and other leaders to get together and make agreed decisions reflecting the will of the entire community. This resulted in the convening of the first All India Muslim Conference in Delhi on 31 December 1928 and 1 January 1929. In his presidential address the Aga Khan summarized the problems facing the Muslims and indicated the way to deal with them. On 1 January the conference passed a resolution listing its basic demands: residual powers in provincial hands; separation of Sind from Bombay; full autonomy for the North-West Frontier Province; reforms in Baluchistan; transfer of power direct to the provinces; separate electorates; special Muslim weightage in all political bodies; constitutional sanction for the enforcement of basic rights; safeguards against communal legislation; adequate Muslim representation in ministries; proportionate Muslim representation in the public services; and amendment of the constitution only with the concurrence of the provinces. These demands, made at the most representative gathering of Muslim leaders in the history of Muslim India, became the charter of Muslim rights for the next six years.

In the meantime the official inquiry was under way. The Simon Commission paid two visits to India: the first lasting from 3 February to 31 March 1928, and the second from 11 October 1928 to 13 April 1929. Its report was published in May 1930. The first volume was a survey of Indian political, communal, constitutional, administrative, financial and educational systems, and an examination of the problems facing the country. The second, published a fortnight later, set forth the proposals for constitutional reform.

This was followed by three Round Table Conferences convened in London by the British Government to determine the contents of the future constitution on the basis of the report's proposals. The first opened on 10 November 1930. The Congress was absent because it insisted that the conference must not discuss whether India should or should not receive responsible self-government but must shape a constitution on the assumed basis of a free India. All other parties attended. The Muslims were represented by the Aga Khan, who was elected the leader of both the Muslim delegation and the entire British Indian delegation, Muhammad Iqbal, Jinnah, Zafrullah Khan and others. Most of the work was done through the Federal Structure Sub-Committee, and slowly the proposed federal plan took shape (this must have been a matter of considerable satisfaction to the Aga Khan who, as I show in the following section, had been advocating a federal system for India since 1918).

The second conference opened in the autumn of 1931. The Congress was present in the sole person of Gandhi. The communal problem was seriously tackled, and the Aga Khan, acting as the unofficial spokesman of all minorities, had long conversations with Gandhi. But the Mahatma refused to consider any compromise until the Muslims accepted the Nehru Report in its totality. As a result all the minorities, except the Sikhs, drafted a joint demand of claims and the Aga Khan presented it to the British Government as their irreducible minimum. However, the second conference ended on a dismal note. No agreement was reached on the Hindu–Muslim issue, and it was clear to all that the British Government would have to arbitrate.

This was done by the Prime Minister, Ramsay MacDonald, on 10 August 1932, in what came to be known as the Communal Award. Its terms were roughly as follows. In Hindu-majority provinces the Muslims received, as in the past, seats in excess of their population ratio. In Bengal, where Muslims formed 55 per cent and Hindus 43 per cent of the total population, Muslims received about 48 per cent and Hindus 39 per cent of the total number of seats in the provincial assembly. The Europeans of Bengal were given excessive representation. In the Punjab, where Muslims formed 57 per cent, Hindus 27 per cent and the Sikhs 13 per cent of the population, Muslims were given 49 per cent, Hindus 27 per cent and Sikhs 18 per cent of the total provincial seats. The evil spirit of the Lucknow Pact was not exorcized.

The last conference, meeting from 17 November to 24 December 1932, was brief and unimportant. The Congress was again absent.

The results of the long labours of the three conferences were collected, sifted and summarized in a White Paper issued in March 1933. It faithfully translated the measure of agreement reached at the conferences. Parliament debated it on 17 March. A joint committee of both houses of Parliament was then appointed to consider the White Paper. Constitutionally this body was exclusively composed of members of Parliament, but 20 representative Indians from British India and 7 from the States were appointed as assessors to the committee. The 5 Muslim co-optees were the Aga Khan, Sir Zafrullah Khan, Sir Abdur Rahim, Sir Shafa'at Ahmad Khan and Sir Abdul Halim Ghaznavi. The committee was at work from April 1933 to November 1934, and finally reported to Parliament on 22 November 1934. The report was debated in the House of Commons from 10 to 12 December and in the House of Lords on 18 December. The second reading took place in February 1935, and after the third reading the India Bill finally reached the statute book on 24 July 1935.

The federation set up by the Government of India Act of 1935 was of the closer rather than the looser type. Hindu unitarianism had prevailed, particularly in the composition of the federal legislature. The Muslim League found the federal scheme "fundamentally bad", "most reactionary, retrograde, injurious and fatal . . .", and rejected it. However, it undertook to work the provincial part of the constitution "for what it is worth". The Congress turned down both parts of the Act, but decided to contest elections and to wreck the constitution "from within".

Provincial elections were held in early 1937 and the Congress won majorities in eight provinces. The Muslim League won only 103 out of a total of 482 Muslim seats, the remaining seats were not won by the Congress but by other Muslim parties or groups; the Congress captured only 26 Muslim seats. Out of a grand total of 1,711 seats the Congress won only 762. Further, out of a total of 1,289 non-Muslim or "general" seats the Congress won only 736. In simpler terms, the Congress could only speak for less than half of the total number of voters.

These results shocked the Muslim League out of its complacency. Jinnah, who had recently returned from exile in England, took up the task of reorganizing, popularizing and strengthening the League. His success was reflected in League victories in the by-elections: between 1937 and 1945 out of seventy seven by-elections held in the provinces it won fifty five, Independent Muslims eighteen, and the Congress only four. Between 1934 and 1945 there were eighteen by-elections in the centre, out of which the League won eleven, Independent Muslims five, and the Congress only two.

The Congress was in office in eight provinces from July 1937 to October 1939. It refused to form coalitions with the League or to take into the cabinets any League member of the assembly. Instead of accepting the fact that the Congress did not represent the Muslims, it launched a "Muslim mass contact" campaign, appealing to them to forsake the League and come over to the Congress. Simultaneously, Jawaharlal Nehru declared that there were only two powers in India that counted, the British imperial rule and the Congress (other parties "do not count"), and asked the Muslims to decide which to support and join. The argument backfired, and Muslims flocked around Jinnah in ever increasing numbers. Further, the working of the Congress governments did not conform to the kind of parliamentary system envisaged in the 1935 Act. A high command was established, consisting of Abul Kalam Azad, Rajendra Prasad and Vallabhbhai Patel, and all provincial ministers were made responsible to it. It could act and decide without any reference from or to the Provincial Parliamentary Party or the Provincial Congress Committee.

The Muslims experienced the full force of Hindu rule. Proceedings in the assemblies were opened with the singing of the Hindu song "Bande Mataram". The Congress tricolour flag was flown over local administrative buildings. Congress committees issued all kinds of orders. In some districts Congress police stations were opened and the Congress police investigated crime. The Congress opened a "military department" to raise and train a "national army". In the United Provinces Government schools Hindi replaced Urdu as the medium of instruction. Muslim boys were ordered to worship (*puja*) Gandhi's portrait.

The Muslim reaction to Congress rule may be said to have led directly to the idea of Pakistan. From 1935 to 1937 Jinnah had opposed the 1935 constitution because it did not concede responsible government at the centre. After the experience of Congress rule in the provinces he had to revise his views. If this kind of provincial autonomy was extended to the centre, Congress rule over the whole of India would be unavoidable. And a Congress-dominated central government would nullify the autonomy of Muslim provinces. Where lay the remedy? A very weak centre might have satisfied the Muslims, but the Congress was adamant on a strong centre. In the face of these possibilities the Muslims refused to have any centre at all. If the Hindus wanted a strong centre, let them have it. But then the Muslims must have their own separate centre. This was partition – the Muslim reply to Hindu unitarianism. This was Pakistan – the Muslim reply to Hindu hegemony.

But to imagine that Muslims had never thought, however vaguely, of having a state of their own before 1940 is to misread Indian history. The idea of some kind of territorial re-arrangement, re-organization, re-demarcation, division or partition of the subcontinent along religious lines had been around since the middle of the nineteenth century. Some of the suggestions had come from the British, and some even from prominent Hindu politicians. The best known among the Muslim contributors were Iqbal, Chaudhri Rahmat Ali, Sir Sikandar Hayat Khan, Sayyid Abdul Latif and Mian Kafayat Ali ("A Punjabi").

In December 1930, presiding over the annual session of the All India Muslim League at Allahabad, Iqbal suggested the amalgamation of the Punjab, Sind, Baluchistan and the North-West Frontier Province into a large Muslim province in a truly federal India. But he did not talk of partition. In January 1933 Chaudhri Rahmat Ali of Cambridge not only argued for the separation of the four provinces named by Iqbal (plus the state of Kashmir) and their making up a new independent Muslim state, but coined a name for it: "Pakstan" (later "Pakistan"), which was an acronym of "P" for Punjab, "A" for Afghan or North-West Frontier Province, "K" for Kashmir, "S" for Sind, and "Tan" for Baluchistan. Sir Sikandar Hayat Khan, the Prime Minister of the Punjab, proposed the division of India into seven "regional zones". Latif of Hyderabad Deccan presented his "zonal" scheme. But the only detailed plan which foretold the 1947 partition was put forward by Mian Kafayat Ali, writing under the pseudonym of "A Punjabi". All these people were considering a Muslim north-west; Rahmat Ali demanded the creation of a second Muslim state in the north-east embracing Bengal and Assam, to be called Bang-i-Islam or Banassam or Bangistan. He also wanted the territories of the Nizam of Hyderabad in the south to be formed into another Muslim state to be called Usmanistan.

The Muslim press in India – and its readers – had been talking about some sort of a Pakistan since at least 1928, but the Muslim League, and especially Jinnah, were very late converts to this solution. It was only on 24 March 1940 that the League passed a resolution, at its annual session in Lahore, demanding a partition or a confederation (the wording is very ambiguous and confused). The word "Pakistan" was not used, but within a year the general public interpreted the Lahore Resolution to mean complete separation, and christened the hoped-for country "Pakistan".

Why did the Muslims demand Pakistan, and why in 1940? The Pakistan scheme was proof of the desperate apprehension with which Muslims regarded the prospect of Hindu domination. The League policy in asking for a division of the country was a direct answer to the Congress policy of persisting in a unitary nationalism and in the rule of the majority. If the Hindus wanted a strong centre and were not prepared to compromise on it, the Muslims did not want a centre at all. If the Hindus believed in the rule of the majority, the Muslims denied that they were a minority.

World War Two had broken out a little before the Lahore

Resolution was passed. The Congress was not co-operating with the government and was demanding radical political changes without delay. The League declared its willingness to help the war effort but warned that no future constitutional arrangement which neglected Muslim security would be acceptable to it.

The greatest victory of Muslim nationalism came in 1942, when the British War Cabinet accepted in principle the idea of Pakistan. The draft declaration brought by Sir Stafford Cripps to India in March contained a provision whereby any province could stay out of the proposed Indian Union, with the right to form its own independent government. This "non-accession clause" was a major, if not a complete, concession to the Pakistan demand. Though the League rejected the offer on the ground that the clause did not go far enough to produce the Pakistan it wanted, the fact remains that within two years of the Lahore Resolution the British Government officially and publicly accepted the principle of a partition of India.

After the failure of the Cripps mission (the Congress, too, had rejected the offer) the Congress was frustrated. Its bid to control India had come to naught, leaving it impatient and bitter. The result was the disturbances of August and September 1942, which Gandhi called an "open rebellion" and historians the "quit India movement". The revolt failed and all the Congress leaders were sent to prison, giving Jinnah a rare opportunity to consolidate the League. In Jinnah's opinion the revolt was a Hindu attempt to win India for the Hindus when the British were busy fighting a war; it was as much anti-Muslim as anti-British.

For the two years, from 1942 to 1944, when the Congress leadership was in prison (Gandhi was comfortably installed in the Aga Khan Palace in Poona), the Muslim League was building itself into a powerful party. A great majority of the Muslims now wanted Pakistan, and were seen to be wanting it. When Gandhi secured his release in the late summer of 1944 he saw no alternative to negotiating with the League.

The path to negotiation was first prepared by C. Rajagopalacharia, a front-rank Congress leader who alone among the Hindus was advocating a *rapprochement* with the League on the basis of partition. He prepared a formula in July 1944 which conceded the principle of Pakistan under two conditions: partition would come after the British withdrawal and it would be contingent upon the favourable outcome of a plebiscite of *all* inhabitants of the areas claimed by the Muslim League. The Gandhi–Jinnah talks took place in Bombay in September 1944, but failed to reconcile the differences between the two leaders. The heart of the matter was that the Muslims did not trust the Hindus, and refused to accept Gandhi's word that partition would be effected when the British had departed. Jinnah wanted his Pakistan then and there, before the British went, and had serious doubts if the Hindus would keep their word once India was free and the Congress was in power. Jinnah was also not ready to accept a plebiscite of *all* voters: it was the Muslims who demanded Pakistan, not non-Muslims.

In the following year another attempt at reconciliation was made, this time by the government. All political leaders were summoned to a conference in Simla by the Viceroy, Lord Wavell, and the official idea was to discuss the formation of an Executive Council (entirely Indian except for the Commander-in-Chief) from amongst the Indian parties "in proportion which would give a balanced representation of the main communities, including equal proportion of Muslims and Caste Hindus". The attempt failed because Jinnah not only wanted parity between the Muslims and the Hindus (which was conceded) but also insisted on the Muslim League nominating all Muslim councillors (which was not conceded).

The fact that the Congress accepted the principle of parity between Hindus and Muslims was a great victory for the League and a vindication of the two-nation theory. Hindus and Muslims were two separate nations coming together for the time being in the Viceroy's Council. The Muslims were no longer a minority asking for, or being fobbed off with, a debatable measure of representation: they were a nation entitled to equality with the other nation, the Hindus.

At least a partial reason for the failure of the Simla Conference was that both the Congress and the League had made claims about their representative standing unsupported by electoral evidence. No general election to the central legislature had been held since 1934, and none to the provincial assemblies since 1937. The balance of political power had shifted so much in ten years that new elections were imperative.

These elections were fought on the simplest conceivable programmes. The Muslim League contested to vindicate two elementary points: that it represented all Indian Muslims and that Pakistan was the only solution to the Indian problem. The Congress stood for an opposite principle: independence without partition and a united Indian nationalism. The results were very clear: the League won every single Muslim seat in the central legislature and 428 out of the possible 492 in the provinces; the Congress had similar success in the non-Muslim constituencies. The results were also confusing. The deadlock deepened. One party had stood for a united India and received strong support. The other had called for a divided India and had also received strong support. The cleavage ran as deep as ever.

In a final effort to reconcile the irreconcilables the British Government sent a Cabinet Mission to India in March 1946. It was headed by the Secretary of State for India, Lord Pethick-Lawrence, and its two members were Sir Stafford Cripps and A. V. (later Lord) Alexander. It found discussions with the leaders unfruitful, and published its own recommendations on 16 May.

The Cabinet Mission plan, as it came to be known, ruled out Pakistan as a practical possibility and suggested a Union of India controlling foreign affairs, defence, communications, and the finances required for these subjects. All other powers would belong to the provinces, which would be free to form groups with group executives and legislatures, and each group could determine which provincial subject should be taken in common. Any motion in the Union legislature which raised an important communal issue would require the consent of a majority of the representatives from each of the two major communities. The constitutions of the Union and the group were to be subject, at ten-year intervals, to reconsideration if demanded by any province. The three groups of provinces were: (a) Madras, Bombay, the United Provinces, the Central Provinces and Orissa; (b) the Punjab, North-West Frontier Province and Sind; and (c) Bengal and Assam. A constituent assembly, consisting of 292 members from the provinces and 93 from the native states, was proposed. Following the convening of the Constituent Assembly, the representatives of each of the three groups were to meet separately to decide the nature of their group constitutions. After this action the group representatives were to reassemble in a single body for the drafting of the Union constitution.

On 6 June the Muslim League accepted the plan, in the hope that it would ultimately result in the establishment of Pakistan. On 25 June the Congress accepted the long-term plan with reservations on certain vital points, but refused to accept the short-term plan of entering the interim government. On 16 June the Viceroy had announced that if any of the major parties refused to come into the government, he would proceed with its formation in co-operation with the party or groups that were prepared to join it. But when the Congress rejected the short-term plan on 25 June, the Viceroy, instead of forming a government with the help of the League and other parties which had accepted the whole plan, postponed the formation of the interim government. The League took this as a breach of promise and an unnecessary concession to the Congress.

At the same time, the Congress leaders were making intemperate speeches defining the position of the Congress in the plans for the transfer of authority in India. Jawaharlal Nehru declared that his party's actions in the Constituent Assembly depended entirely on its own free will. The Congress president supported him by announcing that the Constituent Assembly would be sovereign and would legislate for a united, not divided, India. These statements reduced the Congress's acceptance of the long-term plan to nonsense. The Viceroy had also failed to keep his word about the formation of the interim government. Muslims felt that their worst fears were being realized and that they were facing a Hindu-British front. On 27 July the Muslim League reversed its acceptance of the plan and announced that the time had come to resort to "direct action" to achieve Pakistan.

Meanwhile, the Congress had changed its mind and accepted the short-term plan. The Viceroy at once invited it to form the interim government, and this administration took office in September. The Muslims protested and put up black flags atop their houses and shops. It was not till 15 October that the League revised its decision and entered the interim government.

The Constituent Assembly was scheduled to hold its first meeting on 9 December, but the League asked for its postponement so that discussions could be held on the vexed question of the grouping clause. The Congress interpreted this provision to mean that each province had the right to decide both as to its grouping and as to its own constitution. To overcome this impasse the British Government invited the Viceroy, Jinnah, Liaquat Ali Khan, Nehru and Baldev Singh to come to London to settle the controversy. The talks failed, and the British Government reaffirmed that the Muslim League's interpretation was the right one, viz., that the decision of the assembly's sections on provincial constitutions and grouping should be taken by a simple majority vote of each section. But the Congress still refused to accept the official construction, and demanded that the League should either enter the Constituent Assembly on the Congress interpretation of the grouping clause or resign from the interim government. The League refused to quit the government and boycotted the assembly on the ground that it was the Congress that had refused the official interpretation of the grouping clause.

Faced with such an acute difference of opinion, and unwilling to compel the Congress to accept the official interpretation, the British Government announced on 20 February 1947 its intention to withdraw from India by June 1948; and it replaced Wavell with Lord Mountbatten as Viceroy.

When the new Viceroy reached India on 22 March, he found the country in a state of virtual civil war. His appointment was greatly welcomed by the Congress and his relations with Nehru were very good even before his arrival (they had met earlier in Malaya). He proved a good friend. After meeting all major leaders he drew up a plan for the division of India and transfer of power. On 10 May he showed it to Nehru, and to no other leader. Nehru was furious and insisted on substantial modifications. Therefore, V. P. Menon, a South Indian Hindu constitutional advisor to the Viceroy, was asked to draft a new plan immediately with the Congress objections in view. Such a plan was ready in exactly four hours on 21 May 1947. Both Lord Ismay, the Viceroy's Chief of Staff, and Sir George Abell, the Viceroy's Personal Secretary, opposed the new scheme, but Mountbatten put all his weight behind it and threatened to resign if it was not accepted by the Cabinet. He had his way, and the India-Burma Committee of the Cabinet approved it without the alteration of a comma. Attlee and his Cabinet sanctioned it in a Cabinet meeting which lasted exactly five minutes.

The final plan made according to Congress wishes was announced on 2 June in Delhi as the British offer. According to it, the Muslim provinces not represented in the Constituent Assembly would vote to determine whether their constitution was to be formed by the existing Constituent Assembly or by a new one. On 3 June both the parties accepted the plan, and on 4 July the Indian Independence Bill was introduced in the British Parliament, becoming law on 15 July. Power was formally transferred to the two new Dominions on 15 August 1947.

By no means had the Aga Khan's concentration on India and European peace prospects meant a lack of interest in the continent and people of Africa. The European powers had partitioned Africa at the conference held in Berlin in 1884–5. In the following few decades the task of colonization was completed, the fruits of imperial advance were reaped and consolidated, and the continent was incorporated into an international economic system shaped and controlled by the Western conquerors. The twentieth century saw unprecedented social and economic changes which transformed the entire scene and revolutionized African societies: transportation networks, monetization of economies, marketing structures, urbanization, migration from the rural areas, rise and spread of a Western system of education, import of Western values, birth of a working class, and the emergence of a new and untraditional élite which had received Western education and had been exposed to Western values. The various rebellions and constitutional movements which appeared on the political scene in the 1940s and 1950s to wrest the control of affairs from the colonial masters were the logical results of the awareness created among the people by the new education and values brought into the continent by the West.

In different fields and on different occasions, but with a consistence born of a vision, the Aga Khan spoke about, commented upon, advised on and tackled the problems of the African people with his usual diplomatic skill and long experience of dealing with the British and other policy makers. Race relations, African development, educational improvement, economic advance, Muslim interests, patriotism – nothing escaped his attention. References are made to all these matters in the following pages. Here it is sufficient to remember that the Aga Khan lived through this entire period of change, convulsion and human advance – he became the 48th *Imam* of the Ismailis in 1885, the year of the imperial partition of Africa, and died in 1957, the year Gold Coast (now Ghana), became the first British colony in Africa to acquire independence.

The Statesman

In spite of his moderate opinions and his firm refusal to join the extremist critics of British rule in India, the Aga Khan had a sure grasp of the complexities of the political situation and the problems awaiting the attention of both the Indians and the British.

Contemplating the contours of Indian discontent in the early part of this century, he wrote, "The flight of time has been rapid in India's history, and it is still too little realized that each succeeding generation demands an advance on what its predecessor knew and enjoyed. It is this advance or progress which India has achieved under British rule that creates one of the problems for British policy." *Sati* (the practice whereby a wife threw herself upon the funeral pyre of her deceased husband) was prohibited and a ban was imposed on slavery, torture and mutilation. "The tendency of these interventions is to raise the standard of humanitarian feeling and sentiment. It is thus idle to express surprise when the Indian himself having imbibed these feelings, shows in his Press and in his life, that he wishes to live up to Western standards. The educational policy of the Government of India adopted in response to the persistent urgings of Sir Charles Wood, and dating from 1854, is largely responsible for modern ambitions and the longing for a larger place in the government of their own country."[1]

Some of the suggestions he made for the removal of this discontent were startlingly fresh. He called upon the government to change the rules of appointment and transfer of British officials serving in India, with a view to making those men more knowledgeable, almost experts, about their own area or territory. A civil servant or engineer or doctor who made his home for the duration of his stay in India in one of the provinces would inevitably be more cognizant of its problems, more friendly with its inhabitants and more interested in its welfare, than his colleagues or predecessors who arrived and left at regular short intervals.

The Aga Khan tendered this advice in the context of education. The Government ought to educate the Indians to make them better citizens. But at the same time, it should also educate those who tended the machinery of governance and kept the whole mechanism in good trim. "The aphorism that education never ceases is true", he wrote, "or should be true, not only of the Indian student, but also of those English officials who do such excellent work throughout the Indian Dependency. I have written of the necessity for uniformity of standard and equality of opportunity in education throughout each province. Could it not also be arranged that upon entering the Indian Civil Service the young officer should be notified that, save in exceptional circumstances and cases, his life's work will be confined not only to the particular province to which he is posted, but as far as possible to one section of the province? This will encourage and justify the civilian in studying local languages and customs in much more detail than is at present possible. A great deal would thus be done to promote that personal contact between the British administrators and the Indian people of their districts, on which the future progress and contentment of the country largely

---

[1] "Some Aspects of Indian Reforms", *National Review*, December 1909.

depends. There would flow from this closer knowledge greater sympathy, coupled with better understanding of the aims and objects which the more advanced Indians have in view. . . . In this way both in the realm of education and of administration the government have it in their power to standardize and organize British India. Equality of education and unformity of standard will have been combined with a most desirable system of keeping the Indian administrators in touch with the people and the problems best known to them."[1]

It will surprise those who insist on seeing the Aga Khan as nothing but a loyal subject of the British Empire to know that he had always been a strong advocate of self-government for the subcontinent. He gave this demand such a high priority that in the only full-length political testament he wrote in the winter of 1917–18 he devoted one of his longest chapters to a discussion of the reasons justifying the Indian demand for self-rule.

The British should not, he said, view the support given to them by Indians during World War One as an acquiescence to whatever political system they chose to impose on India, but as an intent of friendship based on equality of treatment and sharing of power. This attitude of sympathy and sanguine expectation "cannot last unless changes are introduced in the administration so as to give the people a fuller share and voice in the control of affairs in their own country".[2]

He viewed Indian demands in the context of what was happening in the world at large. "China and the Russias are republics, with nominally the most democratic forms of government, and Persia and Turkey both claim to be considered constitutional monarchies. Thus, in India alone we have a Government that is not only in practice free from internal parliamentary control, but is actually based on the principle that final decisions are in the hands of an administration not responsible to the people, although some opportunities for criticism are given in the Viceregal and provincial legislatures. The contradictory position of the Government leads to its being open to attack from all quarters, and yet to its being considered anomalous that Indians, alone of the great Eastern peoples, should have no control over their administration." Now there was a general feeling "throughout the length and breadth of India that, when the cause of liberty as represented by the Allied armies has led

---

[1] "India's Education and Her Future Position in the Empire", *National Review*, July 1911.
[2] *India in Transition*, June 1918.

humanity through victory to peace, the structure of Indian administration also may be brought into line with the spirit of the times and a reasonable share of control and supervision be given to the Indian public".[1]

He gave yet more examples of lands and territories marching on the road to democracy, and wondered how Great Britain could possibly discriminate against India. "If we turn to the Native States", he said with some exasperation, "and to the fully or semi-independent countries, such as Afghanistan and Nepal and the Arabian principalities, we find a general recognition on the part of the authorities that the time is coming for sharing their powers with the ruled. The best administered of the Native States and most of the princes desire to establish some form of legislative or other constitutional government. . . . In Afghanistan some attempt, howsoever nominal, has been made by the present King to lay the foundation of a representative institution. In fact everywhere in South Asia we find local forces striving, if sometimes unconsciously, after forms of administration more or less modern in character and leading to association and co-operation between the sovereign power and the nation. It follows that however excellent the present administration of India may be, however efficient and suited to the conditions of the recent past, it is not for the people of England to deny to their great Eastern Empire those forms of constitutionalism which were first developed in Britain and with the manifestations of which, whether in infancy or vigorous growth, England has always sympathized in the case of other countries on the European, American, and Asiatic continents."[2]

In 1913, he had declared that for him self-government was "an ideal involving many decades of effort towards self-improvement, towards social reform, towards educational diffusion and towards complete amity between various communities."[3] In 1918, he regretted that there were some statesmen in England who were "ready to trust Japan and accept her as a full equal, exhibiting a strange lack of confidence in the King's Indian subjects, for which there is no single justifying fact in history."[4] He wanted the British Empire of the future to "confer full self-government on the peoples she has trained for the responsibility".[5]

[1] *Ibid.*
[2] *Ibid.*
[3] Speech at the Fifth Annual General Meeting of the London Muslim League, London, 14 July 1913.
[4] *India in Transition*, 1918, p. 292.
[5] *Ibid.*, p. 293.

More than a quarter of a century later, and on the eve of the independence of India, he warned the British that it was neither politic nor moral for them to impose a constitution on India. It was for the people of the country to decide and determine their future. "It has been suggested", he said in March 1945, "that Britain should make an immediate announcement to the effect that a year after the end of hostilities, power in India should be handed over to the Indian political parties provided that they reach agreement between themselves. Failing this agreement, Britain, it has been suggested, should make an award to India of Dominion status by Act of Parliament and draw up a constitution, according to British ideas. I cannot deprecate the latter suggestion too strongly; it would be the ultimate humiliation. You cannot force ideals on a people from without, and it would be far preferable for Britain herself to insist upon retaining governing power and responsibility, as at present, than to try and force her essentially foreign ideals permanently on India's growth. This must come from the people of India themselves ... to impose a constitution from without would violate the self-respect of all parties."[1]

But these parties were separated by geography, race, religion, language and political ideals. The Aga Khan was aware of the fact that the happy consummation he desired was being frustrated by two major factors. India's political advance to self-government, self-determination and ultimate independence was retarded by her multi-dimensional heterogeneity and the Hindu–Muslim conflict.

To take the religious clash first, the Aga Khan was, from the beginning of modern politics till about 1945, a consistent supporter of Hindu–Muslim co-operation. Again and again, whether he was addressing a purely Muslim meeting or a general Indian gathering, he emphasized the urgent importance, the vital necessity, of communal peace and harmony. He used every argument to state his case: political, economic, social, religious.

"I have no hesitation in asserting", he warned the Muslim League in 1910, "that unless Hindus and Mohammedans co-operate with each other in the general development of the country as a whole and in all matters affecting their mutual interests, neither will develop to the full its legitimate aspirations or give full scope to its possibilities. In order to develop their common economic and other interests, both should remember

---

[1] Interview with the *East African Standard*, Nairobi, 26 March 1945.

that one is the elder sister of the other, and that India is their common parent. . . . We must determine what are the interests that we have in common with the Hindus, and co-operate for their advancement; then remember the measures necessary for the removal of our peculiar ills, and again help each other in removing them."[1]

At the end of the same year, he told *The Times of India* that "he considered no catastrophe so great as disunion and rupture between the two great communities" which "were component parts of a body politic, and creatures of one God. Hindus and Mohammedans were like two arms of a nation – they could not sacrifice nor injure one without weakening the other. Their united efforts were necessary for the good of the country, for its peaceful and orderly development . . . it was the sacred duty of both sides to work whole-heartedly, and with single devotion, for promoting measures that would secure the lasting welfare of the country." He considered "no sacrifice too great, no efforts too arduous, to secure friendliness between the sister communities. . . . They required each other's co-operation, good-will, and practical help in promoting social and industrial measures." He promised to "do what lay in his power to advance the noble mission of conciliation: for India could not develop to its full, legitimate, and natural dimensions until all forces worked harmoniously as a whole, and until all warring elements were set at rest once and for all."[2]

In the course of a lecture delivered in London in mid–1911 he declared that his ideal was "the building up of an Indian nationhood in which religious and racial differences will be largely forgotten and overshadowed by the sentiment of geographical and political or national unity". The Muslims of India "are bound to incline to self-organization and self-expression" on grounds of history, sentiment, morality and religion. But "at the same time, the great economic developments in progress and the intellectual forces of modern civilization must work upon their minds in favour of the evolution of Indian nationality. The task of statesmanship will be to reconcile these apparently opposing factors, or, at all events, not to allow them to come into conflict injurious to the common interests and the general welfare."[3]

Addressing the London Muslim League in mid–1913 he even

---

[1] Inaugural Address, All India Muslim League, Delhi, 29 January 1910.
[2] Interview, *The Times of India*, Bombay, 23 December 1910.
[3] Lecture, London, 3 July 1911.

went to the extent of asking the Muslims to voluntarily give up ritual cow slaughter in order to win the hearts of the Hindus. The Muslims must realize "how far they can go in evoking and strengthening Hindu goodwill by voluntarily abandoning the public slaughter of cows for sacrifice". The question was mainly economic, and it could be tackled by committees composed of Muslims and rich Hindus which would raise subscriptions for the purchase of other animals to be sacrificed in substitution of kine. The two communities should also make friends on the social level. Where inter-dining was not possible because of Hindu caste prohibitions, the two should meet in games and sports. "Play is instinctive in young life in India as elsewhere. I believe that with due organization there can be spread among our youth everywhere the *camaraderie* of the playing ground, and that social knowledge and goodwill is to be attained in India largely along the lines of the physical culture of our young people."[1]

He repeated his suggestion about cow sacrifice before the largest and most representative Muslim assemblage in December 1928. Delivering his presidential address at the inaugural session of the All India Muslim Conference in Delhi, he said that the origin of ritual animal sacrifice, made to emulate and remember the great sacrifice of Abraham, showed that cows were not sacrificed by the early prophets and communities, nor was the sacrifice of a bovine enjoined in any religious text. "How many of our Hajis have sacrificed cows in Arabia, the home of Islam?" he asked. He quoted the example of Amır Habibullah, the ruler of Afghanistan, who had discountenanced the practice. He asked the '*ulema* to ponder the point and guide the community. But the least that the Muslims could do was to abstain from parading the cow in public places before slaughtering it. Many other communities ate beef, but they did not hurt the sensibilities of their neighbours by parading the animal, sacred to and adored by the Hindus, before eating it.[2]

No Muslim leader could go further, and none did, in his respect for Hindu religious sentiment, and in his efforts to persuade his people to cultivate and befriend the Hindus, even at the cost of a major act of self-abnegation by promising to forego a well-established local ritual convention.

Diversity formed the second hurdle in the way of Indian constitutional evolution, and the Aga Khan offered the solution of federalism to remove it. But a federal arrangement was to be

---

[1] Speech, London Muslim League, London, 14 July 1913.
[2] Presidential Address, All India Muslim Conference, Delhi, 31 December 1928.

preceded by a radical and far-reaching re-organization of the provinces.[1]

He rejected the idea of subdividing the existing provinces into a large number of self-governing states. Small administrative units would "narrow down" the national effort. At the minimum the province must be equal to a medium European state. The Bengal Presidency, as composed in 1918, was "a good example of suitable and reasonably homogenous area" to receive federal autonomy. Burma was too ethnically distinct and integrated to be split. In all other major provinces readjustment was necessary. A few districts of the Central Provinces should be merged with Bihar. The Hindi-speaking districts of the Nagpur division were to form part of the United Provinces; some western districts of the latter were to be given over to the Punjab on grounds of affinity. With the disappearance of the Central Provinces its Marhatti-speaking divisions would fall to Bombay. The Madras Presidency was to stay unchanged, except that its most north-western districts would go to Bombay. Of course, Bombay would lose Sind; and Sind, Baluchistan and the North-West Frontier Province were to be merged to form a new large province to be called the Indus Province with Quetta as its capital. In terms of language, Bombay would contain Marhatti- and Gujerati-speaking populations, and Madras the Tamil- and Telugu-speaking people. Elsewhere each province would be a linguistic unit. "Everywhere beyond the areas where it is the principal vernacular Urdu would be the recognized home tongue of the Mohamedans." Such a scheme of redistribution would produce "much greater approximation than at present to provinces which would honestly be called nationalities, each having an importance and coherence ranking with those of at least some European States."[2]

In 1924 he pointed out that one of the reasons for the failure of the Montagu-Chelmsford reforms was the fact that some of the provinces under dyarchy were "miniature Indias, in the sense that they lack the characteristics of being linguistic and economic units". The existing configuration resulted in "costly administration and unnecessary friction."[3]

With her vast population, varied provinces and races and religious differences, a unitary government for India was evidently impossible. Already, under an administrative system in which the executive was not responsible to the people and an

---

[1] See p. 61 below.
[2] *India in Transition*, June 1918.
[3] Article, London, 13 April 1924.

elaborate bureaucratic system was firmly in place, the provincial governments had been increasingly complaining of excessive interference and of being kept in leading strings by the Government of India. On the other hand, under a federal arrangement, "the diversified problems of education, sanitation, public works, commerce and industry would be solved by each State in a natural, healthy way". Each would develop itself sufficiently to become an "independent and worthy" member of the South Asiatic Federation which the Aga Khan now proposed[1] (and to which I will turn a little later). This was written just before the Montagu-Chelmsford Report was published. Years did not change his conviction, and on the eve of the appearance of the Simon Report he again warned that "unless the findings of the Commission are based on an association or federation of Indian free States . . . then, God help them! They will simply be reaping more Dead Sea fruit."[2]

The creation of this "internal federation" was to mark the beginning of the formation of a much wider confederation. Afghanistan would be the first country to seek association with it. Then the group of small principalities from Arabia and the southern littoral of the Persian Gulf would ultimately become members of a union "that would ensure peace and liberty, freedom and order to the south of Asia". Persia herself would be attracted. Then the northward thrust of the federation would in time take it to the boundaries of China when Nepal, Bhutan and Tibet attached themselves to it; in the south, Ceylon would naturally be a member. The making of this great federal fabric was to be without any compulsion, direct or indirect. "In a word", he concluded, "the path of beneficent and growing union must be based on a federal India, with every member exercising her individual rights, her historic peculiarities and natural interests, yet protected by a common defensive system and customs union from external danger and economic exploitation by stronger forces. . . . We can build a great South Asiatic federation by now laying the foundations wide and deep on justice, on liberty, and on recognition for every race, every religion, and every historical entity."[3]

In a detailed criticism of the Nehru Report in October 1928 he reverted to the Indian problem of her future constitutional and political system. He rejected the proposal of a unitary and

[1] *India in Transition*, June 1918.
[2] Interview, *Daily Express*, London, 1 May 1929.
[3] *India in Transition*, June 1918.

non-federal India made by the Indian National Congress and the Hindu Mahasabha in the Nehru Report. "The country", he said, "must accept in all its consequences its own inevitable diversities, not only religious and historical, but also national and linguistic." Advancing from the conventional federal principle, he now prescribed a more radical cure for the heterogeneity inherent in India. This was his significant and promising plan of Free States of India, based on the model of the German Empire of the pre–1918 years. "Each Indian province must enjoy to the full the freedom and independence of, say, Bavaria, in the years before the Great War. The Indian Free States would resemble the self-governing British Dominions in being ultimately held together by the bond of monarchy, represented by the present British Sovereign and his heirs."

He was confident that with his proposal, if honestly accepted by all parties, "almost all the difficulties in the way of a Swaraj [free] India would sooner or later be overcome". Each free state, he pointed out, "would be based, not on considerations of size, but on those of religion, nationality, race and language – plus history". For example, Burma would be one state; East Bengal (Muslim) and West Bengal (Hindu) two separate states; all the Marhatta territories would form one state; where a distinct race, like the Gujeratis, occupied a relatively small area it would still receive the status of a free state. The Muslim provinces of the north and the west would coalesce and make "one important free state".

The creation of these free states would largely solve the problem of the minorities. The compact bodies of Muslims in the north-west and the east would have free states of their own; where they were in small minorities they would have some guarantees of fair play "in the fact of propinquity by language and residence to their Hindu neighbours, and also by being too small numerically to bid for political control". Moreover, these states would not be mere provinces liable to be overruled by a central government in which the Hindus had an unalterable majority. "They would be secure from all kinds of interference, except in matters in which they would be freely associated with other states and . . . these would be few and far between." Each of the larger native states, like Hyderabad, Kashmir or Mysore, could be a free state in its own right; groups of smaller ones, like those of Kathiawar, Rajputana or Central India, could "confederate" among themselves and enter the union as free units. The Aga Khan emphasized the great advantage of the scheme for the

Muslims. "By freeing the Muslim majorities in the North-West and East from ultimate Hindu control it will give them something worth having. Glaring injustice to any community is improbable, because nowhere in the free states of India will one nationality, race, religion or historical unit be at the mercy of a semi-foreign majority dictating its orders from a distance."[1]

Four days later he explained that these free states shall have their own armies in time of peace as well as their own railways. He could not conceive, he wrote, that the great native states or the Muslim provinces would enter the proposed system on any other terms.[2]

This federation or association of free states would be "equal to the other units of the British Empire as it exists at present", and each state would possess "economic and military freedom". The territories would be "nationalistic free States [created] on historical and linguistic foundations", and as such would eventually remove the Hindu–Muslim conflict.[3] British India, he again pointed out a little later, was "ramshackle" in its grouping. "I cannot conceive of any final and satisfactory solution of the Hindu-Muslim question except by the establishment of federalism on nationalistic, racial, and linguistic principles." It is significant that he called the Marhattas and the Sindhis, and by clear implication all such groups, nations.[4]

In spite of his earnest appeals and endeavours for amity and peace between the Hindus and Muslims, the Aga Khan was keenly aware of the depth and sharpness of the differences separating the two peoples. On several occasions he pointed out the historical and other factors which created the conflict, thus presenting a reasoned and logically developed theory of two nations on which, later, the Muslim League was to base its demand for a Pakistan and, still later, the subcontinent was to be divided at the time of independence.

Referring to the communal riots of 1927–32, he said that they were due largely to "the action of the dominant Hindu political organization in endeavouring to force its will upon the Musulmans, in obstructing the Administration, and in raising the standard of civil disobedience, whereby political ill-will has been created. Moslem citizens who have resisted the tyranny of boycotts

---

[1] "A Constitution for India: II", *The Times*, London, 13 October 1928.
[2] Letter, *The Times*, London, written on 17 October 1928.
[3] Interview, *Daily Express*, London, 1 May 1929.
[4] "British Policy in India", *The Times*, London, 7 November 1929.

and *hartals* have been attacked and have suffered severe loss in trade and property."[1]

It was in 1902–4, he recalled, that he had begun to realize that the Indian National Congress, the only active and responsible political organization in the country, was proving itself incapable of representing the Muslims or dealing adequately or even justly with their needs and aspirations. The reason was that the pressure of Hindu extremism was too strong. "Already the artificial unity which the British Raj had imposed from without was cracking. Deep-seated and ineradicable differences expressed themselves once political activity and aspirations had advanced beyond the most elementary stage. The breach was there – in Hindu intransigence and lack of perception of basic Muslim ideals and hopes. I did all I could to prevent the breach being widened. I maintained a campaign of remonstrance with Sir Pherozeshah Mehta . . . I begged him to use his influence and make Congress realize how important it was to win Muslim confidence; but all to no avail."[2]

Between 1902 and 1905, he wrote, the Indian National Congress, "by its blindness to legitimate claims and aspirations, and by its persistence in its ridiculous habit of choosing Muslim yesmen from Madras and Bombay as its representatives on the Viceroy's Legislative Council, lost a great opportunity which was not to recur". These were critical years "in that vast and complex process which brought about, in little more than forty years, the partition of the Indian subcontinent".[3]

This realization of the dimensions of the conflict led the Aga Khan to mount a campaign in favour of Muslim separatism. This was done simultaneously on two different levels. He led a deputation of prominent and representative Muslims to the Viceroy in October 1906, which argued for a political and constitutional recognition from the official quarters of a separate identity for the Muslim community. In the December of the same year, with Nawab Salimullah of Dacca and Nawab Muhsin-ul-Mulk, he founded the All India Muslim League. Between 1906 and 1909 he concentrated solely on fighting for the attainment of separate electorates, which he regarded as a sure constitutional manifestation of a separate identity for the Muslims.

Both these steps – the demanding of separate electorates and the formation of the Muslim League – had suggested themselves

[1] Letter, *The Times*, London, 7 June 1932.
[2] *Memoirs*, 1954.
[3] *Ibid.*

to him during his visit to Aligarh in 1906. He communicated his ideas to Muhsin-ul-Mulk, who arranged for the Simla Deputation. This "was the starting point of the recognition of the principle that the important Muslim minority in this country should have its fair and legitimate share in the administration of the country",[1] for "Lord Minto's acceptance of our demands was the foundation of all future constitutional proposals made for India by successive British Governments and its final, inevitable consequence was the partition of India and the emergence of Pakistan".[2]

The deputation had won the sympathy and support of Lord Minto, but the translation of its demand into parliamentary statute was in the hands of John Morley, the Secretary of State for India. All the evidence that we have shows that it was entirely due to the persistent and deft efforts of the Aga Khan and Sayyid Ameer Ali in London between 1907 and 1909 that Morley and the British Cabinet were persuaded, against their will, to concede separate electorates to the Muslims. The struggle during the making of the Minto-Morley reforms was, as the Aga Khan recorded in his reminiscences, nothing short of laying the foundations of Pakistan.

The arguments which the Aga Khan set out with lucidity and passion in equal measure during this campaign of persuasion and conversion give us a unique opportunity to grasp his thinking. He still believed in a future united India, but one in which the Muslims had a place worthy of their past history and present position. "But while holding the ideal of a united people in India with strength and earnestness, I hold no less strongly that in framing the new political order of things statesmanship must take account of the wide differences which separate Hindus and Musulmans at the present time. These differences are not only religious, they are historical and physical, and in the latter respect, at least, they soon become marked, even in the case of recent converts to the Moslem faith. The changes of dietary habits, outlook, and social life generally consequent upon such conversion soon tell upon body and mind, as has often been pointed out. When I reflect upon the great distinctions between the two races – distinctions more or less known to every one familiar with India – I have to admit that fulfilment of the ideal of homogeneity lies in a future so distant that it is quite beyond me to predict the date of its arrival." The "existing divisions will

[1] Inaugural Address, All India Muslim League, Delhi, 29 January 1910.
[2] *Memoirs*, 1954.

be widened instead of being bridged if at the present stage, by political machinery provided by the Sovereign power, one element in the population is placed in a position to dictate its will to the other elements. An Act of Parliament cannot weld into one, by electoral machinery, two nationalities so distinct as the Hindus and the Mohamedans. The former is a vast conservative and widely-varying federation, while Islam is a proselytizing and unifying faith, so closely corresponding in doctrine and ritual with Judaism that it is much nearer in spirit and origin to Christianity than it is to Hinduism. With such vast differences existing, it is certain that if one element gets excessive political power, or is in a position to dictate its will on the other, it will always not only be liable but compelled by religious and social circumstances to exert that authority."[1]

He told the British Government that "it was impossible anywhere, and least of all in a country like India, to work a constitutional scheme satisfactorily with one large and important section of the people disappointed and left without real representation, and another section exultant and triumphant because they had been permitted to attain a virtual monopoly of political representation".[2]

In his *Memoirs* he summarized the hostility with which he had to contend before getting Morley to accept the system of separate electorates. "John Morley, with his liberal background and outlook, of the purest theoretical and academic kind, was extremely reluctant to accept the principle of separate electoral representation for the Muslims. It went against the grain of his character. . . . For Syed Amir Ali and myself, 1907 was a period of what I can best describe as guerilla warfare, whose aim was to keep Morley up to the mark. We won in the end, but it was hard going."[3]

Because of Hindu opposition and British reluctance the case for separate electorates had to be pleaded again in 1918, at the time of the Montagu-Chelmsford reforms, and once again in 1930–35 when the last reforms fashioned by the British were on the anvil. On each occasion the Aga Khan was the foremost among those who argued for the continuation and enlargement of the concession granted in 1909.

In 1918 the Aga Khan explained that his scheme of a provincial reorganization in India was not inconsistent with a separate elec-

[1] Interview, *The Times*, London, 14 February 1909.
[2] Speech, London Muslim League, London, 24 June 1909.
[3] *Memoirs*, 1954.

toral system. Statesmen legislate to meet actual rather than ideal conditions, he said. "The various religions, communities, castes, et cetera, within each province have very much in common, something national in effort and aspiration, that will meet the difficulty of separate communal representation in practical working and in time. On the other hand, the smaller communities by being assured from the first of their voice in affairs will feel growing confidence in the autonomous system, and the self-respect and self-confidence so necessary to the backward classes in India will steadily grow. There will be awakened in them an enthusiasm for great public interests that now lies dormant, and an increasing fellow-feeling with the leading communities."[1]

During the three Round Table Conferences he went on trying to convince the Hindu delegates – and, on one occasion, Gandhi himself – of the value of separate electorates to the Muslims and other minorities, but here he was tilling barren soil. However, he won the final battle both in the conference, when the Prime Minister, Ramsay MacDonald, gave his Communal Award, and in the Joint Committee on Indian Constitutional Reform where he was assisted by men like Zafrullah Khan and Abdullah Yusuf Ali.

He told the Indian press in February 1934 that "the present communal electorates would have to be accepted by all the parties concerned", and that "it would be a sheer waste of time and energy to strive to get the Communal Award altered, so long as an equally good if not better alternative scheme, which would satisfy all sections of political opinion, was not put forward before the country".[2]

In presenting the case for separate Muslim electorates the Aga Khan was doing nothing less than arguing in favour of a two-nation theory according to which the Muslims of India formed one nation or nationality and the rest of the Indians another such group.

Already in 1905 he had come to the conclusion that "our only hope lay along the lines of independent organisation and action, and that we must secure independent political recognition from the British Government as a nation within a nation".[3] In 1907–9, in the course of his campaign during the making of the Morley-Minto reforms, he had referred to the Indian Muslims as a nationality. In 1928 he asserted that the Muslims of India "are not a community, but in a restricted, special sense a nation

[1] *India in Transition,* June 1918.
[2] Press interview, New Delhi, 7 February 1934.
[3] *Memoirs,* 1954.

composed of many communities and [a] population totally out-numbering the total even of the pre-war German Empire."[1]

In his *India in Transition*, 1918, he set out a plan of a huge federation of South Asia with India as its nucleus. He began with the assumption that India, "with her vast population, her varied provinces and races, her many sectarian differences (brought to the surface by the present search for the lines of constitutional advance)", would never be fit for "a unilateral[2] form of free government. Constitutional reform should be so worked out that the provinces were groomed ultimately to make up a genuine Indian Federation. ". . . for some years to come each Indian province in the critical stages of federalism, must have a constitution that provides, on the one hand, for an independent and strong executive, responsible to the Viceroy and the Secretary of State for tenure of office and appointment; and, on the other, for elective assemblies to control finance and legislation. Thus will be built up the future United States of India within the British Empire."

Coming to the question of the shape and size of the provinces he proposed some very significant changes. As we noted earlier he was strongly opposed to what he called "the suggested sub-division of the existing provinces into a considerable number of self-governing states". The general criterion he had in mind was the unit of provincial self-government being equal "at least to a medium European state". Bengal, as then constituted, was a good example of a "suitable and reasonably homogeneous" area for federal autonomy. Punjab, Sind and the Indus Provinces were cited as other examples.[3]

He believed that "by such a scheme of redistribution there would be much greater approximation than at present to provinces which could honestly be called nationalities, each having an importance and coherence ranking with those of at least some European States". This "internal federation" would then slowly develop and expand into a South Asian Federation embracing a very large area.[4]

In this scheme the Aga Khan is as yet far from presenting or defending the two-nation theory (that was to come later). He is still thinking along the lines of territorial nationalism and

[1] Presidential Address, All India Muslim Conference, Delhi, 31 December 1928.
[2] He was using the word "unilateral" in its old sense; today we would call it "unitary".
[3] See p. 53 above.
[4] *India in Transition*, 1918, pp. 37–46.

regional loyalties. He believes that the Indian provinces would, according to his plan, mature into "nationalities". From the Muslim point of view, the most significant suggestion is for the creation of a large Muslim province, by amalgamating Sind, Baluchistan and the North-West Frontier Province. Iqbal was later to develop this idea into a scheme for a yet larger Muslim province including the Punjab. Still later Chaudhri Rahmat Ali was to go beyond both the Aga Khan and Iqbal in proposing a completely independent Muslim federation of all these north-western provinces plus Kashmir to be called Pakistan.

But ten years on, the Aga Khan recommended a substantially different plan in which religion and history took the place of territory as guiding principles, and the setting up of a Muslim state was indicated. Apart from the sweeping force of events which had the strength to thaw the chill off the most conservative ideas still held by many Muslim politicians, the immediate cause of this change in the Aga Khan's views was the publication of the Nehru Report. The Indian National Congress and the Hindu Mahasabha, in co-operation with some minor and insignificant groups, had produced this report and declared it to be the blueprint for the future constitution of the subcontinent. The framers of this Nehru Constitution had, with studied arrogance and incredible shortsightedness, dismissed from their consideration all Muslim safeguards which were by then a part of the established arrangements and hardly open to renewed controversy. They had also rejected the Muslim demand for a genuine federal structure, not realizing in the zeal of their 'nationalist' faith that Muslims were already on the point of forsaking even federalism and embracing partition as the only acceptable solution of the minority problem in India.

In response to the Nehru Report, the Aga Khan wrote two articles for *The Times* in which, using unusually strong language, he attacked it as impracticable, shortsighted and silly; it was an attempt by the Hindus to keep the Muslims out of the mainstream of Indian political and national life for all times.

Enumerating the major failings of the report, he feared that the establishment of a unitary government would aggravate all the most serious problems of Indian politics; in addition, it would reduce the Native States to mere districts. On the Muslim question, the report did not contain anything even worth considering. "It is difficult to conceive how serious-minded people, knowing the facts of the present situation . . . can imagine that the Muhammadans as a body are ever likely to accept the proposals of the

Report." Muslims were not prepared to give up the existing guarantees and accept, in their place, an all-India government, very much on the lines of the British imperial structure in New Delhi, yet without its safeguards. Political freedom meant that "peoples should govern themselves and not have an outside authority imposed on them – whether it be that of a British electorate or that of an Executive controlled by an Indian Parliament at Delhi or Simla, inevitably accentuating the dominance in India as a whole of a particular racial or cultural portion".

Some of the consequences of adopting the constitution prescribed by the report would be far-reaching and even disastrous. Burma, not wishing to be dictated to by a Hindu India, would demand separation and the British would find it difficult to refuse it. The future territorial or political unity of India would be imperilled, probably beyond salvage. When British control was gone it was not conceivable that "great and compact races like the Mahrattas, the Bengalis, or the Muhammadans of the north-west and Sind would accept the control of a Central Executive and Legislature". Once the authorities in Delhi began to dictate to peoples which did not share the policies and aims of the centre, "the aggrieved party would be justified, at least where it is territorially preponderant, in insisting on its freedom, and this demand would be based on the very principle of self-determination which was now being invoked against the continuance of British rule. The demand for 'self-determination' can express itself in many forms against even a Swaraj majority among strata of peoples as varied in their outlook and standards as are the peoples of India."

The criticism levelled against the Nehru Report by the Aga Khan was not merely negative. After indicating the serious and more glaring weaknesses of the report, he made his own constructive proposals aimed at solving the communal and regional problems facing India. He took the pre–1914 Bavaria as his model for framing the future arrangements. "Each Indian province must enjoy to the full the freedom and independence" of old Bavaria. The provinces would thus be converted into "Free States", resembling the self-governing British Dominions, and "ultimately held together by the bond of Monarchy, represented by the present British Sovereign and his heirs" (the reader will do well to remember that this was the exact configuration of the British Commonwealth till 1948, when India and Pakistan demanded a change). The existing provinces were not to be accepted as entities for this treatment. Extensive re-casting and re-grouping were called for, and this was to be done on new principles. "Each free state would be based, not on considerations of size, but on those of religion, nationality, race and language – plus history." He then specially referred to the Muslim areas and looked forward to a state of their own. ". . . the Muslim provinces of the North and the West would probably coalesce and make one important free state." He made it clear that these free states were not going to make up an Indian federation: that would not have been a very novel idea, and events and convictions had already rendered it obsolete. "The free states would not be mere provinces with Legislatures and Executives liable to be overruled by a Central Government in which the Hindus would have a permanent majority. They would be secure from all kinds of interference, except in matters in which they would be freely associated with the other states."[1]

Evidently the Aga Khan had made a long journey since 1918. This is the most radical plan we have got from any influential Muslim figure so far. Its radicalism is also its realism. It must be remembered that in 1928 India was not a federation. Federalism had first been suggested as a possible solution of Indian diversity simultaneously by the Aga Khan himself in his *India in Transition* and by Edwin Montagu, the Secretary of State for India, in the report he had prepared with Lord Chelmsford, the Viceroy of India, in 1918.

The great merit of the Aga Khan's proposal of 1928 is that it looked beyond the coming federation and fixed its gaze on an alliance which could be so loose as to be non-existent. In practical terms India was to be divided into a number of near independent states. Some of them would combine together to make a large state. All of them would be associated in an alliance, but this association was to be free and voluntary and only in those matters which were willingly, and without any pressure, put into the pool by each free state. It is implied that once British rule was withdrawn, this alliance would cease to function.

In ascertaining the point of origin of the idea of Pakistan, it must said that the Aga Khan proposal came very near to it. Once the principle of the creation of free states had been established and put to work, he thought it probable that the Muslim provinces in the north-west would merge to make a large free state. This is more than Iqbal was able to foresee in his much-quoted and much-vaunted presidential address to the All India Muslim

---

[1] "A Constitution for India", *The Times*, London, 12 and 13 October 1928.

League annual session held in Allahabad in December 1930. But both Iqbal and the Aga Khan did not mention the eastern wing of India. In the case of the Aga Khan, perhaps there was no point in making a specific reference to eastern India because under the principle enunciated by him Bengal would be a free state, and obviously with a Muslim majority.

The most detailed and graphic espousal of Muslim separatism and nationalism came in a broadcast made by the Aga Khan and addressed to the Americans in 1931. He pointed out that the Muslims of India, more numerous than the 62 million people of Germany, made up one-fifth of the total population of India in 1880, one-fourth in 1930, and would be one-third "before our children are middle-aged men". They were not aliens to India, but they "differ from the Hindus in most matters which can divide one set of people from another". He then recounted these differences in words which Chaudhri Rahmat Ali was to employ with slight modifications fifteen months later in justification of his demand for the creation of a "Pakstan" (the original word coined by Rahmat Ali, later changed to "Pakistan"): "They differ in customs, in habits, in laws, and above all, in their food and in their clothes. They also differ in cultural and economic ideals." The gulf was therefore more than a mere religious one. It was greater than the one separating Protestants and Catholics in Ireland, or even the French Canadians and the English Canadians in Canada.

The Aga Khan proceeded to enumerate more factors which set the two peoples apart. Islam disallowed usury while Hinduism imposed no ban on interest on capital. The result was that over many years the Hindu had become the capitalist and the Muslim the labourer or the tiller of the soil. In most places the Hindu majority was overwhelming and likely to tyrannize and oppress the minority. "We have been accused of looking beyond the frontiers of India and not concentrating all our political patriotism on our Motherland. This is an unfounded accusation. While we are a world-wide brotherhood, while we share the joys and sorrows of Muslims throughout the world, while our spiritual brotherhood is complete with them, politically we have no other country and no other patriotism except that of India."

He went on to say that Muslims wanted such a federal constitution as safeguarded their interests. They want "something that will save them their ideals from being submerged". They were asking for an adequate share in the federal legislature and the federal administration. Further, they claimed self-determination and "fully autonomous" administrations for all racial and linguistic areas, and "particularly for those areas which have a majority Muslim population". It should be their own decision, freely arrived at, whether or not they wanted to retain the separate electorates they now possessed. They "will resist to the last any attempt which, under colour of democracy, places them at the mercy of any other section" of the population.

He concluded with the declaration that "the Muslims will, however, fight shoulder to shoulder with their Hindu brothers for a Constitution which will give India a stable Government of the people, by the people, for the people, for the equal good and advancement of all – and not for the advantage of any particular caste or creed, which would hold the others in its grasp".[1]

It must be noted in passing that this was precisely the policy that the Muslim League pursued till early 1940 before opting for a political solution by partition. Like Jinnah, the Aga Khan was not yet, and not for several years to come, convinced that a division of India on a religious basis was desirable or unavoidable. Jinnah came to such a conclusion in 1940, the Aga Khan about five years later than that. Yet the Aga Khan showed greater realism and constancy by refusing to make any compromise on the issue of separate electorates, on the necessity of reorganizing the provinces, and on the desirability of a truly federal form of government for India.

We must now retrace our steps to take note of another kind of proposal made by the Aga Khan in the 1920s. Surveying the state of Muslim political disarray in the subcontinent, he was anxious to encourage and build up the unity of Muslim India. Naturally, as one of the founders of the All India Muslim League, he looked to it for effecting a united front. But after 1912–13 the leadership of the League had gone to people who were nearer to the Congress and more optimistic about the generosity to be expected from it than was the Aga Khan himself. Since 1919 the League had virtually ceased to function as a major party and had surrendered its public life and importance to the All India Khilafat Conference. The Aga Khan regretted this development because the Khilafat Conference, in close alliance with the Congress and a few small pro-Congress and anti-League groups, was concentrating all its attention and energies on the Turkish issue. There was no party left to look after Muslim interests within

---

[1] Broadcast Address to the United States of America, London, 27 September 1931.

India. He believed that a separate organization was necessary for "attaining progressive union in the community" and in time to have "a great influence on Moslem life and thought". He appealed to the Muslims to bestir themselves and revive the League. "I implore my fellow religionists not to allow the League to become a half-dead institution; if necessary they should enlarge and broaden its constitution from a purely political into a general body for safeguarding and developing Islamic ideas and civilization in this country."[1] This was in 1923.

By the end of 1927, when the Muslim League split into two sections (the Jinnah League and the Shafi League), the Aga Khan was so disappointed that, at least for the time being, he abandoned the hope of a united political party of the Muslims of India. Instead he thought of a better alternative – better in the sense of enjoying irrefutable authority, unquestionable spokemanship and electoral credentials. In December of that year he called upon all the Muslim members of the central and provincial legislatures to "constitute a permanent Moslem governing body, which shall direct the political activity of the community and be in a position to speak with authority and enter into binding compacts both with Hindus and with the British Government". He was of the opinion that the presence of such an organized body, "with binding authority with the masses", was a pre-requisite for laying a solid foundation for Anglo-British confidence, inter-communal peace and smooth constitution making.[2]

This was an eminently sensible suggestion, and it is a matter of astonishment that the plan had not occurred to anyone else. Such a body could be a powerful nucleus, a think-tank and a general headquarters of a popular, well-organized mass party. This signalled the birth of the idea of the All India Muslim Conference.

Planning for the Conference went on apace during 1928 and it had its inaugural session on the last day of that year in Delhi. The Aga Khan, who had inspired and urged its formation, was elected president. There is no exaggeration in his claims, made nearly thirty years later, that it proved to be "one of the most important in the long series of such assemblies which marked the road towards total and final independence for the whole subcontinent. It was a vast gathering representative of all shades

[1] Interview, *The Times of India*, Bombay, 7 April 1923.
[2] Manifesto, Bombay, 29 December 1927.

of Muslim opinion. I can claim to be the parent of its important and lasting political decisions."[1]

The Aga Khan's presidential address to the Conference summarized the major political developments of the day and showed the way to greater unity within the Muslims – and to the minimum and definite guarantees and concessions without which any future constitution of India would not be acceptable to the "nation".[2] Under his guidance, almost according to his dictation, the Conference passed a resolution spelling out the basic principles which were to underly the future constitution of India if it was to be imposed on the Muslims. "The principles which we had enunciated were to be our guiding lights henceforward in all our encounters with British or Hindu representatives and negotiators, with the Government of India or with the Congress Party, in every discussion of schemes of reform and new projects for the administration of the country. We now had our code-book, and we did not intend to deviate from it."[3] At the Round Table Conferences, in private meetings with Gandhi and other Hindu delegates, in the sessions of the Joint Committee on Indian Constitutional Reform, during the acrimonious public debate in India on the Communal Award, in the course of the discussions about the interpretation of the Government of India Act of 1935 – on every occasion the Muslim leaders and spokesmen carried a copy of, or made references to, the first resolution of the Conference and challenged or rejected any deviation from its terms.

The Muslim Conference had brought together on one platform every Muslim who mattered in Indian public life (except Jinnah; but he was soon acting at the Round Table Conference, as a valuable and loyal member of the Muslim team under the Aga Khan). Yet an emaciated and half-dead Muslim League continued to eke out a precarious existence. Iqbal's name gave it some respectability when he presided over its annual session at Allahabad in December 1930, but generally it had lost all influence among the policy-makers in India and Britain and all support among the rank and file of Muslims. However, the Aga Khan was so obsessed with the idea of bringing about a complete Muslim unity that he repeatedly tried to effect a merger of the League and the Conference.

In December 1931 he launched a three-pronged attack on the

[1] *Memoirs*, 1954.
[2] Presidential Address, All India Muslim Conference, Delhi, 31 December 1928.
[3] *Memoirs*, 1954.

existing political dualism. In a long letter to *The Times* he declared that ''we are now a compact and homogeneous body, united by a programme which has brought Moslems of different Provinces and varying interests on to a common platform, and has provided them with an instrument for united political expression. The All India Muslim League, founded a quarter of a century ago, did a most useful service by training our young men in political work, and inculcating in them a deep and abiding purpose to assist the development of their community... A later organization, constituted on a different basis and doing useful work, is the All India Moslem Conference. Conflict between the two bodies has been avoided hitherto by the good sense, tact, and reasonableness of the leading members of both organizations. But I am confident that it is not in the best interests of the community to maintain two organizations. They should be amalgamated and together form an organization to be called the United Moslem League Conference... The proposed amalgamation should serve to focus Moslem political thought and concentrate within itself the energy, ability, wealth and influence of the community throughout India. I have written to my fellow Moslems that we cannot afford to dissipate our energies at a time so critical in our history, that division and disunion may ruin the prospects of a lasting settlement of the claims of Indian Moslems... I believe the next two years will be the most critical in the history of India that we of the present generation have known. If Muslims remain solid and well organized, if they act as disciplined soldiers and follow the policy of their main organization with cheerful zeal, they will succeed in maintaining their due position in the Indian body politic, and will play a part in the development of their country that is consonant with their great past and their present importance as by far the largest of the Indian minorities.''[1]

He took two further steps on the same day. In a manifesto dispatched to the Muslims of India he said, "Islam in India can exist and advance only if and when all its sons are willing and eager to follow the lead of their political organizations. I am therefore most strongly of the opinion that Moslem leaders should immediately hold a joint meeting of the working committees of the two bodies [the League and the Conference], frame rules for a common organization, and organize branches in every part of India. Unless we do this, we shall never be able to achieve what we have been striving so anxiously to realize. So far as the programme is concerned there is, in my opinion, no material

[1] Letter, *The Times*, London, 16 December 1931.

difference in the political purpose of either body. The amalgamated political organization of which I have written must not be content with a central executive committee. The work of organizing branches should be taken in hand and every effort should be made to keep in constant touch with the feelings and desires of the masses. In these days of extended franchise, work among the *intelligentsia* is not in itself sufficient. A centre and, possibly two or three, centres should be established for training young men for political work."[1]

He also sent a telegram to Sir Muhammad Yakub saying, "The Muslim League had done and is doing great work in creating political consciousness and it is impossible to exaggerate its work in political development. I have done my best for the Muslims through both organizations, and I believe that the Muslims cannot afford two organizations with identical programmes. Conflict between the two organizations has hitherto been avoided by the tact of the leaders. I am convinced that the time has now come for the amalgamation of the two organizations and that amalgamation is absolutely imperative. I suggest that the amalgamated body be called the United League Conference [*sic*], and that it should focus political life by serving real Muslim interests."[2]

Three years later he seems to have changed his mind for unstated reasons. He told the Muslim Conference leaders that "I was very keen on amalgamating the Muslim Conference and the Muslim League two years ago and had asked several of my friends to do their best to achieve this object. I am, however, now convinced that the All India Muslim Conference is all right, and that amalgamation, if it is to come, must wait. This can only come some time after the inauguration of the reform."[3]

I must now retrace my steps to describe the Aga Khan's role in the making of the reforms of 1935. At the first Round Table Conference, in the autumn of 1930, he was elected leader of the Muslim delegation which contained such distinguished persons as Jinnah, Sir Muhamad Shafi and Zafrullah Khan. The delegation made its headquarters at the Ritz Hotel in Piccadilly where the Aga Khan used to stay whenever he was in London. Soon afterwards the entire British Indian delegation elected him its Chairman.

[1] Manifesto, *The Times*, London, 16 December 1931.
[2] Telegram to Sir Muhammad Yakub, London, 16 December 1931.
[3] Address to the All India Muslim Conference Executive Board, New Delhi, 15 February 1934.

Since at least 1919 the Aga Khan had been advocating a federation for India in which the federal arrangement would be as
"open" as practicable, with the constituent provinces and states
determining the quantum of their own autonomy and the scope
of the powers to be surrendered to the centre. In 1928 he had
taken a very significant and radical step further in suggesting a
confederation of Free States of India consisting of reconstituted
provinces and states. This confederal plan would probably not
have been acceptable to the British, and certainly not to the
Hindus, but at the Conference he pursued to a successful conclusion his conviction that "whatever the temporary difficulties
and risks involved in a federal scheme, it still offered the best and
the most acceptable solution of India's political problems, that it
offered an opportunity which might never occur again, and that
if it required compromise to make it effective, that would be a
small price to pay for its obvious and numerous advantages".[1]

On behalf of the Muslim delegation he asked for the following
guarantees: a truly federal constitution; the Muslim majorities in
the Punjab and Bengal would not be turned into minorities;
delinking of Sind from Bombay and its establishment as a separate province; the raising of the North-West Frontier Province to
the status of a full province; and statutory reservation of a certain
proportion of the places in the Army and in the Civil Service for
Muslims. He told the Hindu delegates that if they agreed to these
assurances the Muslims would in their turn offer them a united
front against the British. "I even went further and offered, as a
special concession, unity of command under a chosen Indian
leader whose orders we would bind the Muslim community to
accept." The Hindus were adamant in refusing to consider any
Muslim proposals. The Aga Khan believed that the failure of the
first Round Table Conference (and, by a successive series of
stages, the ultimate partition of India) was due to the Hindu
delegation's refusal to accept his offer. He was sure that Tej
Bahadur Sapru and Srinivasa Sastri wanted to accept "in their
heart of hearts" the Muslim proposals but that they were afraid
of their Hindu colleagues and, above all, of the Hindu Mahasabha.[2] The Congress was absent from the first conference.

When the second conference opened, the presence of Gandhi
(as the sole delegate of the Indian National Congress, and in his
own view expressed openly, the only genuine and true Indian
delegate) inspired the Aga Khan with the hope that now the

[1] *Memoirs*, 1954.
[2] *Ibid.*

Hindus would "appreciate the fact (and act upon it) that to make a combined front of Hindus and Muslims would in itself be a major step forward". A few hours with Gandhi blew away all his hopes.

Gandhi and Sarojini Naidu (the Hindu poetess) met the Muslim delegation at the Ritz at midnight (the date is not given). As a symbol and summary of Gandhi's attitude towards the most genuine and sincere offers of co-operation, even self-abnegation, the Aga Khan relates the following opening of their conversation. "I opened it by saying to Mahatmaji that, were he now to show himself a real father to India's Muslims, they would respond by helping him, to the utmost of their ability, in his struggle for India's independence. Mahatmaji turned to face me. 'I cannot in truth say', he observed, 'that I have any feelings of paternal love for Muslims. But if you put the matter on grounds of political necessity, I am ready to discuss it in a co-operative spirit. I cannot indulge in any form of sentiment.' This was a cold douche at the outset; and the chilly effect of it pervaded the rest of our conversation. I felt that, whereas I had given prompt and ready evidence of a genuine emotional attachment and kinship, there had been no similar response from the Mahatmaji."[1]

Negotiations were bound to fail in the light of the inflexible stand taken by Gandhi. He sought to impose a first and fundamental condition: that before asking for any guarantee the Muslims must accept the Congress interpretation of Swaraj as their goal. The Aga Khan felt that Gandhi might "have seen his way to accept our viewpoint" but the Hindu Mahasabha leaders were putting too great a pressure on him.[2] This is a generous estimation of the Mahatma's role.

As the talks continued, recalled the Aga Khan, "the hair-splitting became finer and finer, the arguments more and more abstract: a nation could not hand over unspecified powers to its provinces; there was no constitutional way of putting a limit on the devices by which a majority could be turned into a minority – fascinating academic issues, but with little or no connection with the real facts and figures of Indian life". In the end, little was achieved. Gandhi returned to India. The "sum total of all our work was a vast array of statistics and dates, a great many speeches, and little or no positive understanding".[3]

In June 1932 the Aga Khan reiterated and summarized the

[1] *Ibid.*
[2] *Ibid.*
[3] *Ibid.*

Muslim demands in a letter to *The Times*. In the Punjab and Bengal the comparatively small numerical majority should be given due weight because Hindus would be in an overwhelming majority at the centre and in no fewer than six other provinces. The central government should undertake to meet any deficit in the separated province of Sind. Muslims must have at least one-third of the British Indian seats in the federal legislature; which was actually far less than they agreed to at the Kashmir Conference in respect to the Hindu minority of that state under the proposed constitutional reforms, although Muslim interests were more vital and their percentage in British India was much higher than that of the Hindus in Kashmir. The rulers of the Native States should agree on a convention whereby such a proportion of state seats in the federal legislature may be reserved for the Muslims so that their total strength in the house does not fall below one-third.[1]

In 1933 the Aga Khan was able to unite the entire British Indian Delegation behind a Joint Memorandum, drafted by him and some of the delegates, which was then submitted to the British Government. This document, he says with justified pride, "for the first time in the history of Indo-British relations put before the British Government a united demand on behalf of all communities, covering practically all important political points at issue. It propounded what would have been, in effect, a major step forward – the penultimate step indeed before Dominion status. By it we sought to ensure continuity in the process of the further transfer of responsibility . . . It was a claim for the transfer to Indian hands of practically every power except certain final sanctions which would be reserved to the British Government. Had a constitution been granted along these lines, later critical situations . . . might all have been much less difficult. Had this constitution been fully established and an accepted and going concern, it would have been in due course a comparatively simple operation to lop off those reserve powers which in our draft marked the final stage of constitutional devolution."[2] But the Congress disowned it, and for this reason the British Government was compelled to reject it.

In the meantime, the Aga Khan continued to press the British over the matters of Sind and Bengal. He assured the Muslim leaders that he "will leave no stone unturned till I find that separation [of Sind] becomes an accomplished fact . . . I am

[1] Letter, *The Times*, London, 7 June 1932.
[2] *Memoirs*, 1954.

convinced that its people have not had a government of their own for generations past. It would be a terrible blow if the province was made a Chief Commissioner's department."[1] He told the Bengali Muslims that theirs was the "premier country of Islam in the world. I say advisedly, 'of Islam in the world', because there is no other country in the world where you have such a large Muslim population concentrated in such a small area as in Eastern Bengal." He was hopeful that Muslim Bengal would play its proper part in Indian politics after the federation was in place.[2]

By 1935 the Indian Reforms Act had been passed by the British Parliament. The Aga Khan did not have a high opinion of it. It "left far too many loopholes for British interference, and indeed actual decision, on matters which every Indian patriot believed should have been solely for India to decide . . . Its grossest failing was that it offered no foundation on which to build . . . Neither did the Act supply an impetus to any effort to bridge the rift between Hindus and Muslims; and in the testing times of 1942 and 1946–47, the emptiness in the Act were glaringly revealed. By its reservations and by its want of clarity about the real meaning of Indian independence, the 1935 Act made a United India an impossibility. It had to be set aside and the effort made to build up Indian independence from scratch. Then it became harshly clear that Indian unity was impossible, unless it were based on extremely wide federal, or confederate, foundations."[3]

There is not much in the Aga Khan's works on Indian (or any other) politics during the years of the Second World War. He was living in Switzerland whose strictly neutral government did not approve of its guest residents making political statements. When the war ended and the dust settled the partition of India was on the horizon. But the Aga Khan was not persuaded of the desirability of a division till quite late. He met Gandhi for the last time during his visit to India in the winter of 1945–6. Up to that point he had hoped that some compromise would be effected and a truly federal government established with Hindu–Muslim co-operation. The meeting with the Mahatma put all such hopes to rest. "Now I see clearly that I was wrong," he wrote in 1954; "amputation was the only remedy."[4]

---

[1] Speech at a dinner hosted by Muslim legislators, Bombay, 22 February 1934.
[2] Speech at a luncheon given by Muslim legislators of Bengal, Calcutta, 28 February 1934.
[3] *Memoirs*, 1954.
[4] *Memoirs*, 1954.

In Search of World Peace

By definition a statesman is a man with a vision who can stand, gaze and penetrate the mists of time to see what mankind needs today to make its tomorrow more agreeable and worthwhile. In the times in which he lived, the Aga Khan was convinced that a peaceful international order was the only guarantee not only of the security and happiness of the world but of its very existence and survival. He was an internationalist by conviction, observation and experience. Conviction taught him patience, persistence and honesty of intention. Observation gave him an insight into human nature. Experience made him read other people's minds and showed the way to the objective.

Armed with an understanding of the forces of history, a grasp of human psychology, the strength of his own belief in a revealed religion, and a deep acquaintance with the way of the world, he decided to approach his goal from three directions. The chief lever which moved history, though many were not aware of it, was the broad cultural environment in which men lived. In the Orient throughout the ages – and also in the Occident up to the seventeenth century – it was personal faith that moulded the life of man, teaching him how to live in this world and how to prepare himself for the next. The modern age, however, had made man a political animal far more thoroughly than Aristotle had intended to aver in his definition.

This analysis persuaded the Aga Khan to mount a three-pronged offensive in his campaign to bring peace to the world. In the cultural field he emphasized the need, and prescribed the means, for co-operation, understanding and amity between people: learning foreign languages, studying literature other than one's own, travelling, raising the standard of education, improving the health of the common man, expanding external trade, and beating down racial bias and discrimination. In the religious sphere he pleaded for Hindu–Muslim unity in India, (he was a very late convert to the idea of a partition of the sub-continent, after all avenues of collaboration and corporate living had been closed by Congress arrogance and Hindu obduracy), for a Christian–Islamic understanding in the West, for a deep respect to be shown to all faiths, and, in his own religion, for the achievement of the pan-Islamic ideal, and also a Shia–Sunni *rapprochement*. These broad means for bringing humanity together, or at least closer, are dealt with below in the sections on "The World of Islam" and "The Conciliator". Here I propose to consider his contribution to the making of world peace during

the years of his close association with the Disarmament Conference and the League of Nations.

The Aga Khan entered the world of international diplomacy in
1932 with impeccable credentials. During the preceding eighteen
years he had been a keen observer of the international scene,
and a friend or acquaintance of most of the men who were now
destined to play a major role in the shaping of world politics.
He was a perceptive reader of leading European and American
newspapers and magazines. He was equally conversant with the
current of passing events and the problems facing the policy
makers. With these intellectual advantages he combined the
social graces of a royal lineage, generous hospitality, and a flair
for cultivating friendships and retaining the affection and loyalty
of his colleagues.

He was initially nominated second-in-command to Sir Samuel
Hoare (later Lord Templewood) in the Indian delegation to the
Disarmament Conference Geneva in 1932. Hoare left Geneva
during the early stages of the conference, and the Aga Khan
became the chief spokesman. Directly upon his arrival he set
about building a substantial base for negotiations by renewing
old friendships, seeking and making new contacts, entertaining
lavishly, and winning the confidence and trust of the chief representatives of the major powers. To Arthur Henderson, the
British permanent president of the conference and a Labour
Party statesman, he extended an invitation (which was accepted),
to come and stay at his villa at Antibes as often and for as long
as he liked. The two men had many intimate conversations, and
Henderson sought and valued his host's advice on several knotty
points. The Aga Khan soon established affable relations with
the military adviser to the German mission, General (later Field
Marshal) Werner von Blomberg (who was not averse to talking
to him freely, and sometimes scathingly, of the men who were
then ruling Germany). Most important of all, he struck up a
rapport with the Soviet Foreign Minister Maxim Litvinov who,
anxious to establish contacts with the West after more than a
decade of Soviet isolation, found in the Aga Khan a sympathetic
listener. The Aga Khan must have appeared to him a unique
medley of the East and the West.

The Aga Khan hosted dinners at which the chief delegates and
their advisers mixed freely, shed (or at least tempered) their
prejudices, indulged in small intimacies (which lessened national
animosities) and bridged, however temporarily, political and doc-
trinaire differences. He exercised his legendary charm through

accustomed *bonhomie,* good food, beaming smiles and a flawless use of the language of international intercourse.

He tried very hard, but the tide of events was flowing against him. There prevailed on the surface a mood of optimism which he could not fully share. The major powers were not prepared to make "a more strenuous and a more realistic effort", which the circumstances demanded. The European world was passing through many "harassing and disillusioning happenings", the ominous consequences of which he drew to the attention of his fellow delegates with eloquence and poignancy.[1] The conference fell far short of what it had set out to achieve, but its long sessions provided the Aga Khan with an opportunity to tell the world his thoughts on the prospects for international peace and how it could be won. It also gave him an opportunity to prepare himself for his later role in the League of Nations.

In perspective, the journey that the Aga Khan made from the lobbies of the Disarmament Conference to the halls of the League of Nations was a logical step from preparation to achievement. Soon after his appointment to the Disarmament Conference he was nominated the chief Indian representative at the 1932 session of the League of Nations: this bubbling cauldron of international rivalries and distrusts could not have given the Aga Khan a moment of respite. Seven years earlier, in 1925, he had declared, "The League of Nations is a child of an aged mother, the Old World Imperialism that led to the conflict begun eleven years ago. In consequence the infant is sickly and weak, but it lives and may grow."[2]

By 1932 the task of peacemaking was becoming more formidable, intractable and perplexing. The world had descended from disarmament to collective security, and during the Aga Khan's years with the League the alternative choice was reduced to individual self-defence. Germany was to leave the League in 1933. Maxim Litvinov was to preach the indivisibility of peace to his fellow delegates. The spokesman of Japan, Matsuoka, was to make graceful speeches in Geneva while his country invaded Manchuria. Italy, within a few years of signing a treaty of "friendship, conciliation and arbitration" with Abyssinia, was to attack and occupy the empire of Haile Selassie. New nations, some of them from Asia and Africa, were to swell the League's member-

---

[1] The words in quotation marks are the Aga Khan's; *Memoirs,* 1954, pp. 241, 242.
[2] Quoted in Stanley Jackson, *The Aga Khan: Prince, Prophet and Statesman,* London, 1952, p. 151.

ship, only to discover that the organization's preoccupation with European affairs amounted to a neglect of their own problems (a sentiment the Aga Khan was to express in unmistakable phrases from the floor of the League in 1935).

Working at the League in these disheartening conditions, experience taught the Aga Khan how to handle difficult situations with ease, if not success. His courage enabled him to speak with a frankness not expected from a non-European delegate representing a country which was still a colony. His geniality saved him from making enemies. His tact postponed, but could not avert, some crises. His reputation for fairness and broad-mindedness gained his appeals attention and respect. His forbearance nipped some approaching disasters in the bud. His personal popularity and charm solved many minor tiffs and unpleasantries. He waded through a slush of problems and a tangle of snags with optimism. But his optimism could not of itself alter the course of events. He struggled hard to salvage Europe from the excesses of its own chauvinism. And though, at the end, the Continent decided to wage war, the Aga Khan's pointed and vigorous warnings against such action left a bright spot on the records of the League of Nations. At the fourteenth plenary session of the League he said:

"We have found that armaments still hold sway and that the feeling of insecurity still persists. It is by no means certain that the war to end war has been fought and won. On the moral side we must set ourselves to remove the paralysing effects of fear, ill-will, and suspicion. On the material side it is absolutely essential that the non-productive effort devoted to warlike preparations should be reduced to the bare minimum. In distant India, no less than in Europe, the World War created a host of mourners and left a legacy of bitter tragedy. Over a million of my fellow-countrymen were called to arms, of whom more than fifty thousand laid down their lives. India's own scale of armaments allows no margin for excessive uses. The size of her forces has to be measured with reference to the vastness of her area and the diversity of her conditions. The fact is so often forgotten that the area of India is more than half that of the whole of Europe, and her population nearly one-fifth of that of the entire globe. There is a cry going up from the heart of all the peace-loving citizens of every country for the lessening of their military burdens, for a decrease of the financial load which those burdens impose, for the security of civil populations against indiscriminate methods of warfare, and above all, for security against the very idea of war."[1]

When the Sino-Japanese dispute was brought before the League of Nations the Aga Khan, on his own initiative, suggested to the British Foreign Secretary, Sir John Simon (later Lord Simon), that he should be given an opportunity, as an Asiatic, to negotiate personally with the representatives of China and Japan with a view to bringing them round to an amicable settlement. He was authorized to carry out his plans, and had several conversations with the two contestants. The talks broke down, but his solo and sincere effort demonstrates the lengths, both official and private, to which he was prepared to go to obtain world peace.

Similarly, when the Abyssinian crisis erupted he told Anthony Eden, "If you want international politics to have a foundation of justice, if you want the League really to be what it is supposed to be, if you want to give it a chance to grow into a real society of nations, deciding matters of right and wrong among themselves, then here is an outstanding case which must be tackled. Here there is no valid excuse of any kind. There is no large Italian minority in Ethiopia deprived of their independence or their civic and economic rights. Here is a case of open and inexcusable aggression. And the remedy is in our hands. *All we need do is shut the Suez Canal.* Or if we must have sanctions, let them be applied to oil as well, and thus make them a reality and put some teeth into them. But I still think the best solution is a simple, unanimous resolution by the League to close the Canal."[2] His advice was disregarded, and the League of Nations proceeded to pass inane resolutions in favour of empty sanctions.

The Aga Khan was discouraged and disillusioned, yet he did not let his hopes turn to ashes. Sanguine by temperament and training, burning with a desire to devote the last drop of his energy and talent to the cause of peace, he persisted in his exertions. When he was elected President of the League in 1937 he was perfectly aware of the perils accompanying the position. "This election", he declared, "honours my country, whose sole philosophy is attuned to the fundamental principles in which the League of Nations is grounded ... If we can do something to bring about a more equitable adjustment of things in economic

---

[1] *Memoirs*, 1954, p. 241. From his speech delivered at the fourteenth plenary session of the League; the Aga Khan considered this passage of such importance that he reproduced it in those memoirs.

[2] *Ibid.*, p. 258. Italics in the original.

and social life, no less than in politics, the better it will be for our neighbours, and we shall have helped the League on the long road that lies before us – the peaceful removal of the causes of war and the establishment of the unchallenged empire of peace throughout the world."

It is a sad commentary on the political ambitions and moral ineptitude of the men who ruled Europe in the 1930s that the Aga Khan's powers of conciliation, diplomatic urbanity and high prestige failed to stem the tide of aggression. The fault lay with those who refused to listen to him and let their greed overtake their prudence, not with the man who beseeched, cajoled, begged, appealed and warned.

The Aga Khan's role as a peacemaker was judged accurately in 1939 by a contemporary Indian prince, the Maharajah of Bikaner. "His achievements in many different and varied fields have earned for him a unique position in the political and social life of today. A farsighted statesman whose advice is sought by the highest authorities in the Empire... the Aga Khan is undoubtedly one of the most spectacular personalities of the age ... As becomes one of his descent and affiliations, His Highness, though a genuine patriot, is a true citizen of the world. His interest in humanity is not circumscribed by narrow geographical considerations. Equally at home in the capitals of Europe as among his own compatriots in India, the Aga Khan is a bridge between the East and the West, a connecting link between the two main civilizations of the modern world. His mission in life may justly be described as that of bringing the East and the West nearer to each other through understanding and sympathy."[1]

The Conciliator

As we have seen, the Aga Khan was a unifier and a peacemaker. The ideal of unity was a means to a peaceful world. He was a citizen of this wide world and rejected narrow loyalties, political or economic.

He did not believe in narrow nationalisms. His constant advice to the Indians – Hindus and Muslims – living outside India was to be model citizens of their chosen land. He told the Indians who had settled in Burma that it was "right and proper" that they should accept it as their domicile "with all their heart". They

[1] Maharajah of Bikaner, Foreword, dated 4 May 1939, in N. M. Dumasia, *The Aga Khan and his Ancestors*, Bombay, 1939, pp. v–vi.

must cultivate the Burmese and openly discuss with them their problems, make friends with them, and do everything for the benefit of the country. He hoped that if "his words helped to bring those who had made this country their home nearer to those whose home it was, alike for civic, economic and political co-operation, he could say he had spent a very useful and happy afternoon".[1]

This attitude did not change even in the case of South Africa where the Indians were living under severe conditions. Though they might be rightly proud of their great Indian cultural tradition, yet once they had come here their allegiance, no matter what the country did to them, must be "wholly and in toto" to South Africa. This was right because they lived there, most of them had been born there, all of them received their sustenance from there, and most of them would die there. They must look upon the country as their own and upon themselves as its "humble servants". Their guiding thought should be its glory. Only then would they have the right to say that, in spite of what had gone before, they wanted fairplay in the future.[2]

In the case of East Africa he went to the extent of declaring that though local agriculture held forth almost unlimited promise and the Indian settlers could guide their African brothers in its improvement and extension, yet he did not want more agriculturists to arrive there from India. There were already as many Indians as the land could accommodate.[3] The future prosperity of Tanganyika had to be built from within "on the foundation of African prosperity, with Africans their own proprietors". He warned the Indians, "you will get nowhere if you regard Tanganyika as a sort of plantation from which the crop is to be exported and for which Africans provide the labour".[4]

To his own community, the Ismailis, he gave the same message in no uncertain terms: in 1926, in an address in Mombasa, he called upon his followers and other Indians to regard Kenya as their home and not to repatriate to India the profits they made in their country of domicile.[5] A quarter of a century later, speaking in London, he repeated the advice. It was to the countries in which they chose to make their homes that the Ismailis

[1] Speech before the Burma–India Chamber of Commerce, Rangoon, 6 March 1934.
[2] Speech before the Natal Indian Congress, Durban, 16 August 1945.
[3] Interview, *East African Standard*, Nairobi, 26 March 1945.
[4] Interview, *Tanganyika Standard*, Dar-es-Salaam, 2 August 1945.
[5] Addresses before the Ismaili community, Mombasa, 1–7 April 1926.

owed their loyalty and affection. They should identify themselves with their new homes if they wanted to prosper in the years to come. They could not continue to live in Africa if they failed to win the esteem of the African people. He quoted the example of the Indians in Burma, who did not look across the border but considered themselves a part of that country. "Whatever country you choose to live in, work for it, mix with its people, achieve its outlook, and keep religion in its proper place – in your soul. In Africa the day will come when the people of that vast continent will want to know who foreigners are, and it is the people who have made the country their home who are going to have the best opportunities in that country. For that day prepare yourselves." He did not even want them to call themselves Asians in Africa. "When you live permanently in a country you become a member of that country."[1]

The loyalty which he was demanding from the Ismailis on behalf of the country of their domicile was even defined as a *religious* duty by the Aga Khan. It was "a fundamental point in your religion that wherever you be, whatever the state where life and honour are protected, you must give your entire loyalty and devotion to the welfare and service of that country".[2]

The Aga Khan's emphasis on peaceful mixed racial and religious living (between Asians, Africans and Europeans, and between people of different faiths) was derived from the unhappy East African scene where, especially in the 1930s and 1940s, race relations were characterized by a great deal of conflict. The Aga Khan advised all the parties involved in the strained situation – Europeans, Asians and Africans – not to hate and fear one another. "White, black and brown are complementary members of a common body politic", he underlined in a speech in Dar-es-Salaam.[3]

His anxiety to create harmonious relations between and among the different races living together was one aspect or channel of his great ideal of world peace. He was not only a cosmopolitan in his own life (which might have been by chance or circumstance) but a messenger of cosmopolitanism for all peoples and nationalities. A citizen of the world himself, he wanted a world at peace.

He hated war or anything leading to it. If he had total power, he said, it would be his first duty to make impossible "the over-

[1] Speech at a dinner of the Aga Khan Students' Union, London, June 1951.
[2] Speech at his Platinum Jubilee ceremony, Karachi, 3 February 1954.
[3] Speech at his Diamond Jubilee celebrations, Dar-es-Salam, 10 August 1946.

whelming calamity of another world war, and to rectify the acknowledged errors" of the Treaty of Versailles. The first essential would be the abolition of national armies and navies. He was aware that the ultimate sanction of all authority was force, but the force he would provide to keep peace would be internationally owned.[1] Concern for humanity was, in his opinion, the most fundamental motive for creating world peace: "Indeed, all the problems that fall to the League [of Nations] may ultimately be reduced to one – that of man, and the dignity of man." It was this fact that gave the League's work its true significance and a permanent value. "The tribulations of one people are the tribulations of all. That which weakens one weakens all. That which is a gain to one is surely a gain to all. This is no empty ideal. It is a veritable compass to guide right the efforts of statesmen in every country and of all men of goodwill who, desiring the good of their own people, desire the good of the whole world."[2]

The League of Nations did not, however, win his complete approval. Giving his views as a spokesman of India, he said that his country was troubled by the League's "lack of universality, the incompleteness of its composition and the tiny representation of Indians in its organisation". The League was giving far too much attention to Europe and European interests.[3]

He presented a more detailed critique of the League in 1947; it must be read in the context of his own involvement: he was India's chief representative at the League from 1932 onwards and the president of the organization in 1937. He found the League to have been too much of an ideal and too little of practicality. "The League Covenant was a perfect instrument – for angels. Human beings, with their passions and weaknesses, with their loves and hatreds, with the long traditions of autonomy, national sovereignties, of former wars and jealousies, could never have worked the Covenant successfully over long periods." The League could not solve the German question. It failed in the Far East. It did not stop Italian aggression. It was very strong in dealing with third rate questions and still more so in removing the least cause of dissatisfaction for France, Britain and Russia." The absence of America, Japan and Germany made it impotent. It had been powerless from the very beginning. By about 1938 it had lost even its prestige. He forecast no better future for the United Nations Organization, which appeared to him as power-

---

[1] "If I were a Dictator", a broadcast talk, London, 11 November 1931.
[2] Speech at the League of Nations, Geneva, 6 October 1937.
[3] Speech at the League of Nations, Geneva, 13 September 1935.

less as its predecessor. "Excellent on paper, ideally perfect in its fine adjustment of regulations, it is impotent the moment it touches the fundamental rights of any State that has the power and energy to challenge its decisions. Gradually it is leaning to open opposition among the Great Powers and their friends and clients or to make-believe, face-saving resolutions that lead nowhere." If this continues, "sooner or later we will find the Great Powers settling things among themselves, either at the cost of the small fry, or with such bitterness after each so-called pacific settlement of a thorny question as to make future warfare a probability first, a certainty later".[1]

Among the suggestions he made to improve the prospects for a peaceful world was a redrawing of the boundaries of some parts of the world. He was convinced that peace and goodwill between neighbours was very difficult to maintain if ethnic and linguistic groups were torn asunder, whether by a Napoleon or by a President Wilson (the British did the same in India and Africa). A "general world-wide recasting of existing political units" would not be necessary, but certain areas needed attention: central Europe, the Balkans and Asia. Germany and Austria would become one nation-state, and any "truly Germanic" territory acquired by others in the past would be restored to it. Hungary would get back its lost areas through a plebiscite. The will of all doubtful zones in the Balkans would be ascertained by a free vote. Whenever racial and cultural unity had existed in the past, the peoples concerned should be allowed to unite or remain united. "In a word, aggressor States would be compelled to disgorge, and the map of Europe would be re-made on cultural and voluntary lines." The same policy would be pursued in the Middle East and Central Asia. The Persian and Turkish races of the Middle East should be re-united under one strong government covering each. The regions of Central Asia would be re-formed into States on cultural and racial lines.[2] He had already proposed a radical reorganization of the provinces of India. A few years later, and a year before the Second World War broke out, he appealed for the revival of the idea of a United States of Europe suggested by Briand and Stresemann; if this were done, "ninetenths of the dangers to civilization would disappear".[3]

World peace could also be achieved by a general disarmament, by a limit on the destructive power of air bombardment, and by

[1] "Can We Stop the Next War?", *Sunday Post*, Nairobi, 16 November 1947.
[2] "If I were a Dictator", a broadcast talk, London, 11 November 1931.
[3] Speech at the Empire Exhibition, Glasgow, 8 July 1938.

a restriction on the use of weapons of warfare which may "broadly be classed as aggressive in their purposes". But only a very effective kind of international co-operation could achieve and maintain such disarmament. He pointed out several problems which would have to be faced and solved: the composition of an organization to direct the forces under the command of the world authority, and the processes and procedures of its functioning; the mechanics of the power necessary for prompt and decisive action to be taken by the central body of the world authority; the ability to use international force against the more powerful members; the means of taking vital decisions – by majority vote or a unanimous vote; and the place where the proposed international force would be stationed or distributed regionally in sensitive or troubled areas.

Disarmament and international policing involved, or rather assumed, a juridical machinery in existence behind the political decision-making. A judicial organ was needed, which drew on the best representatives of the nations. Gradually, the Aga Khan was led to the idea of something like a world government. "The central authority, acting as a whole, would have to exercise, more than merely judicial or advisory function. If confronted in various areas with vast internal forces of discontent, it might in its ultimate state be called upon to carry out rectifications, re-alignments and re-adjustments in accordance with the wishes of the peoples most vitally concerned." This was, of course, a matter to be given careful thought.

For the immediate needs of the world, it was necessary to use and develop to the full the instruments already available. Disarmament in its widest sense, "the neutralization of war, the security and peace of mankind", could be and must be taken in hand. "There is a cry going up from the hearts of all the peace-loving citizens of every country for the lessening of their military burdens, for a decrease in the financial load which those burdens impose, for the security of civil populations against indiscriminate methods of warfare and, above all, for security against the very idea of war."[1]

During the debate in the League of Nations on the China–Japan conflict the Aga Khan pointed to another means of international goodwill: awareness of historical and intellectual give-and-take. Speaking in his capacity as a delegate from India, he said that his country had a tradition of friendship with both

[1] Speech at the Conference for the Reduction and Limitation of Armaments, Geneva, 19 February 1932.

parties to the dispute. "China is our good neighbour in the north and in the east, and with her province of Turkestan we have had, since time immemorial, friendly cultural and economic relations. India has behind her a long history of intimate association with China and Japan. The mutual influence of the three countries in religion, in art and in literature has endured since time immemorial. . . . Just as the Indian Buddha has influenced Chinese and Japanese thought, so the great Confucius has left his living and eternal mark on India. . . . Memories are long in the East, and India will have memories of all she has given and received in interchange with Further Asia, and cannot now be backward in pressing earnestly the cause of reconciliation in the spirit of the thought which has inspired the three countries alike."[1] In this way education of the right kind and content could be employed gainfully not only to achieve enlightenment within national borders but also to bring nations closer to one another in understanding and amity.

Another avenue to be explored in search of international peace was economic regeneration and exchange. If the time was not ripe to deal with military disarmament directly, the problems could be tackled indirectly through monetary and economic means. The accessibility of raw material could be ensured to all the nations in genuine need of it. Barriers of economic nationalism could be broken down before they became barrages of war. So far, the so-called law of nations had been used to "strengthen the title deeds of the 'haves' against the 'have-nots' ";[2] justice demanded the "pooling of the earth's resources for the welfare of mankind".[3]

To fight for the self-interest of the developing nations was really to fight for international peace, because their improvement was in the best interests of the world. Any economic set up which ignored these people would lead to another collapse of the international security system.[4] This warning was given two months before the Second World War ended.

Democratic Values

There are two passages in *India in Transition* which set the pattern for the Aga Khan's unshakeable belief in democratic values. In

[1] Speech at the League of Nations, Geneva, 8 March 1932.
[2] Speech at the League of Nations, Geneva, 29 September 1936.
[3] Broadcast talk, Bombay, 17 January 1939.
[4] Interview, *East African Standard*, Nairobi, 26 March 1945.

both he argues for a wider franchise for the Indian masses and the cultivation of a democratic system of government.

The first runs: "If there is one thing which modern history proves, it is this: that unless the government and the governing classes take up the task of raising the masses of the people gradually, but surely, thus founding the fabric of the commonwealth on the widest and deepest basis possible, namely, the whole of the population, the State renders itself liable to years and years of anarchy and disaster, and perhaps to dissolution."[1]

The second reads: "The greatest mistake made in the successive reconstitutions of Indian provincial legislatures has been that of limiting the right of representation, in practice if not always in theory, to what may be termed the privileged classes – the best-educated and richest sections of the population. Owing to this serious error the national conservatism necessary to the evolution of a normal modern State, and in India characteristic of the man at the plough, has been artificially prevented from making its voice effectively heard. An exaggerated mid-Victorian form of Liberalism, natural to the classes that now form the narrow electorates, has been dominant. Taxation and representation have not gone together. The provincial legislatures have been far too small to be really representative bodies in such large areas."[2]

These sentiments were not aberrations of mind or expressions of expediency. On numerous occasions the Aga Khan pleaded for more power to the masses, for the participation of the rural population in policy-making and law-making bodies, for making political parties grassroots organizations, for a continuous process of consultation between the leaders and the people, for bringing women into public life and the electorate, and for broadening the base of political governance. Such utterances from the lips of an aristocrat of aristocrats sound strange and unfamiliar. They also shatter the popular image of the Aga Khan as loyalist and sycophant, whose blinkered vision ignored rents in the imperial fabric which deserved criticism. Truth is stranger than fiction.

In his 1927 manifesto he appealed to the Muslims of India to replace the old self-constituted political bodies with an organization which was in constant touch with the electorate. The purpose was to "place the guidance of our people in their own hands".[3]

[1] *India in Transition,* June 1918.
[2] *Ibid.*
[3] Manifesto, Bombay, 29 December 1927.

In 1928 he told the All India Muslim Conference that the great lesson of modern history was that "only those nations succeed and only those policies lead to national greatness, which are based not on ideas or ideals of a few leaders, however eminent, or of a few thinkers, but on the general consensus of views and opinions of the people. The time has come when the leaders should keep their ears to the ground and ascertain the views and wishes of the masses." Political parties of today and tomorrow shall have "to evolve a truly representative body to look after and further the desires of Muslims of India". "The greatest service you can render to your people would be to organize the Muslim members of each and every [Legislative] Council into a body where exchange of views and ideas and communication of the same to the electors as well as the reception of the general desires of the masses, would remain the main purpose and object. . . . If we had such a body, I for one should sleep in peace; for I would know that many political theories would most certainly be made by them and not by anybody else for them. From now onwards we must ever remember, even in this Conference, not what are our own individual political preferences but what are the aspirations of the Muslim masses in this country."

He continued his advice in even firmer accents. "You are part of [the people]. It is your duty to interpret as far as you can their wishes, their aspirations and their ideals, till such time as our political organization is sufficiently advanced to let the people carry out their own wishes. . . . You must avoid forcing your own preferences when they clash with what we believe to be the real wishes of the mass of the people. The policy to be pursued during the immediate years, I would once more emphasize, must not be based on our personal views and predilections, but on what you know to be the general desires of the people to whom you belong."[1]

The historian of Muslim India will be hard put to discover a parallel page, with even half the cogent appeal, earnest articulation, and firm purposefulness of the above in the papers of the Muslim League or any other party.

The Aga Khan had not yet finished his counsel to the Muslim Conference. Addressing its Executive Board four years later, he emphasized the absolute necessity of "making the people and the electorate the real base and true foundation of all political power and organization". He wanted the Board to be "responsive

---

[1] Presidential Address, All India Muslim Conference, Delhi, 31 December 1928.

to public opinion and responsible to a representative assembly of the people". "There must be", he concluded, "a real living and vital link between the Muslim Conference at the top and the Muslim people at the foundation, otherwise it [is] bound to degenerate into a mere debating society."[1]

To Muslim politicians of every variety and persuasion he gave the same advice. All Muslim parties should "illuminate and educate public opinion among the Muslims".[2] During his next visit to India in the winter of 1934–5, he added an economic dimension to his appeal when he asked the leaders to listen to and cultivate the masses. The "main work of the future now lies in the countryside" where the task of economic amelioration awaited their attention. "It is no use thinking of politics unless it be to observe economic ends. The surest way to command the vote is to serve the voter, and unless our organizations are ready to serve the voter, they cannot hope to claim to have a bright political future before them. This work is humanitarian no less than political, but when dealing with the masses all things tend to merge into one another." Every party should have district centres whose duty shall be "to take the message of help and service to the countryside, and help the cultivator and the ignorant labourer with information, advice, the organization of co-operative enterprise and development of cottage industries".[3] Three days later, on another occasion, he again exhorted his audience to "work for the voter and to give him proper guidance." The legislators must get power but "use it for the betterment of the people whose representatives they would be and whose happiness and comfort in life would be their sole consideration".[4]

The Aga Khan favoured a democratic set-up not only in political parties but also in academic and research organizations. He told the Islamic Research Association of Bombay that he wanted the "full and complete control of such an institution to belong to those who subscribe in it".[5]

For a person so concerned with the will of the people it was necessary to emphasize the role and importance of the press.

[1] Address to the Executive Board of the All India Muslim Conference, New Delhi, 15 February 1934.
[2] Speech at a luncheon, New Delhi, 14 February 1934.
[3] Statement to the press, New Delhi, 5 February 1935.
[4] Speech at a luncheon, New Delhi, 8 February 1935.
[5] Speech at the Islamic Research Association, Bombay, 18 January 1939.

The Muslim press needed to be improved and extended.[1] It was the duty of the Muslims to keep their voice strong and effective through an efficient and far-reaching press. He wanted the *Star of India*, an evening daily of Calcutta, to bring out a Bengali edition, and wished Bengal to have a good Bengali daily. "The newspapers of the future", he said, "will mould the destinies of the country, and there must be a paper which can reach the widest possible public."[2]

His appreciation of a competent press was not confined to verbal expressions and good advice. When Muhammad Ali decided to bring out his *Comrade* he could not embark on the venture without the Aga Khan's promise of financial support, a promise which he kept in spite of the fact that the two leaders were not on the best of political terms and had at least once clashed in public on policy matters. The *Star of India*, probably the finest Muslim English-language newspaper of its age, was sustained by grants from the Aga Khan. He may also have aided and supported some other journals, but no direct information about this is available.

If it is surprising to see the Aga Khan moved by the spirit of democracy, it is astonishing to find him likewise impelled by socialism. He seems to have come to the socialist path via his interest in democratic politics and his concern for the rural masses. We must remember that in India an overwhelming majority lived off the land, the Muslims even more so than other communities. Uplift of the peasants and the labourers was only possible through some sort of socialism, however one defines the doctrine. On at least two occasions he came down clearly in favour of choosing socialist and leftist means to raise the standards of the common man and to bring him into the mainstream of both political and national life.

"Nothing is more significant in world affairs in our time", he wrote in 1925, "than the eagerness with which, in every free land, organized labour has thrown its influence on the side of peace and international goodwill as the sure means of human prosperity and happiness. The manual workers recognize that these blessings are dependent on peaceful solution in an age of wonderful scientific developments which in war may bring destruction on multitudes in a single hour." If the British Empire were given a broad base of mutual and equal service regardless of race, "we may see the fulfillment of the dream of the Socialist

[1] Letter, *The Times*, London, 16 December 1931.
[2] Message to the *Star of India*, Calcutta, 26 February 1934.

poet . . ." This is followed by six lines of poetry from an unnamed poet.[1]

To the Muslim leaders of India he explained that the issue of the future was "principally one of the economic freedom of the masses". He quoted with approval the example of the Soviet Union as proof of the failure of private effort. The legislative assemblies must take up the betterment of the masses as their foremost duty. "This was the work before everyone in the country. The social betterment of the masses could only happen by Socialism when every component part worked for the entire social fabric, and it was only through the political field that the nation could achieve its aim."[2]

In the field of education he advocated some form of state intervention. This is not to suggest that the Aga Khan did not favour private effort. It would be fair to indicate that in the task of promoting development, he viewed private and public efforts as complementary.

In Africa peaceful economic development and race relations were the two principal problems which attracted his attention. During his visit to Tanganyika in August 1945, he urged the Colonial Government to undertake comprehensive and energetic planning for the advancement of the African. To his mind the prosperity of the indigenous people was the key to the progress of the entire country.[3]

The discriminatory treatment meted out to the Indians domiciled in South Africa drew his wrath because it went against his convictions about political democracy and social equality. In unusually strong terms he described the plight of these Indians, attacking the authorities who allowed or countenanced such treatment. "Our fellow subjects, who are there maintaining an unequal struggle in a heroic manner that commands our admiration are wilfully subjected to persecution, insults and indignity and are branded with the undeserved stigma of an inferior race." This was a matter of the prestige of the whole Indian population. Their passive resistance "amid untold privations and sufferings, with patience and martyrdom" was an example to "those here who are not ashamed to have a recourse to measures that have brought infinite shame and disgrace to India". If no better method was available to make the Colonial Government see the injustice and cruelty of its acts, the Indians must ask the

[1] Letter, *The Times*, London, 3 August 1925.
[2] Speech at a luncheon, New Delhi, 8 February 1935.
[3] Interview, *The Tanganyika Standard*, Dar-es-Salaam, 2 August 1945.

Government to stop all indented labour to South Africa as a "mild step of retaliation".[1]

The average Indian, he wrote elsewhere, felt "pained astonishment" at the spectacle of the British Government appealing in vain for justice to be done in South Africa. Now there was the added danger that in East Africa a handful of white settlers might repeat some of the injustices which had already made of South Africa "a running sore" in the relations between England and India.[2] Twelve years later, in a public speech in Bombay, he painted the life of the Indians in South Africa in moving words. "It means forty years of humiliations inflicted upon them of harassing legislation and ordinances, of offensive rules and regulations, of constant pin-pricks and of many bludgeon blows borne with characteristic patience, with forbearance, with fortitude." During these long years the Indian leaders in South Africa and in India had made a succession of concessions, giving up their inherent rights for the sake of peace and in order to save the Indians out there from total ruin. "Not only the claims of a common Imperial Citizenship, not only the respect which their willing services to the cause of the development of South Africa but many promises have been forgotten."[3] Manifestations of racial prejudice were as hard for the Aga Khan to accept as the loss of political rights, avoidable economic deprivation, or the exploitation of the rural poor by the urban rich. His ideal was a society in which all men and women could live with dignity and self-respect.

Educational Ideals

Education was the ruling passion of the Aga Khan's public life. Nothing angered him more than an inefficient and wasteful educational system. Nothing pleased him more than the establishment of schools and colleges. In the twilight of his life, looking back at a long and distinguished career marked with many achievements, each of which alone would have satisfied a man of high ambition, he was content to say that in his own opinion one single achievement which gladdened his heart and that his single greatest success was the creation of the Muslim University of Aligarh.

[1] Inaugural Address, All India Muslim League, Delhi, 29 January 1910.
[2] "Indian Muslim Outlook", *Edinburgh Review,* January 1914.
[3] Speech at a public meeting, Bombay, 15 January 1926.

Throughout his writings and speeches we find a constant emphasis on the importance of education. It was the most urgent and essential duty of the community, and neither Indians, who had little power, nor the British in India, who had almost all, could escape this responsibility. The fundamental cause of the extreme poverty of India was the ignorance of the great majority of the people. "Has not the time come for taking a bold and generous step towards some system of universal education suited to the conditions of the various provinces of the country?" he asked the Viceroy in the Legislative Council in 1903.[1]

The diffusion of education was a question of life and death for India, and on it no compromise could be tolerated. Money was scarce, but care ought to be taken that an undue proportion of what was available was not swallowed up by buildings. "A slowing of the pace in order to wait for good buildings and other conditions of an ideal state of things would be a crime against the young life of India and her future generations."[2] He considered illiteracy as a menace to people and government alike. Its sinister consequences were poverty and disease.[3]

His critique of the Indian educational system was wide-ranging and comprehensive. The universities were mere examining boards. College life as it existed in Oxford and Cambridge was not known here, depriving the students of the most effective method of education. Moreover, education only touched the fringe of the vast population. In the West nations were making progress through the application of science to industry, which meant that industry, to be successful, had to be managed by skilled men. In India, on the contrary, science was harnessed to production, and people were generally given only elementary education, with a selected few receiving training in technical trades. The number of people receiving a significant level of education was very small. This virtual absence of education, and the resulting ignorance of the people, produced many evils – including the political discontent with which the government had then to deal with a strong hand. An expanded system of education would remove the discontent, create civic awareness, improve the economy, and eradicate caste and religious prejudices.[4]

The universities were producing a large number of persons

[1] Budget speech, Council of the Governor General, Calcutta, 25 March 1903.
[2] *India in Transition*, June 1918.
[3] *Memoirs*, 1954.
[4] "Some Aspects of Indian Reforms", *National Review*, December 1909.

just sufficiently educated for taking up government appointments. When the supply exceeded the demand, as it often did, these people had nothing to do. Reform must commence at the top and at the bottom at the same time. The standard of degrees should be raised and made uniform in all provinces. Every area ought to have the same facilities for education. The primary schools should be placed within easy reach of the people, or the means of reaching them should be improved. Each province should be divided into educational districts, determined by the number of primary schools in each area. The best students from these primary schools should go to the secondary school or college; and the most promising of the college students should be selected for the university. Before a student entered the secondary school his parents should indicate the calling they preferred for him, and the remainder of his educational course should be directed towards fitting him, generally and specifically, for that vocation. The university must be residential and situated at a good distance from the crowded city. Facilities for sports and recreation should be ample and free.[1]

In a country like India, where many financially independent mature men wanted to gain more knowledge, there ought to be a few degree-granting universities which would cater to their needs by providing for every age and class, at moderate fees, regular lectures and courses in different fields of study. An added advantage of these kinds of universities would be that many well-to-do people would join them and, appreciating the benefits, may be moved to render them substantial financial help.[2]

The Aga Khan gave education the same priority as national defence, calling for the same sacrifice. "Just as certain generations in Europe, namely, those of 1790 to 1815, and of the present day, have been called upon to bear the immense sacrifice of guarding the future of their countries from foreign aggression and military subjection, so the present generation in India must make greater sacrifices than would have been requisite but for past neglect, to deliver her from the grip of ignorance, poverty, and disease."[3]

One of the major functions of a university is research, and the Aga Khan's wide-ranging study of education did not miss its importance and existing weaknesses. He regretted that far too

[1] "India's Education and Her Future Position in the Empire", *National Review*, July 1911.
[2] *India in Transition*, June 1918.
[3] *Ibid.*

94

many unsuitable men were put to laboratory work. This produced poor results. Only men of proven ability should be vested with the responsibility of research and then provided with the fullest means for investigation. "In this way scientific research and progress would be revitalised with the fire of individual genius." These scientists would then be offered the highest material and social prizes, respect and titles. Those who showed a natural inclination for original thought and work would be placed in positions where they could pursue their research not only in the sciences, but in history, literature and economics.[1]

No communal barrier stood in the Aga Khan's way. He was, in 1902, probably the first Muslim to propose that there should be two Indian universities, one for the Hindus and one for the Muslims.[2] In 1913, while receiving the Deputation of the Hindu University of Benares, he declared his belief that "in a vast country like India every movement that gave greater intellectual variety to the country made the country richer and greater in colour and variety. The very fact that ancient Hindu learning and Hindu social life and sacred Hindu literature would be brought out to move and guide the young minds must surely be for the greater good of the country. With the intellectual development of youth it would bring out the higher side of life." Eminent literary men would emerge from such universities, and every facet of human life would be developed – intellectual, spiritual and religious. These centres of learning and intellectual endeavour would in time turn out more tolerant Indians.[3]

The Aga Khan was not afraid to tackle the thorny and controversial question of the medium of instruction. He realised that many people, especially in Bengal, wanted English to be the language of learning for a long time to come, and that in north India there were those who favoured Hindi as both the general medium of higher instruction and the national language. The Muslims had similar ideas in respect of Urdu. In the name of patriotism he asked the Hindu leaders to refrain from imposing Hindi on the rest of the subcontinent. The centralizing policy of the Mughal emperors had broken up their empire. But it was a saddening fact that the people of the United Provinces were still inclined to claim for their area the title of "the real India", and to consider the great provinces of the south and east as mere

[1] "If I were a Dictator", a broadcast talk, London, 11 November 1931.
[2] Presidential Address, All India Muhammadan Educational Conference, Delhi, 1902.
[3] Speech, Bombay, 23 February 1913.

addenda. If this spirit were carried into the linguistic field it would strike a fatal blow at the prospect of a federated, vital India of tomorrow. The example of Switzerland belied the fear that plurality of languages weakens national unity. "Let all the main Indian languages and their literary potentialities receive the fullest encouragement, with universities devoted to them when possible. . . . Philological science long ago taught us that languages are the natural expression of a people's inner life and mentality. To artificially force some to adopt the idioms of others is nothing but a cruel injustice only appropriate to the ideals of Prussian Kultur. Pragmatism and vital character and quality are the essential needs – not imitation of some external ideal of unity."[1]

Outside India, too, the Aga Khan preached the gospel of education. His principal advice to the Indians settled in South Africa was to take up the cause of education with zeal and energy. He told them that, despite racial discrimination, no one could stop them from raising the educational standard of every Indian boy to that of the level of the European. The wealthy members of their community could make it possible for the poor among them to receive high-quality education. He advised them to send their boys to British or American schools. "In the long run this education will go further than any amount of other action in bringing about a better understanding of your qualities as citizens of South Africa."[2]

If the Aga Khan's interest in the education of the Indians was a passion, his concern for and involvement in the diffusion of knowledge among the Muslims was a crusade: it is significant as it is symbolic of his lifelong *jihad* against ignorance that his first appearance on the national stage in India, when he was only twenty-five, was at the All India Muhammadan Educational Conference in 1902. On this occasion he equated education with the future of the nation. "We are", he said, "if I understand the purpose of this Conference aright, considering what in modern times are the ideals we must hold before our people and the paths by which they can attain them; and upon the right answer to these questions depends no trifling matter, but nothing less than the future of Indian Muslims."[3]

The Muslims must enlarge the sphere of education where it

[1] *India in Transition,* June 1918.
[2] Speech before the Natal Indian Congress, Durban, 16 August 1945.
[3] Presidential Address, All India Muhammadan Educational Conference, Delhi, 1902.

existed already and must create it where it was absent. Scientific education was vital, but that did not mean the neglect of the humanities. Muslim interests as well as the sentiment of communal harmony made it necessary that a knowledge of not only English, Arabic and Persian, but also of Sanskrit literature, should be attained, so that the community could come in contact with the sources of Hindu civilization and the roots of Hindu society. Referring to the encouragement to learning and science by the Prophet of Islam, he reminded his audience of the *hadith* exhorting the Muslims to travel as far as China in their search for knowledge.[1] Of the "two great aims" which he put before the Muslims in their domestic policy, the first was "to alter the position of affairs under which they are justly described in the recent Government pronouncement on Moslem education as 'educationally backward' ". They could not play an adequate and satisfactory part in the "great developments of Indian life now in progress" unless their educational attainments were of the same standard and quality as those of other communities.[2]

The Aga Khan considered education a religious duty imposed by the Quran on every Muslim. This was, in his case, neither a metaphor nor a slogan, but a logical deduction from the verses of the Book of God. His arguments on this point deserve close inspection.

Islam is fundamentally a natural religion. Throughout the Quran God's signs (*ayat*) are referred to as natural phenomena, the law and order of the universe, the exactitudes and consequences of the relations between natural phenomena in cause and effect. The stars, sun, moon, earthquakes, fruits of the earth and trees are repeatedly mentioned as the signs of divine power, divine law and divine order. In the Verse of Light the divine is described in terms of the natural phenomenon of light. During the great ages of Islam, Muslims did not forget these principles of their religion. By the end of the seventeenth century, however, they had forgotten them, and henceforth knowledge passed on to – and was developed by – Europe, while the Muslims stuck to their ceremonies and rituals. The downfall of Islam, not only in political power but also in learning and intellect, was the logical outcome.

What can be done to stop the rot? "If the present method by which the *'ulema* being brought up on one line of studies and

[1] Speech at a reception given by the Anjuman-i-Islam, Bombay, 10 January 1910.
[2] Speech at the London Muslim League, London, 14 July 1913.

the scientific youth on a different one continues, the disaster will come because there will be a fundamental misunderstanding in the outlook of intellect and faith in the soul of the nation." Christianity was saved in Europe because during and after the Renaissance the universities consisted of faculties of natural studies as well as of divinity. "The atmosphere of science permeated the atmosphere of Christian divinity studies and the atmosphere of the Christian divinity studies permeated the atmosphere of the scientific studies, [and] thus both grew and developed together." In this way Christianity adapted itself to science, though it is far from being a religion of nature or reason.

On the other hand, Islam, which is a religion of nature, drifted away from science which is nothing but the study of the laws and orders of nature listed in the Quran. The drift continues. "The only practical hope I see is that all your universities in Pakistan should have a faculty of Islamic religious and philosophical studies attached to ordinary curriculum for post-graduate students, who alone could be recognized as 'ulema." If the religious doctors and the general students are products of two different systems and schools, "there is no unity of soul without which there can be no greatness". "Unless our universities have the best graduate 'ulema schools for men brought up in the same atmosphere as the science students, realizing the fundamental truth that Islam is a natural religion of which the ayats [verses] are the universe in which we live and move and have our being, the same causes will lead to the same disastrous results."[1]

Every level or stage of education was equally important in the view of the Aga Khan. Sound primary education was the foundation of a society. "No solid superstructure can stand safely on softer soil." If the masses did not have rudimentary instruction, they could not produce or encourage leaders competent to raise the nation to its legitimate sphere of power, influence and usefulness. It was the "colossal" ignorance of the masses which prevented the Muslims from "uniting themselves in a spiritual union and of brotherhood such as must be our essential aim and ambition".[2]

Primary education must be imparted in the native and natural language of the student. This principle touched the issue of the rights of the minorities. There could not be free and primary education for one language and complete illiteracy for those who

[1] Letter to the President of Arabiyya Jamiyyat, Karachi, 4 April 1952.
[2] Inaugural Address, All India Muhammadan Educational Conference, Bombay, 4 December 1911.

spoke another. "I beg of you to realize fully that the system of primary education, unless it is free and compulsory, and provides a safeguard for teaching the vernacular, will injure your community more than any other. Besides, such a system is doomed to be an inevitable failure."[1]

Institutions of secondary education among the Muslims were of a poor quality. There were a large number of Muslim and Islamia and other schools and colleges throughout India, but most of them were inferior to similar schools and colleges run by the government or by other communities. The All India Muhammadan Educational Conference should, through a process of co-ordination, bring about a "unity of ideal and work" among these institutions. If their standard was not raised immediately, their students would always lag behind the others.[2]

A useful and sensible programme of educational uplift would note the following: primary education should not only be free and universal but also sufficiently practical to be of use to agriculturists and labourers. It should take into account the fact that an immense proportion of those attending the primary schools did not proceed beyond that stage, and planners should design the curriculum accordingly. Generally there should be no redundance or superfluity in the system. The secondary system needed a twofold development. Extension and improvement should be effected in the facilities available for proceeding to a course in the arts, while the "modern side" of science and technology should be urgently developed. The quality of teachers must be raised; in the meantime students in certain special courses must obtain their instruction abroad, and for this purpose the number of government and private scholarships had to be multiplied. Students should be sent not only to England and Europe but also to the United States and Japan, so that "they may learn the various processes in the lives of the great industrial commonwealth". Those who had received commercial training should be helped by co-operative societies to open businesses, not only in Europe and America but in Africa and Asia in order to find markets for indigenous Indian products.[3]

The Aga Khan was a great believer in the highest quality of education and training in science and technology. This kind of instruction, he said, must be one of the "main practical

[1] *Ibid.*
[2] Presidential Address, All India Muhammadan Educational Conference, Rampur, 21 February 1936.
[3] Inaugural Address, All India Muslim League, Delhi, 29 January 1910.

objects of our energy and ambitions".[1] Not satisfied with the one College of Science in the Aligarh Muslim University, he urged the Muslim Educational Conference of 1936 to create "a great institution" like the College of Technology to teach engineering, electronics and "all the sciences applied to life and actual work". This was so important that the scheme should not be left "in the stage of discussion and thought and idea"; this was the "immediate task" before the conference, the Aligarh University and the people.[2] Nothing was done in this direction, and ten years later, in 1946, he again reminded the Court of the Aligarh University that "the world of the future depended upon science". Once again he implored them to establish a great scientific research institute, to be located in Karachi so that it could attract students from South Iran, Afghanistan and East Africa (if he were younger he would have collected money for it himself, as he had done for Aligarh many years ago). Now was the time to act; or the future certainly "would not be one in which the Muslims could hold their own."[3] Still nothing was done.

Twice he appealed to Pakistan to translate his dream into a reality. In early 1950 he implored the Quaid-i-Azam (Jinnah) Memorial Fund to establish an Institute of Technology to perpetuate the memory of the maker of Pakistan.[4] A year later he asked the University of Dacca in East Pakistan to create an institute on the model of the famous Zürich Technological School.[5] The dream remains unrealized.

Management science is a relatively new field of study even in Europe and America. But the Aga Khan, with his consuming passion for the uplift of the Muslims through every educational avenue, asked the curriculum makers in 1936 to include it as a subject of study. What he called "pure and practical commercial education", to distinguish it from the instruction available in schools and institutes and college of commerce, was the "science of exchange and business organization", which should be taken up particularly by the people of the land coasts of Muslim India. European trade and commerce had developed to its existing efficiency and scope because of its mastery of this branch of

[1] Speech at the Anjuman-i-Islam, Bombay, 11 January 1910.
[2] Presidential Address, All India Muhammadan Educational Conference, Rampur, 21 February 1936.
[3] Speech before the Court of the Aligarh Muslim University, Bombay, 9 March 1946.
[4] Message to the Quaid-i-Azam Memorial Fund, Karachi, possibly February 1950.
[5] Speech, University of Dacca, Dacca, 28 January 1951.

knowledge. Once the technique of banking and allied practices was mastered, the path to commercial prosperity and social progress would open up.[1]

At this time he also drew the attention of the Muslims to another useful practice: career planning. He pointed out that in Europe there were "career masters" who tried to discover the natural inclinations of pupils (from infancy to undergraduate level) for various walks of life. A three-dimensional exercise was necessary if the Muslim educationists were to benefit from this Western example. Processes and procedures must be devised by which the student, his teacher and his parents were in constant contact with one another while planning the pupil's future. "Those who are naturally inclined to some particular work or who are of practical type of mentality, should be brought in touch, as early as possible, with such intellectuals as will develop their particular qualities."[2]

Finally, the Aga Khan turned to the question of the Urdu (or Persian or Arabic) script. Having established that primary education ought to be given in the language of the student, and foreseeing that at some time in the future university education might also adopt Urdu as its medium of instruction, he must have reflected upon the quality of the script in which Urdu was written. He has given us no details of his process of thought, only its results. Both Urdu and Persian scripts presented serious difficulties in the primary stages of education and the leaders and educationists ought to deliberate on how to improve and simplify the way the language was written.[3]

The Aga Khan's concern for Muslim education was not limited to India. He advised the Muslims of South Africa to improve their educational attainment even though the facilities open to them were not adequate. To overcome this difficulty he suggested the opening of night classes wherever there was a group of Muslims living together. There they must study books on Muslim history and literature so that they could, through the Western door of the English language, enter "the palaces of Eastern culture".[4]

But, next to India, his main area of interest lay in the eastern part of Africa. Before 1914 he had made a financial contribution

---

[1] Presidential Address, All India Muhammadan Educational Conference, Rampur, 21 February 1936.
[2] *Ibid.*
[3] Presidential Address, All India Muslim Conference, Delhi, 31 December 1928.
[4] Speech before the Transvaal Muslim League, Johannesburg, 12 August 1945.

to the creation of the Gordon Memorial College in Khartoum, the first college in the Sudan and the forerunner to the later University of Khartoum. In 1945 he told the East Africans that he did not want them to repeat the tragedy of India where graduates earned less than a servant tending his master's horse, and where men could not make use of the education they had received and could also not adapt themselves to other work. The remedy lay in an emphasis on agricultural, technical and vocational training which would turn out useful citizens with a sound, practical background as well as the more academic aspects of education.[1]

One of the great ambitions of the Aga Khan during his declining years was to help set up an international Muslim university in East Africa. There was no good institution which the young African Muslims could attend and still remain loyal to their faith. He had been told that while the young Christian boys graduating from the Makerere College in Kampala, Uganda, had become a source of strength to Christianity, the Muslim boys had returned as propagandists of Communism and anti-religious tendencies. The hour had arrived to think seriously of establishing a university in the region for all races and communities of Muslims along the lines of the Aligarh or Beirut universities. Though it would be primarily an Islamic university to serve the Muslims of East, Central and South Africa, it must also be a world Islamic university: funds should be contributed by the whole Muslim world, and he would double whatever was collected; boys and girls from China to Morocco would be on the roll of this institution.[2]

Like the great school of technology in Pakistan, the pan-Islamic university of East Africa has also remained a distant goal. However, his efforts led to the establishment of an institute for technical education for Muslims at Mombasa, Kenya. He donated £100,000 to the project, and insisted that its doors be open not only to the Arab population of the area but also to the indigenous Muslims.

The Aga Khan's greatest dream was, however, fulfilled. The Aligarh University was his lasting joy and pleasure which he called his greatest service to Islam.

It was in 1902 that he began to see the vision of a university in which the Muslim youth of India could cultivate – besides the modern sciences – a knowledge of its glorious past and religion,

[1] Interview, *East African Standard*, Nairobi, 26 March 1945.
[2] Speech at the East African Muslim Conference, Mombasa, 28 July 1946.

and receive more attention to character – building than to examination passing. It would be a residential university, like Oxford and Cambridge, and it was bound to serve more lands than India alone. Muslim India had a legitimate interest in the intellectual development of the Muslims of Turkey, Iran, Afghanistan and other countries. The best way to help them was to make the Muhammadan Anglo-Oriental College of Aligarh into a "Muslim Oxford". All the Muslim countries would then send their best students there, not only to master modern studies but also to cultivate a spirit of honesty and self-sacrifice which were the hallmark of the Muslims of the first century of Islam. It would "restore the faded glories of our people", and "arrest the decadence of Islam". And "if we are not willing to make sacrifices for such an end, must I not conclude that we do not really care whether the faith of Islam is dead or not?"[1]

The proposed university was to aim high: "We want to be able to give our Muslim youths not merely the finest education that can be given in India, but a training equal to that which can be given in any country in the world." Why should the Muslim student of the future be obliged to go to Britain or Germany to attain eminence in any branch of scholarship? The expectation was that in time Aligarh would be able to command the same respect among the *literati* as Berlin or Oxford, Leipzig or Paris. And "we want those branches of Muslim learning, which are too fast passing into decay, to be added by Muslim scholars to the stock of the world's knowledge". Above all it would be for the Muslims "an intellectual and moral capital; a city which shall be the hope of elevated ideas and pure ideals; a centre from which light and guidance shall be diffused among the Muslims of India, aye, and out of India too, and which shall hold up to the world a noble standard of the justice and virtue and purity of our beloved faith. Gentlemen, do you think that the restoration of the glory of Islam would be too dear at one crore [ten million] of rupees?"[2] It was a stirring appeal, indeed for a worthy ideal, which would touch the right chord.

He returned to the subject two years later. The university would have the highest standard of learning. The place would combine, in the instruction it imparted, scientific training with moral education – "that indirect but constant reminder of the eternal

---

[1] Presidential Address, All India Muhammadan Educational Conference, Delhi, 1902.
[2] *Ibid.*

difference between right and wrong which is the soul of education". The existing Indian universities divorced learning from religion, and this was not acceptable to the Muslims, who wished to save the Muslim identity from being pressed out of existence by a mechanical imitation of the West. "We have a history in which noble and chivalrous characters abound; we have a religious past so full of heroic figures that direct contact and communion with them could not but improve and give our youth early in life that sense of the necessity for self-sacrifice, for truthfulness, and for independence of character without which instruction and knowledge are, from the national point of view, worthless." Other histories had great heroes and noble characters, but they were alien to the Muslims. Muslim history had figures who lived and moved very much as the Muslims of the present age do in their home life. Any academic contact with them could not but ennoble the students and strengthen their character, and thereby strengthen the character of the nation. Until this was achieved, the graduates would not be able to remove "those degenerate customs that keep us not merely amongst the backward, but amongst the fallen". Pernicious social customs had crept into the religious life of the people so insidiously and deeply that even moderately educated Muslims did not know the difference between such customs and the injunctions of the Prophet; Islam was now being held responsible for these accretions. The planned university could and would remove this libel from the name of Islam and its followers. "I earnestly beg of you", he concluded, "that the cause of such a university should not be forgotten in the shouts of the market place that daily rise amongst us."[1]

In 1910 he reminded the Trustees of the Aligarh College that his connection with it had been from the first a labour of love, and that "among the various interests and pursuits that occupy my time none is so dear to me as the services I can render the College". He added: "Unfortunately the wretched state of my health has so far prevented me from doing all I should otherwise do for Aligarh, and above all has prevented me from carrying out my cherished dream of coming and passing a few weeks quietly in your midst every year and conversing freely, not only with the trustees and the professors, but with the students as well." The ideal before them was to make this institution a great

---

[1] Speech, Muslim Educational Conference, Bombay, 1904.

centre of research and learning and "a source of moral influence for the Mussalmans."[1]

Three days later he put his plans before the annual session of the All India Muslim League. A Muslim university was vital to the nation because "without a sincere and deep but unobtrusive and charitable faith, without that childlike feeling of dependence on the Unseen Power of which the visible universe is but a sign, our youth can never develop their highest and noblest faculties, their spiritual and emotional qualities. It would be a residential university, forming the character, training the intellect, satisfying the emotions through the medium of a loving and charitable faith, imparting discipline through sports, and providing that intangible atmosphere which a good university breathed. It would be an educational centre and an intellectual capital to which all Muslims could turn for light and guidance. In order to come in touch with what is best in the ancient Hindu civilization Sanskrit would be a part of the curriculum. The object of the university is not to gratify mere sentiment or vanity; we believe it to be necessary for the true development of our principles and the ultimate spiritual unity of our faith."[2]

The remainder of the story of the making of Aligarh is best told by the Aga Khan himself in his reminiscences. Right from his first visit to Aligarh "I was on fire to see [its] scope widened and its usefulness extended, and to find the money for it". The pursuit of this ideal led "to years of arduous and all-demanding toil, the journeyings, the speech-making, the sitting on committees, the fight against apathy and the long, long discussions with those in high places" ... "But we may claim with pride that Aligarh was the product of our own efforts and of no outside benevolence." ... "I suppose that I was a sort of one-man 'ginger group' on behalf of the project of converting Aligarh into a great Muslim university." He persuaded the Viceroy, Lord Hardinge of Penhurst, and Sir Harcourt Butler, Education Member of the Viceroy's Executive Council, to favour the project, extracted concessions from them and made some compromises.

The Aga Khan undertook a strenuous tour of the subcontinent with two purposes in view: to convert the critics of the idea of a university to his own opinion and to collect funds. It was hard going: his health was poor; the area to be covered was as large as Europe. "These were years of unrelenting hard work. For days

---

[1] Reply to the address of welcome from the Trustees of the MAO College, Aligarh, 26 January 1910.
[2] Inaugural Address, All India Muslim League, Delhi, 29 January 1910.

and weeks at a time, it seemed, I lived in railway trains. In every town the train stopped I would address Muslim gatherings on the platform of the railway station. At every opportunity I preached the cause of Aligarh." Assisted by his principal aide and private secretary, Maulana Shaukat Ali, (whose oratory and unbounded energy proved invaluable), the tour ended with three million rupees in the bag – an immense sum in those days – to which the Aga Khan added his own contribution of a hundred thousand.

It would be appropriate to end this section with the Aga Khan's own words. "Now when all is said and done, when I look back on all that the Muslim University of Aligarh has stood for and achieved in the past forty years, this is without doubt one of the facts of my life which I can record and contemplate with real and abiding satisfaction. I do not want only to stress its political consequences, momentous as these have been. Where else than in a Muslim university would it have been possible to establish and maintain, alongside and fully integrated with the libraries, the laboratories and all the facilities essential for a full under-standing of our world and our time, a true centre of Islamic faith and culture, in which can be expounded and practised the principles of our religion, its universality and its real modernity, its essential reasonableness, its profound spirit of tolerance and charity and respect for other faiths? That I played my part in establishing such a centre is for me one of the happiest, most consoling, and most fortifying thoughts to take into old age."[1]

Social Reforms

The Aga Khan's great interest in education was only one manifes-tation – although the most important – of his concern with the general uplift of society. As social improvement, to be effective and permanent, must start at the bottom, the earliest stirrings of his social conscience were caused by the pitiable condition and needs of the rural masses. His perception of the situation in India made him offer a new and wider definition of the generally accepted term of "untouchables" (which was then, and has been since, reserved for the lowest Hindu caste). "In India", he wrote in 1918, "so widespread is the poverty of the people that, judged by Western standards, an overwhelming majority, and not the outcastes alone, can be described as depressed or submerged. Long familiarity with this all-pervading poverty, however, leads to

[1] *Memoirs*, 1954.

the application of these terms on the basis not of poverty, but of membership of the 'untouchable' communities. Henceforth, if the task of national improvement and consolidation is to be taken in hand, we must give a wider meaning to the description of 'depressed' than that of the mere position of a number of inferior sections in relation to the Hindu caste system."[1]

There were many problems faced by the people working on land which required attention. The peasant was illiterate, ignorant, unhealthy and poor. Since he could not read or write he did not understand the meaning of contracts he was making. Hence the exorbitant rates of interest he paid to the money-lenders and bankers. The members of the Legislative Council should prepare a scheme having for its objects a decrease in the rate of interest, expansion of education at the elementary level, and an introduction of the principle of co-operation in distributing the products of agriculture.

The Aga Khan made an interesting suggestion: in Europe local councils had appointed agricultural lecturers who toured a given area. A similar system should be instituted in India, with experts communicating with the peasant in the latter's vernacular, informing him of the latest developments in agricultural science, of modern practices of tilling, sowing, watering, crop growing and harvesting, and of the uses of manure, etc. Besides these technical advisers, a class of travelling lecturers should be created, who would explain the commercial and business side of agriculture.

The eradication of poverty from among the land workers required innovative measures. The government could not lend to individual tillers for reasons of book-keeping, collection of the capital sum and the fixation of the interest. But it could approach the co-operative societies and enter into some arrangements whereby, on certain conditions, these societies or kindred bodies lent money at a cheap rate and the government made loans to the societies for this purpose. If the scheme worked successfully, the bankers, facing semi-official competition, would be forced to lower the rate of interest chargeable to the peasant.[2]

It was unwise and impracticable to leave all the chores of amelioration to the state. It was also the duty of the Hindus and Muslims of the country to come to the aid of the toiling peasants, hit by poor returns, ravaged by famines, and impoverished by

---

[1] *India in Transition*, 1918, p. 244.
[2] "Some Aspects of Indian Reforms", *National Review*, December 1909.

their own social customs and thriftless habits. They could be saved from the clutches of the usurer through elementary education, and from erratic rainfall by the extension of irrigation. But these were no more than palliatives. The real and lasting salvation of the cultivator lay in co-operation. "Co-operation to secure cheap credit and wipe off the burden of hopeless debt that hangs round the necks of our *ryots*; co-operation to secure cheap and efficient distribution; co-operation in the introduction of agricultural implements and so profit by the lessons of our Research Institute and experimental farms – this is the only agency that can permanently benefit our backward agriculture."[1]

India would one day become a living industrial force, but agriculture was currently of the greatest importance to its economic well-being. Scientific methods must be applied to agriculture and to the improvement of cattle breeding. The peasant should not be forced to sell his produce before he could get an equitable return on his investment. A further benefit of these reforms would be that, with agriculture becoming an attractive profession, fewer young people would migrate to the cities in search of a precarious living, and ultimately this might remove or at least decrease the political and economic unrest in the country.[2]

Agricultural education could offer one key to the solution of these problems. "The present divorce between practical agriculture and theoretical education on one hand and between scientific agriculture and primitive cultivation on the other is worthy of our serious attention. An immense bridge must be found to cross this wide gulf.... What I ... want to see is that the Muslim tenant and the Muslim landlord should be graduates of the Imperial College of Agriculture, or at least they should be able to understand what the graduate of agriculture says."[3]

The Aga Khan gave similar advice to the Indian residents in East Africa, insisting that they should explore the avenue of agriculture instead of adding to the number of commercial and clerical workers. In Kenya a lot of land remained undeveloped, especially near Lake Victoria. The country needed and could easily support a large agrarian population. The scope was even greater in Tanganyika than in Kenya because of the comparatively

[1] Inaugural Address, All India Muslim League, Delhi, 29 January 1910.
[2] Interview, *The Times of India*, Bombay, 28 December 1928.
[3] Presidential Address, All India Muhammadan Educational Conference, Rampur, 21 February 1936.

small indigenous population and large areas awaiting development.[1]

The cultivator might have been, and probably was, particularly depressed, but other strata and sectors in society also presented a pitiful sight – "extreme poverty, hunger and nakedness, emaciated and enfeebled bodies and ignorance". Such people could be called human beings by courtesy only. In addition to economic backwardness they were also intellectually backward."With this denial of divinity in mankind, there is the denial of human brotherhood, and we have developed intolerance in matters religious and sectarian. The whole economic, social and religious fabric calls for immediate relief – uplift of the weak – economically, intellectually and culturally, so that there may be left no one to be called downtrodden."[2]

He saw conditions of poverty also among South African Muslims, and marked out for them certain specific areas for improvement. Education, of course, came first; but the eradication of some minor daily habits could also promote Muslim well-being. He put his finger on two of these. "The greatest danger to every Muslim citizen – I have not the least hesitation in saying it – is alcohol. Time has shown that it is an injury to you; an injury to your person; an injury to your health." Islam had put a ban on it because it carried greater evil than good. In the community he was addressing it was "a very grave danger", a "terrible poison", and it must be avoided at all costs. Then he came to the habit of smoking. It was not forbidden by their religion, but few could deny its economic risks and health hazards. "What would you think of a man who went about the streets burning up ten-shilling notes? You would call him a mad man, wouldn't you? But people go around buying cigarettes and burning them." In the opinion of many doctors, smoking was bad for one's health. It was better to avoid it.[3]

Social reform in all Muslim countries was a thing dear to the Aga Khan's heart. Co-operative enterprise along modern scientific lines could help to remove the destitution, hunger and economic distress. The ensuing social progress would relieve the rural masses of their existing state of misery. Principles and practices of modern sanitation and hygiene should be adopted. "Physical fitness and mental ability are necessary conditions of progress. This economic and social progress would constitute an

[1] Interview, *East African Standard*, Nairobi, 26 March 1945.
[2] Speech, New Delhi, 17 February 1936.
[3] Speech before the Transvaal Muslim League, Johannesburg, 12 August 1945.

important factor towards permanent political freedom of the Muslim people. It is our belief that a free and progressive Muslim world, a land which commands the very centre of the world's intercontinental traffic, and which possesses an important wealth in raw materials will constitute an important stabilising factor in the world peace of tomorrow."[1]

For the economic progress of Pakistan, a country which he considered the hope of the Muslim world, he prescribed savings for capital investment. If real independence was the object in Pakistan, or indeed any Muslim country, the present generation must be willing and ready "to reduce welfarism and consumerism to the very limit". Offering the Soviet Union as an example, he called for national effort to reduce consumption and increase capital investment to enable Pakistan "in 20 years, [to] build up the elements of a free system, independent alike of communism and colonialism".

The Government of Pakistan might make and implement its own plans to this end. But let every citizen realize the importance of investment, and, guided by the authorities, divert it to the production of capital goods. If such an effort was not made, "a time might come when, for its very survival, it [the country] may be compelled to try some form of compulsory investment such as in Russia. The alternative to that would be total economic dependence on either one or the other of the two capital investing countries, viz., America or Russia." Here he used an argument from religion: the statesmen and religious leaders ought to know that "the soul and the body are interdependent and indeed are one in life". They should prevail upon their people to wake up to the necessity of constant investment. "With the standard of life already low and precarious, it is difficult to forego the immediate advantage. But not to forego it will mean future loss."[2] The Aga Khan's advice was not heeded, and his fears came true: Pakistan, refusing to make any effort to raise itself, ended up as a daily supplicant at the doorstep of the United States.

Social reform was impossible without the co-operation and participation of women who constituted half the population, and who played a crucial role in sustaining the fundamental and conserving values by which the society wished to live.

The Aga Khan took equal interest in the emancipation of

[1] *Glimpses of Islam*, 1944.
[2] "Economic Development in Pakistan and other Muslim States", lecture in Karachi, 1 February 1952.

Muslim as well as non-Muslim Indian women. His views and reflections about the place of women in society are so startlingly fresh that some of them need to be reproduced at length.

"Biologically the female is more important to the race than the male. While average women are capable of earning their own livelihood like men, they are the guardians of the life of the race, and only through their natural constitution are they able to bear the double burden. Experience shows the strong probability that the active influence of women on society, under free and equal conditions, is calculated not only to bring about practical improvement in the domestic realm, but also a higher and nobler idealism into the life of the State. Those who know Muslim society from within readily admit that its higher spiritual life owes a great debt to the example and influence of women. Today, as in the lifetime of the Prophet, probably the majority of devout and reverent followers of His teachings are women."[1]

"No progressive thinker of today will challenge the claim that the social advancement and general well-being of communities are greatest where women are least debarred, by artificial barriers and narrow prejudice, from taking their full position as citizens. Hence it is with deep sorrow that the admission must be made that the position of Indian women is unsatisfactory, that artificial obstacles to their full service of the commonwealth are every-where found, and that, from the point of view of health and happiness alike, women suffer needlessly through chains forged by prejudice and folly... These and other social evils have so handicapped India that it is impossible to conceive of her taking a proper place in the midst of free nations until the broad principle of equality between the sexes has been generally accepted by her people. The present abrogation of this principle is the more to be deplored since the natural intelligence and ability of Indian womanhood are by no means inferior to those of their emancipated sisters."[2]

To all Indian societies – be they in East Africa, South Africa, or India itself – the Aga Khan's message was to educate the girls. He wished to found female schools and colleges, to send women to universities, and give them an equal place in the educational sphere. "Personally, if I had two children, and one was a boy and the other a girl, and if I could afford to educate only one, I would have no hesitation in giving the higher education to the girl." The man could concentrate on manual effort to earn a

[1] *India in Transition*, June 1918.
[2] *Ibid.*

111

livelihood, but the woman had to maintain a home life and to bring up the children. Her influence in the family was enormous, and the future of the generation "depended upon her ability to lead the young along the right path and instruct in the rudiments of culture and civilization".[1]

To the Indians in Natal he said that in the standard of education there should be equality between the two sexes. It was only when a nation could summon to its service both men and women to run the domestic and social life and look after economic and secular activities could fulfillment and greatness be achieved. Britain could not have won the Second World War, nor the Soviet Union completed its Revolution, without the contribution made by their women. If all the ordinary but essential advantages and facilities were brought to "our mothers and sisters and daughters", society would make great advances.[2]

The Aga Khan was also an eloquent supporter of female franchise. When Indian women were not lacking in natural intelligence and had given ample proof of their success in such worldly affairs as management of property, it would be a pity to deny them the vote. "It would be a signal advantage to the State to have both the intuition and the naturally conservative influence of women operating in political life. . . . No scheme of political reform based on the co-operation of the people with the rulers can or will succeed, if it is vitiated by the radical defect of closing the door to women on the irrational ground of sex, and not accepting equal qualifications as conferring equal rights." He also felt that the inclusion of women among the electorate and in the councils would make it difficult to defend, renew or enact socially unjust laws.

"We must not build up", he proceeded, "the fabric of the autonomous State on weak and one-sided foundations. I am confident that an assembly to the election of which Indian women had contributed would keep nearer to the facts and needs of life, to the real and actual in the country, than one selected by men alone. . . . Is it to be maintained that the women of India are less capable than the men of realizing the need for sacrifice [demanded by public life]? Or are we to impose on them the acceptation of responsibility to society at large without participation in the political shaping of the State? The progressive modernization which depends on co-operation and understanding between the rulers and the ruled will be impossible in

[1] Speech before the Transvaal Muslim League, Johannesburg, 12 August 1945.
[2] Speech at the Natal Indian Congress, Durban, 16 August 1945.

India unless women are permitted to play their legitimate part in the great work of national regeneration on a basis of political equality."[1]

It must be borne in mind that these demands were made in 1918, when even the most radical among the 'ulema were not prepared to send the women out of the home, when the other kind of 'ulema were arguing that Islam did not sanction female franchise and did not allow women to sit in a legislative assembly, and when there was no Muslim woman, and only one or two Hindu women, in public life.

In 1919 the Southborough Committee on Franchise, one of the instruments which prepared the Montagu-Chelmsford reforms of that year, rejected the extension of franchise to women. Lord Southborough himself was surprised at the volume of evidence in favour of giving women the vote, but he disregarded it, calling it so much political idealism. The Aga Khan, in a letter to *The Times*, castigated him and other British administrators of India. "It seems he [Southborough] has forgotten that the world is governed by ideas, and that true progress is rooted in idealism." He rejected the official explanation that women in *purdah* would find it difficult to visit the polling booths to cast their vote by recalling that *purdah*-observing ladies regularly went to the law and registration courts, gave evidence in relation to the transfer of property and visited other offices when the need arose. It was "ludicrous" that there would be anything revolutionary in their coming to record their vote once in three years. Similarly, he found Sir James Meston's statement that female enfranchisement would present many practical and social difficulties "an instance of the regrettable fact that while many conscientious British officials spend their working lives in administrative duties in India, they never enter into a real understanding of the life or aspirations of the people – national, social, or religious". His rebuke continued. "It is painful to Indian readers that men who have attained high distinction in the Civil Service should have to be seriously asked if they would be shocked at the inclusion of women in the electorates. No Indian, not even the most conservative, will be shocked by the proposal that now that the sacred right of enfranchisement is to be given on a substantial scale to men, women should share it, just as they share the sacred rights of property." He disagreed with Southborough and Meston that very few women would exercise the franchise. But that was not the issue. "The question is one of justice, and not of the degree

[1] *India in Transition*, June 1918.

to which the right would be used." And if the official view was to be followed to its logical end, the women of India should be deprived of the rights to property and equality before civil law which they had enjoyed for centuries. The Aga Khan concluded with a stinging reprimand. "I feel it my duty to the hundreds of venerable and sensible *purdah* ladies of position I know in India to register this protest against the obsolete views of men who have attained to place and power in India, but who have never taken the trouble to know the people among whom they do office work."[1]

Islamic Modernist

In the last section I outlined the scope of the social and economic reforms urged upon the Muslim community by the Aga Khan. He wanted the Muslims to translate the spirit of the message of Islam into concrete activity, so that every Muslim man and woman would be living proof of the verity of the teachings of the Prophet as conveyed to him by Gabriel. These prescriptions for the good of society made up, so to speak, the mundane aspect of a life lived according to certain beliefs and convictions.

But such advice did not exhaust the guidance needed by the Muslims. In the diverse – but essentially interrelated – fields of law, jurisprudence, theology and spiritual thinking there were concepts and values crying out for interpretation, re-interpretation, elaboration and understanding, so that Muslims could live at peace with their conscience in the modern age without forsaking the fundamentals of their faith. This brings us to the religious ideas expressed by the Aga Khan; and taken together they place him firmly among the modernists of the past two centuries. Like Shah Waliullah, Sir Sayyid Ahmad Khan and his Aligarh school, Sayyid Ameer Ali, Iqbal and Ghulam Ahmad Parwez, he attempted to steer the ark of liberalism through the rocks of reaction. Before comparing the Aga Khan with these thinkers it is relevant to provide the reader with a short account of their principal views.

The liberal tendency in Indian Islamic thought can be traced back to Shah Waliullah (1702/3–63), an enlightened Sunni scholar-reformer of exceptional perspicacity who argued for a return to the original purity of the faith. His importance lies in the fact that he combined the skills of scholar, theologian, jurist, social reformer and economic thinker. His learning and insight

---

[1] Letter, *The Times*, London, 8 August 1919.

led him to emphasize the need for *ijtihad* (individual reasoning) and the re-opening of its doors which were closed shut by the consensus of the medieval conservative *'ulama*. He was critical of the contemporary *'ulama*, who had reduced religion to a collection of formal rites and rituals which he deemed to be not only outside the scope of *sharia* but also un-Islamic. To the philosophy of social reform he made the startlingly refreshing contribution of the theory of economic justice. Islam aimed at the creation of an ideal society, and this social purpose was impossible to fulfill without far-reaching economic reforms. He is the first thinker in modern Islam to underline the importance of improving the condition of the common man: today he would be called a socialist. In opposition to Shaikh Ahmad Sirhindi, he stood for amicable relations between Sunnis and Shias. He founded a seminary in Delhi which trained a large number of *'ulema*, including his own sons, who carried his message to all corners of the subcontinent. His family continued his mission, and his influence on all succeeding thinkers and scholars has been immense.

For the Sunni Muslim Sir Sayyid Ahmad Khan (1817–98), the rise of the West and the coming of British rule posed three challenges: evaluation of Western civilization, rationalization of the basic data of faith, and meeting the challenge of Christian missionaries. He responded to them by studying Christian apologetics, writing a sympathetic commentary of the Bible (indicating his religious pluralism), offering a well-constructed rationalist scholasticism (in the tradition of the *Mu'tazilah*) and reconciling religion and science. He founded the Scientific Society in 1864 to popularize Western science and inculcate an interest in it among the Indians. He established the Muhammadan Anglo-Oriental School in 1875 (made into a college in 1878 and which became the Muslim University of Aligarh after his death) to spread education among the Muslims. He created the Muhammadan Anglo-Oriental Educational Conference in 1886 (renamed successively the All India Muhammadan Educational Congress, All India Muhammadan Educational Conference, and All India Muslim Educational Conference) to enable leading politicians, teachers, *'ulama*, scholars and men of culture to meet and reflect upon the educational, cultural, intellectual and social problems and needs of the community. To publicize his views, and those of his supporters and sympathizers, he began publishing a journal called *Tahzib-ul-Akhlaq*.

According to Sayyid Ahmad Khan, religion equals ethical criteria, which equal truth, which equals human nature as understood by reason, and natural laws, making Islam a religion of nature. Believing that personal interpretations of the Quran by each individual Muslim were valid in both literal and symbolic realms, he proceeded to expound his interpretation. *Wahi* (divine inspiration) and reason are identical, and revelational law is consonant with human rationality. There are no miracles in Islam. Angels and *jannat* (good and evil spirits) are properties of created things. *Hadith* (the words of the Prophet) is not binding in law or in *sharia*. Polygamy and slavery are not permissible. Simple interest is allowed, compound interest is probably not. *Ijtihad* (individual reasoning in religious matters) is an inalienable right of every Muslim. *Ijma'* (consensus) is unacceptable in the classical form, where only the *'ulama* can exercise it.

Among Sayyid Ahmad Khan's close associates were men like Muhsin-ul-Mulk and Chiragh Ali, who wrote in the *Tahzib-ul-Akhlaq* and elsewhere, giving an equally radical, bold and forward-looking interpretation of Islam.

Sayyid Ameer Ali (1849–1928), an *athna-ashari* Shia thinker of Arab-Iranian origin and leader and a friend of the Aga Khan for many years, was a distinguished jurist, judge and historian. Through personal example and fine scholarship he did much to eradicate many of the Western-Christian misreadings and misapprehensions of Islam. Most of his writings seem to aim at effecting Shia-Sunni amity. The Shias believe in the pontifical *khilafat* of the first three righteous Caliphs and the apostolical *imamat* of the fourth Caliph, Ali, in whom the apostolical and pontifical authorities came together. The absent or hidden messianic *imam* is an apostolical *imam*. The Ottoman Caliph was a pontiff of both Shias and Sunnis. Ameer Ali has strong *Mu'tazilah* sympathies, and rejects the inhibiting externalism of the Ash'arite school. According to him, certain Quranic injunctions are only relevant to the Prophet's day and age. Ethical humanism is the essence of *din*. There is greater stress on charity and benevolence than on justice. Muhammad performed the dual role of prophet and statesman. Islam disallows both polygamy and slavery. Any Quranic disabling injunction against women is temporary and relevant to the Arabs of that age. Quranic injunctions are generally of two kinds: permanent or eternal, and temporary or expedient. *Ijma'* is at the same time a source of law through legislation and a constitutional check on the sovereign or executive.

Sir Muhammad Iqbal (1877–1938) is not only the greatest poet produced by Muslim India and one of the greatest in world literature, but also an eminent thinker in his own right. He presided over the All India Muslim League in 1930, attended the Round Table Conference, and in 1932 presided over the All India Muslim Conference. His lectures on the reconstruction of religious thought in Islam and the bulk of his Persian poetry provide us with the corpus of his thought.

Iqbal is the philosopher of movement, both in relation to the universe and to man's life. The universe moves from chaos to order and is in a process of continuous becoming. Parallel to this, the individual moves and progresses to higher levels of achievement and consciousness through conquest of the forces of nature. Human action is defined as the organization of man's potentiality for movement directed towards the conquest of nature. But, while movement in nature is amoral, in man it is ethical and purposive. God describes Himself as *ahsan al-khaliqin* (the best of the creators), which implies that other creators are possible. Man can be a creator through progression and development of his potentialities, culminating in the *insan-i-kamil* (the perfect man). History is always moving forward; there is no historical recurrence or cycle. History is also the collective memory of a people. The conservation of specific values or traditions of a culture is a historical activity which should not be confused either with revivalism or simply looking backwards. Animals evolve through instinct, men through reason. The exercise of reason is a religious duty, and in the juristic sphere becomes *ijtihad*, which is the principle of legal advance in Islam. Muslim law is neither unalterable nor sacrosanct, not even an essential element of Islamic faith. Laws passed by a legislative assembly amount to *ijma'*, and the legislative procedure itself amounts to *ijtihad*. Social justice and the eradication of economic exploitation are the two ideals of an Islamic society.

Ghulam Ahmad Parwez (1903–85), a Sunni civil servant turned thinker, carries Iqbal's radicalism even further, and from the late 1930s onwards acts as a foil to the traditional and conservative *'ulama* class, especially to Abul 'Ala Maududi. He bemoans the fact that the *'ulama* have reduced Islam to a *madhab* (a ritualized form of religion) and confined it to the domain of the Spirit, leaving all aspects of man's worldly life in the hands of secular forces. In reality, Islam is a *din* (way of life), and its *only* authoritative source is the Quran. An elected parliament is empowered to interpret the Quranic injunctions and freely exercise *ijtihad* in the light of the general principles enunciated in the Quran. The *fiqh* laws inherited from the classical lawmakers are not binding on the legislature. Justice is the primary attribute of an Islamic society which has, as its bounden duty, to provide the basic necessities of life to every citizen. Land reform and collectivization of the major means of production are imperative. Acquisition of excessive wealth by private individuals cannot be allowed. Monogamy is the normal form of marriage approved by the Quran. The Quran also closed the door on slavery for all times to come.

It is easy to see, from the above summary, the many connections between the ideas of the Aga Khan and those propounded by these thinkers. The Aga Khan was neither a philosopher, nor a theologian, nor the head of a religious political party. Yet he was a leading modernist in Indian Islam. He led and guided the liberal majority of Indian Muslims through his involvement with and influence on the All India Muslim Educational Conference, the All India Muslim League and the All India Muslim Conference – three institutions which spoke on behalf of the Muslims of India. His modernizing influence extended to other Muslims residing in Africa and Britain. This makes his achievement in the realm of religious ideas and reform even greater.

The Aga Khan's emphasis on reconciliation between Shias and Sunnis bears comparison with Shah Waliullah and Ameer Ali. His deep interest in the welfare and future of the Islamic world recalls the efforts of Ameer Ali and Iqbal, as does his defence of the *khilafat* as an institution advantageous to the entire *ummah* of Islam. The top priority he gave to education and the part he played in the making of the Aligarh University were an extension of the lifelong mission of Sayyid Ahmad Khan, and ran parallel to Ameer Ali's success in opening schools all over India. His exhortation that political parties must develop grassroots support, should remain in constant touch with the electorate, and ought to attend to the needs and requirements of the masses, and his demand for a wider franchise reflected his belief in the Islamic injunction of *shura* (consultation), a conviction he shared with all the reformers mentioned above. In asserting the importance of science and scientific education in the modern age, he was reinforcing the views of Sayyid Ahmad Khan, Chiragh Ali and Iqbal. His economic ideas for the uplift of the agricultural masses, the amelioration of the labourer, the eradication of poverty, removal of all forms of exploitation, the prevention of concentration of wealth in a few hands, and the spread of social justice, bear comparison with Shah Waliullah, Ameer Ali, Iqbal and Parwez. In calling for the emancipation of women and the

118

widening of their franchise he echoed Ameer Ali and Parwez, and went far beyond Iqbal's vague and conservative ideas on the question. He was one with Shah Waliullah in arguing for the parallel moral and material progress of the Muslims, and with Ameer Ali and Iqbal in urging Westernization, modernization and constitutional advance. The Aga Khan's reformist programme was also in step with those presented by Khairuddin Pasha of Tunisia, Shaikh Muhammad Abduh of Egypt, and the Turkish modernists of the second half of the nineteenth century and the first quarter of the twentieth century. He also shares most of his interpretations of the Quran with those of another of his Indian friends, Abdullah Yusuf Ali.

Turning now to the major tenets of the Aga Khan's religious thought, his understanding of the central principle of God's message is beautifully expressed in his brief explanation of the phrase *Allah-o-Akbar.* "Here we find on one side divinity, on the other side infinity. For what is the greater – time, space, the starry heavens, intelligence, knowledge? – wherever existence goes there His greatness extends. Greatness here, to anyone who understands the implications of the Arabic language, does not mean 'greatness' as literally translated into English. It means that everything else is within the womb of the greater – everything else is maintained and sustained by Divine Power, including the furthest spaces of imagination."[1]

The Aga Khan believed in Islam as a religion of nature, not only because of the hundreds of references in the Quran to natural phenomena and objects but also because its laws are nature's laws and God's miracles are the very law and order of nature.[2] All the dogmas and doctrines of Islam are "ultimately based on the regularity and order of natural phenomena, on the natural inclination of human beings for survival and reproduction, while the religion of the West, Christianity, is based on a miraculous event and faith in miracles, that is to say, a break in that very regularity to which the Holy Koran refers on a thousand occasions". Today Islam is perhaps the farthest away from control over nature while the West harnesses it. In India Sayyid Ahmad Khan and Muhsin-ul-Mulk were the first to realize that it was this command over nature and its forces that gave power and strength to human beings. The Quran frequently

---

[1] Foreword, Qasimali Jairazbhoy's biography of the Prophet, Geneva, September 1934.
[2] Letter to the President of Arabiyya Jamiyyat, Karachi, 4 April 1952.

refers to the fact that we are surrounded by God-given gifts that we should comprehend and from which we can profit.[1]

Islam is as much a religion of reason as of nature; indeed the concepts of reason and nature are co-extensive: natural laws are rational laws. "Genuine Islam is in perfect agreement with reason, and none of the real acquisitions of reason can be contrary to it. It is able to assimilate modern sciences and methods, without allowing them to interfere with the Faith and Muslim tradition."[2]

Islam is an affair of everyday minute, like breathing. The Quran says, "In Him [God] we live and move and have our being." God is the Sustainer. He sustains us always and everywhere. The true Muslim is ever conscious of this fact, and in daily existence and the ordinary course of business he will pause to get into direct touch with his God. Many in the West, who are nominally Christian, regard God as infinitely removed from them and their affairs. But our faith is that God is ever-present, ever-creative. He watches us at all times. When a Muslim breaks from his everyday routine to pray, there is no feeling that he is passing from one mood, much less from one world, to another. Formal observance of prayer, however, still has its own value. "I think it is well that a man should make a habit of formal prayer . . . for protection and in thanks. But, I place emphasis on the continued direct relation between God and man." The Westerners and others have remembered the messengers of God but forgotten the message. "You think that we have forgotten the message of Christ? That is where we disagree with you. We think that we are the true Christians, and that your Church distorted the message." Islam also teaches us "to accept God's will joyfully, to acclaim what happens to us as a benefit, however much it may seem to the irreligious a misfortune. . . . 'It is the will of Allah', it is said by us of Islam, not with sad resignation, but with pious hope."[3]

The Aga Khan's personal view of Islam is summarized in the following advice he gave to the Muslims: to seek satisfaction, not in the flux of circumstances, but within oneself; to be resolute, self-controlled, independent, but not rebellious; to seek communion with the Eternal Reality which is our God; to be at once entirely oneself and altogether at one with the Eternal; to endeavour to suit one's desire to the event, and not the event to one's desire; and not to lament one's position with regard to those above; to congratulate oneself that one is better off than

---

[1] "This I have Learnt from Life", *Dawn*, Karachi, 3 February 1954.
[2] *Glimpses of Islam*, Lahore, 1944.
[3] "Is Religion Something Special?", undated.

those below. To look upon the world in this manner, is to see it not as a prison but a garden – a marvellous garden, the garden of the Lord. Feast the eyes on the miraculous beauty of the earth; all these gifts are freely given to those who have open eyes, open hands and an open heart, provided that the eyes are clear and the hands and the heart are strong. The society in which we live cannot bring happiness; society can provide a space to breathe and freedom to move in it; real happiness does not depend on surroundings, it depends altogether and exclusively on oneself.[1]

Determinism, or what the West has always called fatalism, is rejected by the Aga Khan in words which brook no misunderstanding. The Quran insists on freedom of the will and individual human responsibility. It was al-Ash'ari's great but misapplied genius which stamped Islam with that doctrine of fatalism which so discourages effort.[2]

Formalism and verbal interpretations of the teachings of the Prophet are in absolute contradiction with the history of the Prophet. In fact, his Divine Message is the channel of our union with the Absolute and the Infinite. It is only necessary to establish once again our spiritual faith.[3] For the scholars of Islam there are two duties to perform: research aimed at bringing to light the vast treasures of Muslim history, literature and philosophy; and interpretation, even critical interpretation, which must be fearless and have only one objective – truth.[4]

The age demands a reinterpretation of the Muslim faith. Religion, science and philosophy have to be seen as one integral whole, not three disparate and opposing forces. We should bring about the intellectual reconciliation of Islam with modern philosophy, science and other disciplines. Muslims have fallen in the world because they have placed their belief in formalities, in fact outformalized the formal. This does not mean that the faith of Islam is not true. It only means that our interpretation of Islam fails us. However unpalatable it may be to the conservatives, the task of reinterpreting Islam shall have to be taken in hand, so that Muslims shall be able to hold their own in the face of modern life. A faith that can be believed in by some of the

[1] "My Philosophy of Happiness", undated.
[2] Presidential Address, All India Muhammadan Educational Conference, Delhi, 1902.
[3] Message to the Islamic World, London, 14 March 1934.
[4] Speech at the Islamic Research Association, Bombay, 25 February 1935.

greatest philosophers of the world can never be in contradiction with the best thought of the present.[1]

The doors of *ijtihad* were never shut. According to the principle of *ijma'* the interpretation of the precepts and laws which regulate our lives, and are laid down in the Quran and the *hadith*, can be undertaken at any time and by any generation. *Ijtihad* is a personal and living search which can be undertaken within the general limits of the Divine Message. The suppleness of Muslim law enhances its value, and its broad lines have room for vigorous growth and adaptation to changing and unforeseeable circumstances. This law must, therefore, be freed of the rigid character given to it by ancient codification. If the modern readers of the Quran study it and reflect upon it, without being blindly attached to ancient exegeses, the Book would inspire them to a revival of religious thought and action. The corpus of *hadith* has to be seriously and critically scrutinized with a view to freeing it from posterior deviations and infiltrations.[2]

The above summary of the Aga Khan's religious opinions will give the reader an idea of where he stood in modern Islamic thinking. In the application of his views and interpretations to contemporary and current problems he was consistent.

The Aga Khan was dismayed by the presence of sects and subsects, divisions and sub-divisions, which had crept into Islam.[3] His advice to Muslims of all denominations was to avoid the plague of sectarianism. He himself practised to perfection what he preached. From the high rostrums it was his privilege to occupy – the All India Muhammadan Educational Conference, the All India Muslim League, the leadership of the Muslim Delegation to the Round Table Conferences – he did not utter one word or make one gesture which would show his Ismaili connection. In India, where sectarianism was rampant and was destroying the political power of the Muslims, it was delightful to see the leaders and the commonality of every sect, schism and school accept the Aga Khan as an unqualifiedly *Muslim* leader. He lived up to the image his people had of him. He supported the continuation of the Sunni *khilafat*, even at the cost of his reputation in modern Turkey. He even called for a final Shia–Sunni reconciliation.

Unlike some Shias, the Aga Khan was not reluctant to pay high tribute to the three "righteous" Caliphs and to Sunni leaders

[1] Presidential Address, All India Muhammadan Educational Conference, Rampur, 21 February 1936.
[2] *Glimpses of Islam*, Lahore, 1944.
[3] Speech, Muslim Educational Conference, Bombay, 1904.

and men of religion. He recalled "the high standard of duty, morality, truthfulness, justice and charity that was general in Arabian society during the glorious reigns of Abu Bakr and Omar". Omar was to him a model of what a Muslim ruler ought to be. "Omar was removed at the most important moment in the history of Islam when vast additions had been made not only to the Empire but to the wealth of every individual Moslem. And he was, above all, the one man whose intense piety and faith and justice made him not only obeyed by all, but made him above everything the model of perfect manhood to the Moslems. The rising generation . . . lost in Omar in that critical period that example of saintly virtue."[1]

He told the Muhammadan Educational Conference of 1904 that "Muslim history is full of heroic characters or men, who lived and moved very much as the Muslims of today in their home life do, that contact with them could not but ennoble. Muavia and Walid are as statesmen not eclipsed either by Caesar or Augustus; and where can you find in the annals of any dynasty, whether European or Asiatic, a more saintly sovereign than Omar ibn Abdul Aziz or a more exemplary Emperor than Hisham ibn Abdul Malik."[2]

Nearly half a century later he referred to the dynamic and glorious Umayyad period of Islamic history and drew the Pakistanis' attention to "the free social and intellectual part played in the life of Arabia during the first century by Imam Husain's daughter Sakina" and other women.[3] A year later, speaking in Dacca, he expressed the hope that Pakistan would take for her model the first century of Islam which was its finest age.[4]

His love for Islam led him to make the suggestion that the Muslims should attend to the needs of the untouchables of India with a view to elevating their social status, bringing them enlightenment and easing their entry into a "cultured Civilization".[5]

The Aga Khan established more than one insurance company in India and East Africa and impressed upon the Muslims that insurance was perfectly lawful in Islamic *sharia*. He told them of its benefits: far from being a form of gambling, as some people

---

[1] Presidential Address to the All India Muhammadan Educational Conference, Delhi, 1902.
[2] Speech at the Muhammadan Educational Conference, Bombay, 1904.
[3] Address to the Pakistan Institute of International Affairs, Karachi, 8 February 1950.
[4] Speech at a public meeting, Dacca, 28 January 1951.
[5] Speech, London Muslim League, London, 14 January 1913.

thought it to be, it was like "locking up an iron safe at night in order to protect its contents".[1] He asked the Muslim League to follow up Sayyid Ameer Ali's suggestion about *wakf-alal-aulad,* so that Muslim families could be "protected against the impoverishing influence of constant and vexatious sub-divisions".[2]

Looking upon Pakistan as "this greatest child of Islam", the Aga Khan gave sage advice to her Muslims. He was anxious to prevent a clash between the conservative and modernist elements. He warned that if a middle way was not found while there was time, "there is almost a certainty that the day will come when the progressive elements faced with the dangers of being left far behind amongst the nations of the world, will clamour and demand a secular state, or decay". Now was the time to build up "that free Islamic state mentality of toleration, mental and spiritual charity, forgiveness towards each other, on one side, and, what Quran and the Tradition [*hadith*] both insisted on, namely, that nature is the great daily book of God whose secrets must be found and used for the well-being of humanity".[3]

He was aware that many, both in the West and the East, had not favoured the emergence of a new Muslim country, and were now trying to paint it as a medieval theocracy simply because its people wanted to call it an Islamic State. This was an act of misconstruction and misunderstanding by the enemies of Islam and those "who do not want to face facts". Raising his voice (he was addressing a public meeting), he said, "I want to tell them that a Muslim State does not mean hostility against anyone". A truly Islamic country implied the pursuance of the ideology of equality and kindly treatment for all.[4]

If Pakistan was an Islamic country, this did not mean that she was hostile to non-Muslims. "Nothing could be farther from the truth." Under a truly Islamic state there could be "no loading of the dice against any section of the people". He did not favour the idea of Pakistan's adoption of the "subsequent centuries" of Islam as a guide. It was the first century of Islam which had demonstrated the greatest unity among Muslims, and this "infant" State's urgent need was for unity and solidarity. Her

---

[1] Speech at the Eastern Federal Union Insurance Company, Calcutta, 1 March 1934.
[2] Inaugural Address, All India Muslim League, Delhi, 29 January 1910.
[3] Broadcast on Radio Pakistan, Karachi, 19 February 1950.
[4] Speech at a public meeting, Dacca, 28 January 1951.

model could be no other than the age of the Prophet and his companion-rulers.[1]

The most eloquent epitome of the Aga Khan's belief in the creative and spiritual power of Islam is contained in the following two paragraphs which occur in the last chapter of his reminiscences, written three years before his death. Referring to the countries of East and Central Africa, he noted:

"Wherever the indigenous population is Muslim there is remarkably little racial antagonism or sense of bitterness against the European, in spite of the European's obvious economic superiority. Islam, after all, is a soil in which sentiments of this sort do not take root or flourish easily. This is not a shallow and fatalistic resignation; it is something much more profound in the essence of the teaching of Islam – a basic conviction that in the eyes of God all men, regardless of colour or class or economic condition, are equal. From this belief there springs an unshakeable self-respect, whose deepest effects are in the subconscious, preventing the growth of bitterness or any sense of inferiority or jealousy by one man of another's economic advantage.

"Islam in all these countries has within it, I earnestly believe, the capacity to be a moral and spiritual force of enormous significance, both stabilizing and energizing the communities among whom it is preached and practised. To ignore Islam's potential influence for good, Islam's healing and creative power for societies as for individuals, is to ignore one of the most genuinely hopeful factors that exist in the world today."[2]

Turning to the world of Islam in which he lived, and finding it very different from what the *ummah* should be, he was anxious to discover the reasons for its downfall. One factor struck him immediately: the Muslims had lost touch with the central message of their faith. Islam was a religion of nature and reason. The Quran imposed upon its followers the principal duty of observing, studying and controlling nature through an understanding of the laws of nature, which were also axioms of reason. During the great age of Islam they had used this principle. But by about the end of the seventeenth century, while the European renaissance and scientific revolution rapidly advanced its knowledge of nature – the very message contained in the Quran – and thereby its control of nature, the Muslims were content with their rites, rituals, ceremonies and formalism, neglecting the active,

[1] *Ibid.*
[2] *Memoirs*, 1954.

primary principle of their faith. In spite of their humble prayers, their moral standards, their kindliness and gentleness towards the poor – substantial virtues in themselves – there was constant deterioration in their learning process, intellectual prowess, scientific progress and mental curiosity. They went down in the world. Why? "Because we forgot the law and order of nature to which the Quran refers as proof of God's existence and we went against God's natural laws. This and this alone has led to the disastrous consequences we have seen."[1]

With anguish in his heart he warned the Pakistanis, and through them the Muslims of the world, that if we continued to look upon Islamic principles as mere rites and ceremonies, and forgot the real message of God's natural phenomena, then "not only Europe but China and India will go so far ahead of us that either we will become like North Africa, humble protectorates, or we may have, like Turkey, to throw over much that is most valuable and precious in our mental outlook". What could be done to avoid the disaster? The immediate need was to bring together the religious education of the *'ulema* and the general education of a university graduate into one stream where intellect and faith, science and belief, went hand in hand. The prospect meanwhile was bleak. "Alas, Islam which is a natural religion in which God's miracles are the very law and order of nature drifted away and is still drifting away, even in Pakistan, from science which is the study of those very laws and orders of nature."[2]

At a critical time in the history of the *ummah* the Muslims were giving greater thought to the study of their classical discoveries and achievements and less to current endeavours. The "Allama" theory of knowledge blinkered their sight; all wisdom belonged to the past; all worth achieving had been achieved; the future consisted of remembering the past, not of building over it, extending it, enriching it. This put a stop to all political, economic and cultural advance. It is true that the Greco-Arab period had produced some of the greatest intellectual giants the world has seen. "But while we were satisfied to look at the world through the eyes of our giants, the West insisted on more and more pigmies sitting one over the other on top of the giants' shoulders till their accumulated height was infinitely greater than that of the original giant on whom they had built their foundations."[3]

Living in an age which had witnessed some of the greatest

[1] Letter to the President of Arabiyyah Jamiyyat, Karachi, 4 April 1952.
[2] *Ibid.*
[3] "This I have Learnt from Life", Karachi, 3 February 1954.

scientific and technological discoveries and advances in history, the Aga Khan realized that the Muslim world could not even commence its march towards social and intellectual goals unless it understood the importance and value of science and turned its energies to mastering it. He himself had demonstrated his personal belief in science as early as 1897. In that year Bombay was struck by a serious outbreak of bubonic plague. The general population, ridden by superstition and blinded by ignorance, refused to be inoculated against the disease. The Aga Khan broke the taboo by getting himself inoculated in public. This action was not merely aimed at setting an example to his Ismaili followers; it was also a visible affirmation of his faith in modern science. "I took care to see", he recalled in his reminiscences, "that the news of what I had done was spread as far as possible. My followers could see for themselves that I, their Imam, having in full view of many witnesses submitted myself to this mysterious and dreaded process, had not thereby suffered. The immunity, of which my continued health and my activities were obvious evidence, impressed itself on their consciousness and conquered their fear."[1]

Neglect of science took the Muslims to the position where they were "almost at the last stage, almost at the last hour, between a final collapse and revival . . . Is the Muslim world at last going to turn its thought and culture to what is the fundamental teaching of the Holy Koran and the meaning of all Muslim sectarian interpretations of our Holy Book, namely, knowledge gained by the observation and questionings of the world which Allah Almighty has given to us and in which we live and move and have our being? Is that blessing to remain in the hands of others to be further developed? Incredible new powers are attained while we remain humble followers and in truth condemned even to lose our individuality. It is for the public of Pakistan, and indeed of the Muslim World, to adjust its cultural foundation to the study and ultimate victory over the forces of nature ever at our disposal through science, and thus once more, as in the first thousand years of Muslim history, we will be in the vanguard of mankind."[2]

Another source of worry for the Aga Khan was the future of Islam in Africa, where the Muslims were surrounded by a vast non-Muslim population and also faced the full force of European Christian, chiefly British, imperialism. The indigenous Muslims

[1] *Memoirs*, 1954, p. 38.
[2] "This I have Learnt from Life," Karachi, 3 February 1954.

in Africa were politically ill-equipped, economically unfledged, educationally unprepared and socially and culturally weak. They could not stand alone against the might of the numerous Christian churches and missions; opportunities to convert other Africans to Islam were practically nil. If the Islamic world did not come to the rescue of the African Muslims, the tragedy of Islamic Spain might well be repeated in East and Central Africa. It must organize efficient support and arrange for proper religious education.[1]

Overwhelmed by the prospects for Islam in East and Central Africa, the Aga Khan was moved to make an emotional speech before the East African Muslim Conference in 1945. "I am going to put to every one of you here, without exception, one simple question – a question which I have very often put to myself. This question ... I am as convinced as I am sitting here and facing you ... will be put to you as it will be put to me on the Day of Judgement... This will be the final and decisive question and on this you will fall or you will be saved... 'What did you do to save Islam in Central Africa?' " Those who spoke of the great glories of Islamic history had forgotten the history of Spain – where Islam ruled in magnificent splendour for over 600 years – and what befell it there and in Sicily. "And if you do not wake up now – this is the last opportunity – history may repeat itself here also ... Well, if you have to save Islam in this part of the world, you should help and raise the Africans, Arabs, Swahilis, and Somalis ... We must give help to those who are most exposed to danger. If worse comes to worse, Indians can go back to their own country, but the bulk of Africans will have to face it here, and it is to place them on a basis which will remove future danger and give them the possibility of becoming so numerous as to save Islam."

He then made a few specific and concrete suggestions to save the situation. First, there must be a permanent organization to do what had to be done. Second, they should have an African Muslim ally. The main leadership, now or in time, must belong to the African Muslims; the Indian Muslims in Africa were their friends and brothers. Third, the conference should select several hundred people from amongst the local population and send them to Britain, India, America or Egypt to study law, medicine, liberal arts, theology and religious propaganda. This group would serve, expand and save Islam in the region. Fourth, mosques must be constructed where needed, and schools should be attached to

[1] *Glimpses of Islam*, Lahore, 1944.

128

them, imparting both religious and secular education. Fifth, the African Muslims ought to be persuaded to attend the government schools in large numbers; if such schools were not available, they should ask for them. Finally, the work of conversion must go on apace, so that the maximum number of Africans would be attracted to the fold of Islam.[1]

It was the Aga Khan's ideal that the African Muslims should attain the same status as was being enjoyed by non-Muslims. "Unless you reach the same social and economic standard as others have done", he admonished them, "you will pass yourselves as second class people and others who steal an advance on you will look down upon you and you will have to look up to them. For this reason, you have got to help your African and Arab and Somali and Swahili co-religionist to attain a place of honour and respect in the society."[2] The same message and the same appeal were addressed to the Muslims of Tanganyika.[3]

In the following year (1946) the Aga Khan returned to the subject. He was distressed to see that "our African brothers-in-faith were living in the most appalling condition," without adequate provision for education, without an institution to look after their welfare, and without an organization to protect their rights. It was, he said, the sacred duty of every Muslim to make all possible sacrifices to "ameliorate the terrible state of their less fortunate brothers-in-faith". Geography and race were no barriers in Islam, and mutual love and sacrifice tied together all the faithful.[4]

In 1945 he had tried to goad the East African Muslim Conference into action by frightening them with the example of Spain. In 1946, he quoted the happenings in India "during the last 75 or 100 years" to the same purpose. If the African Muslims were not helped, "there will be two kinds of citizens in Africa. There would be Brahmin Christians and Shudra Muslims and the inevitable result will be that the African Muslim will be left outside the sphere of education and knowledge, of science and modern outlook, and he will be chained down in the economic sphere and generally he would be going down and down like the Aborigines of India did 400 or 500 years ago."[5]

[1] Speech at the East African Muslim Conference, Mombasa, 16 June 1945.
[2] Speech at the East African Muslim Conference, Mombasa, 17 June 1945.
[3] Speech before the Tanganyika Muslim Association, Dar-es-Salaam, 22 July 1945.
[4] Interview, *The Observer*, Nairobi, June 1946.
[5] Speech at the East African Muslim Conference, Mombasa, 27 July 1946.

He matched the word to the deed. By 1945 the East African Muslim Welfare Society had been set up under his patronage to improve the lot of the African Muslims. To encourage the collection of funds, he pledged that for every pound given by the non-Ismaili Muslims he would donate an equal sum. Up to July 1957, his personal contribution to the Society amounted to £200,000, enabling it to build a number of schools, health clinics and mosques in Kenya, Uganda and Tanganyika (now Tanzania).[1]

The World of Islam

The Aga Khan was affiliated to the Shia branch of the Islamic faith and, more significantly, was the hereditary *Imam* of the Ismaili community which is a branch of the larger Shia community. His passion for the unity of Islam, however, overruled sectarian considerations. His affection for Ottoman Turkey and his anxiety for the continuation of the *khilafat* illustrate this passion: he was prepared to criticize the highest in the land, to alienate his best friends, and to take on the British Empire, in order to defend his convictions.

The story begins in 1913, with his declaration that the Indian Muslims felt that it should be a matter of great importance to Britain that Turkey continued to hold sway as an independent power in Asia, and with the warning, addressed to the British, that the break-up of Ottoman domination in Asia would expose the Western route to India to attack by other European powers.[2]

In January 1914 he criticized the British Prime Minister, Herbert Asquith, for his public condemnation of the Ottoman reoccupation of Adrianople and his request for its withdrawal. Hearing the premier's words the Indian Muslims asked in vain what British interests would be served by turning Turkey out of Adrianople and installing the Bulgarians against the wishes of the inhabitants. "Why should England", the Aga Khan asked, "have gone out of her way to support Bulgarian aggression in Thrace, contrary to the strong wishes of her Muslim subjects, and to local sentiment and interests?" Defending the Young Turks, he said, "It is not fair to judge the administrative capacity of a people unversed in the great art of constitutional government when they are engaged in a life-and-death struggle, brought upon them in the first instance by the unprovoked aggression of one of the Great Powers of Europe . . . they must be judged by their powers

[1] Souvenir of the Muslim Welfare Society, Kampala, n.d. (? 1959).
[2] Speech, London Muslim League, London, 14 July 1913.

of statesmanship when there is some recovery from the exhaustion of the fighting and tumults of the last two years, and the great and difficult work of reconstruction has been entered upon."

He then quite accurately forecast the state of the Middle East in the case of the Ottoman Empire's disintegration. France would lay claim to Syria, Germany to Anatolia with northern and central Mesopotamia, Russia to Kurdistan and Armenia, and Great Britain to Arabia and southern Mesopotamia. The British empire would be brought into closer contact with the great European powers whose large armies would be less dependent on sea for their communications. The route to India would be even more exposed to danger. "For these reasons", he advised Britain, "a strong and stable Turkish Government in Asia ought to be a cardinal principle of British international policy."

The interest of Muslim India in the future of Turkey was justified on the grounds of the sentiment of Islamic unity, and the British critics were snubbed for their failure to understand it. "The Indian Muslim does not ask for the surrender of any British interests; he simply points out that these interests are in accord with Muslim sentiment and wishes. Yet his incursion into international politics is frowned upon in reactionary Anglo-Indian quarters as if it were in some mysterious and inexplicable way disloyal. People who make these charges might reflect that the Mussulmans of India gain absolutely nothing for themselves, in any material or political sense, from the preservation of the Muslim States; they are simply animated by the sentiments of unity and brotherhood above referred to, which are stronger than these unsympathetic and unimaginative critics can realise."[1]

When the First World War was over, and the peace treaties were being prepared, and British politicians were making no secret of their anti-Turkish feelings and schemes, the Aga Khan (often in collaboration with Sayyid Ameer Ali) tried to convey Muslim sentiment to the British public and to warn the British Government against taking steps which might cause widespread and long-lasting unrest in the Middle East and India. To rob Turkey of Constantinople and Thrace, to give her seaports to other countries, to cut her access to the sea and the markets of the world, to penn up six or seven million Muslims on the plateau of Anatolia and to place the rest of the country under subjection to alien races, would not be a settlement; it would be "a real tragedy and the gravest of blunders". The result would be to

[1] "The Indian Moslem Outlook", *Edinburgh Review,* January 1914.

isolate Turkey from all other Muslims, to debar her from intercourse with the international community, to deny her all chances
of progress and development, to sow the seeds of discontent and
"cruel racial wars and feuds", to cause perpetual unrest in the
whole of Asia, and to create "unquenchable bitterness" in the
hearts of Muslims all over the world. Muslim India had been loyal to
the Empire during the war. And now, "to appease the ambitions
and 'earth-hunger' of certain nationalities whose help in this war
can hardly be compared with the sacrifices of the Mussalman
soldiers brought to the cause of England, we have turned their devotion, to put it mildly, to something akin to embitterment". The
Indian Muslims' feelings for Turkey were a "living and universal
sentiment, and must be counted as a factor in practical politics" . . . "Is it wise, is it statesmanlike, to treat this living sentiment
in the way, we are told, the Peace Conference proposes to do?"[1]

When the infamous Treaty of Sèvres was signed the Aga Khan
called it unjust and cruel and attributed the disorder in Persia
to it. He thought that the Greek invasion of Turkey could not
succeed without the backing of the Allied Powers, and if it failed
the part of the treaty affecting the Turkish territory assigned to
Greece would be rendered null and void. He advised the Allied
governments to revise the treaty with good grace.[2]

Two months later he took up the issue again. The question of
the treatment of Turkey, he said, was really a test of whether or
not India was in the full sense of the term a partner in the
Empire. This was a matter in which, whatever the general
imperial obligations, Indian wishes should not be a secondary
consideration. A new treaty with Turkey must be signed "on lines
acceptable to Indian sentiment". Such a step would "constitute
the first united attempt of England and India to apply to a
great Imperial problem the principle of Swaraj, which is now
universally acknowledged to be the Indian goal".[3] Four months
later, he urged upon the new Viceroy, Lord Reading, to press the
British Government to leave Greece alone and to enter into a
new treaty with Turkey which would satisfy the Muslims. The
latter could never consider Constantinople or the *khilafat* safe
unless Eastern Thrace and Smyrna remained under complete
Turkish sovereignty.[4]

[1] Letter (with Sayyid Ameer Ali), *The Times*, London, 2 August 1919.
[2] Press interview, Bombay, 22 January 1921.
[3] Speech at a luncheon given to bid farewell to Lord and Lady Reading,
London, 13 March 1921.
[4] Telegram to the Viceroy of India, London, 8 July 1921.

In November of the same year, in a long letter to *The Times*, he put the Turkish and Indian Muslim case before the British public. There was no justification for the attitude of "passive neglect" adopted by the Entente statesmen which had permitted the Turkish question to drift until it had become a "definite danger". The way the Turks had been treated had aroused "the most intense exasperation throughout the whole of Islam". It had also created many difficulties for Britain in Asia. It had compelled the Turks to cultivate the Bolsheviks of Russia. It had alienated the Persians, for though they were Shias "the inner unity of Islam is a fact which non-Muslims can hardly realize". It had stalled an agreement with Afghanistan.

There could be no doubt about the deep interest of Muslim India in the welfare of "the most important Muhammadan State in the world". It did not want to see Turkey blotted out, and it feared that "such is the aim of Turkey's enemies". It was true that Great Britain defeated Turkey in the war, but only with the help and support of the Indian army. India, therefore, was justified in arguing that her views ought to receive attention in the matter of a Turkish peace settlement. "It is so easy to do reasonable justice to Turkey, so dangerous for the well-being of India to let the misunderstanding grow and grow until it hangs like a dark cloud over all the countries between the Maritza and the Ganges."

What was the way out? The "least possible basis" of a permanent settlement was to restore to Turkey her sovereign rights in Anatolia and Asia Minor. Greece had decided to appeal to the sword, and the beaten Turks had cut her down to size. She should immediately effect a complete withdrawal from Asia. Secondly, Constantinople must remain in Turkish hands. Thirdly (and all Muslims of all sects gave it high priority), the Sultan-Caliph should be freed from "the scarcely veiled bondage" in which he had been put. The humiliations heaped upon him had caused "the most intense grief and anger in all Muhammadan communities". In brief, the Turks must have an opportunity to evolve a free national state. "The Turks cannot be extinguished, and if they are left as they are today they will struggle for years until they have recovered their rights." Nor would Indian Muslims wait quietly for justice to be done to Turkey.[1]

In the autumn of 1922 Andrew Bonar Law, barely two weeks before entering office as Prime Minister, wrote a letter to *The*

---

[1] Letter, *The Times*, London, 8 November 1921.

Times, arguing that a British "withdrawal" from Turkey would have been "regarded throughout the whole Mussalman world as the defeat of the British Empire" and, further, that dangers would have arisen "as a consequence of what would have been regarded as British impotence in the face of a victorious Turkish army". The Aga Khan put the Conservative statesman right. Had the British withdrawn, he wrote, far from looking at it as a weakness Muslims worldwide would have seen in the act a strong man's generosity "in ceasing to bar the way to the return of the Turks to their national home". Bonar Law had shown "a distressing misconception" of Muslim feeling. "I cannot tell you how great will be the shock to Muhammadans to find that a universally respected statesman like Mr. Bonar Law, who has been the leader of a great political party, and who may fill the highest office, so completely misunderstands Muhammadan psychology, and, in particular, holds in such low esteem the intelligence of His Majesty's loyal Muhammadan subjects throughout the Empire." The Aga Khan then contrasted British and French attitudes to the advantage of France. The French and the Italians had withdrawn from Chanak without suffering any loss of face among the Muslims. "The prestige of France in the world of Islam never stood higher than it does today. In all my life I have never known any Western Power so highly honoured among Muhammadans as is now the case with France . . . Would not the Viceroy's task in India have been greatly facilitated if British policy in the Near East had been more closely on the lines followed by France?"[1]

He continued this pressure on British public opinion in his writings and speeches and through long and frequent conversations with men in high places, until the Treaty of Sévres was replaced with the Treaty of Lausanne in July 1923. He was immensely pleased with the new treaty and exulted that "for the first time in history a Treaty has been signed on behalf of a Muhammadan nation upon absolutely equal terms with the Great Powers of the West". The treaty "reflects the greatest credit upon the steadfast leadership of Ghazi Mustafa and the patient diplomacy of Ismet Pasha". Now Turkey would become an independent and compact national state. "The fetters which so long held her enchained have been struck off." Foreign governments or nationals would have no special privileges in future. No foreign troops would stay on her soil. The *khilafat* would be maintained. The capital city had been returned to its rightful owners, and so had been Adrianople and Thrace. This "highly

---

[1] Letter, *The Times*, London, 9 October 1922.

134

satisfactory settlement" was due to the Turks' "own sacrifices and their own courage and fortitude", but also to the goodwill of "the peoples" of Great Britain and France.[1] He was careful not to give any credit to the British Government.

He then turned to post-Khilafat Movement India's attitude to the post-war new Turkey. The Khilafat agitation was now obsolete and could serve no useful purpose. The Muslims of India should now turn their energies to helping Turkey "to bind her wounds and to recover her lost property". "The best advice that I can give to all Muslims, both in India and elsewhere, is to do their utmost to assist this new national Muhammadan State in its hour of need. This can best be done, not by talking politics, but by taking practical steps. Turkey has suffered grievous losses, and her people require direct aid. We ought to send from India special missions to restore sanitation, to bring back health, and to encourage movements for child welfare ... Let us therefore leave politics alone, and turn ourselves to the task of offering such help as we can to the new State, which will assuredly become the brightest star in Islam."[2] The Indian Khilafat Movement leaders paid no heed to his words; nor, as far as I know, did other Muslim leaders make similar suggestions.

In England the Aga Khan, now relaxed after his exertions on behalf of Turkey and Islam, took this opportunity to explain to the British public and eκlite the reasons for the sympathy of the Muslim world for Turkey. The British were ignorant about everything concerning Islam; this duty had to be performed by someone. During the making of the post-war peace settlements, Allied and American statesmen claimed that they were fighting for certain fundamental principles of justice, nationalism and freedom. Such pronouncements had a profound effect on the peoples of Asia, and the Turks and Muslims throughout the world expected a peace which would leave Turkey intact and free and provide for the Arabs at least the possibility of a united Arab federation. During the last few months of the war certain men in power in the Allied countries had made authoritative statements which encouraged such expectations. When, therefore, the Treaty of Sèvres was imposed on Turkey, in disregard of the principles laid down while the issue of the war had still to be decided, "nothing could be more inevitable and natural than the keen disappointment and indignation of the Muslim world". The treaty made Turkey a vassal state, put under a virtual over-lordship

[1] Message to the Muslims on the Lausanne Treaty, Lausanne, 27 July 1923.
[2] *Ibid.*

of the Allies, and deprived of "every shred of real independence". Then Turkey, "with the support of the whole of Islam, rose as one man and, after immense sacrifices and sufferings, for which history scarcely affords a parallel", won its own freedom and independence. "If Turkey has won her way in the field and in the international council chamber to a position in the world which she had not held for generations, she has done so by the self-sacrificing devotion of her sons to national ideals ..."[1]

The Turkish question had had two aspects, both of keen concern to the Aga Khan: the danger of the dismemberment of the Turkish land and the risk to the status and authority of the Sultan-Khalifa. The first was averted by the Treaty of Lausanne. The second was removed surgically by the Turks themselves by abolishing the *khilafat* and overthrowing and exiling the Emperor. Before the second step was taken the Aga Khan (with Ameer Ali) wrote a letter to the Turkish Prime Minister, appealing for the retention of the *khilafat* as a unique, historical and necessary Islamic institution. As both the authors were Shia who, by their doctrine, did not believe in or even acknowledge the Sunni concept and reality of *khilafat*, it is pertinent to look closely at the points they made in favour of their argument.

As "consistent friends" of the new Turkey, they "noticed with the greatest regret that Islam, as a great moral and cohesive force, is losing among large sections of the Sunni population, owing to the diminution in the Caliph's dignity and prestige, its weight and influence". Coming to the theological-cum-political issue involved, the letter said, "In the Sunni communion, we need not point out, the spiritual headship forms the link which binds the followers of Islam as a vast congregation. When the Caliphate was in peril from outside attacks, Musalman feeling all over the world was violently agitated." The Muslims of India gave their support to Turkey, believing that in fighting for her independence she was fighting also for the "preservation intact of the institution which symbolized Muslim solidarity". The Indian Khilafat Movement had done much, and had suffered much, on behalf of the Turks. There was now no intention at all to curtail the powers or interfere with the business of the Grand National Assembly of Turkey. What the authors of the letter did "respectfully urge is that the religious headship of the Sunni world should be maintained intact in accordance with the Shariyyet. In our opinion, any diminution in the prestige of the Caliph or the elimination of the Caliphate as a religious factor from the Turkish

[1] "The New Moslem World", *Edinburgh Review*, October 1923.

body politic would mean the disintegration of Islam and its practical disappearance as a moral force in the world." The Caliph-Imam "symbolizes the unity of the Sunni Communion: and the fact that he is a member of the Turkish people and is a descendant of the founder of the Turkish nation gives to Turkey a position pre-eminent among Islamic nations. For fourteen centuries, it has been the cardinal principle of the *Ahl-i-Sunnat,* and on this, we believe, is the *Ijmaa-i-Ummat,* that the Caliph, the Vicegerent of the Prophet, is the Imam of the Sunni congregations, and that between him and the general body of worshippers, there is a nexus which knits together the *Ahl-i-Sunnat.* This mystical element cannot be eradicated from the Muslim mind without creating discord in the world of Islam."

The letter concluded, "For these reasons, among others equally cogent, we, as the two friends of Turkey, respectfully urge upon the Grand National Assembly and its great and far-sighted leaders the imminent necessity for maintaining the religious and moral solidarity of Islam by placing the Caliph-Imamate on a basis which would command the confidence and esteem of the Muslim nations and thus impart to the Turkish State unique strength and dignity."[1]

For his exertions on behalf of the Islamic world, the Aga Khan was accused by the Turks of being a British agent and a friend of the monarchist and other anti-revolutionary parties in Turkey. In refutation of the first charge, he declared that he had not discussed the matter contained in the letter, "directly or indirectly, with any Englishman, official or unofficial". He had, he reminded the Turks, supported the Turkish cause during all the previous years; he had lectured to the British public, and for this had been attacked with asperity in some British quarters. How could he have agreed to take this step on British instigation?

As to the second charge, he said that since the Armistice he had had "no relationship of any sort or kind with any Turkish party or individual that has been in opposition to the Angora Government". In fact, "I have always held that Republican institutions are particularly well suited to purely Islamic societies". Far from wishing the new Turkey ill, "I yield to none in the desire to see it consolidated so as to be beyond menace from any quarter, internal or external."

He took this opportunity to explain a Shia *Imam'*s support of a Sunni institution. He underlined the fact that this desire to

---

[1] Letter (with Sayyid Ameer Ali), *The Times,* London, 24 November 1923.

see a flourishing and great Turkey "is in no sense inconsistent with another life-long belief as one who, while belonging to the Ismailiah school of Islam, yet follows the tradition of Ali and Hassan, his eldest son – viz., that the essential unity of Islam is of far greater importance than any sectarian differences".

He gave another argument in favour of Turkey's retaining the *khilafat*. It was an honour and a privilege for Turkey, but it was also in the interest of Islam. It would avoid the "raising of issues which would lead to eager aspirations and jealousies in ambitious quarters" (as actually happened). Therefore, the Caliph should stay in his place, and should receive from all Muslim states headed by Turkey, "at least general homage and veneration equal to that which Catholic States voluntarily offer to the Pope". This practice had historical parallels in Islam: in Baghdad during the later Abbasid period, and in Cairo during the Abbasid *khilafat*.[1]

But, once again, the Aga Khan's plea on behalf of the Islamic world was unheard in Angora, and the venerable and ancient institution, which had commanded, at the least, the emotional loyalty and public esteem of Muslims throughout the world, was abolished.

The unity of the Islamic world, to which the Aga Khan referred throughout his involvement with the Turkish issue, was not merely an argument to prove a point or to cause discomfort to the West: it was a conviction that bordered on obsession. Throughout his speeches and writings this is one subject to which he returns again and again, with his vision undimmed and his vigour undiminished.

The emancipation of the world of Islam from colonial rule was his wish as far back as 1919. He asked for the application of the Wilsonian principles of reconstruction and self-determination to Islamic countries. "Where the Muslims have been long established, where they are a majority, or even a large minority, they should not be exposed to proscription in, or the monstrous idea of expatriation from, the countries where they have been settled for centuries." With the end of the "terrible nightmare of Tsardom" in Russia, the Wilsonian principles should be applied to the liberated Muslim countries of Central Asia and the Caucasus. Persia ought to receive the same treatment. "Moral ideals know no boundaries of race or faith, and we ask for justice for Islamic no less than for other communities."[2]

---

[1] Letter, *The Times*, London, 16 December 1923.
[2] Speech at a banquet in honour of Lord Sinha, London, 7 March 1919.

Any injustice or cruelty inflicted on a Muslim country caused him pain, just as any Muslim achievements gave him joy.

When the Spanish authorities subjected the Moroccan rebels in the Riff to severe reprisals, he appealed for funds on behalf of the British Red Crescent Society to help mitigate the misery of the women and children of the area, the non-combatant population, and the sick and the wounded, and to relieve the hardships of the Spanish prisoners.[1]

Afghanistan's entry into the League of Nations was to him a "memorable occasion". The event went part of the way to averting the danger of the League becoming an exclusively Western and Christian organization. Afghanistan was not only an Islamic nation, but also one with which seventy million Indian Muslims shared their blood, their languages, their culture and, of course, the "glorious brotherhood of Islam".[2] Egypt's entry into the League drew his deep satisfaction. "Today the crowning seal is set on Egypt's re-assumption of her ancient and glorious sovereignty." Once again it was Egypt's links with Islam and Muslim India which made the occasion particularly welcome to him. To the Muslims of India the Egyptians were not "aliens or strangers, but brothers with the same culture, the same religion, the same outlook on the world."[3]

The Aga Khan saluted the new state of Pakistan as "this greatest child of Islam".[4] He appreciated the significance of East Pakistan (now Bangladesh) much more shrewdly than did the contemporary or later rulers of Pakistan. He called its Dacca University "one of the greatest hopes for the future, not only for the people of Pakistan, but for Islam" ... "What America was to England and Spain, we can almost certainly say that East Pakistan is for the Muslims of this subcontinent."[5] It was "the most important part of the greatest Muslim State in the world".[6]

He reflected on Muslim India's interest in the world of Islam. With the downfall of Islam as a political power and European colonialism closing in to fill the vacuum, the Indian Muslim, "instead of holding out the outposts of Islam in the East, sees around him nothing but Muslim societies in a far greater state

[1] Letter (with Lord Lamington and Sayyid Ameer Ali), *The Times*, London, 17 October 1924.
[2] Speech in the League of Nations, Geneva, 27 September 1934.
[3] Speech in the League of Nations, Geneva, 26 May 1937.
[4] Broadcast on Radio Pakistan, Karachi, 19 February 1950.
[5] Speech at the University of Dacca, Dacca, 28 January 1951.
[6] Speech at a public meeting, Dacca, 28 January 1951.

of decay than his own". He looks upon India "more and more as the hope of his political freedom and as the centre that may still raise the other Muhammadan countries to a higher standard of civilization".[1] On the other hand, he could not help but remain a part of the world community of Islam. He was determined not only to maintain his cultural affinity with India, but also to remain culturally related to Muslims worldwide.[2]

The real goal of all the efforts of the Aga Khan was the unity of Islam based on religious, cultural, economic and historical ties. The aim of everything he did or said or thought was the forging of Muslim interrelationships on the foundations of a shared faith and its values.

His belief in the "inherent solidarity of those who profess and call themselves Muslims" never wavered. Wherever they might live, they had "a fellow-feeling and an interest in each other's welfare". This was but inadequately realized in Europe where the strong sentiments of Islamic unity were not understood. There were years when the mind and heart of Muslim India were full of nothing but the thoughts of Turkish tribulations and Iran's problems.[3]

Awakened to national consciousness by the new education he was receiving, the Indian Muslim was lifting his gaze above the Himalayan ramparts and beyond the waters of the Indian Ocean to see an essential unity with his fellow-believers in other lands. He "shares the glorious heritage not only of the Koran ... but of the history and philosophy of Arabia, the incomparable poetry of Persia and the romances and legends of Egypt and Morocco and Spain". The result was a new consciousness of the soul. "Drinking from these imperishable springs, Muslims, whether Turks, Persians, Arabs or Indians, and whether or not they have also come to the Western wells of knowledge, are bound together by a certain unity of thought, of sentiment, and of expression. The feeling of brotherhood thus engendered is not dammed up within the confines of devout faith. On the contrary, agnostics and atheists of Muslim origin have felt the Turkish and Persian misfortunes just as much as the most orthodox mullah. To ask why the Indian Mussulman, blessed with a beneficent rule, should concern himself so much about international issues affecting co-religionists, is as futile as asking why men on the rack of torture cry out with physical pain ...

[1] *India in Transition*, June 1918.
[2] Presidential Address, All India Muslim Conference, Delhi, 31 December 1928.
[3] Speech at the London Muslim League, London, 14 July 1913.

Shias have been moved by these emotions no less strongly than Sunnis. All sections of the Muslim world are moved by a deep sentiment, originally called into being by the Prophet's summons of all the faithful into one great brotherhood and welded through the centuries into a lasting bond by a common faith, a common literature, a common outlook, and a common history."[1]

Every sincere Muslim believed in the "theory of the spiritual brotherhood and unity of the children of the Prophet". It was "a deep, perennial element in that Perso-Arabian culture, that great family of civilizations to which we gave the name Islamic". It connoted "charity and goodwill toward fellow-believers every-where from China to Morocco, from the Volga to Singapore". It meant "an abiding interest in the literature of Islam, in her beautiful arts, in her lovely architecture, in her entrancing poetry". It also meant "a true reformation – a return to the early and pure simplicity of the faith, to its preaching by persuasion and argument, to the manifestation of a spiritual power in indi-vidual lives, to beneficent activity for mankind". It assumed a sharing of grief and pain. "A famine or a desolating fire in the Muslim quarters of Kashgar or Sarajevo would immediately draw the sympathy and material assistance of the Mahomadan of Delhi or Cairo." New developments – modern civilization, the spirit of liberty, and a general awakening of the East – were giving a new fillip to this "spiritual and cultural Pan-Islamism".[2]

By 1923 Turkey and Afghanistan were free to manage their own affairs. Persia was independent, though foreign capitulations were still there. Egypt had regained a part of her sovereignty. These states were "united by the ties of a common civilization and religion, and by that general similarity of ideas and manners which, though modified by local conditions, prevails throughout Islam". But Europe did not understand the phenomenon of the great sympathy of the Muslim people for each other. Therefore it feared an imaginary political pan-Islamism, a bogey of its own creation. No combination of Muslim states was "aspiring to curtail, under the banner of pan-Islamism, the independence or individuality of any non-Muslim State". They only sought to develop their own independence and individuality to the maximum on national foundations. The nearest parallel to this in Europe was that of the three Scandinavian states of Norway, Sweden and Denmark.[3]

[1] "The Indian Moslem Outlook", *Edinburgh Review,* January 1914.
[2] *India in Transition,* June 1918.
[3] "The New Muslim World", *Edinburgh Review,* October 1923.

One of the arguments given by the Aga Khan in his campaign of reducing the Indian military budget was that there was no possibility of India's going to war with her adjacent countries because the only neighbours of any military consequence were Muslim states and their independence was a question of "very great importance" to the Indian Muslims.[1]

He had ''unshaken faith in Islam which is the greatest unifying, civilizing and fraternizing influence in the world". Interested politicans were misnaming the unity of Islam and Pan-Islamism and misrepresenting them as a political bogey. The reality was that Islam was "a great cultural and spiritual force for the unity of the world and the fraternity of the nations".[2] One illustration of its force in action was the bonds between the Indian and Egyptian Muslims. Any one of each country, whatever his economic background or social class, when visiting the other country, would feel immediately at home. Even if he did not understand the language of the other, "the similarity of custom and habit of brotherly feeling and of religious faith, will make him feel that he has not left his own country".[3]

There was a danger to Islamic unity in an open or hidden clash between the conservative and progressive elements in Muslim countries. In Turkey such a conflict had ended in the establishment of a secular state. In Egypt the Ikhwan were at loggerheads with the governing classes. In Indonesia the Dar-ul-Islam was ranged against the establishment. It was vital to discover a healthy, acceptable middle way, as it existed in the first century of Islam.[4] Without this the Muslims would not be able to bring about a spiritual and intellectual unity. In answer to a question about the materialization of "the idea of Islamistan", he repeated his views on political pan-Islamism. "What do you mean by Islamistan? Do you mean by it intellectual, religious and cultural unity or political unity? If you mean political unity, how can that be? All the Muslim countries want their independence. Some day, perhaps, there might be a sort of federal arrangement. But that is far away in the future."[5] That was the closest he came even to entertaining the idea of a political unity in the Islamic world.

---

[1] "Optimism and Goodwill", *Sunday Express*, London, 13 April 1924.
[2] Address to the Executive Board of the All India Muslim Conference, New Delhi, 15 February 1934.
[3] Speech at the League of Nations, Geneva, 26 May 1937.
[4] "The Future of Muslim States in the Background of History", lecture delivered in Karachi, 8 February 1950.
[5] *Ibid.*

Sectarian differences could not stand in the way of the unity at which he was aiming. Each sect and sub-sect should understand the other "under the general brotherhood of those who say '*la ilaha illallah Mohamed Rasul Allah*' " (the words of the Muslim confession of faith). "Pan-Islamism does not mean that one gives up one's own historical interpretation of Islam, but that one accepts that of the other brother Muslims as an equally earnest endeavour to put to practice the Faith in God and the Prophet (S.A.W.) which illuminates and which, we hope, will save all Muslim Souls."[1]

He wanted to utilize every opportunity and institution to further this unity. In 1911 he was promoting the establishment of a Mosque Fund to construct a mosque in London. In his appeal he did not confine himself to enumerating the usual advantages and uses of a mosque, as a *mullah* would have done. He hoped that every Muslim student and visitor would attend the mosque and thus play his own part in bringing Muslims of the world together and thus strengthening the bonds of solidarity. The rich and the poor alike, as the educated and the uneducated, would come to the House of God, and this experience of Islamic brotherhood would help to remove ancient prejudices.[2]

Another path leading to greater Islamic unity lay in economic regeneration and co-operation. The Aga Khan evolved the idea in an indirect way. As all the Muslim states were then (in 1933) economically backward or politically constrained, he appealed to the British and European people to enlarge the scope of their trade and business relations with them. British traders learned Spanish and Portuguese to promote their interests in Latin America. Why didn't some of them, particularly the younger section, learn Persian or Arabic or Urdu? This linguistic acquisition was bound to create an intellectual and spiritual understanding between East and West. Its practical and commercial advantages would, of course, be substantial. Commercial travellers in India and the Middle East would imbibe the culture of those areas and thus improve their knowledge of the world. The lands with which they did business would gain much materially. The Muslims of India could act in this venture as coadjutants and partners; they could help the British as well as their co-religionists throughout the Middle and Near East.[3] The ultimate

[1] Message to the East African Muslim Welfare Society, Evian les Bains (France), 10 July 1954.
[2] Lecture on the Muslims of the British Empire, London, 3 July 1911.
[3] Speech at the National League, London, 2 July 1933.

objective was to develop the Muslim regions and at the same time bring them together through the instrumentality of the Indian Muslim partners of the British trading business.

Next to the faith of Islam it was its culture and civilization which offered the brightest prospects for unity. The Aga Khan was a great admirer of this culture both for its own inherent worth and for its role as a unifier of all Muslim communities and regions. Without this culture the world would have been a poorer place to live. "The fact that King and Darwesh (beggar) were both called Shah showed the true brotherhood of Islam."[1]

As an Iranian it was a matter of pride for the Aga Khan that his country had contributed magnificently to the glories of Islamic culture. This he called Iran's role in strengthening the spiritual forces of human existence, meaning by "spiritual forces" not something simply religious or other-worldly, but "anything that deals with man's life of the spirit here and now on this earth and in this life". Whatever one's belief in the future of the soul, there was "one impregnable central fact in existence: that here and now, in this world, we have a soul which has a life of its own in its appreciation of truth, beauty, harmony and good against evil". Iran had perfected this soul of man.[2]

People should realize that Islamic civilization was the first to appreciate "art for art's sake, beauty for beauty's sake and literature for literature's sake" – an outlook which had been largely overlooked in Greece and Rome. At its very best, Islamic culture and civilization pursue this aesthetic principle, whether the sphere is religious or political or economic.[3]

The Aga Khan was convinced that a better understanding by the West of Islamic culture would not only bring about a valuable understanding between the West and the East, thus helping in the cause of world peace, but would also indirectly promote Islamic unity. The world of culture, he said, had lost much by the inadequate knowledge in the West of many of the greatest treasures of Eastern literature and philosophy. Art had an advantage over the written word: vision was the same everywhere; language was not. The East had become acquainted with the literature of the West, but the West had not reciprocated to any significant degree. Scholars liked E. G. Browne, R. A. Nicholson and Sir Denison Ross were giving pleasure to their own people

[1] Speech at a dinner, New Delhi, 17 February 1936.
[2] Lecture on "Hafiz and the Place of Iranian Culture in the World", London, 9 November 1936.
[3] Speech at the Islamic Research Association, Bombay, 18 January 1939.

through their translations and other works, but a vastly greater effort was required.[1]

Was the great poetical treasure house of Iran fated to remain something belonging only to Iran and a fringe of India, and a closed book to the Western world? "Is Europe, is America, is the West so rich in the joys of the spirit, in its immediate satisafaction with life, that it can afford to close its doors to what Iran has to offer in the highest spiritual satisfaction to mankind? In these days of intensive nationalism – nationalism of a kind that wishes to turn even art, beauty and goodness into national possessions – is this immense lesson of Iran to be forgotten? Iran in its language, in its culture, in its highest soul expression, has taken to its bosom and freely accepted the contributions of Greece and India, the immense stream from Islam, Arabia and the Turkish race. It has assimilated the best of each in order better to express its yearning after truth and beauty. Is this fundamental influence not to be brought into the service of the highest culture of the West?"[2] He reflected: ". . . science had reduced space almost to nothing . . . a conscious effort was needed to bring the East and the West together, so that with the shrinkage that had taken place over the physical part of the earth, cultural and moral and spiritual expansion might take place to meet it."[3]

The single most radical suggestion the Aga Khan made in the interest of Islamic unity was that Pakistan should adopt Arabic rather than Urdu as her national language. The advice was earnestly given, in the context of a national controversy and the international turn of events. His arguments against Urdu were novel, cogent and powerful.

He confessed that his opinions would mortally offend important sections of the population; but he would be "a traitor to Islam" if he let this opportunity pass without placing before the "people of this powerful and populous Islamic nation" his own views on the subject. "The language of a nation is not only the expression of its own voice but the mode of interpretation with all other human societies." Before it was too late, before a "tragic and deadly" step were taken, his brothers in Islam should give ear to the words of an old man, he pleaded.

First, India had not made Urdu its national language. Had she done so, there might have been some excuse for Pakistan to

[1] "Persian Poets", *The Times*, London, 22 September 1934.
[2] Lecture on "Hafiz and the Place of Iranian Culture in the World", London, 9 November 1936.
[3] Speech at the Royal Central Asian Society, London, 31 October 1934.

follow suit in order to make a bridge of contact and under-standing between the two countries. But now that India had opted for Hindi, the Pakistanis' choice of Urdu would in no way help their relations in India (this was addressed specifically to the Urdu-speaking migrants in Pakistan from the United Provinces, Delhi and Bihar) or fortify the Muslim minority living there.

Second, howsoever the Urdu lovers might add Arabic and Persian words to their language, the fact would stand that the syntax, the form and the fundamentals of Urdu were derived from Hindi.

Third, Urdu was the language associated with Muslim decline and downfall in the subcontinent. During the Pathan rule it was yet unborn. Under the Mughals it was not the language of the educated classes. The court language, the medium of adminis-tration and education and culture was Persian. The early Mughals spoke Turkish. The Hindu intelligentsia wrote and used Persian, not Urdu, till the early nineteenth century. Till Macaulay's time, Persian was the language of Bengali upper classes, and of the courts in Bengal and all other provinces. It was a historical fact that Urdu became the language of Muslim India after its down-fall. All its poets belonged to the age of decline of Muslim power. The last and greatest of them, Iqbal, "with the inspiration of revival", gave up Urdu in favour of Persian. In the Aga Khan's presence in London, Iqbal had once said that he had adopted Persian because it had been associated with the greatness of the Islamic epoch and not with its misfortunes. "Is it right that the language of the downfall period should become the national language of what we hope now is a phoenix-like national rising? All the great masters of Urdu belong to the period of greatest depression and defeat."

Fourth, the Urdu language was, at a certain stage in Indian history, a legitimate attempt at reconciliation; a language of Hindi derivation, with additions of Arabic and Persian words, it was intended to create a better understanding with the majority com-munity of that period, the Hindus. Now, however, the subcontinent was divided into two independent nations – and both sides accepted partition as final.

Fifth, Urdu was not the natural or national language of the population of Pakistan. It was certainly not the tongue of Bengal where the majority of the Muslims lived; nor of the Pathan prov-ince, nor of Sind, nor of the Punjab.

Finally, Urdu was born in the Mughal camp. The camp followers – the vast Hindi-speaking horde attached to the imperial
court – adapted and borrowed Arabic and Persian words ad hoc,
fitting them into the syntax of their own language, just as many
English words were later to find their way into the common
tongue and become a part of a new form of Urdu called Hindustani. "Are you going to make the language of the Camp or of
the Court your national language of your new born realm?"

After disposing of the case for Urdu, he came to the points in
favour of adopting Arabic as the national language of Pakistan.
Every Muslim child learnt to read the Quran in Arabic, whether
he lived in Quetta or in Dacca. Arabic was the language of the
Quran, and therefore of Islam. The Prophet's traditions (*ahadith*)
were in Arabic. The highest manifestation of Islamic culture in
Spain was in Arabic. All Pakistani children had to learn a
modicum of Arabic. Further, from the practical and worldly point
of view, Arabic would give the Pakistanis immediate contact not
only with the forty million Arabic-speaking people of the heart-
land but with another sixty million more-or-less Arabic-speaking
people in Africa. From the Atlantic, in the north of Africa, to
Nigeria and the Gold Coast (Ghana), Arabic was known to the
upper classes. In the east, some knowledge of it was possessed by
parts of the Muslim populations in Zanzibar, Tanganyika, Kenya,
Uganda, Somalia, Madagascar and Portuguese East Africa. On
the other side of Pakistan, the eighty million Muslims of
Indonesia and Malaya and the faithful of Ceylon, were acquainted
with Arabic to a varying extent. Was it not right and proper that
Pakistan, with its central geographical position, forming a bridge
between nearly a hundred million Muslims of the East and a
hundred million of the West, should make Arabic its national
language? She should not isolate herself from all her neighbours
and from the world of Islam. Arabic, as a universal language of
the Muslim world, would unite the *ummah*; Urdu would divide
and isolate. "Gentlemen, brothers in Islam, people of Pakistan,
people of every province", he pleaded, "I appeal to you, before
you take the final and what, I unfortunately must say, I consider
the fatal jump down the precipice, please discuss and let all and
everyone contribute their views. Take time and think over it.
Once more I appeal, to those whom I have offended, for Islamic
charity in the discussions that inevitably will take place, and all
others to look facts in the face historically and the present world
of today."[1]

---

[1] Speech before the Motamar-al-Alam-al-Islami, Karachi, 9 February 1951.

Had this advice been accepted, who knows, the 1971 disaster in East Pakistan might have been averted, the rising tide of Sindhi nationalism dammed, and the chaos in the educational system avoided – to mention only the domestic scene. But political power was in the hands of the Urdu-speaking microscopic minority settled in Karachi; the press was on their side; and the Punjab had long ago surrendered its linguistic and cultural autonomy. Arabic had as much chance against Urdu as Islam had against narrow nationalism and democracy against military ambition.

Viewing the Empire

The image of the Aga Khan so lovingly fashioned by the Indian, British and American historians and scholars – as an agent of imperialism, a sycophant, a blind supporter of foreign rule in India, an enemy of self-government or self-rule for the peoples of the subcontinent, a pillar of the British Empire, etc. – dissolves completely before historical reality. This stigma has been attached to many Muslim leaders who commanded unquestioned respect and popularity among their own community. I want to take this opportunity to lay this ghost once and for all. My argument rests upon three points. The Muslims of India, belonging to all periods and affiliated to nearly all political parties and movements, supported British rule when it came to a choice between it and Hindu rule which would last for ever; their minority status in India *vis-à-vis* an overbearing and hostile Hindu majority left them no alternative. The Hindus themselves, even of front-rank nationalist variety, were not always as anti-British as their biographers and Indian historians would like to present them to posterity. The declarations and writings of the Aga Khan himself offer convincing refutation of this accusation. Let me take up these points one by one.

I do not think it would be far from the truth to say that in the period 1860–1947 (the only years of political British rule) a majority of the top-ranking Muslim leaders in India were convinced that it was in the interest of their community to co-operate with the British rulers. There was hardly any political or political-cum-religious party or any organized group of Muslim intellectuals and men of religion which, at one time or another, hesitated to express its loyalty to the government, on some occasions in language quite nauseating.

A brief review of this current of feeling will substantiate my contention. The deep loyalty which Sir Sayyid Ahmad Khan entertained for the British, and which he upheld as a virtue and preached as a necessity, is well known to every student of modern Indian Muslim history. But some of the lesser-known expressions of it need to be recorded here.[1] On 1 November 1858, when Queen Victoria's royal declaration to India was read out at a *durbar* in Allahabad, Sir Sayyid wrote, "Undoubtedly God's hand rests upon the head of our Queen Empress. Undoubtedly this beneficent declaration has been issued under Divine inspiration [*ilham*]."[2] In 1884, in toasting W. S. Blunt, he said, "We hope that wherever you went [in India] you found our community [*qaum*] loyal to the British Crown and well-wishers from its heart [*dili khairkhwah*] of Queen Victoria, the Empress of India. . . . British rule was established in India at a time when poor India had become a widow and was in need of a husband. Therefore, she herself chose to make the English nation her husband, so that they could join together to form one body according to the concordat of the Gospel . . . The English nation came to our vanquished country as a friend, not as an enemy . . . It is our wish that English rule should last in India, not just for a long time but eternally. This desire is for the good of our own country, not for the English nation."[3]

In the same year, during his tour of the Punjab, he delivered lectures in which his praise of British rule was the prevailing theme. One example should suffice. "I have not rendered any service to the Government. In whatever I have done I have merely carried out the instruction [*hukm*] of my holy [*pak*] religion and true Prophet. Our true Prophet has ordered us to obey, to wish well and to be loyal to the government under which you are living. Thus, whatever service I have been able to render to the government has really been a service to my faith."[4]

In 1911 the influential Lahore newspaper, *Paisa Akhbar*, wrote, "Over ten crore [one hundred million] followers of Islam are loyal to Emperor George. This number is greater than the combined populations of the three largest Musalman States, viz.,

---

[1] Most of the sources quoted here are originally in Urdu. I have rendered them here in a literal translation, even if the result is stylistically clumsy, because I want to convey the flavour and nuance of the original word.

[2] *Maqalat-i-Sir Sayyid Ahmad,* Lahore, Vol. 9, 1962, p. 106.

[3] Cited in Altaf Hussain Hali, *Sir Sayyid Ahmad Khan ki Kahani, Sir Sayyid Ahmad Khan ki Zabani,* comp. Ziauddin, Lahore, 1982, p. 71.

[4] *Sir Sayyid Ahmad Khan ka Safarnamah-i-Punjab,* Lahore, 1961 reprint, p. 65.

Turkey, Iran and Afghanistan. On this basis the British Empire is known as the world's greatest Islamic monarchy [*saltanat*]."[1]

Maulana Zafar Ali Khan, the indomitable editor of the *Zamindar* of Lahore, who prided himself on his love of Islam and his hatred of Christian rule over India, wrote to King George V in an open letter on 22 November 1934, "Sire, I fully know the deep feelings of the eight crore [eighty million] Musalmans of India who accept Your Majesty as their emperor."[2]

In 1935 the Ahrars, one of the most ardent pro-Congress nationalist groups ranged against the Muslim League, were receiving help from the Punjab Government and especially from its Criminal Investigation Department, of course for a *quid pro quo*.[3]

Iqbal's writings provide us with several proofs of his deepseated and unconcealed allegiance, even obsequiousness, to the British. On Queen Victoria's death on 22 January 1901 (which day was also the *id-ul-fitr*), he composed an elegy of 110 couplets, praising the deceased Empress, paying servile tributes to her, grieving for the loss, and calling her death a *muharram* for the Muslims of India.[4] The poem was published at government expense. Encouraged by official approval, Iqbal himself translated it into English under the title of "Tears of Blood".[5]

In reply to an inquiry made in 1910 by Ali Gohar, Secretary of the Anjuman-i-Islamiah Hazara, in the *Paisa Akhbar*, whether it was advisable for the Indian Muslims to participate in the proposed World Islamic Conference to be held in Egypt, Iqbal argued against such participation, and added that "the peace and freedom enjoyed by the people of India because of British rule were denied to other countries... The Message of God

---

[1] *Paisa Akhbar*, Lahore, 22 June 1911.

[2] The letter was published in full text in *Zamindar*, Lahore, 22 November 1934. On 25 November it was read out to a large gathering at the Friday mosque in Aligarh.

[3] This is the evidence of Sir Fazl-i-Husain; see *Diary and Notes of Mian Fazl-i-Husain*, ed. Waheed Ahmad, Lahore, 1977, pp. 141, 165.

[4] Full text in *Sarod-i-Raftah*, eds. Ghulam Rasul Mehr and Saiq Ali Dilawari, Lahore, 1959, pp. 183–91. It must be explained to the non-Muslim reader that *Muharram* is the month of mourning in the Islamic calendar for all Muslims, and particularly for the Shias, because of the tragedy which occurred in this month at Karbala in Iraq when the Prophet's grandson, Imam Husain, was butchered along with his family by the army of the Mu'awyah ruler.

[5] See Munshi Din Muhammad, *Kitab-i-Yadgar-i-Durbar-i-Dilli Tajposhi 1911*, Lahore, 1912, p. 507; Sayyid Nazir Niazi, *Dana-i-Raz*, Lahore, 1979, p. 361, and *Iqbaliat* (Journal of the Iqbal Academy of Pakistan), July–September 1988, p. 13.

[Quran] enjoins upon the Muslims to live in peace and amity; they are not even permitted to consult each other in secret".[1]

On 22 June 1911 the coronation of King George V was celebrated by the Muslims of Lahore at a gathering in the Royal Mosque of the city, and among the speakers was Iqbal who emphasized the Muslims' bounden duty to bear allegiance to the ruler of the day. "The goal of the Muslims is not rulership [*saltanat*]", he said, "but the maximum spread of their religion, and under British rule this is permitted."[2] In May 1918 the Punjab Government convened a meeting in the Town Hall of Lahore to collect funds and encourage recruitment for the war. The Governor of the province, Sir Michael O'Dwyer, was in the chair. Iqbal delivered a speech in praise of the virtues of the British Empire, and then recited a poem swearing sincere and unselfish obedience and true fealty, offering the sacrifice of his own life if that could save the Empire, and praying for the grant of an eternal lease to British rule.[3] In a couplet of 1925 he paid homage to Sir Malcolm Hailey, the Governor of the Punjab.[4]

In July 1931, in a letter to Sir Francis Younghusband, he wrote, "I shall have no objection to be ruled by the Hindu if he has the tact and the ability to govern, but I can't worship two Gods. It must be either him alone or the British alone, but not the two together."[5] On 24 November 1932, in a speech delivered at a reception given in his honour by the National League of Britain in London, he said, "Muslims have courage and have always shown loyalty and affection to Great Britain."[6]

Lesser men were echoing the same sentiments. Iqbal's teacher Shams-ul-Ulema Mawlawi Mir Hasan, issued a *fatwa* (religious edict) in favour of loyalty to the British, calling their rule kind, just and a gift from God, and concluding with the remark that it

---

[1] *Paisa Akhbar*, Lahore, 21 July 1915; this was a reprint of his written opinion given in August 1910 and published in the issue of 22 August 1910.

[2] *Ibid.*, 24 June 1911.

[3] *Ibid.*, 5 and 11 May 1918 gives an account of the proceedings of the meeting. The poem "Punjab ka Jawab" is reprinted in *Sarod-i-Raftah*, pp. 55–57; it first appeared in the *Wakil* of Amritsar, 11 May 1918.

[4] Faqir Syed Wahiduddin, *Rozgar-i-Faqir*, Lahore, 1950, p. 173. The couplet ran: "*Punjab ki kishti ko dia us né sahara/Tabindah hameshah rahe Hailey ka sitarah*'.

[5] The letter, originally published in *The Civil & Military Gazette* of Lahore on 30 July 1931, is reproduced in *Speeches, Writings and Statements of Iqbal*, ed. Latif Ahmed Shirwani, Lahore, 3rd. rev. ed., 1977, p. 207.

[6] Reproduced in *Letters and Writings of Iqbal*, ed. B. A. Dar, Lahore, n.d., p. 70.

was a matter of pride to be born under such a government.[1]
Maulana Shibli Naumani, one of the most highly respected *'ulema*
and men of letters, while welcoming the Governor of Agra and
Oudh to his Nadwah in 1902, assured the guest that "we look
upon our loyalty and goodwill [*khairkwahi*] to the Government
as our religious duty".[2] A history of the Deoband School, published in 1917, carried the following exhortation: "Every virtuous
Musalman [*momin Musalman*] is requested that he must [*zarur bil
zarur*] pray, day and night, standing and sitting, in short every
moment and instant [*her lahza aur sa'at*], for the rule under
whose governance every person is leading a life of luxury and
ease [*'aish aur aram*] and on account of whose gift of freedom
the garden of Islam is green and fruitful – Oh God: thou keepest
it in power for ever and ever."[3] It must be remembered that the
Deoband School was firmly allied to the Indian National Congress, preached the doctrine of a united Indian "nationalism",
opposed the Aligarh Movement at every step, and opposed the
creation of Pakistan until 1947.

In 1887 Khwaja Altaf Hussain Hali, the well-known poet and
literary critic, wrote a eulogy of British rule in which he offered
a prayer that God may always keep the family of the ruler in His
safekeeping and the ruler may always keep India under his
shadow [*saiah*].[4]

The Nadwaht-ul-'Ulema was established with the express
purpose of bringing together all the doctors of religion of Islam
so that they could play their true part in the progress and advance
of Islam in India. The foundation stone of the college (*dar-
ul-'Ulum*) of the Nadwah was laid by the Lieutenant Governor of
the United Provinces of Agra and Oudh on 28 November 1908.
Describing the function Shibli Naumani wrote with pride, "Our
eyes have witnessed the glitters of [many] fantastic spectacles,
many pageants of authority and might [*jah-o-jalal*], the
enthusiasm and zeal of [many] conferences and societies, many
congregations where moving sermons were given and homilies

---

[1] This was done in a speech delivered on 4 April 1897 in Sialkot at a meeting
to celebrate the Diamond Jubilee of Queen Victoria; see Dr Syed Sultan
Mahmud Husain, *Allama Iqbal kek Ustad Shams-ul-Ulema Mawlawi Syid Mir
Hasan: Hayat-o-Afkar*, Lahore, 1981, pp. 77–79.
[2] *Wakil*, Amritsar, 14 November 1902.
[3] Muhammad Rafi, *Deoband ki Sair aur us ki Mukhtasar Tarikh*, Delhi, Shawwal
1335 A.H. (1 September 1917).
[4] *Kulliat-i-Nazm-i-Hali*, ed. Dr Iftikhar Ahmad Siddiqui, July 1968, pp. 353 ff. The
poem is entitled "Marsia Malikah Victoria", 1901. The eulogy was presented to
Queen Victoria on behalf of the Anjuman-i-Islamia of Lahore.

[*wa'z-o-pand*] were preached, but what we saw on this occasion was more astonishing, more strange and more inspiring [*bil asar*] than all these. This was the first time that turbans and Turkish caps were together. This was the first time that the revered [*muqaddas*] 'ulema were bowing respectfully and with gratitude in their hearts before a Christian ruler. This was the first time that the foundation stone of a religious school [of Islam] was being laid by a non-Muslim. The Pulpit of the Prophet's mosque was also the work of a Christian." The address written in Arabic presented to the Lieutenant Governor declared that "religious tolerance is a characteristic feature of the British Government", and submitted that "we maintain it as our belief that loyalty to the Government is our proven stance. Through the 'ulema produced by this school Muslims will advance in their obedience and submission to the Government."[1] About the speech made by the Lieutenant Governor in reply to the address of welcome the 'ulema of Nadwah said, "Each and every word of it is Water of Life [*ab-i-hayat*] for the Nadwah."[2]

In 1928 the Maharajah of Mahmudabad, speaking at the All India Muslim League annual session in Calcutta, said, "The application of the doctrine of independence in the sense of the severance of British connection is, to my mind, a hopelessly unworkable proposition. India's place in the British Commonwealth is a valuable asset and, in my judgement, it will be a folly to destroy this precious commodity with our own hands. It is my conviction that there is plenty of room for growth, development and expression of Indian nationalism within the orbit of India's connection with England."[3] The Maharajah's personal and political predilections marched together. His residence was named "Butler Palace" after Sir Harcourt Butler, the Lieutenant Governor of the province.

There is no evidence available yet that the Punjab Unionist Party, which ruled the province for two decades and kept the Muslim League out of the Punjab with conspicuous success was a British creation; but only an addle-pated historian will call it an anti-British group. Sahibzada Sir Abdul Qayyum Khan, the

---

[1] For fuller details see *al-Nadwah* (journal of the Nadwaht-ul-'Ulema), December 1908, pp. 1–4.

[2] *al-Nadwah*, November 1908, p. 6; the journal was then edited by Shibli Naumani and Habib-ur-Rahman Khan Shirwani.

[3] *The Times of India*, Bombay, 27 December 1928. Jinnah paid a warm tribute to the Maharajah of Mahmudabad at the meeting: "I can assure you that among Mussalmans there is not a truer friend of the Muslims nor a greater well-wisher of the Muslim community than the Maharaja."

maker of modern North-West Frontier Province and its first Prime Minister, had served the British administrators of the province as their *munshi* and agent throughout his official career and showed his loyalty in every respect after entering public life. The same can be said of nearly every important politician and minsiter in every province of India.

I think the above examples, chosen at random, should suffice to convince even the most sceptical reader that the Aga Khan's was by no means a singular case of a very loyal subject of His Britannic Majesty's imperial dominions showing appropriate respect to his masters. Nor, in this, was he speaking for a lunatic fringe of the Muslims of India, nor for a minority of Muslim politicians. On the contrary, he was very much in the mainstream of Indian Muslim political and religious thinking. The myth that the Muslims were loyal because they were toadies and anti-nationalists can easily be shown to be a false assumption by looking at the predicament in which Muslim India found itself at the time of the commencement of British rule, and then throughout the course of Indian politics. The following considerations are relevant to this inquiry.

During the testing days that followed the revolt of 1858 Muslims were convinced that their only salvation lay in practising loyalty. Sayyid Ahmad Khan foresaw that the Muslim minority was no match for the progressive Hindus, and that if it also alienated the sympathies of the rulers its ruin would be complete. He brought forth many arguments from his religious study and social experience in justification of his pro-British attitude. This might have been a conscious or unconscious rationalization of his political views, but there is no doubt that Sayyid Ahmad passionately believed in the desirability, practicability and necessity of a Muslim–British understanding.

With the foundation of the Indian National Congress in 1885 the Muslims redoubled their efforts to prove their loyalty in fear lest the Congress might be accepted as representative of all educated Muslim opinion. They were alarmed by the Congress and what it stood for, for any advance towards self-government would imply their relegation to the position of an insubstantial minority. During the Hindu unrest of 1905–11 they supported the government unstintedly. The greatest test of Muslim constancy came in 1911 when the partition of Bengal was annulled. Muslim India was shocked and some leaders talked of extreme retaliatory measures. But even in this crisis the tradition of years prevailed and the leading Muslims, though irate and indignant, instructed their followers not to agitate against the decision. The Aga Khan issued a similar appeal.

After the 'disloyal' interlude of the Khilafat Movement the old habit reasserted itself and at the Round Table Conferences Muslims were by and large so co-operative as to evoke from the Congress the charge of being reactionaries and toadies. In 1931 just before the opening of the second conference, a striking article appeared in the *Empire Review* which stands as a faultless testament of Muslim loyalty. The author's background under-lined the significance of what he said. It was written by Maulana Shaukat Ali, one of the famous Ali brothers who had led the Indian Khilafatists into a virulent campaign against the British. Now as a delegate to the conference, he made a stirring appeal for Muslim–British friendship. "We both need each other", he wrote. "We should grasp that hand and Islam would stand with Britain, a good and honourable friend, a brave fighter and a staunch ally . . . Should Hindus and Muslims live together a thou-sand years, there is no chance of the two cultures merging into one. This is adamant, bedrock fact, which cannot be glossed over . . . At the back of every Muslim mind, based on our experi-ence of the last fifteen or twenty years, is the fear that Great Britain had lost something of her old virility, and that she may let us down . . . We want no handicap against anybody, including the British."[1]

What lay behind such expressions of loyalty? What was the philosophy of loyalty? Was there indeed any coherent thought behind it at all?

First, loyalty was the safest course of action for a minority which was backward and helpless. Either it could co-operate with the Hindus, which it would not, or it could keep on good terms with the rulers. To alienate both the present and the future rulers would have been unmitigated folly.

Second, paradoxically the fact is that the Muslims, universally characterized in the West as a militant body, were the only consti-tutionally-minded group in India. Without trying to resolve this paradox (which may have been a reaction to the unsuccessful Mutiny), we must notice that the Congress was, except in the first few years of its existence, an agitational organization. *Satyag-raha* was often portrayed as a peaceful movement; but to break the laws of a country is unconstitutional, whether the deed is

---

[1] Shaukat Ali, "An Appeal from the Muslim World to the British People", *Empire Review*, November 1931, pp. 807–9.

done by making women volunteers lie down on the road or by leading a band of mutinous riflemen. In fact, *Satyagraha* is more deadly – for it is planned and cold-blooded – than open agitation which may be due to the heat of the moment. Muslims were not fond of agitating, first under the influence of Sayyid Ahmad Khan, and later under that of Jinnah, both of whom were, for different reasons, almost constitutional martinets.

Third, the Muslims were sceptical both of the genuineness of the Hindu agitation and of the likelihood of its successful outcome. The agitation was for greater democracy, which to the Muslims meant greater oppression. The agitation was also unlikely to achieve its end because the rulers were strong and because all India was not on the side of the agitators. It was thus both unwise and fruitless to stand with the agitators and incur the displeasure of the government.

Also, most Muslims appreciated the fairness with which they had been, or were being, treated by the British. Between the Hindus and the British they chose to trust the latter, and on the whole found that this policy paid dividends.

In terms of religion, Christian rulers were closer to the Muslims than were the idol-worshipping Hindus. As religion was a vital factor in the awakening of their nationalism this affinity tended to throw the Muslims on to the side of the British.

In social matters, again, the Muslim found himself in more congenial company among the British. The two could, and did, intermarry, interdine and intermix in society without disagreeable taboos. With the Hindu one was always on one's guard against breaking some caste restriction or polluting a Brahmin household. Social mixing is as essential an ingredient of friendship as aloofness is a creator of misunderstanding.

The educated among the Muslim community were greatly influenced by English literature, history, philosophy and art. This intellectual and academic deference paved the way to political loyalty. The British ruled the country and held power and patronage in their hands. The Muslims, as a minority, wanted safeguards, and the British alone could grant them. The Islamic injunction of obeying the ruler of the time may have weighed with a section of the Muslims. Disobedience to those in authority is not permitted unless the ruler interferes with the religious rites of the Muslims.

Finally, Britain was the greatest "Muslim Empire" in the world, and had intimate relations with all independent and semi-independent Muslim states. As the Indian Muslims formed a part of the world Muslim community it was important for them to remain on good terms with Britain.[1]

Thus the Aga Khan was not ploughing a lonely furrow, nor echoing a minority view, in choosing to work within the framework of British connection. His policy of co-operation defined and reflected the essence of Indian Muslim politics. He was a realist who was convinced that, given the ground rules of current politics and the minority status of the Muslims, the protection of Muslim rights and the advance of their interests lay in co-operation with those in authority who could fulfil Muslim needs and demands rather than in confrontation with the only source of power and arbitration.

Nor were the Hindus themselves as consistent and steadfast in their anti-British and anti-imperialist opinions and activities as they would like others to believe. The Congress itself, during its early years, was a completely and unashamedly loyal body, and at every annual session passed a resolution in praise of British overlordship. Many Indian nationalists and patriots of impeccable credentials cultivated the British Viceroys and Governors with unremitting zeal. Does that make them toadies?

A few parallels between the actions of the Aga Khan and those of some eminent Hindu nationalist leaders culled from modern history confirm the point I am trying to make here.

The Aga Khan was convinced that British governance of India was beneficent; so did all the leaders of the first generation of the Indian National Congress and of the Indian Liberal Federation throughout its career. The Aga Khan, however, never allowed any Englishman to preside over any session of the All India Muslim League or the All India Muslim Conference; but we know that the Indian National Congress gloried in the leadership of Hume and Wedderburn. The Aga Khan received many titles and honours from the British court; so did such elder statesmen of the Congress as Surendranath Banerjea, such liberal leaders at the top of the tree as Tej Bahadur Sapru and Chimanlal Setalvad, and such literary giants as Rabindranath Tagore. The Aga Khan was a Privy Councillor; so were Congressmen like Srinivasa Sastri and Hindu Mahasabhaists like M. R. Jayakar. If these decorations

---

[1] The last two pages have been drawn from my *The Making of Pakistan: A Study in Nationalism*, London, 1967, pp. 70–5. The reader will find scattered references to the subject in my *A History of the Idea of Pakistan*, Lahore, 1987, 4 vols.

make a traitor of him, then the highest ranks of Indian nationalism reeked of treachery.

The Aga Khan asked the Muslims of India not to rebel against British rule with the argument that a Christian government which did not interfere with the performance of their religious rites and ceremonies was accepted and that India was not a *dar-ul-harb*. Shah Abdul Aziz said the same thing, and a majority of highly respected *'ulema* repeated it for over a hundred years. During the Second World War the Muslim League, under Jinnah, resolved to co-operate with the official war effort. Does that make all these Muslim religious leaders agents of imperialism? In the First World War Mahatma Gandhi (and the British Empire had no greater enemy than he) accepted a decoration from the government for (of all the things) helping in the recruitment of Indian soldiers to fight in defence of the Empire. Gokhale was as liberal a Hindu as any that India has produced, and his ideas aligned with those of the Aga Khan so closely that he chose the Muslim leader for the bequest of his political testament. The Aga Khan used his friendship with Lord Minto to get separate electorates for the Muslims, and he was dubbed a loyalist by the Hindus and their British friends. Jawaharlal Nehru made friends with Lord Mountbatten so that India could get Kashmir and an edge over Pakistan in the 1947 dispensation and yet his reputation as a great and sincere leader of the independence movement has never been sullied by any reference to his unusual relations with the Mountbattens. Gandhi sent Birla and a special emissary, Sudhir Ghosh, both in secret, to convey his wishes to Labour leaders like Sir Stafford Cripps, Lord Pethick-Lawrence and Clement Attlee, and to extract their sympathy for the Hindu point of view. Nobody has ever called the Mahatma a loyalist. The Aga Khan used his influence in high places in Britain to protect Muslim rights in Turkey and India. He was called a communalist and a parasite of an alien race.

One can go on adding to this motley of parallels and contradictions. The point I want to make is that any Muslim leader in India standing guard over the interests of his community and fighting on behalf of it was a communalist in the vocabulary of Hindu national politics. The Muslim leader went to the British Government for the redress of his wrongs and the fulfilment of his political ambitions because, first, the Hindus and the Congress did not listen to him, and, second, it was the only ruling power in whose hands lay the gift of concession. But he was a loyalist, because he chose to approach the British rather than beg to the Congress and the Hindu Mahasabha (all these parties could give him was the Nehru Report). Both the Muslims and the Hindus were suppliants at the doorstep of an imperial ruler, and both courted the source of power for their own ends. Had the Aga Khan been a loyalist, the entire British Indian delegation to the Round Table Conference would not have chosen him as its leader and spokeman.

Historical judgement should be (but not always is) based on facts, not myths. The facts, in this case, are the words and deeds of the Aga Khan. His actual activities and pronouncements are the only measure by which he should be judged. In the preceding sections I have indicated, with direct quotations, how strongly he criticized the British for the educational system they had established in India, for failing to give enough seats to the Indians in the army and the civil service, for withholding wider powers from the legislative councils, for neglecting rural development, for failing to protect Indian rights in South Africa and Kenya, for denying Indian women their right to vote, for signing an unjust peace treaty with Turkey, and, on the whole, for not inducing reform at a faster pace. He was unhappy with the structure of bureaucracy in India and said so in strong words to the Royal Commission on the Indian Public Services. His role in the making of the 1919 Act, and his fight on behalf of reforms in the Joint Committee on Indian Constitutional Reform, where he exchanged candid words with Churchill, fail to show a loyalist at work.

If all that is not enough to counter his detractors, let us hear more from him about the weaknesses, errors and follies of the British, and the nature and character of their rule in India.

He did not mince words in chastising the British for their record in India. In 1905 he reminded the British that "the present rulers of India have found themselves therein either by conquest, or force of circumstances, or by the will of Providence, but certainly not by the will of its peoples".[1]

When, on 19 September 1914, Lloyd George, the Chancellor of the Exchequer, in a recruitment speech in London, likened Kaiser Wilhelm of Germany to the Prophet of Islam, the Aga Khan was incensed at the solecism; his riposte could not have been more strongly worded. "...the Chancellor of the Exchequer may not be able to reciprocate the veneration for the founder of our faith, which we are taught from our child-

[1] "The Defence of India", *The Nineteenth Century and After*, September 1905.

hood, to give to the founder of the Christian faith, but he might at least show towards him the respect and reverence we all accord to the memories of the great sons of Christendom who do not belong, so to speak, to our religion like the founder of Christianity does."[1]

In 1918 he wrote that British rule in India "has been criticized, and rightly criticized, for having allowed the twentieth century to dawn and grow without having grappled fully with the illiteracy general in India, and with the insanitary environment of the masses so bad that avoidable deaths are counted by the million every year, while the standard of the physique of the masses is deplorably low. The various modern departments of State that lead towards social betterment and social welfare in the West have still to be organized. The Indian public conscience demands that British rule should come into line with progressive modern ideas and tackle illiteracy and other social problems left for too long unsolved."[2]

Having thus dealt with the Government of India, he went on to castigate the British Parliament and Government. "India's want of confidence in the making of the theory that the people of England are her ultimate owners is not based on merely national pride or purely idealistic reasons." The continuance in office of the Secretary of State for India was dependent "far less on the relative merit and advantage of his services to India than on the exigencies of party convenience, or on the verdict of the electors on subjects having no relation to India. His salary has not been placed on the British estimates, and the control of Parliament over Indian affairs has been more nominal than real." The House of Commons gave inadequate attention to the many misfortunes of India. "How many debates", he asked, "how many critical divisions, how many proposals to share the sacrifice in the battles against cholera and malaria, plague and poverty, do the pages of Hansard record? How often, with what devices, and with what power, has the House of Commons discussed the need for overcoming illiteracy in India? In what general sections of Parliament have votes been affected in any appreciable degree by the terrible poverty-famines or poverty-plagues of that distant country?"[3]

His next target was the conservative opinion in England which

[1] Speech at a meeting of the Indian Volunteers Committee, London, 1 October 1914.
[2] *India in Transition*, 1918.
[3] *Ibid.*

rejected any constitutional advance for India on the grounds of India's supposed political extremism or anarchism. This, in his opinion, was nothing less than "tragic non-comprehension". The tiny lunatic fringe which believed in extremist measures to extract reforms from reluctant British troops was being given too much importance. For the British and their parliament to allow their sense of justice to be deflected by this small body of political opinion was "at once so inequitable and so wanting in the sense of proportion as to be wholly inconsistent with British political tradition". Those who barred the way to Indian reform could not challenge this view. "It is not surprising that the belief is entertained in India that they use this horrible fact [extremism in India] as a handy argument and weapon to beat back her legitimate aspirations towards a worthy place in the Empire ... To maintain that the system of the last sixty years must be continued in the interests of law and order is to wholly misunderstand the spirit and aspirations of enlightened Indian opinion." "If such counsels are listened to and no substantial instalment of reform is proposed to Parliament", then, after the war, the Indians would place the situation before the British electorate. "Counter agitation on the part of conservative elements in England, leading to contentious argument at the hustings, is to be deprecated" – that would leave behind bitter memories.[1]

In 1920 came a stinging attack on British policy in the East. The Indians had discovered that "the views of the Government of India, still less Indian public opinion, count for little or nothing in the settlement of Imperial policy in the East. The Indian point of view, whether official or otherwise, appears to be almost entirely disregarded". He went on, hardening his language in the process, "Between the convictions I have personally felt and the wild and reckless ventures undertaken in the name of Great Britain in the Near and Middle East since the armistice, there is a great gulf. That gulf is widened by the general policy underlying the recommendations of the Esher Committee, which seems to contemplate some sort of active British hegemony of the Middle East, with the Indian Army, rather than the British Army, as its sword and buckler." He "profoundly disagreed" with the Committee's proposal that henceforth the Indian Army should be used at will outside India at the bidding of the Imperial General Staff, in pursuit of objectives regarding which India would never be consulted. This policy was wrong and hazardous. British statesmen seemed to him to have some "vague and

---

[1] *Ibid.*

cloudy" ideas about the supposed value and necessity of the measures they were undertaking in the Near and Middle East. "For the sake of imaginary British interests, they are frittering away real and immediate interests." How could it be believed that British advocacy of the League of Nations was sincere when the Esher Committee made the "open and naked suggestion of preparations for military enterprises and activites" in that area? Was, then, British praise of the League mere lip service?[1]

Next, he assaulted British policy in India. "People in Great Britain do not seem to understand how widely the British promise of ultimate Dominion *status* is mistrusted by Indians." They did not seem to know that even Edwin Montagu was often attacked in India on the grounds that he never really meant what he said, though he had been the mouthpiece of the Declaration. In any case, whatever the future constitutional advance might be, it was not "right or proper" that India should be asked to bear heavy financial and military burdens, and to maintain an army far beyond her own requirements to enable the British to use these forces, without her consent and beyond her shores, to "further the vain and grandiose dreams (or rather nightmares!) of a few statesmen and soldiers six thousand miles away". He warned the British that a high taxation of India for such military purposes implied a policy which might eventually prove disastrous to British–Indian relations.[2]

Other points made by the Aga Khan were no less critical of British rule in India. If Bolshevism ever came to India, part of the blame would rest on Britain. If she continued to fritter away Indian men and money in other lands she would create a discontent in India in which Bolshevic propaganda would find a congenial home. There would be dangerous times when India concluded that her soldiers who had gone to Europe in 1914 to defend British liberty had merely established a precedent for the use of Indian troops "to destroy such liberties as may be left in Central and Western Asia". A discontented India with no trust in British promises would be a gift to Bolshevism.[3]

Britain, he proceeded to advise, should tread very carefully in Mesopotamia (her objective was to hold the entrance to the Persian Gulf). Mesopotamia would make her own future sooner or later without British intervention or influence. "The one thing certain is that the people of Mesopotamia will never find their

---

[1] "British Policy in the East: I", *The Times*, London, 5 November 1920.
[2] *Ibid.*
[3] "British Policy in the East: II", *The Times*, London, 6 November 1920.

own salvation while their country is full of British and Indian soldiers. Whether they settle down or not, it is not the duty of either Great Britain or of India to impose strange systems upon a people whom they have professed to rescue, who have shown them that they now wish to be left alone, and who are fighting for what they believe to be their freedom." He reprimanded those British statesmen who said that the country would collapse if Britain did not go in, telling them that "these ancient lands are not likely to collapse", and reminding them that they had said the same thing in 1879 and 1880 about Afghanistan, when actually the Afghan nation "instead of collapsing, found new strength when the British retired from Kabul and Kandahar".

On the British interest in Mesopotamian oil deposits he taunted his readers with a personal reference. "I may mention that I am a considerable shareholder in companies which hope to exploit the oil of Mesopotamia; but personally I do not expect either the British or the Indian taxpayer to put his hand into his pocket, in order that my income may be slightly increased, and I think it wrong that Mesopotomia should be a burden on the taxes."

He also asked Britain to withdraw all her forces from Persia and to establish friendly diplomatic and commercial relations with her. This could be done far more easily than the British public were given to suppose. Bolshevism would never spread among the Persians "provided the exploitation of the masses of the people by a small minority of prominent persons, who are bolstered up by British arms, is terminated".[1]

Nor did he fail to castigate the British for their racist attitude in Kenya. Unless the relations of the British settlers with the Indian population were put on a sound footing "great and indeed incalculable injury may be done to the interests of the Empire as a whole". The reaction of Indians in Kenya to any high-handedness might spread to the Indian subcontinent.[2] He hoped that the India Office would take the necessary precautions and steps, but the Indians [of India] should not let the matter slip away and should give their full support to the deputation headed by Srinivasa Sastri. "Many thoughtful people in England realized the damage done to British prestige and the Empire by the behaviour of the whites in Kenya," but the resolution of the diffi-culty was really in the hands of the Indians. If they could carry on a vigorous propaganda campaign in England things might

[1] *Ibid.*
[2] Letter, *The Times of India*, Bombay, 23(?) January 1923.

be on the mend.[1] He called the situation deplorable, but was glad to notice that on this issue there was complete unanimity among Indians – "Hindus, Mahomedans, Parsis, Indian Christians, extremist or moderate". They [Indians resident in Kenya] were being asked to "consent to become second-class citizens in such a country and to accept a subordinate and humiliating position. I consider this very unfair and derogatory to the self-respect of Indians and we must fight this matter to a finish till justice has been done to our cause."[2]

Indians did not subscribe to racialism. In India there was very little hostility to the Englishman as an Englishman or to a European as such. But there was a widespread impression that India had a stepmotherly government "from which her interests get full play only when there are no interests nearer home for the authorities in Whitehall to conserve". When such interests arose India's "wishes go to the wall". He cited several examples of this. The treatment of Indians in Kenya was one. Another was the disregard of Indian sentiment on the question of a just and equitable peace settlement with Turkey after the First World War. Still another was that the final word in regard to military matters and frontier policy did not rest with the people of India, or the Government of India, or even the Secretary of State for India, but with the War Council and the General Staff in Whitehall. "There is loud complaint that, at the cost of the Indian taxpayer, the strength of the Indian garrison and its composition are related to the requirements of the Empire, as a whole, rather than to India's own needs."

The Indians did not like the excessive defence expenditure imposed on them to fulfil purely British needs. The resulting heavy taxation was "obnoxious" because it represented so much unproductive expenditure. If the money being spent on this "excessive insurance" could be diverted in the years of peace to economic development, "the wealth of the country would so increase that in a few years the Army Budget could be adequate to the most exacting of reasonable standards without straining the public patience".[3]

Nor was cultural assimilation with the West acceptable to the Indians. They were ready to follow England in science, industry, hygiene, sports and such things, but "we take our stand on our

[1] Press interview, Bombay, 14 March 1923 published in *Civil and Military Gazette,* Lahore, 17 March 1923.
[2] Press interview, *The Times of India,* Bombay, 7 April 1923.
[3] "Optimism and Goodwill", *Sunday Express,* London, 13 April 1924.

own culture in the realm of the spirit". Indians, be they Hindu or Muslim, "are no less proud than Englishmen of their own traditions and teachings in religion, philosophy, poetry, romance and art".[1]

He stated, in a speech in New Delhi in 1936, that Indians were not fairly treated in the dominions and colonies: at home they lived under gross economic inequality, "extreme poverty, hunger and nakedness, emaciated and enfeebled bodies and ignorance". They could only be called "human beings by courtesy" and were intellectually depressed.[2]

In its leading article of 22 October 1951 on "The Middle East", *The Times* called Islam "an intolerant religion which teaches the duty of shunning foreign influences". The Aga Khan took the journal to task in the strongest language possible. The remark, which was both untrue and unfair, "shows a lamentable dearth of knowledge regarding Islam and its legal and religious principles, even among leading writers of the leading journal of the west". Islam taught toleration to its followers, and Islamic history had lived up to it, so that even the smallest Christian and Jewish minorities survived and practised their religion during the thousand years of Muslim rule. The level of Christian tolerance was shown in Spain where, after the Christian conquest, the Muslims received a treatment which they had not given to any minority in any Muslim dominion. How can the Europeans be so ignorant of the early Muslim rulers' patronage of studies of Greek and Roman culture and philosophy and medicine and of their assimilation with Islamic knowledge? The modern sense of nationalism, which had been acquired by Muslim countries from the West, had no connection with Islam. "If there has been violent reaction against the West in some of the Muslim countries, the reason is to be found in the attitude and behaviour of the Westerners, their ignorance, and want of respect for the faith and culture of Islam, of which the reference to that faith in your leading article is a typical and usual example . . . if the Atlantic nations and the West generally want better relationship with the Muslims, the solution lies in their own hands, and this can be done only if they change their mental attitude and cultivate better understanding of the Muslims' material needs and the loyal recognition of the high quality of their national culture and the purity of their faith."[3] Strange words from a toad-eater!

[1] Letter, *The Times*, London, 3 August 1925.
[2] Speech in New Delhi, 17 February 1936.
[3] Letter, *The Times*, London, 3 November 1951.

The Man

Thanks largely to his mother, the Aga Khan received good education in his early years, and though he did not attend university either in India or Britain, this thorough grounding stood him in good stead throughout his long life. He built on it through wide reading and through his conversations with educated people. Those who knew him well or met him for serious discussions report that they found him knowledgeable, well-read and very well informed. History, religion, literature and international affairs were fields which attracted him most. His ability to read Persian, Arabic, English, French and German (and probably Italian) gave him an opportunity to read wider and study the views of more people than most other educated persons.

As a man of culture it seems that his first love was – not surprisingly – Persian poetry. He was of Iranian origin, Farsi was his native tongue, and the home in which he was brought up had a strong ambiance of Persian culture – Persian poetry was recited and quoted round the dining table; Persian proverbs were frequently cited. In his adult life there were so many calls upon his time that he was not usually able to concentrate on any intellectual subject and write seriously on it. But his passion for Persian poetry forced him to make time for some reflection and writing.

Persian poetry, in his opinion, had a message for mankind which every poet had expressed in his own idiom – "man's greatest of all treasures, the greatest of all his possessions, was the inherent, ineffaceable, everlasting nobility of his own soul. In it there was for ever a spark of true divinity which could conquer all the antagonistic and debasing elements in nature". This faith in the soul of man, he emphasized, was "not simply a religious or mystic faith but an all-embracing and immediate contact with a fact which, in every human being, is the central fact of existence".[1]

He found time to share his love for Hafiz with the world. The universality, lyricism and passion of this greatest Persian poet of the *ghazal* genre appealed to him above everything else. For anyone conversant with the Farsi language and the layers of meanings of its words, "whatsoever a human being's mood, emotions, and thoughts may be, he can turn to Hafiz for the highest pleasure and inspiration". In the problem of solving

---

[1] "Hafiz and the Place of Iranian Culture in the World", lecture, London, 9 November 1936.

the riddle of the universe, "from the highest theism to the most realistic materialism, every point of view has been more beautifully expressed in Hafiz than anywhere else. Every mood, every human thought, is given in language of supreme lyrical beauty".

Hafiz's appeal was universal. He was liked, understood and enjoyed by every class of men in the Muslim East, from the humblest to the highest and most intellectual. In his own lifetime he was read by all literate men from the Bay of Bengal to Kashmir, and from Central Asia to Egypt. "Today his empire in these regions is still supreme." In him we could find "thoughts, ideas, expressions that would illuminate the fundamental conceptions of even such abstract hypotheses and speculations as those of, say, Einstein, [Sir James] Jeans, or Whitehead . . . his supreme genius enabled him to lay such splendid foundations that place can be found within his universal temple for almost any later development".[1]

He was "by far the greatest singer of the soul of man". In him we can see "all the strivings, all the sorrow, all the victories and joys, all the hopes and disappointments of each and every one of us". In him we find "contact, direct and immediate, with the outer universe interpreted as an infinite reality of matter, as a mirror of an eternal spirit, or indeed (as Spinoza later said) an absolute existence of which matter and spirit alike are but two infinite modes and facets". That explained why, throughout the Muslim world, his *diwan* was used as a book of divination (*fal namah*).

Hafiz was well acquainted with philosophy, history, poetry and literature. "In each verse [of Hafiz's poetry], with the intense concentration of thought and wisdom so singularly his own, he has produced in amazing variety facts of truth and beauty, of meaning and wisdom." For this reason he was the national poet, the national hero, of Iran. He was the prophet of universal human convictions – appreciation of beauty, love, gentleness and kindliness; of the value of human beings; of glory and splendour and joy of the universe; the wonder of communion with nature.

In the turmoil and tribulations of the modern age, when man seems to have lost his direction and place in the universe, there is room to turn to Hafiz for guidance. "For if ever there was a time when we needed the universality of Hafiz as a guiding light

[1] "Persian Poets", *The Times*, London, 22 September 1934.

that is today when there are forces that threaten the roots of humanity."[1]

The Aga Khan was a keen admirer of Qa'ani, whom he rated as "one of the greatest poets Persia has produced", and placed next to Hafiz and Firdausi. He was a modern poet. Like D. H. Lawrence and Andreκ Gide he wrote on themes of sex in supremely lyrical language, but in entirely physical terms. This should not blind the reader to the "wealth of beauty and depth of thought" in his *qasidas* – a form which he used to express his perceptions of nature. In this he was the Wordsworth of Iran and in his poetry were to be found many varieties of "Tintern Abbey". The Aga Khan suggested that some European orientalist with a good command of Persian should translate, in the spirit of Edward Fitzgerald, his most famous *qasida* about the person of God which begins with the words: "Nehani az nazar ay be nazir az bas aayanasty."[2]

Qa'ani, "one of the very greatest poets that the Iranian race has ever produced", interpreted nature "with a wealth of variety, a strength and beauty, which I doubt can ever be surpassed". What drove people to read him was the fundamental honesty of his outlook on life and the universe, the sincerity of his belief in the beauty and goodness of nature, the music and joy of his verses, and the passion of his conviction that life is a great, noble and splendid experience, every minute of which should be treasured as the greatest of God's gifts.[3]

The Aga Khan strongly recommended the study of oriental literature for its healing calmness. In a world of "troubled temper" there was one path which led to internal solace and peace – the contemplation which "only the sublimity of [the] highest form of prose and poetry can give". Reading or reciting the gems of this literature would "contribute to the ushering in of that frame of mind which alone could save mankind from a disaster greater than anything of the past". Such passages would prove an antidote to the venom of today, and "fill your heart with liquid sunshine, and the enchantment of their soulful beauty will linger as a rhythmic melody amongst mankind bringing into

---

[1] "Hafiz and the Place of Iranian Culture in the World", lecture, London, 9 November 1936.
[2] "Persian Poets", *The Times*, London, 22 September 1934.
[3] "Hafiz and the Place of Iranian Culture in the World", lecture, London, 9 November 1936.

life 'The Great Purpose Of Peace' – that Peace that rests on the earth, but like a rainbow lifts its head to heaven".[1]

It has been said that a man who loves poetry cannot have a bad soul. The Aga Khan must have had a beautiful soul which could appreciate man's highest and noblest expression of beauty in such memorable phrases.

The Aga Khan was also noted for the readiness and generosity with which he acknowledged the ability and stature of his political colleagues – in the cut-throat competitiveness and insensate selfishness of modern political life such decency and generosity are hard to come by. This attitude reflected his cultural background as well as the spirit of the time.

Sayyid Ameer Ali – his close colleague, friend, mentor – was highly praised by the Aga Khan. Many years after Ameer Ali's death he still remembered his great services to Islam, and called Ali's book, *The Spirit of Islam*, a "great monument". But his greatest service, as he had told Ameer Ali often, had been a short and concise explanation of Islam, which people had forgotten since long. "I wish the people of Pakistan could find it again and make its study compulsory for religious training in all Muslim schools, whatever the sect or sub-sect."[2]

The Aga Khan paid a magnificent tribute to another distinguished colleague, Abdullah Yusuf Ali, author, historian and, above all, translator and commentator of the Quran in English. In the 1930s, the London *Spectator* asked some leading persons to give a short and brief expression of their idea of religion. Yusuf Ali tendered a concise commentary of the *ayat-ul-kursi*, the "Verse of the Throne" in the Quran. "I was then in Geneva, but Mr. Yusuf's *tafsir* was so beautiful, rational and soul-inspiring that for weeks all kinds of people, even some of the most distinguished figures of Europe, came up to me and said, 'Is it real Islam?' "[3]

Chaudhri (later Sir) Muhammad Zafarullah Khan was by far the ablest Muslim at the Round Table Conference. During his years at the conference and the Joint Committee on Indian Constitutional Reform he and the Aga Khan worked very closely. The Aga Khan came to respect the many qualities of his intellect and character. In 1936, at a dinner given by the Indian Muslim

---

[1] Preface to Sirdar Ikbal Ali Shah's *The Coronation Book of Oriental Literature*, London, 1937.

[2] "The Future of Muslim States in the Background of History", lecture, Karachi, 8 February 1950.

[3] Presidential Address, All India Muslim Educational Conference, Rampur, 21 February 1936.

legislators in the Aga Khan's honour, he addressed the following words to Zafarullah: "Your spokesmanship won the admiration of every one, not only of your countrymen, but also of British statesmen. I have known statesmen in Europe and can honestly say that among any gathering of statesmen, you would have taken the very front rank and position. There are few instances of men in this land, where youth is so handicapped, having risen at the age of 44 to the highest position open to your countrymen, and everyone of us feels that in the Federal Government you will be a light to follow and that you may be the Prime Minister some day."[1]

The Aga Khan also held Gokhale, Sir Pherozeshah Mehta and Mrs Sarojini Naidu in high esteem. In spite of his clash with Gokhale during the making of the Morley-Minto Reforms, when Gokhale was putting pressure on Morley to reject the Muslim demand for separate electorates while the Aga Khan and Ameer Ali were doing the opposite, the two statesmen developed such mutual respect, and became such good friends, that just before his death Gokhale entrusted the Aga Khan with his last political testament. Sir Pherozeshah, a Parsi from Bombay, was in the confidence of the Aga Khan. The two did much for the city of Bombay, and it was to Mehta that the Aga Khan complained of Congress stubbornness and obduracy *vis-à-vis* the Muslims. At a public meeting held in Mehta's memory he paid the dead leader many tributes, and later spoke warmly about him in the Foreword he contributed to Mody's biography of Mehta.

He found Sarojini Naidu a fascinating personality. "She was one of the most remarkable women I have ever met, in some ways as remarkable as Miss Nightingale herself." She was "a real poet, who wrote strongly and tenderly of love and of life, of the world of the spirit and the passions. In that linking of tenderness and strength which was her nature there was no room for malice, hatred, or ill-will. She was a vigorous nationalist, determined that the British must leave India and her destiny in the hands of India's children, yet her admiration for Western civilization and Western science – above all for English literature – was deep and measureless."[2]

But his highest praise was reserved for Jinnah. The creation of Pakistan would have been inconceivable without his "iron will and lion courage". His memory would remain for ever in the hearts of the people of Pakistan and the general body of Muslims

[1] Speech at a dinner, New Delhi, 17 February 1936.
[2] *Memoirs*, pp. 226–7.

throughout the world.[1] His career was "brilliant and epoch-making", and his memory was imperishable. "Of all the statesmen I have known in my life – Clemenceau, Lloyd George, Churchill, Curzon, Mussolini, Mahatma Gandhi – Jinnah is the most remarkable. None of these men in my view outshone him in strength of character, and in that almost uncanny combination of prescience and resolution which is statecraft." He attained "immortal fame as the man who, without an army, navy, or air force, created, by a lifetime's faith in himself crystallized into a single bold decision, a great empire of upwards of a hundred million people". On one crucial occasion when the Cabinet Mission plan was offered to India, the Congress leaders, with "incredible folly", rejected it, or rather they put forward "dubious and equivocal alternative suggestions, which so watered the scheme down that it would have lost its meaning and effectiveness", Jinnah stood rock-like, and in that one decision, "combining as it did sagacity, shrewdness, and unequalled political *flair,* he justified – I am convinced — my claim that he was the most remarkable of all great statesmen that I have known. It puts him on a level with Bismarck."[2]

Another feature of the Aga Khan's personal life was a very individual view of Islam as his faith, and of its spiritual and aesthetic dimensions. In his judgement religion and spiritual happiness were the highest values in life. "A man must be at one with God." This was the fundamental question: "Are you in harmony with God? If you are – you are happy."

Appreciation and enjoyment of the glories of nature was part of his religion. "All those sunrises and sunsets – all the intricate miracle of sky colour, from dawn to dusk. All that splendid spendthrift beauty. As a very rich man treasures the possession of some unique picture, so a man should treasure and exult in the possession – his individual possession – of the sights of this unique world. Those glories are his from dawn to dusk, and then – and then comes night – 'a night of stars – all eyes'. . . . I look up at night and I know – I *know* the glory of the stars. It is then that the stars speak to us – and the sense of that mystery is in our blood."

Painting is linked with nature. The "man who has been blind to the beauty of nature may have his imagination quickened by seeing the visions of great artists. He may come to see that dawn and dusk make glorious even the drab pavements of a town."

[1] Message to the Quaid-i-Azam Memorial Fund, Karachi, February (?) 1950.
[2] *Memoirs,* 1954.

Poetry has a special place in one's life. It is the "voice of God speaking, through the lips of man". If great painting "puts you in touch with nature, great poetry puts you in direct touch with God".

To be one with God was important. "Those who accept the normal responsibilities of life, with all the chances of minor annoyance and utter catastrophe, may know many small griefs and much great sorrow – that is why I call their joys dependent – but, if they are at one with God and have lived manfully, behind the mask of sorrow, bitter though it may be, their souls will be at peace."[1]

It is imperative to remember that this was written in his mid-fifties when he had still another twenty-six years left to live, not at the close of life when thoughts are wont to turn to the meaning of one's faith for self-justification or solace. In his *Memoirs* he reflects on his religious convictions and persuasions at some length and with deep feeling. These passages provide us with an authentic source for a study of his view of Islam. The following paragraphs, drawn from these passages, tell us a great deal about his personal faith and some of its esoteric and mystic dimensions.

"It is said that we live, move, and have our being, in God . . . when we realize the meaning of this saying, we are already preparing ourselves for the gift of the power of direct experience." Rumi and Hafiz, the great Persian poets, have told us that some men are born with "such natural, spiritual capacities and possibilities of development, that they have direct experience of that great love, that all-embracing, all-consuming love, which direct contact with reality gives to the human soul". Even those among us who lack this capacity can make up for its absence by worldly, human love for individual human beings; and they should respond to it with gratitude and regard it as a blessing and a source of pride. "I firmly believe that the higher experience can to a certain extent be prepared for, by absolute devotion in the material world to another human being. Thus from the most worldly point of view and with no comprehension of the higher life of the spirit, the lower, the most terrestrial spirit makes us aware that all the treasures of this life, all that fame, wealth, and health can bring are nothing beside the happiness which is created and sustained by the love of one human being for another. . . . But as the joys of human love surpass all that riches and power may bring a man, so does that greater spiritual love

---

[1] Interview, *Daily Sketch*, London, 2 November 1931.

and enlightenment, the fruit of that sublime experience of the direct vision of reality which is God's gift and grace, surpass all that the finest, truest human love can offer. For that gift we must ever pray. Now, I am convinced that through Islam, through the ideal of Allah, as presented by Muslims, man can attain this direct experience which no words can explain but which for him are absolute certainties.... I am certain that many Muslims, and I am convinced that I myself, have had moments of enlightenment and of knowledge of a kind which we cannot communicate because it is something given and not something acquired."[1]

Once man has understood in the real sense the essence of existence, "there remains for him the duty, since he knows the absolute value of his own soul, of making for himself a direct path which will constantly lead his individual soul to and bind it with the universal Soul of which the Universe, and much of it as we perceive with our limited vision, is one of the infinite manifestations. Thus Islam's basic principle can only be defined as monorealism and not as monotheism." The Aga Khan then provides a perceptive and penetrating commentary on the phrase "Allah-o-Akbar", words which all Muslims repeat when praying or on other occasions in their daily lives. "There can be no doubt that the second word of the declaration likens the character of Allah to a matrix which contains all and gives existence to the infinite, to space, to time, to the Universe, to all active and passive forces imaginable, to life and to the soul. Imam Hasan has explained the Islamic doctrine of God and the Universe by analogy with the sun and its reflection in the pool of a fountain; there is certainly a reflection or image of the sun, but with what poverty and with what little reality, how small and pale is the likeness between this impalpable image and the immense, blazing, white-hot glory of the celestial sphere itself. Allah is the sun; and the Universe as we know it in all its magnitude, and time, with its power, are nothing more than the reflection of the Absolute in the mirror of the fountain."[2]

Commenting on the duties of Muslims he wrote: "The healthy human body is a temple in which the flame of the Holy Spirit burns, and thus it deserves the respect of scrupulous cleanliness and personal hygiene.... All men, rich and poor, must aid one another materially and personally. The rules vary in detail, but they all maintain the principle of universal mutual aid in the Muslim fraternity. This fraternity is absolute and comprises men

[1] *Memoirs*, 1954, pp. 170–1.
[2] *Ibid.*, p. 175.

of all colours and of all races: black, white, yellow, tawny; all are the sons of Adam in the flesh and all carry in them a spark of the Divine Light."[1]

When the shades of this earthly existence were closing on him, he wrote: "Never in my long life – I may say with complete honesty – have I for an instant been bored. Every day has been so short, every hour so fleeting, every minute so filled with the life I love, that time for me has fled on far too swift a wing. A mind that is occupied, in health or in sickness, with things outside itself and its own concerns, is I believe a perpetual source of true happiness. In ordinary prayer, as we in Islam conceive it, adoration of the beloved fills up every nook and cranny of the human consciousness; and in the rare, supreme moments of spiritual ecstasy, the light of Heaven blinds mind and spirit to all other lights and blots out every other sense and perception."[2] Only a man of extraordinary personal faith and convictions could have written this at the end of his life.

The Aga Khan believed that "man must never ignore and leave untended and undeveloped that spark of the Divine which is in him. The way to personal fulfilment, to individual reconciliation with the Universe that is about us, is comparatively easy for anyone who firmly and sincerely believes, as I do, that Divine Grace has given man in his own heart the possibilities of illumination and of union with Reality. It is, however, far more important to attempt to offer some hope of spiritual sustenance to those many who, in this age in which the capacity of faith is non-existent in the majority, long for something beyond themselves, even if it seems second-best. For them there is the possibility of finding strength of the spirit, comfort, and happiness in contemplation of the infinite variety and beauty of the Universe."[3] He concluded: "Life in the ultimate analysis has taught me one enduring lesson. The subject should always disappear in the object. In our ordinary affections one for another, in our daily work with hand or brain, we most of us discover soon enough that any lasting satisfaction, any contentment that we can achieve, is the result of forgetting self, or merging subject with object in a harmony that is of body, mind, and spirit. And in the highest realms of consciousness all who believe in a Higher Being are liberated from all the clogging and hampering bonds of the subjective self in prayer, in rapt meditation upon and in

[1] *Ibid.*, p. 176.
[2] *Ibid.*, p. 307.
[3] *Ibid.*, p. 334.

the face of the glorious radiance of eternity, in which all temporal and earthly consciousness is swallowed up and itself becomes the eternal."[1]

The Aga Khan's advice to his heirs sums up his philosophy of religion. "I would counsel my heirs to seek satisfaction, not in the flux of circumstances, but within themselves; I would have them resolute, self-controlled, independent, but not rebellious. Let them seek communion with that Eternal Reality which I call Allah and you call God! For that is the twin problem of existence – to be at once entirely yourself and altogether at one with the Eternal. I say that you should endeavour to suit your desire to the event, and not the event to your desire."[2]

A counsel of perfection? Perhaps yes. The secret of happiness? Certainly.

Achievements and Legacy

It is impossible to sum up the contribution of the Aga Khan to modern history in a page or two without reducing the effort to a monotonous and jejune inventory of speeches, decisions and actions. He played so many parts, over such a long period and on so many different stages of public life, that we are called upon to judge an age, not an individual.

In the context of Indian politics the Aga Khan was simultaneously a moderate and a radical, a conservative and a revolutionary, a warner and an adviser. He lectured the British in England on the discontent in India and the problems of imperial rule in their own idiom and language, not in the rhetoric and accent of Indian politicians. He acted as a spokesman for India in England, and a bridge of understanding between the rulers and the ruled. He prescribed education to the Indians as a giant step forward in both political advance and social uplift. But education was equally needed by those Britons who aspired to rule India from the comfortable yet demanding seats in the Indian Civil Service. The candidates should be obliged to study Indian culture, languages and history as subjects for the competitive examination. During their career they should spend most of their service in one province, in order to know the people and perceive their problems, and should, over the years, develop

[1] *Ibid.*, p. 335.
[2] "My Philosophy of Happiness", article, n.d.

sympathy for the region, friendship of the local population, and loyalty to India.

He was probably one of the first Indians to see the vision of a federal India and to expound its virtues. The vastness, diversity and heterogeneity of the subcontinent demanded a federal constitutional structure. Had the Hindus pondered over his 1918 suggestion they might have saved the unity of India in 1947. But they were bent upon ruling the country as a unitary state with their own overwhelming majority in most of the provinces and in the powerful centre. Ten years later what they offered to the minorities in the Nehru Report draft constitution rejected every argument presented by the Aga Khan and every demand made by the Muslims.

His riposte to the Nehru Report's unitarianism was the 1928 proposal of Indian Free States, which, if worked out by the Congress, would still have kept India together in 1947 with Muslim Free States inside a confederal arrangement. At the same time this scheme was a foreshadowing of the idea of Pakistan. He was also one of the earliest exponents of the two-nation theory, declaring the Muslims to be a separate nation or nationality. However, it is important to remember that he came round to this view after years of efforts and appeals for Hindu–Muslim co-operation. It was only when he was disappointed with Hindu intransigence and political developments that he moved to the separationist camp.

For the protection of Muslim rights and the encouragement of Muslim aspirations he fought with courage, consistency and tenacity from 1902 till 1934 – annoying some British politicians, like Morley, making new friends, organizing the London Muslim League, and collaborating with another great man, Sayyid Ameer Ali, to break the will of Whitehall. Between 1906 and 1947 the Muslims of India organized themselves twice in order to fight their case: in 1906 under the All India Muslim League and in 1928 under the All India Muslim Conference. The Aga Khan was the founder and president of both. It is significant that the making of the Morley-Minto reforms was preceded by the birth of the All India Muslim League, and the 1935 reforms by that of the All India Muslim Conference. Between 1930 and 1934 he was fighting on two fronts. In India he was preaching the gospel of unity to the Muslims and pleading for a merger of the League and the Conference. In Britain he was arguing with the British in favour of a federal and democratic constitution for India which safeguarded the legitimate rights of the Muslims. During these years his words carried considerable weight because, apart from his personal contacts and influence, he sat at the Round Table Conference and the Joint Committee on Indian Constitutional Reform in three capacities: as a delegate of Muslim India, leader of the Muslim Delegation, and leader of the whole British Indian Delegation.

In spite of his royal background and aristocratic lifestyle he was at heart a democrat. Again and again he asked the Muslim parties and leaders to go to the masses – to understand their problems and opinions, to reflect their feelings and aspirations and to open a network of local branches. On the broad front of Indian constitutional advance he was in favour of consistent progress towards a democratic and popular system of government, but with the overriding proviso that the Muslim minority did not suffer any abridgement of its liberties and freedoms.

The 1920s witnessed the rise of education in the Muslim world. Mustafa Kamal Atatürk in Turkey, Raza Shah in Iran and Amanullah in Afghanistan were prescribing the same medicine for the ignorance and backwardness of their peoples. Muslim India was more fortunate in that Sir Sayyid Ahmed Khan had laid a solid foundation in the previous century, and had also bequeathed his message to a body of sincere, loyal and energetic leaders capable of developing his ideas and enlarging his legacy. Two men in particular, Muhsin-ul-Mulk and the Aga Khan, worked incessantly to advance the cause of Muslim education. Muhsin-ul-Mulk died in 1907, but the Aga Khan brought his Aligarh inheritance to its full flowering. His heroic efforts on behalf of the MAO College, and later the Aligarh University, were his finest hour. But he was not a dogmatic and unimaginative schoolmaster. He was the first Muslim to suggest the establishment of a Hindu university and to enumerate its advantages and benefits. But he also warned the Hindus of upper India against the dangers of imposing Hindi on the rest of India: this would strengthen the fissiparous tendencies already at work in that vast land of disparities and diversities and might lead to a break-up.

In social reform his ideas were ahead of his age. Hardly any other Indian politician, Hindu, Parsi or Muslim, gave as much attention as he did to the improvement of agriculture, the needs of the rural masses, and the advance in agricultural education. Emancipation of women was a strong plank of his reformist programme.

As a religious thinker and activist he was a successor to Sir Sayyid Ahmad Khan and Ameer Ali and in the direct line of the liberal modernism which could be said to have originated with Shah Walilullah and ended with Iqbal and Ghulam Ahmad Parwez. He stood squarely with the modernists on all significant issues, offering original ideas of his own. As far as I know, he was the only important Muslim who saw the need and underlined the importance of educating modern students of sciences and arts and the future religious doctors ('*ulema*) at the same place and to the same level. For as long as the making of these two intellectual segments of society was not brought into one educational stream, a fundamental and catastrophic schism in the body politic and social fabric of Islam would continue and fester.

His concern for the safety and unity of the Islamic world ruled most of his ideas and dictated most of his public activities. He was completely devoted to the ideal of making the Muslims strong in their faith and respected in the world, ever progressing, ever living up to the demands of the Quran. Wherever he found the future of Islam in danger, as in Africa, he suggested remedial action and extended his aid and comfort. The finest example of his true love for Islam was his interest in the future of Turkey. To ensure the continuance of an independent and strong Turkey, which could serve as the centre for the whole Islamic world, he was prepared to make the ultimate compromise: though a Shia, he accepted as desirable, lawful and necessary the existence of the Sunni institution of *khilafat*, for the sake of the future glory and greatness of Islam.

For such a resolute and unwavering believer in the unity of the Islamic world, the culture and civilization of Islam were not only great achievements in themselves and made up the intellectual and moral contribution of Islam to the history of the world, but were to be used in the service of Islam in two ways. First, the Muslim peoples themselves should be made aware of their inheritance, so that they could enjoy it and derive benefit from it, and look the world in the eye, and above all, seek and find in it avenues leading to unity. In the second place, he made an earnest appeal to the Western man to know and understand this Islamic gift to mankind in order to stretch his mental horizon and include in it something more than Greek and Roman achievements, and through this wider comprehension of human endeavour to bring international and inter-religious amity closer to realization.

World peace was one of the ideals of the Aga Khan even before he entered the council chamber of the League of Nations. He hated war, and all his eirenicons had one goal: to see mankind live in an atmosphere of mutual understanding and goodwill. He was anxious that every means of bringing about this desirable state of affairs ought to be used: education, negotiation, disarmament, knowledge of various literatures and cultures, and economic collaboration.

In the pursuit of his ideals the Aga Khan was not afraid to incur criticism or even popular wrath. In spite of being an admirer of the beneficent aspects of British rule, he did not hesitate to attack the way in which the Empire was being run. He was equally ready to take on the highest in Britain when he judged that Islam was in danger, or that Muslim India was being denied its rightful place, or that the colonial and dominion governments were maltreating their Indian populations. The myth of "Aga Khan the arch loyalist" has no historical warrant.

A good example of his singlemindedness and frankness was his call to the Pakistanis to drop Urdu as their national language and replace it with Arabic. He thought he was giving good advice and the risk of public ire did not deter him. The reaction was strong, emotional and publicly expressed. A storm of severe criticism blew his advice away. But he is not known to have recanted or regretted his suggestion.

In his personal views of the meaning and end of life the Aga Khan attached the greatest importance to the genuineness of faith and to its manifestations in nature, art and poetry. The beauty of nature fortified our faith in Divine creation. Art reflected nature. Poetry was the voice of God speaking to man through man. What mattered in the end was inner spiritual happiness – and that came from an honest acquiescence to God's dispensations, in containment of desire, in appreciation of nature, and in love of mankind.

What is the Aga Khan's legacy to the world? He deeply influenced the political and historical evolution of the Indian subcontinent. He safeguarded the future of Islam in South Asia by organizing the Muslims of India, fighting for their rights and identity, and showing them the path to Pakistan. He helped to save Turkey from dismemberment and humiliation by compelling the Allies to abandon the Treaty of Sévres and make a new peace settlement in Lausanne. He carried on the work of Sir Sayyid Ahmad Khan in the field of education, and almost singlehandedly established the Aligarh University. He tried to inculcate in the minds of his followers (meaning *all* Muslims not just the Ismailis) the virtues of education, social reform and economic advance through hard work. He attempted to protect the poor and ignorant peasantry from exploitation and general neglect. He financed and encouraged several newspapers and journals, thus giving a voice to the public and a democratic dimension to politics. To Indian and African Muslims he showed a liberal and modernist path which would enable them to live in the contemporary world with honour and self-respect, and without having to surrender the substance of their faith. He did everything in his power to bring about unity in the Islamic world, to awaken the Muslims to the quality and amplitude of their culture, to persuade the West to know and understand oriental literature, and, through all these things, to create an East-West *entente*, international amity and world peace.

This imperfect world of ours has not yet produced a statesman – nor even a saint or a prophet – whose achievements equalled his ambitions. Man's reach is always shorter than his vision, his fulfilment always lower than his expectation, his success always less than is intended. And that is how it should be. Otherwise we will have a perfect world, with our oars rested and all our restless roaming and journeying at an end. To strive is to be human, and some try to be something more than human.

The impact of the Aga Khan's personality and ideas was deeper in some places and on some people than in other regions and on other societies. On the whole, the Aga Khan left a legacy which only the *future* historian can fully comprehend. In the meantime, the Muslims, and many others, should be content that he appeared when he did.

Though his mission in the service of Islam and mankind is not yet realised, he has passed on to his progeny his intellectual interests, social conscience and love of Islam. The Aga Khan IV is following in the footsteps of his grandfather to a degree exceptional in hereditary succession. With a different background and living in a vastly different age, he cannot play the political role of the grand old man. But in other respects he seems to have taken up the affairs and preoccupations of Sir Sultan Muhammad Shah. He is the greatest legacy that the subject of this Introduction has left to his people and to the world, and without some mention of him this treatment of his grandfather will remain incomplete.

His Highness Prince Karim Aga Khan IV is the son of Prince Aly Khan and Princesss Taj-ud-Daulah. Born in Geneva, Switzerland, on 13 December 1936, his early childhood and school days were spent in Nairobi, Kenya. He went on to attend Le Rosey School in Switzerland for nine years before going up to Harvard

University, from where he graduated with honours in Islamic history in 1959. On 11 July 1957 he succeeded his grandfather as the 49th hereditary *Imam* of the Shia Ismaili Muslims. In 1969 he married Begum Salimah, who was born in New Delhi of English parents and was brought up in India. They have three children, one daughter and two sons.

He could be considered an architect of modern Ismaili institutions. On assuming the *imamate* of the Ismaili Muslims he set out to expand, develop and adapt to modern conditions the institutions he had inherited from his grandfather, with a view to their playing a new role in the service of independent nation states. He has introduced rationalized, professional and modern expertise and management into these institutions, and given them an international basis. He has, in addition, created a number of new institutions, such as the Aga Khan Foundation, the Aga Khan University, the Aga Khan Fund for Economic Development and the Aga Khan Trust for Culture.

The Aga Khan IV has a keen interest in virtually every field which was dear to his predecessor – education, social reform, economic development, democracy, East-West understanding, and the unity and culture of the faith and especially its architecture. His ideas on these subjects are worth studying both for their inherent worth and for the thread running from them back to the thoughts and ideals of Sir Sultan Muhammad Shah.[1]

To take education first, he has been arguing for its relevance and necessity at all levels. Education will expose the civil servants to new concepts, instruct the common citizen in sanitation and health, and train the school children in basic building skills.[2] He is aware of what lack of resources and attention has done to education in the Third World: over-crowded classes, scarcity of textbooks, teachers with low social status and poor salaries, and an inevitably low standard of instruction. Industrialized nations no longer recognize the academic qualifications gained in that part of the world.[3]

---

[1] In this section all quotations and paraphrases are from the speeches of the Aga Khan IV, and the footnotes cite their sources. All these speeches have been printed and issued by the Aga Khan Secretariat in France. Unfortunately, they have not been collected in a book and made available to the general reading public.

[2] "Rural Housing", speech at an international seminar sponsored by the Association of Builders and Developers, Karachi, 16 March 1983.

[3] Speech on Development Activities of the Aga Khan Foundation in Pakistan at a luncheon hosted by the Foundation and the Aga Khan Social Welfare Institutions, Islamabad, 22 March 1983.

He recalled that during the heyday of Islam, "everywhere, whether in the simplest mosque schools or in universities, teaching was regarded as a mission undertaken for the service of God". Endowments financed all education, and no time limit was set for the pupil to finish his studies. "Above all, in keeping with the precept of the Quran, there was freedom of inquiry and research. The result was a magnificent flowering of artistic and intellectual activity through[out] the *Ummah*." All the ancient universities of Europe "received a vital influx of new knowledge from Islam"; later other centres of learning, including those of North America, benefitted from this borrowing. Explaining the twofold character of knowledge in Islam, he said, "There is that [knowledge] revealed through the Holy Prophet and that which man discovers by virtue of his own intellect. Nor do these two involve any contradiction, provided man remembers that his own mind is itself the creation of God. Without this humility, no balance is possible. With it, there are no barriers. Indeed one strength of Islam has always lain in its belief that creation is not static but continuous, that through scientific and other endeavours, God has opened and continues to open new windows for us to see the marvels of His creation." After a reference to the abysmally low standards of the universities of the Third World, he quoted Ibn Sina on the continuing round of travels of the intellect, and proceeded: "It is these journeys of the mind which our students must make, for what is the study of science but man's endeavour to comprehend the universe of God's creation, the immediate world around him and himself? The laws of science are not bounded by cultures, nor should there be any basic conflict between loyalty to high academic standards and the service of practical development needs." Finally, he emphasized another vital accompaniment of education. "Academic freedom is in the truest spirit of Islam. Without it excellence cannot be achieved. From the start of my grandfather's association with the Muslim University of Aligarh he insisted that it should 'preach the gospel of free inquiry, of large-hearted toleration and of pure morality'."[1]

He is convinced that education must relate to the needs of the nation. "There must be a relationship between the kind of education provided and the requirements of the country's

---

[1] Speech on the occasion of the Aga Khan University Charter Presentation Ceremony, Karachi, 16 March 1983.

economy and demography."[1] He underlines this by bringing out the close connection between the Islamic concept of education and intellect and the future needs of the community.

"The Divine Intellect, 'Aql Qul', both transcends and informs the human intellect. It is this intellect which enables man to strive towards two aims dictated by the Faith : that he should reflect upon the environment Allah has given him, and that he should know himself. It is the light of intellect which distinguishes the complete human being from the human animal, and developing that intellect requires free inquiry. The man of Faith who fails to pursue intellectual search is likely to have only a limited comprehension of Allah's creation. Indeed, it is man's intellect that enables him to expand his vision of that creation. Eleven hundred years ago, Al-Kindi wrote, 'no-one is diminished by the truth, rather does the truth ennoble all'. I quote that great Muslim scientist and thinker because his words are as relevant to higher education today as they were during the first flowering of Islamic civilization. If the frontiers of physics are changing, it is due to scientists discovering more and more about the universe, even though they will never be able to prove its totality, since Allah's creation is limitless and continuous. I apprehend that in certain educational institutions respect for tradition has restricted academic study to the accomplishment of the past. However, our Faith has never been restricted to one place or one time. Ever since its revelation, the fundamental concept of Islam has been its universality and the fact that this is the last revelation, constantly valid, and not petrified into one period of man's history or confined to one area of the world.... The Holy Koran's encouragement to study nature and the physical world around us gave the original impetus to scientific inquiry among Muslims. Exchanges of knowledge between institutions and nations and the widening of man's intellectual horizons are essentially Islamic concepts. The Faith urges freedom of intellectual inquiry, and this freedom does not mean that knowledge will lose its spiritual dimension. That dimension is indeed itself a field for intellectual inquiry."[2]

In consonance with this view, spelling out the future plans of the Aga Khan University, he said that the University was committed "to advancing society by educating its most talented

---

[1] "Social Institutions in National Development: The Enabling Environment", speech, Nairobi, 6 October 1982.

[2] Speech at the inauguration of the Aga Khan University Faculty of Health Sciences and the Aga Khan University Hospital, Karachi, 11 November 1985.

people". It sought "models for pursuing that advancement in ways that reconcile the ethics of Islam with the infinitude of possibilities that characterizes the modern Western world. Islamic ethics offer that stabilizing framework that will allow our societies to benefit from those possibilities without being unnecessarily confused or unbalanced by them."[1]

In the sphere of social reform and economic development the Aga Khan has inherited his grandfather's emphasis on rural uplift and health-care, which he has supplemented with his deep concern for economic development. "There are those . . . who enter the world in such poverty that they are deprived of both the means and the motivation to improve their lot. Unless these unfortunates can be touched with the spark which ignites the spirit of individual enterprise and determination, they will only sink back into renewed apathy, degradation and despair. It is for us, who are more fortunate, to provide that spark."[2] He has justified his interest in the material improvement of his people with the fact that Islam is a total religion "touching on all aspects of a Muslim's life". As the *Imam* his first care is of course the spiritual well-being of his flock, but he has also a continuous concern with their material and physical progress.[3] He explains the point further: "Seen against the background of Christian religious tradition, it might appear incongruous that a Muslim religious leader should be so involved in material and mundane matters of this world. It is not an Islamic belief, however, that spiritual life should be totally isolated from our more material everyday activities."[4]

Like his grandfather, as Prince Karim Aga Khan has himself declared more than once, the "issue of improving the living conditions of the poor has long been of the deepest concern" to him. It is said that even today inadequate development is being directed towards the uplift of the rural population. In both the rich and the poor countries the rural masses have to abide by decisions made by the urban intelligentsia. The world has recently been talking a great deal about the need of dialogue

---

[1] Speech on the occasion of the Fourth Convocation of the Aga Khan University, Faculty of Health Sciences and School of Nursing, Karachi, 16 November 1991.

[2] "Housing and Development", speech at the inauguration of the Aga Khan Baug, Versova, 17 January 1983.

[3] "The Private Sector in Economic Development: The Enabling Environment", speech, Nairobi, 7 October 1982.

[4] "The Role of Private Initiative in Developing Countries", speech to the Swiss-American Chamber of Commerce, Zurich, 14 January 1976.

between the rich North and poor South, but it is of equal urgency to initiate a "free, constructive and continuing dialogue" between the rural and urban populations of the Third World.[1] The national planners and decision-makers are out of touch with the rural masses, and there is no interaction between the two strata of national life. As a result, international and bilateral aid programmes impose thinking derived from Western urbanized economies rather than focusing on rural improvement and uplift.[2] The solution of the Third World lies in increased production, and the only way to achieve this is to enlarge the scope of both local and international investment in rural development.[3]

But giving more resources to the peasant is pointless without improving his health so that he can work harder. Hence the Aga Khan's stress on the need for medical facilities and health-care not just in small towns or slum quarters of cities, but also in rural areas. Health management is an important but generally ignored dimension of health-care, according to the Aga Khan. The patient referral systems pose several questions. "Are there adequate links between the smaller, intermediate and large institutions and between urban and rural health centres? Can the poor afford the costs of being referred to a higher echelon? Do doctors refer patients up the line when they should?"[4] The challenge of health-care, he points out forcefully, is one of management, not of values.[5]

Housing is an important component of social reform because the poor and lower-middle-class people face this problem in both villages and towns. The Aga Khan has created a low-cost housing project on the periphery of Bombay and a trust for a similar purpose in Pune. In 1980 he sold the Aga Khan's hereditary official residence on Malabar Hill, Bombay, to provide the bulk of the funding for the Muniwarabad Charitable Trust which financed and executed these housing schemes. This must have been a major sacrifice because the family was deeply attached to

---

[1] "Rural Housing", speech at an international seminar sponsored by the Association of Builders and Developers, Karachi, 16 March 1983.
[2] "Planning for Development in the Third World", speech at a luncheon hosted by the Aga Khan Foundation of Canada, Toronto, 27 April 1983.
[3] Speech on the Enabling Environment at a dinner given by him in honour of the President of the Republic of Kenya, Hon. Daniel T. Arap Moi, Nairobi, 7 October 1982.
[4] "Social Institutions in National Development: The Enabling Environment", speech, Nairobi, 6 October 1982.
[5] "The Role of Hospitals in Primary Health Care", speech, Islamabad, 22 November 1981.

the old house in which three Aga Khans had lived. An interesting feature of the future plans of this Trust is a "reasonable social mix so that the better educated and better-off people" are allotted some plots so that they can "provide stimulus and guidance to those people who are less socially advantaged".[1]

Sir Sultan Muhammad Shah had been a pioneer of insurance business in Muslim India and East Africa, telling the Muslims that insurance was perfectly legal and valid in Islamic law and establishing more than one insurance company. The money collected on the occasions of his Jubilees had helped to launch the Jubilee Insurance Company and the Diamond Jubilee Investment Trust (now Diamond Trust). The Aga Khan has modernized and expanded these enterprises and made them national institutions. In East Africa the vast majority of policy holders are now indigenous.[2]

For the economic development of society the Aga Khan has fashioned a new concept of what he calls the "enabling environment", without the existence of which private and even voluntary effort has little chance of flourishing. The conditions necessary for this environment are "political stability, democratic institutions, a framework of law which protects all citizens and a constant dialogue with [the] Government and parastatal organisations on national objectives".[3] Various ingredients contribute to this environment – "reliance on the rule of law and a system of laws which in itself encourages enterprise and initiative. Democratic institutions. Protection of the rights of citizens. These are what encourage investment, encourage good managers to remain, encourage doctors and nurses and teachers to want to serve their country, rather than to migrate as soon as they are skilled. The creation and extension to all areas of the nation's life of this enabling environment is the single most important factor in Third World development. It is as critical to national growth as sunlight is to the growth of plants."[4] In 1986 the Aga Khan Foundation, in collaboration with leading international development agencies and the Government of Kenya, organized

---

[1] "Housing and Development", speech at the inauguration of the Aga Khan Baug, Versova, 17 January 1983.
[2] "The Role of Private Initiative in Developing Countries", speech at the Swiss-American Chamber of Commerce, Zurich, 14 January 1976.
[3] "The Private Sector in Economic Development: The Enabling Environment", speech, Nairobi, 7 October 1982.
[4] Speech on the Enabling Environment at a dinner hosted by the Aga Khan in honour of the President of the Republic of Kenya, Hon. Daniel T. Arap Moi, Nairobi, 7 October 1982.

"The Enabling Environment Conference" in Nairobi, Kenya. Its aim was to explore the role the private sector could play in promoting development in sub-Saharan Africa.

This plea for creating a desirable milieu for economic growth is also a thinly disguised appeal to the Third World rulers to put their political house in order. The Aga Khan must be painfully conscious of the threat posed to the social fabric by the crumbling democracies and burgeoning military and civil dictatorships in Asia and Africa. He can only hint at the dangers present in the situation, as he did in Peshawar by saying that "ordinary people find it hard to associate themselves and their own fortunes with those of their Governments".[1]

The above is a very abbreviated account of the Aga Khan's theoretical framework for promoting economic and social development. It is pertinent now to cast a quick glance at the practical results of this thinking. In 1984 he established a central institution, the Aga Khan Fund for Economic Development, whose goals and operations are similar to those of the various national and international economic development agencies currently in existence. The novel feature of the endeavour is that by far the greater part of the Fund's financial support is in the form of equity; this decreases the developing countries' dependence on loan finance, thus averting a debilitating debt burden. Further, equity investment also frequently carries with it a technology transfer. In this respect the Fund is superior to all other development instruments which the West and the Western-dominated international bodies have devised for the purpose of helping the poor nations.

The Fund has absorbed the Industrial Promotion Services group of companies, which was established in 1963. It now operates in two countries in Asia, four in Africa, and in Canada, and promotes industrial, financial and tourism projects by harnessing together modern management, advanced technology and local know-how. By 1989 it had launched over one hundred enterprises, ranging from building materials and textiles to mining and tourism facilities. It also participates in the creation of development institutions, for example the Industrial Promotion and Development Company in Bangladesh.

The Aga Khan Foundation was established in 1967 to promote

[1] Convocation Address at the University of Peshawar, Pakistan, 30 November 1967. The country was then being ruled by Field Marshal Muhammad Ayub Khan, who had overthrown a democratic government in 1958.

social development through philanthropic activities. It is a completely non-denominational organization, and its activities include programmes related to education, health, nutrition, rural development and the management of renewable natural resources. It also finances scholarships and training programmes, and at times makes grants to individuals for study and travel. It seeks to promote human resource development and collaborates with over thirty international development agencies. In 1982 the Foundation established the Aga Khan Rural Support Programme, a catalytic private agency with primary emphasis on stimulating income-generating opportunities for the rural poor. So far it has been functioning in the northern areas of Pakistan and in the Gujerat State of India.

The largest product of the Foundation is the Aga Khan University, whose Faculty of Health Sciences is situated in Karachi. The Aga Khan has described the four most important and urgent aims of the University as follows. First, the University will "build on its strengths in maternal and child health", conduct research into problems which "strike the most vulnerable of Allah's people", and aim at being "one of the world resources in health problems of mothers and children". Second, it will enter the vital field of allied health sciences and try to reduce the shortage of laboratory technicians, radiologists, physiotherapists and "a host of other professionals who complement the physician". Third, it will promote continuing education. Medical education never ends for a true professional. The University's own graduates and other doctors in Pakistan and other developing countries would be provided "short courses, seminars and workshops to keep pace with new discoveries, technologies, and pharmacology". Finally, the University will attend to the "field of research and training in health policy and management: the study of health economics, epidemiology, and the management sciences that will be of value to the policy maker as well as to the future manager of health programmes and institutions". The University, he insisted, "must aim to produce the leaders in health policy as well as in medicine".[1] As an international university it plans to establish new faculties in other countries.

The Aga Khan Health Services, one of the largest private health agencies in the developing world, is made up of a network of health institutions and projects, and operates over two hundred

[1] Convocation Address at the First Convocation Ceremony of the Aga Khan University, Faculty of Health Sciences, Medical College, Karachi, 20 March 1989.

health-care centres, diagnostic clinics, dispensaries and five general hospitals. A parallel organization, the Aga Khan Education Services, sponsors a host of educational institutions and programmes in many parts of the world.

What Sir Sultan Muhammad Shah did for some of the Indian Muslim newspapers the present Aga Khan has done for the East African press. In 1957 he entered the publishing field in Kenya in association with the *Sunday Times* of London, the *Globe and Mail* of Toronto and *The Times* of Ceylon (now Sri Lanka). Newspapers in English and Swahili (later also in Luganda, a local language of Uganda) were issued, voicing the national point of view of the emerging nations of East Africa. By 1976 the company, Nation Printers and Publishers, had grown to be one of the largest free newspaper and publishing groups in independent black Africa, reflecting African political thinking expressed by Africans. *The Daily Nation* is today the most widely circulated newspaper in Kenya. In 1994 the Company launched a regional weekly paper called *The East African*.

As a newspaper owner, the Aga Khan has definite ideas on how to run the press and improve the profession of journalism. An upholder of free inquiry, he believes that "disciplined, mature and responsible private ownership is the most effective means of managing a newspaper". He also seeks to lift the tone of the press in the Third World through coherent action by the media and governments of the industrial world to make their managerial and technological know-how available, "structural exchange" of editorial expertise (making journalism a profession in the truest sense), and refusal of the media to become too closely involved with their governments. In elaboration of the last point, he notes that many journalists in the Third World have left the profession altogether for lack of respect, harassment, oppressive official regulations, and the inability of the press industry to offer career satisfaction or the earning potential of other professions.

There is some validity, he says, in the complaint that the press of the industrialized countries reports on the less affluent nations "superficially, condescendingly, sometimes inaccurately, and without proper social, cultural, economic and political background". The "channels and the content" of international communications are a monopoly of the North, and in this respect many people of the South feel "as powerless as they had been under colonial rule". The Western press has been particularly insensitive to the religious feelings of the Muslims. "As a Muslim, one of the seven hundred million, I live in daily astonishment about the incomprehension of Islam and its peoples. Some Western media have perpetuated misconceptions which stick like shrouds to the bones of historical skeletons. . . . The fact is that the quality of reporting from abroad is often unacceptably low, and there is need to re-think how to select and train these all-important correspondents and foreign editors and sub-editors. . . . Exchanges – as in the twin newspaper idea – having a Muslim, for example, nearby a foreign editor to explain Islamic concepts – could help infuse this process with a new spirit of co-operation."[1] (The reader will recall Sir Sultan Muhammad Shah's strictures on *The Times* for presenting a distorted and false view of Islam in one of its leading articles).

Like his grandfather, Prince Karim Aga Khan is a great admirer of the record of Islamic civilization and, like him, a sad man when he compares the past with the present. Once a land had been conquered by the Muslim armies, he reminded a university audience, the intellectual élite took over and governed the state. In their time the Muslim centres of learning produced the finest scholars, physicians, astronomers and philosophers. "Today where are we? . . . Throughout my journeys I have been deeply pained to see the lack of initiative" in educational matters. "I am afraid that the torch of intellectual discovery, the attraction of the unknown, the desire for intellectual self-perfection have left us . . . what is the point in undergoing untold misery for political independence if the result is no better than abject dependence intellectually and economically on one's old political masters?"[2]

He wants the Muslim youth to develop the underlying values of their faith. "This fearful chase after material ease must surely be tempered by peace of mind, by conscience, by moral values, which must be resuscitated. If not, man will simply have converted the animal instinct of feeding himself before others and even at the expense of others, into perhaps a more barbaric instinct of feeding himself and then hoarding all he can at the cost of the poor, the sick and the hungry." If Islamic society has to avoid becoming a replica of the West "a thorough rediscovery, revitalization and reintegration of our traditional values must be achieved. They must be drawn forth from under the decades of foreign rule which have accumulated like thick sets of paper that

---

[1] Speech at the 30th General Assembly of the International Press Institute, Nairobi, 2 March 1981.

[2] Presidential Address at the first anniversary of the Mindanao University, Philippines, 24 November 1963.

have rested for generations on top of the finest oriental painting, making the edges turn yellow, but the centre piece remaining as colourful and lively, for us to discover, as when it was originally completed. . . . It is of fundamental importance that our own traditional values and attitudes should permeate our new society. . . . It must never be said generations hence that in our greed for the material good of the rich West we have forsaken our responsibilities to the poor, to the orphans, to the traveller, to the single woman. The day we no longer know how, nor have the time nor the faith to bow in prayer to Allah because the human soul, that He has told us is eternal, is no longer of sufficient importance to us to be worthy of an hour of our daily working, profit-seeking time, will be a sunless day of despair."[1]

Once again echoing the thoughts of his grandfather, the Aga Khan told the people of Pakistan that in the past much of the dynamic power of Muslim society had come from the leaders of the faith and religious doctors. The identity between the religious leaders and the intellectual élite of the empire was a perennial source of strength both to the faith and to the rulers. "How many aspiring mullahs or imams today enter secular universities and obtain degrees in secular subjects? And, vice-versa, how many university graduates, after completing their degrees, turn their lives to directing the flock of the faithful? . . . in future I believe it will be in our society's interest to have a much wider platform in common between our religious and our secular leaders." The religious leaders must be fully aware of the contemporary secular trends, including those of science and technology, and the academic or secular élite must be well acquainted with the history, scale and depth of the leadership exercised by the Islamic empire of the past in all fields.

It is "through the creation of such a new élite, inspired by, and widely read in, everything related to our heritage, that there must come about a revival in Muslim thought". The educational system should begin to re-introduce in its curricula the work and thought of great Muslim writers and savants, so that "from the nursery school to the university, the thoughts of the young will be inspired by our own heritage and not that of some foreign culture". At the end he warns that "a society without a strong sense of its own identity has time and again in human history proved to be well on the way to decay", and impresses upon his audience that "the need to break finally with the immediate and

[1] Convocation Address at the University of Peshawar, Pakistan, 30 November 1967.

largely alien past, and to rebuild on the foundations of our historic greatness is more than a condition of further progress; it has now become an urgent necessity throughout the Muslim world".[1]

The greatest love of the Aga Khan has undoubtedly been Islamic architecture. Due to personal predilection, or perhaps the fact that architecture subsumes in itself all the other interests near his heart – rural development, social reform, Islamic heritage, cultural unity – for nearly thirty years he has been speaking on behalf of the cause of Islamic architecture, extolling its greatness, and the need and desire for its revival and adaptation in the present age.

He told the University of Sind that for five centuries Muslim architecture "led the world in concept, in design, in finish and even in structural ingenuity. . . . And yet what is being done today to develop our own Islamic architecture of the twenty-first century? Practically nothing. Our office buildings, our schools, our hospitals, our banks and insurance companies – nearly all are copies, monkeyed and mimicked from styles and designs which have been imported. I ask you today to think about this: is it really impossible to adapt for our modern needs those magnificent finishes and building materials so widely used in our past?"[2]

His main concern is the physical form that the Islamic world of the future will assume. What will be the look and shape of the houses, places of work, gardens, parks, markets and mosques? How will these buildings "affect our perceptions of the world and of ourselves?" And, most importantly, "will the Islamic environment of tomorrow be identifiably ours?"

Architecture is not merely an art form. In Islam it is as much an aspect of our daily life as it is a manifestation of aesthetic taste. It is a dimension of our life as a whole, in which no seam divides the spiritual from the secular and the internal from the external. "Islam does not deal in dichotomies but in all encompassing Unity. Spirit and body are one, man and nature are one. What is more, man is answerable to God for what man has created. Many of our greatest architectural achievements were designed to reflect the promises of [the] life hereafter, to represent in this world what we are told of the next. Since all that we see and do resonates on the Faith, the aesthetics of the

---

[1] Convocation Address at the University of Sind, Hyderabad, Pakistan, 6 February 1970.

[2] *ibid.*

environment we build and the quality of the social interactions that take place within those environments, reverberate on our spiritual life." Today, in all that Muslim countries are building, the "wonderful distinctiveness of Islamic architecture is disappearing. . . . There is such homogenized blandness, that one is left with few visual clues to know where one is or who the people of this place might be". The new "structural symbols of power in our world have not sprung from our spirit, from our understanding of who we are, or what we believe, but have been merely copied from foreign images of political and commercial power" . . . "Can this be the world of the people who built the mosque of Cordoba? Of the people whose marvellous urban systems in Isfahan are still studied by the city planners? The people who created the Mugal gardens of Kashmir?"

The Muslim world of today is putting up its structures with such speed that there is little time for reflection on the far-reaching impact of these fabrics on the minds and spirits of the people who will live and work in them. "But to build is to affect the world for a long time. Buildings conceived in haste to meet pressing needs will be negative presence for years ahead." The contemporary scene is heart breaking. "Throughout the Islamic world there is a thirst for the images of modernity, of material progress, the symbols of power. The colonial rulers are gone, the structures they left behind, the courts and residences and legislatures they built and from which the rulers governed, have long been occupied by our own leaders. Now the need is for new symbols, and they are being imported complete and intact without adaptation, without filtering out the inappropriate, without perhaps even asking the question whether they could, or should, be different. There is little time. The treasures of our past are being destroyed. . . . Should we allow future generations of Muslims to live without the self-respect of our own cultural and spiritual symbols of power, to practise their faith without also being reminded by that sense of scale in relation to the universe around us which is so particularly ours?"

Islamic architecture centres on the serenity of form. A balance is created through the use of geometrical principles, and stability, tranquillity and equilibrium are thus effected. The architectural style is modest: there is no domination, pride, grandiloquence, lordliness, or naked power. "The superiority of man-made structures over natural environment is a concept alien to Islamic belief . . . The desire to bring to this world some of the beauty of the hereafter acted as a constant barrier to the discordant or the haphazard in Islamic styles." This architecture frames the space, by defining each area, by supplying a physical context for each activity, and by separating privacy and community, light and shadow, small and large, and interior and exterior. The corridors and passages connecting these spaces supply an element of formality, even solemnity.

Nature is made a partner in Islamic architecture. Cooling systems in classical buildings used only sun and wind for power, thus helping to preserve an ecological balance. The partnership with nature produces strong kinaesthetic experience: "air currents touching the skin, the sound of moving water, the touch of varied surface textures, the richness of colour and the play of light and shade upon the vision, the scents of plants in the courtyards, are touches of the paradise to come".

This heritage cannot be abandoned. It has to be recalled, used, adapted. "We must begin with a new visual language for our future environment, one generated from within Islam, not devised abroad."[1]

He develops his argument further in a later treatment of the theme. Environment moulds life in more ways than we realize, and for Muslims it is "a particularly critical matter". They believe in an "all-encompassing unity of man and nature". Therefore, their architecture was a part of their daily life, their thinking, their ethos, with an internal momentum and rhythm of its own. This explains the fact that "although in time the great Islamic Empires fell, as did the Empires of Greece and Rome, of China and Japan, the Muslim culture they sustained was not affected in a parallel way to those others, since the Faith itself remained strong, and for many Muslims the concepts of what was desirable in a building continued to be inspired by the Faith".

But modern times have upset the order of a thousand years. First colonial rule and then the economic domination of the West have swept away the old moorings. The new structures, both official and public, are mere copies of their Western originals. The vernacular architecture of the rural people has been eroded. Mud walls, stone buildings and wooden houses have been replaced by concrete walls and corrugated iron roofs, because the ordinary citizens look upon those Western materials as modern and desirable, notwithstanding their unsuitability for hot

---

[1] "Islamic Architecture: A Revival", speech at the Asia Society, New York, 25 September 1979. See also his speech at the presentation ceremony of the second Aga Khan Award for Architecture at Topkapi Palace, Istanbul, 4 September 1983.

climates. On the monumental level some attempt has been made to construct buildings in the Islamic style, but the result is nothing more than a mimicry of the Islamic glories. "Adding a dome and towers to a downtown office block does not make it either Islamic or appropriate."

What is required is a reconciliation of Western technology with traditional cultures in a creative way. The overriding consideration is that the architectural environment of the Islamic countries must enable the ethos of their civilization to express itself, as well as give that sense of national identity and integrity which the leaders of the freedom movement sought when they were leading their people to independence.[1]

The Aga Khan has taken several steps in order to achieve these ideals. On a broader basis he has established the Aga Khan Trust for Culture to support, encourage and promote projects, research and training, and other such scientific and creative activities which "foster a better understanding of Islamic civilization and contribute significantly to the physical, cultural and intellectual environment in the developing countries of Asia and Africa".

Architecture has received more specific attention. He has created the Aga Khan Award for Architecture which seeks to recognize architectural excellence in the Islamic world. Its aim is to nurture within the architectural profession, in its related disciplines and in society as a whole, a "renewed understanding of the vitality of Islamic culture while encouraging architecture appropriate to the rapidly evolving context of the twentieth century". Up to half a million United States Dollars are presented every three years to completed architectural schemes. It is the richest architectural prize in the world. In 1979 he established the Aga Khan Programme for Islamic Architecture at Harvard University and the Massachusetts Institute of Technology. He has also sponsored the publication of the quarterly *Mi'mar: Architecture in Development*, whose first issue appeared in 1981. It is the only international architectural journal with a professional focus on architecture and design in the developing world.

The Aga Khan also wants to utilize architecture to develop a better understanding between East and West. His aim is to make a bridge, a constructive relationship; but the West must first "cease to look at the Islamic architectural heritage simply as a matter of scholastic interest and admiration". He has appealed

---

[1] "Islamic Architecture: Concerns and Directions", speech made on the occasion of receiving the 1984 Thomas Jefferson Memorial Foundation Medal for Architecture at the University of Virginia, Charlottesville, 13 April 1984.

to the West to give to Islamic architecture "recognition of a different dimension, a dimension of the future. Enhance it, enrich it and enliven it, put at its disposal your talents, your knowledge and your creativity".[1]

Finally, Prince Karim Aga Khan's perception of Islam has much in common with that of his grandfather. In his own words, "the correct interpretation of our office [*Imamat*], and of the faith which guides it, is that man must not shy away from the material endeavour in the name of his faith. On the contrary, he must be enterprising, contributing of his best to his family and the society in which he lives, so long as the content of his endeavour is within the terms of our social and moral conscience and so long as the objectives of the enterprise are equally acceptable".[2] Islam is an all-encompassing faith, and it gives direction to every aspect of man's life. It urges us to "lead a balanced life, one that strives to accommodate both material progress and spiritual well-being".[3] It establishes a moral framework within which material endeavour is to be encouraged, and this equips us with a social conscience.[4]

The Aga Khan's fullest and finest exposition of his understanding of Islam and its relevance to the contemporary world was made in a speech delivered in 1976 at the International Sirat Conference in Karachi. Islamic society in the coming years, he suggested, will find that our traditional concepts of time – a limitless mirror in which to reflect on the eternal – will become a shrinking cage, an invisible trap from which fewer and fewer will escape; while in the West the anchors of moral behaviour no longer hold firm the ship of life. Continuing the theme, Prince Karim said: "In the face of this changing world, which was once a universe to us and now no more than an overcrowded island, confronted with a fundamental challenge to our understanding of time, surrounded by a foreign fleet of cultural and ideological ships which have broken loose, I ask, do we have a clear, firm and precise understanding of what Muslim society is to be in times to come? And if, as I believe, the answer is uncertain, where

[1] "Islamic Architecture: A Revival", speech at the Asia Society, New York, 25 September 1979.
[2] "The Aga Khan Social Welfare and Economic Development Institutions in India", speech at a luncheon given in his honour by the Federation of Indian Chambers of Commerce, New Delhi, 14 January 1983.
[3] "Social Institutions in National Development: The Enabling Environment", speech, Nairobi, 6 October 1982.
[4] "The Aga Khan Social Welfare and Economic Development Institutions in Tanzania", speech, Dar-es-Salam, November 1982.

else can we search than in the Holy Quran, and in the example of Allah's last and final Prophet?"[1]

There is no excuse or explanation for delaying the search for the answer to this question. The ordinary Muslim, with demands on his time multiplying, has less and less opportunity to look for an answer. It is the religious leaders and the élite who have to find it and give it to the common citizen. But we must remember that the Islamic world covers such an amazing range of historical, ethnic and cultural backgrounds that a monolithic answer may not be available. On the other hand, we must avoid that degree of diversity which makes Muslim countries oppose one another or makes them too divided to face common enemies.

"Let me return, now, to the question of what Muslim society should seek to be in the years ahead," he said. "Islam is a way of life. This means that every aspect of the individual's daily existence is guided by Islam: his family relations, his business relations, his education, his health, the means and manner by which he gains his livelihood, his philanthropy, what he sees and hears around him, what he reads, the way he regulates his time, the buildings in which he lives, learns and earns."

The modern age, he suggested, provides the Muslims a unique opportunity to unite, and also to ensure that the society in which they live is that which they have defined and chosen for themselves. But this can only be done with the help of our own men and women who have achieved positions of eminence in the wider world. They must be persuaded to return home so that we can benefit from their knowledge, learning and work. Most of them stay abroad, or return only to leave again, because their own countries and governments fail to give them the support and encouragement necessary for them to work or teach in their own environment. All meaningful endeavour, all original thinking, all authentic research must be encouraged.

Concluding his address, Prince Karim said: "The Holy Prophet's life gives us every fundamental guideline that we require to resolve the problem as successfully as our human minds and intellects can visualize. His example of integrity, loyalty, honesty, generosity both of means and of time, his solicitude for the poor, the weak and the sick, his steadfastness in friendship, his humility in success, his magnanimity in victory, his simplicity, his wisdom in conceiving new solutions for problems which could not be solved

---

[1] Presidential Address at the International Sirat Conference, Karachi, 12 March 1976.

by traditional methods, without affecting the fundamental concepts of Islam, surely all these are foundations which, correctly understood and sincerely interpreted, must enable us to conceive what should be a truly modern and dynamic Islamic society in the years ahead."

The virtues of a grandson have erected the noblest mausoleum in memory of his grandfather's life-long dedication to nurturing respect for human dignity. A legacy enriched by ripe wisdom and good fortune endures through felicitous heredity.

1

IN THE DAYS OF MY YOUTH

A Chapter of Autobiography

15 August 1902

Reminiscences of the last twenty-five years – memories of grandfather – brief *imamat* of father – fostering care provided by mother
– early educational background – interest in racing and sports –
first visit to England and Germany – visits to Ismaili followers –
representative institutions – hope for the development of the industrial and manufacturing resources of India.

Though we of the East are generally credited with maturing and
passing to the sere and yellow leaf earlier than man [men] of
Occidental race, we are not, if mine is the customary experience,
much given to retrospect while still on the right side of thirty,
and it seems to me that two or three decades hence (when, no
doubt, *M.A.P.* will be maintaining its great popularity) would be
a more suitable time than the present for me to write on "The
Days of My Youth." However, in reluctantly accepting an invitation to be numbered among the contributors to the series, I
feel that, though I may not have much of interest to say, I have
the advantage over many of my predecessors in this gallery of
being under no obligation to be silent as to the years only just
left behind, because the Rubicon of early manhood is passed. Yet
so deep are the impressions sometimes left on the plastic mind
of a child, that I can – without any great effort of memory – go
back nearly a quarter of a century.

In those days I was taken to race meetings in a big coach, there
to survey with childish interest a bright and moving scene, in
which my aged grandfather was invariably the central figure. It
was in the later forties that Hasan Ali Shah, then in the meridian
of life, left Persia, where he had filled high satrapies, and settled

in India, to the great gratification of the vast number of Ismailis residing in that country. And yet, more than three decades later, I was privileged, as a grandchild, to hear from the lips of the old man eloquent the [sic] and stirring tales of days when the nineteenth century was young, and to see him on race-days riding about the grandstand on a led horse, partially blind, and weak from the weight of over fourscore years, but, for the time, roused to new life by the associations of his principal pastime. He passed away in his eighty-ninth year, to the sore grief of a grandson then only six.

My father, Aga Ali Shah, was destined to hold the spiritual leadership of the great Ismaili community for fewer years than his predecessor had decades. When only ten I was left fatherless, and with the weight of this hereditary responsibility upon me.

Happily, however, I had the inestimable, and, in the circumstances, essential advantage of receiving the fostering care of a gifted and far-seeing mother, the daughter of the famous Nizam-ud-Daulah, who renounced the life of the Persian Court to spend his days in religious retirement. She took care that I should continue the education commenced under my father's guidance.

I had already been grounded in Arabic and Persian literature and history, and, first inspired thereto in childhood, to this day I take a special interest in historical studies connected with the early Caliphs. Under my English tutors I gained an attachment, which also remains with me, to the writings of the more stirring and eloquent of the English historians and of the foremost novelists – particularly Gibbon and Thackeray and Dickens. I cannot say that Western poetry has greatly appealed to me, though I make an exception in the case of Fitzgerald's "Omar Khayyam," which I regard, after frequent comparison, as superior to the original.

I have inherited something of my grandfather's interest in racing, to which has been added a keen enjoyment of out-door sports. This was stimulated to no small degree by our popular cricketing Governor, Lord Harris, from whom, as from his immediate predecessors and his successors, I have received unvarying kindness and consideration. I am specially fond of golf and hockey, and am glad to have done something to popularise the latter sport in India by giving two tournament cups, annually played for one by schoolboys and the other by civil and military teams. Golf is a favourite pastime of Anglo-Indians, and stands in no need of stimulation.

During the portion of the year I spent at Poona, it was frequently my privilege to play over the Ganeshkhind links, by invitation of Lord Northcote, our present statesmanlike and philanthropic Governor. Amid the manifold and pleasant engagements of what would in happier circumstances have been the Coronation season, I have been able now and again to get out of town for a little golf. Amongst other English links with which I am acquainted I may mention those of Wimbledon, Ranelagh, Deal, and Walmer. I have also had some very pleasant motoring experiences, and hope to take back to India some cars to enjoy on the broad, well-kept roads in and about the Deccan capital that exhilarating pastime, by way of change from the cycling and horseback exercise which I daily take.

From my earliest years I have thought to place a high value on the rule of Great Britain in India, and to reverence the august lady in whose name it was then conducted. I felt it to be no small honour, therefore, when not only my own followers but the Mahomedan community generally, at a mass meeting held in Bombay under my presidency to vote an address to the Queen-Empress on the completion of sixty years' reign, deputed me by acclamation to take the address to Simla, where, along with others, it was received in durbar by Lord Elgin.

But still greater honour was mine in the following year, when I paid my first visit to England, and was invited to dine and sleep at Windsor Castle. I had often been told of the deep interest Queen Victoria took in her Eastern empire, but must confess to astonishment at the close knowledge of Indian problems and deep abiding sympathy with her subjects there which Her Majesty displayed during the conversation I was privileged to have with her.

It was then that I was first presented to his Majesty, King Edward, whose gracious kindness to me both on that occasion and during my present visit will ever remain engraven on my memory.

I was but a boy when the Duke and Duchess of Connaught were in India and the cordiality and kindness they then showed towards me have been continued to this day. It was on the occasion of my previous visit to Europe that I was presented to the Emperor William at Potsdam and received from his Majesty the Order of the First Class of the Crown of Prussia.

It is my pleasurable experience to travel extensively during the winter months amongst my followers, not only in India, but along the Persian Gulf littoral, in Arabia, along the East Coast of Africa, in the further East and elsewhere. I am proud of the industrial and commercial progress they are making as of the sincere attachment manifested to British rule by those of them who live under its protection.

This spirit was inculcated by my grandfather and my father, both of whom exerted their authority on the side of Government measures on occasions when ignorance or prejudice led to a misunderstanding of them. It has been my humble endeavour to follow the traditions thus established, not however as a mere family convention, but as the result of settled political convictions, based upon much reading and on personal observations in many lands. It is sometimes said that now so much is heard of the self-governing colonies there is a danger of India being overlooked in current discussion of schemes for closer union of the dominions of the King.

But whatever changes the next few decades may bring, I am persuaded that India will ever hold the greatest place in any scheme of Imperial consolidation. What the peoples of India have to do is to prove themselves worthy, by whole-hearted patriotism of that place. In saying this I do not mean that the time is near at hand when advanced political institutions should be granted to India . . . Even on some European nations which could be mentioned representative institutions sit badly. The Anglo-Saxon race, like the Roman Empire in its best days, has a genius for the art of government, whether of itself or of others; but the success of representative institutions in Anglo-Saxon lands is no proof of their suitability to Oriental conditions.

The present system of administration in India must be occasionally adjusted to changing circumstances, but in the main it is the best system for the country that can be devised. It secures individual freedom and equality before the law. It is this freedom and equality of legal protection that the people value, and, given that, they care little or nothing for political power. I believe the great mass of my fellow-countrymen to be thoroughly well content with the "pax Britannica." This could never be the case if the power of government were used arbitrarily and despotically, but so long as the settled legal forms of government and those principles of individual liberty on which the administration is framed are closely adhered to, all will be well so far as public contentment is concerned. India has in the past few years passed through dark trials which it was not within the range of human achievement to avert. Let us hope that the cycle of bad seasons is almost at an end, and that the people, stimulated by the aid a larger resort to technical and manual instruction will afford – a matter on which I expressed my opinion at length to an interviewer for British India Commerce two or three years ago – will be enabled to promote their material well-being by further development of the industrial and manufacturing resources of the country.

In the past few weeks the greatness and the glory of the British Empire have been demonstrated in the kaleidoscope of the world's metropolis, where have been gathered together representations – unparalleled in their completeness – of its diversified character and interests. I think I can speak for my brother Indian visitors when I say that Britain's greatness has been even more markedly demonstrated in these six anxious weeks of waiting than if the postponement of the Coronation had not been rendered inevitable. The illness of his Gracious Majesty has shown the fortitude with which the British people can bear sudden and almost overwhelming trial, as also the unqualified degree to which the Throne stands broad-based upon the people's will. During the days of danger our joy was sadly marred, and to many of the functions arranged in our honour, with lavish hospitality, we went with heavy hearts. But the Indian representatives, from the greatest chief to the humblest soldier, will return with a prouder sense of British citizenship than they have ever before possessed. The story of the glory and glamour of these wonderful days will flitter down to every bazaar and village in the Eastern Empire, carrying a message of loyalty to the most ignorant.

Source: Naoroji M. Dumasia, *A Brief History of the Aga Khan with an Account of His Predecessors, the Ismailian Princes or Benefatimite Caliphs of Egypt*, the Author, Bombay, 1903, Appendix III, pp. 168–76.

According to Dumasia, "In *M.A.P.* for August 15, the Chapter of Autobiography under the heading of 'In the Days of My Youth', is contributed by his Highness the Aga Khan." But he does not tell us what the *M.A.P.* stands for. The text shows that this piece was written in England.

The reader should collate it with the account of his early years given by the Aga Khan in his *Memoirs* published fifty-two years later.

2

MUSLIM EDUCATION IN INDIA

Presidential Address to the All India Muhammadan Educational Conference

Delhi: 1902

Advantages which Muslims of India possess – schools needed to teach boys and girls the Faith and modern secular science – Muslims have neglected industry and commerce – the moral disease among Muslims not congenital but acquired – high standards in Muslim society during the reigns of Abu Bakr and Umar – causes of the moral disease prevalent today – one solution: foundation of a University, "an intellectual and moral capital".

My first duty and pleasure is to thank you for the honour you have done me in asking me to preside at the meeting of the Conference. To sit in this chair is a signal honour of which any Muslim may be proud, but you have conferred upon me a very particular distinction in inviting me to be your President in this Imperial city and upon this historic occasion. For this honour, gentlemen, I tender you my deep and sincere thanks.

As, gentlemen, you have given me the right to speak in your name, I will lose no time in giving expression to a sentiment which is, I know, in the hearts of all of us. On behalf of the Mahomedan Educational Conference I welcome the guests and delegates who have come from a distance – I thank them that they have borne the discomfort of so much travel in order to confer by their attendance distinction upon this meeting.

And, in particular, I wish to offer the thanks of this Mahomedan assembly to those distinguished Governors of Provinces and Rulers of great States who have promised to honour this occasion with their presence, the fact that our great statesmen and administrators, amid the burden of public cares, should find time to show their interest in the religious, educational and social problems of a community, not their own, confers upon this assembly a very conspicuous honour, for which our heart-felt thanks and gratitude are due to their patronage.

It is, indeed, a matter of surprise as well as congratulation that any one of all this distinguished company should have entered this modest building at all, when a few paces from here all the pomp and splendour of this glorious Empire is unrolled before our dazzled sight. Never before have the Princes of India shone forth in so superb a pageant, never have we beheld, concentrated with equal magnificence, all the might and splendour of the Empire of India, and never have the antique battlements of this Imperial City witnessed the proclamation of so great or just an Emperor.

That you have attended this Conference at all, in spite of all these splendid attractions, is due, I believe, to the fact that, though education is our theme, we are deliberating upon something more important than the suitability of this or that textbook, or this or that course of study. We are, if I understand the purpose of this Conference aright, considering what in modern times are the ideals we must hold before our people and the paths by which they attain them; and upon the right answer to these questions depends no trifling matter, but nothing less than the future of Indian Moslems.

We are undertaking a formidable task when we attempt to correct and remodel the ideals of our people. But for the task before us, we Indian Mussalmans possess many advantages; we have the advantage of living under a Government which administers justice evenly between rich and poor and between persons of different creeds and classes; in the second place, we enjoy complete freedom to devise plans for the amelioration of our people. We have no reason to fear that our deliberations will be abruptly closed if we propose schemes of education other than those approved by Government. We know that no book and no branch of knowledge will be forbidden to us by official command; and, lastly, we know that, under the protection of British rule, we shall be allowed to work out to the end any plans for social and economic salvation which we may devise. Our wealth will not excite rapacity, nor our advancement in learning awaken the jealousy of our rulers. More than all this, we are members of a polity in which the opportunities for advancement in wealth and learning are greater, perhaps, than in any country in Asia, if only we have the energy and wisdom to make a right use of those opportunities.

These are privileges which our co-religionists in Turkey or Persia, who are not British subjects, do not possess. In those countries the opportunities for growing wealthy in commerce and industries or in the independent liberal professions can hardly be said to exist, and in both of them the pursuit of learning and freedom of thought are fettered by restrictions. We Moslems of India, therefore, enjoy unparalleled advantages, and we occupy among our co-religionists a unique position, and, if we properly utilize them and realise our duties, we ought to lead the way and constitute ourselves the vanguard of Islamic progress throughout the world. Here in India we can develop our own ideals of society, we have freedom in which to deliberate upon them, and we have security from internal and external enemies. We may carry our plans to maturity without fear of internal trouble or external aggression. Our brethren in Turkey and Persia must give their first thoughts and unceasing attention to military preparations and diplomatic arrangements, lest, whilst they are evolving schemes of progress, illiberal and autocratic European States should swallow up their independence, and thus they should at one blow lose for ever all chance of future development. But we, who live beneath the liberal rule of England, have here all the chances that a people require of developing our own individuality according to our own ideas.

And now, gentlemen, let us direct our attention to a question with which your Conference is intimately concerned, namely, how have the Indian Moslems taken advantage of the chances which Providence has placed in their way? We must all acknowledge with shame and regret that so far we have failed. Throughout the whole length and breadth of India how many national schools are there in existence which educate Moslem boys and girls in their faith and at the same time in modern secular science? Is there even one to every hundred that our nation needs and which we should have established had we been like any other healthy people? There are, indeed, a certain number of old-fashioned Maktabs and Madrassahs which continue to give a parrot-like teaching of the Koran, but even in these places no attempt is made either to improve the morals of the boys or to bring before them the eternal truths of the faith. As a rule, prayers are but rarely repeated, and when said, not one per cent. of the boys understand what they say or why.

Let me take another example of our failure to fulfil our obvious duties towards our co-religionists. During the recent famines no national effort was made to save Moslem children or to bring up to [sic] the Moslem orphans of famine-striken parents in some special technical or elementary school. This surely was a public duty which could never have been neglected in a healthy society.

Again, in Mahomedan society, we too often hear futile laments over the loss of political power, but we must remember that in the modern world a monopoly of political power, such as Moslems once held in India, is neither possible nor even desirable. Now that general liberty is given to all, the monopoly, or even a desire for the monopoly, of political power is both immoral and of no benefit. The just man does not even wish to possess privileges to the necessary exclusion of others. On the other hand, a desire for industrial and financial pre-eminence is perfectly legitimate because it is obtained by the free competition of the energies of individuals without which rapid progress is perhaps impossible. But here again our community has signally failed to take advantage of that peace, justice and freedom which we all enjoy under British rule. We have neglected industry and commerce just as we have neglected every other opportunity of progress.

This general apathy which pervades every walk of life is the sign of a moral disease, and what I will ask you to consider with me today are the causes of this terrible disease, and I will especially invite your attention to this point. Are the causes of this disease, to use a medical phrase, congenital and necessary, i.e., are they part of the faith or are they accidental and acquired? That this disease is accidental and no necessary development of the faith, is shown not only by political progress made by Islam during the first twenty-five years of the Hijra, but by the high standard of duty, morality, truthfulness, justice and charity that was general in Arabian society during the glorious reigns of Abu Bakr and Omar, and this high standard prevailed, mind you, amongst men whose early youth had been passed either like the Koraish aristocrats in the lazy and dissolute society of Mecca before the conquest, or like the rank and file, in Bedoin brigandage, in revengeful murder and in deeds of violence. Islam made heroes of such men, not only in the battlefield but in the more difficult daily sacrifices of [a] healthy and patriotic society. As a body they were law-abiding, just, full of charity, and true to their engagements, so that the conquered Persian peasants looked upon their just Arab conquerors as a godsend, very much as the Indian agriculturists welcomed the English whenever they overthrew a corrupt and cruel native State from 1760 to 1858.

So Islam, as a faith, when it was best understood, did not lead to apathy but to extraordinary devotion and self-sacrifice which it elicited even from such wretched material as the dissolute and immoral Meccan aristocrats of the days of ignorance; for these very men under the purifying influence of Islam distinguished themselves above all the Arabs by their loyalty and devotion. Witness the way in which the great Khalid and Amru, son of Al Ass, conquerors of Syria and Egypt, respectively, accepted the judgment of Omar and Othman in such a remarkably patient and uncomplaining fashion when removed from governments which they had founded and commands of troops whom they had led to glorious victory. Both these men were actuated by profound moral obedience to authority and devotion to duty, and yet both had been in their youth like the usual worthless Meccan aristocrats.

All this shows that Islam does not necessarily lead to apathy and want of devotion to duty. We must, therefore, consider what the real causes are of this supineness which we are compelled to recognize as universal in Moslem society of today, a supineness all the more remarkable under the benign rule of England, where a little self-sacrifice would enable us to achieve greatness; for through greatness in modern times consists in pre-eminence in learning, wealth, and such pre-eminence we might attain with constant effort [sic].

I believe that this disease cannot be assigned to any one single cause, but I will, with your permission, enumerate four causes which, in my judgment, have had a paramount influence in introducing this apathy, this moral torpor, into Moslem society; and you will notice that all the causes of which I speak have been in operation for a very long time.

For the first cause I must go back to the very early days of our faith. The disastrous murder of Omar was an irreparable misfortune. Omar was removed at the most important moment in the history of Islam when vast additions had been made not only to the Empire but to the wealth of every individual Moslem. And he was, above all, the one man whose intense piety and faith and justice made him not only obeyed by all, but made him above everything the model of perfect manhood to the Moslems. The rising generation who had suddenly found themselves possessed not only of Empire but of enormous wealth, when every Arab was richer than he had ever dreamed it possible, lost in

Omar in that critical period that example of saintly virtue on a throne which is perhaps amongst every people, modern or ancient, one of the most precious assets of society.

The very absence of Omar at that period was itself a loss which no impartial historian who has studied Moslem society of that period, can possibly doubt, however he may believe that history is influenced by general causes rather than by individual characters. But when his successor was assassinated and again the next head of the Moslem world had to contend against rebellion, a new element forced its way into Islamic society which has curiously not often been noticed by even the best historians, although its effects are visible to this day in the apathy which we are discussing. Many of the most intimate friends of the Prophet and the most pious and distinguished of the "companions" doubted which side they should take in the civil wars, and how they should act so as not to be responsible for any harm that might come, and so were led to adopt the most dangerous principle of all. They retired each into his private home and did not use their influence one way or the other, but passed the rest of their lives in prayer and pilgrimage. This example has ever since been unconsciously followed by some of the best and purest in every Moslem society. The most genuine and the most moral of Moslems often tell you, as they have a thousand times told me almost in identical terms at Constantinople or Cairo, at Bombay or Zanzibar, that as long as they spent their energies in prayer and pilgrimage they are certain that though they do not do the best, yet they do no harm, and thus they give up to prayer and pilgrimage the lives which should have been devoted to the well-being of their people.

It is to this class in India that I appeal and desire most earnestly to impress upon them my conviction that, if they continue in their present attitude of aloofness, it means the certain extinction of Islam, at least, as a world-wide religion. We of this Conference appeal to the pious for their co-operation and assistance, and we warn them solemnly and in all earnestness that, if they give all their time to prayer and their money to pilgrimages, the time will come when that piety, which they so highly prize, will pass away from our society, and (for want of timely assistance at this most critical period) not one of our descendants will know how to pray or put any store upon the merit of pilgrimage. It is to this genuine class of pious men that we appeal here; let them come forward and take their legitimate place in the advancement of their co-religionists and in the moral and religious education of their brethren and children. In the strenuous life of modern times, a people that does not get help from its most pious and most moral sections has as little chance of success as a man who tries to swim with his arms tied behind his back.

A great, but silent, crisis has come in the fortunes of Islam, and unless this class wake up to the altered conditions of life and to the necessity of superintending and educating the rising generation, the very existence of Islam is at stake. This class of pious Moslems must understand that what Islam now demands of them is that they should surrender to the training of the young a portion of the time hitherto given to prayer and a portion of the money hitherto spent in pilgrimages or celebrations of martyrdoms, long since past, which only help to keep alive those terrible sectarian differences which are one of the misfortunes of Islam. The example of the Prophet and of Abu Bakr and Omar and Ali should convince these pious people that the first duty of a Moslem is to give his time to the service of his nation and not merely to silent prayers.

A second cause of our present apathy is the terrible position of Moslem women ... There is absolutely nothing in Islam, or the Koran, or the example of the first two centuries, to justify this terrible and cancerous growth that has for nearly a thousand years eaten into the very vitals of Islamic society. The heathen Arabs in the days of ignorance, especially the wealthy young aristocrats of Mecca, led an extremely dissolute life, and before the conquest of Mecca the fashionable young Koraishites spent most of their leisure in the company of unfortunate women, and often married these same women and, altogether, the scandals of Mecca before the conquest were vile and degrading. The Prophet not only by the strictness of his laws put an end to this open and shameless glorification of vice, but by a few wise restrictions, such as must be practised by any society that hopes to exist, made the former constant and unceremonious companionship of men and strange women impossible.

From these necessary and wholesome rules the jealousy of the Abbassides, borrowing from the practice of the later Persian Sassanian kings, developed the present system ... which means the permanent imprisonment and enslavement of half the nation. How can we expect progress from the children of mothers who have never shared, or even seen, the free social intercourse of modern mankind? This terrible cancer that has grown since the 3rd and 4th century [*sic*] of the Hijra must either be cut out, or the body of Moslem society will be poisoned to death by the permanent waste of all the women of the nation. But Pardah, as now known, itself did not exist till long after the Prophet's death and is no part of Islam. The part played by Moslem women at Kardesiah and Yarmuk, the two most momentous battles of Islam next to Badr and Honein, and their splendid nursing of the wounded after those battles, is of itself a proof to any reasonable person that Pardah, as now understood, has never been conceived by the companions of the Prophet. That we Moslems should saddle ourselves with this excretion of Persian custom, borrowed by the Abbassides, is due to that ignorance of early Islam which is one of the most extraordinary of modern conditions. As if the two causes already mentioned were not enough to strangle Mahomedan society, the Abbassides set a terrible example of personal ambition which has left a deep impression on Islamic history. These unworthy relatives of the Prophet, ever jealous of the superior merit of the Ommiades, to whom they had sworn allegiance, beaten time after time in the field, made an unholy alliance with the newly-conquered men of Khorasan, led them astray by the so-called traditions in praise of their own family (invented by the thousand to mislead the newly-concerted [*sic*] and non-Arab Moslems who understood little of the liberal and democratic spirit of Islam), and with the aid of these allies overthrew the house of Ommia. This example of treachery for the sake of self-aggrandizement, coming from a family nearly related to the Prophet, throws great light on the fact that, time after time for the sake of furthering individual or family ambition, Moslems have sacrificed the welfare of their Sovereigns or States or peoples, for it is easy for those who are not naturally pious to forget the welfare of the nation for the sake of their own advancement.

The fourth cause of the general apathy of modern times which we are considering is undoubtedly the doctrine of necessity. No fair or reasonable-minded person who has read the Koran can for a moment doubt that freedom of the will and individual human responsibility is there insisted upon, but Abul Hassan Alashari (a direct descendant of that Abu Musa who was responsible for the fiasco at the arbitration at Doomah) – Abul Hassan, whose piety and learning and genius cannot be doubted – has placed the stamp of his unfortunately misapplied but great genius on Islam and given to Moslem thought that fatal fatalism which discourages effort and which has undoubtedly been one of the principal causes of the non-aggressive spirit of modern Islam. It was not till about the year 200 A.H. that the question of Jabr or

Taqdeer, i.e., freedom of the will or necessity, began first to agitate Moslem thought. Had the matter come before the world of Islam during the Caliphate of some good and virtuous Caliph who was universally respected, and whose piety and faith were beyond doubt (such, for instance, as the saintly and exemplary Omar-ibn-e Abdul Aziz) an authoritative judgment in favour of freedom of the will would have finally laid this question at rest, but unluckily this true doctrine of Islam found, for its champion, Mamoon. Now, Mamoon's extraordinary ideas and very curious behaviour towards some principles of the Shariat had made the pious suspicious, and the very fact that Mamoon was the champion of the doctrine of the freedom of the will was enough to make the pious prejudiced against all those who held, and rightly held, that this was a fundamental doctrine and that no society that accepted fatalism and carried it to its logical conclusion could possibly succeed. It is the fashion to place all the responsibility for the downfall of Islam to Chengiz and the Tartar invasion.

But in my humble opinion – an opinion held also by many of the most learned who have given the matter serious study – it was, first, the bad example and selfishness of the Abbassides; secondly, the fatal system . . . with its restrictions on the intellectual development of the women; thirdly, the constant and silent withdrawal of the most pious and moral Moslems into a life of private prayer and devotion; and, lastly, this doctrine of necessity, that brought about our downfall. I say it was in my opinion these four causes that have brought Moslem society down to its present low and degraded level of intellect and character. How low we have fallen, one can easily find out by comparing Moslem general intelligence of today to that which exists even in the most backward of Slavic-European States. If this downward tendency is not arrested, there is danger that the best minds amongst the present-day Moslems in India will be brought up without any knowledge of the purity and beauty of Islam, and this loss will mean the certain estrangement of all the ablest of the community and the consequent loss of character, honesty and devotion amongst the intelligent, and this will mean, further, that our intellectual and social leaders will not possess the moral qualities most necessary for permanent success.

If, then, we are really in earnest in deploring the fallen condition of our people, we must unite in an effort for their redemption, and, first and foremost of all, an effort must now be made for the foundation of a University where Moslem youths can get, in addition to modern sciences, a knowledge of their glorious past and religion and where the whole atmosphere of the place (it being a residential 'Varsity) may, like Oxford, give more attention to character than mere examination.

Moreover, Moslems in India have legitimate interests in the intellectual development of their co-religionists in Turkey, Persia, Afghanistan and elsewhere, and the best way of helping them is by making Aligarh a Moslem Oxford, where they can all send their best students not only to learn the modern sciences, but that honesty and self-sacrifice which distinguished the Moslems of the first century of the Hijra. Gentlemen, it is not only my opinion, it is the opinion of all the best minds that guide Moslem thought in India, that such a University would restore the faded glories of our people. There is no doubt of the efficacy of the remedy, the element of doubt lies in the preparation of it. Will the Mussalmans of today exert themselves so much as to found such a University? Have we so wholly lost the noble disregard of self, the generous devotion to the good of Islam which character-ized the early Moslems, as not to be able to set aside some of our wealth for this great cause? We are sure that by founding the University we can arrest the decadence of Islam, and if we are not willing to make sacrifices for such an end, must I not con-clude that we do not really care whether the faith of Islam is dead or not?

Gentlemen, I appeal to all of you who hear me today to give not only your money, but your time and your labour to this great end. And especially I would most urgently adjure those who, in obedience to the precepts of our religion, give large sums in the way of God to consider whether it is not more in accordance with the commands and examples of the Prophet to help their Moslem brethren than to undertake pilgrimages and celebrate costly anniversaries.

The sum which we ask for is one crore of rupees, for we propose to establish an institution capable of dealing with the enormous interests involved; we want to be able to give our Moslem youths not merely the finest education that can be given in India, but a training equal to that which can be given in any country in the world. We do not wish that in future our Moslem students should be obliged to go to England or Germany if they wish to attain real eminence in any branch of learning or scholarship, or in the higher branches of industrial and technical learning. Now, we want Aligarh to be such a home of learning as to command the same respect of scholars as Berlin or Oxford, Leipsig or Paris. And we want those branches of Moslem learning, which are too fast passing into decay, to be added by Moslem scholars to the stock of the world's knowledge.

Above all, we want to create for our people an intellectual and moral capital; a city which shall be the hope of elevated ideas and pure ideals; a centre from which light and guidance shall be diffused among the Moslems of India, aye, and out of India too, and which shall hold up to the world a noble standard of the justice and virtue and purity of our beloved faith.

Gentlemen, do you think that the restoration of the glory of Islam would be too dear at one crore of rupees? If you really care for the noble faith which you all profess, you can afford the price. Why, if the Moslems of today did their duty as did the Moslems of the first century, in three months you would collect this money to pay for the ransom of Islam. Bethink you that there are in India 60 million Moslems, and of these at least ten million, or one crore, can afford one rupee a head; from the head of every Moslem family we only ask for one rupee, whereas we all know well that there are people who can pay Rs. 1,000 or Rs. 10,000 with ease.

Gentlemen, these are facts; if our ideal is not realized, it will be because the ape within has swallowed the angel; it will be because, though we profess veneration for the faith and for the Prophet, it is but a lip-loyalty that will not make this small sacrifice to revive in its purity the glorious faith of Islam.

Source: Naoroji M. Dumasia, *A Brief History of the Aga Khan with an Account of His Predecessors, the Ismailian Princes or Benefatimite Caliphs of Egypt*, the Author, Bombay, 1903, Appendix V, pp. 184–202.

Dumasia is wrong in calling it "Presidential Address to the Mahomedan International Conference". It was, in fact, the Aga Khan's presidential speech at the fifteenth annual session of the All India Muhammadan Educational Conference held at Delhi. The Aga Khan was to preside over the Conference once again in 1936 (see Document 162 in this book).

The Conference, which changed its name several times, was established in 1886 by Sir Sayyid Ahmad Khan with the title of Mahomedan Anglo-Oriental Educational Conference "for the general promotion of Western education in Muslim India, for the enrichment of Urdu through translations of indispensable scientific works, to exercise political pressure for the acceptance of Urdu as the secondary language in all government and private schools, to emphasize the necessity for educating women as essential for the balanced intellectual development of future generations, and to formulate a policy for the higher education of Muslim students in Europe, who were discouraged from marrying abroad in order that they should remain involved with the problems of their own land of origin." (Aziz Ahmad, *Islamic Modernism in India and Pakistan, 1857–1964*, Oxford University Press, London, 1967, pp. 37–8).

On the Conference see MAO Educational Conference, *Majmua-i-rezolushanha-*

i-dihsala, 1886–1895, 1896; S. H. Bilgrami, *Addresses, Poems and other Writings of Nawab Imad-ul-Mulk Bahadur (Sayyid Husain Bilgrami, CSI)*, Hyderabad Deccan, 1925; "The Muslim Educational Conference", *Calcutta Monthly*, September 1899; A. Hameed Hasan, "The Mahomadan Educational Conference", *Indian Review*, January 1908; "Mahomadan Educational Conference", *The Civil and Military Gazette*, 4 January 1908; "Muslim Gatherings", *Indian Review*, January 1913; "The Muslim Gathering", *Indian Review*, January 1914; M. C. Chagla, "The Thirty-second Mahomadan Educational Conference", *New Review*, January 1919; "Muslim Educational Conference", *Indian Review*, January 1925; "Muslim Educational Conference", *Indian Review*, January 1931.

THE FINANCES OF INDIA – I

Budget Speech in the Council of the Governor General

Calcutta: 25 March 1903

The burden created by the salt tax – income tax exemption – vast majority of Indian children do not receive elementary education – need for universal primary education and increased grants devoted to higher literary education – reduce the military budget – grant members of the Imperial Cadet Corps commissions in the Indian army – integrate native defence into Imperial defence and eliminate wastage of resources – systematic education for the benefit of India.

My Lord, I must first most cordially congratulate the Government of India on the financial results of the year, which I venture to say prove that there is a steady though slow progress in the material prosperity of the country, and I must acknowledge the wise, liberal and sympathetic manner in which the Hon'ble the Finance Minister has dealt with the various economic problems relating to this Empire. It is almost needless for me to assure Your Excellency that there is universal joy, gratitude and satisfaction throughout India that Your Excellency's Government has in the same year reduced both the most pressing taxes which fall on the shoulders that are least able to bear the burdens of Empire. I must also add that it is almost universally hoped by the people of this country that the present reduction of the salt-tax is the beginning of a series of annual reductions that will in a few years totally wipe out this tax, which by its very nature presses with undue severity on the poorest of the poor, while it practically does not affect the rich and the well-to-do. My Lord, as to the raising of the income-tax exemption to Rs. 1,000 per annum, there is no doubt that it will be a great boon to the lower middle classes, and all I beg to add is the hope that Your Excellency's

Government may be in a position next year to raise the limit to Rs. 1,200 a year and thus carry out the suggestion made by the Hon'ble Sir Montagu Turner last year.

My Lord, as to the various items of expenditure, it is in my humble opinion a cause of regret that year after year passes and no serious effort is made out of the Imperial Exchequer to raise the standard of intelligence of all classes throughout India. In this age of severe competition the more intelligent and the better educated peoples will slowly but surely gain the capital of the ignorant nations, and as the natural and necessary result of their better mental equipment become the creditors of the backward peoples. My Lord, is it right that under these circumstances and in this age the vast majority of Indian children should be brought up without possessing even the rudiments of learning?

My Lord, while the British Government in the United Kingdom and the Governments of all the Australian Colonies and of not only great Powers like Germany, France, Austria-Hungary, Italy and the United States, but of such nations as Japan, Mexico, Peru, Portugal, Spain, Roumania, Serbia and Bulgaria, have adopted compulsory and free primary education for all, the number of illiterates in India according to the census of 1891 was 246,546,176, while those who could read or write was only 12,097,530. My Lord, has not the time come for the commencement of some system of universal primary education such as has been adopted by almost every responsible Government? The extreme poverty of this country has recently been much discussed both here and in England, and all sorts of causes have been found and given to explain the undoubted fact. But, my Lord, in my humble opinion the fundamental cause of this extreme poverty is the ignorance of the great majority of the people, and I venture to add that if by some miracle the angel of peace descended on earth and the military establishments of the Powers disappeared like a mirage and all the gold and silver of Africa and America flowed into this country, yet as long as the present general ignorance of the masses prevailed, in a comparatively few years we would find that the precious metals had returned to the earth and the saving from the military taxes blown into the air in the form of lights and fireworks.

My Lord, with the ever present fact that this country is advancing very slowly as compared to Europe and America, has not the time come for taking a bold and generous step towards some system of universal education suited to the conditions of the various Provinces of the country?

217

Again, my Lord, great efforts are being made in Europe and America towards making higher technical and scientific education general and popular. My Lord, I respectfully venture to suggest that numerous establishments be founded all over India teaching the people by the most scientific and modern methods how to convert the many dormant resources of the country into capital, and even with all this extra expenditure for primary and technical education there ought to be also an increase in the grants devoted to higher literary education, so that the intellectual and moral development of the people may keep pace with its increased material prosperity.

My Lord, it may well now be asked, where is the money to come from? My Lord, I am one of those who feel profoundly convinced that the first duty of the Government of India as the guardians of this country to the people of India is to maintain the military power of this Empire at such a standard of numerical strength and efficiency as to make not only the success of a war with Russia a foregone conclusion but so as to prevent even the most chauvinistic of Russian Tsars from interfering with our many legitimate political and commercial interests in the various independent Asiatic States that border our vast and extended frontier. My Lord, however, if methods could be found by which, without reducing either the effective strength of the Army in time of war or from its efficiency as a military instrument, [the] Government could at the same time reduce the burden of the military budget, I think no considerations of trouble or labour in bringing about such a result ought to be allowed to prevail as against the fact that it will enable the Government of India to devote so many millions a year towards a system of national education. Here I may say, my Lord, that I recognize that no reduction in the number of British troops in India is for the present possible. But with the Indian Army the case is different. First of all, if short service was introduced and a system not only of regimental reserves but of a permanent territorial reserve was formed, it could be brought about that though the peace establishment of the Indian Army and its cost would be less than at present, yet its effective strength in time of war would be greater. This is the system adopted by almost every European Government, including Russia and Turkey, and also by Japan. My Lord, another step which I would respectfully urge not only from the standpoint of economy but also from that of political expediency as also in the interests of justice is that a certain and limited number of the scions of the noblest houses of India such as have passed through the Imperial Cadet Corps be granted commissions in the Indian Army. Your Excellency, by creating the Imperial Cadet Corps, has shown not only your generous sympathy with the aristocracy of India, but by an act of far-seeing statesmanship demonstrated your anxious solicitude that honourable careers may be open to the younger members of ruling families and the noblest houses of India. But, my Lord, the formation of the Imperial Cadet Corps has not only caused general rejoicing and gratitude specially amongst the aristocracy, but also has raised hopes that some at least of the most successful cadets will be nominated to commissions in the Indian Army. I most earnestly beg of Your Excellency that, if possible, a definite undertaking be given that at least some of the most successful cadets will thus be given commissions so as to fulfil the expectations that have been formed. My Lord, to permanently exclude all the upper classes of British India from ever serving their Emperor in the defence of their own country is, I venture to submit, incompatible with those noble principles of justice and generosity which have all along been accepted as determining the character of British rule in India.

There is one more suggestion in this connection that I would like to make in common justice alike to the taxpayers of British India and the Rulers and subjects of Native States. The suggestion is that after the glorious and soul-stirring ceremony held at Delhi it will be an act of wise statesmanship not to allow the spirit of solidarity and common interest which was witnessed there to remain unutilized for the welfare of the empire. My Lord, as things stand at present, the Imperial Army is bound to defend not only British India but the whole country, including the Native States. This, I submit, is unjust alike to the people of British India as also the Rulers of Native States, for the burden of meeting the entire expenditure of the Imperial Army falls at present exclusively on the taxpayers of British India, while on the other hand the Rulers of Native States – representatives of ancient and warlike dynasties, in whom the cherished traditions of a chequered past are still preserved – are precluded from taking their legitimate place in the defence of this great Empire. Of course, my Lord, I am aware of the existence of the Imperial Service Troops, but their numbers are much smaller than the proportion according to population that would have to be maintained by the Native States if in India there was a system of recruiting according to population or territorial extent. My object in mentioning this is not to suggest that an additional burden be imposed on the shoulders of Native States nor that any Imperial bills be presented to the Rulers of these States for payment. But when, my Lord, as at present, a large irregular armed force is maintained by the various Rulers and a large expenditure is borne by their subjects, it is (specially after the great Imperial ceremony at Delhi, when the collective devotion of the whole of India to the person and throne of the King-Emperor was declared to the world) clearly to the welfare of both the Imperial and feudatory Governments to bring this armed but practically wasted force not only to the highest standard of efficiency but also to bring it within the system of Imperial defence, of course under the direct peace and war command of His Excellency the Commander-in-Chief.

My Lord, to make such a force really efficient and to win for it the confidence of the public, of course it would be necessary to place a small number of carefully picked British officers in charge just as has been done with such unique success in the case of the Egyptian Army. My Lord, what has been carried out in Egypt in spite of the great difficulties connected with the British occupation of that Province and in spite of the constant intrigues of some of the Great Powers and the interference of Turkey, the Suzerain of Egypt, ought to be done easily enough with the Native States whose Rulers one and all deem it their greatest privilege to be under the paramountcy and protection of British power. My Lord, I admit this proposal as submitted on the present occasion will appear to be the crude and visionary fancy of an irresponsible dreamer, but the presence at the present moment at the head of the Indian Army of the great and most distinguished General who carried out those remarkable reforms in the Egyptian Army and raised even the despised fellaheen to be trustworthy and loyal troops worthy of fighting by the side of the flower of the British Army emboldens me to hope that this proposal may commend itself to Your Excellency's Government. My Lord, this method of placing the whole of their forces under the direction of the Imperial Commander-in-Chief and under the control of superior officers nominated by the Imperial Commander-in-Chief was accepted after the unification of Germany by the Rulers of Saxony, Wurtemberg, Baden and all the other smaller States of the German Empire. Yet the Rulers of these States had been up till then Rulers of International Sovereign States and the equals of the Kings of Prussia. But with Imperial unity it was at once accepted by all as a self-evident axiom that there could be no particularism in military affairs. What was found necessary by all the Rulers of German States is, I venture to suggest, equally necessary in India, only even more so. Here there are no International Sovereigns, no equal allies, but one and all feudatories and tributaries, proud to acknowledge in a spirit of whole-hearted loyalty and devotion the absolute paramountcy of the Imperial Government. My Lord, then why should this particularism in military affairs, which means in practice burdening the Imperial Exchequer with maintaining a larger force than its proper share and at the same time burdening the treasuries of the feudatories with the cost of a force that is practically useless for its only use, namely, Imperial defence, be allowed to continue? My Lord, such a system as has been suggested above would of course add enormously not only to the influence of the Rulers of these States, but would make them important participators in the responsibility and privilege of fighting for their Emperor and defending their own country. My Lord, I fear that this suggestion may perhaps be misapprehended in certain quarters, but I would appeal to the patriotism of the Rulers of the Native States and ask them to consider whether such a course will not in the end be found to be the best and highest interest of all – preventing a considerable waste of resources which are sadly needed in the present state of the country for the great work of national education and bringing appreciable relief to the Exchequers of both the Imperial Government and the Native States. Of course, my proposition implies that in proportion as the irregular troops of Native States are brought under the supervision of British officers to the standard of efficiency and included within the regular system of Imperial defence, the Indian Army maintained by the Imperial Government will be correspondingly reduced.

My Lord, every care must of course be taken that such reorganized troops of each Native State would wear the uniforms of their own State and carry the colours of their Chief and all the traditional emblems associated with each princely House. The Chiefs, moreover, would be able to command the allegiance of the troops not merely as Rulers but also as their Honorary Commanders. I think, my Lord, such an arrangement will greatly enhance the dignity and prestige of the several Chiefs. Again, my Lord, if the personal inclination of the Rulers was, as it probably in the great majority of cases will be, towards an active military life, he could by studying military science become also the active Commander of his troops and with the advice of the British officers supervising his troops be able to command his own men in time of war. This would be, if I am right, analogous to the position of the German ruling Princes towards their own particular army, and what has been done with such conspicuous success in Germany may, there is every reason to hope, be achieved with equal success in India. My Lord, the spirit of unity which moved the German Princes during the ceremony held in the Hall of Mirrors to this day breathes through the German system of defence. Is it too much to hope that that spirit of loyalty and devotion, which was so evident in the great ceremony at Delhi, may live for ever in India as an active force in our system of Imperial defence, and out of it may come not only a greater military power under the control of the Imperial Government than at present but also release for both the Imperial Government and the Native States the resources by which they can through systematic education raise the whole standard of general intelligence and advance the moral welfare and the material prosperity of this great country?

Source: *Abstract of the Proceedings of the Council of the Governor General of India Assembled for the Purpose of Making Laws and Regulations*, Vol. XLII, Calcutta, 1903, pp. 91–7.

The Aga Khan was the first speaker in the debate after the Hon'ble Sir Edward Law had moved that the Financial Statement for 1903–4 be taken into consideration. He was followed by the Raja of Sirmur.

4

THE FINANCES OF INDIA – II

Budget Speech in the Council of the Governor General

Calcutta: 30 March 1904

Russian expansion – India must be alert and prepared – the burden of Imperial defence must be borne equitably by the Imperial Government and the Princely States – every chief should contribute some money towards Imperial defence – advantage of instituting an Imperial Cadet Corps – give commissions in the Indian Army to successful cadets – appoint others as officers of the Imperial Service Troops – foster the ideal of a united country among the princes.

My Lord, I congratulate Your Excellency's Government on the prosperous condition of the finances of India as exhibited by the Budget Statement for the coming year which the Hon'ble the Finance Minister presented to the Council last week. A careful study of that statement has convinced me that there has been during the past year a steady, though slow improvement in the economic conditions of the country.

My Lord, last year, at the close of the great and very weighty speech Your Lordship was pleased to deliver on the occasion of this same discussion, you drew attention to the great and momentous changes that were taking place throughout Asia – changes that were certain to affect the political and military interests of this great country, and Your Lordship was pleased to say that "they require that our forces shall be in a state of high efficiency, our defences secure and our schemes of policy carefully worked out and defined. Above all they demand a feeling of solidarity and common interest among those (and they include every inhabitant of this country from the Raja to the raiyat) whose interests are wrapped up in the preservation of the Indian Empire both for the sake of India itself and for the wider welfare of mankind". The prophecy has come true sooner than most of Your Lordship's hearers last year expected. We now live in stirring times and hear the din and clash of arms in North-Eastern Asia. A Power that has been looming larger and larger on this Continent and has made the boundaries of her possessions almost contiguous on the North-west to the boundaries of India or of countries in which the people of India are vitally interested has now become a permanent menace to this country. History teaches us that the Muscovite when prevented from expansion on one side of his frontier naturally turns to another where he fancies the forces of resistance to be in less capable hands (witness expansion in Central Asia after the failure of Russian designs in the Balkans in 1878); so the fact that the Power that threatens the peace of this country seems to be failing in expanding in the Far East is the very reason why we should not feel more secure or less anxious about our defensive forces. We hear from all sources that troops are being massed in Central Asia. Misunderstanding the pacific disposition of the British Government and the perhaps too frequent occasions on which that Government gave way to her pretensions, Russia thought the time had come to use menaces when cajolery had failed. I refer to the communications which passed between the Russian Ambassador and Lord Lansdowne (which were recently published) regarding Thibet. They indicate that we must be constantly on the alert and be ever ready to defend ourselves if we wish to secure to this country the blessings of peace. It is, in fact, a necessary condition of our immunity from foreign invasion that our military power and organisation should always be in a state of high efficiency so as to remove from our neighbour the temptation of interfering with us. At such a juncture it seems to me necessary to consider whether the burdens which this state of constant preparedness and high efficiency entails on the Government of India are borne fairly and equitably by all those who are benefited thereby and whose possessions thereby are safeguarded against foreign intrusion. In order to ascertain this I venture to give a few figures. Roughly speaking, two-thirds of India proper is under the direct control of the Government of India and one-third of it is under the Government of the Feudatory States. At the same time, according to the Census of 1901, the population of the Native States was one-fourth of the entire population of India. The military expenditure of the Government of India has risen (and I for one do not grudge a penny of it) to £18,250,000. So for purposes of Imperial defence and in order to protect from invasion this country, one-third the area and one-fourth the population of which belongs to the Native States, the Government have no option but to spend quite 25 per cent of the entire revenues of British India. Now let us consider whether and to what extent these States contribute towards this Imperial defence. Their aggregate revenues amount to well over £15,500,000 a year. Now, if the burden of Imperial defence were borne by the Imperial and the Feudatory Governments equitably, that is, proportionately to their revenues, the annual contribution by these Native States ought to be considerably over £3,500,000 a year. Now what do they contribute? In 1888 many Chiefs offered assistance in the defence of the North-West Frontier by placing large sums of money at the disposal of the Supreme Government. The offers of money were declined. But being renewed in another form, viz., as offers of troops for Imperial service, such renewed offers were at once willingly accepted by [the] Government. A scheme (which, my Lord, was then really in the nature of an experiment) was organised by which it was expected that the States would be able to render efficient aid to the Supreme Government in times of emergency by providing Imperial Service Troops capable of taking their place in line with the regiments of the Imperial Army. When the scheme was started it was believed that quite 25,000 would be supplied, and unless I am greatly mistaken some such number was promised. But there was one flaw in the scheme. From a delicacy of feeling (a delicacy of feeling that was then justified since the scheme was an experiment only) [the] Government left it entirely to the Chiefs to provide or not provide Imperial Service Troops and thereafter to maintain the same number or more or less according as their patriotism dictated. The result of this voluntary system has been what was to be expected. Some have (as the figures laid on the table of this Council by Sir Edmond Elles prove) actually reduced their troops, and the total number of effective troops is now under 15,000. The generous enthusiasm which has hitherto animated many of the patriotic and far-sighted Chiefs and induced them honourably to carry out (and in some cases like that of that great, wise and patriotic Prince His Highness Maharaja Scindhia more than carry out) their original promises to the Supreme Government may unfortunately not be shared by their successors. Moreover, while some of the Chiefs like His Highness the Maharaja Scindhia and the patriotic rulers of the Rajputana and the Punjab States and of the States of Bhownaggar, Jamnagar and Junagad in Kathiawar maintain a considerable number of Imperial Service Troops, there are others (by no means unimportant or petty rulers) who do not maintain even one Imperial Service trooper. They thus altogether escape the burden of bearing their fair share of Imperial defence.

But, my Lord, my arguments for organising a system by which each State should set aside a settled proportion of its revenues for maintaining Imperial Service Troops is not based on a mean desire to make the subjects of the Native States contribute towards Imperial defence in order to save the British Indian taxpayers from paying more in the future. It is as much in the interests of the Rulers of the Native States that they and their armies should take an active, important and honourable part in the great work of Imperial defence as it is in the interests of the Supreme Government. Companionship in arms will more than anything bring about that feeling of solidarity, of unity and of devoted loyalty to the Emperor that is the aim and object of every one of the Protected Princes of India. Such a system would add enormously to the importance and the responsibilities of the Feudatory Chiefs. It would open honourable and suitable careers (as officers) for the hereditary Sirdars, Thakores and Nobles of each and every State. My Lord, if properly carried out this scheme need not add anything serious to the financial burdens of the Native States, nor reduce the amounts now devoted by Rulers of such States towards useful civil improvements. The Chiefs have always maintained and still maintain a large army of their own, amounting to nearly 100,000 men, which is, I am sure, always at the service of [the] Government for purposes of Imperial defence. I have, however, no hesitation in saying that for these purposes such heterogeneous bodies of 'mere men with muskets' would be quite useless. These men differently or rather indifferently armed, drilled and equipped would be absolutely incapable of fighting against the trained forces of a European foe. The maintenance of such bodies of men, which can only by courtesy be called armies, is an utter frittering away of the resources of the country and dissipation of its means of defence. I would therefore respectfully suggest that [the] Government should propose to the Chiefs that they should in a given number of years disband these men, who are useless for all purposes except for empty show, and that every Chief should contribute a definite percentage of his revenues towards Imperial defence. I am sure there is not one Chief so wanting in patriotism as to object to such a fair proposal. On the contrary, I am certain that the loyal and patriotic Princes who assembled last year at Delhi would be only too eager to adopt such a proposal. The whole scheme of Imperial Service troops was originally an experiment. If the experiment has been successful, why should it not be extended? The so-called armies of the Chiefs would be replaced by men who would add to the glory of their rulers and who would be worthy of fighting by the side of the flower of the British army. The States which now spend large sums on useless bodies of men dignified by the name of armies will get a genuine Army of which they may well be proud without any serious addition to the expenditure side of their Annual Budgets. If these reorganised troops are to be of any use and able to take their place in line with the regiments of the Imperial Army, they must be under the immediate and direct control of the Commander-in-Chief. There would be nothing in this arrangement in any way injurious to the right of the several Ruling Chiefs. Even the Sovereigns of the various German States, who are the equal allies of the Kings of Prussia and in no way subjected to their Emperor, when they joined the Imperial Confederation in 1871 placed their troops under the Imperial Commander-in-Chief. In fact, unless these reorganised troops were under the direct command of the Commander-in-Chief during peace, it would be impossible to place any reliance on their efficiency, and the Commander-in-Chief could never depend on their being as good as the troops that were trained under his direct control and supervision. The Commander-in-Chief would appoint inspecting officers to such reorganised troops, while the Ruling Chiefs would retain command of their own corps, who would, of course, carry the colours and the emblems of each princely house, and if the tastes of the Prince made him turn to an active study of military subjects then of course such a Prince would naturally be not only the *de jure* but the *de facto* Commander of his own troops, receiving only his *military* orders from the Commander-in-Chief. My Lord, this scheme may appear of little value since no ruler has suggested it. But I think it is but my duty to explain that these suggestions are not my own original ideas but that I have borrowed them more or less from various Princes who attended the Delhi Durbar last year and the Coronation Ceremony in 1902. I have no right or authority to use their names. But so much I think I have a right to ask every one here to assume, that there is no Prince so wanting in patriotism and loyalty as to reject these suggestions without giving the matter careful and sympathetic consideration. My Lord, the suggestions I have just ventured to make are both rough and crude, but it is for the Ruling Chiefs and the Government of India to evolve some permanent system by which the Feudatory States may enjoy the privilege of sharing with the

Government of India the power of adequately defending this great country. My Lord, there has been recently a tendency to maintain transports only. I fear it is not quite in keeping with the dignity of a powerful State that entertains hundreds of useless but costly soldiers of its own to refuse to keep any active Imperial Service Troops on the ground of expense and offers to maintain transports only. Transports are undoubtedly essential, but from the point of view of those who wish to see the bonds of common interest between the Imperial and Feudatory States tightened it is a backward step when lancers and infantry are changed into transports. Of course let it be clearly understood that I suggest that the present useless armies should be converted into one corps of efficient Imperial Service Troops in every State and not that the present men should be kept on as well as additions made to the Imperial Service Troops. The rich zamindars who enjoy impartible estates and thus are specially cared for by the State may well be invited to maintain a certain amount of transports. Carts and ponies will, no doubt, entail a certain initial expense, but afterwards such transports during peace time will cost practically very little or nothing, since they will easily earn enough to pay for the expenses of maintenance.

My Lord, I feel it but my duty to thank Your Excellency for establishing the Imperial Cadet Corps of Native Princes and Nobles. This excellent institution was a desideratum, and among the many and great benefits which Your Excellency's Viceroyalty has already conferred upon this country, I would look upon it as one of the greatest. If Your Excellency will permit me to say so, it was a brilliant idea conceived in a happy moment and carried out to the great gratification of the Native Princes and Nobles. Their rank, traditional prestige and natural tastes debar them from every but a military career, and that Your Excellency has, by embodying the corps, opened the possibility of a military career to them proves your deep personal interest in their welfare. They yield to none in loyalty and attachment to their beloved Emperor and country, and such an institution, the credit of initiating which justly belongs to Your Excellency, affords them a unique opportunity of serving both. At no inconsiderable expense to themselves, many have come forward and volunteered for such service. But permit me to say that at present there is no certainty as to the future of the cadets. May I venture at this stage to ask whether the time has not yet come when a few commissions in the Indian Army may not be annually given, say, to three or four of the most successful of the Imperial cadets, who one day may be the pride of their country and achieve that glory which their forefathers had attained in byegone days. Is it too much to ask that three or four of the cadets, who might pass all the necessary tests and in whose character and integrity the commandant of the corps might repose absolute confidence, be nominated by the Viceroy, with the sanction of the Emperor, to commissions in the Indian Army? My Lord, while the Government of India trusts any young Indian, whatever his antecedents, whatever his character, who happens to get a certain number of marks at a competitive examination, to administer districts that often equal in size and population European Principalities, while the Government of India trust tens of thousands of every class and of every community to wear as sepoys the honoured uniform of the Indian Army, is the Government yet unable to see its way to trust even one of the Emperor's Indian subjects with the honour of being a regular commissioned officer? But I am sure that mistrust or want of confidence is not the cause of this singular omission. I rather put it down to the innate conservatism of the British race that is satisfied to leave things alone until it becomes such a grave scandal that its removal becomes an imperative duty. The same spirit of conservatism left our University reforms though badly needed in the background until Your Excellency's Government with characteristic benevolent energy and courage of conviction carried the measure of much-needed reform by the great Act which passed into law only the other day. My Lord, there are some objections to this scheme which I have often heard and which I will venture to try and dispose of. In the first place it is asserted in some quarters that there is no young man in India whose educational and moral training fits him for being an officer. This may have been true in the past. But since the formation of the Imperial Cadet Corps we have a right to expect that a few of the cadets after three or four years' training under the direct supervision and constant care of commanding officers may be deemed worthy and capable of receiving a commission. Even if after three or four years' training under such favourable conditions as prevail in the Imperial Cadet Corps, if there is not yet one noble youth worthy of being an officer, then, my Lord, there must be something so radically wrong and incredibly defective in the moral or intellectual fibre of the Chiefs and nobles of this country that the sooner Chiefs' Colleges and Cadets Corps are abolished the better for all. Another objection raised is that these cadet officers would crowd the Indian Army and thus change its character! If it was suggested that a competitive examination should be held and such as passed

229

the test should be one and all enrolled as officers of the Indian Army, then I admit it might change the character of the army and none would be more strongly opposed to it than myself. Even if it was suggested that ten officers should be appointed every year, I should still oppose it. But, my Lord, the appointment of three or four a year could never change the character of the army. At the end of twenty years, even if there was no natural wastage, their number would be eighty in the whole of India. But we all know that when we take wastage into consideration, we should find not eighty but probably fifty in twenty years. Now, my Lord, I do hope this will not be called a wild, visionary or immoderate scheme. A third argument against the scheme that has come to my ears is the difficulty about messing. However, a large section of His Majesty's subjects have no caste rules whatsoever, nor have they any religious prejudice about dining with Europeans. I refer, of course, to the Muhammadans. We also know that a large and very rapidly growing number of Mahratta, Rajput and Sikh princes do openly dine with Europeans, Jews and Muhammadans. I think there would be no difficulty under this head. Another objection is that these cadets would be as Commanders superior to European officers. However, no one is insane enough to propose that cadets should be directly given commands of battalions and squadrons or be specially promoted. It would take a score of years at least before any of them got command of his regiment, and I am sure that after twenty years' comradeship in a regiment where he would have already won the respect and friendship of his European brother officers, they would willingly serve under an ex-cadet. One other objection is that the European officers would not welcome Indian brother officers. I am sure it is only those who do not know the British officer that can accuse him of such blind racial prejudice. The officers of the British and Indian Army are the pick and the flower of the manhood of England. They are the cream of society. Gentle, just and noble alike by birth, tradition and temperament, they judge men not by their race and colour or creed, but by their intrinsic merits. If the cadets were well selected – and it is absolutely essential to the success of the scheme that every scrutiny and care should be taken that none except those of high moral and intellectual calibre should be selected – then, I for one am quite sure that ex-cadet officers would very soon be as popular as any European officer in their regiments, provided, of course, they behaved themselves properly and acted up to a high and model standard of duty. There is no doubt that in due time some of them would prove to be ideal officers. I have tried to meet all the objections that I have ever heard and I have asked only for a moderate and reasonable concession, a concession which, I hope, will, if made, prove to be a boon which will be gratefully accepted and acknowledged. I do hope that there is no one here who considers this suggestion of mine as wild, visionary or impracticable. My Lord, you have won the everlasting gratitude of the people of this country by your generous endeavours for the improvement of the Indian educational system in all its branches, the advancement of the agricultural classes, their relief from perpetual and harassing indebtedness, and your noble desire for the restoration of ancient monuments, which both Hindus and Muhammadans prize so highly, and also by taking up the question of much needed police reform, railway and irrigation improvements and many other reforms in the administration of this country too numerous to mention. Now that Your Excellency has removed so many abuses, conferred such numerous boons upon the people, will not Your Excellency settle this difficult question in the interest of the cadets, who owe their existence to Your Lordship's foresight. My Lord, I am appealing to one who has not only been a great ruler but who has proved himself an exalted but none the less devoted and true friend and patron of the princes, chiefs and nobles of India.

My Lord, the Members who are not recommended for nomination to this Council by public bodies are at a certain disadvantage here, for their words are naturally supposed to come from them alone, and rarely carry the same moral weight with the Government as do the suggestions of their more fortunate Colleagues – the recommended Members. All the same, I think I am right in saying that when I earnestly appeal that three or four Cadets – and I appeal only for three or four – should be selected after a most careful and rigid scrutiny by the Viceroy for commissions in the Indian Army, I have behind me the sympathy and approval of every prince, Chief and noble in India. My Lord, there seems to be no reason why such cadets as may qualify themselves by capacity, zeal and industry and also win the respect and affection of the Commandant of the Corps, should not be rewarded with commissions in the Indian Army. If such a prospect is ever held out to them, as the reward of an exemplary moral character and of diligent study, I am sure that the scions of the best and noblest of all the families in India would flock to the Cadet Corps and [the] Government would prove and convince the people of this country that their Emperor has full faith in their unflinching loyalty to him and treats all his subjects alike. The remaining less successful cadets could be appointed as officers of the Imperial Service Troops. Regarding the question of Imperial Service Troops and of affording to all the Native States an opportunity of contributing towards their maintenance, I feel confident that such an opportunity will be eagerly embraced by those States. It will enable them to prove that the Chiefs are worthy of being Your Excellency's colleagues in the government of this country as Your Lordship so felicitously described them. It will show to those outside our frontiers whom it may concern that India no longer consists of segregated units with different aims and inconsistent aspirations. It will weld together and consolidate those units into a homogeneous and harmonious whole and foster and realize the ideal of a united country in the minds of these princes. They will have the proud satisfaction of knowing that, come what may, they and their troops will stand shoulder to shoulder with the armies of their Emperor and present a bold and united front to the enemies of their country, and that they have at their back the world-wide Empire based on liberty, justice and righteousness of which both the Raja and the raiyat may well thank heaven that they form a part.

Source: *Abstract of the Proceedings of the Council of the Governor General of India Assembled for the Purpose of Making Laws and Regulations*, Vol. XLIII, Calcutta, 1904, pp. 491–9.

The Aga Khan spoke immediately after Gokhale, and he was, as in the preceding year, followed by the Raja of Sirmur.

5

THE TRUE PURPOSE OF EDUCATION

Speech at the Muslim Educational Conference

Bombay: 1904

Welcome to the delegates – the significance of the Conference – pessimism in the Muslim world – Muslim conferences are a sign of progress – unity among the delegates – the true objects of education – Muslim aspirations for a university – the purpose of the university – the richness of Muslim history – a Muslim atmosphere in the institution.

The assembly to his mind represented all that was best in the Muslims of India. It expressed that awakening sense of their fallen position after a glorious past; it expressed dissatisfaction with their present intellectual, moral and social position; and it expressed the longing desire to regain the intellectual freedom which Muslims enjoyed during the first two centuries of their era. Pessimism was not the force, said the Aga Khan, that had drawn them there that day. Pessimism in the Muslim world was nothing new. It had been, unfortunately, the dominant impulse in such intellectual life as Muslims had had during the last century. Pessimism dominated all modern Persian, Arabic and Turkish poetry. What but pessimism could explain those feverish but constant references to Andalus, to Seville, to Toledo, to Cordova. The forces that had made these annual conferences successful, nay a necessity for the Muslims of the day, were other than pessimistic.

Speaking of the blessing of the British rule, the Aga Khan said:

"I think I am right in saying that one of the forces that has drawn us willy-nilly into assembling here is a growing hopefulness and spirit of optimism amongst our co-religionists in India – a sense of hopefulness directly and entirely due to British rule. Providence has given us a government that guarantees justice; intellectual and religious liberty; personal freedom; a government that gives a clear field and no favour, that constantly, by its acts, reminds us that fitness is the only test, and that for the fit there are no artificial obstacles. We must, if we wish to lead, concentrate all our energies on acquiring those arts that prove fitness under civilised conditions. At last we see signs of dawn. At last we see the dim light of dawning reason. It will be hours yet – in the life of a people decades are but hours – before the sunshine of knowledge penetrates into our homes, but still we see the signs of dawn."

Of the importance of the Conference, His Highness said:–

"Friendly critics have said that we have held many conferences, made many speeches, and many addresses have been delivered, many resolutions passed but that results are still wanting, and that still we Muslims remain behind whenever we are compared with other Indian nationalities on the educational test. This criticism expresses but half the truth. Such critics forget that for us these Conferences are signs of progress. Could a Conference such as this have been held in Bombay 20 years ago? I think not.

"A great historian has said that if St. Paul or Gautama Buddha visited St. Peter's or the Chief monastery of Lhassa or Kandy, they would not at first realise what was the object of the magnificent ceremonial they would there behold. But if the Prophet saw Santa Sophia or the Musjids of Delhi to-day he would find the ceremonial the same as it was in his day at Mecca and Medina. This is true of the ceremonial. But what about the personnel? How different the case is there. The sects, the sectarian differences, the divisions and sub-divisions that have crept even into the simple and clear faith of Islam – how they would pain and surprise the founder?

"However, here for the cause of learning, for the cause of progress, is an assembly where, thank God, differences are forgotten. Here we see once more the unity of early Islam. Is this not progress? Is this not a great step towards salvation? It is a fortunate circumstance that at last we have awakened to the necessity of knowledge.

"There are some dangers ahead and I venture to draw your attention to some of them which we can now guard against. It would be the greatest of all our misfortunes if we now mistook instruction for education and the mere power of passing examinations for learning. It is for this reason that the thoughtful welcome the reform of the Universities which the Government of India now contemplates. It is for this reason that the far-sighted amongst the Muslims of India desire a University where the standard of learning shall be the highest and where with scientific training there shall be that moral education – that indirect but constant reminder of the eternal difference between right and wrong which is the soul of education. It is a source of regret for many of us that in the Indian Universities there is that divorce between learning and religion which, especially in the case of Muslims, will, I fear, lead to disaster. Gentlemen, most Muslims, I think, would most gladly welcome a Hindu University, at Benares; we would gladly welcome another at Poona, a third in Bengal or Madras. But because there is evidently no desire on their part to have a sectarian University with a Brahminical atmosphere, it is absurd to deny us a University at Aligarh with affiliated colleges all over India. Another reason why we require a Central University where our individuality may not be lost for the sake of turning out a mechanical imitation of a European is this: we have a history in which noble and chivalrous characters abound; we have a religious past so full of heroic figures that direct contact and communion with them could not but improve and give our youth early in life that sense of the necessity for self-sacrifice, for truthfulness, and for independence of character without which instruction and knowledge are, from the national point of view, worthless.

"It may be said such noble characters also abound in the histories of Greece and of Rome; what need for the study of the history of Arabs? Yes, Englishmen and Frenchmen, the direct successors of Romans, they can and do feel that the glorious characters of Roman history belong to them in a very real sense. Not so for the Muslim youth of this country. For most of us, even the noblest of them remain to the end but distant figures without any direct attraction. Yet Muslim history is so full of heroic characters or men, who lived and moved very much as the Muslims of today in their home life do, that contact with them could not but ennoble. Muavia and Walid are as statesmen not eclipsed either by Caesar or Augustus; and where can you find in the annals of any dynasty, whether European or Asiatic, a more saintly sovereign than Omar Ibn Abdul Aziz or a more exemplary Emperor than Hisham Ibn Abdul Malik? Direct contact with such great characters could not but strengthen the character of our youth and thus the character of our people. We may have crowds and battalions of graduates – it does not follow that they will be self-sacrificing men who will remove those degenerating customs that keep us not merely amongst the backward, but amongst the fallen. Those painful and those pernicious social customs that have so crept, in the course of centuries, into our religious rites that now even Muslims who are by no means uninstructed, do not know the difference between such customs and the commandments of the founder. Islamism is wrongly supposed to be responsible for such customs. It is for this, gentlemen, that I beg of you to give a thought while yet there is time towards the methods by which you propose to educate your youth. It is for this that I beg of you, gentlemen, to remember that we are a M.A.O. educational and not an instructional conference. It is for this that I beg of you that the cause of a Central University – a University which, please Heaven, may rank some day with Oxford and Leipzig and Paris as a home of great ideas and noble ideal – a University where our youth may receive the highest instruction in the Sciences of the West, a University where the teaching of history and literature of the East may not be scamped over for a mere parrot-like knowledge of Western thought, a University where our youth may also enjoy, in addition to such advantages, a Muslim atmosphere, – I earnestly beg of you that the cause of such a University should not be forgotten in the shouts of the marketplace that daily rise amongst us."

Source: Naoroji M. Dumasia, *The Aga Khan and His Ancestors*, The Times of India Press, Bombay, 1939, pp. 184–8.

The Aga Khan made his speech in his capacity as Chairman of the Reception Committee for the annual general session of the Muslim Educational Conference held in Bombay city. The president of the Conference for this year was Badruddin Tayebji.

On the general problem of Muslim education in India see John R. Mott (ed.), *The Muslim World of Today*, London, 1925; An Indian Mohamedan [Nawab Sayyid Sirdar Ali Khan], *The Indian Muslims*, London, 1928; Zia-ud-Din, *Muhammadan India: Its Today and Tomorrow*, Lahore, 1897; Nawab Abdul Lateef Khan, *A Short Account of My Public Life*, Calcutta, 1885; Abdullah Yusuf Ali, *Muslim Educational Ideals*, Lahore, 1923; M. M. Zahuruddin Ahmad, *Present Day Problems of Indian Education, with Special Reference to Muslim Education*, Bombay, 1935; Sayyid Amir Ali Bilgrami, *English Education in India*, Madras, 1902; F. K. K. Durrani, *A Plan of Muslim Educational Reforms*, Lahore, n.d.; Sayyid Nurullah and J. P. Naik, *History of Education in India During the British Period*, Bombay, 1943; Arthur Mayhew, *The Education of India: A Study of British Educational Policy in India, 1835–1920, and its Bearing on National Life and Problems in India Today*, London, 1926; Liaquat Ali Khan, *Muslim Educational Problems*, Lahore, 1945; Abdul Karim, *Muhammadan Education in Bengal*, Calcutta, 1900; M. Azizul

Huque, *History and Problems of Muslim Education in Bengal*, Calcutta, 1917; Syud Ameer Hossein, *A Pamphlet on Muhammadan Education in Bengal*, Calcutta, 1880; Philip Hartog, *Some Aspects of Indian Education Past and Present*, London, 1939; Herbert Birdwood, "The Queen as a Muhammadan Sovereign", *National Review*, December 1897; M. Abdul Halim, "The Problem of Muslim Education", *Journal of the Muslim Institute*, January-June 1909; A. N. Hydari, "The Problem of Muhammadan Education", *Indian Review*, January 1918; H. J. Lane-Smith, "Illiteracy Among Indian Muslims", *Muslim World*, April 1919; Chaudhri Shahabuddin, "Muslim Educational Ideals", *The Civil and Military Gazette*, 21 October 1923; A. Rahman, "Our Educational Institutions", *Muslim Revival*, September 1933; and Abdullah Yusuf Ali, "What is Wrong with Education?", *Muslim Revival*, September 1935 (reprinted from the *Hindustan Review*).

6

THE DEFENCE OF INDIA

An Article

London: September 1905

Reasons for his interest in the defence of India – the Russian threat – boundaries between India and Russia – need for buffer states – the British presence in India through conquest or by force of circumstances – majority of Indians appreciate British rule – Russia could exploit the disaffection among the Indians who resent British rule – proposals for neutral buffer zones – the British should refrain from acquiring predominance in the neutral zones – instead win confidence of countries like Afghanistan – implications for the army of a contiguous border with Russia – make use of local resources to strengthen the Indian army – reorganise the troops of the native States and utilise them for India's defence.

I owe an apology to the readers of this influential Review for placing before them the following observations. It may well be considered extremely rash for a non-military man to express any opinion on such a technical subject as the one which I propose to treat in this paper, knowing, as I do, that the ablest men in the service of this Empire, and some of the most instructed of our public writers have made the subject a life-long study, and have devoted their most careful attention to it, more especially since the first Afghan war. For another reason also an apology is, I think, due from me to my readers, since, although acquainted with it from my childhood, the English language is not my mother tongue, and it may perhaps be hazardous for me to give expression to my thoughts and views in a language that is not my own. My excuse for doing so is that for more than eight years I have studied the question of the defence of India in its wider aspects with great care, and I may add that I have read, and in some cases re-read, most of the valuable books, articles, and despatches which have at any time been published on the subject. Moreover, being myself an Asiatic, I have not only had opportunities of visiting many of the regions which form the landward boundaries of India to the west, north, and east; but I have regularly received from people in those climes various kinds of information that do not ordinarily reach the ears of the soldier or the statesman.

For the same reason I have had the good fortune of becoming acquainted with the state of political affairs in Arabia, Persia, Mesopotamia, Afghanistan, and Chinese Turkestan. Knowing the political condition of the peoples of those countries, I have been irresistibly led to the conclusion that the maintenance of British rule in India is of vital necessity for the welfare of its 300 millions of people. It was this conclusion which turned my attention to the interesting problem how to safeguard India not only against foreign invasion, but also against the equally dangerous process, in the long run, of the increase of foreign moral influence within her borders. There are, if one carefully considers the matter, only two Powers which can ever really dangerously threaten British rule in India: China and Russia. The other European Powers in Asia, and also the Japanese, depend on the sea for their communications, and so long as British naval supremacy is assured, they can never become sources of real danger to India. The Asiatic States, with the exception of China, have, on the other hand, neither the population nor the resources for ever becoming a real menace to India . . .

We may, therefore, devote all our attention to Russia, since she alone has shown a desire to extend her dominions towards India. As a rodent gnaws ceaselessly through every barrier and obstacle placed in its path, and whenever disturbed or interrupted, stops gnawing for a time only to resume it with all the greater vigour – so Russia has gnawed her way through Central Asia, drawing ever nearer and nearer to the frontiers of India. One of the favourite methods in this process with which we have become familiar has been the sending of 'scientific expeditions' to the regions marked down for conquest. Another has been the employment of natives of the country coveted for the purpose of weakening its indigenous Government, and then when the fruit had become ripe to pluck it. Sometimes, indeed, as on "the bloody day of Geok Tepe," Russia has advanced with a big army; but, although the method has varied, the result has been the same, and it has gratified Russia's tremendous desire to come southwards, and right on to the Indian frontier.

Those who in any way have taken part in the discussion on the question of our relations with Russia in Asia may be divided, roughly speaking, into two main classes. Each of these classes may consist of several subdivisions differing from each other in questions of detail, but we need only concern ourselves with the two main bodies enunciating opposing principles. The first is composed of those who advocate a "forward policy" so that the boundaries of Russia in Central Asia may become contiguous to those of the British Empire of India on the west and north; and, perhaps, also, on the north-east. In India these persons are known as favouring what is called "a running frontier" with Russia.

The second class of authorities advocate the interposition of a wide neutral zone – really independent buffer States – between the possessions of Russia and the boundaries of India proper. I frankly confess that I belong to the latter class, and I will here state my reasons for this, briefly, but without any reservation.

It must ever be remembered that the position of England in India is essentially and fundamentally different from that of the French Government in France, or of the German in Germany, or even of the Russian Government in Central Asia. The Power that rules in France and Germany is not alien to the people. The nation in those countries, if dissatisfied with its Government, whether it be a confederation of dynasties as in Germany or a Republic as in France, can change it and set up some fresh system. But in such cases it would always be only the *form* of the Government and the *personnel* of the administration that would be changed. Without going into the question of a "social contract" on which some philosophers based the origin of every Government, it is enough for our purpose to say that the indigenous government of every country must owe its origin, or is assumed to owe its origin, to the expressed or implied consensus of its people, or of the large majority of them. The Government which exercised authority in England after the Norman conquest may at its inception have been foreign; but in the course of centuries the rulers and the ruled have become welded and fused into one people and one nation. Thus to-day it cannot be said that the ruling dynasty in Great Britain is a foreign dynasty, or that Great Britain is governed by foreign rulers. Similarly the Hapsburgs, the Hohenzollerns, and the Romanoffs, and in Persia the Kajjars, and in China the Manchus, may or may not have been foreigners in those countries when they began to rule; but now not one of those States can be considered to be under foreign rule in the sense in which India is at the present time. The present rulers of India have found themselves therein either by conquest, or by force of circumstances, or by the will of Providence, but certainly not by the will of its peoples.

Nor is there any likelihood of the rulers and the ruled, within the next few centuries, becoming fused or welded into one nation or one people in the European sense of the words. To begin with, there is no Indian nation at present, and even if in time the peoples of the country get fused into a single nation, they will differ too much in colour, race, and climatic characteristics ever to become one with their English fellow subjects. For the last half century a belief has been gaining ground in this congeries of races, which has now deepened into a conviction with the majority, that alien as the British rule is in India, it is the best of all the governments that the country has ever possessed, and that under its tutelage India has prospered, and its peoples advanced in a manner unapproached during any period of the past. Beyond a doubt the majority of the Indian peoples are convinced of the benefits of British rule, and feel devoted loyalty to the person of their Emperor.

But among 300 millions of people, there must be naturally some who . . . could be seduced from their loyalty to an alien Government, and would fall easy victims to the intrigues or the specious promises of Russia, if once that country became a neighbour of India, and if its railways were united with the Indian lines. It must be remembered that the Russian official classes are perfect adepts in intrigue, and that they would be profuse in making promises as to a coming millennium for all Asiatic races under Russia. Even already some Russian intriguers who have reached India have promised the establishment of a thousand native dynasties.

But even if Russia did not lend herself to intrigue, her very presence on the other side of the boundaries of India would be a disturbing element, for it would unsettle the native mind and create new hopes and new aspirations. It was Lord Dalhousie who said "We enjoy peace because we are strong." This remark is as true to-day as it was more than half a century ago. But the causes of strength are not merely military, moral, and economical[*sic.*]. One main cause is the absence of another strong and rival Power in the immediate vicinity, and having its boundaries contiguous to those of India. Russia, in Central Asia, has but 10 millions of Asiatics to govern, while England in India has 300 millions. Knowing what Russia is, I say that if her territory lay immediately on the other side of the Indian frontier, it would prove a very hotbed for fostering sedition and disloyalty in India. Moreover, the constant and unrestrained intercourse that would necessarily follow between that territory and India would result in the spreading of such sedition and disloyalty throughout India as might lead to constant troubles, and eventually to the weakening of the authority of the British Government, and possibly even to its overthrow.

For these reasons certain regions west, north, and east of India should be kept as buffers between that country and Russia, and Russia should be made to understand distinctly that any overstepping of the limits which may be thus set to her ambition would be treated as a *casus belli*, and would be followed by hostilities. Great Britain should also make up her mind to fight once for all to keep Russia out of the neutral zone or buffer region.

What are the regions that we must keep Russia out of? Since the object of keeping her away from these regions is not essentially military, but rather fundamentally to prevent her disturbing India, we must carefully consider what are the lands that do influence Indian thought, and that are near enough to be frequented by Indians. For reasons historical as well as geographical, because these lands have been closely associated with the destinies of India, I would suggest that the regions to be kept as a neutral zone should begin with Mesopotamia in the extreme west, and include the Shat-ul-Arab, the Hassa, and Oman along the western shore of the Persian Gulf. Coming further east, the whole of Persia, south of Azerbaijan, Teheran, and Khorassan, forms an essential part of the buffer region, as also does the kingdom of Afghanistan. I would also include the southern districts of the present province of Chinese Turkestan with the important towns of Yarkand and Khotan, Thibet, and lastly the two Chinese provinces of Szechuan and Yunnan.

I have now named the territories which it appears to me to be necessary to preserve as a neutral zone for the security of India. Possibly these may be considered too extensive, and a more restricted area may be deemed sufficient, and certainly it may be allowed that some of the regions indicated can be left untouched and undefined for the present. But whatever is considered necessary and sufficient should be declared "a neutral zone" after due deliberation by England as a whole, and not by a single party, and the Empire should unanimously accept that decision as a sort of Monroe Doctrine for Asia to be defended and enforced at all hazards by "war from pole to pole" (to use the words of the great and distinguished author of *Russia in Central Asia*) against any European Power that directly or indirectly sought to predominate over any part of the zone thus defined.

However, England, in order to enforce the policy of a neutral zone, must herself observe the self-denying ordinance, and not allow herself to be led by the advocates of a forward policy, or those officers who are tired of Afghan arrogance and Persian and Chinese pusillanimity, into acquiring a predominant position in any part of the neutral zone under one pretext or another. If, for example, instead of interfering with the affairs of Afghanistan, and constantly fretting because we have no railways and no politicals in that country, or seeking to forcibly extend "influence" there, we took care to inform its ruler and people that we should be ready to defend them if attacked by any foreign Power, but that otherwise we should let their country severely alone, and that we were resolved to follow the policy which in Lord Lawrence's time was known as "masterly inactivity," we should inspire them with confidence and win their friendship. Surely it was a man without the sense of humour who evolved the principle of forcing people into friendship, as advocated by some of the forward school. Again a want of knowledge of human nature is evident in people who maintain that Orientals respect only such men and Powers as bully them. Passionate though silent hatred, not respect, is the consequence of the high-handed use of force, and the breaking up of treaties, even amongst Oriental peoples.

The conquest and acquisition by England of territories beyond India proper is far more dangerous to us than the absorption of those lands by Russia would be. In the first place, we should have to fight the invader far away from our natural base, which is in itself a great drawback, as has been demonstrated by history both modern and ancient. Secondly, the population of the conquered countries would be at heart hostile to us; for though their Governments might be bad, they were in a sense national Governments, and they would make common cause with the invader, however foolish and shortsighted such a course might appear, just to get revenge on those who had upset their national institutions. These annexations would even furnish a further cause of moral disturbance in India . . . To my mind the right policy is to insist that the territories constituting the neutral zone should remain inviolate, and free from aggression by any Power, and that they should be independent in fact and in name. The policy that I advocate is precisely the same as that pursued by the United States towards the South American Republics. If we consistently follow this policy, if the Conservative party will dissociate itself from the extreme "forward school" that wants to turn Afghanistan into a "native State," and southern Persia into a "Malay State," if the Liberal party will sever its policy from the ultra-altruists who invite Russia to the doors of India – then the would-be invader of India would, in the first place, have to subjugate portions of the neutral zone before advancing upon India, and their populations would naturally fight for their own freedom, and to that extent would be our allies and fight our battles. Then our assistance would be received with gratitude, and without any suspicion of our good faith.

Another absolutely important reason for our pursuing the policy of neutral zones and buffer States, and of preventing the extension of either the Russian or the British Empire till they meet, is that while our present army in India is nearly – though not quite – sufficient for our needs, it would, in the case of a "running frontier," require to be at least three times its actual strength. Although she had only the extreme eastern frontier of Russia as her neighbour, Japan kept a force of a million men ready. The Imperial forces in India all told are now less than a quarter of a million. If we trebled the army in India, we should have to treble the European troops as well as the native sepoys. To find men for that purpose would be a feat that no Herculean Secretary of State for War could do without a tremendous increase of pay for Mr. Tommy Atkins. But even assuming that men for such an enormously increased English army were by great increase of pay to be found, who, out of a lunatic asylum, would venture to say that India could bear the strain of a trebled military budget?

If any India within our powers of conception could not pay for the increased army that would thus have become necessary not through any fault of its own, but because its rulers had chosen to extend their conquests beyond its frontiers, without allowing the peoples of India a voice in the matter, would the British taxpayers consent to contribute a mere bagatelle of some 25 or 30 millions sterling a year? It would be the men sent out indirectly by the British taxpayers to govern India that would decree and make these new conquests, and theirs would be the doubtful honour and glory thereof, and theirs the responsibility and liability of retaining and safeguarding the new conquests. I who have lived in England off and on for many years, and even went out of my way to study not only the ruling classes but the taxpayer, the man *par excellence* who, personally unknown, is yet the mainstay of the Empire – I know the average British taxpayer fairly well. He will ungrudgingly pay for a predominating navy, and will give, perhaps with a wry face, the necessary millions for a *just sufficient* army. But, I think, when a new annual bill of 30 millions sterling was presented to him, he would curse the people who had taken his peaceful Indian frontier up to the menacing lines of Russia, and he would refuse to pay this enormous and senseless fine.

India could not pay for the increased military expenditure, and John Bull would not.

Even if the present system of voluntary enlistment were replaced by conscription, such a change would not mend matters. To begin with, it is doubtful if a conscript would ever do garrison work on foreign soil, thousands of miles distant from home and friends. Secondly a conscript army must be a short-service army, and the increased portion of the British army would be needed not in England, but opposite the Russian lines on the Asiatic frontier. As it is, with a comparatively long-service army, the waste and expense of transport is enormous, and once real short service of two years was introduced, as would have to be done on the adoption of conscription, then the constant change of drafts would become such a terrible waste, for it would be annual, that millions would be thrown away in merely bringing and taking away the troops to and from India. Above all, even limited conscription is not yet popular amongst the English masses, and though, I think, for home defence it would be a good thing, still, a conscript army in India would, I am persuaded, be found impossible.

We are thus forced back to the policy of a neutral zone and buffer States. But, as I have already said, such a policy must be honestly and disinterestedly carried out, and above all must be rigidly enforced against every delinquent. For the successful carrying out of such a policy, we require, though a much smaller force than for the other policy of a "running frontier" with Russia, a thoroughly efficient army, and also the proper husbanding of the fighting forces of India. We are exceptionally lucky in having at this moment one of the greatest of European soldiers, and one of the ablest organisers the world has seen since Carnot, in Lord Kitchener at the head of the Indian army. If he is given a free hand, and, above all, left in India long enough to finish his great work (for even he can do little if he has to vacate his post after five short years), then, with a comparatively small increase in the expense of the Indian army, we shall have a force well able to carry out the policy of maintaining neutral zones beyond India.

Besides the regular army maintained at the cost of British India, there is a great deal of fighting material and other resources in India which are at present absolutely frittered away. I refer to the thousands of men in uniform shouldering antiquated weapons, who are kept up by the native States. These States are protected from attack by each other, and also against foreign invasion, by the strong arm of the Indian Government. Under these circumstances it is utterly useless and extravagant to maintain these unorganised and undisciplined hordes. These States pay a small tribute to the Indian Government, totally disproportionate to the expense they would have had to incur for the maintenance of an army sufficiently strong to make them secure against attack by their neighbours or by a foreign Power, as well as to the outlay of the Indian Government directly and indirectly for that purpose.

The Indian Government in common fairness to the British Indian taxpayer should order these useless hordes to be disbanded. Some portion of these troops do police duty; but for this they should be replaced by regular and recognised policemen and gendarmes. For the serious business of the defence of India against foreign invasion, which is as much a duty and a necessity for the native States as it is for the Indian Government, every State must be made to keep a certain number of Imperial Service troops in proportion to its revenue, and also no troops but those for Imperial Service should be permitted. These corps should be considered part of the regular army, and placed under the commander-in-chief. Their headquarters, however, should be left in the States that pay for their maintenance, and the respective corps should carry the emblems of their princely houses. Every year they ought to be exercised and brigaded with the British army, and they should have on the establishment European inspectors. The regimental officers of all grades should be appointed from native nobles who had been trained in the Imperial Cadet Corps. The troops of the native States thus reorganised would be a material addition of strength to the fighting power of the country, and would, there is little doubt, acquit themselves in actual war against a foreign foe with as much credit as the regular army.

This very question was raised in the Supreme Legislative Council some years ago, but nothing seems to have come out of the discussion. As probably nine out of every ten chiefs would heartily approve of such a patriotic change, which would increase their importance and usefulness, it is high time that the question should be seriously taken up by approaching the native States in a proper and definite manner. Perhaps a committee composed of several princes who can "think imperially," some civilians, two or three military officers, and perhaps a few independent individuals not in the services, might be formed to make a scientific and thorough study of the question, and prepare a scheme for the effective utilisation of the armies of the native States in the defence of India.

The spirit of the ruling chiefs of India is, I think, made clearly apparent by an anecdote relating to one of the greatest and most powerful of her ruling princes, which I venture to repeat. It was at the time of the last Delhi Durbar, that one morning I saw H.H. Maharaja Scindia of Gwalior riding with a single trooper in close attendance. In answer to a casual question from me as to whether the trooper was one of the Imperial Service troops, his Highness replied that "all his troops, without any distinction, were for Imperial Service, and that he himself was an Imperial soldier."

I am afraid I have already trespassed too much on the patience of my readers; but I feel that I owe a duty to both India and England, countries that seem, by Providence, to be so designed that their welfare and happiness can only be complete when they are thoroughly united. I have pointed out what I consider the greatest danger to our Indian Empire – namely, the extension of the frontier up to that of Russia . . .

Source: *The Nineteenth Century and After*, London, September 1905, pp. 367–75. The journal, a prestigious and influential monthly, was at this time edited by James Knowles.
Much was written, then and later, on the nature, scope and ramifications of the imperial clash between the British Indian Empire and Russia. A short selection: Lady Betty Balfour, *The History of Lord Lytton's Administration, 1876 to 1880, Compiled from Letters and Official Papers*, London, 1899; John Adye, *Indian Frontier Policy: An Historical Sketch*, London, 1897; G. J. Alder, *British India's Northern Frontier, 1865–1895: A Study in Imperial History*, London, 1963; Olaf Caroe, *The Pathans, 500 B.C.-A.D. 1957*, London, 1958; Richard Temple, *The Story of My Life*, London, 1896, 2 vols; John Strachey, *India*, London, 1888, rev. ed 1894; Muhammad Anwar Khan, *England, Russia and Central Asia: A Study in Diplomacy, 1857–1878*, Peshawar, 1963; D. P. Singhal, *India and Afghanistan, 1876–1907: A Study in Diplomatic Relations*, St Lucia, 1963; A. P. Thornton, *The File on Empire: Essays and Reviews*, London, 1968; and the following unpublished theses: A. W. Preston, "British Military Policy and the Defence of India: A study of British Military Policy, Plans and Preparations During the Russian Crisis, 1876–1880", London, Ph.D. 1966; Bhag Singh, "Anglo-Russian Relations in the Middle East since 1907, with special reference to India", California, Ph.D., 1935; G. S. Papadopoulos, "England and the Near East, 1896–1898", London, Ph.D., 1950; R. R. J. Mulligan, "Great Britain, Russia and the Straits, 1908–1923", London, M.A., 1953; R. L. Kirkpatrick, "British Imperial Policy, 1874–1880",

Oxford, D.Phil., 1933; and M. J. Jennings, "Anglo-Russian Relations Concerning Afghanistan, 1882–1886", London, M.A., 1953.

7

A BILL OF MUSLIM RIGHTS

The Memorial Presented by a Muslim Deputation to the Viceroy of India

Simla: 1 October 1906

Benefits conferred by British rule on the population of India – British policy in India – deference to the wishes of the people and the diversity of race and religion – the numerical strength of the Muslims in India – the position accorded to the Muslim community should be commensurate with its numbers and political importance – Muslims have been law-abiding – Muslims value representative institutions but consider the community's representation inade-quate – plea for adequate Muslim representation in the Gazetted, Subordinate and Ministerial services of the provinces, Municipal and District Boards, Senates and Syndicates of Indian Universities, Provincial Councils and the Imperial Legislative Council – appoint-ment of Muslims to the Judiciary and to the Executive Council.

To
HIS EXCELLENCY THE RIGHT HONOURABLE
THE EARL OF MINTO,
P.C., G.C.S.I., G.C.I.E., G.C.M.G.,
Viceroy and Governor-General of India.
MAY IT PLEASE YOUR EXCELLENCY,

Availing ourselves of the permission graciously accorded to us, we the undersigned nobles, jagirdars, talukdars, merchants, and others, representing a large body of the Mohammedan Subjects of His Majesty the King-Emperor in different parts of India, beg most respectfully to approach Your Excellency with the following memorial for your favourable consideration.

2. We have no need to be reminded of the incalculable benefits

conferred by British rule on the teeming millions belonging to divers races, and professing divers religions, who form the population of the vast continent of India. Nor can we forget the chaos and misrule from which British arms extricated us when the country was a prey to an innumerable host of adventurers bent on rapine and plunder. We have good reason to be grateful for the peace, security, personal freedom, and liberty of worship that we now enjoy, and, from the wise and enlightened character of the Government, we have every reasonable ground for anticipating that these benefits will be progressive and that India will, in the future occupy an increasingly important position in the comity of nations.

3. One of the most important characteristics of British policy in India is the increasing deference that has, so far as possible, been paid from the first to the views and wishes of the people of the country in matters affecting their interests, with due regard always to the diversity of race and religion which forms such an important feature of all Indian problems.

4. Beginning with the confidential and unobtrusive method of consulting influential members of important communities in different parts of the country, this principle was gradually extended by the recognition of the right of recognised political or commercial organisations to communicate to the authorities their criticisms and views on measures of public importance; and, finally, by the nomination and election of direct representatives of the people in Municipalities, Local Boards, and – above all – in the Legislative Chambers of the country. This last element is, we understand, about to be dealt with by the Commission appointed by Your Excellency at the initiative of His Majesty's Secretary of State for India, with the view of giving it further extension; and it is with reference mainly to our claim to a fair share in such extended representation that we have ventured to approach Your Excellency on the present occasion.

5. The Musalmans of India number, according to the census taken in the year 1901, over sixty-two millions, or more than one-fifth of the total population of His Majesty's Indian Dominions; while if the Native States and Burma were excluded from the computation and a reduction made for the uncivilized portions of the community enumerated under the heads of Animists and other minor religions, the proportion of Musalmans to the whole population of British India would be found to be approximately one-fourth. In these circumstances, we desire to submit that, under any system of representation, extended or limited, a min-

ority amounting to a quarter of the population – and in itself more numerous than the entire population of any first class European Power, except Russia – may justly lay claim to adequate recognition as an important factor in the State. We venture, indeed, with Your Excellency's permission, to go a step further than this and urge that the position accorded to the Musalman community in any kind of representation, direct or indirect, and in all other ways affecting their status and influence, should be commensurate not merely with their numerical strength but also with their political importance; and that, in estimating the latter, due weight should be given to the position which they occupied in India a little more that a hundred years ago, and of which the traditions have naturally not faded from their minds.

6. The Musalmans of India have hitherto placed implicit reliance on the sense of justice and love of fair dealing that has always characterised their rulers and have in consequence abstained from pressing their claims by methods that might prove at all embarrassing; but earnestly as we desire that the Musalmans of India should not in the future depart from that excellent and time-honoured tradition, recent events have stirred up feelings, especially among the younger generation of Mohammedans, which might, in certain circumstances and under certain contingencies, easily pass beyond the control of temperate counsel and sober guidance.

7. We, therefore, pray that the representation we herewith venture to submit, after a careful consideration of the views and wishes of a large number of our co-religionists in all parts of India, may be favoured with Your Excellency's earnest attention.

8. We hope Your Excellency will pardon our stating at the outset that representative institutions of the European type are, entirely opposed to the genius and traditions of Eastern Nations, and many of the most thoughtful members of our community look upon them as totally unsuitable to the social, religious, and political conditions obtaining in India. Since, however, our rulers have, in pursuance of their own immemorial instincts and traditions, found it expedient to give these institutions an increasingly important place in the Government of the country, we Mohammedans cannot any longer, in justice to our own national interests, hold aloof from participating in the conditions to which their policy has given rise. We must therefore acknowledge with gratitude that such representation as the Musalmans of India have hitherto enjoyed has been due to a sense of justice and fairness on the part of Your Excellency and your illustrious

predecessors in office, and the heads of Local Governments by whom the Mohammedan members of Legislative Chambers have with scarcely one exception been invariably nominated; but we venture to submit that the representation thus accorded to us has necessarily been inadequate to our requirements and has not always carried with it the approval of those whom the nominees were selected to represent. This state of things had, in existing circumstances, been unavoidable; for while, on the one hand, the number of nominations reserved to the Viceroy and Local Governments has necessarily been strictly limited, the selection, on the other hand, of really representative men has, in the absence of any reliable method of ascertaining the direction of popular choice, been far from easy. As for the results of selection, it is most unlikely that the name of any Mohammedan candidate will ever be submitted for the approval of Government by the electoral bodies as now constituted, unless he is prepared to forego the right of private judgment and undertake to vote with the majority in all matters of importance. We submit that a Mohammedan elected on these terms necessarily ceases to represent his own community and becomes a mere mandatory of the Hindu majority. Nor can we, in fairness, find fault with the desire of our Hindoo fellow-subjects to take full advantage of their strength and vote only for members of their own community, or for persons who, if not Hindoos, are pledged to vote for the interests of the Hindoo community. It is true that we have many and important interests in common with our Hindu fellow-countrymen, and it will always be a matter of the utmost satisfaction to us to see these interests safeguarded by the presence in our Legislative Chambers of able supporters of these interests, irrespective of their nationality. We Musalmans have, however, additional interests of our own which are not shared by other communities and these have hitherto suffered grievous loss from the fact that they have not been adequately represented. Even in the Provinces in which the Mohammedans constitute a distinct majority of the population, they have too often been treated as though they were inappreciably small political factors that might without unfairness be neglected. This has been the case, to some extent in the Punjab; but in a more marked degree in Sindh and in Eastern Bengal, where Mohammedan interests have suffered, owing partly to the backwardness of the community in education, for which they are not wholly to blame, but still more to their ignorance of the arts of self-assertion and political agitation.

9. Before formulating our views with regard to the election of

representatives, we beg to observe that the political importance of a community to a considerable extent gains strength or suffers detriment according to the position that the members of that community occupy in the service of the State. If, as is unfortunately the case with the Mohammedans, they are not adequately represented in this manner, they lose in the prestige and influence which are justly their due. Our first prayer, therefore, is that Your Excellency will be graciously pleased to issue strict orders that, both in the Gazetted and the Subordinate and Ministerial services of all Indian Provinces, a due proportion of Mohammedans – to be locally determined – shall always find place. Orders of like import have, at times, been issued by Local Governments in some Provinces, but have never, unfortunately, been strictly enforced, on the ground that qualified Mohammedans were not forthcoming. This allegation, however true it may have been at one time, is no longer tenable now, and wherever the will to employ them is not wanting, the supply of qualified Mohammedans, we are happy to be able to assure Your Excellency, is greater than any possible demand.

10. As Municipal and District Boards have to deal with important local interests, affecting to a great extent the health and comfort of the inhabitants, we shall, we hope, be pardoned if we solicit, for a moment, Your Excellency's attention to the position of Musalmans thereon before passing on to higher concerns. These institutions form, as it were, the initial rungs in the ladder of Self-Government, and it is here that the principle of representation is brought home intimately to the intelligence of the people. Yet the position of Musalmans on these Boards is not at present regulated by any guiding principle capable of general application, and practice varies in different localities. The Aligarh Municipality for example, is divided into six wards, and each ward returns one Hindoo and one Mohammedan Commissioner, and the same principle, we understand, is adopted in some other Municipalities, but in many localities the Musalman tax-payers are not adequately represented. We would, therefore, respectfully suggest that local authority should, in every case, be required to declare the number of Hindoos and Mohammedans entitled to seats on Municipal and Local Boards, such proportion to be determined in accordance with the numerical strength, social status, and local influence of either community – in consultation, if necessary, with their leading men.

11. We would also suggest that the Senates and Syndicates of Indian Universities might, so far as possible, be similarly dealt

with; that there should, in other words, be an authoritative declaration of the proportion in which Mohammedans are entitled to be represented in either body, whether by selection or nomination or both.

12. We now proceed to the consideration of our share in the Legislative Chambers of the country. Beginning with the Provincial Councils, we would suggest that, as in the case of Municipalities and Local Boards, the proportion of Mohammedan representatives entitled to a seat should be determined and declared with due regard to the important considerations which we have ventured to point out in paragraph 5 of this Memorial; and that the Mohemmedan members of District Boards and Municipalities, and the Registered Graduates of Universities, should be formed into Electoral Colleges, and be authorised, in accordance with such rules of procedure as Your Excellency's Government may be pleased to prescribe in that behalf, to return the number of members that may be declared to be eligible.

13. With regard to the Imperial Legislative Council, whereon the due representation of Mohammedan interests is a matter of the utmost importance, we would solicit:–

(1) That in the cadre of the Council, at least, one member out of every four should always be a Mohammedan.

(2) That, as far as possible, appointment by election should be given preference over nomination; and that in any case the majority of members should be appointed by election.

(3) That for purposes of choosing Mohammedan representatives, Mohammedan members of the Provincial Councils and Mohammedan Fellows of Universities should be invested with electoral powers to be exercised in accordance with such procedure as may be prescribed by Your Excellency's Government in that behalf.

14. The methods of election we have ventured to suggest are necessarily tentative: they may even be found, in certain respects, defective; but they are the simplest and the least complicated of the two or three that have occurred to us in the very limited time at our command. But, provided the choice be left free and unhampered in the hands of respectable and educated Mohammedans, we shall have no hesitation in accepting any other method that may be considered more practicable.

15. We have reason to believe that the generality of Mohamme-dans in all parts of India feel it a grievance that Mohammedan Judges are not more frequently appointed on the High Courts and Chief Courts of Judicature. Since the creation of these Courts only three Mohammedan lawyers have held these honour-able appointments, all three of whom have happily justified their elevation in a most signal manner. It is not, therefore, an extrava-gant request on their behalf that, whenever possible, a Mohammedan judge should be given a seat on each of these Courts. Qualified lawyers, eligible for these posts, can always be found – if not in one Province, then in another, and seeing that a Bengalee Judge sits on the bench of the Punjab Chief Court, there should be no objection to a Mohammedan, provided he is qualified being transferred from one Province to another.

16. There has lately been some talk, we understand, of the possible appointment of one or more Indian members on the Executive Council of the Viceroy and the India Council in England. Should such appointments be contemplated, we beg that the claims of Mohammedans in that behalf may not be overlooked. More than one Mohammedan, we venture to say, will be found in the ranks of the Covenanted and Uncovenanted Services fit to serve with distinction in either of these august Chambers. We have at this moment, a retired Judge of the High Court of Calcutta, domiciled in England, who, by his ability as a lawyer, his standing as a scholar, and his reputation as an experi-enced and versatile man of the world, cannot fail to be an ornament to the India Council: we mean Mr. Syed Amir Ali, in whom the Mohammedans of India repose the fullest confidence.

17. In conclusion, we beg to assure Your Excellency that in assisting the Musalman subjects of His Majesty at this crisis in the directions indicated in the present Memorial, Your Excellency will be strengthening the foundations of their unswerving loyalty to the Throne and laying the foundations of the political regener-ation and national prosperity, and Your Excellency's name will be remembered with gratitude by their posterity for generations to come.

We have the honour to subscribe ourselves,
Your Excellency's
Most obedient and humble servants,

Source: Nawab Imad-ul-Mulk Bahadur (Syed Hossain Bilgrami, c.s.i.), *Speeches, Addresses and Poems*, Government Central Press, Hyderabad Deccan, 1925, pp. 139–44.

The address was drafted by Bilgrami. I have included the address in the Aga Khan's works because it was he who read it out and presented it to the Governor General and Viceroy of India, Lord Minto, on 1 October 1906 in Simla on behalf of the Muslims of India. The great and far-reaching impact of this memorial is brought out in the constitutional changes and political developments of the years 1906–9. It gave voice to and encouraged Muslim separatism in the country, procured for the Muslims separate electorates and led directly to the establishment of the All India Muslim League.

As the Viceroy's reply to the memorial was the first British official recognition of a separate Muslim identity in India it is reproduced below:

"Your Highness and gentlemen, – allow me, before I attempt to reply to the many considerations your address embodies, to welcome you heartily to Simla. Your presence here today is very full of meaning. To the document with which you have presented me are attached the signatures of nobles, of Ministers of various States, of great landowners, of lawyers, of merchants, and of many other of His Majesty's Mahomedan subjects. I welcome the representative character of your deputation as expressing the views and aspirations of the enlightened Muslim community of India. I feel that all you have said emanates from a representative body basing its opinions on a matured consideration of the existing political conditions of India, totally apart from the small personal or political sympathies and antipathies of scattered localities, and I am grateful to you for the opportunity you are affording me of expressing my appreciation of the just aims of the followers of Islam, and their determination to share in the political history of our Empire. As your Viceroy I am proud of the recognition you express of the benefits conferred by British rule on the diverse races of many creeds which go to form the population of this huge continent. You yourselves, the descendants of a conquering and ruling race, have told me today of your gratitude for the personal freedom, the liberty of worship, the general peace and the hopeful future which British administration has secured for India. It is interesting to look back on early British efforts to assist the Mahomedan population to qualify themselves for the public service. In 1782 Warren Hastings founded the Calcutta Madrassah, with the intention of enabling its students 'to compete on more equal terms with the Hindus for employment under Government'. In 1811 my ancestor Lord Minto advocated improvements in the Madrassah and the establishment of Mahomedan Colleges at other places throughout India. In later years the efforts of the Mahomedan Association led to the Government Resolution of 1885 dealing with the educational position of the Mahomedan community and their employment in the Public Service, whilst Mahomedan educational effort has culminated in the College of Aligarh, that great institution which the noble and broad-minded devotion of Sir Syed Ahmed Khan – (applause) – has dedicated to his co-religionists. It was in July, 1877, that Lord Lytton laid the foundation-stone of Aligarh, when Sir Syed Ahmed Khan addressed these memorable words to the Viceroy: 'The personal honour which you have done me assures me of a great fact, and fills me with feelings of a much higher nature than mere personal gratitude. I am assured that you who upon this occasion represent the British rule have sympathy with our labours. To me this assurance is very valuable and a source of great happiness. At my time of life it is a comfort to me to feel that the undertaking which has been for many years and is now the sole object of my life, has roused on the one hand the energies of my own countrymen, and on the other has won the sympathy of our British fellow-subjects, and the support of our rulers, so that when the few years I may still be spared are over, and when I shall be no longer amongst you, the College will still prosper and succeed in educating my countrymen to have the same affection for their country, the same feelings of loyalty for the British rule, the same appreciation of its blessings, the same sincerity of friendship with our British fellow-subjects as have been the ruling feelings of my life. (applause)'. Aligarh has won its laurels, its students have gone forth to fight the battle of life strong in the tenets of their own religion, strong in the precepts of loyalty and patriotism, and now when there is much that is critical in the political future of India the inspiration of Sir Syed Ahmed Khan and the teachings of Aligarh shine forth brilliantly in the pride of Mahomedan history, in the loyalty, commonsense, and sound reasoning so eloquently expressed in your address.

"But gentlemen, you go on to tell me that sincere as your belief is in the justice and fair dealings of your rulers, and unwilling as you are to embarrass them at the present moment you can not but be aware that 'recent events have stirred up feelings amongst the younger generation of Mahomedans which might pass beyond the control of the temperate counsel and sober guidance'. Now I have no intention of entering into any discussion upon the affairs of Eastern Bengal and Assam, yet, I hope that without offence to any one I may thank the Mahomedan community of the new Province for the moderation and self-restraint they have shown under conditions which were new to them and as to which there had been inevitably much misunderstanding, and that I may, at the same time, sympathise with all that is sincere in Bengali sentiments. But above all what I would ask you to believe is that the course the Viceroy and the Government of India have pursued in connection with the affairs of the new Province – the future of which is now I hope assured – (applause) – has been dictated solely by a regard for what has appeared best for its present and future populations as a whole – irrespective of race or creed, and that the Mahomedan community of Eastern Bengal and Assam can rely as firmly as ever on British justice and fair play for the appreciation of its loyalty and the safeguarding of its interests.

"You have addressed me, gentlemen, at a time when the political atmosphere is full of change. We all feel it would be foolish to attempt to deny its existence. Hopes and ambitions new to India are making themselves felt; we can not ignore them, we should be wrong to wish to do so. But to what is all this unrest due? Not to the discontent of misgoverned millions – I defy anyone honestly to assert that; not to any uprising of a disaffected people. It is due to that educational growth in which only a very small portion of the population has yet shared, of which British rule first sowed the seed, and the fruits of which British rule is now doing its best to foster and to direct. There may be many taxes in the harvest we are now reaping, the Western grain which we have sown may not be entirely suitable to the requirements of the people of India, but the educational harvest will increase as years go on, and the healthiness of the nourishment it gives will depend on the careful administration and distribution of its product. You need not ask my pardon, gentlemen, for telling me that 'representative institutions of the European type are entirely new to the people of India' or that their introduction here requires the most earnest thought and care. I should be very far from welcoming all the political machinery of the Western world amongst the hereditary instincts and traditions of eastern races. Western breadth of thought, the teachings of Western civilization, the freedom of British individuality, can do much for the people of India. But I recognise with you that they must not carry with them an impracticable insistence on the acceptance of political methods. (Applause).

"And now, gentleman, I come to your own position in respect to the political future; the position of the Mahomedan Community for whom you speak. You will, I feel sure, recognise that it is impossible for me to follow you through any detailed consideration of the conditions and the share that community has a right to claim in the administration of public affairs. I can at present only deal with generalities. The points which you have raised are before the Committee which, as you know, I have lately appointed to consider the question of representation, and I will take care that your address is submitted to them. But at the same time I hope I may be able to reply to the general tenor of your remarks without in any way forestalling the Committee's report. The pith of your address, as I understand it, is a claim that in any system of representation – whether it affects a Municipality, a District Board, or a Legislative Council in which it is proposed to introduce or increase an electoral organisation – the Mahomedan Community should be represented as a community. You point out that in many cases electoral bodies as now constituted can not be expected to return a Mahomedan candidate, and that if by chance they did so it could only be at the sacrifice of such a candidate's views to those of a majority opposed to his own community whom he would in no way represent; and you justly claim that your position should be estimated not merely on your numerical strength but in respect to the political importance of your community, and the service it has rendered to the Empire. I am entirely in accord with you. (Applause). Please do not misunderstand me, I make no attempt to indicate by what means the representation of communities can be obtained, but I am as firmly convinced as I believe you to be, that any electoral representation in India would be doomed to mischievous failure which aimed at granting a personal enfranchisement regardless of the beliefs and traditions of the communities composing the population of this continent. (Applause). The great mass of the people of India have no knowledge of representative institutions, I agree with you gentlemen, that the initial rungs in the ladder of self-government are to be found in the Municipal and District Boards, and that it is in that direction that we must look for the gradual political education of the people. In the meantime I can only say to you that the Mahomedan Community may rest assured that their political rights and interests as a community will be safeguarded in any administrative organisation with which I am concerned, and that you and the people of India may rely upon the British Raj to respect, as it has been its pride to do, the religious beliefs and the national traditions of the myriads composing the population of His Majesty's Indian Empire. (Applause).

"Your Highness and gentlemen, I sincerely thank you for the unique opportunity your deputation has given me of meeting so many distinguished and representative Mahomedans. I deeply appreciate the energy and interest in public affairs which have brought you here from great distances, and I only regret that your visit to Simla is necessarily so short."

(Earl of Minto, *Speeches by the Earl of Minto, Viceroy and Governor General of India,* Calcutta, 1911).

The memorial was signed by the following persons:

1. His Highness Aga Sir Sultan Muhammad Shah Aga Khan, G.C.I.E. (Bombay).
2. Shahzada Bakhtiar Shah, C.I.E., Head of the Mysore Family, Calcutta (Bengal).

3. Honourable Malik Umar Hayat Khan, c.i.e., Lieut., 18th Prince of Wales' Tiwana Lancers, Tiwana, Shahpur (Punjab).
4. Honourable Khan Bahadur Mian Muhammad Shah Din, Barr.-at-Law, Lahore (Punjab).
5. Honourable Mawlawi Sharfuddin, Barr.-at-Law, Patna (Bihar).
6. Khan Bahadur Sayyid Nawab Ali Chowdhury, Mymensingh (Eastern Bengal).
7. Nawab Bahadur Sayyid Amir Husain Khan, c.i.e., Calcutta (Bengal).
8. Naseer Husain Khan Khayal, Calcutta (Bengal).
9. Khan Bahadur Mirza Shujaat Ali Beg, Persian Consul-General, Murshidabad, Calcutta (Bengal).
10. Sayyid Ali Imam, Bar.-at-Law, Patna (Bihar).
11. Nawab Sarfraz Husain Khan, Patna (Bihar).
12. Khan Bahadur Ahmed Muhayyuddin Khan, Stipendiary of the Carnatic Family (Madras).
13. Mawlawi Rafiuddin Ahmad, Barr.-at-Law (Bombay).
14. Ebrahimbhoy Adamji Peerbhoy, General Merchant (Bombay).
15. Abdur Rahim, Barr.-at-Law (Calcutta).
16. Sayyid Allahdad Shah, Special Magistrate and Vice-President, Zamindars' Association, Khairpur (Sind).
17. Mawlana H. M. Malak, Head of Mehdi Bagh Bohras, Nagpur (C.P.).
18. Mushir-ud-Dawlah Mamtaz-ul-Mulk Khan Bahadur Khalifa Sayyid Muhammad Husain, Member of the State Council, Patiala (Punjab).
19. Khan Bahadur Col. Abdul Majid Khan, Foreign Minister, Patiala (Punjab).
20. Khan Bahadur Khwaja Yusuf Shah, Honorary Magistrate, Amritsar (Punjab).
21. Mian Muhammad Shafi, Barr.-at-Law, Lahore (Punjab).
22. Shaikh Ghulam Sadiq, Amritsar (Punjab).
23. Hakim Muhammad Ajmal Khan, Delhi (Punjab).
24. Munshi Ihtisham Ali, Zamindar and Rais, Kakori (Oudh).
25. Sayyid Nabiullah, Barr.-at-Law, Rais, Kara, District Allahabad (U.P.)
26. Mawlawi Sayyid Karamat Husain, Barr.-at-Law, Allahabad (U.P.)
27. Sayyid Abdur Rauf, Barr.-at-Law, Allahabad (U.P.)
28. Munshi Abdus Salam Khan, Retired Sub-Judge, Rampur (U.P.)
29. Khan Bahadur Muhammad Muzammillullah Khan, Zamindar, Secretary, Zamindars' Association (U.P.), and Joint Secretary, MAO College Trustees, Aligarh (U.P.).
30. Haji Muhammad Ismail Khan, Zamindar, Aligarh (U.P.)
31. Sahibzada Aftab Ahmad Khan, Barr.-at-Law, Aligarh (U.P.)
32. Mawlawi Mushtaq Husain, Rais, Amroha (U.P.)
33. Mawlawi Habibur Rahman Khan, Zamindar, Bhikampur (U.P.)
34. Nawab Sayyid Sirdar Ali Khan, son of the late Nawab Sirdar Daler-ul-Mulk Bahadur, c.i.e., Hyderabad (Deccan).
35. Mawlawi Sayyid Mahdi Ali Khan (Muhsin-ul-Mulk), Honorary Secretary, MAO College, Aligarh (U.P.)

On the Simla deputation and memorial see Mary, Countess of Minto, *India: Minto and Morley, 1905–1910*, London, 1934; B. R. Ambedkar, *Thoughts on Pakistan*, Bombay, 1941; Sayyid Ameer Ali, "Dawn of a New Policy in India", *The Nineteenth Century and After*, November 1906; H. A., Letter, *The Englishman*, 10 October 1906; "Muslims and their Claims", *The Englishman*, 19 November

1906; "Simla Deputation", *Economist*, 6 October 1906; "The Forces of Loyalty", *The Times*, 26 September 1906; "The Muhammadan Memorial", *The Times*, 1 October 1906; "The Muslim Deputation", *The Englishman*, 2 October 1906; Abdullah Yusuf Ali, "The Indian Muhammadans: Their Past, Present and Future", *Journal of the Society of Arts*, 4 January 1907; "Muhammadan Address to Lord Minto", *Imperial and Asiatic Quarterly Review*, January 1907; and E. E. Lang, "The All India Muslim League", *Contemporary Review*, September 1907.

8

SOME THOUGHTS ON INDIAN DISCONTENT

An Article

London: February 1907

The concept of "the changeless East" is misleading – "practical" discontent in India – reflected in the Indian press – vernacular press and the feelings of the masses – causes of the unrest – influence of external factors – the importance of internal factors – the theory that British rule has impoverished India not valid – nor the official view that efficient administration and increased wealth will prevent discontent – other theories: lack of sympathy among British administrators; absence of social intercourse between brown and white; and the perception of the British as conquerors – Muslims desire a special system of representation and a university at Aligarh – force alone is not enough to assure British supremacy – changes in the offing: Berlin–Baghdad railway; the Russian railway; the awakening of China – Britain should win the affection of her Indian subjects – advantages of such a policy – dangers of giving power to some individuals and communities – ordinary Indians desire to come up to the level of the white people – the importance of social reforms – the role played by the Sovereign in Britain in social uplift – the proposal for a non-political Regency in India and its advantages – this step should be above party politics.

"There is no idea more misleading than that embodied in the phrase 'the changeless East'. Age-worn Asia is no more exempt from the laws of change than the rest of the world." These wise words of the Indian correspondent of the *National Review* should be taken to heart by all who wish to understand the difficult problems connected with India, and, above all, that problem of problems which is perhaps the most difficult of all connected with the great dependency – the relations of the brown and white races.

It would enormously simplify the task of ruling India, not only justify, but with the contentment of the people, if Englishmen in general, and the individual who is the final arbiter of the destinies of the British Empire, viz., "the man in the street," in particular, took to heart and ever remembered some other words of the same correspondent.

> "Lord Curzon truly said, on the eve of the day on which he laid down the crushing burden of the office of Viceroy, that the one great fault of Englishmen in India is that we don't look sufficiently ahead. If we did, we should foresee that our patriarchal conception of our rule must ultimately be slowly modified in various respects. It is not enough to say that the ryat at the plough typifies India – that truism has too often led policy astray."

It is the odd 20 per cent. (one must bear in mind that this odd 20 per cent. reaches a total over 50 millions of men) of alert, receptive, but often ill-balanced minds who have to be also considered.

I venture to say that before approaching the study of Indian problems – provided that we wish to arrive at conclusions intellectually just, and not merely cause the verbal overthrow of views repulsive to us personally – we should bear in mind the words of the correspondent already quoted, and abandon once for all the method of deducing political actions from abstract principles, and accept frankly the sound method of induction. Then, and only then, will we find results other than the bitter fruit of discontent. We must cross-question history, not merely put leading questions to periods useful to our foregone conclusions. If, with such principles as our guides, we approach the present position of political affairs in India, and the general relations of the brown to the white race, what do we find?

A sentimental loyalty to the Crown and the Flag, and a practical discontent – a discontent that though not disloyal has yet in it the germs of danger. I know that this will be denied, that I shall be told that my assertions do not prove the fact, and that my observations have been limited and faulty. We will, however, appeal to life, and we will go direct to its manifestations. I suppose it will be accepted that general experience goes to prove that the opinions of a people, especially if they are without representative institutions and government, are in the long run reflected by its Press. But even here we must follow the inductive method. It is quite conceivable that in a country of comparatively small size certain small corporations may make a "corner" of the news-papers, and air opinions that belong to a class by buying or commercially boycotting the journals of their opponents, and in this way represent for years views of a minority as those of the mass of the people. But has this been the case in India? Far from it; the Indian vernacular Press is owned by numberless proprietors, and not by any means *entirely* by Bengalese or Brah-mins, as some would have us assume! Almost all are full of discontent, though in varying degrees. Had they bought out those that were ostentatiously started to end their mischief, we might then allow it to be assumed that the power of capital had silenced the voice of the millions. But such "loyal" papers do exist, only they are without healthy circulation, and nobody takes them at all seriously. Their general popularity ceases to exist the moment they become "loyal", and then they become the well-nursed but sickly children of some generous millionaire, prince, or small corporation. They know not the joys of good health enjoyed by their hardy cousins of the disaffected camp. If we leave the Press and go to the man for observation the results are similar. The difficulties are infinitely greater. To begin with, no individual can observe 300 millions of his fellow creatures; but even then if any one makes it his business to mix with the poorer classes and listens to them patiently he will come to the conclusion that most of what one reads in the vernacular Press is thought of and talked about by the public. Of course, here we must take the opinion of the observer on trust. However, such are my own conclusions, drawn from observations in Bengal, the Bombay Presidency, and the Punjab, and I venture to prophesy that if a few independent Englishmen would come out and give to India for five or six years (one in each province) the same amount of thought and patient observation, that Mr. Bodley gave to France, they would come to conclusions similar to mine – viz., that the vernacular Press does represent the feelings of the masses. Of course, we have all often heard the assertions about the dumb millions not having any sympathy with the Press, and the discontent being in no way that of the masses. We must examine this assertion with care and patience. It is comforting, but is it like the opium-eater's paradise – an unwholesome dream, destined to end in a dreary headache, or is it like the North Sea breeze, an exhilarating reality?

To begin with, if these millions are *dumb*, how on earth did any one come to know that they were contented and happy? Dumbness does not mean the silent ecstasy of supreme joy; it means the inability of intelligible articulation. If, however, we look into the question more thoroughly, and reason from observations of actions, the only form of reasoning open to us, since "dumbness" prevents questioning, we shall soon find that these very dumb people are the backbone of the disaffected. To begin with, human nature being what it is, and the influences of childhood and early associations being so very powerful, surely if the dumb millions had such a wonderful amount of contentment a fair proportion of their numbers that had learnt the secret of speech would show some of their original preferences? Now we will turn to the reality. Almost all the most disaffected and discontented come from families and classes that are or have been "dumb". Amongst the articulate who come from the "talking" classes – the merchant, the lawyer, or the city broker – one often finds individuals who are satisfied. But when the early associates have been "dumb" the result is invariably extreme disaffection. A little observation of men will prove this. Surely if discontent was only the speciality of the articulate classes the result would have been the other way round? We will not discuss this point further. We will accept the evidence of the Press and of almost all non-official observers – English, foreign, or Indian. As for the insignificant, but noisy race of Indian optimists, generally well-born gentlemen, who are to be found in India in the anterooms of Government Houses and Residencies, who are ready to assure us that all is for the best in the best of all possible worlds, we will only hope that our rulers will remember that to indulge often in the sweet words of such men is as dangerous to clear views and thought as the contrast use of poisonous *apéritifs* to digestion.

I will now examine the causes usually asserted as the causes of discontent, and the remedies generally suggested, hoping that by the dispassionate examination of every suggested cause and remedy we may not only diagnose the disease rightly, but find a curative specific. Some loyal Indians hastily assert that the prevailing ferment is the result of Lord Curzon's seven years of active and energetic administration. They also are ready to assert that until Lord Curzon came out the average Indian did not think much about the government of India, and that the mass of the people had not been taught to think about any political ruler above the collector of his district, and that Lord Curzon so

impressed the native mind with the importance of the government of India to his own well-being, and so drew attention to
the fact that the government of India was – as far as internal
affairs went – an autocratic despotism, that the Indian began to
inquire for himself, and wonder why one man, the occupant of
a distant palace, and not of his race or blood, nor his hereditary
ruler, should have the power to so change – for better or worse
– his affairs, and be able to make such changes in his personal
mode of living as he willed. This explanation is clearly insufficient. No man in his senses will assert that the general
discontent and ferment of today were never heard of in the latter
nineties, and the dreams – silly day-dreams, no doubt, but still
the dreams – of the masses, of certainly some provinces, of today
were known in the last years of the last century. But it must be
remembered that the germs of all that has come to life today
existed then, and long before the first years of the twentieth
century. Again, it must be remembered that the last years of Lord
Curzon's rule have been years of extraordinary unrest in Asia.
The Chinese boycott of American goods, the assurance of the
continued integrity of China, the commencement of the Reform
movement in that country, the success of Japan against Russia,
and the certainty that the Far East will remain Asiatic, have deeply
impressed the Indian mind. Lastly, and above all, the comparative
success of the revolution in Russia, the collapse of autocracy and
the granting of votes to the Tartar Muhammadans and the Jews,
have turned the heads of other Asiatics, otherwise calm, wise,
and sane people. All these events occurred during the last years
of Lord Curzon's Viceroyalty, and those who look upon today's
unrest as the result of the rule of one individual may well be
advised to ponder on all these world-events, and be asked to say
if they think it was within the range of possibility for a Viceroy
of India, however absolute, to prevent any one of the above-
mentioned occurrences. No one man could have done that,
perhaps not even the Emperors Nicholas and William.

We must not, however, accept the theory that the present
unrest is *due* to these external movements. No greater mistake
could be made. Unless the soil of the country contained the
germs of the malady of discontent, all such foreign movements
would have only raised curiosity, but not that general sense of
discontent that is today apparent. All historical examples indicate
that though the outward signs of discontent may be due to
external influences, the existence itself of discontent cannot possibly be due to foreign causes. To understand the question, "Why

is the Indian of today discontented?" we must turn our gaze towards the internal movements of India and study the acts of the central Government. Perhaps the fearless application of the inductive method when considering the acts of the Government of India and the present state of civilisation in that country will show us the primary cause of the unrest that is today apparent to all, except the willingly blind. Is this primary cause to be found in the most quoted of the so-called "faults" of British rule in India?

Let us examine them and try to see if they are really such as to cause disaffection and, if so, if they are remediable ... We will examine some of the measures suggested by various Indian and European thinkers for changing the ferment and perhaps discontent of today into a healthy affection that shall, when united with the loyalty to the Throne which today undoubtedly exists, make of India as surely and truly a source of strength to the Empire as Scotland or Ulster.

One school of thinkers, of whom Mr. Hyndman and Mr. Naoroji are the extremest and best known representatives in England, and who are more or less followed by the leaders of the Congress Party in India and by some of the English politicians and thinkers who have taken an active and sympathetic interest in Indian affairs, maintain that British rule has greatly impoverished India and that the country is getting poorer every day. This is an enormous question, and volumes have been written on both sides. We must, however, remember that the grand arguments used by Mr. Hyndman and his friends are purely deductive, and that after assuming general laws – just as did the old schoolmen – they try and arrive at necessary conclusions about the growing poverty of India. We cannot for a moment accept such *a priori* reasoning nor its conclusions. The question, "Is India getting poorer or richer?" must be studied *ak posteriori*; we must take the general standard of living, the volume of trade, the habits of the people, and many other facts into consideration, then compare carefully the facts of today with the records of the past and the oral traditions of the people, and thus arrive at conclusions, not so clearly necessary as the *a priori* ones arrived at by Mr. Hyndman and the best known Congress leaders from assumed premisses, but infinitely truer and more resembling the actual facts. I venture to defy any one to prove on historical and economical facts that India is getting poorer. We have many grounds of comparison. There is the case of Upper Burma, where native rule disappeared only within our own times, and where comparisons with the past can be easily made.

According to the *a priori* methods of the poverty-of-India school, the Burmans must be daily getting poorer and poorer, the standard of life must be deteriorating, and the Burman's power of exchanging his commodities, rights and services must be falling off. All the so-called "drains" on India that are supposed to have bled India to famine have been now at work in Upper Burma for nearly twenty years. We therefore ought to see the beginning of the effects. The Burman ought to be spending a little less on his household and find some difference in his domestic economy. *A priori* reasoning from Mr. Hyndman's assumptions leads us necessarily in this case to the same conclusions bravely arrived at and constantly proclaimed *re* India. Now has that been the case in Burma? Not at all; on the contrary. All and every sign of greater wealth and of greater general prosperity is to be found in that province. Any individual who will give his time to the study of Upper Burman economic affairs will be surprised at the marvellous results of British rule in the material prosperity of the inhabitants. I venture to say that comparison of the facts of today as to the life of the people with the past in every province of India will prove that the *a priori* reasoners have been greatly at fault in their conclusions, and that the continent is in every way more prosperous than it ever was. If we compare the British Indians with the subjects of the native States, the result is in no way such as to support Mr. Hyndman's theories. It must also be remembered that under the present arrangement the British Indian subject pays for the greater part of the army that protects the subject of the native States as well as himself. Thus it would not be surprising if the British Indian was not as well off as his "protected" neighbours. No doubt certain classes, such as the agricultural labourers and the small farmers, have not benefited as much by British rule as the traders, labourers, and the urban population generally. But, in comparison with their forefathers, I cannot conceive that any one (who is familiar with the social history of India, during the reign of the Moghuls for instance) will maintain that the agricultural classes have got poorer.

I cannot conceive an impartial student who knows about the facts of the past denying an actual and very material improvement. Personally, after years of study and perusal of various Persian books, reports, &c., of the Moghul period, I feel profoundly convinced of a general and progressive increase of prosperity in India even amongst the rural population. Nor am I alone in this conclusion; the great majority of English officials in India, whose knowledge of the economic position of the masses is unrivalled, are of the same opinion. Many Indian publicists, some of whom, like the late Sir Syed Ahmed Khan, were the children and in their youth the contemporaries of people who had known Moghul rule, have often proclaimed that the standard of living and all the general signs of prosperity have increased. No doubt conclusions arrived at by the study of facts have not the prim neatness of those arrived at by *a priori* reasoning. But since when has political economy become a geometric science? Surely it belongs to the inductive sciences, and conclusions drawn, howsoever hesitatingly, and with as many exceptions as possible, from facts, are worth all the syllogisms of Mr. Hyndman and his friends? We cannot put down the discontent of today to the impoverishment of the people; this is, I think, undeniable.

However, we must not assume, as some officials and optimists of the Anti-Congress Party assume, that because the masses are slowly but surely getting richer there can be no real discontent.

This hasty assumption has led to a theory that I fear is a very real source of danger: certain European thinkers assume that as efficient administration will increase the prosperity of the Indian, and as material prosperity will increase contentment, all that the Government of India has to do is to improve the method of administration and develop the resources of the country, and then it has nothing more to worry about and can rest assured of love and fidelity. Such a one-sided, such a short-sighted view of human nature would be ludicrous were it not so dangerous. Surely such thinkers forget that men do not live by bread alone, and that emotions and sentiments play as important a part in life as material wants and necessities Nor will any number of gorgeous ceremonies like the Durbar at Delhi, *plus* any amount of quick-service trains and cheap telegrams and good canals, satisfy the complicated desires and dreams of the Indian of today. All these things will appeal to one side, and one side only, of human nature. Not even a cynic, unless he be a fool, would suggest that sentiment can be altogether forgotten in a European country or altogether satisfied by magnificence. The sooner Englishmen learn that human nature in India does not consist entirely of abdomen and eyes, the better for all concerned; the sooner Englishmen realise that the very railways and canals and efficient administration that raise material needs and satisfy them directly by making wealth more general raise moral and sentimental needs indirectly which they are unable to satisfy, the better for all concerned. Is it wise in the long run to forget such sentiments, to pooh-pooh them as mere bunkum? Can any Government be considered permanent and safe as long as such sentiments remain unsatisfied? Does general wealth, the result of efficient administration, strengthen or weaken such sentiments? Far be it from me to run down efficient administration. It is one half of life certainly, but is it all life? Will a rich community require a greater or a lesser share in its government? History points to the fact that the very poorest and the most miserable have rarely rebelled, and that political discontent is much more likely to appear among those who have a competence but who do not possess the political and social advantages that they desire and their neighbours enjoy. The French Revolution was not made by the down-trodden peasants, the only people who bled under the old economic *régime*; the leaders of the revolutionary movement in France came from the middle classes; from the very classes that had gained most under the old *régime*, from the classes that supplied the *Financiers* and *Intendants*, who more than all the nobles and the Court benefited by the misery of the peasants. Every child knows what classes supported Cromwell and the Parliamentary party. Even today from what sources are recruited the leaders of anarchy in Europe? Are the most dangerous anarchists of Italy Sicilian or Neapolitan peasants nursed into hatred of society by misery and poverty? or do they not come from Milan, Ancona, and Turin, and the prosperous North? Are they the sons of labourers and the submerged tenth of industrial Italy? Many other examples could be quoted to prove that mere material prosperity, the result of efficient administration, will not stop discontent. Far from it. The more wealth there is, the more leisure will there be; the more leisure, the more time for that half-thinking, half-dreaming state that usually precedes revolution. Small grievances that in the midst of grinding poverty and inefficient administration are borne and patiently attributed to the nature of things or to Divine wrath or justice, become unbearable in a society that has been used to efficiency and been made wealthy by it. Feelings of hate and revenge will in some hour when they are least expected and most dangerous break out from a materially prosperous but disaffected people. The wealthier such a population is, the more dangerous will it be if it ever rebels.

I fear that neither the Congress theory of increasing poverty as the cause of discontent, nor the official one of only efficient administration, *plus* slow and sure increase of wealth, as remedy, take in all the facts of India and human nature. They are alike wanting. The impoverishment theory is not true to the facts; the so-called remedy takes into consideration only half the facts, and deliberately forgets all the sentiments and all the aspirations that history and daily experience alike prove to be as equally needed by men as all the material comforts of life. In fact, the more successful the remedy, the greater will the disease be; the more efficient the administration, the lighter the taxes, the greater the wealth, the less will you find that readiness to accept being governed and ruled by mere commands from Viceroy or Executive Council that you found in the days of poverty and ignorance.

Let us now turn to other so-called faults of British rule, faults usually pointed out by some distinguished foreign visitors and by some non-Congress Indian thinkers. It is constantly asserted that Englishmen are unsympathetic in India, that Tommy Atkins quarrels with the lower classes, and that the occasional rows in railway carriages, hotels, &c., between Indians and Englishmen lead to ill-will. It is further insinuated by many foreign visitors that the absence of social intercourse between the brown and the white race accentuates political differences and makes grievances that otherwise would not be noticed appear of great importance. These two points we will deal with one after the other. Many officials assign a great deal of the discontent to the attacks made upon Indians by some Englishmen. Now what are the facts as they appear to the impartial student who compares them with similar incidents in other parts of the world? Do French and German and American private soldiers never, late at night, when returning to barracks, quarrel with some chance passer-by? Is it quite unknown in England that in garrison towns sometimes a soldier hits a civilian when both are influenced by drink? Were such attacks ever more numerous in India than in European and American countries? The 9th Lancers incident, had it happened outside Lille or Breslau, would have undoubtedly been investigated by the police; but who would have dreamt of giving it any exceptional importance?

As to the second criticism of Englishmen in India so often made by foreign visitors and by some Indians, impartial consideration of the facts will show them as wanting in foundation and reasonableness as the first one we have been discussing. The foreign visitor who arrives, and day after day visits European houses and goes from city to city without meeting a single Indian gentleman, begins to assume that there are no natives whom he can meet on grounds of social equality; accidentally somewhere he meets an Indian gentleman or lady as well educated as himself, and at once he hastens to conclude that the English in India deliberately keep away from natives. He does not know that in India people are still living in compartments; there is less social intercourse between Mahomedan and Hindu or between Rajput and Parsi than between any of these races and the English in India. If there is aloofness, it is much more due to the Indian not unnaturally preferring his own section of the community to the others. As to the Indians who complain about not having enough intercourse with Englishmen, they are generally men who (probably for the most honourable reasons, such as breaking some caste rules) are not readily received by their own people, and thus wish to know the English, who, not being conversant with Indian customs, are shy to mix with them. Yet, even as things are, Englishmen, and Englishmen alone, receive and have friends amongst all classes and races. Where is the Hindu or Mahomedan who has so many devoted friends and admirers amongst all races as the late Sir J. Woodburn had in Calcutta, or Sir Lawrence Jenkins has in Bombay? Such men, respected and looked upon with affection by all races, are no doubt rare in India; but they are rare in every country. However, they prove that when the Hindu and Moslem and Parsi and Sikh and Rajput do find a common friend it is invariably a noble-hearted Englishmen, and that there is none of that want of sympathy with Indians socially on which some people constantly insist.

According to others – for we have not come yet to the last of those suggested causes of the unrest of today – the explanation lies in this fact, that India is a conquered country, and, whatever her foreign Government may do, the very nature of that rule will make it unpopular. To see if this theory will explain the facts let us turn to the history of India. Was ever India conquered as Gaul or Britain were by Rome? Was there ever such a place as India before various causes unified vast territories under the Crown of England? Were the Moghuls a national dynasty like the family of the Mikados in Japan? From the very first day when the East India Company began that career of conquest till today have we a single instance where Englishmen as mere conquerors attacked Indians? Throughout they were in alliance with the natives of the country. Princes and peasants alike turned by instinct to the white race for help against the internal and external enemies who were then fighting over the remains of the Moghul Empire. More native troops fought for England in the dark days of the

Mutiny than against her. To describe a confederation built on such lines as a conquered country is to forget the origin of British rule.

We have now come to the end of our hurried examination of various suggested causes of discontent and of some remedies, such as more efficient administration and slow growth of material prosperity. We have found them insufficient either to explain the facts or to prevent the mischief. Before venturing to suggest what I consider to be the cause, and a remedy for the unsatisfactory position of affairs in India, I must explain why it is necessary to change the system, and why its continuance will in the long run endanger British rule. The fact that the fighting races, such as Sikhs, Rajputs, Goorkhas, and Mahomedans, have not so far been affected by the form of discontent known in the older British provinces cannot be a source of comfort to us. We will begin by taking the Mahomedans, because they are probably the most compact and numerous body who have kept themselves aloof from political movement. There is danger of the Mahomedan attitude being misunderstood. It is not, as some people fondly imagine, mere opposition to concessions on the part of the British Government towards the Indians. It is a desire to have changes introduced different from those advocated by the Congress representatives. We will take two instances. Mahomedans are no more satisfied than Hindus with the present system by which the Government of India and the local Governments name their representatives to the various legislatures. But instead of wanting mere territorial representation which they consider alike unsuited to the religious and racial differences and to the present state of moral civilisation, they require a special system of representation, which their spokesmen have already placed before the Government of India. Though they do not want the present official majority to be reduced, and the power of the Government over legislation brought down to the mere veto of the Viceroy or Governor (an evil system which they firmly believe will leave all legislative power to the majority of elected members); they still desire to have larger legislative bodies. Again, they are anxious for a university of their own at Aligarh. Their leaders constantly assure them that the future of their faith and the revival of their artistic and literary powers depends upon it. This does not mean that they welcome the making of higher education more expensive. If the Mahomedan rank and file are once convinced that their aloofness from the agitation of today means that it will lead to the mere marking of time, and perhaps even reaction, I feel convinced that no amount of influence from the leaders and the elders will keep them from joining the Conservative section of the Congress Party. My reason for mentioning these things is merely to prove my contention that the attitude of the Mahomedans does not justify a mere negative position on the part of the Government, and that their particular and detailed objections to the representative system asked for by the Congress Presidents annually do not weaken the forces of discontent, for such are due to general causes and not to the details of any system.

As to the Sikhs, Rajputs, Goorkhas, it is only a matter of time before they think as Bengalese and Mahrattas, &c. The railways, posts, telegraphs, and canals that efficient administration introduces are influencing even these races. Their stolidity has so far kept them a great deal outside the political movement, but even that is giving way before the communications and schools of today. The Punjab is a case in point. It would be impossible to exaggerate the change that has come over the political feelings of its inhabitants within the last seven or eight years. Lahore is politically becoming a suburb of Calcutta. Nor can feelings be changed except by the removal of their radical cause. I fear those who get some comfort from the so-called opposition of these races to the discontented section of British Indians are, unless the discontent itself is removed, destined to a rude awakening.

The belief, not often expressed, but ever remembered by some of those thinkers who really guide the policy of England towards India, we are compelled to discuss and criticise here. Unfortunately want of space obliges me to do so hastily. It is thought that though the majority of natives be dissatisfied, and though the ranks of the discontented be increased by the addition of other classes and races, it does not really matter as long as England maintains a strong executive in the country, and is strong enough materially to compel obedience in India. It is shortly stated that the foundation of British rule is the military and naval power of England, *plus* the energy of English Viceroys, civilians, &c., and the excellence of the local communications. One of the most thoughtful of the journals published in the English language (the *Times of India*) recently said, and rightly, that, whatever the amount of discontent in India, there was as little likelihood of physical danger to British rule as of India being buried under snow. It went on to give expression to the central idea which I am now trying to examine, and said that it was because the rulers knew their overwhelming strength that they did not often talk about it, and did not care seriously for the noisy demonstrations of the natives.*

This view of the matter is undoubtedly true. If we consider the immediate state of political affairs, it is no more than the stubborn fact. Though no thinker can ever forget the ethical and moral questions raised by reliance on force, we will in this paper try to show that even from a purely material view mere strength is insufficient to hold India permanently. Undoubtedly if we take a short view of the question, if we think in years and decades, force alone is ample to assure British supremacy. But if we take long views of things . . . the conclusion is different.

Apart from the grim possibilities of foreign war, it should never be forgotten that the overwhelming strength of England is greatly due to the isolated position of India. That vast country is at present practically an island. Turkey and Persia (both feeble States) play the part of non-conductors on the west; on the north Afghanistan and Chinese Turkestan and Thibet, and on the east China herself, prevent that contact with living forces and movements which would revolutionise matters. Things cannot continue for ever in this ideal state. Three forces even now are at work, and any of them would be ample to cause great changes. Germany may well reach Baghdad with her Anatolian Railway. Though I cannot conceive of any danger to England from the Indian Mahomedans through the so-called Pan-Islamic movement, yet the effect produced on the Indian mind generally, and especially on the disaffected classes, by the presence of a Great Power so near would be enormous. A railway to Baghdad, even if it came no nearer, would necessarily make the Gulf a great centre of Indian commercial activity. The opportunities that such intercourse would offer to the great and vigorous Power that built that railway of intriguing with the discontented in India, should there be differences with England over Holland, South America, or some Mediterranean country, would be enough to unsettle the native mind and to require a vastly greater white garrison if England is to keep India by force alone.

Secondly, sooner or later, whatever the result of the present revolution, the Indian and Russian railways will somehow or other meet. Whatever be the state of Anglo-Russian relations, and whatever the form of the Russian Government, the power of the

---

*I am writing this paper on board ship in the Yellow Sea, and thus am quite unable to verify any of my references to various articles, speeches, &c. However, I do not believe that I have misrepresented the meaning of the particular article in the *Times of India* to which I have referred.

discontented party in India will be at once enormously increased, for the isolation that makes the Government of India resemble that of Rome in having no neighbours and being for its subjects the only possible Power would disappear.

Thirdly, we have the possible awakening and development of China. One need not be a believer in the Yellow Peril to imagine a China, assured of her continued national existence through her own strength, carrying on a great commerce and freely communicating with India through Szechuan, Yunan or possibly even Thibet. That too would change the whole nature of that enormous superiority which is absolute today. Nor will it at all help England to build the connecting railways herself and to directly or indirectly own the intermediate States to meet Russia at Herat, Germany at Mosul or Aleppo, Japan and others on the Yang-Tse, if India is discontented and held by force alone. For such is the commercial activity of the Indian, and such his ability to underlive as well as overlive his Arab, Persian, and Afghan neighbours, that what is happening today in Burma and Baluchistan would come to pass; gradually the natives of such newly conquered States would become intellectually Indians, and would be, were India discontented, affected by the same poison. Were a railway carried through Afghanistan, in a few years the Afghans would be as much affected by what may come to be known as the Indian movement as the subjects of the Nizam and the Gaikowar. The only result of such extension of British power would be, were India discontented and held by force alone, that, instead of having three hundred millions of discontented Asiatic subjects, she would have three hundred and fifty or four hundred millions, and, instead of meeting her neighbours far away from their base, she would meet them on their base. Those who care not for the contentment of India's native population forget that the disintegration of such a polity is sure to happen the moment it meets external forces. This impact may be felt through war or commercial competition and exchange or mere influence of ideas. Whatever the details, the foundations of a purely forcible Government will not stand the dissolving forces introduced by constant contact with external policies. There could be only one scientifically perfect method of permanently occupying India in spite of the permanent discontent of her races. Had she a temperate climate, and were her races wanting in natural vitality, her native population might vanish like some other weaker races under Anglo-Saxon dominion. In the case of India such a result is out of the question. With the exception of a few so-called aborigines, her people are free from those natural weaknesses that lead to racial death. We are now forced to the conclusion – though we could bring forward many other arguments in support of our contention – that, taking really long views, as thoughtful men should when discussing matters of such importance, it is necessary for England to possess the affection or at least to prevent the hostility of her Indian subjects if she wishes to rule the country permanently.

Nor is it by any means what I may be permitted to call a "hopeless case." Were one to select the most disaffected men in India to-day and approach them, ninety-nine out of each hundred would say frankly that they greatly preferred what has been by Mr. Gokhale described as the "Colonial Ideal" to one of separation as their national dream. The vast majority of the other 1 per cent., some of whom openly encourage anti-British ideals, will not deny that they would much prefer the Colonial ideal, but that, as they consider it hopeless, they are compelled to go in for the extremest of all possible views. This phenomenon in itself, this clinging of all to some dream of connection with England, shows that there is no really insuperable difficulty, if the matter were dispassionately considered, in bringing an end to the discontent. Race instinct is not the dividing line. And since it is possible for England to possess the affection of her Indian subjects, is it not worth her while at whatever cost – except, of course, honour and safety – to win that love to which she has so many splendid claims? The advantages would be enormous. Were the people of India as mentally satisfied and contented with British rule as they are emotionally loyal to the Throne of England, England alone of all the Great Powers could with safety be permanently free of conscription as understood on the Continent. Were India satisfied, England could safely devote more of her resources towards the improvement of the condition of her working classes, and introduce with greater ease such social reforms as old-age pensions, &c., for which the majority of her people seem so anxious, for the princes and people of India would, moved by patriotic reasons, take a far more active and real interest in the military state of their country than they do at present. England would then possess in India a source of man-power which, *plus* her sea-power and wealth, would make her the only absolutely invulnerable State in the world – far more so even than the United States.

How can India be contented? Shall we accept the Congress programme at once? Before we can do so we must understand clearly what the pith of that programme is. We must take off the silver coatings and look at the actual pill these gentlemen offer us. Now the main recommendation of the Congress is this: The Government of India's legislative power and its financial authority – which in the long run means all her rights and strengths – should be handed over, by perhaps gradual steps, to the people of the country, and the executive should be made mainly Indian. Will the security of British rule and the honour of England allow her to accept this programme? . . . In putting forward my reasons for this belief I will arrive at what I firmly believe to be the real cause of discontent, and what can be in that case its only possible remedy. For if the real power was given over to the people's representatives how would they use it? Would they be satisfied to be led by a very few who are like Mr. Gokhale and many of the accomplished leaders in Bengal, not only intellectually distinguished, but free from all those social prejudices that are the real curse of India? No one who knows the average graduate will think so. Whatever the material or educational test of the franchise, the result would be, under the present state of social civilisation, that power would fall into the hands of individuals or communities who, while in many things abreast of the century, are in other things full of prejudices against the lower classes of their countrymen, unworthy of the days of the Tudors. It must not be forgotten that many of those who are demanding the highest political rights deny at this moment to their own dearest and nearest female relatives the simplest of human rights. If the elected legislators were really powerful, we can well anticipate the type of laws that would satisfy the "educated electors." In such a contingency the dissatisfaction of the masses and of the social reformers with English rule, the new "Parliament," and the new laws would be ever so much greater than today, and infinitely more justifiable. Are we, then, to put the blame on the people who are so full of prejudices, and address them: "Use the liberties you already possess – make them general, you shall then have more"? Such a cold and unsympathetic attitude would be alike unjust and unreasonable. These prejudices have existed so long that, without the indirect help of the Government, they may well take centuries to disappear. Dissatisfaction is not owing to the absence of political concessions made to the people, but to the fact that the public do not see themselves getting appreciably fitter, notwithstanding all the universities, schools, &c., for ever exercising reasonable political power. It must not be imagined that because the lower and middle classes of the towns and villages, the 20 per cent. that count most in India, do not talk of the Queen's proclamation, they have never heard of it or have forgotten it. Certainly the word proclamation is unknown to most of them. But there is a very distinct idea that when the late Queen-Empress assumed the government a distinct promise was made that no difference except "fitness" would exist between her Indian and English subjects, and that step by step everything would be done to raise the brown to the level of the white. The very schools and colleges that became general after 1858 the poor Indian vaguely associated with this policy of improving him. Now fifty years have passed; the schools have done wonders. Yet he knows that, whatever his intellectual powers, he is not very much nearer than before 1858 to the level of his white ruler morally. He is disenchanted, and the necessary result follows – discontentment.

He wants to know when the first earnest steps in raising him morally will be taken. The official answer is cold and distant. The business of the Government is merely to keep law and order; it has no more to do with other improvements than with religion. Quite so. But the Indian qualifies the word business with the adjective direct. The direct business of all Governments is to keep law and order. But indirectly every Government (no Government more so than that of England herself, through the example of her Sovereign) encourages those who work amongst the people for the moral and social improvement of the masses. Even the Government of India as at present constituted does a little by the conferring of honours on philanthropists to encourage social reform. The question is one of degree. Does the Indian Government as at present constituted possess any individual or department that can efficiently help towards the betterment of the social condition of the people? Can a political Viceroy already crushed with the affairs of State take that constant interest in various movements for social reform that should be taken if such improvement is to be due to his influence? Has he the time to encourage or initiate such movements? Of all the reforms carried by successive Viceroys since 1877 probably none will appear to the historian of such real benefit to the people as the medical aid offered by what is known as the Lady Dufferin Fund. It would not be difficult to suggest at least a hundred similar social movements that, with the same encouragement and attention from similarly exalted quarters, would be as beneficial to India as what will be ever associated, through Lady Dufferin's activity, with Lord Dufferin's administration. Nor can reform movements, if they are to be efficient and include the many needs of the people, be left to the influence of a consort only. They require the guidance of the representative of the Crown, and his whole time and thought. The delicate nature of such work makes it impossible for a department or councillor to carry it out. It requires the prestige and the influence of the highest authority. However, these are not the only disadvantages. The example of a political Viceroy working night and day at political affairs and sparing odd moments only from his very short hours of recreation for helping social reform is catching. Naturally many of the best minds in India, many of the most selfless of her sons, whose real province of labour is the betterment of their own castes, unconsciously influenced by the example of the Viceroy, give up their time and thought to political matters. How impossible political reform is while social and racial prejudices continue is the cardinal fact of Indian life. Thus a deadlock arises. Both the English and Indians, who are busy inventing solutions for political problems, forget that no such can be effective under present social conditions. Even in England, which is a nation generations ahead of India, the influence of the Crown used for the benefit of the masses had and has as much to do with the general raising of the standard of civilisation as all the laws passed by Parliament. The stupendous voluntary work done for improving the condition of the people in that country is essentially due to the example of the chief of the State. Again, England enjoys the great boon of having a head of the State who is above all political parties, and who enjoys the loyalty of all. In India there is no individual who, being above political and sectional questions, can ever attract such universal and unifying veneration. Of course, we have the Emperor. But he is not on the spot, and he is represented by one who is intimately associated with and primarily responsible for political decisions, and who is, and will be, as intelligence becomes more general, even more freely criticised. His acts and speeches may sometimes raise feelings that are not such as should be felt for the representative of a universally beloved Sovereign. Nor can it be reasonably expected that the present system can have any other result.

What is the remedy? To the writer's mind there is one and one alone that can assure the natural, gradual, and healthy growth of political freedom in India and unite her for ever to England by sentiment, gratitude, and self-interest. That remedy was suggested by one who is not only one of the most important of India's ruling princes, but who enjoys the confidence and the esteem of the Indian public to a remarkable degree – the Gaikowar of Baroda. His Highness, at the Bombay Social Reform Conference, after an exhaustive review of the state of civilisation in the country, rightly said that one remedy alone could put an end to the present state of affairs. That was to change the constitution of the Government of India – to abolish the political Viceroyalty and to institute a non-political Regency, with a descendant of the Sovereign as a permanent Prince Regent. I am compelled not to enter into the detailed examination of the many political and other advantages of such a change of system alike to England and India, though I hope to resume the consideration of such on some future occasion. However, certain aspects of the question I am forced to inquire into, howsoever hastily, in order to show that there is nothing really impossible about it. The Imperial Titles Act was an instalment of a policy towards India that can be crowned only by some change such as advocated by the Gaikowar. The two principal criticisms of that proposal we are forced to consider. The first one shows the slovenly thinking that is responsible for half the mischief in India. It was actually suggested that the Indian, being an Oriental, could not understand a non-political and irresponsible ruler, that such an authority would not be in keeping with the genius of Eastern races, and that he would constantly associate the Prince with the acts of his advisors. What wonderful wisdom! What knowledge of Oriental history! What was the actual position of an hereditary Hindu raja before the country was influenced by the Tartar or Turkish conquerors of Kashmir, and before the Mahomedan invasion, when new ideas (entirely new, and due to Islam) as to the position of the ruler were introduced into India? The raja, unless he happened to be a usurper or the immediate descendant of one, was the head of society, the representative of the Divine. In his name and by his grace the administration was carried on. But the officers of the State were responsible for political affairs, and they were criticised by the people. Nepaul is today an example of a perfect Hindu polity very little influenced by Islam. Her ruler holds exactly the position that is naturally given by the Hindu mind to the Divine representative, his Sovereign. The political authority is carried on by the Ministers. Again, Japan was for centuries, and would have been even now but for foreign influences, reigned over by irresponsible but unusually reverenced emperors ... To describe systems that prevailed usually in ancient Hindu States, and even now prevail in all the countries influenced by Buddhism, as un-Oriental merely shows the self-satisfied ignorance of such critics.

The second criticism was that the attacks of the native Press would then be directed against a member of the Royal Family. As for this, were a Prince sent out as Viceroy, and the office remained, as at present, a political and responsible one, no doubt the Prince Regent too would be freely criticised like Viceroys at present. But the whole point is that the office would be changed as well, and the Regent would be as little responsible for any act of his advisors as the King-Emperor. Under such an arrangement it is quite inconceivable that the Indian Press should make attacks on the representative of their Emperor. The political work done under the present system would be entrusted to a Prime Minister sent out every five or six years from England, who would be the President of the Executive Council.

Amongst the many advantages of such a system would be the fact that the influence of the Civil Service Members of the Council would be considerably increased indirectly. Any one who knows the splendid work of that service, and their true, though not advertised, sympathy with India, would welcome this increase. Another great advantage would be that while the dangers of responsible Government would be avoided, the disadvantages of the autocratic rule of today, already out of date, would disappear; for the Prime Minister, not having the prestige of being Viceroy, would be more thoroughly criticised by his Council than at present, and his hasty decisions would never appear before the public. Above all, the Government would have the advice, the knowledge, the experience of the Regent to guide them; for, of course, as in all constitutional countries, the Ministry or Council would have, when submitting their measures, to explain clearly all their reasons to the Regent. Of course, the Regent must be a very near relative, son or grandson, of the Sovereign. Coming out to India at about the same age as a Civil Servant usually does, for some thirty years' Regency, the Prince can retire from office soon after he is fifty. Round the Regent slowly would gather all the most earnest men of India, chiefs and princes downwards. Political questions would receive the amount of interest and importance due to them, and not, as at present, practically monopolise Indian public life. The Regent, being free from political cares, would put himself at the head of all movements, social, literary, economic and artistic, that improved the relations of all sections of society, that destroyed racial and religious particularisms, that helped to amalgamate the parts into a healthy whole. Sympathy the Government of India lacks, because its Constitution prevents its members from having the time to take an active interest in the emotional life and social progress of the people. The Prince would soon get to be acquainted with the life of the people considered as a whole. The social reforms carried would, being due to the guidance of the Regent and the free choice of the people, be the best possible school for learning the secret of political freedom that India can ever possess. The Prince's interest in national life as a whole would elevate it by attracting to its service many of the best brains now wasted in the arid field of political controversy. Political changes so constantly prayed for would then come naturally, and be welcomed alike by India and England, for they would be the result of mutual understanding.

One may say with as much certitude as such contingent judgments admit that under such a Regency India can be governed for eighty or ninety years *at least* without any political change in the real character of its government, and with benefit alike to her own people and to the Empire. Even then the political changes which came would be gradual, and would not in any way anticipate the moral ideas of the country, for voluntary social reforms would have preceded all others. And the government would be, in the meanwhile, not merely the exercise of authority by superior force, but the exercise of such rights by a Regent who would possess the love of all classes. England would regain, as one improvement after another assured the people of the benefits of her rule, that contentment which pessimism has now stolen from her. And the imagination of the people of India, once so powerfully impressed by the superior benefits of British rule, would again be, like the intellect of those races, impressed by the superior and disinterested political morality of her rulers.*

Will Englishmen ever consider these questions impartially and act on their merits, or will the innate conservatism of the race prevent them from such bold political speculations? Will the great Liberal Party take the first steps towards preparing the Indian subjects of the King for taking their proper place in his Empire? Or will the party that is deeply interested in federation and union of the Empire remove the canker of discontent in India by giving that country a Government suited to her present state of development, and thus, by crowning the work of the two Conservative

*When English rule was at first established it appealed to the imagination of the people through its two great principles – absolute religious toleration and equal justice. However, the people have now become so used to these two things that they look on them as matters of course, and the lower classes especially have become incapable of conceiving of an intolerant or an unjust Government. Their very ignorance has helped to make them forget the state of affairs that prevailed in the eighteenth century and earlier.

Governments of 1858 and 1876, strengthen the Empire? Let the Indian pray that it will be no party matter, but that England as a whole will take this most important of all her measures for raising, in the fullness of time, the greatest of her foster-children to the level of her own daughter nations.

Source: *National Review*, London, February 1907, pp. 951–72.

The journal, a monthly of conservative views, was at this time edited by L. J. Maxse.

9

ADVICE TO THE MUSLIM LEAGUE

Inaugural Address to the Deccan Muslim League Meeting

Poona: 12 August 1908

The new forces affecting India – what patriotism and love for India mean – violent disturbances arrest the forces of progress – unification of India a slow process – alternatives to British rule: internal anarchy or unsympathetic foreign domination.

My dear Mr. President. It was my earnest desire to attend the first meeting of the League of Moslems of the Deccan, and to discuss with them the questions which must be stirring all thoughtful, patriotic Indians at the present juncture. But unfortunately business of the most urgent character has called me away; I can only briefly write the views which I should have liked personally to put before the League.

The times are such when no true Indian patriot can remain silent. We find the country in the grip of new forces, quivering with new emotions. Amid much that is good we see, alas! a growing indiscipline and contempt for authority, striving after change without perceiving whither that change would lead us, and the setting up of false and impracticable constitutional ideals which will mislead the unthinking. No man who loves his country, as we do, can stand idly by, and see India drift into courses leading irrevocably to disaster.

I have referred to the duty of patriotic Indians. What do we mean by patriotism? Love of one's country. This is no cold and abstract sentiment, like the love of beauty and the arts. It is a constant and fixed desire, like the longing for health and strength – it is a passion which fills our lives and colours all our ideals, aiming always at serving our country and maintaining its laws and institutions. In India, patriotism, and love of country, must mean the desire to see its people happy and prosperous and contented; its soil and natural resources developed; its intellectual life quickened, ennobled by example, stimulated towards progress. But these ends – ends which must be the goal of every true patriot – can only be reached by the processes of development and evolution working on natural lines. Violent disturbances arrest the growth of the forces which make for progress, perhaps for generations.

But these processes of evolution and development, which are the fundamental bases of national progress, imply the existence of a strong, just and stable Government: a Government strong enough to resist external aggression and maintain internal order: a Government powerful enough to protect the interests of the weak against the pressure of the strong, and prevent minorities from being crushed by the weight of powerful majorities: a Government which will secure justice and equality of opportunity for all. In Europe and America, the various races have been moulded into homogeneous States by centuries of combined self-sacrifice and by unity of ideals. It took a century to weld Norman and Saxon into England; another six centuries to amalgamate England and Scotland into Great Britain. Ten centuries elapsed between the death of Charlemagne and the dissolution of his premature Empire, and the union of the German States under one head. Even in America, built out of ready-made European human materials, union came only after one of the fiercest wars in the history of the world. In India no such union as is essential to the creation of a strong, independent, homogeneous State is possible without centuries of consolidation. Even if we assume that the forces tending to unification are quickened by the machinery of modern civilisation, generations must pass before India is a nation. In very truth we can detect no signs of the advent of that unity which is the first essential to the creation of a modern State.

Is it not abundantly clear then that until such unity is attained the maintenance of British rule is an absolute, a paramount necessity? India must have a strong and effective Government. Great Britain alone can give her the protection and guidance which are essential to her progress and prosperity... Assuming that ["Swaraj"] were possible of attainment, it would, by throwing the country into inextricable confusion, arrest the march of all those forces which are steadily, if slowly, pressing India forward in the paths of industrial, economic, social and intellectual advancement. But we all know that neither now nor in the perceptible future is "Swaraj" possible of attainment.

There is no alternative between British rule and internal anarchy or some other form of foreign domination. Will any man who can think clearly say that any other form of foreign domination could do for India a tithe of what Great Britain has done in the past: would hold out the prospect of a tithe of the progress which is possible under British rule in the future?

Let us look these facts squarely in the face. If we do we cannot fail to see that until the Indian peoples are so united that out of them can be fashioned a homogeneous, independent State, British rule – not only a titular supremacy but a vigorous force permeating every branch of administration – is an absolute necessity. Therefore, I put it to you that it is the duty of all true Indian patriots to make that rule strong. I do not mean strong in the physical sense. That is the duty of Great Britain, which she is perfectly able to discharge. Moreover, Great Britain's mission in the East is not and never has been one of force, but of the peace and liberality, which have brought the tens of millions in Asia the comfort, the prosperity, and opportunities of intellectual advancement which they now enjoy. No! I mean strong in its hold on the mind, the affection, the imagination of the peoples of India. This is a duty which lies not only upon Muhammadans, but equally upon Hindus, Parsis and Sikhs, upon all who are convinced of the benevolence of British rule. If there are any amongst the less thoughtful members of the Hindu community who think they can snatch temporary advantage by social supremacy, let them pause upon all they would lose by the withdrawal of that British control under which has been effected the amazing progress of the past century.

These are the patriotic ideals which, I think, should animate the Muhammadan community at the present juncture. Recognising, as we must do, that British rule is essential to India – that it is the only rule which can preserve us from internal anarchy or unsympathetic foreign domination, that it is the only rule under which India can march steadily along the paths of peace, contentment, and moral and intellectual progress by which we have advanced so far – let us bend all our energies to making that rule strong in its hold upon the imagination and affection of the people of India. Ours must be no lukewarm patriotism, no passive unemotional acquiescence in the established order. It must be a living, controlling, vitalising force, guiding all our actions, shaping all our ideals.

Here in the Deccan we should pursue these ideals and combat the disruptive, retrograde forces at work in no sectarian spirit. Rather, should it be our task to persuade by precept and example those Hindus who have strayed from the path of true progress to return to it. But because I see so clearly the chaos and retrogression which threaten India from the growth of some of the new forces we find at work, because I shudder at the anarchy, the loss, the moral and material suffering which must befall our country if they are allowed to spread, I say from the bottom of my heart that it is the duty of all true Indian patriots not only to accept British rule as the indispensable condition of natural advancement, but to make the strengthening of that rule the fixed purpose of their lives.

Source: *The Civil and Military Gazette*, Lahore, 18 August 1908.

This first meeting of the Deccan League was held at the Band Cottage, Poona, on Wednesday, 12 August 1908. Delegates from all the important districts of the provinces and leading Muslims of the city of Poona were present. Mawlawi Rafiuddin Ahmad was in the chair, and at the end of his speech he announced that the Aga Khan had accepted "the offer of permanent Presidentship of the League, made to him by your Committee". As the Aga Khan was unable to attend, his inaugural address was read out to the session by Rafiuddin Ahmad.

10

THE PROBLEM OF THE MINORITIES IN INDIA

Interview with The Times

London: 14 February 1909

The ideal remains of a united people of one nationality – but differences between Hindus and Muslims must be recognized – unifying tendency introduced by British rule – one element in the population should not be placed in a position where it can dictate to the other – separate Muslim electorate means sending representatives to an exclusively Muslim electoral college – the principle of minority representation should be applied to other small communities and extended to local government – a Muslim member in the Executive Council – Hindus cannot speak for the whole of India.

The ideal for my country to which I look forward is that of an eventually united people of one nationality among whom religious differences, now so acute, will have the minor significance in social and political life they have, for instance, in the United States between Christians and Jews. There can never be, perhaps, so close an affinity between the various communities in India as between Catholics and Protestants in England, who, after all, are both believers in the main tenets of the Christian faith. But while holding the ideal of a united people in India with strength and earnestness, I hold no less strongly that in framing the new political order of things statesmanship must take account of the wide differences which separate Hindus and Musulmans at the present time. These differences are not only religious, they are historical and physical, and in the latter respect, at least, they soon become marked, even in the case of recent converts to the Moslem faith. The changes of dietary habits, outlook, and social life generally consequent upon such conversion soon tell upon body and mind, as has often been pointed out. When I reflect upon the great distinctions between the two races –

distinctions more or less known to every one familiar with India – I have to admit that fulfilment of the ideal of homogeneity lies in a future so distant that it is quite beyond me to predict the date of its arrival. If there is some tendency in the desired direction, it is the result of the unifying change wrought in India by British rule – of internal peace and security unknown before; of resources of civilization, such as railways and municipal water supplies, compelling some abrogation of the fetters of caste; of economic developments involving the co-operative work of different elements of the population; and of equality in law of all classes, in regard to the protection of person and property. These factors, though met by strong opposing forces, will, with other favouring conditions, slowly but surely do the work of unification, always provided there is no forcing of the pace by artificial stimulus prescribed from above, or, in other words, by political machinery created by the Sovereign Power.

The British Government has hitherto been most careful to maintain a neutral attitude as between one religion and another, and it has thus been in a position, moral as well as physical, to keep the peace when conflict, involving public disorder, has been threatened or has broken out. In this way the Government has created an atmosphere favourable to the spread of the spirit of real intellectual toleration. But the growth of this spirit is a work of time, and existing divisions will be widened instead of being bridged if at the present stage, by political machinery provided by the Sovereign power, one element in the population is placed in a position to dictate its will to the other elements. An Act of Parliament cannot weld into one, by electoral machinery, two nationalities so distinct as the Hindus and the Mahomedans. The former is a vast conservative and widely-varying federation, while Islam is a proselytizing and unifying faith, so closely corresponding in doctrine and ritual with Judaism that it is much nearer in spirit and origin to Christianity than it is to Hinduism. With such vast differences existing, it is certain that if one element gets excessive political power, or is in a position to dictate its will on the other, it will always not only be liable but compelled by religious and social circumstances to exert that authority. It is not that the leaders of the Hindu majority want to do us injustice, but they will be compelled by circumstances to use to the full the political supremacy over us they may possess. They have to take into account the crude and often fanatical notions of the unlettered throng. Even now, with the control of the executive authority entirely in neutral British hands, there are occasional

outbreaks of rioting between the two communities, and such outbreaks in all probability would be much more frequent and much
more serious if an idea prevailed that political power held by
one of the contending parties was being turned to racial account.
It has to be remembered that while educated men may be
expected to have no real sympathy with riotous intolerance, pressure may be brought to bear upon them by less-instructed family
connexions and other co-religionists, and that usually, owing
to neglect of female education, their own wives belong to the
uneducated, and sometimes to the fanatical, portions of the
population. Under ordinary conditions this liability to pressure
might not greatly matter, but at times of stress these unhappy
social influences will be felt. Thereby the gulf would be widened.
So from the very point of view of promoting a united India
eventually, and the happiness of the country now and hereafter,
we Mahomedans must protest against any features of the proposed constitutional reforms which may work injustice.

[I have] read with keen interest and appreciation the speeches
on the subject of Mr. Ali Imam at the Amritsar Conference [of
the All India Muslim League] and of Mr. Ameer Ali in London,
as also the communications the latter had made to *The Times.*

I can cordially endorse their respective statements of the Mahomedan position, and I am glad it has been put so clearly to Lord
Morley. I trust his lordship will take an early opportunity of
making definitive his intimation that he may be willing to
concede the principle of an exclusively Mahomedan electorate
sending their representatives to an exclusively Mahomedan electoral college. Unless this modification of the original plan is
effected there cannot be a fulfilment of the pledge given to the
deputation I introduced to Lord Minto more than two years ago,
that the rights and interests of the Moslem community would be
safeguarded in any administrative reconstruction in which his
Excellency might be concerned. As to the suggestion that Mahomedans should be at liberty to elect members of other
communities to represent them in the electoral colleges, the
same right being given to Hindu and other electors, I am of
opinion that while this might be done eventually without grave
disadvantage, such a step would be most premature in existing
conditions, and having regard to the business and social pressure
which might in that case be put upon electors. For some years
to come it should be laid down that members of the Mahomedan
electoral colleges (I assume that the colleges are to be separate)
should themselves be Mahomedans.

[The Aga Khan went on to express keen regret that Lord Morley, while admitting the necessity for taking into account modifying local circumstances, desires to adhere to numerical strength as the main factor in determining the number of representatives of the different communities.] Upon a strict proportional basis the Musulman representation will be absolutely inadequate. It must be sufficient, taking into account the balance of parties, to be of real importance as a political factor. I quite agree with Mr. Ameer Ali that the many millions of outcast Hindus whose very touch and even their presence is defilement for the "twice-born" Brahmin cannot with justice be reckoned among the peoples whom high-caste Hindus can properly claim to represent. Moreover, in fixing electoral proportions regard must be had to the tendency revealed in the last three decennial census reports for the Moslem ratio to total population to increase while the huge Hindu ratio tends to diminish. For my part I see no reason whatever why the principle of minority representation should not be applied to minor communities as well as to the Mahomedans. On the contrary, I strongly favour such representation as an act of justice, and had health and strength permitted I would have drawn earnest attention to this respect of the subject. The difficulties in the way are not so great as has been suggested, for it so happens that in almost all cases the great bulk of the smaller communities are collected in provincial areas, where their distinct representation can be easily arranged for. To give but two examples, the Sikhs are mainly centred in the Punjab, and the Buddhists in Burma or on its confines. No one who studies the subject can fail to be struck by the wide divergencies in ethnographic characteristics between one province and another. In view of these conditions, it seems to me that the only procedure by which the interests of authorities can be safeguarded is for the legislative seats in the respective provinces to be apportioned not by mandate from Whitehall, but by the executive authority of the Viceroy in Council and the respective local Governments, nor should such apportionments be confined to the seats on the Legislatures. The principle should be extended to local self-government in all its forms; and all the way through, on rural boards, on municipalities and on the Councils there should be representation of Mahomedans by Mahomedans.

[His Highness went on to say that he had noted with disappointment Lord Morley's statement that he could not assent to the proposition that if a Hindu is appointed to the Executive

Council a Mahomedan should also be appointed, and *vice versa.*]
The Secretary of State has said that in making any recommendations to the Crown he will go upon the principle of appointing
an Indian as such, and not as a Hindu or Mahomedan. This is
all very well in theory, and would be satisfactory if there were to
be found qualified men able to represent and trusted by both
communities; but bearing in mind the enormous differences
between them at this stage, it is scarcely too much to say that the
Indian who could represent both has yet to be born. As to
the objection that to give two out of six "ordinary" seats to Indians
would be a serious step, I consider that this difficulty might be
met by appointing both a Hindu and a Mahomedan to be advisers
of the Viceroy and the Council without portfolio, but with the
same emoluments as the members of the Council. Such appointments would, of course, be additional to the existing Council,
and the arrangement would be more analogous to the precedent
of two Indian appointments to the Council of the Secretary of
the State to which Lord Morley referred as an advantage. The
presence among the Viceroy's colleagues of two Indians not
absorbed in the charge of a department, but able to give advice
from their knowledge of the Hindu and the Mahomedan mind
respectively, would give to the deliberations of the Government
of India a leisured element such as exists in the English Cabinet,
wherein men whose experience and knowledge is valued but who
are free from heavy departmental work are available as holders
of such offices as those of Lord Privy Seal, Lord President of the
Council, and Chancellor of the Duchy. For my own part, I feel it
would be better to have no Indian representation on the Executive Council than that it should be representative of only one of
the leading communities.

The fact is that no reform scheme for India can yield satisfactory results which does not deal with conditions as they exist
today. It is futile to introduce methods that might be appropriate
to the conditions of 50 years hence. They are bound to break
down and to retard the growth of that national feeling which is
to be desiderated. If present conditions are duly recognized,
Hindus and Mahomedans will more and more come to see that
they have many common interests, and thus will be evolved a
spirit of homogeneity which can only be checked by premature
and artificial methods of unification imposed by legislative and
executive mandate. Now is the opportunity for leading Hindus
to show a true spirit of patriotism and good will by recognizing
that Mahomedan misgivings as to the original scheme are just

and reasonable. They should frankly abandon the untenable claim that they speak for the whole of India, and they should recognize that the minority representation to which many of them agree in theory can [*sic*] be real and effective without the changes for which the Mahomedans have asked. By adopting such an attitude they will do far more to lay the foundations of eventual Indian nationality than by clamouring for adhesion to methods which, designed no doubt to advance that end, will in reality greatly retard it.

Source: *The Times*, London, 15 February 1909, and *The Civil and Military Gazette*, Lahore, 14 March 1909.

The making of the Morley-Minto reforms is described and analysed in the following works: *Papers Relating to an Imperial Advisory Council and Provincial Advisory Councils*, London, 1907, Cd. 3710; *Advisory and Legislative Councils...*, London, 1908, 3 vols, Cd. 4426, 4435 and 4436; *Representation of Muhammadans on Legislative Councils*, London, 1909, Cd. 4652; London Muslim League, *The Indian Muhammadans and the Reforms*, London, n.d. (? 1909); John, Viscount Morley, *Recollections*, London, 1917, 2 vols; Mary, Countess of Minto, *India: Minto and Morley, 1905-1910*, London, 1934; K. K. Aziz, *Britain and Muslim India*, London, 1963; S. R. Wasti, *Lord Minto and the Indian Nationalist Movement, 1905 to 1910*, Oxford, 1964; and Stanley A. Wolpert, *Morley and India, 1906-1910*, Berkley and Los Angeles, 1967.

11

RECENT DEVELOPMENTS IN INDIAN POLITICS

Letter to the London Muslim League

London: 23 February 1909

Representation of elements with a steadying effect on Indian politics – members of "Constitutionalist Party" could take a broad and dispassionate view of public questions – Indian advice to the Governor should not be one-sided.

The Chairman, in giving the toast of "The Aga Khan", read a letter from His Highness, written in the event of his being precluded from attending the luncheon, stating that he desired to supplement the views he had already expressed by calling attention to the abnormal conditions which had come into existence in India of late. They made it necessary in the vital interests of empire that the elements which exercised a steadying effect on Indian politics should be strongly represented on the new Councils.

"We all know," continued His Highness, "that ideas inconsistent with British rule have recently gained ground among the people. There can be little doubt under such circumstances that the members who would be returned will not all belong to the party of Moderates. The exaggerated criticism to which the policy and measures of [the] Government would in all probability be subjected at the hands of the very advanced sections would have a most mischievous effect on the population. This can be counteracted only if the Constitutionalist Party among the non-official members of Councils is sufficiently strong to represent matters in their proper light, and to take a broad and dispassionate view of public questions. With regard to the Executive Council of the Viceroy and of the provincial Governors, I wish to make one observation in addition to what I have already said – namely, that Indian advice on the governing bodies, to be of practical value, should not be one-sided." (Cheers).

Source: *The Civil and Military Gazette*, Lahore, 19 March 1909.

The London Muslim League gave a luncheon to meet the Aga Khan on 23 February at the Westminster Palace Hotel, London. But the guest, who had been in indifferent health for many past months, had been ordered to take a period of complete rest in a nursing home. Yet, he planned to leave the home for a few hours to attend and speak at the luncheon. But his doctors advised against it, and Sayyid Ameer Ali, the president of the London Muslim League, read out to the assembled guests a letter from the Aga Khan's medical adviser regretting that he was not in a fit condition to come to the party. Ameer Ali, in giving the toast to the Aga Khan, read out a letter which the latter had sent from the nursing home. This brief letter is reproduced here.

Among those present at the luncheon were Lord Avebury, Lord Ronaldshay, Sir Raymond West, Sir Charles Crostwaite, Sir George Birdwood, Sir Henry Cotton, Sir George Mackenzie, Sir A. T. Arundel, Sir William Bigge, Sir Percy Bunting, Sir M. M. Bhownaggree, J. D. Rees, T. Hart Davies, T. J. Bennett, C. E. Buckland, Major Syed Hasan, C. A. Latif and Ibn-i-Ahmad.

Ameer Ali's speech on the occasion is worth reproducing. He said that at this important epoch in Indian administration the Mahomedans felt that neglect to keep their claims before Government and the public might permanently and seriously prejudice their interests. They had cordially welcomed the principle of the projected reforms in the conviction that their legitimate rights would be adequately and substantially guarded in applying details. He held that they had not put forward any undue claims or made any demand which could be looked upon as encroaching on the just rights of any other community. (Cheers).

Although the Viceroy had admitted the justice of their claim to a share in political privileges commensurate not only with their numbers but with their historical and political importance, it had been assailed from many not altogether uninterested quarters. He would remind them that the East India Company acquired its rights to three of the richest provinces under a grant of a Mussulman sovereign – (cheers) – and today the Mahomedans of India were connected by ties of race, religion, and traditions with the whole of Western Asia and Northern Africa right away to the Atlantic. Throughout those vast regions England occupied an unchallenged position as the champion of Justice and fair play. (Hear, hear). He went on to observe that the Mahomedans supplied soldiers to the British-Indian Army to a larger extent than the communities who expected to profit most by these reforms. In the social economy of the country their upper classes occupied an acknowledged position of weight and influence beyond their actual numbers.

Repudiating the suggestion that the Mahomedan attitude towards the reforms had been inspired by racial or religious antagonism, the Chairman declared that their educated men were anxious to live in harmony and work in concord with their fellow countrymen, co-operating with them, as with the servants of the Crown, for the common good. At the same time they could not shut their eyes to the divergences which had divided and still divided the rank and file of Hindoos and Mahomedans – divergences which ramified in all directions, entered into all the minutiae of life, and made of them, in fact, two distinct nations. These two absolutely antithetical systems had existed side by side for ten centuries, with, on the whole, great toleration from each to each without amalgamation. It was quite erroneous to liken the differences between them to those between Roman Catholics and Protestants. Hindus and Mahomedans were not the followers of two sects or communions, but of two wholly distinct systems – distinct not only in their religion and institutions, rites, and observances, but even in their food and dress. Hinduism was a vast conservative federation, hedged round by stringent rules of caste. Mahomedanism was democratic, tending towards Socialism, and opening the door to all comers. So long as there was no fancied or real encroachment on either side there was much good will among the lower *strata*, and among the better minds and educated classes there was real friendship. But any attempt to drive the smaller into the bigger camp would only lead to discord and strife. (Cheers). It was only by recognizing the differences between the two nations and their equal importance as factors in the administration of the country, and by not allowing the interests of the one to be subordinated to the interests or ambitions of the other that the impending reforms could be made successful. (Cheers). The proposals as they originally stood caused much dismay among the Mahomedans in all parts of the country, it being felt that unless there were substantial modifications the Mahomedans would be placed in a state of permanent subordination to their fellow-countrymen, a position they could not accept. (Cheers). Lord Morley's courteous reception of the recent Moslem deputation had unquestionably eased the situation, and there was now an expectant attitude.

Proceeding to urge that a system of proportional representation would be wholly unsuited to the conditions of Indian life, the Chairman said that vast masses of low-caste tribes and communities who either disclaimed the designation or were nominally Hindus were included in the Hindu figures, and the claim was made that the proportion of representation should be based upon these figures. The transparent injustice of the suggestion did not seem to strike the partisan mind. After giving illustrations of the difficulty of fixing representation in India on the bases of numerical proportions, Mr. Ameer Ali said that, irrespective of the question of balance of parties important for the even working of the State machinery, it was only just and equitable that the representation of the two communities should be determined on consideration of policy and local circumstances. (Cheers). For his part he could not conceive how separate electorates or adequate representation of the Mahomedans in the Councils could possibly prejudice the interests of the other communities. Both patriotism and policy, it might be supposed, would impel their fellow-countrymen in general to concede such reasonable demands as some of their best men, he believed, were inclined to do. In regard to the Viceroy's Executive, the Mahomedans thought that the introduction of one Indian alone, however capable and qualified, who must necessarily belong to one or the other community, would not, in the absence of a thorough spirit of compromise among the population at large, prove satisfactory. It would give rise to frequent complaints of unfairness and prejudice, and would be detrimental to the interests of the State. When the deputation raised this point, Lord Morley gave them a friendly admonition meant to show their mistake in mooting a question that might make difficult the carrying out of a generous resolve. But in stating the Mussulman view the deputation had no *arriere pensee*, no 'tactics' in mind, 'dubious' or otherwise. (Laughter and cheers). On the contrary, they sought to assist the Government, so far as lay in their power, in the solution of a great problem. An Eastern sage had said that 'It is treason to keep the truth from the King'. They would have been false to their sovereign and their people if they had refrained, on account of timidity or 'tactics', from stating clearly and explicitly the feelings and opinions of the Mussulmans. (Loud cheers). (*The Civil and Military Gazette*, Lahore, 19 March 1909.)

The Right Honourable Sayyid Ameer Ali (1849–1928), was the fourth son of Sayyid Saadat Ali of Mohan, Oudh. Educated at Hoogly College. Called to the bar at Inner Temple, 1873. Lecturer in Muhammadan Law, Presidency College, Calcutta, 1873–8. President, Committee of Management, Mohsin Endowment, 1876–1904. Member, Committee of Inquiry into the affairs of the ex-King of Oudh, 1879. Magistrate and Chief Magistrate, 1878–81. Member, Bengal Legislative Council, 1878–83. Tagore Law Professor, University of Calcutta, 1884. President, Faculty of Law, University of Calcutta, 1891–2. Member, Imperial Legislative Council, 1883–5. Judge, Calcutta High Court, 1890–1904. Member, Judicial Committee of the Privy Council, 1909–28. Honorary LL D, University of Cambridge. Honorary Doctor of Laws, University of Calcutta. Honorary D.Litt., University of Aligarh. Author of *Critical Examination of the Life and Teachings of Mohammed, Spirit of Islam, Ethics of Islam, A Short History of the Saracens, Personal Law of the Muhammadans, Muhammadan Law* (2 vols), *Students' Handbook of Muhammadan Law*, joint author of *The Law of Evidence Applicable to British India, Commentary on the Bengal Tenancy Act* and *The Code of Civil Procedure*. Wrote several articles on Islam and India in British journals.

On Ameer Ali, see K. K. Aziz, *Ameer Ali: His Life and Work*, Lahore, 1968; Badruddin Ahmad Bogra, *The Bengal Musalmans or a Short Sketch of Muhammadan Life in Bengal*, Calcutta, 1885; C. E. Buckland, *Bengal Under the Lieutenant Governors: Being a Narrative of the Principal Events and Public Measures During their Periods of Office from 1854 to 1901*, Calcutta, 1901, 2 vols; Marquess of Dufferin and Ava, *Speeches Delivered in India, 1884–1888*, London 1890; *Eminent Musalmans*, G. A. Natesan, Madras, n.d.; J. N. Farquhar, *Modern Religious Movements in India*, New York, 1915, rev. edn, 1919; Almeric Fitzroy, *Memoirs*, London, n.d., 2 vols; Julius Germanus, *Modern Movements in Islam*, Calcutta, 1932; H. A. R. Gibb, *Modern Trends in Islam*, Chicago, 1947; *Indian Judges: Biographical and Critical Sketches (with Portraits)*, G. A. Natesan, Madras, n.d.; Viscount Morley, *Indian Speeches (1907–1909)*, London, 1909; John R. Mott (ed.), *The Moslem World of Today*, London, 1925; Wilfred C. Smith, *Modern Islam in India: A Social Analysis*, Lahore, 1943, London edn, 1946; Murray T. Titus, *Indian Islam*, London 1930; Felix Valyi, *Spiritual and Political Revolution in Islam*, London, 1925; S. R. Wasti, *Lord Minto and the Indian Nationalist Movement, 1905 to 1910*, Oxford, 1964; Samuel G. Wilson, *Modern Movements among Muslims*, New York, 1916; and S. M. Zwemer, E. M. Wherry and J. L. Barton, *The Muhammadan World Today: Being Papers Read at the First Missionary Conference on behalf of the Muhammadan World Held at Cairo, April 4–9, 1906*, London, 2nd edn, 1906.

There is no study in existence in any language and of any size of Ameer Ali's religious ideas. And he still awaits a biographer.

12

THE MUSLIM PROBLEM IN INDIA

Speech at the First Annual General Meeting of the London Muslim League

London: 24 June 1909

Numerical strength of the Muslim community in India – their welfare and progress are of concern to the entire Islamic world – the London League's work for the Muslim cause – Muslim loyalty to Britain – Muslim demand for an equitable share in the constitutional privileges being granted to Indians – Indian reforms doomed to failure if pledges made to Muslims are not fulfilled – loyalty to the British sovereign – fusion of Hindus and Muslims cannot be imposed.

The Aga Khan said that many people in this country, even in circles usually well-informed, hearing of the Musulman "minority" in India, failed to realize that it numbered at the last census nearly 62 millions; that its percentage to the total population of India had been steadily rising since the decennial enumeration begun nearly forty years ago; and that it now constituted $21^{1}/_{4}$ per cent. of the total – a figure exclusive of the numerous and martial border tribes included within the political frontier of the Indian Empire. Not only was it the case that the Musulmans to be found within the administrative limits of the dependency substantially outnumbered the entire population of Germany, but their welfare and progress was a matter of concern to that vast brotherhood known as the Islamic world, stretching in unbroken line from the Asiatic seaboard of the Pacific to the African coast of the Atlantic, and numbering considerably more than 250 millions, or 15 per cent. of the entire human race. (Cheers). The King-Emperor had far more Mahomedan subjects than any other Sovereign. In spite of the deeply-rooted prejudices and difficulties that they had to meet, the members of the

298

[London] branch [of the All India Muslim League], by force of sound argument and indisputable fact, had succeeded in convincing the fair-minded people of this country [Britain] that the Indian Moslems, though they might be unversed in the arts of rhetoric, were entitled to consideration. (Cheers). The soundness and justice of their claims in connexion with the reforms had been recognized by an overwhelming proportion of the leading organs of public opinion, and particularly by the foremost of them all, *The Times.* Yet this fact, encouraging and gratifying in itself, had been used against them in unlooked-for quarters. He was never more astonished than when he read in *The Times* of March 6 a message of the Special Correspondent in India stating that high officials in Northern India were expressing alarm as to the advocacy that the claims of the Mahomedans were securing. The "alarm" arose from a fear that such advocacy might "produce an undue exaltation in the minds of Mahomedans". (Laughter). Had these high officials forgotten that throughout the storm and stress of the last few years the Musulmans had remained unswerving in their devoted loyalty to the King-Emperor? (Cheers). They had never indulged in violent agitation, nor had they adopted reprehensible methods of attracting attention to grievances, real or nominal. They had not claimed "self-government", whether on the so-called "colonial basis" or any other. They had remained law-abiding when, in some parts of the country, they were under strong provocation to resent and resist actively the illegal pressure put upon them by persons who seemed bent on undermining British authority. (Cheers). They had asked nothing more than an equitable share in the constitutional privileges now being granted to the Indian peoples. If the independent advocacy of such a demand had caused misgivings in certain official quarters it could only be because the troubles of the last few years had tended to distort the perspective open to them, and because sinister influences were at work. They had been looking through the wrong end of the telescope (Laughter), and it was to be hoped that their apprehensions would in the future be apportioned on juster lines. Undoubtedly early in March there was widespread satisfaction among the Musulmans arising from the specific and unreserved announcement that Lord Morley had made a few days before, that their claims in respect to the electoral system would be met "to the full". But he had not found in any Indian newspaper, whatever its politics, or in his large correspondence from India, one iota of evidence that the Musulmans were at that time "exalted above measure" (Laughter). There was certainly no danger of undue exaltation at the present moment. Notwithstanding the pledges given by the Viceroy to the deputation which he had the honour to introduce nearly three years before, and Lord Morley's pledges of the present year, the Musulmans were even now, when the eleventh hour was far spent, still called upon to press for the practical recognition of their rights. They had still to urge their claims for simple justice; they had still to press the arguments and reasons that had been officially accepted long ago without qualification – accepted, that was, so far as words went.

The measures which the Government of India was about to take fell far short of the promises given. At Oxford the other day, Lord Morley claimed to have fulfilled the pledges given to the people of India; but unhappily this could not be said to be the case so far as the special pledges to the Mahomedans were concerned. Speaking with a full sense of responsibility as president of their [All India Muslim] League, and after fully weighing his words, he said unhesitatingly that if in the final shaping of the plans of the Government those pledges were not carried out to the full, in the spirit as well as in the letter, the Indian reforms were doomed to failure (loud cheers). It was impossible anywhere, and least of all in a country like India, to work a constitutional scheme satisfactorily with one large and important section of the people disappointed and left without real representation, and another section exultant and triumphant because they had been permitted to attain a virtual monopoly of political representation.

Because they declined to accept such a position with complacency, they were spoken of as "Separatists". As a matter of fact no community in India excelled their own in working for the cause of true unity among the Indian peoples . . . When the time was ripe they would be ready to co-operate and unite with any section that did not contain elements of hostility, whether open or covert, to the strength and permanence of the rule of their Sovereign, or to the British agency in India by which it was repesented. Subject to the acceptance of that indispensable condition, the Indian Musulmans had no intention or desire to hold permanently aloof from any feature of, or element in, Indian public life. But fusion could not be effectively brought about by legislative or administrative *fiat* – it must come along the lines of natural evolution; and that evolution must be social and industrial, as well as political. (Cheers). He rejoiced to think that that necessity was recognized by the best minds among the Hindu thinkers of today, being strongly emphasized, for example, by

Mr. Justice Sankaran Nair in his last presidential address at the Indian Social Conference. He would appeal to the leaders of Hindu political thought generally to adopt that sound view in the shaping of their policy; to admit the soundness of their position; and thus to co-operate with them in a policy which, rightly understood, so far from retarding, would hasten the day of evolutionary unity of the Indian peoples. They simply asked that indisputable facts should be recognized in rearing the new electoral fabric. (Cheers).

Source: *The Times*, London, 25 June 1909.

This should be read with Sayyid Ameer Ali's letter to *The Times*, written on 14 May 1909 and published in the issue of 20 May.

13

ACCEPTANCE OF THE MORLEY-MINTO REFORMS

Telegram to The Times

London: 15 November 1909

Endorsement of Lord Morley's reforms

I consider new regulations respecting Council constitute fulfilment pledges made to Muslims, and far in advance of earlier proposals. I strongly recommend them to loyal acceptance by Indian Muslim fellow-subjects. Trust all Indian parties will work spirit mutual goodwill make the new rights granted a success. I propose to address you on the subject in fuller detail by letter.

Source: *The Times*, London, 16 November 1909.
    An almost identical telegram was sent by Sayyid Ameer Ali on the same date, and it appeared in *The Times* on 16 November; see its text in K. K. Aziz, *Ameer Ali*, p. 326.

14

MUSLIMS AND THE MORLEY-MINTO REFORMS

Letter to The Times

London: 16 November 1909

Regulations under the Indian Councils Act not ideal – but Indian Muslims will accept them as fulfilling the pledges made to them earlier – the representation of landowners is complicated – the principle of Muslim participation in the general elections – one day Indians will be united into one nationality – Muslims ready to co-operate with the British and show goodwill to the other communities.

In confirmation of the brief telegram already sent to you, I write to set forth in detail my reasons in welcoming, both personally and in my capacity as president of the All-India Muslim League, the settlement of Muslim claims in respect to representation in the Viceregal Legislature embodied in the regulations under the Indian Councils Act now promulgated. I feel I can do so consistently with my public declarations at a time when fears were entertained by the Mussalmans that the Government was disinclined to adhere fully to the pledges which were made by the Viceroy to the representative Muslim deputation I headed in October, 1906, and which were repeated even more specifically by the Secretary of State in February last.

It would be idle to pretend that the regulations now issued give us all that we could have desired, or that they constitute an ideal solution to the problem. But I regard them – and have every reason to anticipate that my people will regard them – as a real fulfilment in the case of the Supreme Legislature of Lord Morley's pledge of the grant to us of a number of seats in excess of actual numerical strength, and election of our own representatives to the Councils in all stages. The essential point is that our interests as a most important element in Indian life are to be safeguarded; and that being clear, the vast majority of the Indian Mussalmans will not, I am persuaded, stand out in the spirit of Shylock for every jot and tittle that can be read into the pledges. At a time when greatly extended powers are being trusted to the people, a discontented and impracticable spirit would be unworthy of the traditions of the Indian Mussalmans.

The plan propounded by my friend the Hon. The Raja of Mahmudabad in the summer had some advantages over the present scheme. It was upon a much simpler basis. It guaranteed nine Mussalman seats as against the eight definitely provided now. It had the support of a large number of responsible Mussalman landowners in Northern India, and, with certain modifications, it was endorsed by the London branch of the [All India Muslim] League in a representation submitted with my full concurrence. On the other hand, the accepted scheme had the great advantage of conserving in a somewhat fuller degree the principle of separate Mussalman representation. There will be an elected representative of the Mussalman community in Madras, Bombay, Bengal, and the United Provinces, and Eastern Bengal and Assam; and – pending the formation of a suitable electorate in the province – a Muslim will be nominated to represent the community in the Punjab. This will give six distinct and separate Mussalman seats to represent the community in the majority provinces, as has all along been asked. It is in respect to the landowners' seats that the system becomes, perhaps, unduly complicated. At the first election, and alternately at subsequent elections, the Mussalman representatives will be a landowner elected by the zamindars of Sind and one nominated (or on later occasions elected) to represent the Punjab landholders. At the intermediate elections – the second, fourth and so on – the Mussalman landowners of the United Provinces and of Eastern Bengal will each return a representative. The arrangement is confusing, and stands in the way of continuity of the services of capable representatives. But I recognise the advantages of a system of alternation in preventing either the Hindu or the Mussalman landowners of the province concerned being left permanently unrepresented. I also see how difficult it would be in the case of the Bombay Presidency to constitute a homogeneous landowning constituency in the absence of some method of alternation. Incidentally, this difficulty points to the justice and reasonableness of the consistent Mussalman claim to the creation of separate constituencies.

The arrangements I have outlined assure a total of eight Mussalman representatives in the Supreme Legislature. I should have been glad to see a further seat assured by the hypothecation of one of the nominations reserved to the Viceroy for a Mussalman member from the North-West Frontier Province and Baluchistan. However, I trust that, in practice, there will be such nomination in the event of the Muslims failing to return any candidate in the general elections. I recognise that there is a possibility of their securing a seat or two in the general electorate, as, for instance, when a majority of the unofficial members of the Punjab or Eastern Bengal Legislatures are Muslims. I rejoice that the arrangements made introduce the principle of Mussalman participation in the general elections. My public declarations throughout have shown that, while I regard separate Mussalman electorates as a very real necessity of existing conditions, I look forward to a time when the various sections of the Indian population will be a united people of one nationality. Though the Mussalmans cannot hope to win more than a seat or two, at best, they will welcome the opportunities for association with other communities that will be provided in the general electorates.

It is both our bounden duty and our privilege to live and work with the Hindus and other Indian races as loyal subjects of the Imperial Crown. The plan now published does not give the Mussalmans all they could wish, but it will be accepted unreservedly, I hope, as an earnest of our readiness to co-operate with our rulers and to help them in their difficult task of introducing the principles of constitutional government in so diversified a country as India, and also as exhibiting our cordial goodwill towards other communities. It is our earnest hope and cherished expectation that a reciprocal spirit will be shown in other directions. The keeping open of this controversy after a final decision of [the] Government has been reached could only be advised by responsible leaders of a community if the alternative had been a political extinction. Happily, such an alternative is not presented, and it behoves all parties to receive this grant of liberalizing institutions with gratitude, and to do all that lies in their power to make the new arrangements successful. For my own part, I shall feel that any contribution I may make, or have made, to this end will constitute the greatest service it has ever been my lot to render my community.

My confidence that the plan now adopted will be accepted and carried out loyally by the vast majority of the Indian Mussalmans is confirmed by the information that reaches me that so earnest and foresighted a leader of the community as my distinguished friend Mr. Ameer Ali, the president of the London branch of the [All India Muslim] League, is prepared to recommend this course.

Source: *The Times*, London, 18 November 1909.

A day earlier *The Times* had published a letter from Sayyid Ameer Ali on the same theme, which had been written on 15 November. For the text of Ameer Ali's letter see K. K. Aziz, *Ameer Ali*, pp. 327–8.

15

SOME ASPECTS OF INDIAN REFORMS

An Article

London: December 1909

Many writers on India have only a superficial knowledge of Indian problems – the political structure of the Indian government – blessings brought by British rule – yet discontent exists – Indians would prefer British to German rule – possibility of German expansion – impact of British rule – ambitions of the Indians – state of education and literacy – condition of agriculture – agricultural education – systematic elementary education needed – the credit system in rural areas – agricultural indebtedness – how the standard of living of the farmers might be raised – travelling agricultural lecturers – cheap credit – co-operatives – political stability and capital investment – the role of the press – education will eliminate prejudice and bridge gulfs.

The complexity of modern life and the multiplicity of subjects which form the range of modern politics prevent the systematic study of some of the questions which cluster round the Imperial burden of Great Britain.

And whilst I make no apology for addressing my fellow citizens within that Empire, I do sincerely enter a caveat against one novel feature, unfortunately present to-day. It is the custom for persons all and sundry to visit the various districts of the Empire, and on returning home to publish a book upon their experiences of two or three months. No sane man can say that it is a bad thing for such journeys to take place. But equally no sane person can believe that two or three months' tour can give more than a most cursory knowledge of the problems and history of the area visited.

Perhaps no portion of the Empire has suffered more in this

respect than India. Almost every year there are issued to the British people what purport to be up-to-date books on India, containing crudely formed opinions set out with all the zeal of the enthusiastic traveller, but with little or none of the sifted knowledge of such a person as the trained Civil Servant, to whom the problems of India present most difficulty.

Much of the information is culled from the annual Government Reports, which the travellers, alas, in so many cases, read for the first time in India – yet of which the supply presented annually to the British Houses of Parliament shows a steady increase. If the same attention to these excellent annual reports were a tithe of that which is given to those of Canada and New Zealand, we of the Indian Empire would indeed be proud. It is not my intention within the compass of this short article to deal with more than one or two points, but I hope to direct British attention to some of the real problems of India.

It is hardly disputable that where discontent is constantly showing itself, there must be some cause for it. Just as restlessness in a human being indicates the approach of some ailment, so discontent points to some rankling sense of unfairness. India as we know it to-day has been governed and developed under what is known as the Government of India Act of 1858, by which the Secretary of State for India is invested with all the powers of the old East India Company, being assisted in his Administrative work by a Council of not less than ten persons. This Council has no initiative authority. In all matters relating to foreign policy, or policy towards native States, or in matters in which secrecy is necessary, the Secretary of State can act on his own authority. The Secretary of State is thus the supreme power as regards India, and being at a distance from the Dependency for which he is responsible, must consequently act on the information which reports give him, with such assistance as the members of his Council can supply.

This system in the hands of the present Secretary of State [Morley] has been slightly altered by the addition of one Indian gentleman to the Viceroy's Council, and of two others to the Secretary of State's Council.

It is undeniable that India has under the system of 1858 made great progress, and has, whilst making progress, been learning something of the art of government. She has also learnt that under the rule of Great Britain property is secure – justice is meted out to all, while the Indian frontiers have not been crossed by a hostile foe. Peace, security, and justice are no mean achievements for any system of Government. But when there is allied to this a sympathetic and powerful Government, a condition of affairs exists for a series of Dependent States unprecedented in history.

Yet, in spite of all this, restlessness and discontent exist. What are the causes of this? And what can be done to avert the causes which have produced these feelings of irritation?

One obvious question is whether the inhabitants of India could expect better treatment from any other European nation? Would they, for instance, be better off under German administration with all its cast-iron regulations in matters of health, police, law and military organisation; would they be happier under a German official who would have to learn all the intricacies of native custom and caste, and native law, who would bring to the consideration of these questions no knowledge, no experience, such as the Civil Servants of India now possess. They could not for one moment prefer such a prospect to the system now existing – yet the Germans are a most methodical, most persevering race, who could undoubtedly hold India and most certainly would rule India with skill and determination.

But the moment we consider the possibility of a change of Government in India from one set of European to another set of European rules and codes – we are dismayed at the thought of such a change. It would be a change from the known to the unknown, from rule by a race which has been identified with the East in general and with India in particular for centuries – to the rule of a nation whose knowledge of the East is as limited as her hold on India is unknown. Yet there is a danger that a power like Germany, even though largely ignorant of Indian customs, might because of her man-power be able to supplant the present European rulers. Man-power is after all the final arbiter of any question. The capacity to bring up more men for a final tussle must ultimately control any situation.

Germany with sixty-six millions within her own Imperial sway, but having in all about eighty millions of children in the world, has a larger capacity in numbers than Great Britain with her forty-five millions in own Island sway, and some fifty-five millions in all within her Imperial Dominions. Is such a *fort* new to Imperial Britain, or is it spurned as an impossible one? As race-power grows, as commerce demands new openings, as the ambition of a people swells, so surely does the consideration of such possibilities commence. The great Powers of the world are those whose population increases. These are: The Chinese

Empire; the United States of America; the German Empire; the Russian Empire. The day of monster States has come and monster States mean vast numbers of men of the same thoughts, same interests, same principles, same desires. Are the interests, the desires of Indians as recently expressed, the same as those which are now expressed on behalf of Great Britain? If the interests and the desires of the governed and Governors are hostile, then some collision must take place, a collision that will, whatever its immediate results, end disastrously for both.

The form in which this collision will take place is more or less immaterial. The paramount question is why affairs have drifted into the position in which they now are.

To the writer the outlook on the future is not gloomy; the present troubles rather appear to be the outcome of certain characteristics of the British system and these characteristics are not necessarily permanent. The interests and desires of the two parties are not irreconcilable. The Indian, taken as a whole, is a man of sensitive nature, open to persuasion, responsive to sympathy, wishful to be friendly, and desirous to be taught. He resents strongly any action or treatment which seems to indicate that he is of an inferior race – or a negligible quantity – but fifty years of life under British institutions has made him trust in the inherent justice and fairness of British rule.

The flight of time has been rapid in India's history, and it is still too little realised that each succeeding generation demands an advance on what its predecessor knew and enjoyed. It is this advance or progress which India has achieved under British rule that creates one of the problems for British policy. British law protects the moral and social types that have grown out of the native religions, and has paid and does still pay respect to the Hindu conception of the family, a conception which differs widely from that of European nations. The prohibition of suttee and of infanticide has no doubt introduced changes of a grave character into Indian life, whilst Government action has been exercised in native States in the direction of putting down like practices, in addition to slavery, torture, and mutilation. The tendency of these interventions is to raise the standard of humanitarian feeling and sentiment. It is thus idle to express surprise when the Indian himself having imbibed these feelings, shows in his Press and in his life, that he wishes to live up to Western standards. The educational policy of the Government of India adopted in response to the persistent urgings of Sir Charles Wood, and dating from 1854, is largely responsible for modern ambitions and the longing for a larger place in the government of their own country.

It should not, however, be thought that the educational advancement of the Indians is solely due to the work of the colleges and schools. Railways, telegraphs, posts and good main roads have each done their part in bringing about this feeling of national unity.

The universities, which form the pinnacle of the educational system, are largely modelled on the methods that once obtained in the University of London, which means that they are merely examining boards in secular subjects, and do not take up much active work outside the examination room. College life in India may be said not to exist as it is known at Oxford or Cambridge. Hence one of the main features, and perhaps the most effective method, of education is not given to the Indian student. It is true that education at present only touches the fringe of the great population of India. The total number of graduates and under-graduates in arts, law, medicine, engineering and Oriental languages for all the Provinces of India was, in 1906–07, only 9457, of which number 3306 were in the Madras Province, 2124 were in the Bombay Province, giving a total for the two Provinces of 5430, or more than half the total number of graduates and under-graduates for the whole of India. This is a ridiculously small number out of a population of 293,000,000 of people.

In considering the education question in India, regard must be had to the end at which we are aiming. In Western lands the cry is almost universal that the only way in which any nation can hope to maintain its position is by the application of science to industry, a phrase which may be understood to mean that industry, to be successfully carried on, must be managed by skilled men, not only in the administrative department, but also in the manufacturing and distributive departments.

What is being done in India is to harness science to production, by giving her people a sound elementary education, and then selecting from the pupils those whom it would be beneficial to train for technical trades, and those whom it would be better to send to professional callings.

It will have been noticed that as regards university graduates the numbers proceeding to the degree stage is very small. From which it may be deduced that the numbers of pupils in other classes of education must also be small. This unfortunately is the case. The total population of India is 293,000,000, of which there were in 1901 between the ages of five and twenty, the following:

Age	Males	Females	Total
5–10	20,831,085	19,895,462	40,726,547
10–15	18,880,658	15,568,718	34,447,376
15–20	12,942,322	12,017,853	24,960,155
Totals	52,654,065	47,480,033	100,134,078

This Table shows us that more than a third of the population is of school age, yet the number of children attending the primary schools is under 4,000,000; that is only one child in twenty-five is being educated during that period of its life when it is most open to receive instruction, and when its mind is in the most plastic condition. Similar information is also disclosed in the census of 1901, which tells us as follows:

	Total	Illiterate	Literate
Males	149,442,106	134,752,026	14,690,080
Females	143,972,800	142,976,459	996,341
Total	293,414,906	277,728,485	15,686,421

This Table shows that only one person in every eighteen of the population is literate.

It must not be thought that these figures can be construed into an attack on the Government of India. The contrary is the real fact – the number of schools is increasing, the number of scholars attending is on the up grade. But the task is gigantic and needs much detailed organisation, much expenditure of money, both of which are not at the present moment beyond the reach of the Indian Government. But certain results must naturally follow from such a position as is disclosed here. The industries of the country cannot progress so rapidly as they might, because of the lack of education of those engaged in them. It is impossible to harness science to industry until the workers are possessed of scientific training.

Take the greatest industry of the country, agriculture, and compare the position as it is and as it might be. Much light is let in upon the question of education from the following quotation: "One of the hindrances to the further progress of technical education arises from the deficiencies in the system of general education upon which it must rest and for which it cannot be substituted." (Page 3, C.D. 4635, "Education in India.")

This general criticism shows that India suffers as Great Britain did a few years ago, and indicates also that much of her higher education must suffer from the inability of her students adequately to benefit from it, by reason of their bad grounding in elementary subjects. Unfortunate as this may be, even in the higher forms of agricultural education, what must be the position of those vast numbers of illiterate persons engaged in agriculture – India's largest and most important industry. It appears that agriculture supports 191,691,731 of the total population of India, of which number over 155,000,000 are in the Provinces immediately under British rule – and 36,000,000 are found within the areas controlled by the native States. If these figures are analysed more minutely it will be found that 88,000,000 are actual workers in agricultural pursuits, and 103,000,000 are dependent on agriculture for their existence.

Put in another way, out of the total population of India, 65.16 per cent. are supported by, and are dependent on, agriculture for their living. Obviously then the prosperity of India must largely depend on the prosperity of agriculture. Much has been done in recent years for agricultural education, but much of the trouble to-day is due to the vacillating policy of early years.

It was in 1871 that the Land Revenue and Agricultural Department was established by Lord Mayo, but in 1879 it was abolished on financial grounds, only to be reconstituted in 1881 after the disastrous famine of 1880. But as it had no funds, it contented itself with collecting records. It was not until 1892 that an agricultural chemist was appointed on the recommendation of Dr. Völcker.

From this date agricultural education, and the shepherding of it, has commenced in real earnest. Now this department has a civilian Director in each Province, under whom there works an expert Deputy Director, whilst in 1901 the Government of India appointed an Inspector-General of Agriculture. So that the Board of Agriculture, if that term really accurately describes the Agricultural Committee, consists of experts from all over India under the Director. Slight as this sketch is of the development of the department, it will serve to indicate that once the central Government realised what agriculture meant to India, they worked thoroughly and persistently to develop that industry. Side by side with this central development there has been an attempt to found colleges and schools in which agricultural methods and science shall be taught. These colleges exist at Poona, Coimbatore, Sabour, Cawnpore, Nagpur, Lyallpur, whilst in Burmah, at Mandalay, an agricultural college is being built to which there will be attached an experimental farm. Furthermore owing to the munificent generosity of Mr. Henry Phipps, an American gentleman, who gave a donation of £30,000, an Imperial Agricultural College Research Institute has been established at Pusa in Bihar; in 1905 the Indian Government announced their intention of setting aside 20 lakhs of rupees annually for the development of agricultural experiment, research, demonstration, and instruction; and there are not wanting signs that the Government have also larger schemes of development in view. But in order that these beneficent and enlightened methods may have full effect, it is necessary that the elementary education of children of school age should be more systematic. The teaching of the child of elementary subjects such as reading, writing and arithmetic, even if only in his own vernacular, will give him or her, when of an age to work, that little equipment which enables him or her to understand the elements of bargaining and business. To-day the Indian ryot is in many instances utterly unable to appreciate the liabilities he has incurred owing to his want of education, and owing to the same wants many naturally able youths never get an opportunity of improving their position in life.

The agricultural industry of India is financed by two classes of institutions: (1) the native banker, (2) the banks run on European models.

The wealth of the native banker varies according to his environment, and he must not be confused with the banker of the larger towns. The village banker, who advances small sums or sometimes small quantities of grain to the Indian ryots, is a man who as a rule does not seek the fierce glare of publicity which attends modern banking; he prefers to carry on his business in private; this is because he knows full well the condition of his clients, and charges a high rate of interest which frequently borders on the exorbitant.

It must not be imagined that there is only an evil side to these petty bankers' proceedings. The system is suitable to Indian agriculture inasmuch as it enables money to come in small doses to the land – it is unsuitable because of the high interest which is demanded. But mixed up inextricably with the system is the absurd action of the ignorant peasant who insists upon indulging in wild extravagance in connection with marriage ceremonies, and who contracts loans for these purposes at a rate of interest which jeopardises his financial position, and thus prevents him from developing his land and crops as might be done.

The ryot's adhesion to old custom, and his ignorance of business frequently result in the profits of a good year going wholly into the pockets of the local banker, in order that the peasant may clear his indebtedness or at least reduce the outstanding liabilities.

The agricultural indebtedness of India in certain areas has grown to be an evil and consequently has forced the Government to introduce special legislation. One of the most important of these is the granting to the cultivators Government Loans at much lower rates of interest – sometimes made on the joint responsibility of the villagers. These amounted in total to more than two crores of rupees in 1900–01. Good as this policy is, it after all only touches the fringe of the evil because until the ryot can write and read for himself and thus to some extent appreciate the meaning of the contract he is making, little can be done to stop the exorbitant charges of the bankers. Thus if Indian representatives could combine to lay a scheme before the Government which had for its aim and object the lessening of the rate of interest, the increase of education in its elementary forms, and possibly some introduction of the principle of co-operation in distributing the products of agriculture, much would be done to raise the standard of comfort of the Indian ryot, to increase the output of agriculture, to augment the prosperity of agricultural India. This is the more necessary because of the Government's own record, which though good in the past can be expanded and developed on broader lines when the Indian ryot has by education been placed in a position to judge of the blessings of British rule, which once appreciated will give to the Government that support necessary to enable them to proceed once more along the admirable lines of policy which they after years of forethought and consideration have adopted on behalf of the teeming millions which Providence has committed to their care.

Perhaps it would be possible for the Indian Government to adopt the plan which it is understood finds some favour in Great Britain, and also in some Continental countries. Some of the County Councils have appointed agricultural lecturers who tour round a certain fixed area giving addresses or lectures upon agricultural matters. Would it be possible for the Indian ryot to have the benefit of such a class of agricultural lecturers, who would give in popular language, and in the ryot's own vernacular, the latest developments in, and the most recent practices connected with, wheat-growing, cotton, jute, and sugar cultivation?

Such lecturers could also give advice as to the use of manures, and how to get the best results from their application to the soil.

In addition to these technical advisers, it should be possible to have another class of travelling lecturers, who would explain the commercial and business side of agriculture – such as how by co-operation the ryots might be able to sell their products in commercial quantities to the large buyers, and by this means save some of the costs which are imposed upon them by the present system. This is only put forward as a suggestion – but as the practice of selling in commercial quantities is already in operation in Canada and other large wheat-growing areas, and as the English County Councils do now supply lecturers on the points indicated above, it is submitted that what is possible in Canada and the United Kingdom should not be wholly impracticable within the Indian Empire.

Another suggestion which is put forward for the consideration of the Indian Government and the Indian people is that possibly they might arrange some such plan as follows in order to deal with the present unsatisfactory conditions which impede the ryot from obtaining financial assistance. It is recognised that it is almost impossible for the Indian Government to lend to individual ryots. The difficulty of book-keeping and collecting the capital sum and the interest thereon would be enormous. But no such plan is suggested here, but rather that the Indian Government should approach the co-operative societies, or such kindred bodies, and come to an agreement with them that, on condition that these companies or bodies lend money at a cheap rate to the Indian ryot, they, the Government, will be prepared to lend money to the societies or bodies themselves.

Perhaps something like the following might be adopted. The Indian Government, through its agents in each Province, might meet the central board or committee of the local co-operative society, or land company, and ascertain from them how much money the Indian ryots would require for the coming year. Suppose this co-operative society or land company had ascertained that a quarter of a million sterling was required in any district, it should be arranged that the ryot should have the money lent to him at say $7\frac{1}{2}$ per cent., the Government undertaking to lend the quarter of a million to the society or company for say $4\frac{1}{2}$ per cent. The land company or society would be responsible for the collection of the interest and capital of such loan by Government after the sale of the crop.

The reason why the high rate of interest – high that is if

judged by Western standards – is suggested, is because the Indian Government would have to borrow for the whole of India possibly two or three millions, and the Government could not borrow under $3\frac{1}{2}$ per cent.

The first effect of such a plan would be that the bankers would be compelled by competition to lower their rate of interest to the ryot, in order that they might continue in the business of money-lending. This plan would be better from the statesmen's point of view because it avoids the necessity of direct legislation by the Government of India, having as its object the compulsory lowering of the Mahajans' rate of interest.

This policy, coupled with a system of co-operation in the sale of the products of the soil, should place the Indian ryot in a far more prosperous position. And, if at the same time the Government could see their way to adopt a system of agricultural lectures in each Presidency at the spot where the ryot does his work, there would flow from increased knowledge of agriculture, from better organisation in the collection and the distribution of the crops, coupled with easier financial methods of borrowing the necessary capital, that prosperity which would in itself largely mitigate the effects of a famine and certainly lessen the expenditure on famine should that unfortunately occur.

It is from the adoption of such a policy that the prosperity of the bulk of the Indian population can be secured, but it cannot be all give on the side of the Government and all take on the side of the governed.

Those who benefit from the Government's beneficial legislation must do their part. This was summed up as excellently put by Mr. Gokhale when speaking recently at Poona when he said: That the patriotism which in other countries assumes other forms, in India must lead to the loyal co-operation with the Government.

The citizens of India must realise that peace and security can be maintained by two methods: (1) The ruthless and the relentless sweeping of obstacles from its path; (2) by complete confidence between those who work for the Government and those who work for the country.

Confidence is the touchstone of commerce, whilst nothing is so easily frightened as capital. It is capital that India wants, capital for the development of railways, capital for the increase of canals, capital for the augmentation of irrigation. But capital will not go to a country where unrest or discontent is present. Capital has no confidence in a community which is influenced by violent and vehement scribbling in the Press.

It is not unfair to say that the standard of education of a nation or a people is judged by the style and the form of its Press. No greater dis-service is done to a country than for a local or a national Press to continually write in biassed [*sic*] and hyper-critical tone – because in time the irritation which the writer betrays is silently communicated to his readers. The more so is this the case in a country where education is still in a backward condition. It is to the Press in such a country that the Government must look for the spread of those ideas which are sound in policy and fair in the presentation of particular matters of information.

If the Press of India seek now by unfair means to embitter the relations between the Government and the multitude over which it watches, they must not at the same time grumble that the condition of the Indian peasantry is not what it should be.

This condition can scarcely be altered until education in all its forms has been more widely diffused, not only in agricultural areas, but also in the centres of population. The ignorance of the people, the absence of education, are the prime causes of discontent, because when persons do not understand they so easily misrepresent. I am the more confirmed in this view when so distinguished a ruler and Indian as His Highness the Gaekwar of Baroda says: "Sedition and anarchy are due to the absence of education." Anarchy can only bring in its train misery for the millions of India – therefore it is the duty of every citizen to co-operate with the Government in promoting those measures which will once and for all free India from the propagation of its noxious tenets.

The last and most important benefit would be that as education became general caste and religious prejudices would gradually die out. The greatest misfortune of India is that its peoples are divided into compartments and live in compartments. Mohamedans and Hindus, owing to ignorance, and owing to religious and social prejudices due to ignorance, are like two nations apart. The Hindus of the upper and lower castes are equally separated. This division is not only ruinous to the people but in the long run will make peaceful administration impossible. This gulf cannot be bridged by force. No, the work must be done through education, general, elementary and scientific. Religious difficulties and caste disabilities will only become the minor things they are in Europe and America when education teaches the public that such differences are not to be allowed to interfere in their daily lives.

Source: *National Review*, London, December 1909, pp. 577–89.

16

DUTIES OF MUSLIM LEADERSHIP IN INDIA

Speech at a Reception Given by the Muslim Citizens of Bombay

Bombay: 10 January 1910

Reasons for the success of Muslim constitutional struggle – duties of a true leader – the difficulties faced by Muslim leadership – Indian Muslims' relations with Hindus and the Muslims of other lands – improvement of education as an objective for Muslims – the example of Prophet Muhammad – need for stability – rights as a means to an end.

"As you know, it was a hard and difficult constitutional struggle and your representatives had no light task to perform in overcoming prejudices and preconceived notions in some quarters, but I am glad to say that the justice of our cause has prevailed, thanks to the high statesmanship of our rulers and their innate sense of fairplay and to the very powerful support of English and Anglo-Indian journals of exceptional weight, especially of *The Times* and other leading organs of public opinion. Among our staunch advocates were men of great talents and patriotism, with high notions of justice."

"You have been kind enough to refer to me as the leader of the Muslims. It is the greatest honour that any individual can aspire to and that a community can confer, but the mighty responsibility upon any Muslim leader cannot be ignored or lightly treated. Any man in the world can well be proud of being termed a leader of the Muslims, who have made fascinating and romantic history in many countries. But now, what are the duties of a leader? True leadership consists in thinking out a practicable programme of constructive policy consistent with principles of truth and harmony, worthy of the past traditions, and the historical and political situation in the Empire of which Indian

Muslims form such an important part, and in steering them on the right path by persuasion and advice. A leader's function is to restrain any dangerous extremism and to enlighten the people as to what the good of the country requires and to instil in the minds of the public the influence and feelings of humanity and brotherhood. But to construe any such policy for the Muslims of India involves an immense difficulty. The political task of a patriot in European countries like England, Germany and France, with their comparatively united peoples and their healthy and more or less simple past is comparatively easy. Whether he be a Socialist, an Imperialist or a Conservative, a patriot in European countries can concentrate and focus his energies and thoughts and follow certain well-defined principles of policy clearly marked out by the interests of his people according to the lights of his party. But it is not so in India, where the historical past traditions and differences in religion and social customs make the task peculiarly difficult. It is difficult for any Indian patriot to lay the line clearly but it is more so for a Muslim leader, owing to a combination of superficially and apparently conflicting ideals and interests. The task of an Indian Muslim patriot who takes upon himself the thinking out of a policy that is best for his people is peculiarly difficult, for he has to think of seventy to eighty millions of people with internal differences of race, language and colour, and with peculiar institutions in a country which has passed through various vicissitudes and in the midst of a vast Hindu population upon whose welfare the future of Indian Muslims depends.

"Then there is another fact, which makes the Muslim position more complicated. For all time to come Muslim interest is bound up with the progress of the sister communities and it is our duty and privilege to continue on the most cordial and fraternal terms with the vast Hindu population and also with so many other small minorities, each sub-divided into castes and creeds, yet the welfare of every one depending upon the welfare of its neighbours. Again sentiment and love would always attach the Muslims of India to the welfare of their co-religionists outside India, whether they are independent or self-governing communities like those in Turkey, Persia, Afghanistan and Morocco, or whether they are subjects of non-Muslim sovereigns as in China, Russia or France. All these duties, interests and sentiments must have a legitimate place in the ideal life and in the moral and intellectual outlook of Muslims. This presents a formidable difficulty.

"Now to co-ordinate all these interests and to harmonise conflicting elements and to reduce some of those sentiments to their legitimate places and to concentrate more and more on the fundamental duties and interests without interfering in the legitimate sphere of the secondary ones is not an easy matter. And first of all you have to find a practical line of action that will legitimately help forward each one of those ideals. Such are the inevitable difficulties and complications that face anyone who pretends even for a moment to lead the Muslims of India. Of course on this occasion I cannot say much about the practical and constructive policy that may meet all the requirements of the Muslims.

"The duty, sentiments, honour and interests of the people we represent should be all focussed and a course should be determined – one that will satisfy each legitimate aspiration while preventing any from overlapping into another sphere. That course should be laid down with mature consideration, deep thought and consultations with eminent Muslims and non-Muslim English and Indian compatriots of the Muslims. Fortunately, there is one object in front of us to which we can give whole-hearted devotion, being perfectly sure that whatever happens the result of that object will do credit and give satisfaction to all concerned.

"That one object is the improvement of education. The Muslims should enlarge the sphere of education where it exists already and must create it where it is absent. Scientific and technical education in all its various branches such as commercial, industrial and agricultural instruction must be the main practical objects of our energy and ambitions. At the same time the literary side so beautifully known as the Humanities should not be neglected and our interest as well as sentiments make it necessary that a knowledge, not only of English, Arabic and Persian, but also of Sanskrit literature, should exist amongst us so that we may come in contact with the sources of Hindu civilisation and the roots of Hindu society.

"I am glad you have quoted with approval and reverence the example of our beloved Prophet for giving encouragement to learning and science. He encouraged his followers especially recommending them to go to various centres of learning in Rome and China that they might get knowledge and learn to respect the conventions of foreign thought and society.

"The great need of the country is development of its resources amongst which I give the first place to the development of its intelligence and education. But it is impossible that the country should develop if we live in a state of endemic anarchy that destroys the confidence between the rulers and the ruled and which eventually recoils on Society at large. We must not forget that for the first time in the history of India the rulers have made endeavours to share with the people the responsibility of Government. The Government is quite competent to deal with disorders and physical anarchy. It is true [that] the whole of India has protested against the senseless crimes that have recently made a big blot on the fair name of India. But protests and repression are ineffectual and unavailing so long as Society as a whole does not stir itself and take active and vigorous measures to restore healthy conditions and root out the anarchical spirit on its intellectual side. What we want is not protests after the foul deed is done; but we must go deeper and think out a policy to prevent the state of mind that produces evil-doers. We should send out earnest missionaries to preach sanity, to bring misguided zealots to see, through reason and righteousness, the sacred nature of the ties that unite Indian Society and the Government. We must consider ourselves as members of a common brotherhood and we must exert ourselves to prevent the violation of laws of society and humanity in the spirit of the words of the Persian poet Sa'adi: Bani Adam Azai Yakhi Garand. [*sic*]

"One immediate and sacred duty rests upon us all and that is that this institution must be made a permanent living force in the Muslim life of this beautiful city and worthy of the renowned race to which we belong. We must equip it with the latest machinery of education. We should remember that the rights we have obtained are not an end in themselves but are a means to an end in new and economical conditions of the people. Now that we have won certain forms of rights, our objects should be to make good use of the reforms with moderation and wisdom and sincerity and to strive to turn out energy to improve the condition of the people and to advance the progress of the country."

His Highness concluded by saying that he would cherish the most pleasant recollections of that day and he assured them that if ever he was called upon to serve the interests of the community or to further its material prosperity, he would not be found wanting and would consider it a happy privilege to serve them to the best of his power.

Source: Naoroji M. Dumasia, *The Aga Khan and His Ancestors*, The Times of India Press, Bombay, 1939, pp. 174–7.
    On 10 January, in the Anjuman-i-Islam Hall, Bombay, a large and influential

gathering of Muslims entertained and honoured the Aga Khan. A complimentary address from both the Shias and the Sunnis was presented to him "in appreciation of his services in the cause of the country in connection with the Morley-Minto Reforms. The address in the name of both the sects referred to His Highness as their leader. . . . The late Sir Currimbhoy Ebrahim, Bart., read the address, in which it was stated among other things that by his learning and courtesy and the deep and unfailing interest he had always taken in the welfare of the community he had endeared himself to every Muslim heart in India and they were proud to own and acknowledge him their leader."

"The address then referred to his single-hearted devotion to the cause of Muslim progress, social and political, and claimed that his efforts had met with such success as to justify the hope that the future of the Muslims of India had been secured. Recalling his various services the address pointed out that in getting the principle admitted by the Government of India that the position and status of the Muslim should be estimated, not merely on their numerical strength, but with due regard to the political importance of the community and the services it had rendered to the Empire, His Highness had rendered lasting and truly inestimable service to the entire Muslim community of India."

The address continued: "Nor have you worked only for the advancement of the Muslim community but also for the improvement of the condition of the Indians in general. When the first public meeting of protest of the citizens of Bombay against the great hardships and sufferings of the Indians in South Africa was organized, it was to Your Highness that the eyes of everyone turned as the fittest person to preside at such a meeting. Your Highness did preside at the meeting and you have since continued to take the keenest interest in the struggle of the Indians against the unjust rules and laws that unfortunately obtain in South Africa."

"Your munificence and liberality in the cause of Muslim education has justly won for Your Highness the love and esteem of every true Muslim. Our Prophet of blessed memory prided himself on being the 'city of knowledge', and called his son-in-law Ali 'its gate'. 'Acquire knowledge', said he, 'for whoso acquireth it in the way of the Lord performeth an act of charity.' We need scarcely refer further to the many exhortations to acquire knowledge which our Prophet had made to his followers. Your Highness has inherited that love of knowledge and its encouragement which has characterized Your Highness's life from its very childhood. We acknowledge with thankfulness and gratitude your munificent donations and grants to this institution and to the great Muslim institution of India, the Aligarh College." (Dumasia, pp. 173–4).

17

THE OBJECTIVES OF THE ALIGARH COLLEGE

Reply to the Address from the Trustees of the MAO College

Aligarh: 26 January 1910

Financial contribution to the College by Princes and leaders – appeal to others for funds – the ideal of Aligarh – the question of quantity vs. quality – definition of a good Muslim – the European example of self-sacrifice – annual grant to the College.

Nawab Sahib, trustees and gentlemen, – Allow me first to thank you most sincerely for the kind way in which you have received me here, and for the cordial terms in which you have referred to the services I have rendered this institution. I can assure you that my connection with the College has been from the first, for me, a labour of love, and among the various interests and pursuits that occupy my time none is so dear to me as the services I can render the College. You have suggested in your address that I am one of yourselves and that is so. Unfortunately the wretched state of my health has so far prevented me from doing all I should otherwise do for Aligarh, and above all has prevented me from carrying out my cherished dream of coming and passing a few weeks quietly in your midst every year and conversing freely, not only with the trustees and the professors, but with the students as well. (Cheers). I am glad to see that so many Princes, Nawabs, and leaders have lately contributed large sums of money to the college, but our hopes and dreams, I hope periodical dreams, of a mighty university, worthy of Islam in India, depends on not only every Muslim Prince and leader, but the well-to-do of every town and village to come forward and raise this college to the status of a great university. Gentlemen, no one can offer you better advice than what the present Lieutenant-Governor gave you when he was last here, that the ideal before us is to make this institution a great centre of research and learning and a source of moral influence for the Mussalmans.

The object of this College, and in fact its early claim upon the love and affection of Mussalmans, is that it should be not a mere cramming house to turn out employees for Government service, that necessary but relaxing profession, but to produce men morally and intellectually equipped for developing the resources of the country by becoming captains of commerce and industry, leaders of men and the moral teachers of their people. That being the object in view you must not look to quantity but to quality.

Our community is not only backward, morally, intellectually and materially but even more spiritually; in the true sense Aligarh should not only turn out learned and capable men but good Mussalmans, nor can I accept the definition of a good Moslem as one who is merely a perfect formalist. We want amongst the students that atmosphere of self-sacrifice and true devotion and pity for suffering, that sense of dependence and responsibility towards an infinite power, the light of which can only be known through our emotions and whose influence must permeate every moment of our lives. Islam can only be maintained if there is a revival of such spirit. Then only shall we produce men who will be ready to go not only to try to become leaders of the Bar and members of the Executive Councils, not only the far more honourable and mighty members of society known as founders of art and industry, but men ready to sacrifice every material interest, men ready to go and give their lives to the humble and to the lowly without any visible recompense, or men ready to devote their future to the advancement of pure learning.

As you are all aware I have lived many a year in Europe. Though the people of that continent are far in advance of us in material comforts and wealth, yet their material superiority is not so evident, nor did it so impress me as the immense numbers who had sacrificed every personal advantage for the advancement of some ideal not only in England but in so-called materialistic France and Germany. Vast numbers in every village and in every district give up their lives to the service of God, of mankind and of knowledge, nor is this light of self-sacrifice confined to the ranks of believing Christians and Jews. Amongst the so-called agnostics and atheists, I have seen a wealth of true spiritual devotion. If only we could infuse a little of this into the hearts of the Mussalmans of India, we should be very different from what we are to-day. Gentlemen, do all you can to bring that spirit into the youths of Aligarh. That way lies salvation.

Gentlemen, it is with great pleasure that I inform you that I raise my annual grant to Rs. 10,000, and I hope that this is but a step towards a still larger grant later on . . .

Source: *The Times of India*, Bombay, 27 January 1910.

The Aga Khan paid a visit to the MAO College on 25 January. On the following day the Trustees of the College gave a garden party in honour of the distinguished guest at the College Club, made him a life member of the Club, and presented him with an address of welcome. The Aga Khan's reply forms the text of this document.

For the MAO College see Theodore Morison, *The History of the M.A.O. College, Aligarh, from its Foundation to the Year 1903*, Allahabad, 1903; Oscar Browning, *Impressions of Indian Travel*, London, 1903, pp. 151–60; Yusuf Husain, *Selected Documents from the Aligarh Archives*, Bombay, 1967; Theodore Morison, "An Indian Renaissance", *Quarterly Review*, April 1906; Gertrude Bell, "Islam in India: A Study at Aligarh', *The Nineteenth Century and After*, December 1906; and *Aligarh Magazine*, special Aligarh number, 1953–4, Aligarh, 1955.

18

THE AWAKENING OF MUSLIM INDIA

Inaugural Address to the All India Muslim League Third Annual Session

Delhi: 29 January 1910

The awakening of Muslims in India – formation of the Muslim League – separate representation for Muslims a starting point for good relations between Hindus and Muslims – co-operation and use of the opportunity for further advance towards constitutional government – the Councils as a means to improving the welfare of Indians – Muslim aims and interests – co-operation with the Hindus – plea for avoiding narrow political outlook and selfish aims – problems of education, agriculture, commerce and industry – help sought for Indians in South Africa in their struggle for equality – the ideals of the future Muslim University of Aligarh – co-operation with all communities – the system of *wakf-alal-Aulad* – support law and order – blessings of British rule – elevate the quality of Muslim life and hold forth the highest ideals before the younger generation.

Seven years ago I had the honour of presiding at the Mohammedan Educational Conference held in this Imperial city at the time of the historic Proclamation Durbar of His Majesty the King Emperor. During the interval many things have happened, and one of the most gratifying signs of the times is the partial awakening of the Musalmans of India. The recent march of events has been as rapid as it has been momentous; its course is indicated by the enactment in the Indian Empire of what Lord Morley called the "signal transaction", with which benevolent and statesmanlike policy his Lordship's name will be permanently associated – and by the formation of our League. At first the idea of the formation of the League was actually pooh-poohed in some quarters, while in others it did not receive the attention it

328

merited. But as subsequent events have shown, it has more than justified its existence, and I am proud to say that I was one of the originators of the movement. The necessity for the immediate formation of a Muslim League impressed me on the occasion of my visit to Aligarh in 1906, and I communicated the idea to my late and most lamented friend, Nawab Mohsin-ul-Mulk, by whose death we have suffered a serious and irreparable loss. With characteristic foresight, he accepted my suggestion, worked for its attainment, and brought about the Deputation which, waiting on H. E. Lord Minto in 1906, was the starting point of the recognition of the principle that the important Muslim minority in this country should have its fair and legitimate share in the administration of the country. We must not, however, forget that a sympathetic Viceroy whose memory is dear to Hindu and Muslim alike – the Hon'ble Lord Ripon – had in the early eighties laid down the principle of communal representation. For the maintenance of our due share in the political life in this country, and for the removal of an old-standing exclusion, which formed a bone of contention between the Hindus and Mohammedans, the separate electorate for Musalmans was deemed to be an absolute necessity. Now that we have secured it, I hope it will result in a permanent political sympathy and a genuine working *entente cordiale* between the members of the two great sister communities.

Let me make it clear that we have not received any undue perference [*sic*], as has been alleged in some quarters. In fact, we have not got all that we thought was promised or all that we had asked for; but in their final shape, the Reforms were publicly and gratefully acknowledged by us as a fair and reasonable compromise. Here, I must recognize the loyal support which your representatives in England, Syed Ameer Ali and myself, received from practically the whole of the Muslim community; and I must say that without this practically absolute unanimity, we should never have had the fair share of representation in the new Councils to which we are entitled. When the elements of constitutional government were being introduced into India, it was only natural and right and just that we should press for the reasonable recognition of the special interests and peculiar needs of a vast and important community like the Muslims. I am glad our just demand has been recognized. Now that the Reform Scheme has been finally settled and is actually in active operation, we must accept it as final in an appreciative spirit, worthy of our traditions, and try to make the best of it as loyal subjects of our beloved Sovereign the King Emperor and as citizens of India. May I venture also to say most emphatically that it is to the interests of Indians – Hindus and Muslims, Christians and Parsis alike – to accept the Reforms in a spirit of cordial appreciation, and that it now lies with us to do our utmost as enlightened citizens to co-operate with [the] Government and our representatives in the Councils in working them for the common welfare of the people, remembering that if we make a practical and beneficent use of this opportunity, we shall surely, in time to come, get a further advance towards constitutional government. In fact I may say that self-government has come to our very doors. On the other hand, if we waste our time in squabbles over the form of the Regulations, and in general hostility towards what should be regarded as a settled fact, we shall lose the sympathy of our well-wishers in India and England, and the result will be that the growth of liberal institutions, and our slow progress on the long path towards ultimate parliamentary institutions in India, will be greatly retarded. We must also remember that if these Reforms fail, the alternative will not be a more liberal set of regulations, but a return to the *status quo ante* that will check the realization of our aspirations. Public opinion in England scrutinizes India carefully and is watching to see how we discharge the great trust committed to us. Are we Indians prepared to go forward on the road to reform or to recede and disappoint our friends? Do we desire further liberal concessions, or do we wish the curtailment of the rights now at last granted? There can be no doubt as to the reply. Is it not then the duty of all, Hindus as well as Mohammedans, to prove by our conduct and ability that we are capable of making practical improvements in the moral and material conditions of the people, which is after all the aim of wise governments? If we fail in the initial stage, what prospect is there of our obtaining the further liberalization of the rules and regulations at a later stage? A grave duty rests upon us in connection with the new Councils; they are not an end in themselves but are only the means to achieve an end, namely, the improvement of the moral, material and economic condition of our people by the diffusion of education and science, so as to develop the intelligence and humanity of our peoples in the highest sense. If we prove by our knowledge of the conditions of the country, by our zeal and efficiency, that our co-operation is an indispensable factor in the improvement of the administration of the country, then I have no doubt that gradually our area of utility and opportunity and powers will expand. But, if on the other hand, we view the Reform Scheme and the regulations under it in a spirit of obstructive particularism instead of using the wide powers placed in our hands for the conservation and development of those forces which are the dynamic factors in national progress all the world over, then as surely as night follows day, we shall divert the slant of fair wind which ought to drive us far on towards the realization of many of our cherished ambitions.

Now that we Musalmans have striven for and obtained a reasonable recognition of our rights, should we not consider what our aims are, what interests we have in common with our Hindu brethren, and what are the peculiar communal interests which will demand the steady attention of our representatives? Our first and foremost duty is to prove our active loyalty towards our Sovereign and his heirs and successors by our endeavours to strengthen the foundation of British rule in India and its permanence by consolidating the sentiments of loyalty which permeate the land, by taking a ligitimate [sic] pride in the glorious Empire in which we are partners, by uniting the great sister communities through the bonds of sympathy, affection, and a community of interests. And may I plead again for no mere cold calculating loyalty, bound up with a materialistic sense of favours to come; but a warm passionate attachment to the Imperial house under which this country has made such gigantic strides, which has given us the most liberal *raj* the world has ever seen, and which alone guarantees us the peaceful attainment of those grand national destinies that we believe to be in our hand – an attachment to His Majesty's throne and person, and through that to the historic institutions of which he is the head, which shall burn in our hearts and colour all our actions . . . [Our representatives'] function in the Council is of a threefold character. In the first place, they must co-operate, as representative Indian citizens, with other Indians in advancing the well-being of the country by working wholeheartedly for the spread of education, for the establishment of free and universal primary education, for the promotion of commerce and industry, and for the improvement of agriculture by the establishment of co-operative credit and distribution societies, and for the development of all the natural resources of the country. Here indeed is a wide field of work for Hindus and Mohammedans acting together, in forwarding practical measures that must tend to the permanent welfare of the country. In the second place, our representatives must be ready to co-operate with the Hindus and all other sections of society in securing for them all those advantages that serve their peculiar conditions and help their social welfare, for although the two sister-communities have developed on different lines, each suffers from some peculiar weakness in addition to the misfortunes common to general economic and educational backwardness. And then our representatives must watch and promote social measures exclusively for the benefit of their Muslim co-religionists with the co-operation, we hope, of the Hindu members; for we, too, have needs that are not known to them and which we alone can fully understand. We have committed to us the sacred duty of helping forward, with our sympathy and advice and practical help, the interest not only of Indian Musalmans, but also of our co-religionists outside India, whose true and permanent welfare depends, in no small measure, upon the greatness of England and upon the maintenance of the British Empire foremost in the councils of the world.

I have no hesitation in asserting that unless Hindus and Mohammedans co-operate with each other in the general development of the country as a whole and in all matters affecting their mutual interest, neither will develop to the full its legitimate aspirations or give full scope to its possibilities. In order to develop their common economic and other interests, both should remember that one is the elder sister of the other, and that India is their common parent; religious differences should be naturally reduced to the minor position, as such differences have been in America and Western Europe. We must bear in mind that the healthy national unity which we seek to establish will not be promoted but retarded by forgetting the historical and social differences that have made Hindus and Mohammedans what they are to-day. We must determine what are the interests that we have in common with the Hindus, and co-operate for their advancement; then remember the measures necessary for the removal of our peculiar ills, and again help each other in removing them. What is the actual work of those who sit in the different Councils as our representatives, what is to become of the League, what is its legitimate sphere of work? My respected friend the Right Hon'ble Syed Ameer Ali has to some extent defined the proposed division of work of the League, and I fully and cordially agree with him. I need therefore say no more about it than this, that nothing would be more disastrous to our interests than the impression that its work is to be confined to the narrow limits of political activity or the attainment of merely selfish ends. It must embrace catholic interests in their broadest sense. We must ascertain the real, pressing needs of

India; and then devote our attention and energies to satisfying them.

We have then before us a comprehensive programme involving a vigorous, practical, sustained attack on the problems relating to education, agriculture, commerce and industry. I place free primary education for the masses in the front rank. Our aim must be to see that it is not only free and universal but also sufficiently practical to be of use to agriculturists and labourers. In arranging our courses of elementary education, we must keep in mind the fact that an immense proportion of those attending the primary schools do not proceed beyond them, and that they should be so designed that the pupil will fully benefit from the primary schools without reaching the secondary. We must concentrate our energies on primary education in such a way that there shall be no redundance or superfluity, so as to make it of real benefit to the recipients. The agricultural classes should in particular be given such training as will secure them the fruits of their industry. Our system of secondary education stands in need of a twofold development. We should extend and improve the facilities for imparting a sound grounding to those who are proceeding to the Arts Course, and then, on the other hand, we need urgently to develop a "modern" side, which will be complete in itself, and will fully equip the student for a career in the rapidly increasing commercial activities of the country, or for the specialized scientific course, for which there is an ever-growing field. So far we have made little or no progress towards securing that diffused knowledge of science, which is absolutely essential if the country is to take its rightful place amongst the producer nations of the world. Until our teaching machinery is enormously improved, students in these special courses must obtain their instruction abroad, and there is no method better than the multiplication of Government and other scholarships. But we shall not rest content until there are provided in this country facilities for the instruction of its students up to the highest pitch demanded by the stress of modern industrial life. Then when we have our trained men, we have to assist them to develop the economic resources of the country. We must send our boys not only to England and the Continent but to America and Japan, so that they may learn the various processes in the lives of that great industrial commonwealth. Those who have acquired proficiency in commercial training should be helped by co-operative societies to open business not only in Europe and America but in Africa and Asia to find markets for indigenous

Indian products. To foster local industries, to relieve agricultural indebtedness, and to ameliorate the lot of the peasantry and encourage artisans, it is necessary to form extensive co-operative societies under the aegis of the Government.

To obtain the regeneration of Indian arts and industries, either a temporary moderate system of protection, or some corresponding economic expedient should be adopted, so as to prevent the strangulation of these infant industries. We must have ever before our eyes the fact that the great mass of the Indian population is dependent upon agriculture . . . Hindus and Mohammedans have ample scope for improving the lot of the toiling agriculturists, impoverished by the ravages of famine consequent upon drought and their social customs and thriftless habits. Here we have an immense agricultural class; our duty is to make that agriculture pay. By a rational system of elementary education we can keep the peasant from the coils of the usurer; by the extension of irrigation we can reduce his dependence upon an erratic rainfall. But the history of agriculture all the world over tells us that the salvation of the small cultivator lies in co-operation. Co-operation to secure cheap credit and wipe off the burden of hopeless debt that hangs round the necks of our *ryots*; co-operation to secure cheap and efficient distribution; co-operation in the introduction of agricultural implements and to profit by the lessons of our Research Institute and experimental farms – this is the only agency that can permanently benefit our backward agriculture. Then our industrial development must equally claim our united attention. No country in the world can be great or prosperous until its agricultural and industrial activities have been made mutualy [*sic*] dependent on each other. It is commerce and trade that have made European countries prosperous and powerful; and if we aspire to our legitimate place in the British Empire, we must concentrate our mind on our economic development.

Another direction in which the two communities must immediately work together is on the burning question of the Indians in South Africa. Our fellow subjects, who are there maintaining an unequal struggle in a heroic manner that commands our admiration are wilfully subjected to persecution, insults and indignity and are branded with the undeserved stigma of an inferior race. We must all do all in our power to help our compatriots in South Africa. Hindus and Mohammedans have combined there in the common defence of the prestige of the whole Indian population; and the passive resistance they offer, amid untold privations and sufferings, with patience and martyrdom, must set an example to those here who are not ashamed to have a recourse to measures that have brought infinite shame and disgrace to India. If no better method can be found of bringing the Colonial Government to see the glaring injustice and cruelty of their acts to our brethren, we must ask the Government to stop all indented labour to South Africa as a mild step of retaliation. Yet another channel, and even more important for immediate purposes than anything else, in which Hindus and Mohammedans can co-operate with all their powers of mind and will, is the wiping out of the blot on the fair name of India by the extirpation of the anarchical cult. We must send earnest missionaries, form organizations and vigilance committees, and from pulpits and platforms, from mosques and temples, orders must emanate for the prevention of political crime, inflicting social disabilities on sedition-mongers and their disciples. In particular, students must be guarded from the tainted influence of the foolish and insane people who would ruin the country. All these are questions in which loyal and patriotic Hindus and loyal and patriotic Moham-medans can work hand in hand for a common goal with singleness of purpose and awakened conscience.

Now I will come to the questions of separate or exclusive Muslim interests, which, let me at once add, in no way clash with the interests of the great sister community, but still affect us only. Pre-eminent amongst these practical questions is the foundation of a Muslim University at Aligarh. As I pointed out here seven years ago, our youth must be in a position to acquire, in addition to modern science, a knowledge of the glorious past of our religion. Without a sincere and deep but unobtrusive and chari-table faith, without that childlike feeling of dependence on the Unseen Power of which the visible universe is but a sign, our youth can never develop their highest and noblest faculties, their spiritual and emotional qualities. Our university must be a resi-dential university. Like those great seats of learning, Oxford and Cambridge, it will strive to form the character, as well as train the intellect, and satisfy the emotions through the medium of a loving and charitable faith, of discipline, of field sport, and that intangible atmosphere that environs all which is best in university life. It should be the home of our great ideas and great ideals. But it should also be much more: our efforts ought to be bent to the task of making Aligarh a Muslim Oxford – an educational centre and intellectual capital to which all Muslims should turn for light and guidance. We should lay bare before the rising generations the treasures concealed in ancient Arabic lore with a view to developing the spiritual and emotional side of their nature, which in its true sense is now even more backward than our economic condition. In order to enable us to come in touch with what is best in the ancient Hindu civilizations and better to enable us to understand the origin and structure of Hindu thought and religion in its widest sense, as well as to inculcate in us a feeling of respect and affection for our fellow-subjects, and to teach us to consider their customs and their prejudices, Sanskrit and other Oriental literature ought also to be given due prominence in the curricula. The object of the university is not to gratify mere sentiment or vanity; we believe it to be necessary for the true development of our principles and the ultimate spiritual unity of our faith. Commonsense and science alike teach us that we are not independent agents but links between the past and the future; and all that is healthy and glorious in the past should be preserved, taught and understood, because it exercises a beneficial influence on the future. It is therefore necessary that all that is good should be conserved to enable us to hold a spiritual communion with the beloved figures of the Prophet and his companions and with our splendid historic past. To avoid the catastrophe involved in the radical separation of ancient and modern ideals, the university is our great need. Moreover, it is our aim to develop discipline and reverence in our youth, and instil in their minds the principles of toleration, piety and charity, so that they can live in concord and harmony with other races. Our loyalty to the Throne must be absolute, and our relations with the Hindus and all other Indian communities who share that loyalty must frankly be most cordial. Otherwise our political activities will tend to the undoing of both, and ultimately prove detrimental even to the British Power. The true interests of the British Empire can never lie in a policy of 'divide and rule'. Such a policy, as British and Indian statesmen worthy of the name well know, can only weaken their ultimate power and make India a source of anxiety instead of a source of strength.

Whilst we hold fast to our own religious, social, and ethical ideals, whilst we hold equally fast to the separate organization and separate representation which are essential for their maintenance and to secure for our community its due influence in the body politic, it must be the desire of our rulers, no less than of ourselves, to pursue these ideals, to work out our constructive programme, in harmonious co-operation with all other Indians who accept the cardinal principles of our political faith – the ordered development of this country under the Imperial Crown. Time, the opportunities for co-operation in stimulating the social and economic progress of this country, and the diffusion of education will also, I believe, remove the acerbities attaching to the religious difficulties and caste disabilities which sap the foundation of Indian society, so that they will become, in the distant future, the minor forces that they are now in Western Europe and America. If we extend hearty and sincere co-operation in each other's transactions and interests and pursue higher ideals and act with moderation and judicious calm, then I have no apprehension for the future of India.

Now I will say a few words in special support of the suggestions made by my distinguished friend Syed Ameer Ali, the President of the London Branch of this League – whose absence from our deliberations I deplore more than I can say – as to the system of *Wakf-alal-Aulad.* This is again our exclusive interest, but I hope the Hindus will co-operate with us in seeing that Muslim families are not broken into pieces. We must strive to bring about a satisfactory solution of this important question, as it is necessary that Muslim families should be protected against the impoverishing influence of constant and vexatious sub-divisions. I feel very strongly on the subject, with Syed Ameer Ali, and I think this is a question where our Muslim representatives can directly set to work, and thus benefit the community. I fully endorse the various practical suggestions made by Syed Ameer Ali, but I do not wish to tire you out by treading the same ground, as most of you are already familiar with my full agreement with his views on the practical proposals placed before us in his usual forceful manner by the London President.

And now, gentlemen, let me say a final word with regard to the future. We have before us a convincing demonstration of the altruism and liberality of British statesmanship. In the midst of difficulties so great that at times they threatened to overcast the political horizons, undaunted by acts of anarchy in India and those conservative influences that must beset the path of the reformer in every country and in every age, Lord Minto and Lord Morley have turned a bright new page in Indian history. We do not know which to admire most – the courage and sympathy of the Viceroy, or the judgment, intellectual strength and sober liberalism of Lord Morley. But we are confronted by the fruits of their work. We see the representatives of all classes of people in this country brought to the Councils of the Imperial and provincial governments in numbers never before approached. We see these Councils endowed with an authority, with opportunities for making the opinions of its members known and operative, to a degree far transcending any that existed in the past, associating us indeed with the daily administration of the country. The future lies more largely than ever with ourselves. By the measure in which we rise to these responsibilities shall we be judged, will the fortunes of the land to which we are passionately attached rise – or fall. Fully conscious of these opportunities, let me once again earnestly appeal to all to support law and order, remembering the immense blessings British rule has conferred upon this land. Never was the condition of Indians more happy than it is to-day. Never was peace of the country so serene and secure as under the Crown. Fifty years of British rule in India, since it passed to the direct control of the Crown from the East India Company, has changed the entire character and political aspect of the country. We have been secured against strife and disorder. The elevation of the people in the scale of civilization by means of Western training, the development of the country by encouraging foreign capital, the gradual disappearance of social and traditional barriers through the levelling influence of education, the security of life, property and peace, and the dispensation of justice with an even hand to rich and poor alike, the guarantee of freedom of thought and speech, and liberty of press, and above all religious toleration, have all brought about a silent but steady change in the thoughts, aspirations and manners and behaviour of the people. We are at the beginning of a period of renaissance and reform in the social, economic and political life of the people, and by ethical teachings we may inspire our youth and their descendants, with a genuine love of their country and fellowmen. The moral and material and intellectual condition of the population presents a curious and on the whole a favourable contrast with the pre-British period; and in the words of the philosopher-statesman that rules India, the bureaucracy in India has proved to be "a great and splendid machine for performing the most difficult task that ever was committed to the charge of any nation". Indian public spirit is cultivated on Western lines, the intellectual expansion is quickened in a marvellous degree. New hopes and new ambitions have been created as a natural sequence of this instruction, and to meet them British statesmen have wisely resolved to give Indians a far larger share in the administration of the country. No human agency can be perfect in this world and that applies to British rule as to all others; but even if the British Government had no other claim on our affections, these great political concessions alone would entitle them to our deep and sincere gratitude. But they have, as you and I know full well, changed the destiny of the country, set afoot progressive agencies, the end of which is not yet in sight, and brought the country into line with the civilized countries of Europe, proving in the words of the great English poet:

Peace has her victories,
No less renowned than war.

All this is due to the beneficial influence of *Pax Britannica.* Now may I ask whether we have paid our debt to the Empire, to our country and to our community? The community that carried culture to the Pyrenees and to Central Asia, the community that can still recall with emotional pride the greatness of Cordova and Damascus cannot be dead to its sense of duty. I appeal to you with all the force in my power, I entreat you with all the earnestness at my command, to imitate the spirit of those who made Toledo and Baghdad, to dream day and night, to work day in day out, for the noble object of elevating Muslim life so as to hold forth the highest ideals before the younger generation. The task before us is of stupendous magnitude, the path of progress is endless; but if we have at heart the true interests of Islam, no obstacle and no sacrifice will be too great to speed our onward march on the path of progress.

... our immediate aim shall be to make young generations virtuous and efficient and our posterity robust and healthy, so that it may fulfil its legitimate part in the Empire with honour to the race. Let our pole-star be active and unimpeachable loyalty to the Sovereign and the glory of India and of Islam.

Source: Syed Sharifuddin Pirzada (ed.), *Foundations of Pakistan: All India Muslim League Documents, 1906–1947,* National Publishing House, Karachi, n.d. (?1969), Vol. I (1906–24), pp. 94–103.

This address was delivered at the first sitting on the morning of the opening day (a Saturday) of the third annual session of the All India Muslim League held at the Sangam Theatre in Delhi on 29–30 January 1910. Hakim Muhammad Ajmal Khan was the President of the Reception Committee, and after his speech Maulana Syed Ahmad, the Imam of the Juma Masjid of Delhi, recited a few verses of the Quran. Then the Aga Khan gave his address, at the end of which he introduced to the audience the president of the session, Sir Ghulam Muhammad Ali Khan Bahadur, c.i.e., the Prince of Arcot. This ceremony was followed by the Prince's presidential address of the year. As soon as the presidential speech came to an end, Mian Muhammad Shafi announced that the Aga Khan had made a permanent annual grant of Rs. 4,000 to the All India Muslim League besides that of Rs. 1,600 to its London branch.

On the following day, the Aga Khan moved a resolution asking for the election of sixteen vice-presidents, one honorary secretary and two joint secretaries of the League. It was adopted unanimously. Mawlawi Muhammad Aziz Mirza was named honorary secretary, and Haji Muhammad Musa Khan of Aligarh and Mawlawi Sayyid Wazir Hasan of Lucknow were appointed joint secretaries.

On the fourth sitting on Sunday, a resolution, moved by the President himself and adopted without dissent, said that the All India Muslim League "places on record its appreciation of the great services rendered to the Muhammadan cause by His Highness the Aga Khan, G.C.I.E., and assures him of its continued confidence and trust in his statesmanship and in his leadership of the Musalmans of India".

The session ended with three cheers for His Imperial Majesty the King Emperor.

It was in this session that the League decided and announced the shifting of its headquarters from Aligarh to Lucknow.

For the official record of this session see *Proceedings of the Third Annual Session of the All-India Muslim League Held at Delhi*, published by the party on 9 July 1910, reproduced in Pirzada, op. cit., pp. 87–139.

For the All India Muslim League see Muhammad Aziz Mirza, *A Talk on Muslim Politics*, Lucknow, 1910; A. B. Rajput,. *Muslim League Yesterday and Today*, Lahore, 1948; Muhammad Noman, *Muslim India: Rise and Growth of the All-India Muslim League*, Allahabad, 1942; M. R. T., *Nationalism in Conflict in India*, Bombay, n.d. (?1942); W. C. Smith, *The Muslim League, 1942–45*, Lahore, 1945; M. A. Jinnah, *Presidential Addresses of Quaid-i-Azam M. A. Jinnah Delivered to the Sessions of the All-India Muslim League*, Delhi, 1946; I. H. Qureshi, *The Struggle for Pakistan*, Karachi, 1965; Chaudhuri Khaliquzzaman, *Pathway to Pakistan*, Lahore, 1961; Lal Bahadur, *The Muslim League: Its History, Activities and Achievements*, Agra, 1954; Abdul Hamid, *Muslim Separatism in India: A Brief Survey, 1858–1947*, Lahore, 1967; Syed Sharifuddin Pirzada (ed.), *Foundations of Pakistan: All India Muslim League Documents, 1906–1947*, Karachi, n.d., 2 vols; and M. L. Becker, "The All India Muslim League, 1906–1947: A Study of Leadership in the Evolution of a Nation", unpublished Ph.D. thesis, University of Harvard, 1957.

19

BRITISH MONARCHY AND THE EMPIRE

Interview with the Reuters Agency

London: May 1910

Majority of Indians attached to the Royal Throne – it unites Indians with others in the Empire – tribute to King George V and Queen Mary.

Speaking first for myself personally, secondly, as President of the All-India Moslem League, representing seventy million Moslems, and thirdly, on this question, on behalf of all Indians, I gladly pay a tribute to King Edward and to his successor, the new Emperor of India. While a certain proportion of the Indian people has for a long time been clamouring for political rights and equality, it must not be forgotten that 999 out of a thousand, or even a bigger majority, are, and have been, and have never dreamt of being anything but loyally attached to the dynasty and the Throne. Some have regarded the British form of rule as autocratic and not in sympathy with the aspirations of the people of India, but the overwhelming majority even of these critics is passionately attached to the Imperial Throne and dynasty. The Throne is the only object in the Empire which unites us with white British fellow-subjects – a common centre of loyalty and love.

This passionate loyalty to Royalty which is partly due to the traditions and character of Orientals, is also greatly due to the extraordinary sympathy and affection shown by Queen Victoria, by the late King, by the King and Queen, and by the Duke of Connaught towards Indians. Everyone in India knew that Queen Victoria was especially kind to, and fond of, Indians, that she kept Indian servants, and went out of her way to show courtesy to Indian Princes who visited England. Sixty years of such sympathy won her the love and unbounded affection of the people of my country. The late King – although he did not visit India in my time – had always shown a gracious interest in India. It was in his reign that reforms were instituted and the liberalisation of the Indian Government inaugurated, and his name will for these reasons ever have a foremost place in the annals of India.

As to the present King and Queen, it is no flattery or exaggeration to say that during their tour in India they won the hearts not only of those who saw them, but also of the whole population. The fame of their sympathy, kindliness, and simple dignity has penetrated to the remotest and poorest classes. Often I have heard it remarked by people of all conditions that the present King and Queen were the real and true Emperor and Empress of India. By their demeanour they brought it home to all classes that they were not foreign rulers coming to a country of another race, but that, though rulers and owners, they came as belonging to the same people. King George and Queen Mary have won by the right of affectionate conquest the undying love and loyalty of the millions of India, and I firmly believe that in the course of their reign the white and coloured elements of the Empire will be drawn closer together by their common loyalty to the Throne, and will realise how dependent the welfare of the one is to that of the other.

Source: *The Civil and Military Gazette*, Lahore, 3 June 1910.
    The interview took place on the Aga Khan's unexpectedly early arrival in England from India in order to attend the funeral of King Edward VII. The newspaper does not give the date of the interview. Generally an interval of a week or ten days elapsed between the appearance of a news item in the British press and its reproduction in this newspaper. Therefore, I have dated the interview in May.

20

AN AGENDA FOR THE INDIAN MUSLIMS

Interview with The Times of India

Bombay: 23 (?) December 1910

Why Hindu-Muslim unity is essential – ways of achieving it – Muslim sphere of work broad and catholic – the mosque in London – forthcoming visit by the King to India – an opportunity to create a Muslim university.

His Highness the Aga Khan, who arrived in Bombay by the mail *ss. Salsette* today, was interviewed by a *Times of India* representative in regard to the proposal to hold a Hindu-Moslem Conference. His Highness said he welcomed the movement most sincerely. He considered no catastrophe so great as disunion and rupture between the two great communities. He had been insisting for years on the necessity of establishing harmonious relations between them by relegating to the background all racial religious questions. They were all partners in the mightiest and most glorious empire the world had ever seen, they were component parts of a body politic, and creatures of one God. Hindus and Mahomedans were like two arms of a nation – they could not sacrifice nor injure one without weakening the other. Their united efforts were necessary for the good of the country, for its peaceful and orderly development under the aegis of the Crown; and it was the sacred duty of both sides to work whole-heartedly, and with single devotion, for promoting measures that would secure the lasting welfare of the country. He considered no sacrifice too great, no efforts too arduous to secure friendliness between the sister communities. This was a momentous period of great awakening in both the races, and formed a grand oppor-tunity for bringing the two races into closer and more friendly union. They required each other's co-operation, goodwill and practical help in promoting social and industrial measures. The proposed conference must be made a permanent annual institution; they must establish "vigilance committees" in different centres, and establish a common meeting ground for the representatives of both communities. They must work to find out causes of irritation, and take prompt measures to remove them as soon as the least sign of unpleasantness manifested itself. He believed the recent riots at Calcutta could have been easily prevented if the leaders of both sides had taken up the matters in dispute in advance, and taken steps to remove any misunderstanding. Such deplorable occurrences did good to nobody, they retarded peaceful progress, and added to the difficulties of the rulers. The Moslem sphere of work was not confined to the narrow limits of political activity, nor to the attainment of merely selfish ends but it embraced catholic interests in the broadest sense of the term. He was very anxious to see Sir William Wedderburn succeed in his noble mission.

The Aga Khan proceeded to assure his interviewer that if it did not succeed as it ought to it would be through no lack of support or sympathy from himself or his Moslem friends. He would do what lay in his power to advance the noble mission of conciliation; for India could not develop to its full, legitimate, and natural dimensions until all forces worked harmoniously as a whole, and until all warring elements were set at rest once and for all. This was necessary to strengthen the hands of the administrators. He was hopeful of the future and was sure the lustrum of the present Viceroy of India would make for a vast and rapid advance in social and material welfare, the promotion of which was the solemn duty laid on all patriotic citizens.

Referring to the proposal for the establishment of a Moslem mosque in England, the Aga Khan said Moslems had rightly decided to commemorate the brilliant rule of the greatest monarch of the present, or, for that matter of any age, by the construction of a great mosque in London. Lord Ronaldshay and Lord Lamington had already signified their intention to associate themselves in promoting the movement, and Lord Minto would be requested to be president of a committee which was composed of very influential persons.

His Highness next spoke in most sanguine tones as to the enormous possibilities of a great future that lay before the present King Emperor [George V], who, His Highness said, had already made a glorious beginning by efforts for securing unity in his domains with a view to stirring and leading them in the path of moral and material welfare. The announcement of His Majesty's intention to visit India, said His Highness, must stir every Indian to the deepest depth of his heart. The King had already conquered their imagination and their affection by his call for deeper sympathy with his Majesty's Indian subjects, and his famous speech at the Guildhall, after his return from India was still ringing in their ears. Here was an opportunity for Moslems to commemorate the visit of His Majesty to India by raising a suitable memorial. He could conceive no better memorial than the foundation of the Moslem University at Aligarh. By visiting Aligarh College on the occasion of his Indian tour as the Prince of Wales, His Majesty had demonstrated his deep interest in the institution and in the community; consequently it would be the more fitting and appropriate if they took this opportunity of His Majesty's visit to India to create a Moslem University comparable to the great universities of Berlin, Paris, or Oxford. His Highness said that he had unfolded his views about the University on the occasion of the last Coronation Durbar at Delhi, and he had emphasised them last year at the sessions of the Moslem League, and when he proceeded to Nagpur this week he proposed again to bring the proposal before the conference. He was sure the Moslem princes, its great merchants, captains of industry, and rich zemindars would come forward to help them in launching the scheme into existence under the auspices of His Majesty. His Highness thought a beginning could be made if twenty lakhs of rupees were forthcoming to start with, and he announced his intention of giving one lakh of rupees as his share towards the creation of model University bearing the name of King George V. His Highness said that it being a national institution public opinion should be created in its favour, so as to appeal and give an opportunity even to the masses to contribute their mite to it.

Source: *The Civil and Military Gazette*, Lahore, 25 December 1910.

21

LORD MINTO'S VICEROYALTY

An Article

London: January 1911

Tribute to Lord Minto – reasons for the reforms – their main features – Muslim rights and interests – appointment of an Indian to the Executive Council – Lord Minto's dialogue with the Princes and Protected States – relations with Afghanistan – Lord Minto's achievements – some omissions, e.g., the Cadet Corps – no scope for Indians in the army – Indian aristocracy should have access to the army – tribute to Lady Minto.

After a dozen years of almost continuous service as the representative of his Sovereign, first in the great Dominion of Canada, and then in India, Lord Minto has returned to his own country, with the consciousness of duty well and bravely done in the midst of difficulties such as few Indian viceroys have ever had to face. The profound regard and goodwill of the Indian people are with him, for they recognise that in difficult and perplexing times he has displayed not only those characteristics of the true English gentleman which Indians can always understand and appreciate, but also less expected gifts of statesmanship that have been of incalculable value at a critical stage in the history of Britain's rule in India.

Before Lord Minto started for Calcutta, he told his friends at a private banquet in his honour in London that he felt some diffidence in succeeding a brilliant ruler who, in perfecting the machinery of State, had given evidence of abilities and talents which his successor could not hope to emulate; and yet, he added, with a touch of humour, his racing days had taught him that many a race had been won by giving the horse a rest in his gallop. But very soon after Lord Minto's arrival in Calcutta he

346

recognised that mere breathing-space from the overhauling of departments and from strenuous raising of the standards of administrative efficiency would entirely fail to meet the needs of the situation. He saw, as in a lightning flash, that when the people asked for the bread of political advancement they would not and could not be satisfied with the stone of mere administrative efficiency, however valuable the latter might be from many points of view. He saw there must be a positive and not merely a negative policy; that the time had come for conciliating the moderate and loyal classes who were anxious to have a fuller share in shaping the affairs of their country. He saw that they had been discouraged by the long number of years that had passed without anything very definite and practical being done to keep the pledges of an earlier time, particularly those of Queen Victoria's gracious Proclamation.

Not only had nothing been done for many years to interpret these pledges in a broad and generous spirit; but it seemed as though English statesmen had forgotten that they were ever meant to be fulfilled. The position was becoming positively dangerous to the stability of British rule, much more dangerous, indeed, than the anarchical movement that was beginning to appear on the surface of the body politic in India, though so utterly alien to the traditions and outlook of the people. While the anti-British and disloyal section was ready and eager to damage the Government both morally and materially, the vast and loyal solid majority had been so discouraged by the want of any substantial political advancement that there was real risk of their sulking in their camps, and standing aside while the Government addressed itself to the task of repressing the seditious elements. The danger arose from the effect of this situation in assisting the leaven of discontent to work among the masses. In the phrase afterwards employed by Lord Morley, it was necessary to "rally the Moderates," and thus to cut the ground from the feet of those who argued that Government disregard of Indian aspirations justified sullen resentment, if not, indeed, passive or active resistance. It is no exaggeration to say that to Indian observers, British administration seemed in 1905 to be in danger of losing its moral authority over the best elements of Indian society.

Lord Minto realised that, to use his own words, the political atmosphere was "heavy and electric"; that influences were at work which the Government of India could not disregard; and that ambitions had come into existence the justice of which

England could not deny. So far from resenting and seeking to check the political awakening, he saw, as he had told us, that it was but the ripening of the educational seed which British rule had systematically sown. It was, therefore, in no grudging and unwilling spirit that he recognised the signs of the times and attempted to deal with the new conditions. The published papers show that Lord Minto had been in the country only a few months when he penned a minute reviewing the political situation, and appointed a Committee of his Council to give form and substance to the constitutional ideas he had laid down therein. To quote the words of a Simla writer, he seized "with all the enthusiasm of a generous and sensitive spirit upon such hopes, projects and ideas as were already in the air, and made the minute of them which precipitated them into history."

The resulting reforms, evolved after prolonged discussion, public and official, have been accepted with gratitude by all reasonable men as constituting a conspicuous and definite advance in the development of political institutions in India. Their outstanding feature, as all the world knows, is the enlargement and reconstitution of the Legislatures, Imperial and Provincial, and a considerable increase of their powers. In the peculiar conditions of Indian life, the ship of constitutional reform would have foundered as soon as launched if the great Mussalman community had been left without due share in the benefits of the advance; but here Lord Minto's prescience, at the earliest stage in the consideration of the constitutional changes, was of the highest value. He had been in the country less than twelve months when he assured a representative Moslem deputation of his hearty recognition of the principle that the political rights and interests of the community must be safeguarded by distinct representation, and promised that they should be so safeguarded in any administrative reconstruction with which he was concerned. As leading Mussalmans have remarked in an appeal for a fund to commemorate Lord Minto's rule, this declaration "is destined to remain a landmark in the history of Mahommedans, as from that time dates the recognition of their separate political existence in the polity of India." In a few quarters the incorporation of such recognition in the reforms has been animadverted upon. But the principle would not seem to be in need of any defence when Mr. Ramsay MacDonald, M.P., though opposed to it theoretically, has to admit that in respect to the assumption that India, the land, is sacred, "Indian Nationalism is Hinduism"; that "no Mahommedan can enter its

Holy of Holies, where politics are transfigured by the presence of the gods into religious faiths, and where the struggle for civil freedom is transformed into the worship of the Hindu genius." Mr. MacDonald even seems to hint that the absorbing power of Hinduism, written so plainly on the social and religious history of the country, will in time swallow up Mahommedanism in India.* The fact that the rules and regulations for elections to the new Legislatures have, by general admission, worked well proves that no portion of the community has been placed at serious disadvantage by them.

In respect to no feature of the reform did Lord Minto show a clearer recognition of the need for discarding some of the traditions upon which administrative policy had been based than that of opening the Executive Councils to Indians. The proposal to select an Indian for the Viceroy's Executive showed in a most effective manner that the policy of associating the people of the country more fully in its responsible administration was to be a reality and not a sham. Appointments to the Government of India are made by the Crown on the recommendation of the Secretary of State, but we have Lord Morley's own authority for the statement that it was at Lord Minto's "special instigation" that he was contemplating the nomination of an Indian; the step he said would have "the absolute and zealous approval and concurrence of Lord Minto." (House of Lords, December 17, 1908.) Moreover, when the proposal he had thus originated was carried into effect, Lord Minto did all that was possible to ensure its success. The prophecies of some objectors when the new departure was under discussion that the Indian member would be in the Council but not of it, that there would be *arcana imperii* he would not share, have not been fulfilled. Lord Minto took care that Mr. Sinha should be as freely and unreservedly consulted as any other member of the Government; and he has borne testimony to the "absolute fairness and broad-minded patriotism" which has always characterised the advice he so often sought from Mr. Sinha. In this, as in other ways, the late Viceroy may be said to have given concrete form to the new spirit he has infused into the Administration. The old idea of making the machinery as efficient as possible by undivided English supervisory agency and from the English standpoint, has given place to generous trust in Indians of good faith and loyalty, and the enlistment of their active co-operation.

We had further illustration of this attitude in Lord Minto's

*The Awakening of India. Hodder and Stoughton, 1910.

decision to enter into communication with the Ruling Chiefs on the subject of Indian unrest. The replies of the Princes, as Mr. Chirol has pointed out in detail in his "Indian Unrest," showed that they appreciated and reciprocated the confidence reposed in them. Moreover, Lord Minto has carried out a like procedure in his general dealings with the Protected States. His speech at Udaipur in November 1909, was not only an admirable exposition of sound policy on the part of the Paramount Power; it was a faithful transcript of the principles of his own dealings with the States. He has most carefully avoided unnecessary interference in the management of their affairs; he has opposed anything like pressure on Durbars with a view to introducing British methods of administration, preferring that reforms should emanate from the Durbars themselves; he has recognised that "any attempt at complete uniformity and subservience to precedent" must be inimical to truly cordial arrangements; and he has consistently dealt with questions as they have arisen, "with reference to existing treaties, the merits of each case, antecedent circumstances, and the particular stage of development, feudal and constitutional, of individual principalities." By steadfastly pursuing this policy, Lord Minto has drawn still closer the strong ties of sentiment and interest which bind the Native States to the Paramount Power. One of his latest acts in India was to announce to the Maharaja of Benares that in view of his unique position as much more than a *zemindar* he is to be given practically the *status* he has hitherto held honorifically as a Ruling Prince; and that the greater part of his Family Domains will be transferred to his direct rule. From first to last Lord Minto has been, not the stern pedagogue of the Indian Princes, but their steadfast friend and helper, stimulating to high standards of personal conduct and public policy by his confidence in them, rather than by anything like an irritating exercise of authority as the representative of the Emperor.

Nor has the late Viceroy confined the application of this spirit to the Chiefs to be found within the limits of British India. It was a happy inspiration which led him to invite the Ameer of Afghanistan [Habibullah] to make an extended tour in India, combining with it an assurance that there would be no effort to take advantage of his position as a guest of the Government to press for the settlement of given questions on lines convenient to his host. The Ameer crossed the border for pleasure and instruction, and the consideration shown him, together with the absence of a bargaining spirit, made an excellent impression on him which has since borne fruit in various ways. No doubt, Lord Minto had a considerable share in bringing about the change of nomenclature whereby the Ameer is officially addressed with the titular honour due to the undivided sovereignty he wields over the Afghan kingdom. In his dealings with the trans-frontier tribes Lord Minto seems to me to have been no less happy and well advised.

To have accomplished these great ends in the face of deeply seated timidity and prejudice, in contravention of traditions looked upon in some quarters as almost immutable; to have frankly and gladly met the changed conditions of the times; to have breathed a new spirit over the civil fabric of Anglo-Indian administration, even when engaged in the unwelcome and anxious task of cutting out the canker of sedition – these are achievements which will give Lord Minto a place of higher honour on the roll of Indian Viceroys than that assigned by history to some predecessors whose achievements may have attracted much more notice while in progress. The great change has been accomplished in circumstances of exceptional difficulty by an English gentleman who has shown his true nobility by his complete disregard of the arts of self-glorification. It might have been better if, on occasion, Lord Minto had been more careful to maintain the traditional authority of his great office in relation to Whitehall. But the truth is that on constitutional issues of this kind, Indian sentiment has not been stirred. The niceties of "control," "agency" and "initiative" have been regarded not only as capable of due readjustment now that attention has been called to them, but as entirely subsidiary to the dawn of a new spirit in British administration, under the guidance of Lord Minto, with the sympathetic and earnest co-operation of Lord Morley. It is felt that the consummation of that great change will be reached by the epoch-marking visit of the King-Emperor [George V] and his gracious Consort [Queen Mary], the announcement of which has filled the Indian mind with the keenest joy and has given a new impetus to the strong loyalty of the Indian peoples to the person of the Sovereign. It is one of the greatest of Lord Minto's services to the country that he is known to have expressed his cordial approval when he was consulted as to the spontaneous and most gracious desire of his Majesty to give India this special mark of Royal favour. Nothing that I can conceive could more strongly attach the peoples of India to the Empire than this glorious and most statesmanlike decision of his Majesty.

Lord Minto's work for India has been shown to be of such signal advantage that it is with reluctance I call attention to one omission in the application of the new spirit he has infused, but the importance of the subject compels me to say a word thereupon. Lord Minto seems to have taken no serious step to promote the development of Indian co-operation in the very direction where there was more lee-way to make up than in any other. The fact that the late Viceroy is himself a soldier by profession adds to one's feeling of surprise that he seems to have given no heed to the lack of opportunity for Indian nobles and the younger sons of Ruling Princes to serve their Sovereign in the Army. Though necessarily very limited in its scope, Lord Curzon's institution of the Imperial Cadet Corps as a means of training for selected scions of noble houses to secure commissions in the Army was an important step towards remedying this state of things. But Lord Minto, owing presumably to the anxious preoccupations of the last five years, has done little or nothing to encourage or develop the Cadet Corps, and the general question has been left untouched. The case for advancement has been briefly but effectively put by Mr. Chirol in his memorable and invaluable articles, now happily available in his book on "Indian Unrest" (p. 328):

> Whilst, subject to the maintenance of effective executive control, we have extended, and must continue steadily to extend, the area of civil employment for Indians in the service of the State, there would certainly seem to be room also for affording them increased opportunities of military employment. It is a strange anomaly that at a time when we have no hesitation in introducing Indians into our Executive Councils, those who serve the King-Emperor in the Indian Army can only rise to quite subordinate rank. A good deal has no doubt been done to improve the quality of the native officer from the point of view of military education, but, under present conditions, the Indian Army does not offer a career that can attract Indians of good position, though it is just among the landed aristocracy and gentry of India that military traditions are combined with the strongest traditions of loyalty.

Men of wealth and standing cannot be expected to enter the Army so long as the Indian officer in the Regulars can never rise above the position of a squadron or company officer, and has little or no prospect of due recognition of his work and position when his period of active service is completed. That there are grave military disadvantages, likely to be acutely felt in the event of a great war, in a restriction imposed under completely different circumstances more than a century ago, is admitted by British officers of repute. But the disability affects not merely the situation with which Great Britain might be confronted in the course of a great war; it has a most unfavourable influence on the sentimental attachment of the Native Army and on the popularity of recruitment thereto. The English public is liable to forget how great is the importance of the Indian troops in the whole scheme of Imperial defence; and that they must be treated not as a mere horde of mercenaries, but as a National Army upholding the honour and dignity of their Motherland.

That all real command of these 160,000 Indian troops – to say nothing of some 36,000 reservists and certain special forces – should be committed to English officers, and that the latest-joined subaltern from Sandhurst should rank before war-worn Indian officers, constitute a racial disability that cannot be conducive to the zeal and contentment of the native soldiery, and will in time, I fear, undermine the self-respect of the Indian soldier and his moral efficiency and perhaps his loyalty. To a much greater degree than is commonly recognised in Great Britain, the Indian people are led and influenced by their countrymen of high birth and good position; and so far from this absolute racial bar serving as a safeguard, its maintenance is a source of weakness, and must if persisted in, become a source of actual peril. I am convinced that the safety of British rule in India will be greatly increased by substantial and carefully devised measures for extending to the Indian aristocracy in the sphere of Army organisation the confidence and trust shown in the people of the country, and more particularly in the professional classes in the sphere of civil and judicial administration. There are scores of young noblemen lacking definite purpose in life, only too eager to place their inherited military instincts at the service of their King-Emperor, but who are debarred from doing so by the existing archaic limitations. It may be hoped that Lord Hardinge, whose Viceroyalty has begun under most favourable omens, will not only maintain the new spirit of which I have spoken, in the general sphere of administration, but will promote its extension to the Army.

No reference to this new spirit as the animating glory of Lord Minto's tenure would be complete without allusion to Lady Minto's active and whole-hearted co-operation with him in its promotion. Not only has she maintained the tradition of deep practical interest in works of charity and mercy exhibited by her predecessors, but from the Indian point of view she has humanised Viceregal Lodge, Simla and Government House, Calcutta. From the now distant days of Lady Frere, Government House, Bombay, and also the Governor's residence at Poona, have been open to European and Asiatic alike, on terms of social equality. But in Upper India, unfortunately, this had not been the case till Lady Minto became Vicereine. The example she set so quietly and tactfully in humanising the homes of which she has been for five years the chateleine has inevitably been followed at other centres, and thus a further and very important breach has been made in traditions which have served their day, but cannot be defended now that Indian political and social consciousness has been awakened. In every respect Lady Minto proved the right helpmate for the high-minded nobleman whose departure from India is deeply regretted; and like him she will live in the memory and admiration of a grateful people.

Source: *National Review*, London, January 1911, pp. 852–60. The *National Review* was a conservative journal of some influence.

On Lord Minto see Mary, Countess of Minto, *India: Minto and Morley, 1905–10*, London, 1934; John Buchan, *Lord Minto: A Memoir*, London, 1924; S. R. Wasti, *Lord Minto and the Indian Nationalist Movement, 1905–10*, Oxford, 1964; Stanley A. Wolpert, *Morley and India, 1906–1910*, Berkeley and Los Angeles, 1967; Martin Gilbert, *Servant of India: A Study of Imperial Rule from 1905–1910 as Told Through the Correspondence of Sir James Dunlop Smith, Private Secretary to the Viceroy*, London, 1966; M. N. Das, *India under Morley and Minto*, London, 1964; "Lord Minto's Viceroyalty", *Edinburgh Review*, October 1910; Asiaticus, "India: Lord Minto's Viceroyalty", *National Review*, November 1910; and H. H. Dodwell, "Lord Minto as Viceroy", *National Review*, April 1925.

22

THE MUSLIMS OF THE BRITISH EMPIRE

A Lecture

London: 3 July 1911

Numerical strength of Muslims in India – their ties with the British Crown – their importance in the defence of India – the unifying bond of Islam – Muslim self-organization and expression vs. Indian nationality – potential influence of the upper classes – no unifying centrifugal force – need for a head of State – present gulf between the rulers and the ruled – the role a Prince Regent would play – relations between Hindus and Muslims – the All India Muslim League – the London Muslim League's work – education in India – the Muhammadan Anglo-Oriental College – subscriptions for raising the College to a University level – a mosque in London – outlook full of hope – the role the Aligarh University will play in India.

It was with hearty pleasure that I accepted the invitation of the Council of this Festival to speak on the position of the Maho-medan subjects of King George in the British Empire and more particularly in India: for while I feel that there are others better qualified than myself, by reason of frequent participation in the work of the platform to address you, I also feel that it is eminently fitting that in this auspicious Coronation year the sentiments, hopes, and aspirations of the many-millioned Moslem subjects of the King-Emperor should be brought to your notice by one who may at least claim that he has special opportunities to acquaint himself with those sentiments and aspirations . . .

The Indian Census of 1901 records a total of no less than $62\frac{1}{2}$ million Mahomedans, and from the date of the first general Census in that Dependency, twenty years earlier, their proportion to the general population had been steadily rising. While in 1881 out of every 10,000 of population there were 1,974 Mussulmans, the proportion had risen to 2,122 ten years ago. We have still to learn the distribution of the Indian population by religion at the fourth general enumeration in March last; but as the aggregate for the country has risen by $20^1/_2$ millions in the decennium it may safely be assumed that the total strength of Indian Moslems is now much nearer 70 millions than 60 millions.

It is well known to all students of Indian history that the ties binding the Mussulmans of India to the British Crown are of the strongest kind. The *de jure* right of Britain to the three rich provinces of Bengal, Behar and Orissa (as we are reminded by one of the beautiful tableaux in the Indian Court of this Festival) was derived by express grant from a Moslem Sovereign. Subsequently the defeat of Scindia and the release of the Mogul Emperor from Mahratta tutelage sealed the transfer of the rightful title to Indian overlordship from the Mussulmans to the English. As my friend the Right Honourable Syed Ameer Ali has pointed out, the British Government is working to this day with the legacy left behind by the Moslem rulers. "The revenue system still proceeds on lines laid down by the great Akbar. You have still the *laccavi* (the advances to peasants) of the Moguls; you have still the *ryotwari* settlement – the very word *ryot* has been left to you by them." And this close historical connexion has been cemented by the blood of many a Moslem soldier fighting for his British Sovereign. You are well aware that the Indian Mahomedans form a very large proportion of the Native Army – a circumstance illustrated to the vast crowds which witnessed the Coronation Procession and Royal Progress both by the composition of the Indian Contingent and by the coincidence that the King's Indian orderlies this year are Moslems. The Frontier Militia and the independent tribes of the North West Frontier – all valiant fighters – are Mussulmans to a man; and Great Britain has in her friend the Ameer of Afghanistan an ally having at his disposal between 65,000 and 70,000 regular troops, and 20,000 irregulars – all Moslems and all potential elements in defending India from external aggression. Nor must it be forgotten that the lascars who go down to the sea in ships and do business on great waters, thereby contributing greatly to the development of India's ever-expanding seaborne commerce and forming a potential source of strength as stokers, etc., in times of naval warfare, are, almost without exception, followers of the Prophet.

I mention these considerations in no spirit of vainglory but in order that you may recall that history, tradition and present-day conditions contribute to that steadfast loyalty which, as all observers attest, has been shown by the Mahomedans of India under recent circumstances of excitement and unrest. But there is a still greater bond to be referred to – the bond of certain central religious convictions (essentially Semitic) held in common. The Mahomedans are much more closely drawn to the Western world in this all-important aspect of life and thought than they are to their Indian compatriots. They know that there are close similarities between the Old Testament and the Koran and they reverence the name and record of the Founder of Christianity. The existence of the bond will probably be most fully realised in Great Britain than at present when the movement for the erection of a mosque for Mahomedan worshippers resident in or visiting London duly materialises. The Moslems differ greatly among themselves in the stages of their respective advancement, but Islam is so unifying a power that in the respect I have mentioned as in many others, there is identity of sentiment from men of high culture down to the untutored hill tribes. Similarly the bond of Islam unites the Indian, the Arab, and the Persian with the Negro followers of Islam . . .

These considerations cannot be neglected by those who are labouring with earnest purpose for the building up of an Indian nationhood in which religious and racial differences will be largely forgotten and overshadowed by the sentiment of geographical and political or national unity. On historical, sentimental and moral and religious grounds the Indian Mussulmans are bound to incline to self-organisation and self-expression and to the traditions associated with English rule. At the same time, the great economic developments in progress and the intellectual forces of modern civilisation must work upon their minds in favour of the evolution of Indian nationality. The task of statesmanship will be to reconcile these apparently opposing factors, or at all events, not to allow them to come into conflict injurious to the common interests and the general welfare.

In the solution of this great problem of the future the cultured and leisured classes may be expected to be more adaptable to the spirit of the age than the middle and working classes, the rank-and-file on both sides, who have yet to learn the spirit of what is called in Europe toleration – of "live and let live." It has been justly observed that the best way to bring about toleration and mutual understanding in a country like India is to work, not so much up from below as down from above. The upper and leisured classes, who have a degree of influence not adequately understood in this country, should first be brought into harmonious association. That the middle and ultimately the lower classes would follow their example is certain. Of course progress will be slow, comparatively speaking, in a country where the intermarriage of people of differing race on equal terms is practically impossible, and must long remain so. But modern experience has shown that such intermarriage is not essential to a large measure of social fusion. In the United States where the tide of immigration from many countries of Europe provided a similar problem, the social unity exhibited by the settlers has largely nullified racial differences though these are still, in considerable degree, recognised in selective marriage there.

Though some little progress has been made by the educated classes under the unifying influence of English speech, social unity is still a long way off in India. Yet it is by way of social unity that any real development of Indian nationality can best be promoted. One obstacle to its development is the absence of a visible and unquestionable head of Indian and Anglo-Indian society. Hindus, Mahomedans, Christians, Parsis mingle from time to time to go back to their several communal customs and detachments of life, largely because there is no unifying centrifugal force, such as exists in Great Britain in the Person of the Sovereign. Custom and political convenience ordain that Viceroys and heads of provinces should reign only for five years, and in that short period they cannot do more than leave a fleeting impression upon the social customs and progress of the country. The Viceroy may and does invite to social functions, but he is too busily occupied in his vast administrative responsibilities to be in the fullest sense the formative centre of Indian social life. As was remarked in a noteworthy article in the Empire Day edition of *The Times*: "It is admitted by all who know the facts that the Viceroy has a load which is too heavy for one man. Decentralisation is a comfortable word, but the Viceroy is held responsible by Great Britain and by the world, and his load cannot be lightened."

India is not and cannot for generations be vested with any constitutional system such as exists in this country: but there is one element of British Constitutionalism which could be transplanted to India with the most signal advantage, namely, a head of Society not directly responsible for the working of the administrative machinery yet higher in status and dignity than those who hold that responsibility. Such a position can only be taken by a member of the Royal House who would make India his home, going out there as a young man, as the Indian Civilians do, identifying himself with the nation of which he was Regent and from time to time coming back to Europe for his holidays, thus keeping in touch with English sentiment and progress. There is a great and growing desire in India for the visible embodiment of that rule of the King-Emperor to which all classes of the community are intensely devoted. To no section of the population would the change be more welcome than to the Mahomedans, with their traditions of the Mogul Court. The case is well put in the article I have already referred to:

"The Prince Regent would have no political functions and the Viceroy, a Prime Minister of India, appointed for five years, would be responsible to the British Cabinet. In this departure we must not repeat the mistake which was made in education – the mistake which caused the present trouble in India. We must not be content with a cheap and soulless instrument, but must secure the highest and most noble of agencies. This is to be found in a Prince Regent of the Royal House. He would be the head of Society, and would discharge all the social and ceremonial duties which now trench so heavily on the Viceroy's time. . . . The aspirations of Indians are social rather than political, and at present we have no one to lead in social matters. There is a great gulf between the rulers and the ruled. With the best will in the world, the Viceroy and his over-worked officials have no time for things social, and the work which will be added by the reforms will give them still less leisure for social activities. And there is such a glorious field for the leader of Indian society!" The writer goes on to observe that if we want "to give India a social status in the world, if we want to see India bound by golden chains to the British Empire, we must have a Prince Regent as the social leader and arbiter, the fount of honour, and the symbol of continuity, to foster and guide India into the comity of civilised nations."

I make no apology for emphasising this point in a lecture respecting the position of the Indian Moslems, since I hold that their future social development, like that of other communities is largely bound up in this question. The Prince Regent would powerfully and inevitably contribute to that social unity which must precede any other form of unity, whether political or racial. Even with this centrifugal force at work social unity will be a plant of somewhat slow growth; while under the existing conditions I do not see how it can ever come to maturity. A system, under which the Viceroy is the ceremonial and social as well as the administrative head of a vast country with 315 million inhabitants must break down, since the political work of the Governor-General of necessity absorbs, or at least greatly overshadows, the work of the King's Viceroy.

I have indicated that the way of unity is made difficult by the traditions of life among the general population, and by the friction which unhappily occasionally springs up between Hindu and Mahomedan in respect to local usages and circumstances. As a result of discussions when I was last in England between Sir William Wedderburn on the one hand and Mr. Ameer Ali and myself on the other hand, a Conciliation Committee representative of both Hindus and Mahomedans has been formed to work at this problem and I earnestly trust it will be successful in narrowing the area of possible friction, or at least in organising machinery for such friction to be removed by conference instead of being fanned by riotous outbreak. But facts have to be faced; and the fact that many of the people believe in their hearts that real social unity is unattainable affords in itself ample justification – if justification were needed – for the existence of organisations on communal lines, such as the All-India Moslem League.

That the League, while specially responsible for promotion of the welfare of the Indian Mahomedans is always ready to work for the good of India as a whole is demonstrated – to take a case at hand – by the record of the London Branch. Its third annual report, passed at a meeting held within the last few weeks, showed that there has been serious and sustained activity in bringing before Government and the public the questions of the treatment of Indians in the self-governing Dominions, and the grievances they have had to face in British East Africa. Representations have also been made on the important question of widening the opportunities for Indians of position to serve the King-Emperor in the Indian Army. In these and many other ways the League here – and the remark applies equally to the Central League and Indian Branches – has been working for the advancement of the general interests of India, and has been doing so in harmony and concert with the other Indian communities. A similar spirit is manifested in other quarters. Notwithstanding passing troubles from which we have still to emerge, the future of India is destined to be bright, provided the spirit of comprehension and toleration is allowed to grow naturally and that no forcing of this tender plant is attempted.

One of the greatest services that can be rendered to the cause of social unity in India is to give her people the best type of education possible. So far as the Mahomedans are concerned they demand that their education shall not be entirely divorced from the religious and moral teaching or the traditions of the past, handed down to them by pious forefathers. The illustrious Sir Syed Ahmed Khan recognised this need in the principles he laid down for the formation of the Mahomedan Anglo-Oriental College at Aligarh. That College, based on a residential system, has had a most vitalising and beneficent effect upon the ideals and efforts of the Moslems of India. It has met a need which the State colleges, strictly bound by principles of religious neutrality, could not supply; and its alumni have gone forth into the world and won high repute for character and culture. The hope that the college would one day reach the status of a University, and thus become in a fuller sense than at present, the centre of Indian Moslem culture, has long been cherished; and last cold weather a movement was started to provide initial funds to enable the community to submit its petition for a Charter and make a beginning with the project as a memorial of the forthcoming visit of their Majesties to India. The eagerness and enthusiasm with which the Moslems of all parts of India took up the matter was to me a source of pride and thankfulness. I asked for a minimum subscription of Rs. 30 lakhs, (equivalent to £133,333) and within three months this large amount was forthcoming. All classes of the community evinced their practical interest in the movement, for subscriptions came from poor cultivators as well as wealthy land-owners, from the humble trader as well as the Ruling Chief. No one realises more clearly than I do that this is only a beginning and that further sacrifices and effort are called for. But I am confident that these will be forthcoming, for enough has been done to show that the community realises that as the *Times of India* observed the other day, "this University movement is really the index of Moslem sincerity and progress; it is valuable not only for what it effects but for what it symbolises – a reviving consciousness of the destiny of the race, a test of its enlightenment."

The provision of a Mosque in London, to which I made passing reference earlier in this address, is, to my mind, an essential corollary to the University scheme, having regard to the large and growing number of Aligarh students and other young Indian Moslems who came here to complete their preparations for professional, official, or business careers. The two or three years they individually spend in this country, far removed from home and family influence, constitutes a time of testing and peril; and the promoters of the Mosque Fund believe that one of the most valuable of safeguards against shipwreck on this sea of temptations will be the provision of religious facilities such as have been open to the young men in their own land. They are the men who will have the future of their community in their hands, to a very great degree; and a house of prayer for them in the Imperial capital will, we are persuaded greatly contribute to their remaining both good Mussulmans and loyal and self-respecting citizens. It is proposed to attach to the Mosque a reading-room and library, to organise suitable lectures, and to adopt such other measures as may be found best calculated to make it a helpful centre of the best Islamic culture.

Of course the Mosque will not be for the Indian student alone. The fullest right of access will be secured by the Trust deeds to Moslems from any part of the King's dominions or elsewhere in the Islamic world, without distinctions of sect of nationality, or social condition. Both the Sultans of Turkey and the Shah of Persia have subscribed liberally to the Fund, and the great Moslem dominions they rule are represented on the governing body. This house of prayer will be provided alike for the aristocracy of Islam and for the humble lascars who, to the number of some thousands in the course of each year, come to London in the crews of great merchant vessels and spend days or even weeks here awaiting the return journey. The object lesson thus supplied in the brotherhood of Islam will help to remove ancient prejudices and to draw closer bonds of sympathy between the British people and the followers of Mahomed. The Board of Trustees, though preponderatingly Moslem in composition, includes two English noblemen, and there are also influential British sympathisers upon the Committee of the Fund, which is under the chairmanship of the first Moslem to be called to His Majesty's Privy Council – Mr. Ameer Ali. The undertaking is one of Imperial importance, and I am confident that as time goes on it will receive to an increasing degree the sympathy and practical support of English friends of Islam.

Altogether the outlook for the Mahomedan subjects of His Majesty in India is full of hope. The reception accorded the appeal to raise Aligarh to the status of University affords the strongest possible proof that the traditional spirit of the Moslem people is not dead and that the rich and poor, learned and ignorant alike perceive the need for intellectual regeneration and progress if the community is to play its part fittingly and well in the India of the future. There underlies this great movement no thought of a decadent spirit fortifying itself behind a rampart of isolation, but the thought of the true culture which will bring in its train, not only immediate benefit to the community, but adaptation to the reasonable wishes and prejudices of other sections. By the University will be created the atmosphere which will enable the leaders to co-operate for the good of India with all others, of whatever community, who seek her good on lines conserving and consolidating that British administration of the country which alone has rendered possible the dream of Indian nationality.

Source: *The Times of India*, Bombay, 22 July 1911. A brief report was carried by *The Times*, London, on 4 July.
    The lecture was delivered under the auspices of the Council of the Festival of Empire at the Crystal Palace Theatre, London. Lord Avebury was to preside, but he could not come, and his place was taken by Lord Middleton.

23

INDIA'S EDUCATION AND HER FUTURE POSITION IN THE EMPIRE

An Article

London: July 1911

Unrest in Serbia, Portugal, France, South America, South Africa, Egypt and Great Britain – echoes in Asia – signs of conciliation – – majority of the population engaged in agriculture – state of education – G. K. Gokhale's views – widespread illiteracy makes villagers vulnerable – temporary migrant workers – liberal extension of primary education needed – conditions in princely States – Gokhale's bill for free primary education for boys and its implications – poor salaries of teachers – suggestions for educational changes – university education – encourage British administrators to learn local languages and customs – anticipated impact of education on commerce and industry – potential for development is present – salvation of British rule rests on the enlightenment of the masses – provide for a capital outlay for education – India a pillar of the Empire – India's strategic position – education will equip Indians for their future role in the British Empire.

The first decade of the twentieth century will be memorable in history for two great movements of thought, at first sight discordant but in reality the concomitants of each other. The first of these has been a movement of discontented unrest, which, so far from being confined to a few countries, has been world-wide. The waters have been deeply moved in Europe no less than in Asia, and in Africa as markedly as in America, though of course the manifestations of discontent have differed with the varying conditions. To take but a few instances: In Servia [*sic*] and in Portugal the action of the malcontents was drastic and brutal. In France the unrest has been more industrial than political; the workers were enabled at least for a time to plunge Paris into darkness, to dislocate the means of communication, and, more recently, to commit wanton and wholesale destruction upon the vineyards of the south. In South America revolutions have been frequent, and often the downfall of presidents and parties has been accompanied by mutiny and civil war. When the century opened discontent and the conflict of jarring political aspirations in South Africa had issued in a great war, and though that unhappy chapter in history has long been closed and Union has been achieved the problem of the native population is far from solved. In Egypt unrest has been persistent. Even in Great Britain repeated electoral struggles and the proposal of drastic changes in the Constitution have vividly illustrated the restlessness of the age.

It was inevitable that in these days of quickened inter-communication this restlessness in Europe, America, and Africa should find an echo among the vast populations of Asia. The East, though persistently stated to be somnolent and dreamy, has, indeed, outrivalled the West in the last few years as the scene of active movements of a momentous character. The Japanese have forced their way into that comity of Great Powers which has hitherto consisted of the larger European States and America; and their successful encounter with Russia has demonstrated to an astonished world that they have the courage and ability to support their claims. Persia, like Turkey, has been riven with discontent and is evolving Parliamentary institutions. The Arabs have been in rebellion; and, above all, under pressure from the educated classes, China is making use of her strength in unexpected ways, and is stirring with a new life. Finally, in India a spirit of restlessness has accompanied the great social and political changes of recent years. Nothing else could have been expected in view of the enlightenment brought by British rule.

The concurrent movement to which I have referred is the strong and earnest effort of English, American, and other statesmen to bring in a reign of Peace. In England the Liberal Government has renewed and extended the arbitration treaties negotiated by Lord Lansdowne during his successful tenure at the Foreign Office. It has sought to reduce the possibilities of war by international agreement for the reduction of European armaments; and it has, with the full support of public opinion, evinced an eager willingness to submit all causes of friction with the great sister nation of America to arbitration. The advance made in at least the first of these directions has been other than encouraging, but that does not diminish the credit due to the peaceful and noble aims of Liberal foreign policy. The Ministry are also to be praised for extending these pacific aims to the continent of Asia by making an agreement with the Russian Government whereby the Asiatic sources of friction between the two Powers are removed, or at least greatly mitigated. The same conciliatory attitude has been exhibited in Lord Morley's control of Indian administration. He refused to be moved to drastic repressive measures by the extreme alarmists, and no doubt this was largely due to his realisation that the wave of unrest has been almost universal in its embrace, and that it would be folly to expect India, leavened by contact with the democracy of Great Britain, to remain unmoved and somnolent.

To describe the evolution and manifestations of unrest would be to tread well-worn ground, and my purpose is to seek for the points of contact between the British Raj and the teeming millions of India rather than to diagnose discontent... the number of Indians who have Western experience of Western politics is infinitesimal. In the nature of the case this must be so: until the Indian educational system becomes more universal in its application there can be little expectation that the average Indian will gain the knowledge requisite to form opinions of any weight upon public questions. Ignorant prejudices inevitably abound; and it is most lamentable that many of those who pose as the friends of India in the House of Commons and elsewhere are not more guarded and circumspect in their utterances on Indian affairs. They forget that the ordinary Indian ryot cannot count beyond ten, and can only count up to ten because he has that number of digits. It will probably be some time before we know the distribution of population according to occupation as revealed by the census last March, but taking the figures of 1901, when the Indian population was 294 millions, we have these percentages (*Statistical Abstract relating to British India*):

	Nos. supported	Percentage
Agriculture	191,691,731	65.16
Earthwork and general labour	17,953,261	6.10
Provision and care of animals	3,976,631	1.35
Totals	213,621,623	72.61

The "general labour" in these returns is classed as "not agricultural," but in many of the other classifications, such as provision of wood, cane, leaves, &c., and of forage, the work is so closely connected with agriculture as to be scarcely distinguishable there-from. The village communities contain many members not returned as agriculturists whose employment depends on the cultivator, and who are therefore ordinarily supported from the produce of the village fields. Consequently the percentage of 72.61 is far below the actual mark; indeed, according to the *Imperial Gazetteer of India* (1907), "it has been estimated that nine-tenths of the rural population of India live, directly or indirectly, by agriculture." And it is important to bear in mind that only some $31^1/_2$ millions of the Indian people live in towns with a population of 5000 or upwards. The difference between India and England in this respect is forcibly pointed out in Sir Theodore Morison's new book on *The Economic Transition in India.*

Obviously under Indian conditions the facilities for education must be smallest in the rural areas, where nearly nine-tenths of the people live. The cost of erecting schools in each area within reach of the children will be enormous, and it will be most difficult to obtain an adequate supply of efficient teachers. Need we be surprised, therefore, that in 1908–9, with a population going on to 315 millions, the total number of male and female scholars under instruction was less than six millions? The situation was commented on by Mr. Gokhale in his speech to the Supreme Legislative Council on March 18, 1910, as follows:

The statistics of school attendance in the different countries are, in this connection, deeply instructive. To understand these statistics it is necessary that we must remember that the English standard of school-going population is 15 per cent., but that standard presupposes a school period of six to seven years. In England the period – the compulsory period – being from five to seven years, they estimate that about 15 per cent of the country must be at school. It follows therefore that where the period is longer the proportion of the total population that will be at school will be greater, and where the period is shorter the proportion will be smaller. Now in the United States and in some of the Continental countries this period is eight years, whereas in Japan it is only four years, and in Italy it is now as low as three years. Remembering these things, I would ask the Council to note the statistics. In the United States of America 21 per cent. of the whole population is receiving elementary education; in Canada, in Australia, in Switzerland, and in Great Britain and Ireland the proportion ranges from 20 per cent. to 17 per cent.; in Germany, in Austria-Hungary, in Norway, and in the Netherlands the proportion is from 17 per cent. to 15 per cent.; in France it is slightly above 14 per cent.; in Sweden it is 14 per cent.; in Denmark it is 13 per cent.; in Belgium it is 12 per cent.; in Japan it is 11 per cent.; in Italy, Greece, and Spain it ranges between 8 per cent. and 9 per cent.; in Portugal and Russia it is between 4 per cent. and 5 per cent. I may mention in this connection that though elementary education is nominally compulsory in Portugal, the compulsion is not strictly enforced, and in Russia it is not compulsory, though for the most part it is gratuitous. In the Philippine Islands it is 5 per cent. of the total population; in Baroda it is 5 per cent. of the total population; and in British India it is only 1.9 per cent. of the total population.

At the 1901 census there were seventy-five million boys and girls between the ages of five and fifteen, but there were considerably less than six million persons, including those below and above those age limits, in receipt of school or college education. Of the 294 million people in India no less than $277^3/_4$ millions were absolutely illiterate, unable even to sign their names in their vernaculars. Having regard to the slow but steady advance of educational facilities in the last ten years, it may be hoped that the figures of the recent census will show at least some improvement in this respect. But while a vast preponderance of illiteracy prevails, the villagers must be at the mercy of any person who may play upon their ignorance and prejudice. These sentimental and sympathetic rustics are liable to be as clay in the hands of the potter when they listen to the heated rhetoric of the agitator who relies upon exciting prejudices and gives no proof for any statements he makes.

The state of affairs is the more serious as the large centres of population absorb, though often only temporarily, many of the rural dwellers to work in factories, to do domestic service, or to be office messengers. Being illiterate, they may be pardoned for listening open-mouthed in these centres to the utterances of those who pose as the learned of India, and for implicitly accepting their statements. They are thus brought into the ranks of the more or less disaffected; often they are fired with zeal, and on returning to their homes they become missionaries of disloyal and demoralising ideas. Most blameworthy have been the men who, knowing the state of affairs, have not hesitated to lead a seditious campaign. The poisonous seed they have sown can only be prevented from germinating and bearing fruit through a liberal extension of elementary education, giving the masses the capacity for unprejudiced judgment, and helping them to form individual opinions.

It is a mistake to suppose that great blame attaches to the Government of India, because only 1 out of every $17^1/_2$ persons in India is able to read and write. As a matter of fact our British rulers have done magnificent educational work. Critics possessing little or no first-hand acquaintance with Indian problems do not realise the difficulties of the question in an area so vast and with a population so scattered and prejudiced. When we consider what the Indian Government have already accomplished, we can only regard with mingled gratitude and amazement their steadfast persistence and the record of their enterprise.

Of course that enterprise has been exhibited for the most part in British India. The Government have not the same powers in Native States as in the vast areas under British administration. Let us not, therefore, make the mistake of confusing the issue by introducing into the considerations here set out the particular problems of education which the Indian Princes are called upon to solve. Speaking in London on November 21, 1910, the Gaekwar of Baroda said he had tried to introduce education, and even compulsory education, not merely for popularity's sake, but because he believed the spread of education and of schools to be necessary for the progress of India. "Without education and intelligent appreciation of affairs," he added, "no community could hope to progress, and it was the duty of every Government to educate the people as much as possible." Other States may not be so far advanced in this matter as Baroda, but it is a significant fact that within the Native States, which now have an aggregate population of nearly seventy-one millions, manifestations of disloyal unrest have been extremely rare. The replies of the Ruling Chiefs to the Earl of Minto's circular letter asking for their advice and assistance show clearly enough the vigorous methods they would have pursued within the confines of their respective dominions had the same class of trouble and the same methods of agitation been pursued as were followed in British territory.

This aspect of the history of the recent unrest serves to emphasise the duty of the Indian Government to devise a policy of extended education and increased facilities for training students, male and female, for future careers. It is suggested that there should be close observance of two principles – equality in the standard of education and uniformity of practice within the various presidencies and other provinces. Such principles are followed in European countries with most beneficial effects. Surely they might with equal profit be adopted in India. Insistence on a minimum standard of efficiency would not involve any curtailment of the provincial autonomy so jealousy upheld by the local Governments. That the time for a general uniform advance has come is clearly indicated by the circumstance that a leading Indian citizen, Mr. Gokhale, has introduced into the Viceregal Legislature a Bill for compulsory and free primary education for boys. It is not the purpose of this article to take sides in the controversy aroused by this significant action, but an examination of the difficulties confronting Mr. Gokhale's bold scheme may not be out of place.

Mr. H. W. Orange, the late Director-General of Education, in his quinquennial report for 1902–7, stated that there are in British India more than eighteen million boys of an age to attend primary schools, and that in 1907 the number of boys in such schools were 3,630,668 and the number of teachers 140,000. If Mr. Gokhale's Bill were passed provision would have to be made for the primary education of from six to nine million more boys, and of course the number of teachers would have to be proportionately increased. Now it is well known that although there are training colleges for teachers, the standard of the primary teachers in all parts of the country leaves very much to be desired. The question is whether enough is being done or purposed to attract a better class of teachers. At an educational conference held under the chairmanship of Mr. Harcourt Butler, the Member for Education, at Allahabad last cold weather, it was suggested that the salary of the teacher in primary schools should be raised from Rs. 8 to Rs. 12 (16s.) per month. But has not the cost of living in India increased within the last few years in at least the same proportion? As that is so, the profession will continue to be grossly underpaid. Nowadays in India an ordinary groom draws nearly as much as the proposed enhanced scale of pay for teaching. It is not unreasonable to think that the members of a noble profession should be better remunerated than menial servants. If knowledge is to be diffused and the moral and intellectual standard of the rising generation is to be generally improved greater attention will have to be devoted to the nurseries and the nurses. It is in the primary school that the boy will receive many of his first and most lasting impressions; and a very great deal depends upon the example and culture of the master.

The tendency of the higher educational system in India has

been to turn out year by year hundreds of persons sufficiently instructed to take up Government positions and public appointments, a large proportion of whom can find nothing to do, as the supply greatly exceeds the demand. Yet it is universally admitted that the crying need of India to-day is education. Why not, then, commence at the top and at the bottom at the same time? Why not raise the standard of degree, and make it uniform in each of the provinces? At the same time it should be insisted that every area should have the same facilities, proportionate, of course, to population, for education. Take, for example, the Bombay Presidency. The primary schools should be placed within easy reach of the people, or the means of reaching them should be improved. The Presidency should be divided into educational districts, regulated by the number of primary schools within the area. From these primary schools the best and most promising children should be selected to go to the secondary school or college; from thence, in due time, there should be selection of the promising youths to go forward to the university – the culminating-point of an educational course in India. Before a boy entered the secondary school his parents should be required to state their intentions as to his calling in life, and the remainder of his educational course should be devoted, as far as may be practicable, to fitting him, generally and specifically, for that calling. Care should be taken to point out to the parents, before they come to definite decision on the matter, that in view of the economic changes and developments of the day technical and practical knowledge of arts and manufactures is likely to offer far better scope for a career than the crowded professions of law and medicine. Should the youth go forward to the university his final studies there should be the avenue directly leading to the particular trade or profession selected.

It is most important that at the university the young Indian should be provided with accommodation on the lines adopted by Oxford and Cambridge from their institution. In the speeches and writings of educationists such as Dr. Garfield Williams and Dr. Ashutosh Mukerjee attention is again and again drawn to the regrettable fact that the growth in the size of Calcutta has placed the university in a densely populated portion of the town. The university should be some distance from the crowded metropolis, and residential hostels should be built in close proximity to the university buildings. The life of the student should be rendered more attractive and healthy by the provision of gymnasia, racquet and tennis courts, and cricket and football grounds, and other outdoor pastimes should be organised. This policy would remove some of the temptations which now assail the students at a time when they are plastic and impressionable; and on the athletic field they would have opportunities for developing those characteristics which make for a better type of manhood and a higher moral tone. As things are, there is ample evidence that many of the students are compelled by their poverty to resort to quarters where the surroundings are far from helpful. Very often they are fresh from country places and gain their first experience of life in a large town – a life with many hazards and trials – in these crowded and undesirable surroundings, where, removed from the eye of the university authorities, they may be the prey of the sedition-monger. In this way there is a great wastage of the noble potentialities of young manhood. Would it not be better, and far cheaper in the long run, to remove the university to a quiet suburb and plan the buildings and equipment upon more modern lines, with the accompaniment of hostels, gymnasia, and playgrounds? The transfer may cost much; but will not demoralised and sedition-ridden students, the probable missionaries of disaffection, ultimately cost more?

The aphorism that education never ceases is true, or should be true, not only of the Indian student, but also of those English officials who do such excellent work throughout the Indian Dependency. I have written of the necessity for uniformity of standard and equality of opportunity in education throughout each province. Could it not also be arranged that upon entering the Indian Civil Service the young officer should be notified that, save in exceptional circumstances and cases, his life's work will be confined not only to the particular province to which he is posted, but as far as possible to one section of the province? This will encourage and justify the civilian in studying local languages and customs in much more detail than is at present possible. A great deal would thus be done to promote that personal contact between the British administrators and the Indian people of their districts, on which the future progress and contentment of the country largely depends. There would flow from this closer knowledge greater sympathy, coupled with better understanding of the aims and objects which the more advanced Indians have in view. It is admittedly difficult to bring to the Western mind the fact that, notwithstanding the division of six years ago, Bengal Proper, as it is now termed, even when the great areas of the native States are excluded, is almost as large as the United Kingdom. But under the English system of local administration the idea is never entertained of transferring a junior official of, say, the Kent County Council to work within the area of Northumberland Council. Save when they successfully apply for some higher post elsewhere – and these cases are the exception, not the rule – the officials of the local government bodies in England remain in the same county or large borough through their working lifetimes, and gain their promotion there. It follows that they are closely acquainted with the aims and the objects, the hopes and the fears, of the people living within their administrative areas.

There can be no doubt that similar knowledge would be acquired in India if officials were kept not only in the same province, but also for a much longer period than is now usual in the same divisional area of the province. This should at least be done as regards the less important and district appointments, whilst the present practice might be continued, though with much less frequency of transfer, in respect to the higher posts. In this way both in the realm of education and of administration the Government have it in their power to standardise and organise British India. Equality of education and uniformity of standard will have been combined with a most desirable system of keeping the civilian administrators in touch with the people and the problems best known to them.

It may be argued that with all this the problem of commercial and industrial expansion will remain not only unsolved, but almost untouched. My reply is that if, by the diffusion of elementary education, the standard of ideas of the average ryot is raised, and he is brought to understand the rudiments of business, he will be placed on a higher platform than he has ever before occupied. The truism that the luxuries of one generation are the necessities of the next simply means that the standard of life and its requirements are continually rising. The rise is most rapid where education is good and thorough. We may expect, therefore, that there will flow from the education of the Indian the same class of benefits as flow from that of the European. There may be considerable difference in the intensity of the two streams; but the main result of educating the Indian will be the increasing demand he will make upon Indian commerce, and the stimulation of industry such an increased demand will bring.

In my judgment it will be a mistake to attack this great problem of educational diffusion piecemeal. In the long run it will be best and cheapest to face the situation boldly now and to lay out a sufficient sum to meet the main requirements. Of course we shall be told once again that India is poor, and that her resources are not equal to an ambitious programme of educational diffusion. This, no doubt, is true; but does any one believe that India must ever remain in this state? And, considering the great ends in view, is she not equal to carrying on her shoulders for this purpose the burden common to all civilised nations, namely, the burden of a National Debt? Each day the scope of India's advancement is increasing. By scientific treatment land that has been lying fallow for generations is being brought under cultivation. As a conspicuous instance reference may be made to the great additions to the cultivated area in India through the medium of the Punjab canal colonies. New methods for improving the quality and productiveness of the soil are being discovered at the experimental model farms; and the agriculturists are being taught how to turn their land to most profitable account. The co-operative credit societies are doing much to relieve the ryots from what has seemed the irremovable load of indebtedness to the money-lender. Signs of real and steady, if slow, progress are discernible at every turn. The great need for their acceleration is a diffusion of education whereby India's peoples will be enabled to develop and improve economic potentialities. A system of education working up from the bottom and down from the top concurrently must surely find the centre of its gravity and enormously promote the interests of India. Remunerative occupation goes to make a happy people; when they are actively engaged in developing and improving their economic condition they will find no time for devoting thought and energy to movements of doubtful profit to themselves and the country. In short, the salvation of India under British rule rests upon the enlightenment of the masses.

Speaking at the Bankers' Institute in May last, Lord Morley stated that India's indebtedness amounted to 290 millions sterling, and that her assets in public works, &c., were 329 millions. Thus India's liabilities are far more than covered, and in one sense she has no Debt. Why not, then, treat the capital outlay I have suggested for education and the necessary machinery to bring it up to date as an investment on which interest will be paid in the future in the shape of a higher standard of comfort, a greater commercial and industrial skill? With her vast population thus equipped and educated, India will not only offer ample securities for her Debt, but will be a fructifying asset within the Empire, offering to Britain and her dominions the second largest potential market in the world. And it will be a market whose goodwill is certain to be on the side of Britain's sons, because of the boon Britain has conferred. The signs of a steady progress are already visible, and what is now required is to provide the means for acceleration of the progress. Indians will see that such provision, in the shape of a general system of education, is due to the foresight and sympathetic purposes of the British Government. Thus will be revived in the minds of myriads of Indians the feeling of affection for the British Raj against which the Indian agitator will thunder in vain when there is commercial content and an augmentation of knowledge.

Under these circumstances a community with something to lose will be evolved, and it will be naturally slow to risk the substance for the shadow the agitator places before its members. If education has any meaning at all it should have the effect spoken of by Mr. Benson: "It seems to me that the whole progress of life and thought, of love and charity, depends upon our coming to understand each other." Would that the idea under-lying this sentence formed the central thought of all persons to whom there stands committed a share in the care and progress of India. We Indians wish for it, knowing how much both sides have to gain therefrom. The outcome of educational diffusion must be that India will find an increased hope from its ordered uniformity and from the progress following on educational devel-opment. Method and reasoned organisation will at last be harnessed to the life of the people, for whom careers will be opened not only in law and medicine, but in commerce, trade, and Government service, both civil and military.

It is to this, and from this, development of India as part of an Imperial whole that we must look for the means of strengthening her and the Empire at one and the same time. For India must remain one of the pillars of the British Empire – and a most important pillar, because she is to-day the Empire's largest poten-tial market and the greatest reservoir of man-power within the limits of British heritage. That is why the education of her people is so vital: vital because of the future increase of her commerce, vital because of the almost unlimited areas of cultivation within her boundaries, vital because of her defensive strength and as a half-way house to the great self-governing States of South Africa, Australia, and New Zealand. By education there can be trained a people whose past history has proved that they can be fighters and can show a loyalty to their leaders unparalleled in history. Therefore the motto to-day for British and Indian statesman must be, "Educate, educate, educate."

Look for a passing moment at the question of man-power. The

375

British Empire has perhaps fifty-six millions of white men; but these are scattered in four continents – strategically a bad position. Canada could be absorbed by the United States, South Africa overrun, and Australia attacked before sufficient help from the Mother Country could reach them. Yet India could put troops into South Africa as quickly as they could be sent from England; she could land soldiers in Australia long before England could do so; and forces from India could reach Western Canada almost as soon as from England. Still more: India from her vast reservoir can supply thousands where England can only send hundreds. In the noble speech in which he urged conciliation with America Burke said: "Such is steadfastly my opinion of the absolute necessity of keeping up the concord of this Empire by a unity of spirit, though in a diversity of operations."

Never was this great conception more applicable than in this restless age. If by education the myriads of India can be taught that they are guardians and supporters of the Crown, just as are the white citizens of the Empire, then the realisation that India and the self-governing dominions stand and fall together, bound by a community of interests and a common cause to maintain, will have come. Britain and her sons will demonstrate to the world and to herself at the same time that the cement of self-interest, the amalgam of an identity of fate, compels the constituent portions of the Empire to work for the defence of all parts. It is only from the realisation of this identity of interests that Great Britain can remain the foremost of States, for by herself she has not sufficient population to defend her vast commerce and Empire. She can only retain her unique position by frankly securing the co-operation of all her dominions and dependencies in the commercial and perhaps ultimately the military contest between herself and the modern military and naval European and American States. India supplies the men, while the self-governing dominions and the Mother Country supply the energy and directing force. Hence it is imperative to give Indians the education to fit them for their future role in the British Empire.

Source: *National Review*, London, July 1911, pp. 779–92.

24

EDUCATIONAL NEEDS OF MUSLIM INDIA

Inaugural Speech at the All India Muhammadan Educational Conference

Delhi: 4 December 1911

The purpose of a University – the Western model must be modified – keep alive true spirit of Islam – revive intellectual and moral forces – financial aspects – University's constitution – provincial colleges – sound system of primary education – minorities must receive same benefits as majorities – languages of minorities deserve attention – technical and commercial education – science and scientific education – sacrifices needed – examples of Japan and Prussia – precedents of the companions of the Prophet – spirit of self-sacrifice among the Muslims – call for action.

Nine years ago you did me a great honour by electing me to be the President of the M. A. O. Educational Conference held in the Imperial City of Delhi on the historic occasion of the Proclamation Durbar of His late Majesty the King Emperor Edward the VII as the first English Emperor of India, and since then many important transactions have taken place in the history of the country, but there is none of greater dignity than the present visit of Their Imperial Majesties King-Emperor George V and Queen-Empress Mary, to announce in person their Coronation to their Indian subjects. This visit coincides with the date of the inaugural meeting of the Moslem Educational Conference and, therefore, we open our present Sessions to-day under the most auspicious and favourable circumstances. I appreciate the great honour you have done me by electing me to be your spokesman once more, and I will begin my remarks by humbly tendering our most heartfelt and most reverential homage to Their Imperial Majesties the King-Emperor and Queen-Empress on their arrival in this country. We still remember with deep gratitude the inspiring and memorable visit of Their Majesties to Aligarh in March 1906. The present most auspicious visit will, I am sure, tend to unite all the races and different creeds into one great Indian Nation.

From this solemn subject of the King-Emperor's presence in the country I turn to that of the University whose cause we all have at heart. When the King-Emperor, on his accession, replied to the deputation from the University of Oxford he said it was his desire to follow the example of his illustrious father, and of Queen Victoria, "in sustaining and fortifying those acts of learning on whom prosperity, the character and repute of our civilisation largely depend." In that pregnant phrase we see indicated something of the true nature of a University. It is an institution that is meant to teach far more than the knowledge imparted in the lecture-room; if not, it fails in a great essential. The character and prosperity of a people do not depend upon mere book-learning. They require deeper foundations. So it must be our aim in founding our University, not to produce at a great cost merely an institution where the wisdom of the East and the science of the West may be acquired and degrees conferred upon the meritorious, but to found an institution that will play the same part in the life of the Mahomedans of India, as do the great Universities in Europe in the life of the Europeans. But one must remember that to copy any model must mean an ultimate failure; for an institution must be in keeping with the traditions and historic circumstances of the people it desires to serve. We must try and embrace all the best features of the principal Universities of the world, and while accepting the noble traditions of the Institutions of America and Europe, we should ever remember that our first duty is to keep alive the true spirit of Islam. We must ever keep in mind the example of those who have gone before us. The true essence of Islam is its noble teachings, its purity of thought and deed, its ennobling influence and its spirituality which has been misunderstood and ill-used in the last few generations. Let it be for us to make good the wrong, and to show that we at least are not ignorant of the true nature of our beloved faith. It is for us the living to take an inspiration from the past, and to revive the intellectual and moral forces of Islam.

I am glad to see that the great University movement has emerged from the region of doubt and difficulty, and that the initial stage of our great undertaking has been entered upon. But I must plainly say that tremendous, almost super-human sacrifices and efforts must be made by us if we wish to make it a complete and an unqualified success. No great task has ever succeeded without great sacrifices on the part of its promoters. Our deserts will be in proportion to our sacrifices. I am glad to see that we have among us men who realise this fact, and I cordially congratulate you all on the initial success of your under-taking so ably and so tactfully engineered by my esteemed friend the Raja Saheb of Mahmudabad. I beg of you to remember and realise the fact that we must, in the first place, deal with the immediate and practical aspects of the question. If we fail to make the best use of the advantageous circumstances in which we now find ourselves, our efforts will come to naught. That will be a bitter disappointment to all the lovers of Islam. In the first instance, we are confronted with the financial question, and I beg of Princes and peasants, and all the well-wishers of Islam, who have most generously promised to contribute to the funds of the University, to be so good as to send in their subscriptions at once. There is no time to lose. Our position and our hopes are trembling in the balance. They depend upon our finances and the sacrifice we make, but I hope the whole of Islam will rise to the great occasion and rally round and help this great cause without any delay. The minimum sum required must be found immediately. I have faith in my co-religionists and I am sure they will not fail to make the best use of the splendid opportunities that are now within their grasp.

It was with the greatest admiration that I learnt of the work carried on by my friend the Raja Saheb of Mahmudabad and the Constitution Committee [on the proposed Muslim University of Aligarh]. I need hardly say that I find myself in hearty agreement with the principle and details connected with the arrangement of the Constitution. I must also fearlessly assert that according to my humble opinion, we must not be unnecessarily too jealous of giving a little more power of supervision to the Chancellor, for one thing that I am quite certain of is that the influence of the head of the Government of India will certainly be exercised for improvement in the standard of education, and that is perhaps the greatest need of the University. These are the immediate questions before us. I earnestly beg of you not to let this rare occasion slip from our hands, but to make a firm, united and whole-hearted effort to complete this great national work. The immediate and necessary question is the launching of the Univer-sity into existence, but there are great and vitally important questions which cluster round our central movement, and they deserve our careful attention. To make our system of education successful, and to be attended with satisfactory and far-reaching effects, we must rest it on a solid base so that our superstructure may not give way under the stress of higher learning.

I have more than once expressed my opinion that in addition to the University, we must establish first class Provincial Colleges to be affiliated to the great University and prepare men of learning, who may by and by take rank as servants and capable teachers in the University. While advocating the system of higher education, I must also draw your attention to the absolute necessity of a sound system of primary education. No solid superstructure can stand safely on softer soil. In order to raise our people to their legitimate sphere of power, influence and usefulness, we must have a serviceable and extended system of education for the benefit of the masses. It is the duty of the Government to supply primary education to the masses which is beyond the means and scope of voluntary efforts in a vast country like India. I am glad to say that the Government have expressed themselves in favour of free primary education, and are anxious to do what they can in this matter of vital importance to the ryots. I am also delighted that enlightened public opinion has so unmistakably pronounced itself in favour of compulsory universal education.

Gentlemen, believe me no country can ever flourish or make its mark as a nation, as long as the principle of compulsion is absent. The colossal ignorance of the Indian masses militates against uniting them as a nation, and the ideal of a united nation is an ideal, which we must constantly cherish and keep before us, making every endeavour towards its realization. It is this colossal ignorance of the masses which prevents Moslems from uniting themselves in a spiritual union and of Brotherhood such as must be our essential aim and ambition. I firmly believe that primary education should be free and compulsory, and it should be so devised that its benefit may extend equally to the minorities, as to the majorities of the Indian communities. No system of primary education can be deemed satisfactory unless it is so carefully elaborated that minorities receive the same benefits as the majorities. I must cordially welcome the movement for the adoption of compulsion in primary education among the masses, and if it is to be efficacious and serve the noble purpose which it is intended to do, then it must be free from all and any taint of an invidious distinction between one category of poverty and another.

Nothing would be more fatal than forcing the parents of going through an inquisition of their income, and more particularly will this be so in the case of parents belonging to the minorities, and even when they were treated most justly they would constantly feel that they had not received the same benefits as others. This impression should not in any case be created or allowed. If there is to be a limit, then let that limit be Rs. 100 per month. I think it will be disastrous to set any limit. If you fix a limit, let it be only to prevent the rich from receiving free benefits, but great care should be taken to see that it is only the real well-to-do classes who are made to pay. Knowing as I do the rural population, I am convinced that nothing short of a most reasonable and most liberal limit will satisfy them. If a liberal provision is not made in the limit of income of parents, the system would possibly be an engine of injustice and discontent. Hence the greatest possible care should be exercised in drawing a line. Again, it is equally necessary that proper safe-guards should be provided in regard to the teaching of their own languages to the minorities, who should receive an equitable treatment in this important respect. There cannot be free education for one language and utter illiteracy for those who speak another. I beg of you to realise fully that the system of primary education, unless it is free and compulsory, and provides a safe-guard for teaching the vernacular will injure your community more than any other. Besides, such a system is doomed to be an inevitable failure. You stand to gain more by the carrying out of the principle of the Hon'ble Mr. Gokhale's Bill than any other section of the people in India, provided care is taken in the re-adjustment of the details. It is not only as a Moslem that I heartily support the movement for the free and compulsory primary education. You must also remember that we are Indian, and I support the movement just as well as an Indian as a Moslem from a deep conviction of its necessity. I have frequently emphasised the urgent need for a technical and commercial system of education, and I entertain great hopes from the University which may develop into a great centre of scientific teaching together with moral and humanitarian training. If our people take to science and scientific education in the right spirit, the industrial and economic future of our community will no longer be in doubt.

But everything depends upon the sacrifices we now make. We should take a lesson from Japan. If we make such sacrifices as Japan did during the period of its regeneration, or the same sacrifices which the Prussians made after they were once humbled to the dust, we may be certain of our regeneration. We should be prepared to give such sacrifices as have been given by civilized nations, who gave enormous sacrifices of money, time, and thought, and even of many of their cherished sentiments. If we are desirous of attaining our ideal, and reaching the goal of ambition, we must be prepared to give ample sacrifices for the reality of the struggle for existence and national development. The late Marquis Komura, the great Japanese statesman, once told me that during their period of regeneration from 1800 to 1890, every Japanese individual paid in one shape or another, directly or indirectly, a third of his gross income, that is to say, more than 90 per cent. of his average income for the national work and national welfare. The result is that Japan was made what it is to-day. What were the sacrifices which the companions of the Prophets made? What were the sacrifices of the fraternity from the reign of glorious Omar? We all remember with pride the brilliant period in Andelos and Baghdad. We must not forget the spirit of self-sacrifice and self-effacement which made Moslems of the first century immortal in history. We must derive our inspiration from those imperishable names, and strain every nerve to revive the faded glory of Islam. I must frankly tell you that utter and ignominious failure stares us in the face unless we make the necessary sacrifices of our wealth, our income, our time, energies and thought. Will you make it now? Upon your action, and not upon my words or your words depends the future of Islam.

Source: *The Times of India*, Bombay, 5 December 1911. *The Civil and Military Gazette* Lahore, (6 December) published a shorter account of the Aga Khan's speech and the general proceedings of the conference.

The inaugural speech by the Aga Khan was preceded by the address given by Hakim Muhammed Ajmal Khan as chairman of the reception committee. As the Aga Khan could not be present in person Nawab Imad-ul-Mulk was elected president, and the Aga Khan's speech was read out by Maulana Shaukat Ali. The president moved the following resolution from the chair, which was carried with acclamation:

"This conference representing as it does the entire Moslem community of India deems it a privilege to offer its most loyal and respectful welcome to Their Imperial Majesties the Emperor and Empress of India whose august presence in India and at Delhi on the auspicious occasion of their Coronation is a source of real joy and happiness to their subjects, and is pregnant with results of everlasting good to this country, and earnestly prays to God Almighty for the long life and prosperity of the Sovereign and his Imperial Consort who have so completely won the hearts of the people by their royal grace and unique benevolence."

Nawab Imad-ul-Mulk, referred to the Royal visit and described it as the greatest and most auspicious in their national history. He said "Their Imperial Majesties are giving us a practical demonstration of their love for their Indian

382

subjects. They might have honoured Canada with their first visit, they might have gone to South Africa or to Australia: in each and all of these countries their reception would have been enthusiastic and they would have been in the midst of their own people; but they have most graciously chosen to come to us first whichever of their vast dominions beyond the seas they might visit afterwards. They have chosen to honour us first because India is the brightest jewel in their Crown and they know that the loyalty of the people of India is a wholehearted loyalty hedged in by no mental reservation, qualified by no conditions or stipulation coloured, by no distinction of caste or creed."

The president then said that it was the 25th anniversary of the Conference and reviewed its work during the past years and eulogised the services of the late Sir Syed Ahmad. Referring to free and compulsory primary education he said "In my humble opinion you will be making a great mistake if you will allow it to pass altogether out of your hands into those of a State Department. I need hardly tell you how the Musalman children of all classes will be handicapped if suitable provision is not made for their education. We must have schools that will not neglect their special requirements and these schools must be placed to some extent under our own control. In this connection I am tempted to refer to the scheme of free compulsory education now before the Government. Now primary education to be free and compulsory pre-supposes the employment of a very large body of well paid and well trained teachers. If I am not far out in my calculation this will need a recurring expenditure of at least 24 to 30 crores of rupees every year in addition to a non-recurring outlay of some 80 crores of rupees on buildings, furniture, etc. A fresh tax will of course be needed to raise these amounts." The president also referred at some length to the Moslem University scheme and urged for speedy collection of funds. He advocated the adoption of the Oxford and Cambridge model for the University and favoured the idea of grouping all colleges round a local centre. He suggested that the present College, in Aligarh should be divided into two or three institutions and in conclusion referred to the practice of sending students to finish their studies in Europe dwelling upon its advantages and disadvantages.

The Maharajah Gaekwar rose and thanked the Conference for the cordiality of the reception and expressed his great sympathy with the Moslem Convocation and Education movement. His Highness dwelt upon the unity among all classes and creeds and pointed out that it was essential for the national advancement. The Conference adjourned for afternoon prayers.

25

TRANSFER OF THE CAPITAL TO DELHI

A Statement on the Repeal of the Partition of Bengal

Delhi: 17 December 1911

Transfer of capital to Delhi beneficial to the whole country – his own personal views.

The Aga Khan requests me to state that he considers the transfer of the capital to Delhi beneficial to the whole country. He believes that the Muslims, even in Eastern Bengal, will ultimately gain more than they have lost, provided that the admirable work inaugurated beyond the Ganges is steadily pursued and enlarged. The numerical preponderance of Muslims in the re-arranged province gives them opportunities of exerting their influence on a bigger stage. His Highness adds that these views are personal and should not be regarded as coming from him as President of the Muslim League.

Source: *The Times*, London, 18 December 1911.

The statement was given to a special correspondent of *The Times* in India, who put it in his dispatch to the journal sent from Delhi on 17 December.

For the repeal of the partition of Bengal see *Coronation Durbar: Announcement on Behalf of His Majesty the King Emperor . . .* , London, 1911, Cd. 5979; K. K. Aziz, *Britain and Muslim India*, London, 1963; "Delhi Durbar of 1911", *Economist*, 16 December 1911; Asiaticus, "India after the Durbar", *National Review*, April 1912; A. E. Duchesne, "The New India", *Empire Review*, February 1912; Fazalbhoy C. Ebrahim, "The Change of Capital", *Indian Review*, January 1912; J. B. Fuller, "India Revisited", *The Nineteenth Century and After*, September 1912; "India and the Sovereign", *Edinburgh Review*, July 1912; "India and the Empire". *Round Table*, September 1912; C. J. O'Donnell, "Lord Hardinge's Partition of Bengal", *Empire Review*, January 1912; J. D. Rees, "Coronation Concessions in India", *Fortnightly Review*, February 1912, "The Durbar and After", *Round Table*, June 1912; William Wedderburn, "King George and India", *Contemporary Review*, February 1912; Asiaticus, "India: Lord Hardinge's Viceroyalty", *National Review*, April 1916; and Z. H. Zaidi, "The Partition of Bengal and its Annulment:

384

A Survey of the Schemes of Territorial Redistribution of Bengal, 1902–1911", unpublished Ph.D. thesis, University of London, 1965.

26

THE REPEAL OF THE PARTITION OF BENGAL

Statement on the Annulment of the Partition of Bengal

10 February 1912

The recent changes will affect Islam's destiny in India – Muslims
will not lose as a result of the changes – possible results of the
transfer of capital to Delhi – the implications of the partition for
the numerical strength of Muslims in Eastern Bengal and Assam –
their over-riding need is education – Lord Hardinge's promise of
a university at Dacca – ultimate gains and losses of the partition –
advice to the Muslims to welcome the changes.

The recent changes came so suddenly that it is not strange that
the Mussulman public should have hesitated in deciding how it
should receive them. That they will have considerable effect on
Islam's future destiny in India is an evident truism. Yet I doubt
if there be a single individual, outside the small circle of the
authors of these changes, who has not passed through different
emotions since he heard the royal announcement.

I, for one, however, after a careful consideration of every aspect
of the question, have come to the conclusion that the Mussulmans do not lose anything of consequence, while India as a
whole and the Empire will gain considerably. The gain of India
must be the gain of the Mussulmans of India, provided no direct
Moslem interest is attacked. We must take the changes *seriatim*,
look at their probable results, and determine how India, and
then the Mussulmans of India, will be benefited, or otherwise,
by each. The change of capital in itself will have the great advantage for Mussulmans of bringing the Government of India nearer
to the centres of Moslem intellectual activity and to the most
virile portions of the Moslem community in India. It will, in the
next place, bring the Viceroy nearer to the Moslem University,

an institution in the welfare of which as the Chancellor of the University he is directly interested. For India as a whole it will be a great gain that the seat of Government should be, so to speak, in a neutral central position, and removed from any great section of people or province that may have interests of its own not identical with or always friendly to those of other equally great and important sections of people or provinces. For Calcutta, with its great commerce, and tapping as it does the richest 'Hinter-land' of Southern Asia, it cannot be anything more than the loss of the social attractions of [a] Government House.

Then comes the undoing of the Partition. No doubt the Mus-sulmans were in a distinct majority in the province of Eastern Bengal and Assam, and this unique position is now lost. But looking at the position of Islam in India as a whole, I doubt if it will be found that it was a good thing to be in a clear majority in one province and a minority in almost every other. The disad-vantages of such a situation are obvious. Islam in India is one and indivisible. It is the duty of a Moslem to look not only to the immediate interests of his own locality but to those of his co-religionists as a whole. But if we look upon it from a still wider point of view as Indians, we shall find that the old Partition had deeply wounded, and not unnaturally, the sentiments of the great Bengali-speaking millions of India. Anything that permanently alienates and offends the sentiments or interests of millions of Indians, be they Moslem or Hindu, is undoubtedly in itself an undesirable thing and should not only be avoided by the Govern-ment but also opposed by all communities of India. Viewed in this light, the undoing of the Partition which has satisfied the great Bengali-speaking people ought to be in itself a cause of congratulation for all Indians, whether Hindus or Mussulmans, and I think we should all be deeply grateful to His Excellency Lord Hardinge [the Viceroy] for this great act of statesmanship which has removed a grievance from one important section of His Majesty's Indian subjects. From the point of view of the greater good of India and the Empire, the removal of the capital and the undoing of the Partition, or, rather, the creation of two new provinces, have been masterstrokes of statesmanship.

But there still remains the question of the real needs of the Mussulmans of Eastern Bengal and Assam. These needs can all be summed up in one word – 'education'. However, since Lord Hardinge's Government has promised a University for Dacca – a University that we most sincerely hope will be a teaching and residential one – I doubt if there is left unredressed any real grievance of the Mussulmans of Eastern Bengal, provided, of course, that the new Government of Bengal sees to it that the recommendations of the Education Commission of 1882 are carried out both in the spirit and the letter. For with facilities for education provided in the province, the Mussulmans can raise themselves to a position in which it will be impossible for anyone to deprive them of what is rightly their due. Some have no doubt asserted that the new University will perhaps compete with the great Moslem University at Aligarh. Nothing could be more absurd. For the great Moslem University is to be a central residential institution for the elite of the community, while the other is to help forward all those who might be left behind in the race of life by the supersession of Dacca by Calcutta. Competition between two such different institutions would be as absurd as a race between a bird and a fish. Calcutta and India as a whole will also gain educationally, for no university can be really efficient that has to cater for a population of over 100 millions and rush through more than 8,000 examinations. It must necessarily become mechanical.

So resuming the facts, we can put the gains as a neutral and central capital, the satisfaction of the sentimental grievance of the great Bengali nation, and the protection of the only real interest of the Moslems of Eastern Bengal. The loss comes to be limited to the loss of the social importance of Calcutta, but neither the loss of its trade nor of its prosperity.

Under these circumstances, I feel it my undoubted duty to advise my co-religionists to welcome the changes and be grateful to the Government that has initiated them. The need for this is all the greater since the Mussulmans will thus show their real and sincere sympathy with their Hindu brethren of Bengal and their readiness to respect Hindu and Bengali sentiment. Are not the feelings animating the promoters of the Hindu and Moslem University schemes those of fraternal and healthy rivalry? And above all, by working for the success of these great changes loyally, wholeheartedly and without any *arriere pensees*, Moslems will best prove their loyal devotion to their gracious and beloved Sovereign, the King-Emperor, and their loyal appreciation of the sympathetic Government of Lord Hardinge that has removed the great sentimental grievance of the Bengalis and has yet protected, by promising a University at Dacca, all the real interests of the Moslems of Eastern Bengal.

Source: *Comrade*, 10 February 1912.
  The date on which the Aga Khan issued this statement is not confirmed. I

have been unable to discover the origins of this statement. Was it issued to the press, from where *Comrade* picked it up and reprinted it, or sent specially to Muhammad Ali's journal? In any case, the writing of it may safely be attributed to the week preceding its appearance in *Comrade*. The partition was undone in December 1911 at the Royal Durbar held in Delhi.

This issue of *Comrade* also carried a long, very critical comment on the Aga Khan's views. Both the statement and the editorial attack are relevant to the later clash between Muhammad Ali and the Aga Khan.

As far as I know this is the only public pronouncement of the Aga Khan which ran counter to majority opinion in Muslim India. The partition of Bengal in 1905 and its repeal in 1911 should be briefly described here.

Writing to Lord George Hamilton, the Secretary of State for India, in April 1902, on the subject of Berar being put under the administration of the Central Provinces, Curzon had, in passing, mentioned his intention of examining in general the question of provincial boundaries. On Bengal he was definite that it was "unquestionably too large a charge for any single man".

No sooner had his intention to change the boundaries of Bengal been made public than there was an immediate outcry against it. Undeterred by this opposition, which he considered ill-founded and not disinterested, he decided to visit the scene of the trouble itself. Informing his wife of his plan to leave for Chittagong on 13 February 1904, he wrote, "The row about the dismember- ment of Eastern Bengal continues in every accent of agony and denunciation. But so far no argument." His trip to Chittagong, Mymensingh and Dacca convinced him of the case for a change. His chief argument was that Bengal was too unwieldy to be administered properly and conscientiously by one lieutenant-governor. Many among those who bitterly opposed his plan agreed with him in the diagnosis, but prescribed a different remedy. They wanted a governor with an executive council to replace the lieutenant-governor. To one who had for long urged the reduction of Madras and Bombay to the status of other provinces, such a scheme of adding to the number of presidencies was obviously unacceptable.

The scheme Curzon had produced earlier, in December 1903, had proposed the reduction of the population of Bengal from 78,500,000 to 60,000,000. The amended scheme, which he sent to the India Office in February 1905, further reduced the population of Bengal to 54,000,000, of whom 9,000,000 would be Muslims and 42,000,000 Hindus. It handed over to Assam a population which would bring the new province of Eastern Bengal and Assam up to 31,000,000, of whom 18,000,000 would be Muslims and 12,000,000 Hindus. Bengal would consist of 141,580 square miles and Assam of 106,540 square miles. This scheme was sanctioned by St John Brodrick, the Secretary of State for India, in June 1905. The proclamation of the formation of the new province was made in September, and the province of Eastern Bengal and Assam came formally into being on 16 October 1905.

Later events were to show that the Viceroy had misread the temper of the people in his tour of Bengal. He had returned with a firm faith in the righteousness of his resolve and a sincere hope that the reform would be welcome to the people. What actually happened was the exact reverse. He had claimed that his speeches had silenced his critics and his plan had captivated the imagination of the people. In effect, his project started a passionate and sweeping agitation against the partition that was to prove a headache to the British Government, a subject of party politics for the British Parliament, an excellent weapon for the detractors of Curzon, a milestone in the history of modern India and, above all, the beginning of Muslim separatism in Indian politics.

How far was Curzon responsible for these results? He was contemptuously indifferent to the agitation aroused by his scheme. But this attitude cannot be explained by the autocratic character of the Viceroy or by the supreme confidence he had in his administrative genius. In spite of his domineering air he was by no means indifferent to Indian public opinion. On many occasions, when the interests of Great Britain were in conflict with those of India, he had unhesitatingly championed the latter and unmistakably emphasized the importance of the growth of Indian public opinion and the folly of ignoring it. In fact, so consistently and outspokenly did he adopt this attitude that it evoked a respectful protest from Sir Arthur Godley, who could not understand "why what is called public opinion in India should have any more overwhelming weight with Your Excellency's Government or with the Secretary of State than it had ten or fifteen years ago".

Why did a man with such a deep and honest respect for Indian public opinion persist in the execution of his project after he had seen how distasteful it was to the people? His official biographer has one explanation. Curzon was convinced in his mind that his scheme was in the interest of India. He felt that the masses were suffering untold hardships by the existence and retention of old boundaries, mostly drawn as a result of accidents of history, results of battles and whims of kings, and never for reasons of administrative expediency. By doing away with such harmful anachronisms he was, he thought, bringing justice to India. An agitation based on sentiment was not to be permitted to stand in the way of such a noble act. "The fact of the matter is that Lord Curzon reserved to himself the right to decide when public opinion was an expression of views based on sober reasoning and supported by obvious justice and when it was a mere frothy ebullition of irrational sentiment."

A more practical explanation is that Curzon was right when he had found his audience not hostile during his fact-finding visit to East Bengal. Muslims formed a majority of the population of that area, and they naturally welcomed the project of a new province in which they would be the ruling nationality. Thus he was neither factually incorrect nor foolishly optimistic in reporting to Lady Curzon in glowing terms. This is corroborated by later events: the agitation was centred in Calcutta, not in Dacca, and it was more dangerous and widespread in West Bengal than in the new province.

Curzon was the most brilliant proconsul England ever sent out in her long career of empire making. He did many good things in India, and such vital spheres of public policy as education, agriculture, land policy, irrigation, railway administration and ancient monuments, still bear the stamp of his ability and foresight. Such ruthless pursuit of administrative perfection has its own penalties. Men, particularly men ruled by an alien race, forget the benefits bestowed upon them with a generous hand, and remember the tiny slips, the small defects and the passing hardships. Curzon had displeased the Hindus by refusing to recognize the Indian National Congress officially. He had also annoyed the Bengali Hindus by his reforms in the administration of the Calcutta university. When he modified the boundaries of Bengal, his erstwhile enemies were provided with a clear-cut issue on which they could attack the Viceroy. The so-called partition of Bengal was thus made a pretext for giving vent to all the bitterness and hatred the Hindus had been nourishing for so long.

As far as is known, the *Englishman* of Calcutta was the first to suggest that the King should visit India and there be crowned Emperor. It was hoped that this visit would appeal to the Indians, who regarded the sovereign as a deity, and that it would destroy the seeds of discontent. Gradually this suggestion matured, and then the question of boons that His Majesty should declare in India arose. Various suggestions were made. Some thought that it would be a good gesture to admit Indian officers to commissions in British regiments; others prescribed emptying debtors' prisons. The Viceroy proposed two separate major boons: the reversal of Curzon's partition of Bengal and the transference of the capital from Calcutta to Delhi. This was enthusiastically commended by Keir Hardie.

Lord Hardinge, who had succeeded Minto as Viceroy in November 1910, discovered that the partition was severely criticized on all sides yet, in the beginning, he held out no hope of its reversal, though even then Bengalis repeatedly expressed the hope that the King would repeal the measure. In January 1911, however, he received a proposal from Lord Crewe, the Secretary of State, suggesting the possibility of a modification of the partition. Crewe's idea was to create a governorship instead of a lieutenant-governorship, with the capital at Dacca or elsewhere; to form an enclave of Calcutta directly under the Viceroy; and to appoint Commissioners in various divisions of the province. The King was to announce these changes at the Durbar as he was 'strongly in favour of it in principle'. Hardinge consulted his officials and advisers, but all strongly objected to the scheme; and thereupon Crewe let the plan drop. During later months, however, Hardinge became convinced that if partition were allowed to stand very serious trouble would follow. His views became a definite policy after he had received a memorandum from the Home Member of his council, Sir John Jenkins, on 17 June 1911, which urgently argued for the transfer of the capital to Delhi and the reversal of partition, both changes to be announced by the King. Hardinge quickly agreed and drew up a very secret memorandum which was then submitted to his council. No vital objections were raised by the council, and on 19 July the Viceroy wrote a long letter to Crewe containing full details of this policy and a strong plea for its acceptance. Crewe wired back on 7 August giving his full support, and authority to proceed, and urged absolute secrecy till the Durbar. The King was told of this scheme by Crewe himself in the presence of Sir A. J. Bigge. His Majesty accepted it with great keenness. He was very anxious to make the announcement in person and insisted on the need for complete secrecy. Morley and Asquith were told later, and both were deeply impressed with the idea.

In his letter to the Secretary of State, Hardinge expressed his conviction that partition was causing deep resentment among the Bengalis, though he confessed that Eastern Bengal had benefited greatly by the partition and that its Muslims were loyal and contented. One of the arguments he gave in favour of his proposal was that a reversal would bring Hindus and Muslims closer together. Crewe, in his reply, hoped that Muslims would regard with satisfaction the re-erection of Delhi as capital of India, yet emphasized the need to balance the different communities in the new set-up. In his boundless enthusiasm for the new plan he wrote, "I cannot recall in history, nor can I picture in any portion of the civilized world as it now exists, a series of administrative changes of so wide scope culminating in the transfer of the main seat of Government, carried out as I believe the future will prove, with so little detriment to any class of the community, while satisfying the historical sense of millions."

The Coronation Durbar was duly held on 12 December amid brilliant pageantry. The King announced the proposed changes, and said at the end, "It is Our earnest desire that these changes may conduce to the better administration of India and the greater prosperity and happiness of Our beloved People."

Muslim reaction to the reversal of partition was instantaneous, bitter and furious. It confirmed their belief that the Government listened only to clamour and agitation, and a bitter jest, "no bombs, no boons", was passed round among them at Delhi.

27

EDUCATION FOR NATIONAL
REGENERATION

Speech at the Madrasah-i-Anjuman-i-Islam, Bombay

Bombay: 4 March 1912

All evils due to lack of education – need for greater effort – call
to become missionaries in the cause of education – scientific and
commercial education – the example of Japan – representation of
all Muslims in the institution – natural regeneration.

H. H. the Aga Khan, addressing the students after the distribution
of prizes said he need not tell them all the evils from which the
Mussulmans of India suffered, but there was one thing to which
mainly they might be attributed and that was the lack of education. If they wished to find a remedy for any social evil then
education was necessary – moral education, physical education,
or scientific education, but at any rate some form of education.
Perhaps he need not have repeated such a truism in such a
building, because here was an institution, which put it into practice, but to have the results which it should have required efforts
much greater than the efforts which had so far been put forward.
The work which was now being done for the education of the
Mussulmans in India ought to have been attempted 30 years ago,
but progress better late than never, provided they made great
efforts and made up for lost time. His Highness commented with
regret on the fact that only three scholars from the institution
matriculated last year and also on the statement that the number
in the upper standards was very small. He observed that the
numbers should have been much greater and urged all to
become missionaries in the cause of education. He quite
admitted that there was one great danger in any community
taking up higher education on a large scale, viz., the divorce

which had taken place between higher education and commercial activity in the country, but there was evidence that this country was waking up and that a reaction was taking place. The facilities for commercial and scientific education, which would immortalise the present Governor, he hoped would be taken advantage of by far more than at present.

Emphasising how necessary education – and united action in education – is, His Highness pointed to the progress of Japan, which he said had no great reformer, but was a nation of Bismarcks. The only way to remedy the particular evil from which India had suffered so far was in the spread of higher education. In this institution was a great opportunity. It was almost the only school in Bombay, which had unity. Every section of the Moslem community benefitted by it, it was the centre which had brought every section of Moslem society together. Might it long continue to do so! But if they wanted to achieve great results then every individual must do his best to see that as many as possible participated in the benefits of the school and then and then only would there be wonderful results . . . "It is for you to work out your own natural regeneration on your own natural lines of evolution" were His Highness's closing words.

Source: *The Times of India*, Bombay, 5 March 1912.

The full report of the function at the school as carried by the newspaper is as follows:

"The pupils of the Madrasah-i-Anjuman-i-Islam, Bombay, the only Mohammedan High School in the Bombay Presidency, on Monday, evening at the Anjuman Hall, Bombay Road, received the prizes won during the scholastic year from H. H. the Aga Khan. To mark the visit of His Highness Mr. Abdeenbhoy Peerbhoy Danyee gave the school a donation of Rs. 1000 to found a scholarship for a Mahommadan student.

"In the annual report presented by the honorary secretaries (the Hon. Mr. Fazalbhoy Currimbhoy and Mr. Mirza Ali Mahomed Khan), the progress of the school from its establishment in 1880 was traced, and it was shown that the number of pupils had increased during the past year from 600 to 658. The average daily attendance had been between 70 and 83 per cent. The development of the Nagpada branch into a full middle school had especially been serviceable to the young students of the northern part of the city, and had been a thorough success. In the higher classes the extreme poverty of many intelligent boys which cut short their educational careers had to be contended against. The school authorities did their utmost to check this tendency by giving free studentships and on an average no less than 44 per cent were admitted free on the production of a satisfactory certificate of poverty. During the year a donation of Rs. 100 had been received from Lodge Islam, Rs. 200 from Mr. N. V. Mandlik and Rs. 1,500 from Mrs. Shirinbai. Satisfactory progress was reported in the school examinations and it was recorded also that a girls' school had long been under contemplation, but its realisation had had to stand over for the present till sufficient funds were forthcoming and qualified teachers were available. "The Anjuman-i-Islam Schools," the report proceeded, "have been instrumental in carrying the light of learning to some of the poorest of Mahommedan homes in this large and influential city. We cannot, however, help regretting that its efforts have not met with that encouragement, which, we submit, it has a right to expect from its co-religionists. As for our financial position, Government with a grant of Rs. 6,000 a year, the Municipality with a grant of Rs. 5,000 a year, and H. H. the Aga Khan with a grant of Rs. 5,000 a year, are our chief supporters. When the Government grant for Rs. 6,000 a year was first made in 1880, we had a staff of three teachers and a single school where 50 students attended. Since then the school has developed. We have three branches and a staff of 33 teachers with 658 students on our rolls. In our last report hopes were expressed for raising our institution to the status of a College. But in the meanwhile the more comprehensive question of the establishment of a Muslim university arose; and the collection of necessary funds in this connection led to the postponement of the question of starting a Mahommedan college in Bombay for some time to come." Another question which the honorary secretaries thought needed earnest attention was the encouragement among the Moslems of the city of the study of Arabic. To their mind it was sad that throughout the Presidency there should be only four or five Musselmans going on for the various university examinations with Arabic as their second language, but the student was afforded no facilities for taking up the language. The school should encourage the study of Arabic, but the funds were not in a position to bear the burden.

"Sir Currimbhoy Ibrahim, through his son (Mr. Mahomedbhai Currimbhoy) proposed a vote of thanks to the Chairman. 'This is not the first time that His Highness has presided at the distribution of prizes to the deserving students of the Anjuman.' He said: 'It is, however, the first time that His Highness has graced the chair on an occasion like the present during my term of office as President of the Anjuman. I am glad that this opportunity has been offered to me, of expressing on behalf of the Anjuman our deep gratitude to His Highness for the great interest he takes in the welfare of our society, as owing to advanced age I am leaving my office as President of the Anjuman and I take this opportunity to express my thankfulness to the Anjuman for the ready help they have always accorded me. I have tried, to the best of my ability, to do all I could for the furtherance of the objects of the Anjuman, and I hope my work has met with your appreciation and approval. Though I may not remain as your President yet I assure you my interest in the affairs of the Anjuman will never flag and I shall continue to do for it what I can, to maintain the high prestige of the Anjuman-i-Islam, the foundation of which was laid by my late revered friend, the Hon. Mr. Justice Badruddin Tayabjee, and in which work I too had my humble share.'

"The vote of thanks was heartily passed."

28

THE NEED FOR A MUSLIM UNIVERSITY

Interview with The Times of India

Bombay: 8 March 1912

Aligarh University – terms for a Charter – supervision by the Government – finances for the University – target of Rs. 350,000 – trustees of the College – regret at lack of progress – call on Muslims of northern India for sacrifice – urgency of the University movement – importance of education – a voice for Muslims in the counsels of the British Empire – our motto: "work and sacrifice; not talk".

Turning first naturally to the University question, His Highness was emphatic in expressing the opinion that the terms which the Government of India offered for the granting of a charter were fair and reasonable, and no man could honestly say that the Government had treated the Indian Mahomedans at all ungenerously. The supervision which the Government prescribed under the charter was desirable, and he was sure that it would lead to the greater efficiency of the University and conduce to the attainment of the ideals which they all shared. Efficiency and progress were after all what they all desired in their educational system. Asked how the Mahomedan community as a whole regarded the conditions specified for the granting of a charter, His Highness remarked that he believed the members of his community had scarcely realised how advantageous as a whole were the proposals of the Government of India.

Turning next to the financing of the University, His Highness expressed his disappointment at the fact that the funds required had not now been realised. He remarked that unfortunately those who were most backward in supporting the University financially were those who would benefit most materially from its establishment. For instance, the Mahomedans of the Central Provinces had borne their part in the financial burden fully. In Bombay too a splendid response had been made by the local Mahomedans, and almost all the subscriptions promised, which in a majority of cases came from his own intimate friends, had been fully paid. In Northern India, however, the position was less satisfactory. Little had been done by the Mahomedans of the Punjab and not much more in the United Provinces. Now the position was perfectly clear. The Government asked that a sum of Rs. 35,00,000 should be in hand before the charter was granted. This was, in his opinion a fair and reasonable condition. It was true that when he first unfolded his scheme he asked for no more than Rs. 20,00,000; but he was even then careful to point out that with this sum only a very modest beginning would be made, and that once the beginning was made they would realise the necessity of immediately and largely augmenting the University funds. In his presidential speech delivered at the M. A. O. Educational Conference at Delhi in 1902 he asked for one crore of rupees: nor did he now think that this sum was in excess of their real needs. His more modest estimate was fixed for the purpose of getting the movement well established, because he was confident that once a beginning was made they would all realise the necessity of maintaining the University in a high state of efficiency.

What was the position to-day? There was no lack of promises. If, however, all those who made these promises were as earnest in keeping them as they were enthusiastic in making them, more than the requisite thirty-five lakhs of rupees would be in hand now. But all of these promises had not been fulfilled. Some of the leaders of community had played their part, like the eminent patriots they were. The Raja of Mahmudabad and the Raja of Jehangirabad in the United Provinces had, for instance, not only subscribed liberally, but had worked most zealously in inducing others to support the movement. In Northern India as a whole, which would benefit most by the University, because it would be situated within easy reach of the boys, the smallest sacrifices had been made.

Touching for a moment on the educational movement as represented by the Aligarh College, His Highness remarked that there was an increasing complaint that the trustees of the college were almost entirely elected from the United Provinces and that they included a large professional element whose members had not made very material sacrifices for the M. A. O. As an illustration of this he mentioned that Sir Adamji Peerbhoy had contributed more than Rs. 110,000 to the funds of the college and yet not one member of the family had been placed on the Board of Trustees. Whilst he was most anxious not to take a narrow or provincial view of the matter, he could not help reiterating that as the University would be concentrated in Northern India, it stood to reason that the Mahomedans of the Northern Provinces would gain more advantage from it than those of the other parts of the country. If all the trustees of the Aligarh College had made similar sacrifices to the Raja of Mahmudabad and Raja of Jehangirabad, both in giving themselves and in persuading others to give, he was quite sure that the University would be adequately financed to-day. It was to him a source of very sincere regret that although when he left India last year he hoped that by the time of his return all the necessary preliminaries for obtaining the charter would be practically complete, on his return he found that still they were not ready. In fact they had not progressed far beyond the point at which they stood when he left for Europe.

"Now," said His Highness, "our educational needs are so great that serious and sustained sacrifices must be made to satisfy them. Time is precious and it is slipping away; it is indeed most disappointing to find that instead of taking proper and effective action our people are talking, talking, talking. I am convinced if the trustees of the M. A. O. and the leaders of our community in Northern India will concentrate upon missionary effort, all our difficulties will promptly disappear. Surely they cannot expect others to work for them when they, who will reap the largest benefits from the University, do not do their part. How can they expect to reap the fruit if they do not care to sow the seed? A tree can never bear fruit unless it is patiently watered. Let me strongly urge upon my co-religionists in Northern India the enormous importance of putting their hands in their pockets and their shoulders to the wheel in order that our University may be promptly and substantially inaugurated."

In conclusion, His Highness dwelt upon the urgency of this University movement, because until it is well established the Mahomedans of India cannot take up the other great questions confronting them, such as other branches of education and social reform. Indian Moslems, he said, must concentrate on the dominating question before them, namely education. If they were to advance in social reform, it was clear that the way must first be prepared by education and education could not be given in a haphazard manner. They must all make persistent efforts, individually and collectively, for the universal diffusion of knowledge, and they must all be prepared, individually and collectively, to make sacrifices for it. They had a tremendous amount of leeway to make up. Even if they gave their best, it would take a very long time indeed, before they reached the standard of western civilisation. But if they did not do their best, then with the world moving at the pace which was the rule today they would have to abandon all hopes of a great political future and of working out their economic salvation. "There is," added His Highness, "no short cut or royal road to political power and political deliverance. Nobody is more anxious than am I that in the councils of the British Empire my co-religionists should have a voice – a voice to which I think they are entitled when they are fit for it. But how can we expect to have a voice until we have raised ourselves to the standard of those who now control the destinies of the Empire, and how can we equal that standard until we have made great and continuous sacrifices for the cause of education for a generation at least? Fitness and fitness alone can lead us to a great future. We cannot hope to attain our place in the Empire by a miracle; but if we make sacrifices, if we cease talking and really become resolute, determined and generous, then I do not despair of success. I do, however, urge my co-religionists to have patience and to give service, when the reward will be theirs. They must not allow academic questions to loom too largely in their deliberations but must concentrate all their energies and all their thoughts on the advance of modern civilisation by means of education and social reform."

"My word to my co-religionists in India on the eve of my departure is, concentrate on the University, carry it at once to the stage of inauguration, so that we may have a clear road to develop primary, secondary, commercial and technical education amongst our members. There are indeed many projects for the welfare of our community which demand attention; but until the University is inaugurated on what are I repeat the reasonable conditions laid down for the granting of the charter, none of these other important issues which are of vital interest to our community can be taken up. Our motto must be 'work and sacrifice; not talk'."

Source: *The Times of India*, Bombay, 9 March 1912. A slightly shorter report was carried by *The Civil and Military Gazette*, Lahore, on 10 March.

The Aga Khan left India for England on 9 March after his strenuous tour of the country in promotion of the cause of a Muslim university.

For the history and difficulties of the making of a Muslim university in India, see Muhammad Ali, *The Proposed Muhammadan University*, Bombay, 1904; Annie Besant, *For India's Uplift: A Collection of Speeches and Writings on Indian Questions*, Madras, n.d.; Rafiuddin Ahmad, "The Proposed Muslim University in India", *The Nineteenth Century*, December 1898; J. Kennedy, "A Muhammadan University for Northern India", *Imperial and Asiatic Quarterly Review*, October 1898; Theodore Morison, "A Muhammadan University", *National Review*, October 1898; Muhammad Ibrahim Qureshi, "The Proposed Musalman University: A Reply", *Indian Review*, November 1902; "India: Education", *Round Table*, December 1911; M. T. Kaderbhoy, "The Muslim University", *Imperial and Asiatic Quarterly Review*, October 1911; Edward G. Long, "Muhammadan University for India", *Hindustan Review*, June 1911; Arthur H. Ewing, "The Proposed Moslem University for India", *Muslim World*, April 1912; Sayyid Abdul Latif, "The Muslim University Movement", *Indian Review*, May 1916; and Muhammad Ishaq Khan, Letter, *The Civil and Military Gazette*, 23 February 1917.

29

AN APPEAL TO THE INDIAN MUSLIMS TO HELP THE REFUGEES OF THE BALKAN WAR

A Cablegram to the Raja of Mahmudabad

London (?): December 1912

Suffering among Muslim refugees of the war – organize meetings and house-to-house visits for funds.

According all accounts from independent sources, apart from Red Crescent work, terrible, unheard of suffering amongst Moslem refugees. Thousands of women and children dying of cold and hunger, terrible calamity for Islam and humanity. Thousands of innocent little ones daily shivering to death. Pray you at once organise meetings throughout Northern India and Bengal. Appeal to His Highness the Nawab of Rampur, Her Highness the Begum of Bhopal and also to His Highness and the Nobles of Hyderabad. Kindly organise house-to-house visits everywhere and send money collected telegraphically to Right Honourable Saiyad Ameer Ali, who will forward to Constantinople at once for relief of refugees, orphans and widows. Appeal to all Moslems – to all human beings. For God's sake, for sake of Prophet, do not let thousands of Moslems daily die for want of help. See what Russian public subscription has done for the Balkan sufferings. Now or never is time for help. Am broken hearted to see terrible sufferings. Help!

To my Islamic brethren and to all my countrymen I appeal in the name of humanity to rise to the occasion and to extend their helping hand by contributing their mite for the alleviation of the painful suffering of their fellow creatures abroad. The warmth and earnestness with which the people have hitherto responded is gratifying indeed, but the seriousness of the situation demands sacrifice, strenuous efforts and arduous work in a still greater degree. I have no doubt that my countrymen will readily and generously respond to this pathetic cry for relief and I trust that the members of our community will organise local and house-to-house collections in every town and village. It is immaterial whether the money so collected is sent to the Right Honourable Mr. Saiyad Ameer Ali or to the Prime Minister in Constantinople, but the object should be clearly specified. I am doing, and will do all that lies in my power in furtherance of the noble cause and will shortly organise a tour of visits to important places throughout India.

Source: *The Times of India*, Bombay, 9 December 1912.

This appeal formed the text of a cablegram sent by the Aga Khan, presumably from London, to the Raja of Mahmudabad. The Raja released it to the press with the following short statement of his own:

"We are all aware that in the war in which Turkey and the Allies are involved an armistice has now been proclaimed and terms of peace are being considered. Let us all hope that the war has practically come to an end and that further bloodshed will be averted. If that is happily so there will be no further addition to the number of the wounded and the work with which the Red Crescent Society is immediately concerned will soon come to a close. But there has arisen in an acute form the problem of relieving the widows and orphans of those who have been slain and the refugees who have been obliged to take shelter within the walls of Constantinople from numerous places. Their number must be large and their sufferings intense.

"The following cablegram from His Highness the Aga Khan to me indicates the gravity of the situation."

30

INDIA AND THE BALKAN WAR: POSITION OF MUSLIMS

An Article

Bombay: 13 February 1913

India's Muslims disturbed by recent events in Muslim lands – how Muslims of Turkey might be helped – alleviate the suffering of those rendered homeless – let the Sultan and his Ministers solve the question of war and peace – a loan for Turkey – Turkey in Asia should be a strong power – England's absorption of Arabia and Mesopotamia a dangerous proposition – help to strengthen friendship between Britain and Turkey – ideal of self-government for India – duties of Muslims in India.

Ever since the outbreak of the Balkan War, coming as it did shortly after the Tripoli War, the practical absorption of Morocco by France, and the possibility that Persia might be gradually brought under European protection, the position and the sentiments of the Moslems of India have, with ever increasing rapidity, become extraordinarily difficult, sad and unfortunate. On the one hand they realise that their most cherished hope for the permanence of the chief Moslem State and the independence of the two remaining Mussalman States is disappearing; and on the other hand daily they read and hear, and of course they must more or less realise from their own reading of the history of past wars, the terrible happenings in European Turkey. Under these circumstances every Mussalman is not only depressed and sad, but he is anxious, most anxious, to do something to aid his co-religionists. Yet this desire often carries him into an attitude of useless negation – an attitude of mere dislike of the European, suspicion of the Christians, and still inability to put the responsibility for his own misfortune on anybody else. This attitude can be gleaned by anyone who takes note not only of the private conversation of individual Mussulmans of all classes, but who reads between the lines of the various resolutions which have been passed, as well as by the general atmosphere of Moslem gatherings.

Now I may claim that I have studied the Turkish question and the general position of the Mussulman for many years past carefully. I can also say that hardly an important sentence has been written in any of the leading European papers about the war that I have not read, in addition to numberless reports from the charitable organisations at the Front, from the Consuls, and from various Red Crescent doctors and others. Under these circumstances I feel it my duty to offer a few suggestions and ideas as to how the situation strikes one who can claim at least this much – that he has no other motive except the welfare of Islam.

The point that at once strikes us, the immediate question, is, What can we do to help the Mussulmans of Turkey? First we must regard the situation from the point of view of the happiness of the Turks, so as to prevent as far as possible suffering and pain amongst the hundreds of thousands who have been rendered homeless and helpless by the war. This great task is the first and foremost duty of every Mussulman. Secondly, What can be done to make Turkey, as reconstituted by the war, a powerful Asiatic State? The two questions, although interlaced, are in a way really distinct. The first is an immediate question; the second is one for the future. So strongly have I been convinced that our whole efforts should be concentrated on the prompt and effective relief of suffering in Turkey that, while I have been one of the most enthusiastic supporters of the University Movement, I felt it to be my duty entirely to leave that question in other and abler hands amongst the Mussulmans of India, and to devote all my thoughts and the time that I would give to public service to the relief of the sufferers by the war. For the condition of society induced by the war resembles a great famine, though it is infinitely worse. It is a question of life and death. Everything else in life can wait, but when life itself is face to face with hunger and want, there is nothing but immediate relief or death. It would indeed be a terrible thing for the Mussulmans of India, if, through any want of effort on their part, thousands of their brethren in Turkey died. On this point no Mussulman can have any doubt or hesitation: his duty is clear. He must send money – as much as he can – for the relief of the suffering and the wounded; and what is equally important, for the thousands of refugees who are now flocking into Asia Minor from European Turkey and from Macedonia. These refugees want not only food but money to buy seed for the coming season, so as to give them a chance to re-establish themselves in Asia Minor. These are questions of humanity which are urgent and immediate. We can establish a school or a University twelve months hence: we cannot bring to life those who die to-day. Just as when a famine is raging in an Indian district it would be idle to concentrate on some philanthropic work of future utility in preference to the saving of lives, so our immediate efforts must be concentrated on the saving of life. May the Mussulmans of India have the grace to realise this immediate need!

But whilst bending every effort to the relief of distress, surely it is equally incumbent upon us to eschew any policy which may increase and prolong, unnecessarily and uselessly, the sufferings of our co-religionists in Turkey! The Sultan and his Ministers alone can judge of the wisdom of prolonging or terminating the war. They alone are in possession of the facts: they alone can accurately balance the obvious disadvantages of continuing the war with the possible advantages of concluding peace. It does seem to me a cruel addition to the burdens which Turkish stat-esmen have to bear, at this crisis in the affairs of their country, to be harassed by irresponsible advice from Indian Mussulmans who know nothing of the grim realities of the position; and upon whom none of the grievous burdens of the war actually fall. How easy it is to bid others fight for the honour of Islam when here we enjoy the serene comfort of peace and prosperity: how hard it must be for Turkish statesmen to decide, well knowing the consequences of their action, yet driven forward by the tele-graphic appeals of Moslems abroad! His Imperial Majesty the Sultan is bidden do this, or refrain from doing that or the honour of Islam is sold; what right have we to assume that the Padishah is one whit less sensitive on the point of Moslem honour than the Moslems of Lucknow or Lahore, of Madras or Bombay? But he and his Ministers have both the knowledge and the responsi-bility, which none of us here share: their ears are dinned by the cries of the wounded and the wails of the fatherless. As on them lies sole responsibility, with them lies sole discretion unfettered by irresponsible appeals from abroad. Tolstoy and Gladstone both suggested that it would be a good thing for the cause of peace if before a war broke out all the leading journalists were sent to the Front – there would be less Yellow Journalism hankering after war. Well, it would be a good thing if all these hundreds of thousands who are, from here, giving their advice, were forced to make all the sacrifices that the war entails on the people of Turkey themselves. There would be more calm and deliberate advice given. Our watchword is work and sacrifice: let that suffice.

Now we come to the second point, namely what can the Mussulmans of India do for the re-organisation of Turkey, as a great and independent power, after the present war is over. First of all Turkey requires, and must require, a large loan and nothing would show the sincerity of the Mussulmans of India in the interests of Turkey more than the advancement of four or five million pounds to Turkey. But let us at least be practical. The Mussulmans of India are not rich enough and are not in the position to spare the money. Every penny that Turkey receives she must receive in a way that will assure her life in the future.

I am afraid the suggestion of a loan made by the Orient Bank in the form it is advanced is neither feasible nor practicable. Loans without interest are out of the question. If, on account of religious sentiment, no interest is to be touched, there should be a condition by which a loan of 100 would be issued at 75 and repaid at par after five years. The Orient Bank and the other Mussulmans who wish to carry out this scheme should proceed on these lines: Turkey should borrow for five years either at five per cent issued at par or at 75 repayable at 100. These bonds should be sent by Turkey to India; and the various banks here, including the Orient Bank, might sell as brokers only, not as borrowers, while the security would be that of the Turkish Government and not that of the Bank, except of course in the interval between the receipt of the deposit and the delivery of the bonds to the purchasers, which would be very short. The banks naturally would charge their own commission. It is advisable that the loan should be so arranged that even half-sovereign bonds could be issued. Such a loan could be safely subscribed to and safely taken up by the Mussulmans of India and while undoubtedly it would mean sacrifice, for if the same capital were embarked in trade, a greater return would be secured, yet the sacrifice would not be of such a nature as to ruin the millions of India without doing very much for Turkey. The credit of Turkey, especially if peace is soon concluded, is sufficient and there is no danger whatever as to the repayment of the capital in five years.

But now comes a still more important question namely, What is to be the position of Turkey after peace? Whatever happens, whatever the result of the last stages of this war, Turkey must in the future be an Asiatic Power; she must concentrate on Asia. Then comes the greatest of her problems, a problem of life and death to her – whether any Mussulman State is to remain or not. Turkey as an Asiatic Power can live and thrive only if she has the goodwill, friendship and the support of England. England is the only country which has everything to gain and nothing to lose by a strong Turkey in Asia. As it is, the route to India has practically fallen all along the Mediterranean into the hands of foreign Powers, and should Asiatic Turkey, Syria, Mesopotamia and Anatolia become German, French, and Russian, it would indeed be a most serious position for England. Apart from any question of sentiment it is to the interests of England that Turkey in Asia should become strong and prosperous.

I have often heard it suggested that England should herself absorb Arabia and Southern Mesopotamia, but the dangers of such an exposed position, the want of the millions of soldiers to defend it and the hundred and one other difficulties, are so great that it would impose an excessive tax even on the resources of the British Empire. Now here is a great opening for the Mussulmans of India, alike of serving England and Islam. Let them use all their influence – through their loyal efforts, through their goodwill – to bring England and Turkey together and, in fact, to carry out in Asiatic Turkey the spirit of the Cyprus Convention and the policy of Lord Beaconsfield ... At last there is a possibility that the dream of many Mussulmans may come true, and that England and Turkey may become fast and firm friends. But this means an equally important responsibility for the Mussulmans of India. It means that they must say nothing, do nothing, and act in no way that can weaken English confidence in Islam and in the loyalty of the Mussulmans of India. If England is to become the bulwark of Islam, then Islam also must ever be ready to play its part loyally in the welfare and strengthening and defence of the British Empire.

Far be it from me to suggest that the role of Islam in India is to be hewers of wood and drawers of water. We could do Britain and the British people no greater injustice to say that Mussulmans care nothing for the ideal of self-government, within the Empire and under the Crown and Flag. To entertain that ideal is to show that Mussulmans appreciate the British spirit, and desire to pay it the most subtle of flatteries – imitation. But this is an ideal which can be reached only by generations of effort, by generations of self-sacrifice, and any step to precipitate the end by artificial means even by a generation or two would be to do

England the greatest of all injustices – it would force the British people to confuse the only loyalty that is worth having, namely, the loyalty of high-minded, self-respecting subjects, working for the ideals that have been attained in England, with the madness and crime of disloyalty. The stronger our commonsense the more sincere will be our recognition of the fact that the Government of India cannot change its character until new generations, with changed characters and with changed local surroundings and customs, have arisen, alike among Hindus and Mussulmans.

Surely if we look the facts of the situation resolutely in the face, the duty of Indian Moslems in these anxious days is clear. It is first to bend all our energies to the work which cannot wait, the relief of suffering, the care of the wounded, and the rehabilitation of the peasantry who have fled from Macedonia and Thrace to Asia Minor. For this money, and yet more money, is the crying need, not the bemusement of Turkish statesmen, terribly weighted by their responsibilities, by demands for vicarious sacrifices. Then when the war is over, efforts no less sustained will be demanded to help Turkey on her path as a great Asiatic Power. That path will not be easy: covetous eyes are cast toward the territories which must be the home and the strength of the future Turkish Empire. One Power, and one Power only can give Turkey disinterested advice and help in this great work, and that is England. She has no territorial ambitions in Asia Minor or Syria or Arabia or Mesopotamia; all her interests lie in the recreation of a strong and powerful Turkey based on these regions, in order to prevent rivals from being established on the flank of the road to India. What an opportunity lies before the Moslems of India here! By our present sacrifices we can establish an influence with the Turkish Government which will give weight to our sentiments and representations at Constantinople. In this way, we can act as the cement which will unite these two Empires into an irresistible whole, preserving at once to Turkey the opportunity of working out her destiny in Asia, safeguarding the road to India, and returning to the days of the Great Eltchi and Beaconsfield. If that be the outcome of this unhappy war, then we shall find full compensation for the loss of Tripoli and Macedonia in the assured future of a great Turkey in Asia, firmly united with England, and thus both securing her own destiny and averting from the Empire the danger of either a fresh menace or of fresh responsibilities at the very gates of India.

Source: *The Times of India*, Bombay, 14 February 1913.

A very brief summary of the article was carried by *The Times*, London, on the same date, prefaced by the following words of its Bombay correspondent:

"There has recently been an unfortunate development among certain sections of Indian Moslems in their attitude towards the war. Inexcusably extravagant language has been employed at some public meetings – notably at Lucknow and Madras – and there has been a manifest tendency to develop strong anti-British feeling. At this juncture His Highness the Aga Khan has made a notable pronouncement on the situation."

On the Balkan War see Siddha Mohana Mitra, *Anglo-Indian Studies*, London, 1913, pp. 490–504; G. Ward Price, *Extra-Special Correspondent*, London, 1957; Asiaticus, "India: Indian Muhammadans and the Balkan War", *National Review*, March 1913, pp. 179–88; Diplomatist, "Turkey and the Balkan States", *Empire Review*, September 1913, pp. 82–98; Geoffrey Drage, "The Balkan Main Current", *Edinburgh Review*, January 1913, pp. 197–216; Shah Muhammad Naimatullah, "Recent Turkish Events and Muslim India", *Asiatic Quarterly Review*, October 1913, pp. 241–8; Austen Verney, "New Aspects of the Eastern Question", *East and West*, May 1913, pp. 422–30; Homersham Cox, "Turks and Christians", *Modern World*, January 1914, pp. 15–18; Arthur W. Spencer, "The Balkan Question: The Key to a Permanent Peace", *ibid.*, April 1914, pp. 162–74; "The Balkan War and the Balance of Power", *Round Table*, June 1913, pp. 395–424; "The Doctrine of Ascendancy", *ibid.*, December 1914, pp. 70–102; Cyril Falls, "The Balkan Wars, 1912–1913", *History Today*, September 1963, pp. 605–13, Lakshmi Kant Choudhary, "The Balkan Wars (1912–13) and Indian Nationalism", *Political Scientist*, January–June 1966, pp. 59–65; and the following items in *Muslim India and Islamic Review* (London): "Foreign Policy and the Muslims", March 1913, pp. 46–7; Khwaja Kamaluddin, "An Open Letter to the Prime Minister", May 1913, pp. 126–9, June 1913, pp. 164–7 and July 1913, pp. 219–21; Zafar Ali Khan, "The Struggle in the Near East and the Muslim Feeling in India: An Appeal to the British Public", February 1913, pp. 28–32; and Al-Quidwai (Mushir Husain Kidwai), "The Powers and Turkey", May 1914, pp. 168–71.

All India Muslim Conference, Delhi. His Highness the Aga Khan as President with other Muslim leaders, 1902.

His Highness the Aga Khan at the time of the Convocation at Aligarh
University when he received an honorary degree. Quaid-e-Millat, Liaquat Ali
Khan, is seen to the right of the Aga Khan.

Postage stamps issued to mark the Birth Centenary of Aga Khan III.

A keen golfer, the Aga Khan was a familiar figure on the golf courses
when he visited England.

Aga Khan III: A portrait.

His Highness the Aga Khan presiding at a meeting in Bombay held to protest against the treatment of Indians in South Africa. The Quaid-i-Azam Muhammad Ali Jinnah and many other leaders attended this meeting.

The Round Table Conference. The Aga Khan led the Muslim Delegation. Quaid-i-Azam, Muhammad Ali Jinnah is to the left of the Aga Khan, 1931

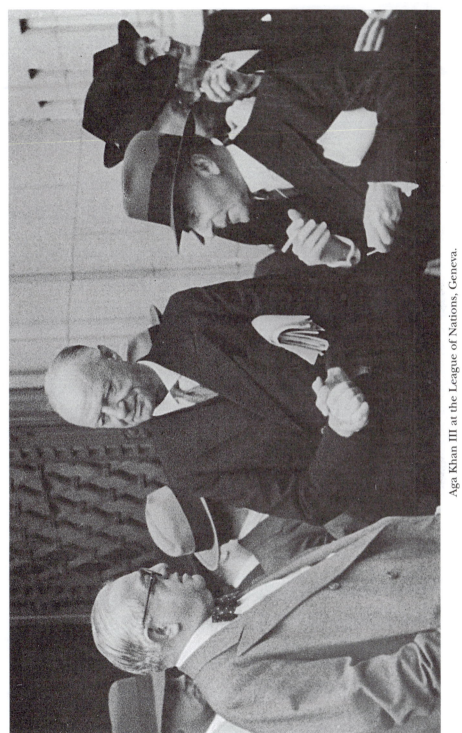

Aga Khan III at the League of Nations, Geneva.

The Aga Khan at the League of Nations.

His Highness Aga Khan III.

31

ON THE NECESSITY OF HAVING HINDU
UNIVERSITIES IN INDIA

Speech at a Function in Honour of the Deputation of the Hindu
University

Bombay: 23 February 1913

Welcome to the deputation – reminder of his own suggestion for
two Hindu universities twelve years ago – room for a movement
for intellectual variety – the higher side of life – lack of men of
letters in India – these universities will produce more tolerant and
loving Indians.

His Highness the Aga Khan, who on rising to speak received an
ovation from the audience, said he had been asked to propose
the resolution which heartily welcomed the deputation of the
Hindu University and congratulated them on the important work
they had done and accorded their hearty support to the same.
He said these were days of short memory, but he reminded them
that twelve years ago, when he had the honour of presiding at
the Mahomedan Educational Conference at Delhi, he had the
temerity to suggest that there should be not one but two, Hindu
Universities and one Mahomedan University. They would, therefore, see that he was one of the early pioneers of the University
movement which was a very difficult problem to solve but which
had now emerged triumphantly from the region of doubt and
difficulty and advanced to a practical stage. These were days of
mourning for the Mahomedan race, but they could not withhold
themselves from a movement which presaged happiness and
peace to Indian minds.

Sir Bhalchandra had said that there had been misgivings as to
the possible narrowing influence of this movement. But he was
sure that in a vast country like India every movement that gave

greater intellectual variety to the country made the country richer and greater in colour and variety. The very fact that ancient Hindu learning and Hindu social life and sacred Hindu literature would be brought out to move and guide the young minds must surely be for the greater good of the country. With the intellectual development of youth it would bring out the higher side of life. Not only the intellectual but the spiritual and religious life, for which India was renowned in the past, would be cultivated in these Universities and develop the boys in perfect men. India had produced a remarkable captain of industries like late Mr. Tata, and mathematicians and scientists like Pranjpe and Bose, but he asked how was it that they were wanting in men who stood high on the literary planes? He hoped the new Universities would enable them to produce eminent literary men. It would enable them to develop every side of men, intellectual, spiritual and religious and turn out more tolerant and loving Indians anxious to sacrifice their lives for the good of their fellow-citizens.

Source: *The Times of India*, Bombay, 24 February 1913.

The full report of the meeting as published in the newspaper is reproduced below:

"A mass meeting of the Hindus of Bombay was held at Madhav Baugh, Girgaum, Bombay on Sunday evening to accord a cordial welcome to the members of the Hindu University Deputation which arrived in Bombay on Friday last... Great enthusiasm prevailed throughout the proceedings which lasted for three hours and a half. There were several admirable speeches made welcoming the new spirit that has come over India and which aims at elevating Indians in social and moral planes.

"Among those present were His Highness The Aga Khan, the Hon. Mr. P. D. Pattani, Sir Narayen Chandavarker, Sir Vithaldas Thakersey, the Hon. Mr. Gokuldas K. Parekh, the Hon. Mr. Lalubhoy Samaldas, Mr. Narotum Morarji Gokuldas, Mr. Tribhovandas Varjivandas, Sir Jugmohandas Varjivandas, Rao Bahadur Keshowji Nathu, Mr. Delvi, the Hon. Mr. Rafiuddin Ahmed, Mr. Kazi Kabiruddin, Mr. J. J. Vimadalal, Mr. V. J. Dani, Mr. Tribhovandas Mungaldas.

"Sir Bhalchandra Krishna was voted in the Chair. In the course of his address he said:- 'When the idea of the Hindu University was broached for the first time, it met with ridicule from some and unmitigated condemnation from others. But every good cause has to pass through such stages and now it must be a matter of pleasure to you to find that those that come forward to curse it have stayed only to bless it and pray for its success.

" 'Ladies and Gentlemen, I do not wish to come between you and the different speakers, and anticipate what they have to say. I shall only refer to an objection raised against the movement. Some of our friends are opposed, and conscientiously opposed, to the movement on the ground of its being in conflict with our national ideal. They conscientiously believe that it will be a reactionary and sectarian University. If the combination of religious with secular instruction and the renaissance of Hindu Culture and Hindu Ideals which are to form the characteristic features of the new University, bring it within the pale of reactionary movements I must admit that the Hindu University is reactionary in that score. But in this connection I cannot resist the temptation of quoting the memorable words of wisdom of a great Bengalee. "Though, education," says the venerable Dr. Rash Behari Ghosh while speaking on this movement, "though education must in a large measure involve moral discipline it cannot be efficient unless it is conducted in a religious spirit. It must rest on truth, on morality, and on reverence. Above all it must have its roots deep down in national sentiments and national traditions." Even Government which initiated the present educational system on secular lines has now come to realise its mistake. The Government Resolution on Education issued only two days ago says "The Government of India while bound to maintain a position of complete neutrality in matter of religion, observe that the most thoughtful minds in India lament the tendency of existing systems of education to develop the intellectual at the expense of the moral and religious faculties," it is just this tendency that the Hindu University seeks to correct among other things. It seeks to preserve all that is best and noblest in Hindu learning and disseminate it along with a knowledge of the Western Science. The association of such men as Dr. Rash Behari Ghosh and the Hon. Mr. Bhupendra Nath Basu, known for the progressive and catholic views, is a sufficient guarantee that the University would not run on reactionary lines. Further the movement is objected to on the ground that it is sectarian. The University though denominational is certainly not sectarian in spirit. Its portals will be open as much to Hindus as to Mahomedans, Parsees or Christians. It will admit students irrespective of caste or creed. The presence of H. H. the Aga Khan, the leader of the Mahomedan Community in India, on the station to receive the Deputation, his participation in to-day's proceedings, and the substantial help he has given to the University Fund are sufficient evidence that our Mahomedan brothers at least do not regard the movement as a rival one. The two Universities are but the two phases of the same national movement. Both the Universities seek to make a National consciousness and quicken the aspirations towards a higher life. One is but the hand-maid to the other. Let me take this opportunity, Ladies and Gentlemen, to offer our sincere thanks to H. H. the Aga Khan and our Mahomedan brothers for the sympathetic interest they have been evincing in the movement and the great help they have been giving us.'

"The Hon. Sir Narayan Chandavarkar said that in the slang language the deputation was called a begging deputation. But it had a higher and nobler purpose behind it, and he would call it a Divine Mission. Sir Bhalchandra had in his speech referred to some people who were at one time given to cursing this movement which had brought the distinguished visitors to Bombay. Sir Bhalchandra had told them that the same gentlemen had learnt to bless it. That was the history of every great movement. His Highness the Aga Khan had asked why in spite of all the progress made during the last 50 or 60 years of English education in India they had not produced one first rate man in literature giving expression to the higher emotion of the people of this land. The answer was obvious. He was not one of those who would join the ranks of those who thought that the educational policy began on wrong lines. All national progress, all political progress and all educational progress rested on definite lines which were marked out by what they would call the Age and Law of Evolution. When the British came into this country and initiated the policy, they had to lay down the lines of their education system. They distinctly aimed at one definite thing, viz., to make them less of dreamers, and more men of action. To make them more practical was the aim which Lord Macaulay had in view. Lord William Bentinck and Lord Hardinge, the great grand-father of the present popular, sympathetic and cool-headed Viceroy, held a similar view. Education in India therefore began on literary lines in order to turn them into practical men. He was one of those who did not at first favour the University movement because he had misgivings as to the direction in which the activities of its promoters would be spent. He was glad that it would not confine itself to the humdrum work of producing men who were only anxious to be successful in commercial and mercantile pursuits, and amass large fortunes from them. He was glad to find that the University would devote itself to research work. What the country required was the spirit of the soul brought out . . . The Hon. Mr. Rafiudin Ahmed, Mr. J. J. Vimadalal and Bai Nanibai Gujjar then addressed the assembly.

"H. H. the Maharajah Bahadur of Darbhanga, in the course of a lengthy speech, said:

'The reasons urged for the establishment of a great Hindu University at Benares have been so often placed before the public that you are now almost quite familiar with them and it will require but little recapitulation on my part to-day to accentuate the statements already made in order to enlist your hearty appreciation and co-operation in the movement. The spirit of education is abroad. There has been a great awakening in our National life. The tide of feeling has been, and is still, rising with great power in favour of the advancement of our youths in the matter of their educational training, rooted and grounded in deep religious principle all the way from the Primary School right up to the University.

'I know that objections have been raised to our Hindu University scheme on the ground that its religious character will make it a sectarian Institution, and that its sectarianism will warp and narrow its functions and belittle its usefulness as an educational force. It is alleged, moreover, that a University such as we propose will tend to breed strife and discord and an antagonistic spirit towards all other religious faiths. You will agree with me gentlemen, that such apprehensions are groundless. I need merely refer you to the cordial co-operation and kindly sympathy which our movement has invariably received from my friend His Highness Sir Aga Khan and his co-religionists, and for which we cannot be too grateful, and I need hardly assure our Mahomedan brethren, that we Hindus on our part entertain the same feelings towards the sister University scheme for Aligarh. Religion is always, and must be, a reconciling force and is, as far as possible, from tending towards the divisions or animosities, and it is one of the charms of University life and this spirit which it breathes, that its training engenders and fosters amongst its cultured students a broad and wide and friendly feeling towards all people of different faiths along with the willingness to work in co-operation with them in any measures for promoting the common good. A cultured, religious University student is one of the most valuable assets a nation can possess. His whole influence is one of the side of peace on earth and good will towards men. The last message which our Gracious King Emperor gave us before leaving our shores and saying farewell to India was this: –

"We fervently trust that our visit may be [sic] God's grace conduce to the general good of the people of this great Continent. Their interests and well-being will always be as near and as dear to me as those of the millions of my subjects in other quarters of the Globe. It is a matter of intense satisfaction to me to realise how all classes and creeds have joined together in the true hearted welcome which has been so universally accorded to us. Is it not possible that the same unity and concord may for the future govern the daily relations of their private and public life? The attainment of this would indeed be a happy outcome of our visit to India." Believe me, gentlemen, that amongst the many factors which will work with potent force for the realisation of our Monarch's desire, not the least will be the sweetening influences which will radiate far and wide from the sister Universities at Benares and Aligarh.

'The Hindu University is to be primarily a residential and teaching University, providing for religious and moral as well as secular education. Its constitution will be drafted on the lines of the Universities like those of Sheffield, Manchester and Birmingham, in which the supreme administrative body is known as the "Court."

'Our University will be equipped with the best Professors and Teachers in the various departments of Theology, Literature, Pure Science, Applied Science, Agriculture, Commerce, Medicine (including Ayurvedic), Surgery, Law, and all other branches of knowledge, and will also provide theoretical, practical and technical instruction for artistic pursuits. It will also provide facilities for original research in all the applications of science. In fact our aim is to make the Hindu University in all respects (adopted to India) similar in educational equipment to the best of those Universities in other countries which have so largely moulded national life and character wherever they have been established. I may mention also that the University shall be open to women, subject to such conditions as the Regulations may prescribe.

'In time, our great ideal in connection with University life and work will be to turn out students who will be men indeed, cultured gentlemen, well fitted through their University training for taking each his part in the position of life to which he has been called. Men who will be god-fearing, full of reverence for the faith of their fathers and the noblest traditions of their race, devoted to our Gracious Sovereign, loyal to the Law and to the social order as all Hindus by virtue of their religion are, and full of sympathy with all good men irrespective of caste or creed. With men like these turned out of our Universities year by year having open minds to receive and assimilate truth from whatever quarter it comes, and ever ready under influence of increasing life to give up all false notions hitherto firmly held. India will be on the high road to take her place amongst the foremost nations of the earth, and her sons will become a tower of strength to the Government of the land, in their stability of character and their example in the political and social life of the country. With these remarks, gentlemen, I heartily commend the scheme for our Hindu University, which I yet hope to live to see as a burning and shining light in our holy City, casting a beneficent radiance over all the land.'

"Pandit Madan Mohan Malaviya then addressed the assembly in Urdu at great length.

"Donations were then announced which included one lakh of rupees already subscribed and paid by Mr. Narotam Morarji Goculdas and his late lamented brother, Mr. Dharamsey. Other donations included Rs. 5,000 from Mr. Tribhowandas Varjiwandas and a like sum from Sir Bhalchandra Krishna. A joint donation of Rs. 5,000 from Sir Vithaldas Thakersey and Mr. Hanaraj Pragji was then announced. A Hindu gentleman, Pandit Mahadev Prashad, a landlord in Mysore, gave 25 acres of land yielding an annual revenue of Rs. 2,500. Several other smaller donations were acknowledged. The proceedings then terminated."

The Hindus of India started a movement for the establishment of a university of their own in 1905. The Benaras Hindu University Act was passed by the

414

Imperial Legislative Council on 1 October 1915. The foundation stone of the university's main building was laid on 4 February 1916 by the Viceroy, Lord Hardinge. The Senate and other bodies met for the first time on 6 and 7 November 1916. The university began to function in 1917 (actually, the Central Hindu College of Benares became a university), and held its first convocation in January 1919. The first Chancellor was the Maharaja of Mysore; the first Vice-Chancellor was Dr. Sir Sundar Lall (knighted in 1917) who died in February 1918 and was succeeded by Sir P. S. Sivaswami Aiyar. For full details see S. L. L. Dar and S. Somaskandan, *History of the Benaras Hindu University*, Benares, 1966.

32

PUBLIC SERVICES IN INDIA

Evidence Given Before the Royal Commission on the Public Services in India

Bombay: 3 March 1913

Views on recruitment to the Indian Civil Service – syllabus – bring Sanskrit and Arabic on the same level as Greek and Latin – encourage Persian literature, Indian administration and Indian history – system unfair to the Indian students – simultaneous examinations in India and England – subjects of Native States should be given opportunity to enter – curriculum for examinations – Indian aspirations for a share in the administration – period of probation – inadequate representation of Muslims in the Provincial Civil Services – salaries in the Provincial Civil Services – a college for Englishmen in India – the question of a fixed percentage of posts for Indians – possibility of recruiting members of Indian royal families – the issue of sending Indians to England for training – granting of scholarships – advantages of teaching Englishmen oriental culture.

PRESENT:

THE RIGHT HON. THE LORD ISLINGTON, K.C.M.G., D.S.O. (*Chairman*).

THE EARL OF RONALDSHAY, M.P.
Sir MURRAY HAMMICK, K.C.S.I., C.I.E.
Sir THEODORE MORISON, K.C.I.E.
Sir VALENTINE CHIROL.
MAHADEV BHASKAR CHAUBAL, Esq., C.S.I.
GOPAL KRISHNA GOKHALE, Esq., C.I.E.
WALTER CULLEY MADGE, Esq., C.I.E.
FRANK GEORGE SLY, Esq., C.S.I.
JAMES RAMSAY MACDONALD, Esq., M.P.
And the following Assistant Commissioners:–

JOSEPH JOHN HEATON, Esq., I.C.S, Judge of the High Court of Judicature, Bombay.

RÁO BAHÁDUR RAMCHANDRA NARAYAN JOGLEKAR, Assistant to Commissioner, Central Division, Poona.

RAGHUNATH GANGADHAR BHADBHADE, Esq., Judge of Small Cause Court, Poona.

M. S. D. BUTLER, Esq., C.V.O., C.I.E. (*Joint Secretary*).

His Highness AGA SULTAN MUHAMMAD SHAH, AGA KHAN, G.C.S.I., G.C.I.E.

Written answers relating to the Indian Civil Service.

27034 (1). What is your experience of the working of the present system of recruitment by open competitive examination in England for the Indian Civil Service? Do you accept it as generally satisfactory in principle? – I accept the present system of recruitment by open competition for the Indian Civil Service as generally satisfactory subject to reservations contained in answers to subsequent questions. I think that the principle of open competition should always be maintained.

27035 (2). In what respects, if any, do you find the present system faulty in detail, and what alterations would you suggest? – I think there should be a change in the syllabus and the marks should be fixed in such a manner as to give no cause of complaint to Indians that they are labouring under a disadvantage. I would give the number of marks for Sanskrit and Arabic on the same level as that for Greek and Latin. I would also encourage a study of Persian literature in the same manner by giving Persian the same marks as French and German. The rudiments of Indian Administration and Indian History, particularly of recent years, should be given a prominent place in the syllabus of studies.

27036 (3). Is the system equally suitable for the admission of "Natives of India" and of other natural-born subjects of His Majesty? If not, what alteration do you recommend? – The system is most unfair to Indian students as for obvious reasons it prevents many deserving and capable students from competing and thus debars them from their proper share in the administration of the country.

27037 (5). If you do not consider the present system of recruitment by an open competitive examination to be satisfactory in principle, please state what alternative you would propose? – I would adopt the system of recruitment to the exigencies of modern times so as to give a wider scope for satisfying the legitimate aspirations of Indians and the fullest development of their talents.

27038 (6). In particular, what would be your opinion regarding a system of simultaneous examinations in India and in England, open in both cases to all natural-born subjects of His Majesty? – I am in favour of a simultaneous examination in England and India. I would give full effect to the House of Commons' Resolution of June 1893 "that all competitive examinations heretofore held in England alone for the appointments to the Civil Services of India shall henceforth be held simultaneously in India and England, such examinations in both countries being identical in nature, all who compete being finally classified in one list according to merit." I would strongly advocate the holding of examinations in India not only for the Indian Civil Services, but for other competitive services as well, such as the Medical, the Forest and the Police. It is unfair that examinations for Indian Civil Services should be held only in England. When the principle of competitive examination for civil appointments in India was introduced sixty years ago, there were no educational institutions in India and therefore it was natural to leave the holding of simultaneous examination in India out of consideration. But the contact of the East with the West has profoundly changed the aspect of Indian education, and during the last half century there has been remarkable educational progress in India. By creating a Special Department of Education, the Government of India have shown their earnest desire to give a vigorous and systematic impetus to education. The establishment of various useful Faculties in recent years, will open up careers to Indian students outside the Government Service and the legal profession, and I, for one, have no hesitation in saying that the Indian Civil Service will in no way be swamped by Indians. Nor will its morale deteriorate in any way. The brightest sons of India – Telang, Ranade, Gokhale and others – were the product of English education in India. As I have said, the simultaneous examination in England and India should be identical in regard to the standard of test, the examination papers, marks, etc. If the Indian Civil Service examination is held in India, it will open the doors to promising and talented students, who, owing to their limited means and the disabilities entailed upon them in consequence of their stay in a foreign land for their studies, and the risks involved in failure, are unable to proceed to England to compete for the Service. It will do away with any feeling of discontent that may exist at the idea that the Indian Civil Service has been kept as a preserve for Englishmen and that the children of the soil are shut out from their proper and legitimate share in controlling the administration of the country.

As I have stated above, there is no fear of the Service being overrun by Indians. At present in the Bombay Presidency, out of 149 posts held by the I.C.S. there are only nine held by Indians, including two Statutory Civilians. This works out at something like 6 per cent. of the Civil posts in the Presidency being held by Indians. Again, in the whole of India, of 1,294 I.C.S. only 56 are Indians and the remaining 1,238 are Europeans. This is a very meagre proportion, and if the simultaneous examination is held in India, I do not think that more than 15 or 20 per cent. at the most of Indians would be recruited by means of the system of competitive examination. I am convinced that the so-called danger of the Service being swamped by Indians is imaginary. The fear that the Service will be overcrowded by Indians is based on the fallacious idea that Indians have the wonderful gift of passing examinations by means of cramming.

27039 (7). What would be your opinion with regard to filling a fixed proportion of the vacancies in the Indian Civil Service cadre by Natives of India, recruited by means of a separate examination in India, or by means of separate examinations in each province or group of provinces in India? If you favour such a scheme, what proportion do you recommend? – I do not think any proportion should be laid down.

27040 (9). If you are in favour of a system for the part recruitment of the Indian Civil Service by Natives of India in India, do you consider that "Natives of India" should still be eligible for appointment in England? – Yes: I think so. I do not think that a very large number of candidates will pass in India through the simultaneous examination and I do not think it expedient or reasonable not to regard them as eligible for appointment in England if they pass the competitive examination.

27041 (10). Would you regard any system of selection in India which you may recommend for young men who are "Natives of India" as being in lieu of, or as supplementary to, the present system of promoting to listed posts officers of the Provincial Civil Service? If the former, what alteration, if any, would you recommend in the conditions governing the Provincial Civil Service? – I think the present system of listed posts should continue: otherwise there would be no incentive to the Provincial Service men for greater efforts if they know that they have nothing higher to look forward to. They would not remain content, if they were depressed by the sense of knowledge that they cannot hope to rise any higher.

27042 (12). Are you satisfied with the present statutory definition of the term "Natives of India" in section 6 of the Government of India Act, 1870 (33 Vict., c.3), as including "any person born and domiciled within the Dominions of His Majesty in India, of parents habitually resident in India, and not established there for temporary purposes only," irrespective of whether such persons are of unmixed Indian descent, or of mixed European and Indian descent, or of unmixed European descent? If not, state fully any proposals that you wish to make in regard to this matter? – I think the subjects of Native States and the aristocratic classes in Native States should be included in the definition so that they might have an opportunity of serving in the British Administration.

27043 (13). If the system of recruitment by open competitive examination in England is retained, state the age limits that you recommend for candidates at such examination, giving your reasons? – I think the present age limit should be retained.

27044 (14). What in your opinion is the most suitable age at which junior civilians recruited in England should commence their official duties in India? – I think 25 is the most suitable age at which junior civilians recruited in England should commence their official duties in India.

27045 (15). What age limits for the open competitive examination in England would best suit candidates who are Natives of India, and for what reasons? Do you recommend any differentiation between the age limits for Natives of India and for other natural-born subjects of His Majesty? – I think the same age as at present. I do not recommend any differentiation between the age limits for Natives of India and for other subjects of His Majesty.

27046 (16). What alterations, if any, do you recommend in the authorised syllabus of subjects and marks prescribed for the open competitive examination? – I would place the classical languages of India on the same footing as the classical languages of Europe in regard to the allotment of the number of marks. I would certainly include Persian and treat it on an equal level with French and German. I would also include a knowledge of rudiments of Indian Administration and Indian History, particularly history of recent years.

27047 (17). Is any differentiation in the subjects for the open competitive examination in England desirable between candidates who are Natives of India and other candidates? If so, state them and give reasons? – I do not think any differentiation in the subjects for the open competitive examination in England is desirable, between Indians and other candidates. I would insist on absolutely the same test for both: though option must of course be allowed in such subjects as modern languages.

27048 (19). Do you consider that a minimum proportion of European subjects of His Majesty should be employed in the higher posts of the Civil Administration? If so, to what proportion of the posts included in the Indian Civil Service cadre do you consider that Natives of India might under present conditions properly be admitted? – I would not fix any proportion. I do not think that the Indian element in the Service would ever be alarmingly great. I would certainly be sorry to see the British character of the administration disappear: but to satisfy the legitimate aspirations of Indians for a larger share in the administration I would throw open to them, when they are found fit and eligible, such appointments as are generally held by Englishmen. They should be promoted to the Commissionership, to the responsible posts in the Secretariats, or even to Lieutenant-Governorship if they are fit and senior.

27049 (20). Do you accept as generally satisfactory in principle the present system under which Natives of India are recruited for posts in the Indian Civil Service cadre partly through the medium of an open competitive examination in England and partly by special arrangement in India? – The recruitment should be by simultaneous examination in England and India.

27050 (21). Do you consider that the old system of appointment of "Statutory Civilians" under the Statute of 1870 should be revived, and if so, what method of recruitment would you recommend? – I am not in favour of the revival of Statutory Civilians.

27051 (22). If the system of recruiting military officers in India for posts in the Indian Civil Service cadre has been stopped or has never existed in your Province, would you advise its re-introduction or introduction, as the case may be, and if the system should be introduced or re-introduced, to what extent, in your opinion, should it be adopted? – No.

27052 (24). What is your opinion of the system by which certain posts, ordinarily held by members of the Indian Civil Service, are declared to be posts (ordinarily termed listed posts) to which members of the Provincial Civil Service can properly be appointed? – I would promote the members of the Provincial Service to listed posts. That would improve the morale of the Provincial Service.

27053 (29). Do you consider that candidates recruited for the Indian Civil Service by open competitive examination should undergo a period of probation before being admitted to the Service? – Yes: one year should be spent either at Oxford or Cambridge, and one year in travelling in Europe or America.

27054 (33). Do you think it desirable to start, at some suitable place in India, a college for the training of probationers of the Indian Civil Service, and possibly of other Indian Services recruited in England? – I think a college started in some suitable centre like Bombay, or Calcutta, would be likely to be more useful for all the Indian Services. I think young officers should not be first of all sent to districts where they are apt to form initial . opinions of India and Indians based on faulty deductions drawn from observing the lower classes of society with whom alone in such districts they are brought into contact.

27055 (45). Do you consider that the exchange compensation allowance introduced in 1893, eligibility for which depends on nationality or domicile, should be abolished, and if so, under what conditions? Should such abolition apply to officers already employed or be restricted to future entrants? – Exchange compensation should not be paid in future. It should be continued to those who get it at present.

Written answers relating to the Provincial Civil Service.

27056 (53). Do you consider that recruitment for a Provincial Civil Service should ordinarily be restricted to residents of the Province to which it belongs? – Yes.

27057 (54). Are all classes and communities duly represented in your Provincial Civil Service? Do you consider that this is desirable, and what arrangements do you recommend to secure this object? – I consider that it is desirable that all classes and communities should be duly represented in the Provincial Service. I do not think that the Muhammadans are adequately represented in the Provincial Civil Service. This should be remedied, especially in the Provinces like Bengal and Sind where the Muhammadan population are in the majority.

27058 (60). Are the existing rates of pay and grading in the

Provincial Civil Service of your Province adequate to secure the desired qualifications in the officers appointed? If not, what alterations do you recommend? – I think the salaries should be increased in view of the improved standard of living and the general rise in prices which has recently taken place in India.

27059 (61). Do you approve of the arrangement by which officers of the Provincial Civil Service holding listed posts draw salary approximately at the rate of two-thirds of the pay drawn in the same posts by members of the Indian Civil Service? If not, what rates do you suggest for the various appointments? – I think they should get the same salary as the members of the Civil Service get for the same posts when they hold them.

His Highness the AGA KHAN, called and examined.

27060. (*Chairman*). Your Highness is in favour of the present system of open competition? – Yes, on principle.

27061. You do not, however, consider it suitable for Indians? – No, not quite.

27062. And to meet this Indian disability you favour the establishment of simultaneous examinations in England and in India? – Yes.

27063. In offering this proposal you make no reservation of any kind in favour of what is called a European minimum? – I do not think it is necessary. I think it is certain that there will always be more than a minimum, so far as I can look ahead.

27064. I take it that you would be sorry to see the British character of the Administration disappear? – Yes, very.

27065. You are convinced that not more than 15 or 20 per cent., at the most, of Indians would actually be recruited? – I do not think anything like that number would be recruited for the present, though I think it might happen some day long ahead.

27066. You would regret it if the European element were to disappear or were to become a negligible quantity? – Yes; I should be very sorry if it came even to one-half or two-thirds.

27067. Holding that view, what is your objection to having the matter put on a clear footing? – I really think the contingency is so remote that it is needless to stir things up. I would "let sleeping dogs lie." I do not see that there is any need of a guarantee. There is no danger of it. But once you found that there was such a danger I should certainly put a guarantee on.

27068. Your main ground for advocating simultaneous examination, apart from the expense to the Indian in going to England, is the educational progress which has taken place in India? – There are many reasons for it, and that is one of them.

27069. That is one of your chief reasons? – No, it is not one of the chief reasons. It is *one* of the reasons.

27070. Do you consider that the advance in education has reached a stage to justify the expectation that some Indian candidates may attain success in the near future in the Indian Civil Service Examination? – That is for the Education Department. On the whole, yes, I think some Indian candidates may get through.

27071. Are you familiar with the standard of education in the Bombay University? – No, I am not really familiar with it, though I know something about it.

27072. Do you know to what extent the standard there would compare with the standard of the Indian Civil Service examination? – No.

27073. Would you be prepared to say whether that standard is as high? – No, probably it is not. I hear that it is so much more difficult to pass into the Indian Civil Service.

27074. If it is not up to that standard, and we have had evidence that it is not in certain branches, would not a candidate to succeed have to go to a crammer? – It is for the student to work very hard at it himself.

27075. So far as I understand you, you do not contemplate that cramming establishments will be instituted in India? – I daresay that in time there will be crammers.

27076. Do you think that the introduction of crammers into India would be to the advantage of India, regarded either from an educational or from a political point of view? – I do not think they would do any harm. It would be one other way of getting knowledge.

27077. It is not a very satisfactory form of knowledge, is it? – I have never been to a crammer myself, and therefore I do not know much about it.

27078. Although you have not been to one, you are probably familiar with the effect of cramming on the educational position of a young man. Would you not run the danger of increasing, to a very considerable degree, the number of what I may term "artificially educated young men"? – I do not think it is very probable.

27079. Do you not think that a large number of Indian young men would manage to get into the Indian Civil Service? – If that happened, then you would put a minimum on, and you would change the way of getting in. The moment the danger arose one would deal with it.

27080. You would be prepared to deal with the danger of a large number getting in? – Yes, if the danger arose, certainly, at the first sight of it.

27081. Do you think that that will be an appropriate moment to deal with the danger? – I really do not regard it as a danger which is so very approximate as to deal with it now.

27082. Assuming that there was a danger, however remote, would you say that it was better to wait until the time had arrived when a larger number of Indian students had been successful in the examination to deal with the situation or would you deal with the problem in the early days when you were instituting the examination? – There are two alternative ways of dealing with it. One is now to take reasonable precautions; and the other is to wait until the danger arises, and then deal with it.

27083. That is my point. You think it is better to wait until the danger arises? – Yes, simply because I think the danger is so remote. I have gone through the Syllabus of getting into it. I think it is very improbable, anyhow for five years, that anybody will get in through India.

27084. You think that, perhaps, in five years individuals might do so? – Yes, they might; and then there would be ample time to deal with the matter.

27085. You do not see any difficulty in the way of imposing a reservation at that particular moment? – I think the principle is admitted by most sensible people that the spirit of the Service, and its numbers, must be British. I admit that most heartily; and that being the case, I do not see why it should not be put in when the danger arises rather than putting it in beforehand.

27086. It is because you have so heartily admitted this that I have asked you whether you do not consider it a wiser and a better policy, in the interests of India, to impose the reservation now sooner than later? – Certainly, if the danger arose there must be this reservation; and it is for Statesmen, rather than for a witness, to say whether it is better to put that reservation now or later.

27087. "Sufficient to the day is the evil thereof"? – Yes. Otherwise, on principle, if there was any danger of its becoming more than 20 per cent. I should certainly be one of the first to ask for legislation about it.

27088. You suggest that there should be variations in the Syllabus of the examination? – Yes; I have suggested some very slight variations.

27089. Variations in the direction of including subjects which would be more favourable for Indians? – I should like to put Persian, with 500 marks, on the same level as French and German. To do so would not be such a very great thing. And I should also like to put Sanskrit and Arabic on the same level as Greek and Latin. With regard to Sanskrit and Arabic, I do not say that it is so very necessary. I do not hold very strong views upon that; but I think that Persian ought to be placed on the same level as French and German.

27090. That, of course, would add materially to the chance of Indians being successful in the examination? – It would not do so very materially. It is only 500 marks, I believe, or something like that.

27091. You are satisfied, I believe, with the present age-limit for the examination? – Yes.

27092. If it could be shown that the present age-limit is unsuitable for obtaining the best British officers, would you favour a reduction of the age? – No, I would not, because I cannot admit the first premises.

27093. You do not agree with the view which some people hold that the age is too high? – No. It is no use bringing boys out as administrators.

27094. You do not regard it as of importance to secure for the Indian Civil Service Indians who are representatives of the various Provinces and communities? – Provinces I have not thought about very seriously. So far as communities are concerned, I do not know; but I would not have any communal separation.

27095. You do not think there would be any difficulty in posting an Indian from one Province to another? – No. I think it would be rather a good thing.

27096. We have had a good deal of evidence during our enquiry to the effect that the Muhammadan community would suffer under a system of simultaneous examination. You do not share that view? – I think as long as you have got examinations it ought to be an open door; otherwise you would go about it in another way.

27097. I observe in your answer to question (54) that you advocate that Muhammadans should be recruited in greater numbers for the Provincial Civil Service? – Yes.

27098. What distinction do you draw between the Indian Civil Service and the Provincial Civil Service in this respect? – First, in the Indian Civil Service the present system does not guarantee any limit, it would be introducing a new principle into it; while, in the Provincial Civil Service, there is more or less a moral understanding that certain Muhammadans get in in practice. That is one thing. Secondly, one expects from a man who has got into the Indian Civil Service (and has had the brains to get in) a certain greater liberality of view than from a man who gets into the Provincial Civil Service. Thirdly, the Provincial Civil Service man has to deal very much with the smaller questions which are not likely to come before Government, or before public opinion, or before the Press; so that he can favour his own people more than a man high up who has to deal with more important questions.

27099. Do you anticipate that Muhammadans will soon stand a fair chance with other classes and creeds in competitive examinations? – No; I think their chance would be worse than it is now.

27100. You ask for an increase in the salaries of the officers of the Provincial Civil Services? – Yes.

27101. And you do so on the score of the improved standard of living, and the general rise in prices? – Yes.

27102. Can you tell us what you would regard as a suitable rise in salaries? – Prices have risen so much of late years. People with fixed incomes are not having a good time now as compared with people who have not got fixed incomes. I think a general rise in salary would be a good thing.

27103. Are you in favour of instituting a time-scale? – What does that mean?

27104. The automatic increase every year of pay in the various grades? – I have not considered it. I may say, however, that I should like to see Collectors get more than they do now, and also Government officers in big towns, and the Secretaries to Government who live in Bombay and Poona. It is absurd that they should get the same pay as they got 10, 15 or 20 years ago. On the other hand, there are places where it is different. The rise in prices is greatest in the towns, and also where new social duties have arisen.

27105. You are not prepared to give us any details; but, generally, you would like to see better terms, as far as salaries are concerned, for the Service? – Yes, for all the officers who live in towns.

27106. (*Sir Murray Hammick*). I should like to ask you a question with regard to the remark you made just now that you thought Muhammadans would be no worse off under simultaneous examination than they are now. Do you not think that out of the number of candidates who go home to prepare for the Indian Civil Service, Muhammadans bear a considerably larger proportion to the total than they would be likely to bear to the total number of students who went up for simultaneous examination in India? – I think that for the first three or four years that might happen; but Muhammadans have woke up to sending boys to school.

27107. You think it would be only temporary? – I think it would be only temporary.

27108. You would agree, first, at all events, that Muhammadans in simultaneous examinations out here would be considerably more handicapped than they are in the examination at home? – Honestly, I believe that for the first few years nobody would get in from simultaneous examination.

27109. So that it would not very much matter? – No; I do not think it very much matters.

27110. I take it that one of your objections to the exclusive way of getting into the Indian Civil Service by examination at home is that you think students who go home run a great deal of risk in their character and so on, by being sent to England to pass their examination, and their having to live under not very good supervision for three or four years before the examination takes place: I suppose that would be one of your objections to the present system? – I say that so far as their being two or three years in England, locked up, working hard at study, merely learning the thing up, they might just as well do it here. They would not, of course, get into touch with European life and people. The only danger I anticipate would be the cramming effect of it.

27111. You do not regard the dangers of student life in London as any great objection? – Those who go up for the Indian Civil Service have to work so hard at it that there is very little time for anything else.

27112. Supposing you cannot get simultaneous examinations, what would you think of the system which has been suggested to us of giving scholarships to selected boys much younger than at present, boys of thirteen and fourteen, and sending them home to public schools in England with, more or less, a guarantee that if they do not get into the Indian Civil Service, assuming their conduct was good, they would be provided for in other Services in this country? If that were possible, what would Your Highness think of a system of that kind? – I should be opposed to it.

27113. Do you think that parents would be ready to send their children home at that age? – Some might, and some might not. Parsees probably would.

27114. What would be your objection to a scheme of that sort? – To begin with, I should say that it was for the parents, those who had made their money, and believed in that. I do not think that it is the business of the State to help parents to give luxuries to their children. I should say, let those parents who believed in that, pay for it. I should not oppose that, but I do not think it is the business of the State.

27115. You would not take the objection that these children would be too much Europeanised, and that they would come back too much out of touch with the people of this country? – I think that parents who are rich people might send their children to England. I would not object to that because when they come back here they will have, more or less, some concern in their own social life here as they would in England. If they have the means let them go; but if they have not the means, I do not see why the tax-payer should pay for it.

27116. I do not understand how you fit in your ages. You would not touch the present age. Do you think the present age is satisfactory? – Yes, I think, on the whole, that it is a good thing. He has time to learn things.

27117. In answer to question (14) you say that you think 25 is a suitable age for Civilians to commence their duties? – Yes, to commence their duties.

27118. But in answer to question (29) you suggest that they should have two years in Europe; that one should be spent at Oxford or Cambridge, and one year in travelling about; and then in answer to question (33) you suggest a college out here? – Yes, a college out here, but only for Englishmen.

27119. That is what I wanted to get out. You intend that Englishmen should only have one year at home instead of two? – Yes, on probation.

27120. One year at home, and then the college for Englishmen here? – Yes.

27121. Do you think it would be a good thing to shut up Englishmen in a college in one central place for two or three years? You say you think that young officers should not first of all be sent to districts where they are apt to form initial opinions of India and Indians based on faulty deductions. If you sent them and shut them up in a college in one part of India, they would not get any association with Indians during that period? – I would suggest about forty or fifty of them going on tour, and looking at the interesting things in the country. For instance, send them up to Agra, and so on, on tour in the same way as they do with the Staff College people. They send them to the battlefields. They would go in the same way, see the country, and learn its history, and so on. I think that would be a good thing; and in that way they would know more about the country.

27122. Probably one great objection to a scheme of that sort is that it would be rather expensive to keep a set of boys here at one college under the supervision of Europeans, and have them sent about the country and to mix with Indians of good society and see interesting places. It would be very nice for the boys, but rather expensive for the Government? – If the Government were ready to send boys to Rugby and Eton for their education, where they would have a good time, I do not see why they should not do as I suggest in this case, for these young fellows would be their own servants, and they would merit more.

27123. (*Sir Valentine Chirol.*) I should like to ask Your Highness further about what you regard as the effect of sending young Indian boys to England at an early age. You have, I suppose, made some observations of your own. You have, probably, followed the careers of a certain number of young men who have passed through that form of education. Do you regard the result as unsatisfactory on the whole of sending boys to England to be educated young, and to have, what we call, a thorough English education? Do you think the results, when they have returned to India, have been unsatisfactory? – Yes, on the whole I think they have. It has not been sufficiently satisfactory as to be remarkable. None of them have shone in any way.

27124. Do you know of instances where it has been remarkably unsatisfactory? – Yes, there is the instance of Arabinda Ghose.

27125. You have not personally come across cases which have been eminently satisfactory? – No, not one.

27126. On the other hand, you are extremely anxious, I understand, to preserve in the administration what is called the "British tone"? – Not only British tone, but Englishmen. I know so far as to say that it must be essential not only that there should be British tone, but that Englishmen must be in a preponderating majority. That, I fully and sincerely admit.

27127. Supposing, for a moment, that you had to assign some limit to the number of Indians whom you think at the present moment it would be desirable to have in the administration of the country, what would be the percentage of Indians which you would be inclined to name? – Now, it is only 6 per cent. which is absurdly small, I think.

27128. Then what would you consider to be reasonable? – For the next few years, I should say 10 per cent.

27129. And then you would have that revised from time to time? – Yes, naturally. Every decade or so it would have to be revised, a slight increase.

27130. But you think that at present 10 per cent. would be a reasonable percentage? – Yes. But as I do not think there is any danger of getting more I am not sure that, as a matter of tactics, it would be a good thing to have it. It is purely a tactical question.

27131. We are engaged in an enquiry which, it is to be hoped, may result in certain recommendations which will be, probably, for a series of years the basis for the recruitment of the members of the administrative services of this country. Do you not think it would be wiser at the present moment to take into consideration those possibilities (if the contingency does not arise, no harm is done) and to settle some sort of basis or limit which would last for a certain number of years, possibly subject to a time-scale on revision, rather than leave the question open, as you suggest, to chance, which would compel (should results arise, which you regard as improbable, but which might arise) the whole thing to be again revised? – In your question you used the words "few years." I think that within a few years it is not only improbable, but impossible. I think that within the next five or ten years it is impossible that there would be anything more than 10 per cent.

27132. Do you think that it is impossible within the next twenty-five years? – Twenty-five years in India is more than a generation.

27133. You must remember, after all, that the last Public Services Commission took place about twenty-five years ago, and therefore one may hope that there will be a certain finality for the recommendation of this Commission covering another generation. Do you think it is absolutely safe to leave that contingency entirely out of our calculations? – This Commission has come out to study the whole problem, but this is only a small question. The moment you see so many Indians coming in, say after ten years, there might be Government Resolutions saying that after such and such a date only such and such a percentage may come in. I would deal with the matter by a Government Resolution rather than by a Commission of this kind.

27134. You think it would be easier for the Government of India to place a limitation, which would probably be unacceptable to many people, simply by way of a Resolution, than it would be for the Government of India to do so backed by the recommendations of a Commission such as ours with the full consideration of His Majesty's Government at home? – I think this Commission might give the Government of India power to move by Resolution. You might say, for instance, in your recommendations that the moment such and such a percentage got in the Government should deal with it.

27135. Going to another point, you are the spiritual head of numerous Muhammadan communities in India, are you not? – Of one sect only.

27136. Numerous Muhammadans? – It is not very numerous in India, it is very small.

27137. It is not a community which is likely to furnish any large *quota* to the classes who may be expected to compete in the simultaneous examination? – Amongst Muhammadan communities, it is a community which, for its numbers, will probably have more in proportion to any other.

27138. I ask you about your own community because you are more closely acquainted with the feelings of your own community than with those of Muhammadans at large. Is your community dissatisfied with the present system of administration of the Government? – No; they are a very loyal community.

27139. Are they not satisfied with the agencies through which the administration is carried on, the agency of the Civil Service? – They think it is a very good service, and all that; but they think there might be a few more Indians in it. That is the feeling, that after six years, 6 per cent. is a very small proportion.

27140. Do they think they would benefit by the possible importation into the administration of a very large Hindu element which has no special interests in common with your community? – Certainly, if you put it that way, a very large mixture of Indians,

– I think the average man would rather be taken aback by it; but a small increase is quite different.

27141. You are anxious to preserve not only the large number of Englishmen, but also the British tone? – Yes.

27142. And you desire, I suppose, that the Indians who enter the administration should be, in regard to what are considered the best characteristics of Englishmen, on a level with them? – Yes, or anyhow, aspiring to have the English spirit in their dealings with affairs.

27143. And you think that that can be as well acquired by education in India as by any education in England? – Looking around me, the men I have seen who have had most of this spirit were men who were brought up by the best Englishmen in India rather than men who have gone to England; so that, judging by that, I say you ought to get it just as well here after so many years. The men who have that desire, who have that spirit, most in their lives, are the men who have spent their early lives here, who have been educated here, and who afterwards went to Europe.

27144. You think that these men you have in your mind are not exceptional, but they are conspicuous representatives of a type which is becoming sufficiently general among the educated class in India? – Yes. What I say is this, that it was only the last generation which began to produce that type, so that probably in the next generation there will be more of them. That type, so far, has been more produced by men who have been brought up here, on the influence of their own family, and people, and religion, rather than by those men who have gone to England for their education.

27145. Looking around generally at the results of western education in India amongst the young men of the present day, I should like to ask you whether you mean that the results are such as to promise a considerable increase in the number of Indians who can share the best characteristics of the English mind and English temper without having been to England? – I think when they are grown up they ought to go to England, when they can draw conclusions for themselves. I think they ought to see English life.

27146. The proposal which has been made by a great many witnesses to us is that opportunities should be furnished for the larger employment of Indians by increasing the number of listed posts to which access is obtained now from the Provincial Civil

Service, and assimilating the position of Indians who have obtained those posts absolutely with the position of Civilians. Is that a recommendation which you would condemn? – In what way assimilating the position to the Civil Service; only in pay, or in what?

27147. That they should on being appointed to what are now called these listed posts become *ipso facto* members of the Indian Civil Service, in the cadre of the Civil Service, with that pay, and, I presume, the pension? – The pension would complicate things very much.

27148. But assuming that complication can be got over, would you condemn that? – Would they have the same prospects afterwards of becoming Commissioners and Members of Council?

27149. That is the hypothesis. They would be assimilated entirely into the Indian Civil Service? – Then it would be a very good thing. It would bring in more from the Provincial Civil Service. It would give chances. Yes, I think it would be a good thing.

27150. Do you think that the proof given by men in the Provincial Civil Service who have worked for a certain number of years, and have shewn in their administrative work the same qualities which we desiderate for the Indian Civil Service, would not afford a better qualification for entering into the Indian Civil Service than any competitive examination? – I think it would be a very good thing to have a certain amount of both sorts.

27151. Will you kindly answer my question? I will put it another way. Do you think that open competition would give a better guarantee for fitness to work in the Indian Civil Service than the fact that a man in the Provincial Civil Service has already for a certain number of years performed the work of his post efficiently, and has actually displayed those characteristics which we all desiderate in the Indian Civil Service? – The man who has displayed that is naturally better. He has given the proof of his efficiency. You see the result of that; while the other, at the best, is a dark horse.

27152. Not that you believe absolutely that open competition is the one way of proving the efficiency of men in the Indian Civil Service? – So many men who have failed in the Indian Civil Service have proved themselves wonderful men at the Bar.

27153. There is only one other question I should like to ask you. I understand that you wish to give Persian literature the same marks as French and German? – Yes.

27154. Of course I need not say that you are quite acquainted with the part which French and German play in the culture of Western civilisation and progress. Do you think that for the purposes of broadening the outlook of a young Indian student and familiarising him with the mind of the West, and with the thought of the Western world, Persian can afford, in any way, the same advantages as German or French? – Not for his mental equipment so far as the West is concerned. If you limit it to the West, no; but if you say for his general mental equipment, allowing that he has had a good education in English, and in the classical history of the West, I think the addition of the humanities of Persian literature would be as useful to him as the extra knowledge of the West which he will get from French and German literature.

27155. It is not that you underrate the value of a knowledge of German and French? – I think that German and French are most excellent for Indians, but I think, especially for Indians, that a certain amount of knowledge of Persian would be of great importance.

27156. You would not describe German as it was described by a witness in Calcutta as a rising language in the way that the Bengali language is amongst Indian languages? – No, I would not.

27157. (*Mr. Madge.*) In your suggestions relating to the recruitment of the Public Service, has this idea occurred to you, that the Commission may have to consider whether the interests of the great masses of this country run in the same direction as those of a small educated class, and that we may have to consider how far the conditions of recruitment bear upon that question? Are they the same in all respects, and if they are not, whether we have not to consider whether the recruitment which would serve one class would serve the great masses equally well? – The welfare of the nation is one and the same, I think.

27158. Do you think that the conglomeration of the peoples we find in India at the present moment constitute a nation in the ordinary sense of the term? – No, not in the European sense of the term, but in the geographical expression which we call India.

27159. But there may be divisions in that Empire, the interests of some portions of which do not run in exactly the same direction as those of others. And here I do not compare one Province with another, the great ignorant voiceless masses on the one hand, and the small educated class on the other. I do not say that their interests are different, but it is quite conceivable that they may be, and that Government, and this Commission, may have to consider the conditions of recruitment with reference to the difference between these two classes? – I think this place is like Russia. There is a small minority of educated people, and a vast ignorant majority, just as in Russia. It is on the same level in a way.

27160. But in Russia you practically have a homogeneous Slave [*sic*] population, which you have not in this country? – I thought you meant that you put the difference between the ignorant and the educated, and not the difference between various communities.

27161. That was the main consideration in my mind. I should like your opinion upon any portion of my question which you would care to give an opinion upon? – I think, roughly speaking, as one speaks in great generalities, that I might say, yes, it is the same interest. In the general sense in which the question has been put my answer is that it is the same.

27162. In your answer to question (4) you say: "I would adopt the system of recruitment to the exigencies of modern times so as to give a wider scope for satisfying the legitimate aspirations of Indians and the fullest development of their talents." Now, apart from any suggestion which you have already made, have you considered any method of enlisting, say, the scions of good families, with local influence? Let me put it in this way. For instance, Lord Curzon started the Cadet Corps, for enlisting in military service: could you think of any scheme for enlisting in the Civil Service men of local influence, who would be a great help to the British Government if they could be brought in? – Something like the Cadet Corps – yes, I think it might be done with advantage.

27163. It would be a great help to us if you, in your position, could give us some suggestion of any method by which that class might be gathered in? – Places like the Rajkumar Colleges might be increased all over India.

27164. As a matter of fact, have students of the Rajkumar Colleges enlisted to any extent in the Indian Civil Service? – Unfortunately they cannot. They are not Natives of India. That is the misfortune.

27165. But you think that if similar Colleges were instituted within British territory we might get hold of men of that stamp?

– Yes, I think so. And if social influence could be brought upon parents and relatives to send their children there, that also would be an advantage; because many of that class, the moment they have sufficient to live upon, have not sufficient incentive to do anything.

27166. Would it be of immense benefit, both to the Government and to the country generally, if public spirit could be developed in that class to the extent of making them join the Indian Civil Service? – I think it would be a very good thing, the very best thing.

27167. Having regard to the fact that for a considerable number of years many students under the simultaneous examination system would not get into the Service, and, on the other hand, even if a large proportion got in, they would be comparatively small in relation to the whole number of students competing, do you think that any dissatisfaction which is now felt would be allayed by your suggestion? – Yes; I think it would shew that it was "a fair field and no favour". It would open the door.

27168. Do you mean that a concession would be made to sentiment? – Yes; and in some cases it would greatly help certain classes. It would very much help some very brilliant boys of comparatively poor parents who are too proud to go and beg from other people in order to pay the expenses of sending their children to England. Now, the only poor people who go there are without much spirit of self-respect. In my position I have constantly had people asking for that kind of thing, help and assistance for sending their children to England, while similarly good people would not do that, for they are too proud to ask. It would give those boys a chance.

27169. With reference to the British tone which you think it desirable to maintain in the Service, do you think we can ever perfect our machinery so highly as not to depend at all upon the personality of the official? – The human equation will always remain. There will always be the human equation. It is one man and another; and it will always make a difference.

27170. There is this about it, that if there were defects in the machinery the personality of the officer might correct that; whereas, if there was a defect in the personality of any officer, no perfection in the machinery would compensate for that? – No doubt a very bad man might spoil any machinery, and a very good man could improve anything.

27171. Is it not a necessary inference from that that it is absolutely necessary to maintain a strong personality rather than merely perfecting machinery that would work automatically? – I am taking the average. The average human being is neither one extreme nor the other; so that good machinery would make the average work better.

27172. With reference to the increase in salaries, of which you are in favour, you have referred to residence in towns? – Yes.

27173. There are two distinct questions, the one is the relative expensiveness of living in towns, and, on the other hand, the general increase in prices all round. Would not an increase in salaries all round be better on the one hand, while a house allowance, or something like that, might be made for town residents? It is not necessary to entangle the two questions. They are quite distinct. One regards the rise in prices everywhere, and possibly we may not come to a conclusion about that until the Prices Commission has issued their Report. Do you not think it is wise, regardless of town residents, to raise the salaries all round with reference to the rise in prices? – No, I do not think so, because, in some districts, although prices have risen as to necessities there has been no great increase in luxuries in the same way as there has been in towns. In districts so-called luxuries have not become *de facto* necessities; so I do not think that that alone would justify a rise.

27174. Would you not really be in favour of a house allowance in towns? – I am in favour of a rise in pay in towns.

27175. Not pay, but house allowance. That would remove them from the general question of the rise in prices? – Yes, I might give house allowance; but I would prefer to give a man a round sum, and let him get along for himself. If he had a house allowance he would be all the time worried as to whether his house was equal, or not, to the allowance he gets.

27176. You have said that districts vary with regard to prices. You do not think you can take in a general view the fact that there has been a rise, it may be more or less in some places, but has not there been such a general rise as to make it desirable to raise salaries? – I think the mere rise in prices has not been sufficiently great to make that necessary; but I think the rise in the amenities of life, in addition to the prices in towns and important places, has been so great that it would necessitate a rise in salaries.

27177. (*Mr. Macdonald.*) With regard to the training of Indians in England from the age of 14, you have expressed general views about it. Supposing, as a matter of fact, this system were adopted, and that we gave scholarships and sent them over to England, and brought them back here as members of the Indian Civil Service, would it, in your Highness's opinion, very largely improve the character of the Indian section of the Indian Civil Service cadre? – I am taking it as an impossibility. I am very much opposed to the whole thing. I think it would be a bad suggestion.

27178. Would you dot your i's and cross your t's by answering that question? Supposing, as a great misfortune, that system were adopted. In your opinion, and from your knowledge of the young men, both Muhammadan and Hindu, who have gone over to England at the age of 13 or 14, do you think that the Indian section of the Indian Civil Service would be much improved? – Judging by those examples which I have seen (of course I have seen only limited examples) there would not be many. I do not think it would be improved, judging from those I have seen.

27179. And so far as objections are taken to the capacities of the existing Indians in the Indian Civil Service, you do not think there would be any improvement if we adopted this method? – What are the objections taken to existing Indians?

27180. I do not want to go into that? – Unless I know what the objections are I cannot answer you.

27181. There are certain objections that they have not got enough of the characteristics of Englishmen, that they are very good officers in many respects, but that in crisis they are not quite so reliable as they might be. I am thinking of the whole bulk of evidence which has been placed before us. The proposal is that in order to eliminate the experience – deficiencies – this scheme should be started. Do you see the position? – It is very hypothetical. The system has not yet been tried. I have no reasons, from the examples I have seen of those who have been brought up in English schools, to imagine that they would be so very different from other Indians of the same age and class. That is all I can go on.

27182. That is all I thought you would be able to say, but I wanted to get it so far as that. With reference to the changes you propose in the Syllabus, I suppose your assumption is that only the Indian candidate would take Persian; or do you assume that the English candidate would also take Persian? – I should like the English candidate to take Persian. I think it would be a very good thing if he took it; but I think, on the whole, an Englishman is much more likely to take French or German.

27183. At the same time, you think it would be far better if English candidates had a little more knowledge of Oriental culture? – Yes, I think it would be a very good thing. It is greatly needed.

27184. Let us look at it from this point of view. If the English candidate, after having spent time in acquiring a knowledge and a sympathy with Eastern culture, should happen to fail in his examination, and never get into the Indian Civil Service at all, that would be rather a bad plan, would it not? – Yes, it would be a very bad plan.

27185. How far would you agree with this conclusion, that it is far better to select your subjects for the open competition from a somewhat less specialised series of subjects, and then give a much longer time for probation after they have passed their open competition, and during that time of probation introduce your English candidates to Eastern civilisation and Eastern culture? – You mean that after he has passed he should get into touch with Eastern civilisation and Eastern learning: that would be one way; and in the case of Englishmen you might give them more marks for Arabic and Sanskrit than for Persian if they took it up.

27186. I should like to get your opinion about it. The theory about this open competitive examination is that when a man fails he has not wasted time in preparing for it which will not be useful in adopting other means of livelihood: that is the fundamental theory? – It would be a good thing.

27187. My suggestion to you, in order that I may get your opinion, is that we ought to rigidly keep to that so far as the open competitive examination is concerned, but that we should meet your point, namely, to bring the Englishman into closer contact with Asiatic culture during the period which we call the probationary period. What I should like your Highness's opinion upon is, do you think the Commission would be well advised if it went upon these lines, that far more care should be taken after he has passed to introduce him to India in all its aspects? – To its intellectual and ,,sthetic aspects, yes. I think it would be very good.

27188. And therefore that we should be, perhaps, better advised if we laid emphasis upon Persian, and all that it stands for in your mind, during the probationary training, rather than lay emphasis upon it before the open competition has been passed? – Yes, I think that would be a good thing too.

27189. If you do that you do not compel the English candidate to waste a certain amount of his time, assuming that he is unsuccessful? – If you say before he passes, I follow. I understand that you put Oriental learning on the same level as, say, the grand tour of Europe. I think that is a very good thing for the European.

27190. Have you thought it out? If you work out the two periods of the candidate's career, before he has passed his open competition, and after he has passed his open competition, but before he goes into active service, if you would draw the line between the period of the open competition and the period of probation, and if you have got the idea that I suggested to you about making the probation a full training in Oriental experience, must not you reduce the age at which the open competition is held? – At present the probationary period is two years. One year you were going to give to Oriental training, as I understand.

27191. At present it is one year? – Well, then, you will have to reduce it, yes.

27192. You would have to increase the probation? – Yes, you will have to increase the probation, and do away with the Oriental learning from the curriculum.

27193. If my mind was running very much upon these lines, your Highness does not see very much objection to it? – I approve of it on this condition, that afterwards there was the Oriental learning. I think it would be a good thing that they should know more about that.

27194. And in that probationary period you would not only bring in Persian, but Indian Economics and Indian History, and Indian Administration? – Yes, and the best literature that existed, the best literature of the country.

27195. There is one question which I should like to ask you, which is germane to this, and I am sure your Highness will assist me by throwing some light upon it. In the Indian Civil Service cadre, in its completeness, you say that the European element must be represented, not merely by men trained in England, but by Englishmen? – Yes.

27196. Then in your idea there should be another section which is not going to be denationalised Indians? – That is so.

27197. But Indians who understand England? – Yes, Indians who understand England, that is so.

27198. Indians who are not palmed off as Englishmen? – Yes, like Englishmen who understand Germany.

27199. Therefore the problem which we have to face, whether we do it successfully or not, so far as the Indian is concerned, is how to select by competition and by subsequent training Indians who will understand English methods, but who will come back to India with their foundations no [*sic*] India. That is a very general proposition. Do I understand that your Highness agrees with it? From that fundamental proposition a great many things follow? – Do you ask, how you would bring that about?

27200. Do you agree that that is the problem? – That is the problem of the country, of course. The question is, how to do it.

27201. You agree with that sort of general idea which I have been putting before you? – Yes: an Indian who actually is an Indian, and has remained an Indian, and yet who has got the spirit of the West, and who realises how an Englishman would look upon things.

27202. (*Mr. Sly.*) How many years have you been President of the Moslem League? – Since its foundation.

27203. In what year was it founded? – In 1906 or 1907, I am not quite sure of the date. It was really formed in 1908. It was being formed between 1906 and 1908.

27204. Can you tell me whether the Moslem League has considered the question of simultaneous examination, or not? – It is being considered by all the branches of the League I believe at this moment.

27205. And by the Central Committee? – They began considering it when I was at Lucknow.

27206. Have they considered it on any previous occasion? – No, not at all; now it is on the tapis.

27207. You contend that under simultaneous examination very few Indians will get in for some years? – Yes.

27208. If that result were to happen, do you think that it will raise any political problem of importance in the country? If this examination was held in India, and it was found that practically no Indians were successful, would there be any great political disappointment in the country? – If they are sensible men, and reasonable, there ought not to be. It is their own fault if they cannot get in.

27209. You say if they are reasonable? – Reasonable and sensible people would come forward and tell them. There would be two sides. When people are reasonable certain men always stand up against them, even in India.

27210. You have suggested to us that instead of the 6 per cent. of Indians who are at present in the Indian Civil Service, the number might be raised to 10 per cent., and gradually increased up to 20 per cent.? – Yes.

27211. In making that recommendation, have you considered the fact that there is at present a certain proportion of Indians already recruited for superior posts, by means of what is known as the listed post system? – I say in addition that I would not take in half of the listed ones already given.

27212. At present the listed-posts held by Indians are about 8 per cent. of the superior posts; and, of course, if we include the inferior posts, the percentage is very much larger. Is the 10 per cent. that you recommend, irrespective of the number of listed-posts altogether? – Yes, irrespective.

27213. Can you give us any maximum that you would suggest for listed-posts and direct recruitment? – There might be one or two per cent. increase of listed-posts and then it could be increased to 10 per cent., and then to 15, and then to 20 per cent. by and by.

27214. But you have not considered the question of percentage by joining the two separate factors together? – No. I have not. It is a very simple sum to work out.

27215. It comes out to rather a surprising result. You have given us an opinion largely in favour of the education of Indians in India preferably to sending them home to England as young boys? – Excuse me, not as an abstract proposition.

27216. Having regard to this opinion of yours, with regard to Indians educated under Western methods in India, failing simultaneous examination, do you think there is any suitable method of direct recruitment to the Indian Civil Service which could be adopted in India? – It could be devised, of course. I have not thought carefully of an alternative method, but it could be devised.

27217. Are you prepared to help us with any suggestion of an alternative method? – The only good one I have so far read is that of Mr. Natrajan's in the *Indian Social Reformer.* I think it is a very good alternative. It is the only alternative I have so far heard suggested.

27218. And that is the one you suggest for our consideration? – Yes, as an alternative. That is the only one so far that I have come across.

27219. In your answer to question (19) you have suggested

that Indians should be promoted to Commissionerships, and even to Lieutenant-Governors if suitable? – Yes.

27220. I wish clearly to understand to what point you refer in your answer. There is no bar at present on an Indian member of the Indian Civil Service rising to those posts? – No, there is no bar: I hope no bar will be placed.

27221. But it is not any change that you recommend? – No; there cannot be any change. You cannot force them to appoint men. If a man comes up, and if he is sufficiently good for it, let him be appointed.

27222. You do not desire any changes upon that point? – No, except that if a man turns up and he is good, by all means appoint him.

27223. He is eligible at present, is he not? – Yes. You leave it as it is.

27224. I wish to understand your scheme of probation and training a little more clearly. For successful Indian candidates for the Indian Civil Service, do you recommend one year at the University? – Yes.

27225. Followed by one year's travel in Europe? – Or in America. I would give him the choice.

27226. And for the English successful candidate what do you recommend? – I rather approve of Mr. Macdonald's idea that his two years should be spent in India more or less studying Indian Literature, and Indian History, and Indian Economics, and travelling about India generally.

27227. Two years in India? – A few months to begin with he might spend outside.

27228. Not spend one year at the University in England? – No. He is supposed to be sufficiently imbued with that.

27229. Then you refer to what you consider to be certain drawbacks in the training of Indian Civil Service men in districts. You say: "I think young officers should not be first of all sent to districts"? – I mean men who have never been in a big city should not be immediately sent to districts.

27230. You think that the first training of European members should be in towns? – Yes, or near a big town; what I call the refined parts of India.

27231. Do you not think that if the European Civilian's training was upon those lines, he would fail very much to get into touch with the ordinary agricultural problems, and peoples of India? –

He is sufficiently young to learn still; and he would not be any older than he is now.

27232. The system hitherto followed has been, as far as possible, to keep them away from large Presidency towns, and send them out into districts so as to get close in touch with the agricultural conditions and peoples of the district. Do you now wish to reverse that policy? – Was it ever a policy, or did it grow up? The fact that he was very junior was the cause of his being sent straight to a small appointment. Naturally he went there. Was it a question of policy?

27233. It was a practice? – Yes, it was a practice.

27234. And you wish to change that practice? – Yes. He is only on probation for two years, and his probation is to be in India.

27235. (*Mr. Gokhale.*) The views set forth in your written answers are, strictly speaking, your own? – Yes, entirely.

27236. At the same time, can you tell us to what extent they are shared by leading members of your community? – What do you mean by "my community"? I suppose you mean by the Mussalmán community of India.

27237. Have you had any means of knowing what views are held with regard to the matter by leading members of the Moslem League? – I have naturally discussed it with all the Mussalmáns of some importance whom I have come across.

27238. In Bombay or elsewhere? – When I was up country at Lucknow I had the opportunity of speaking to them.

27239. To what extent are these views shared by the leading members? – What do you mean by "these views"; which portion?

27240. Those about simultaneous examinations? – On that point I do not think I have heard a single voice against it. Every Mussalmán I have asked about it up country has been in favour of it. Of course I did not cross-examine them as you are cross-examining me. Asking them generally, they were all in favour of it.

27241. That is enough for my purpose. Has the Bombay Presidency Moslem League expressed any opinion, do you know? – I believe it has sent in a written paper, but I have not read it.

27242. Do you know what that opinion is? – No, I have not read it; and I do not quite know what it is.

27243. I believe it is in favour of simultaneous examinations. You yourself advocate simultaneous examinations? – Yes.

27244. And, at the same time, you do not propose to lay down a minimum for Europeans today? – No.

27245. Because you think the danger of Europeans falling below the required number is exceedingly remote? – That is so.

27246. It is really a theoretical danger only? – That is how I look upon it.

27247. And the same theoretical danger exists today? – Yes.

27248. Because if a large number of Indians go and compete in London there is nothing to prevent them? – As a matter of fact, there are thousands who can afford to send their children, but who do not.

27249. The Government have allowed that danger to remain unprovided against? – Yes.

27250. And you would deal with the other danger in the same way? – Yes, exactly. That is why I said that there is no need for putting it down.

27251. I see you insist upon Indians who get into the Indian Civil Service passing the same examination, having the same papers, and the same everything? – Yes.

27252. Is that because you insist that Indians who get into the Indian Civil Service should be on a footing of absolute equality with the English members? – Yes. I think that there should be a fair field. There should be the open door, really, and putting them on the same level.

27253. If Indians were promoted exclusively, or almost exclusively, from the Provincial Civil Service to the Indian Civil Service, and placed on the same level as suggested by Sir Valentine Chirol, do you think they would be regarded as the equals of the English members of the Service? – I think if all men came in on that line, at once the public would say, "Those are the Indians, and those are the Europeans". But, certainly, if some get in exactly like Europeans it would be a good thing.

27254. You would want them to come in in the same way as the English? – That must be natural. There should be no racial bar.

27255. If members come exclusively, or almost exclusively, from the Provincial Service, do you not think there would be something in their previous official upbringing which might militate against their asserting their equality with Englishmen? – I think the exclusion of Provincial Service men would be a great mistake.

27256. You mentioned an alternative scheme suggested by Mr. Natrajan? – Yes.

27257. Will you tell us briefly what that scheme is, because I have not seen it? – I only saw it quite recently. It comes really to this, that M. A. Graduates of the Indian Universities who have got a certain amount of recommendation as to their general character, and so on, from the Principals of their Colleges, and who have got a proper training, might then pass in from that examination quite apart from the Indian Civil Service one; and out of those that pass Government might nominate some.

27258. Government nominates in the end? – I am not quite sure that Government nominates, but it is a system by which at the end few get in.

27259. Is it open competition at the end? – Yes, I believe so. On general lines I thought it was a good alternative. I think the scheme is good.

27260. (*Mr. Chaubal.*) In answer to question (2), I see you advocate the levelling up of the scale of marks as regards Sanskrit and Arabic and Greek and Latin. I suppose you are not particular as to how the levelling up is brought about – either by raising Sanskrit and Arabic to the same number of marks as Greek and Latin or by bringing down the marks for the latter? – I would rather see Greek and Latin brought down, and Sanskrit and Arabic raised a little. I would prefer that, but I do not hold very strong views upon it.

27261. What you want is that they should be on the same level? – I think it would be a good thing, but I do not hold strong views upon it.

27262. You do not strongly hold the view that the levelling up must necessarily be by raising Sanskrit and Arabic, it may equally be done by lowering Latin and Greek? – Yes.

27263. Some questions have been put to you with regard to crammers' institutions starting up in India? – Yes.

27264. Do you know if crammers' institutions in England are patronized by Indians, or do Englishmen go to these institutions? – I have already said that I do not know much about cramming institutions. I have heard most about them from Army Officers who have gone to crammers, so that it must be Englishmen.

27265. I mean Englishmen who have come in as Indian Civil Servants? – I suppose they go to such institutions, but I have never asked them.

27266. I am under the impression that they do go; but I wanted to know from you whether when the Indian Civil Servant comes out here the public find any traces of the evils of his having studied at a crammer's institution. Do you find from your experience of Indian Civil Servants, efficient servants of the Government, that they disclose any of the evils of having studied in the crammers' institutions in the past? – No.

27267. I ask you that because I have heard some Englishmen say that they profited immensely from their education at crammers. Do you think it is easy to start a crammer's institution like those in England? – It would be a tremendous business.

27268. It is a work which would cost an immense amount of money in order to be able to get the same sort of teachers and lecturers as they have at crammers' institutions at Home? – Yes, it would be a very big business.

27269. You have been asked about the policy or the difficulty of posting Indian Civil Service men from different communities? – Yes.

27270. Is it not the policy, generally, of Government to appoint a Bombay man to some other Presidency, and the man who belonged to that other Presidency to some other district? – You said "communities".

27271. The question was put to you whether if a person of one community became an Indian Civil Servant persons of other communities would not object. It is with reference to that that I ask you whether the present policy, more or less, is not that you generally do not post men from the same Presidency? – Naturally, because you want an independent man.

27272. With regard to the fear which I find is very generally entertained about the larger number of Indians, the proportion you are contemplating of 10 or 20 per cent. disturbing the British tone of the administration, you say that out of 1,294 Civil Servants there are at present only fifty-six Indians? – Yes.

27273. Can anybody find out that the British tone of the administration has been in the slightest degree injuriously affected by the admission of those fifty-six people? – No.

27274. Do you suppose that if those fifty-six men were to rise to one hundred there would be a chance of their injuriously affecting the British tone of the administration? – None whatever, even if the number were a hundred and fifty.

27275. As regards this question of the larger employment of Indians in the Service, you were asked whether your community supports the demand by the Indian public for a larger employment. Am I right in supposing that the interests of your community, in this general question of the larger employment of Indians, are identical with those of all the other communities in India? – By "my community," do you mean Mussalmáns, or my own community.

27276. I mean Muhammadans as a body? – All the Muhammadans I have spoken to are in favour of simultaneous examinations with the exception of one Government officer. All the others are in favour of it.

27277. The question is one of such general interest that it does not affect any particular sect or community. The question of the larger employment of Indians in the higher Services is of equal interest to all communities? – Yes, I think so.

27278. You were asked by Mr. Madge about the interests of the ignorant millions and the interests of the infinitesimally small educated portion of the Indian public? – Yes.

27279. Can you understand in what sense the interests of the small educated portion of the Indian public are in conflict with the interests of the ignorant millions? – No, I cannot.

27280. Can you conceive of any direction in which they might be? – I cannot conceive it in this vague way. I can conceive the interests of two individuals of any race being opposed, but I cannot conceive of it in this vague way.

27281. With regard to the larger salaries which you recommend for the Provincial Civil Service in your written answers, you were asked as to whether it would not do if there was a house allowance made for residence in towns. I suppose you are aware that the general body of Government servants in the Provincial Service, although they are themselves serving in the muffassal and not in big towns, still, generally have to keep a residence in town for the education of their children. It was suggested to you that instead of increasing the salaries all round as regards these Provincial Civil Servants, it would do if you gave a house allowance to such of the Provincial Servants as resided in towns. That I think, was put to you by Mr. Madge. I am putting this question to you, whether it is not a fact that in your experience the majority of the Civil Servants, although they are not serving in towns but in tálukas, have more or less all of them residences in the nearest district towns for the purpose of educating their children? – That is so.

27282. And therefore, although they are living in the muffassal, the increase in the amenities of life, and the increase in the cost of living, affect these servants, notwithstanding the fact that they are not residing in towns? – I think in some cases it does. A man must be of a certain age, and advanced to a certain position in the Service, by the time he has the need of sending his children there.

27283. I am putting it in this way to ascertain if a rise in the salaries is not necessary even in the case of persons who may not themselves be serving in a district town? – Yes. I think there might be a slight rise. If he is living in a town he has to entertain, and it is much more necessary.

27284. What I wish to point out is that it must not be considered unnecessary simply on the ground that a man himself is not living in a town? – No, that is not the only reason for considering it.

27285. (*Mr. Madge.*) I should like to say that the suggestion attributed to me was not attributed by me: I was in favour of both increases.

27286. (*Sir Theodore Morison.*) I should like to have your recommendation with regard to Persian made clear. I think you suggested that it should be in the open competition examination before probation? – Yes, before probation.

27287. You agree with the suggestion of Mr. Macdonald that for Englishmen it might be advantageous that they should study Persian during probation? – Yes.

27288. And that therefore for them it was not particularly important that it should be in the open competition? – Yes.

27289. There still remains the question of Indian competitors, does there not? – Yes.

27290. Do I understand that you recommend the introduction of Persian on the ground that it would help Indians, or because Persian contains a literature, as old, as rich, and as good a vehicle of culture as, we will say, Italian? Which of those two is it? Is it on the ground that Persian on its merits is as rich a vehicle of culture as Italian, or is it because Indians know it? – It is on account of its wealth as a language and its historical traditions; and, to a great extent, it would be of great assistance to a Hindu who went into the Service afterwards.

27291. It was agreed to leave that sort of consideration out of the question in talking to Mr. Macdonald, because if a man fails to get in we do not want him to get into a *cul de sac:* the thing is to be on the ground of general education? – Yes.

27292. And as a vehicle of general education, Persian is, in your opinion, fit to stand on a level with Italian? – Yes, I think so.

27293. Therefore it would be differentiated from the Indian Vernaculars which have not such a rich literature? – Exactly.

27294. It is upon its merits as a cultivated language? – Yes.

27295. And if its modern literature does not compare with French and German, it may at least compare with Italian? – Yes.

27296. Arising out of your answers to your written questions, and what has been said around this table, I understand you desire that the Civil Service should remain for some time to come predominantly English? – Yes.

27297. You think it would be a good policy if a certain number of Indians could be advanced to very high posts in the Civil Service? – Yes.

27298. Do I understand that that is the policy which you have mainly in view in your recommendation? – Yes.

27299. If so, are simultaneous examinations the best way of attaining that end? I will put it in another way. Supposing we could devise a scheme which will attain that particular end rather more surely than simultaneous examinations, would you prefer it? If it got a small number of Indians into the higher posts rather than a larger number of Indians without any security that they would rise higher, your simultaneous examinations do not seem to me to offer any guarantee, or any likelihood, of Indians attaining those posts which you have indicated you would like them to attain? – If you could devise a better means I should be in favour of it.

27300. Is it that you want simultaneous examination as some witnesses have said, as being good *per se*, or do you advocate it so as to attain a definite policy, which is that some Indians should rise to very high posts? – I advocate it as a means of arriving at that policy. I think it is a very simple and a very direct way, and it would leave no bitterness afterwards. It will not be like nomination. It will not leave any bitterness afterwards.

27301. My own doubt is whether it will attain that end. With regard to the answer which you gave to Mr. Gokhale, you said that the Mussalmáns you have spoken to have been in favour, generally, of simultaneous examination? – Yes.

27302. Have they generally added a reservation or rider to the effect that they would like a certain number of posts reserved for

Muhammadans? – Those I have spoken to at Lucknow said that they were in favour of simultaneous examinations. They wanted an open door and no favour.

27303. They do not want any posts reserved? – No; with the exception of the one Government official in Bombay which I mentioned. With that single exception they all said that so far as the Indian Civil Service is concerned they did not want any reservation. I was doubtful myself, to a great extent, upon that point, and it was more for my own personal satisfaction that I asked the question.

27304. You found that that opinion was general? – Yes, the opinion was general amongst themselves.

27305. Were they the younger members of the community? – A mixture. Many will probably be witnesses before the Commission, but I do not know. I was at Lucknow at the time.

27306. I understand that your objection to the present system of examination is that the English door is a handicap to the Indians, that it puts the Indian at a disadvantage? – I do not say that that is my chief reason. It puts some deserving Indians at a disadvantage, say poor men of respectability with sons. There are some people that Englishmen least meet with, and they are just the people who avoid officialism. They are not of the pauperized lot, people who would object to taking charity.

27307. At the same weight the Englishman would generally beat the Indian, and therefore there is no advantage in handicapping the Indian? – Exactly. That is what it comes to.

27308. Do you not think that if you want to retain Englishmen in the Service some sort of handicap will eventually be necessary, because it will always be pleasanter for a man to serve his own country than any foreign country? – It is not necessary.

27309. It is not necessary for the Englishman to protect himself for serving in Whitehall, because there will be so little attraction for the Indian to go and serve in Whitehall. If you are going to get an Englishman to serve out of his own country, surely in time you will have to give some sort of preferential advantage, otherwise he is sure to be ousted by the people to whom he is a much greater attraction: more people will compete? – If there was any danger of his being ousted I would reserve at once so many appointments for him.

27310. Are you going to give him any kind of preferential treatment: is there anything less invidious than at present? – We do not want to give him any kind of preferential treatment.

27311. You must either help him to get in, or give him better pay? – I have advocated a general rise in all cities. I think Secretaries to Government, and so on, should have a rise in pay to begin with. Those who get in would not get these appointments for another 25 years; and so for 25 years it would be Englishmen alone who would benefit by an increase of pay. Any increase of pay in the higher posts would benefit Englishmen, and I think it is right that it should be so.

27312. (*Lord Ronaldshay.*) When you were asked what your opinion would be with regard to reducing the age limit for the examination, I think you said it would be no use bringing out boys to this country? – Yes.

27313. I should like to know what you mean more definitely. Would you consider a person of the age of 21 or 22 to be a boy? – I think that a person of 21 or 22 would have no experience; and to be left in a district is a great responsibility at rather a too early period of his life.

27314. Were there any complaints on that score when the members of the Indian Civil Service did come out to this country at that age? – That was a good deal before my time. I think now that the people here are used to more developed men these young people would not carry the same weight as men of more advanced age.

27315. But do you not think, perhaps, that a man who came out at the age of 21 or 22 would come out with an open mind, and that he would find it easier to adapt himself to the conditions out here than a man of 24 or 25? – No; I prefer 25.

27316. After your answers to Sir Valentine Chirol, I am not quite clear in my mind whether you think scholastic examination is the best method or not of testing the capacity of an Indian for administrative work? – I do not know an alternative.

27317. The alternative is selecting men of tried merit and ability from the Provincial Service; and I rather gathered from what you said to Sir Valentine Chirol that you thought of those two methods that of seeing men work in the Provincial Service, and testing their work there, was more likely to prove satisfactory than a mere scholastic examination? – That is to a great extent so. If you limit it to that, I fear there would be an invidious distinction, and you would put up a partition between the two races, which would lead to the needless racial irritation of colour bar in the life of the country. It is for this reason that I think the other door should also be left open. Of course I should prefer guarantees if there were need for them.

27318. Of course I am assuming that the English door would be left open. Even if you promoted men from the Provincial Civil Service, and if you were to institute a system of scholarships, I do not necessarily say scholarships at the school-boy age, but, possibly, scholarships at the University age, which would give Indians greater facilities for passing the examination in England, would not those two avenues into the Civil Service prove satisfactory from an Indian point of view? – I am bitterly opposed to all scholarships. It is not the business of Government to help individuals. It is the business of parents. I am bitterly opposed to anything which pauperises them.

27319. You are opposed to a scheme of scholarships on principle? – Yes. It is not a charitable organisation at all. I am an individualist who regards that with great opposition. On principle I would not consider scholarships. I bitterly resent that peasants and the ryots should be taxed for the children of people who live in town, and that those who have influence with officials should get advantages. I bitterly resent any scholarships of that sort. If anybody wants to help them, let him do it out of his own pocket.

27320. With regard to Indians being eligible for higher posts in the Service, such as Lieutenant-Governorships, and so on, if you had the appointments of Lieutenant-Governorships at the present time, are there any Indians whom you would appoint? – I am sorry I have not got the appointment of them.

27321. I know you have not. I am asking you on the assumption that you had? – When you take the social question as well I should not at present know. Take Bengal. He would have to entertain and so on. As a social question I would not know.

27322. We have to recognise, however unwillingly, that there is a certain amount of antagonism between the two communities in India, the Muhammadans and the Hindus. The question I want to ask you is this. Do you anticipate that there might be in any parts of the country administrative difficulties arising out of a Hindu being posted to a position of authority over a population which was largely Muhammadan? – That has existed now under the present rules for fifty years. It is not as if you were introducing a new principle.

27323. Under the present system does it often happen that you have a Hindu to rule over a Muhammadan population, and *vice versa?* – It has been so. Take the case of a Collector: with three Collectors around who are Englishmen. One is a Hindu and the other is a Muhammadan. The very fact that three were around him and were Englishmen, and were able to keep their places in order, would keep him in check?

27324. I quite admit that; but that is under the present system when there are a very small number of Indians in the higher posts. I am asking on the assumption that if simultaneous examination were established the proportion of Indians must become greater? – I am opposed to anything that would increase it; and I do not advocate guarantees, because there is no need of guarantees at present.

27325. (*Mr. Heaton.*) Supposing we had simultaneous examinations, do you think that those who passed in India would stand any lower in general reputation than those who went to England and passed there? – I think unless they were sent away for two or three years, they would probably: that is, if they had not had the opportunity of living in Europe.

27326. The mere passing of the same examination, if they passed in India, would not put them on quite the same level in the opinion of the public of India? – Not unless they had some European experience afterwards. The expense should come out of their own pockets. To a great extent they would have a position by that time. They would have a stake in the country, and they could borrow, and do other things on their prospects, through Insurance Companies.

27327. Have you considered at all what subjects you would advocate as compulsory subjects, supposing we had simultaneous examinations: perhaps you have not thought of that? – No, I have not.

27328. (*Mr. Joglekar.*) In answer to question (54) you have said – "I do not think that the Muhammadans are adequately represented in the Provincial Civil Service." To what branch do you refer, to the Executive or the Judicial branch? – To both.

27329. On what principle is the statement that they are not adequately represented based? – Look at Sind; look at Eastern Bengal!

27330. What is the principle? – Population, of course.

27331. (*Sir Valentine Chirol.*) I do not quite understand a reply you gave to Mr. Chaubal. Did I understand you to say that you think it is quite impossible that the opinions and desires of the small educated class in India would ever be in conflict with any other community, or with the masses of the population? – It might arise when a portion of the educated community would have class interests against a section of the masses.

27332. (*Mr. Chaubal.*) My question was from the point of view of administration? – I cannot conceive it from the point of view of administration.

27333. (*Sir Valentine Chirol.*) I presume you have modified your view since, as President of the Moslem League, you sanctioned very strong representations to be made with regard to the complete inadequacy of the representation of Muhammadans in the administration? – But that was as far as legislation is concerned, and as far as the lower branches are concerned. In the Provincial Civil Service I strongly held it, and I still hold it. It is only with regard to the Indian Civil Service, where there is at present no such guarantee, that I think that we need not bother about it. But as regards the Provincial Civil Service, I strongly believe to the present day that there ought to be.

27334. The representation of the Moslem League never dealt with the representation of the Muhammadan element of the Civil Service? – No, never. I do not think so, because the Civil Service was not at that time, even three or four years ago, under discussion.

27335. There was quite as much discussion with regard to the Indian Civil Service as there was with regard to the Provincial Service? – But the Provincial Civil Service was always in a state of change and flux.

(The witness withdrew).

Source: Royal Commission on the Public Services in India, *Appendix to the Report of the Commissioners, Volume VI: Minutes of Evidence Relating to the Indian and Provincial Civil Services Taken at Bombay from the 1st. to the 12th. March 1913, with Appendices*, His Majesty's Stationary Office, London, 1914, Cd. 7579, pp. 54–69.

The Commission which was appointed on 5 September 1912 and which reported on 14 August 1915, consisted of Baron Islington (Chairman), Earl of Ronaldshay, Sir Murray Hammick, Sir Theodore Morison (Council of India), Sir Valentine Chirol, Mahadev Bhaskar Chaubal (Member, Governor's Executive Council, Bombay), Abdur Rahim (Judge, Madras High Court), Gopal Krishna Gokhale (Member, Viceroy's Executive Council, died in 1915), Walter Cunny Madge (Member, Viceroy's Executive Council), Frank George Sly, Herbert Albert Laurens Fisher (Fellow and Tutor, New College, Oxford) and James Ramsay Macdonald. Abdur Rahim's name does not appear in the list of members who submitted the Report.

The findings and recommendations of the Commission were published as the *Report of the Royal Commission on the Public Services in India*, His Majesty's Stationery Office, London, 1917, Cd. 8382.

For the history and problems of the public services in India see George

Chesney, *Indian Polity: A View of the System of Administration in India*, London, 1868, 3rd edn 1894; L. S. S. O'Malley, *The Indian Civil Service 1601–1930*, London, 1931; Edward Blunt, *The I.C.S.: The Indian Civil Service*, London, 1937; Philip Woodruff (Philip Mason), *The Men Who Ruled India*, London, 1952–4, 2 vols; Hira Lal Singh, *Problems and Policies of the British in India, 1885–1898*, Bombay, 1963; Ralph Braibanti (ed.), *Asian Bureaucratic Systems Emergent from the British Imperial Tradition*, Durham, 1966 (essay on India by Bernard S. Cohen); Lepel Griffin, "The Indian Civil Service Examinations", *Fortnightly Review*, April 1875; A. J. Balfour, "The Indian Civil Service – A Reply", *Fortnightly Review*, August 1877; Lyon Playfair, "On the New Plan for Selecting and Training Civil Servants for India", *Fortnightly Review*, July 1877; Theodore Beck, "The House of Commons and the Indian Civil Service", *National Review*, May 1894; W. Doderet, "The Training of I.C.S. Probationers and of Junior Civilians", *East and West*, July 1913; H. G. Keene, "The Indian Civil Service", *East and West*, January 1913; E. S. Montagu, "The Indian Civil Service", *The Civil and Military Gazette*, Lahore, 26 and 30 January 1923 (reprinted from *The Times*, London); Henry Wheeler, "Men and Policy in India", *Fortnightly Review*, August 1936; Lord Templewood, "The Men who Shaped a Subcontinent", *Manchester Guardian*, 4 March 1958; Abdur Rahim, "Indians in the Public Services", *Indian Review*, February 1917; "The Services and the Reforms: Their Constitutional Rights", *The Civil and Military Gazette*, 21 September 1921; and the following unpublished theses: S. C. Parasher, "The Development of the Indian Civil Service", Ph.D., University of London, 1947; Muhammad Rafi Anwar, "The Recruitment of Indians into the Covenanted Civil Service of India, 1853–1891", M.A., University of Manchester, 1960.

33

THE IDEALS OF MUSLIM INDIA

Speech at the Fifth Annual General Meeting of the London Muslim League

London: 14 July 1913

Indian Muslim youth in England – leaders of the future – task before the London League – Muslim solidarity – relations between Turkey and Britain – British Empire the bulwark of Islam – Muslims in the Empire can mould British policy – domestic tasks before the Indian Muslims – education – uplift of the depressed classes – meaning of self-government – political and other dimensions of self-government – the example of Japan – relations between different races of India – what Muslims can do – local committees to improve Hindu– Muslim relations – potential influence of sports.

The report presented today justly points out that the young Moslems who come here from India in a steadily-increasing stream will help to form the life of India of the near future. From the point of view of influencing and guiding these young men, the work of such an organisation as this is of very great importance. I doubt whether public opinion here has any conception of the profound significance of the presence in London and in provincial educational centres of so many young men from India. It may be asked what are 300 or 400 young Moslems in comparison with 70 millions of Indian Mussulmans, or 1,600 or 1,700 Indians of various communities in comparison with the 315 millions of Hindustan. The answer is that they are like so many stones thrown into the middle of the placid pool or river each making concentric rings until the brink on either side is reached. Twenty years ago not only the mass of the people but men of standing of what is termed "the old school" looked askance at new-fangled ideas brought by the "European-returned" young men. But now they listen with almost greedy eagerness to any message brought from the West, and are ready to accept in an uncritical spirit the views of their young countrymen who have sojourned here. The day when the educated classes could be spoken of as a "microscopic minority" has passed away; education is already diffused among the middle classes, and with the active encouragement and effort of Lord Hardinge's Government is filtering down to the people at large. The young men sojourning here are the leaders and fathers of the future; though they are to be numbered only by hundreds they represent the hundreds of thousands of men of varying degrees of English education in India seeking to come more and more into touch with European thought and ideals; and, beyond these hundreds of thousands, the millions who are learning to read newspapers and to interest themselves in the world outside their villages. The ideas and messages our youths take back with them from Europe are eagerly listened to, and it is of the greatest importance to India and the Empire that they should here imbibe right ideas and learn the right way of interpreting them. This consideration cannot be lost sight of in estimating the work of the London League, as the report points out, and it is upon this ground that I use the opportunity your committee has kindly provided me to pass over more current details and address myself to problems which go to the very roots of our national life.

When I say that the work of guiding aright the future leaders of Indian Moslem thought is one of Imperial importance I do not confine that word to India alone. The recent Turkish war has demonstrated to the world the inherent solidarity of those who profess and call themselves Muslims. Wherever they may be, Mahomedans have a fellow-feeling and an interest in each other's welfare is inadequately realised in Europe, where the strong religious sanctions of Islamic unity are not properly understood. In India in the last year or two the tribulations of Turkey and of Persia have absorbed the thought of the Moslem people to the practical exclusion of their own immediate affairs and those of India generally. The currents of feeling were very strong, and for a time our people were in danger of losing sight of certain fundamental considerations which they ordinarily hold with tenacity.

Whatever may have been the case in the past when affairs in Macedonia created irritation between England and Turkey, it is clear to thoughtful Indian Muslims that British and Turkish interests are closely identified. They feel that it is a matter of great moment to this country that Turkey should continue to hold sway as an independent power in Asia, and also that Persia should retain whatever remains of her integrity. Obviously the break-up of Ottoman dominion in Asia would expose the Western route to India to attack by other European Powers. Mutual good-will and good understanding between England and Turkey will afford the best possible safeguard against any partition of her Asiatic dominions. I have reason to believe that in view of all that has happened in recent years Turkey is not merely willing but anxious to come more fully within the orbit of British influence. Whatever weight the Indian Moslems may possess in the Islamic world should be used for bringing Turkey and other Mahomedan countries into an attitude of genuine trust in Great Britain. They will thus be doing good service not only to the British Empire but also to their co-religionists in other countries; they will help to fulfil the destiny which has ordained that the welfare of England and of the Islamic world should be closely inter-related, and that if one is weakened the other is weakened also.

Though appearances may sometimes be unpropitious, the British Empire, as was lately observed by *The Times*, is and must be the bulwark of Islam. There are over 100,000,000 Muslims in the British Empire, a total compared with which that of any other Power of Western Europe is small. Whatever is left of independent Mussalman States, in these circumstances they must either more or less gravitate under British influence or lose their position. Needless to say this aggregation of Moslems under the British Empire gives her a great moral asset in the beneficent and mighty part she plays in the world's affairs. At the same time it imposes great responsibilities upon the Indian Muslims, since they have a high destiny to fulfil in their capacity as by far the largest and most important section of the Mahomedan subjects of the Crown. The more steadfast and strong their loyalty is to the British Empire, the more influential they will naturally be in promoting that harmony of interests of which I have spoken and also in the moulding of British policy.

But these international considerations, though vital, should not lead to any neglect in the duties close at hand. In my judg-ment the Indian Moslems should in domestic affairs largely concentrate their efforts upon two great aims. The first of these should be to alter the position of affairs under which they are justly described in the recent Government pronouncement on Moslem education as "educationally backward." They cannot hope to play their part adequately and satisfactorily in the great developments of Indian life now in progress unless their educational equipment is equal to that of other communities. The second great aim should be to help in uplifting and reclaiming the depressed classes. The splendid example which has been set in this respect by Christian missions, and in more recent years by Hindu agencies, have not been responded to by our people. The Mussalmans are doing absolutely nothing to contribute to this essential element in the building up of Indian nationhood. It is high time that they set themselves to work both to elevate the depressed classes and to bring enlightenment and the advantages of cultured civilization to the wild tribes of the jungle and the hills.

Having spoken of Indian nationhood, I may here refer to the adoption by the Committee of the Central League [All India Muslim League] last winter of the ideal of self-government under the British Crown. That ideal, whether on Colonial lines as has been suggested by so many of our compatriots, or in some form "suitable to India," the conditions of which we do not at present conceive and therefore do not attempt to define, must commend itself to thoughtful opinion, if it means, as I take it to mean, an ideal involving many decades of effort towards self-improvement, towards social reform, towards educational diffusion, and toward complete amity between various communities. Given personal and national self-sacrifice for generations to come, some form of self-government worthy of the British Empire and worthy of the people of India will be evolved, and Indians will have won a proud place for their nation in the world under the British Throne. But if it means a mere hasty impulse to jump at the apple when only the blossoming stage is over, then the day that witnessed the formulations of the idea will be a very unfortunate one in our country's annals. We have a long way to travel before the distant goal can be reached, and the voice of wisdom calls us to proceed step by step. The fact that the Central Committee confined itself to favouring some system "suitable to India" shows that at present it is difficult even to define the plan which may be evolved as Indian life develops and expands. Such development, I need hardly say, must be social, material and moral as well as political if a goal worthy of the self-sacrifice involved and of India's place in the Empire is to be reached. We have that extraordinary example of the progress of Japan within living memory to show us that we cannot truly advance upon one side of our national life unless other sides are simultaneously developed. And the motive force must be religious, because for nothing else will vast masses of the East toil on for generations along the path of self-denial.

An element in the new national self-consciousness must be the mutual goodwill and understanding of the different races of India. Unfortunately, as the Report observes, there are parts of the country where the relations of Hindus and Moslems are unsatisfactory. It is eminently desirable that in the provinces and districts where good-will and right feeling exist missionaries should go forth to the less fortunate parts of the country in the effort to bring about good understanding. The Mussalmans have a great opportunity if they will only realise how far they can go in evoking and strengthening Hindu goodwill by voluntarily abandoning the public slaughter of cows for sacrifice. The question as you are aware, is largely an economic one, and much could be done to solve it by committees of Mussalmans and rich Hindus organizing subscriptions for the purchase of other animals to be sacrificed in substitution of kine. Good work could also be done by local committees for bringing Hindus and Mussalmans together in social intercourse. It is true that there are difficulties of caste in the way of taking food together; but no such obstacle stands in the way of games and sports. Years ago in Bombay, Lord Harris revealed to us how much can be done on the cricket field to create good feeling between different races. Play is instinctive in young life in India as elsewhere. I believe that with due organisation there can be spread among our youth everywhere the *camaraderie* of the playing ground, and that social knowledge and goodwill is to be attained in India largely along the lines of the physical culture of our young people – a culture eminently desirable also for the direct benefits it will confer upon coming generations.

Source: *The Times of India*, Bombay, 2 August 1913, which published a verbatim report of the speech. *The Times* of London carried a brief version in its issue of 15 July.

This meeting was attended, by Sir H. H. Shephard, C. E. Buckland, M. A. Jinnah, and Mirza Ali Muhammad Khan among others.

On the London Muslim League see the excellent treatment in M. Yusuf Abbasi, *London Muslim League (1908–1928): An Historical Study*, Islamabad, 1988.

34

RESIGNATION FROM THE ALL INDIA MUSLIM LEAGUE PRESIDENTSHIP

Letter to Sayyid Ameer Ali

Paris: 2 November 1913

Tribute to Sayyid Ameer Ali – reasons for his own resignation – wish to belong to the League Council – historical background to the formation of the League – the principle of separate representation for Muslims – the League should become a national organization – different schools of thought within the League – Muslim representation on municipalities and local boards – primary education and the language question – importance of the London League.

From the remarks I made at the committee meeting of the London All India Muslim League on Wednesday and our previous conversations, you are well aware how profoundly I regret the turn of events leading to your resignation of the presidentship, which you have held with so much wisdom and devotion since the establishment of the League, and for which, I am sure, the overwhelming majority of Musulmans and I, for one, are deeply grateful ... [... in the original – ed.]. I wish you could have seen your way to withhold your resignation until the opinion of the Central Committee in India had been definitely ascertained. I cannot think that the committee would endorse any suggestion which you could look upon as making your position here untenable, for there is on the part of all men in India, both young and old, the strongest sense of indebtedness for your great and unique services to the community.

I am unable, for many reasons, to continue as president of the Central [All India Muslim] League. I have come to an absolutely irrevocable decision to retire therefrom, and I have written already my resignation to the council of the League in India through its honorary secretary. My reasons are numerous, both personal and public. As you are aware, I have had many personal grounds for wishing to take this course for some time past, and your resignation now gives me a golden opportunity of retiring. I will venture to tell you some of my reasons, and I am placing these reasons before Mr. S. W. Hasan, the honorary secretary, to be communicated by him to his council. I am so circumstanced that I am compelled to be out of India for considerable periods every year (next year, for instance, I have to spend six months in Africa), and I have to be very often in Europe, where I have considerable private interests and where I am financially interested in some corporations. Thus, I cannot carry out the duties of president in the way I should like. But I do not propose to sever my connexion with the League; far from it – I indeed wish to belong to its council, and I believe that as an active member of its council, free from the necessarily "judicial" character that attaches to the presidency, I can more effectively contribute my share to the service of the community. In addition to this, I have other minor personal reasons of a purely domestic and family nature. However, all these personal reasons together would not have made me retire from the presidentship if I thought that my continuance would serve the welfare of the community. But I have come to the conclusion that, for reasons which I will now give to you, it is essential for our communal welfare that I should retire.

In order to explain this clearly, I will have to go back to the history of the foundation of the League in India. When in the spring of 1906 I was at Aligarh, foreseeing the coming political movement in India, I suggested to the late Nawab Mohsin-ul-Mulk the formation of a federation or league in order to give our people a political platform and also to prevent their disappearance as a national entity and unity. He immediately agreed, and in the months previous to the formation of the deputation to the Viceroy, he was occupied in preparing the ground. At that time the Musulman community in India, owing to long neglect of all organized interest in politics, had unfortunately fallen into a state of absolute chaos and political non-existence. In these early stages, the foundation of a league in India, with a large number of leaders from the aristocracy and men of strong social and financial position, was absolutely necessary in order to give the organization its weight and its status in the eyes of our Government and the Hindu community. The post of president was necessary so that our organization in India might not die stillborn by too early struggles between different schools of thought in our community. Then came the long and memorable struggle to win the principle of separate representation on Councils, Imperial and Provincial. I, for one, never looked upon the principle of separate representation as a policy but as a necessity for awakening our people to the importance of political life and organization, and, in fact, to give them a platform and the sense of self-reliance. For me, separate representation in the Imperial and Provincial Councils was not a policy but the necessary way of awakening our people from the state of coma and neglect into which they had fallen. In its early stages the League in India had as much need of high-sounding names amongst its officers as a newly-formed company in the city has need of high-sounding titles on its board of directors. Happily, the League has passed through that stage. Thank God, I have lived and seen the infant reach the stage of early manhood. I am profoundly convinced that in India at this stage a permanent president, an official spokesman, a recognized leader, will hamper the natural evolution and development of our community, even if he be always on the spot and fully worthy of such a position.

The League in India must become more and more not a political party but a national organization of the loyal and devoted Moslem community of India, the organization in which all parties must be represented and all schools of thought given due voice. In future, the League cannot have a leader but leaders of parties representing different schools of thought and each trying to convince the community that its policy is the best for India. I do not wish to give these parties question-begging names by calling them Conservative or Liberal, but I will give you two instances of questions on which there must be differences and discussion, and I could easily give you twenty similar examples. In these discussions and differences I, for one, mean to take part and, God willing, I may be the leader of those who agree with me from conviction. One of the two instances is the question of separate representation on municipalities and local boards. There must necessarily be two, or even, three, ways of dealing with this question, and there must be two or three parties to a discussion that will ultimately settle our policy. Another question that must arise is that of primary education and its relation to the local vernaculars and the Urdu language. As these questions arise, there must be differences and discussion, before a settlement can be reached, and I, for one, heartily welcome the fact that our organization in India can now, thanks to the awakening of our people, be freed from the trammel of my presidentship.

Of course, the future of our community in India and of this League depends on the people. This is a truism, but the time has come for our people to realize the truism and its responsibilities. I am convinced that my retirement will help to develop this sense of responsibility and also that my experience will be of greater service on the free bench of the League's council than in the cramped chair of the President. I still think that after the question of the relation of the central and of the London League has been discussed afresh in India, there may be some possibility of reconstruction of the London League on sound lines, but I should not myself be prepared to join the London League as one of its officers on any fresh basis unless I was assured of the sympathy and help, not only of yourself, but also of our wise and elderly friends of weight and standing, who have so well served as its principal officers, and who now retire with you. I cherish this hope of reconstruction because the London League, under wise guidance in the future as in the past, can be made an instrument of the greatest advantage, not only to our community, but to the people of India generally. Therefore, there must be an effort to save it from collapse.

Source: *The Times*, London, 8 November 1913.

On 31 October 1913 *The Times* had announced that Sayyid Ameer Ali was retiring from the presidentship of the London branch of the All India Muslim League, and that the Aga Khan had decided to resign the leadership of the Muslim League in India as soon as practicable upon his return to that country. Now, on 2 November, the Aga Khan wrote to Ameer Ali from Paris giving his reasons for the decision. Passages from this letter were published in *The Times* on 8 November, and these are reproduced here.

The Times of this date also published the following closing passage from the Aga Khan's letter addressed to Sayyid Wazir Hasan, the Honorary Secretary of the All India Muslim League:

"Nearly two years ago, for these very reasons, I tendered my resignation. Unfortunately, just before that time there had been a difference of opinion between me and large numbers in India on the question of the second Partition of Bengal and the Durbar changes. The motive of my resignation was misunderstood, and the community imagined that I was hurt at the criticisms passed on me, and very graciously refused to accept my resignation, which was simply and solely for the reasons I have now told you and from a sense of duty. Then came the Turkish War and all its anxieties and sorrows. I could not go at such a time of pain and distress, and our community's efforts had to be devoted to the single purpose of relieving the distress of the poor Muslims in the Balkans. But now the time has come when the community must wake up and re-organize the League on a popular and sound basis, or it will disintegrate into a self-appointed society of leaders without a following. If I continue longer in the chair of President I shall not be doing my duty, and my conscience compels

466

me to take this step. If you or any other office-bearer of the League wishes to consult me on any matter, whether privately or publicly, my advice is at your disposal. With this explanation, I place in your hands my resignation."

On Ameer Ali see K. K. Aziz, *Ameer Ali: His Life and Work*, Lahore, 1968; and M. Yusuf Abbasi, *Muslim Politics and Leadership in South Asia, 1876–1892*, Islamabad, 1981, and *The Political Biography of Syed Ameer Ali*, Lahore, 1989.

35

INDIANS IN SOUTH AFRICA AND THE EMPIRE

Speech at a Meeting Held to Protest Against the Treatment of Indians in South Africa

Bombay: 10 December 1913

Calamities in South Africa have aroused feelings throughout the Empire – solidarity of public opinion – Britain would not have tolerated similar treatment to Englishmen – British citizens of all colours and creeds entitled to protection – elementary human justice – an Imperial problem – Indians have been patient but now losing faith in Britain – many English people and statesmen sympathize with Indians – plight of the Indians – Indian civilization and ideals – the £3 tax in Natal – demand for a fair treatment for those domiciled – rights of citizenship – a conference needed to solve the problems – Indians in East Africa – the status of Zanzibar – free immigration into East Africa – appeal to the Government of India – likely consequences of non-action.

As the chairman of this public meeting it falls to my lot to echo the feelings of the people of India which the calamities that have lately occurred in South Africa have evoked throughout the length and breadth of this Empire. It is no exaggeration to say that in the modern history of India, it is impossible to find a parallel to the intensity of feeling to which Indians have been stirred by the painful occurrences in South Africa. The solidarity of public opinion in regard to this most difficult and vexatious question is indeed striking, and the fact that the requisition to the Sheriff to convene the meeting is signed by representatives of all the communities furnishes eloquent testimony to the complete unanimity of opinion that prevails in India as to the unjust and harsh treatment to which our fellow subjects in South Africa have been subjected. If such treatment were meted out to Englishmen in any foreign country it would have been treated as a "casus belli." If Disraeli, or Gladstone, or Palmerstone or Bright were alive they would have moved the whole of England by their earnestness and eloquence to see that the fair name of England for justice and equity was kept unsullied.

Everybody has heard about the plundering by a Greek mob of the house of a Jew, Don Pacifico, who was a British subject and a native of the Ionian Islands, and how a controversy about the amount and time of payment of a doubtful claim resulted in the despatch of British vessels to the Pirmus and the seizure of some Greek vessels which nearly brought on a European war. The controversy over the rights of the Jew formed the subject of a memorable debate in the House of Commons, when Lord Palmerstone contended that even the poorest man who bore the name of a British subject should be protected by the whole strength of England against the oppression of a Foreign Government. Lord Palmerstone asked for the verdict of the House to decide whether as the Roman in days of old held himself free from indignity when he could say "Civis Romanusum," so also a British subject in whatever land he might be, should feel confident that the watchful eye and the strong arm of England would protect him against injustice and wrong. The single plea of "Civis Romanus" was sufficient to obtain protection from Caesar's government. As in the case of the Roman citizen, the British subject of whatever creed or colour must be protected by the British Government from violence to his person and property wherever he went. The loyal, patient and silently toiling Indians expect that the fact of their being the subjects of His Imperial Majesty the King Emperor should be a sufficient protection of their rights of citizenship in any British colony. The Indian leaders in South Africa are willing to recognise this delicacy of the relations between the Imperial and South African Governments, but no question of difficulty should be allowed to stand in the way of elementary human justice being done. Public opinion in India cannot believe the statement that the Imperial Government is helpless in the matter.

The problem has assumed an Imperial aspect and what we desire the Imperial Government to do is to allay the feeling of injustice and humiliation which oppresses our minds. For years, the Indians in South Africa have approached some of the burning questions affecting their very existence in that country in a calm and dispassionate manner, free from prejudice and passion or oppositions to authority in the hope that antagonism to their rights of British citizenship may be argued into moderation and persuaded into compromise. But the hope has not yet been realised and their patience is exhausted. The very fact that my distinguished friend, the Hon. Mr. Gokhale, effected a compromise that was so moderate as to provoke the displeasure of some people in India proves how reasonable our fellow subjects there have been. Our brethren in South Africa have been treated as if they were the worst type of Pariah. Before the Boer War, President Kruger's Government chastised the Indian with whips, but the *Times* pointed out six years ago, the Transvaal Government were chastising the Indians with scorpions. As Lord Lansdowne has said, it was the ill-treatment of Indians before the war which called forth vehement protests from Englishmen and eminent statesmen in Great Britain. Not only have all the restrictions of Kruger's regime been maintained in all their severity, but additional and disagreeable disabilities have been imposed upon Indians who have appealed in vain to all the elementary emotions of manhood, and fellow citizenship. It is painfully obvious that the conviction that Great Britain is unable or unwilling to protect her foster children must shake their confidence in the power of the Imperial Government and deal a blow to the prestige of the Empire. We appeal to the sense of justice of the leading statesmen of the Empire to preserve the honour of British Indian subjects lawfully domiciled in a British colony. The sentiment of Empire must begin to lose its meaning, if the Indians in the Transvaal, who have the strongest claims upon British sympathy, find that England is unwilling and pleads helplessness to remove the injustice that is perpetrated on them owing to the colour prejudice of an autonomous colony.

The recent deplorable events in South Africa since the strike commenced have complicated an already grave situation, but that should not be allowed to obscure the main issue. I appeal to you all, and through you to our brethren in South Africa, not to do or say anything which will make the position of the Indian or the Imperial Government more difficult than it is at present. I admit the difficulty of self-restraint, when shocking allegations of barbarity and inhuman treatment towards the Indian settlers in the Colony have been made: but I ask you to hold your breath till an independent inquiry is made. Neither in deed nor word should we betray anything which would savour of malice or racial animosity, for we should not forget that the deep and living sympathy of many Englishmen and of some English statesmen is with us: and we should not jeopardise that sympathy by any indiscreet words or indiscriminate actions . . .

The Indians – men and women, some of whom have been born in South Africa – have been worried, harassed, and tortured by rules, regulations and taxes recognized to be unfair and unsuited to a civilised Government. This has caused bitterness throughout the Indian Empire which is as intense as it is widespread, and to ignore it is neither statesmanship nor justice on which the foundations of the British Empire are broadly based. The Hon. Mr. M. de P. Webb has pointed out in his able contribution to the *Daily Mail* that "the Indian problem in South Africa can only be solved by a frank recognition of the rights as British subjects of those Indians who have already settled there. The further immigration of trade competitors from India can be checked by mutual arrangement and consent but the competition of those Indians who have established themselves in South Africa must be fairly met by civilised manners and not by oppression, exaction and torture which India well never endure."

It is stated that it is not a question of racial prejudice, but an economic one, because the Indian "in South Africa undersells in every branch of commerce the white man, who is forced by society to maintain the position of his caste." Gentlemen, the Indians can boast of a civilisation that was far advanced when South Africa was unknown and even people in Great Britain were in a very early stage of development. Its soldiers have shed their blood for the honour and glory of the British Empire on a hundred battlefields. Indians have imbibed the ideals of freedom, independence and fairplay from the same source, and they rightly recognise – which does credit to their judgment and sense of fairplay – that unlimited Asiatic immigration into South Africa is impossible. The present movement has three aspects to be considered. The first is a £3 tax in Natal. This is a provincial one and affects only Indians in Natal whose indentures have expired. The second aspect is that the Indians who have now organised the Passive Resistance Movement aim at the rights of free movement in South Africa. They are not fighting for the free immigration of Indians in South Africa, but what they are fighting for is that those who have already been domiciled there should be treated in an honourable and civilised fashion. They are not asking for new immigration, and their demand is neither extravagant nor unjust. The third point is the determination of the rights of citizenship of Indians in the self-governing as well as the Crown Colonies, and I think a conference consisting of representatives of the Imperial Government, Colonial Government, the Indian Government and the people of India should be held with a view to settle this whole affair once for all on a satisfactory basis.

The various resolutions that will be moved by different speakers give expression to our views on the subject which has already been discussed threadbare. I will only refer to the resolution protesting against the attempts which are being made to oust the Indians from their position which by dint of industry and aptitude they acquired in Zanzibar and East Africa long before England had acquired any rights in these countries. Whatever excuses may be made by the authorities in England as to their inability to help the cause of Indians in South Africa, they have not even a shadow of excuse for forcing Indians in East Africa to endure a similar treatment unless they wish simply to please a few thousand white settlers in East Africa.

Gentlemen, let us warn our rulers in time not to barter away the prestige of England for justice throughout India in order to please a few white Imperialists – Imperialists of the well known type of Lord Cranworth, whose rabid and bitter attack on Indians in East Africa shows the temper of the White Imperialists to whose tender mercies our people in East Africa are ultimately to be handed over. There is also a persistent rumour – of course with the stereotyped denial that one knows too well – that Zanzibar is to be kindly handed over by Sir Edward Grey to Germany for the sake of some concession on the Shat-ul-Arab and at Bussra. It is high time that even Sir Edward Grey realised that the people of India and their interests should not be sacrificed as if they were mere pawns in the Imperial game; or cattle on an Imperial Estate, India being already referred to by a certain type of white Imperialists as an Imperial Estate. This type of Imperialist in his heart of hearts looks upon us as the livestock in that estate. We have every right to protest against our interests being disposed of in such a summary manner. We must make it clear at once that in the first place we want justice done to our brethren in South Africa already domiciled in that country and their honour and dignity preserved as citizens of the British Empire: secondly, we appeal with all the fervour at our command that the status of Zanzibar be kept intact, and thirdly we want to impress on the Imperial authorities that nothing can be done in British East Africa further to prejudice the position of His Majesty's Indian subjects there or their free immigration into the country without bringing on a struggle worse than that in South Africa. These moderate and minimum demands must be made clear to our rulers in England at any price ...

I venture to make one more appeal, and that is to the Government of India not to allow the status of Indians in East Africa to be changed to their disadvantage. I am convinced that if the state of affairs goes from bad to worse in South as well as East Africa and Canada and other colonies, it will render the task of peaceful Government in India impossible . . .

Source: *The Times of India*, Bombay, 17 December 1913.

Considering the importance and significance of this meeting I reproduce below the report of it given in *The Times of India* of 17 December:

"On Wednesday evening, at a mass meeting which packed the Town Hall to the doors, Bombay joined in the protest that is being made throughout India against the treatment of Indians in South Africa, at the same time thanking the Viceroy and Lord Ampthill for their championship of their cause and appealing to the Government and in the last resort to the King Emperor to intervene on their behalf and also taking advantage of the opportunity to protest against the attempts to infringe upon the liberties of Indian subjects in other colonies.

"The meeting was attended by representatives of every section of the Indian community in Bombay, and on the platform was also a small sprinkling of Europeans. It lasted nearly two and a half hours and was marked by unusual enthusiasm, which was especially pronounced while Sir Pherozeshah Mehta and Sir Narayen Chandavarkar, who had come to Bombay from Indore in order to be present at the meeting, were speaking. There were in all over 22 speakers, but the principal speeches were delivered by His Highness the Aga Khan, who in spite of ill-health took the chair, this being his first public appearance since his return to India, Sir Pherozeshah Mehta, and Sir Narayen Chandavarkar.

"The tone of all the speeches was very similar, and the argument of the Aga Khan that if the same treatment had been meted out to Englishmen in a foreign country as had been meted out to Indians in South Africa it would have been treated as a "casus belli" was echoed by several of the subsequent speakers, as well as His Highness' declaration that the problem was an Imperial one. The Aga Khan, however, sounded a warning note lest there should be a betrayal of anything which would savour of racial prejudice which would jeopardise the sympathy which Indians at present commanded and paid a tribute of praise to the Viceroy for his recent declaration at Madras.

"Most of the speakers who followed His Highness modelled their speeches on similar lines. Sir Pherozeshah, in a vigorous address, said the outlook in India could not be viewed with equanimity if the grievances of Indians in South Africa were not redressed and that controversies of this character brought out more and more the gravity of the white and colour peril. Sir Narayen Chandavarkar referred especially to the marriage question, and declared that the South African Government had given them an example of legal fraud. All the resolutions that were proposed were carried with enthusiasm.

"Among those present at the meeting were: the Hon. Sir Jamsetji Jijibhoy; Sir Dinshaw Petit; Sir Cowasji Jehangir; Sir Narayen Chandavarkar; the Hon. Sir Pherozeshah Mehta; the Hon. Sir Ibrahim Rahimtulla; Mr. Mahomedbboy Currimbhoy; the Hon. Mr. Fazulbhoy M. Chinoy; Mr. H. A. Wadia; Dr. Stanley Reed; Mr. B. G. Horniman; the Rev. Dr. Scott; Mr. Purshotamdas Thakordas; the Hon. Mr. Manmohandas Ramji; Sir Vithaldas D. Thackersey; Mr. H. P. Modi; Mr. Cowasji Jehangir; Mr. Narotum Morarji Gokuldas; Mr. G. Khatav; Mr Pheroz

473

Hosang Dastur; Mr. K. Natarajan, Khan Bahadur Kersaspji Dadachanji and others.

"A number of telegrams were received sympathising with the movement from His Highness the Gaekwar, who contributed Rs. 5,500 to the Transvaal Indians' Relief fund, from the Raja Saheb of Bansda, who gave Rs. 500, from the Maharaja of Panna and almost all important towns in the Presidency. A donation of Rs. 10,000 was announced from the Aga Khan, and other donations announced were:- Sir Dorab J. Tata (in addition to Rs. 5,000 already paid), Rs. 5,000; Lady Tata Rs. 1,000; H. H. The Maharaja of Cooch Behar Rs. 1,000; H. H. the Maharaja of Bhavnagar, Rs. 1,000.

"The Aga Khan, whose election to the chair was proposed by Sir Cowasji Jehangir and seconded by the Hon. Mr. Manmohandas Ramji, recieved an ovation on rising to address the meeting.

"The first resolution stood in the name of the Hon. Sir Pherozeshah Mehta and was as follows:–

'That this public meeting of the citizens of Bombay expresses its entire sympathy with their countrymen and countrywomen in South Africa in the sufferings and privations borne by them in their patriotic and united endeav-ours for the removal of the racial, social and economic disabilities imposed by the recent Immigration Restriction Act.

It promises them the whole-hearted support, moral and material, of the public of this city and of the Bombay Presidency in their righteous struggle against such disabilities and particularly to secure full recognition of the validity of marriages contracted within or without the South African Union according to Indian religious rites; and to obtain the repeal of the iniquitous £3 Tax in Natal on ex-indentured Indians and their wives and children.

It exhorts the people of this country of all classes and creeds to subscribe liberally to the funds that are being collected to help their fellow countrymen in their self-sacrificing campaign in vindication of India's honour and of her peoples' rights as equal subjects of His Majesty the King Emperor.

And it appeals to His Majesty's Government to intervene on behalf of His Majesty's Indian subjects and to insist on the observance by the Union government of those pledges and promises of which the non-fulfilment has compelled the revival of passive resistance; and in the last to exercise the right which vest [sic] in the Crown to veto the Act of which the results are certain to be most injurious to the best interests of India and of the British Empire.'

"The Hon. Sir Pherozeshah Mehta, who was enthusiastically received, at the outset announced that he was not going to make a long speech. For, he added, in the longest speech he might make what could he tell but a thrice told tale of woe and suffering, of patience and resignation, and above all that blessed word moderation, suffered by their fellow countrymen and countrywomen in South Africa, which had stirred their hearts and the hearts of the country to the depths? Sir Pherozeshah referred to a statement which had been made in one newspaper that the agitation had done one thing, which was to show that there were political agitators who, while far removed from the extremists, were perfectly prepared to use all the means in their power to embarrass the Government. The comment Sir Pherozeshah had to make on this statement was that the writer had utterly failed to realise the depth and intensity of the feeling which pervaded the whole country and had failed to realise the sufferings of their fellow men and women in South Africa.

"Asking himself what it was that Indians in South Africa had been – not fighting for – but pleading and praying for, Sir Pherozeshah rapidly traced the trouble from its origin, and declared that it was deplorable that the British Empire should not repress its own subjects from doing what it was ready to resent with all the force of war against foreigners. The effect it would produce upon the loyal people of India was an effect which one could scarcely contemplate with equanimity and a full sense of the benefits of British rule. As to the moderation of the Indian in South Africa, Sir Pherozeshah pointed out that the poor Indian had never commenced by taking up a defiant or aggravating attitude. He begged and prayed and pointed out that he was ready to help the British in the Boer War, and he asked for no more than that he should be allowed the simplest rights of free citizenship. No ear was given to what he urged until, utterly baffled, he resorted to the one weapon which a loyal but firm asserter of the rights of his own country and resort to passive resistance. Sir Pherozeshah spoke of the results of the passive resistance movement and of the modesty of the Indian demands, observing that he was one who had always held, and always would hold, that a subject of His Majesty had a right of free entry and free access to any part of the Empire and that was the reason he had disagreed with some of his friends in India. Mr. [M. K.] Gandhi was a great believer in reason and in argument. He called him an unpractical man, and with all the admiration he had for Mr. Gandhi he disagreed with him on this point. He asked for too little (Laughter). If he had asked for the full rights of every Indian for access to the British dominions and had stuck to the full demand he might have got something. (Laughter). It was a great blunder, but it showed the reasonable character of the campaign led by Mr. Gandhi. He was again at the old game. What was the result? No-one would listen to him, and still Indians in South Africa were asked to practice moderation!

"The situation had developed in a way which had caused intense pain to the people of India, continued Sir Pherozeshah. And they were told, "What can Her Majesty's ministers do in a matter of this character, which concerns the internal government and domestic discipline of a self-governing colony?" They were bound under all circumstances to speak with respect of the high authorities of the Crown, but it was impossible not to tell them that the people of India could not but consider that they had not been granted that protection to the Indian subjects of His Majesty which the ministers of the Crown were bound to accord to the millions of subjects residing in the Indian Empire. It was a piece of singularly good fortune that they had at this moment at the head of the destinies of the Indian administration one who had proved himself one of the greatest and noblest of Viceroys, a man cast in a large mould in every way, a high-minded, a high souled, a large hearted statesman who had fully realised that no sound statesmanship could be founded on anything but justice, righteousness and sympathy. Lord Hardinge had done a service to the English Rule in India by the grave and significant words he spoke at Madras. The people in England did not fully realise the great service he had done, and when they could not but be disappointed by the way in which the ministers of the Crown had been treating the question they found themselves consoled by the thought that the Viceroy had all his feelings for them, all his sympathies for them, and suffered with them.

"It was a blunder of a most serious character that Indians should be allowed to think that while the white race could enter all the fairest places on the earth's surface, at the same time they could lay down the principle that all the other races must not enter the places they had occupied. It became a very serious question, and though they might talk of the yellow peril and the black peril, controversies of this character would bring out more and more the gravity and the reasons of the white and colour peril. Asia and Europe might find themselves confronted with a very serious controversy with regard to this question. He was not a prophet, but he thought that European statesmen had better take warning that while they claimed the right of going over the whole world it was a grave mistake to set out too definitely the policy that they would prevent other races from going into parts occupied by the white races. Lord Hardinge had fully realised the volume of feeling there was in India regarding the treatment of Indians in South Africa, and they must appeal to him to approach if necessary even the foot of the Throne to ask that the veto of the Crown might be exercised and both in the interests of England and India implore their ruler to bring about a reasonable solution of the question.

"Sir Narayan Chandavarkar, in seconding the resolution said the situation in South Africa, the oppressive and inhuman treatment to which their countrymen had been subjected there in the name of law and government was bad enough but the worst of it was that it would do incalculable harm to British prestige if the Imperial Government would not put forth all its power and get the wrong redressed. The South African Government had given them a concrete example of legal fraud, for when a Government promised to maintain existing rights under and by means of a proposed law and then trampled those rights under foot in the name of that very law by employing language to conceal its thoughts and break its faith, it was law legalising fraud. And the comic feature of the situation, – for tragic as the situation was, a question of life and death to British Indians resident in South Africa – it had its humorous side also, the comic feature of the situation was that these marriages were declared illegal because the Union Government professed to have a tender Christian conscience, in favour of monogamy. He had no doubt they all respected that conscience; they venerated the founder of that religion and his apostle who saw in marriage a spiritual fellowship of one soul with another soul. But what would the founder of Christianity and his apostle have said to the South African Pharisees who in his name condemned as a concubine a woman, the sole wife of her husband, merely because the religion according to which she married allowed polygamy! If that was polygamy, with equal ingenuity and Pharisaism they might argue that a Christian marriage was polygamous because it was allowable to a Christian to divorce his only wife and marry another. This sort of cant about polygamy was an insult to law and humanity; for, be it remembered, to the credit of India and Indians that though polygamy was allowed, only eleven in a thousand were polygamous, that was about one per cent.; and the better instinct of India had always been for monogamy and monogamous man had been the object of admiration and imitation, as for instance the hero of Ramayana. The South African policy with reference to British Indians resident there had been a blot on that very civilisation and that very religion whose name the Union Government invoked in defence of their wrongs towards their fellow-countrymen there. It was said and said truly that the cause they had met to further was an Imperial Cause – the cause and the prestige of the British Empire. To say of it that they pleaded for humane treatment for their countrymen in South Africa was to do it but inadequate justice and narrow their vision. There was a larger, nobler, wider and more practical view – the real object and effect of the South African policy which they condemned was to drive the free Indian back to indenture and perpetual slavery within British dominions after what Britain had done to exterminate slavery in every form and written her name in the imperishable book of life, not merely in the pages of history as the champion of liberty and the stern enemy of all Governments that made slaves of God's men, whatever their race. South Africa was now trying to blot out that book and tear those pages and the question of the hour was – "How long shall that go on?"

"The Hon. Sir Ibrahim Rahimtulla, in supporting the resolution, concurred with all that had been said by the previous speakers.

"Mr. Jehangir B. Petit, further supporting the resolution, observed that what they demanded was that once and for all the status of Indians in South Africa and other self-governing colonies should be determined in a way which was compatible with their honour and prestige as citizens of the British Empire.

"The resolution was carried unanimously.

"Sir Jamsetji Jeejeebhoy next proposed:–

'That this meeting conveys to His Excellency the Viceroy its profound grati-tude for the emphatic manner in which he has associated himself with the appeal of His Majesty's Indian subjects to fair and honourable treatment in South Africa, and begs to assure His Excellency that he has greatly strength-ened the foundations of British Rule, in the hearts and affections of the Indian people.'

"The resolution, he said, touched upon the only bright episode in the gloomy tragedy that was being enacted in South Africa at the present moment. When the situation in South Africa assumed an aspect full of danger from more points of view than one, the people of India turned instinctively for help and sympathy to the Viceroy on whom they had learnt to rely with absolute confidence. And they were not disappointed. His utterance had been variously criticised. It had been denounced as factless by those who in their handling of the question had not shown any conspicuous tact themselves. It had been attacked as unstatesmanlike by persons whose conceptions of statesmanship were to say the least, peculiar. But the three hundred millions of India had hailed the pronouncement with feelings of profound satisfaction and gratitude. It had soothed their wounded feelings; it had come as an assurance to them, that at this critical juncture, the Indian people were not entirely voiceless or helpless, but they had at the head of affairs a man who sympathised with them in their trials, who was not afraid to publicly avow that sympathy, nor slow in protesting with all the weight and authority of his high office, against the harsh and unjust treatment of the subjects of one part of His Majesty's dominions by those of another. How greatly this had relieved a situation which had elements in it of danger, would never be fully realised. It was certain, however, that it had done much to restore public confidence in the integrity and sympathy of the Government, and to place on a firmer basis, that deep-seated loyalty of the masses, which was being put to a greater strain than any it had yet received. For this India offered its profound gratitude to Lord Hardinge, and assured him that by his courageous and statesmanlike attitude he had greatly strength-ened the foundations of British rule and brought the throne closer to the hearts of the Indian people. And long after the memories of this bitter struggle had died away, they would recall with thankfulness the great service which the Viceroy had rendered to India and the empire at large. Their thanks were also due to the Secretary of State for India for his recent sympathetic utterance, and they earnestly hoped that he and his colleagues in the Cabinet would not only recognise the justice of their claims, but be also able to secure for them due recognition by the Union Government.

"Mr. Mahomedbhoy Currimbhoy, in seconding the resolution, declared that H. E. the Viceroy had undoubtedly strengthened the foundations of British rule in the hearts and affections of the Indian people by his chivalrous and manly stand on behalf of the people of India. Mr. Mahomedbhoy went on to reply to the criticisms which had been made regarding the Viceroy's pronouncement. Were they to be told, he asked, that while the South African Government was entitled to say and do what it liked in the name of South African public opinion the head of the Government of India should speak with bated breath and whisper humbleness when he pleaded for bare justice for the Indian subjects of the King Emperor domiciled in that colony? Was it well that it should be allowed to go forth to the three hundred millions of the Indian subjects of His Majesty that the head of the Government of India was condemned and criticised by a section of the British Press because he ventured to demand fair play and civilised treatment for their countrymen in South Africa. His Excellency had rendered invaluable service to every part of the Empire by his prompt and timely protest.

"The Hon. Mr. Lalubhai Samaldas, supporting the resolution, said the *Westminster Gazette*, a liberal paper, had said that when diplomats broke loose, there was no limit to which the people went. They all knew what self-restraint the Viceroy had exhibited and he asked who should take up the righteous cause of the Indians if not the Viceroy, who was at the head of the Indian Government?

"The resolution was carried by acclamation.

"Mr. H. A. Wadia moved:–

'That this meeting places on record the feelings of indignation with which the people of India have been filled by the reports of the cruel treatment of their countrymen in South Africa who are taking part in the strikes, and expresses its earnest conviction that nothing short of a full and impartial enquiry into the allegations made, will satisfy public opinion in this country, and respectfully insists that Indians should be adequately represented among those entrusted with the task of carrying out such enquiry.'

"In support of the resolution, Mr. Wadia drew a picture of the sufferings of Indians in the Transvaal. Replying to those who preached moderation to Indians, Mr. Wadia said that those who gave them counsel of moderation had not the honesty to acknowledge that Mr. Gandhi and his followers had refrained from enhancing the trouble of the Union Government by declining to join the strike movement when trouble arose on the gold mines at the Rand. He submitted that the strike of Indians was not a strike against the employers, but it was a protest against the Union Government for not keeping their faith with Indians and breaking their promise given to Mr. Gandhi and others that the £3 tax would be removed. He admitted that there were conflicting statements as to the allegations of barbarity and oppression, but said that was greater reason why a searching enquiry was necessary. It was necessary that Indians should be represented on the enquiry and if the allegations of cruelty were well-founded then those who brought shame on the Empire should be punished. There would be no peace in the country until justice was done to Indians. If the enquiry was granted, the loyalty of Indians towards His Majesty's Government, which was sincere and deep, would be further strengthened by their faith in British justice and British statesmanship.

"Dr. Stanley Reed who seconded the resolution, observed that because he did so in a sentence they must not believe that his sympathy for the cause was not as great as those who had made long and eloquent speeches. What they wanted in this matter was to find out the truth, and that object could be achieved by an enquiry of the kind they demanded.

"Mr. Purshotamdas Thakordas supported the proposition, which was carried unanimously.

"The Hon. Mr. V. J. Patel moved that the best thanks of the people of India be conveyed to Lord Ampthill for his consistent, unwavering and whole-hearted championship of the cause of Indians in South Africa.

"The resolution was seconded by Mr. K. Natrajan and carried.

"Mr. B. G. Horniman next moved:- 'That this meeting protests against (a) the attempts which are being made to oust Indians from their position which, by dint of their industry and aptitudes they have acquired in British East Africa and Zanzibar, and appeals the Government of India to protect the interests of its subjects against the machinations of those who wish to lower their status and to restrict their opportunities in this Crown Colony, and (b) the special restrictions placed on the admission of Indians to Canada, exceeding those applicable to the Japanese and Chinese by means of the law requiring as a condition of admission, immigrants to make a thorough journey from their country of origin to the Dominions, and against the obstacles placed in the way of admitting the wives and minor children of Indians who are domiciled in Canada."

"Mr. Horniman sounded a warning note with regard to what was happening and what might happen in the colonies mentioned in the resolution in connection with the position of the Indian community.

"Mr. H. P. Mody seconded, and Mr. K. T. Kaderbhoy supported the resolution, which was adopted.

"On the motion of Mr. Narotamdas Morarji Gokuldas, a vote of thanks was passed to the Sheriff, the Hon. Mr. F. M. Chinoy, for convening the meeting.

"On the motion of the Hon. Sir P. M. Mehta, a vote of thanks was passed to H. H. the Aga Khan for presiding at the meeting."

On the problem of Indians in South Africa see Mian Fazl-i-Husain, *Indians Abroad: The Hon. Sir Fazl-i-Husain's Statement on the Position of Indians in Africa*, Bombay, 1930; Shafaat Ahmad Khan, *The Indians in South Africa*, Allahabad, 1946; R. M. Hampson, *Islam in South Africa: A Bibliography*, Cape Town, 1964; T. R. H. Davenport, *South Africa: A Modern History*, London, 1977; J. J. C. Greyling and J. Miskin, *Bibliography on Indians in South Africa*, Durban, 1976; E. Hellmann (ed.), *Handbook on Race Relations in South Africa*, Cape Town, 1949; C. W. de Kiewiet, *A History of South Africa: Social and Economic*, London, 1941; E. G. Malherbe, *Education in South Africa, Vol. I, 1652–1922*, Cape Town, 1925; *Vol. II, 1923–1975*, Cape Town, 1977; B. Pachai, *The International Aspect of the South African Indian Question, 1860–1971*, Cape Town, 1971; B. Pachai (ed.), *South Africa's Indians: The Evolution of a Minority*, Washington, DC, 1979; H. J. and R. E. Simons, *Class and Colour in South Africa, 1850–1950*, Harmondsworth, 1969; M. Wilson and L. M. Thompson (eds.), *The Oxford History of South Africa, Vol. II, 1870–1966*, Oxford, 1971; and Robert A. Huttenback, "Indians in South Africa, 1860–1914: The British Imperial Philosophy on Trial", *English Historical Review*, April 1966.

36

THE INDIAN MUSLIM OUTLOOK

An Article

London: January 1914

Crisis in the London branch of the Muslim League – restlessness among Muslims – alleged Pan-Islamic agitation – recent press reports from India – Indian Muslims and intervention by Christian Powers in Muslim lands – roots of Muslim solidarity among all sects – British foreign policy and sentiments of 100 million Muslim subjects of Britain – British support for the Bulgarian aggression in Thrace – Indian Muslims favour friendship between Britain and the Ottoman Empire – need for a strong and stable Turkish government – independence of Persia – railways in Persia – impact of education on Indian Muslims – moderate elements in India – work of the All India Muslim League and the London League – rally the moderates – need to promote economic development – provide opportunities to Indians to study in England – remove disabilities on Indians in South Africa – allow loyal but free criticism – consider the general consensus of opinion.

1. The Preaching of Islam. By Professor T. W. ARNOLD, C.I.E. Revised and enlarged edition. Constable. 1913.
2. Moral and Material Progress of India. Report for 1911–2. H. o. C. 220. 1913.
3. "The Times" articles on Indian Mussulmans. April 19, October 7 and 31, November 8, 1913, and other dates.

During the present winter special attention has been directed to Indian Moslem affairs by an acute crisis in the London Branch of the All-India Moslem League, the organisation which represents the political views of the community.

For more than two years past the Moslems of India, in common with their co-religionists in other countries, have been going through most painful experiences. The Turkish loss of sovereignty in Northern Africa and in the Balkans, the continued disintegration of Persia, the treatment of Indians in South Africa, and certain matters of Indian administration, have all deeply affected Indian Moslems. The resulting restlessness among them has led to much searching of heart among their best friends, while in some quarters exaggerated ideas have been entertained as to the effect of these events upon the hearty loyalty hitherto shown by the community to the British Crown.

Lurid caricatures of the Moslem attitude, such as that drawn in "The Times" of October 7 last by "A Correspondent in India," are to be deplored, since they tend to suspicion and estrangement on both sides. It might well be the duty of a writer anxious to awaken the British public from a fool's paradise to be strident in tone, if his note of alarm was based upon full knowledge and free from prejudice. But this correspondent puts himself out of court as a competent and fair-minded witness in the very first sentence of his communication. He says:

"It is probable that the Balkan war would not have greatly influenced the bulk of Indian Mahommedans had it not been for the efforts of the Pan-Islamic agitators and their organs in the Press."

He does not produce, and I believe he cannot produce, a single quotation to show that there has been a Pan-Islamic agitation in the political sense which his words, taken in connexion with the general tone of his article, seem intended to convey. If he means only that the Moslem Press of India has made the troubles of Turkey a subject of constant lamentation and has strongly criticised the policy of the Concert of Europe in general and of Great Britain in particular in that connexion, I accept the statement, though I take grave exception to the deduction drawn and to the prejudicial form in which it is conveyed. This correspondent might just as reasonably argue that Mr. Lloyd George's land campaign would attract no attention from the agricultural voter if the Liberal Press of England did not keep the question in view; or that the problem of Ulster would be non-existent but for the newspaper notice it attracts. He mistakes cause for effect, and forgets that even a Press so new and crude as that of the Indian Moslems, like the Press of other countries, has to give its readers information on public matters in which they are most interested and must more or less reflect their attitude upon them.

The best answer to his suggestion that the Moslems would have felt no interest in the fate of Turkey if they had not been stirred up by agitators of doubtful loyalty is to be found in the clear-cut statement of the skilful publicist who is the Bombay correspondent of the same journal. Writing in "The Times" of the 19th of April 1913, when Moslem feeling was at its height and had not been mollified by the Turkish re-conquest of Adrianople, he said:

> "Let there be no misunderstanding of the real attitude of Indian Mahommedan opinion towards Turkey. There is much discussion in Europe of the position of the Sultan as Khalif. The Indian Moslem does not recognise the Sultan as Khalif, and offers him no allegiance in that capacity. But he does look upon Turkey as the embodiment of the temporal power of Islam, and he has no desire to see Islam reduced to the position of Israel, a religion without temporal status. This feeling affects all classes." ... "An old Mahommedan friend of mine, a graduate of an English university, assured me that when the news of the battle of Lulu Burgas arrived he felt that the only course for him was to commit suicide."

"A Correspondent in India" contrasts the position now with that of 1897 and admits that there is insufficient ground for the view, then entertained in some quarters, that the great frontier rising was largely attributable to Moslem feeling on the Turco-Greek war. When, however, he goes on to say that internal India was hardly moved by that war, I deny his statement. Moslem India was not indifferent; far from it. It was the only topic of conversation or interest in Moslem society, and every mosque was illuminated throughout India, even in the small villages of the Deccan, to celebrate the success of the Turks. Nor does the "Correspondent in India" take into consideration the great and rapid changes which these sixteen years have brought, including the spread of education among Indian Moslems and the much fuller and more speedy dissemination of foreign news. Moreover, the Ottoman trouble in 1897 was limited to its relations with Greece, and no other Mahommedan State was involved; whereas in the last two or three years the Moslem world has watched with grave misgiving and concern the supersession or control of Mussulman sovereignty by the intervention of Christian Powers in Morocco, in Tripoli, in the greater part of European Turkey, and in Persia. The cumulative effect of these continued losses of Moslem sovereignty on Indian Mahommedans has been reinforced by the spread of Western enlightenment among them.

It is idle for "A Correspondent in India" to lament the passing of the day when the Moslem community, in its apathy and ignorance, did not concern itself with international politics – if indeed that day ever existed. The Hindus have no sentimental interests outside India, apart from those provided by the emigration of co-religionists to other portions of the Empire; their Mecca is Benares; their Holy Waters are those of the Ganges, not of the Euphrates or Tigris. In the days when they alone of the chief Indian communities interested themselves in public affairs it was natural that audible Indian opinion should be confined to the internal affairs of India and her relations with Great Britain. But the Mahommedans, newly awakened to national consciousness by the education England has given them, are not limited in their gaze by the vast ramparts of the Himalayas or by the waters of the Indian Ocean. There is between them and their fellow-believers in other lands an essential unity, which breaks through differences of sect and country, for it is not based on religious grounds alone. Carlyle somewhere says that all men of the English-speaking race are subjects of King Shakespeare, and in the same way all Mussulmans are subjects of the "Arabian Nights." They share the glorious heritage not only of the Koran (which they are taught in early childhood to read in the original Arabic) but of the history and philosophy of Arabia, the incomparable poetry of Persia, and the romances and legends of Egypt and Morocco and Spain. Drinking from these imperishable springs, Moslems, whether Turks, Persians, Arabs or Indians, and whether or not they have also come to the Western wells of knowledge, are bound together by a certain unity of thought, of sentiment, and of expression. The feeling of brotherhood thus engendered is not dammed up within the confines of devout faith. On the contrary, agnostics and atheists of Moslem origin have felt the Turkish and Persian misfortunes just as much as the most orthodox mullah. To ask why the Indian Mussulman, blest with a beneficent rule, should concern himself so much about international issues affecting co-religionists, is as futile as asking why men on the rack of torture cry out with physical pain. That the excitement has not been connected with the question of the Caliphate is shown by the fact that Shias have been moved by these emotions no less strongly than Sunnis. All sections of the

Moslem world are moved by a deep sentiment, originally called into being by the Prophet's summons of all the faithful into one great brotherhood and welded through the centuries into a lasting bond by a common faith, a common literature, a common outlook, and a common history.

Discussing in the new edition of his erudite "Preaching of Islam" the causes of the continued spread of the faith in the almost entire absence of systematic missionary organisation, Professor T. W. Arnold lays stress on the non-political Pan-Islamic movement rendered possible to a degree undreamt of by earlier generations by modern means of communication, and seeking to bind all nations of the Moslem world in a common bond of sympathy:

> "This trend of thought gives a powerful stimulus to missionary labours; the effort to realise in actual life the Moslem ideal of brotherhood of all believers reacts on collateral ideals of the faith, and the sense of a vast unity and of a common life running through the nations, inspirits the hearts of the faithful and makes them bold to speak in the presence of the unbelievers; . . . The spiritual energy of Islam is not, as has been so often maintained, commensurate with its political power."

During the currency of the Balkan war we were needlessly told that Great Britain could not allow her international policy to be dictated by the wishes of the King's Moslem subjects. For this no sane Mussulman asks. It is obvious that a great variety of factors have to be taken into account in the shaping of British foreign policy; but surely one of these, which should be entitled to the fullest consideration is the sentiment of a people, nearly 100 millions of whom are under the sovereignty or protection of King George. It should at least be held as a working thesis for the Foreign Office that when British interests generally coincide with Moslem wishes, the combination is advantageous. But when the Prime Minister publicly lectured the Porte for reoccupying Adrianople by force of arms and warned her to clear out, Indian Moslems asked in vain what British interests would be served by turning Turkey out of Adrianople and installing the Bulgarians against the wishes of the inhabitants. I have a firm conviction that if important British interests were disturbed by Turkish policy – if, for example, we can imagine the Ottoman Government threatening the independence of Holland or Belgium – the Indian Moslems would give no moral support to such a policy, and indeed would loyally uphold England in taking active measures for its frustration. But why should England have gone out of her way to support Bulgarian aggression in Thrace, contrary to the strong wishes of her Moslem subjects, and to local sentiment and interests?

The events of the last two years have not shaken the conviction of Indian Moslems that Great Britain in her own interests should be the friend and supporter of the Ottoman power. It is all very well to say that the Young Turks have forfeited the hopes and good wishes entertained when they overthrew the Hamidian *régime*. It is not fair to judge the administrative capacity of a people unversed in the great art of constitutional government when they are engaged in a life-and-death struggle, brought upon them in the first instance by the unprovoked aggression of one of the Great Powers of Europe. Their dissensions, and at some critical moments their incompetence, have to be recognised; but they must be judged by their powers of statesmanship when there is some recovery from the exhaustion of the fighting and tumults of the last two years, and the great and difficult work of reconstruction has been entered upon. After all, their misdeeds bear no comparison with those of the sanguinary Commune ushering in the Third Republic of France, which has now stood unshaken the test of more than forty years' existence.

Indian Moslems strongly hold that in the reconstructive work before the Constantinople Government the moral support of Great Britain is called for in her own interests. The break-up of Turkey and the partition of her Asiatic provinces must be disadvantageous to Great Britain in any conceivable scheme of distribution. France would lay claim to Syria, Germany to Anatolia with Northern and Central Mesopotamia, and Russia to Kurdistan and Armenia. Great Britain would be left to take Arabia and Southern Mesopotamia, and would thus become possessed of another wild country without possibilities of great development and with a long and exposed frontier. Side by side with this cumbersome and barren increase of territorial responsibility, the British Empire would be brought into closer contact with the great continental Powers whose immense armies would be less dependent on the sea for their communications. The route to India, already removed from exclusively British keeping, would then be further exposed to attack by several other Powers. For these reasons a strong and stable Turkish Government in Asia ought to be a cardinal principle of British international policy. To Mahommedans it is reassuring to know that the above considerations are duly recognised by the just and wise statesman who now rules India. Lord Hardinge won the grateful thanks of the community by the ready encouragement he gave to their practical sympathy with the Turkish troops and people by placing himself at the head of the Red Crescent movement, which was so splendidly responded to by all classes of Moslems. He has further consoled and gratified Mahommedans by the assurance he gave in the Imperial Legislative Council on the 17th of September last, that:

"The British Government, who fully realise the importance of the existence of Turkey as an independent Power, and, in view of the religious interests of the Mahommedans of India, the necessity for the maintenance of the *status quo* as regards the Holy Places in Arabia, are still anxious and ready to help the Turkish Government to introduce reforms and good government, and to consolidate the position of Turkey. There is absolutely no reason why Turkey, while pursuing a steady policy of reforms, should not still be strong and powerful and the second greatest Mahommedan Power in the world."

The Indian Moslems are also grateful to Lord Hardinge for the withdrawal of the regiment of the Central India Horse which was sent to Southern Persia some time ago, and for his recognition in the speech just quoted of the anxiety of the Moslem peoples that no step should be taken calculated to further weaken the sovereignty and independence of Iran. But they feel that Great Britain has been far too complaisant in respect to the arbitrary proceedings of Russia in the north. Mindful of the history of Muscovite absorption of the Central Asian Khanates, they fear that annexation, in fact if not expressly in name, will be the inevitable sequel of Russian policy. If Russia took the north, England would have to make another Afghanistan, much less easily defensible, out of the south. The Indian Moslems are also concerned to see Great Britain taking part with apparent readiness in the formulation of projects for a trans-Persian railway that can benefit only Russia. Great Britain continually claims to be the friend of Persia, and it may be hoped that she will exercise the duties and privileges of friendship by giving moral and financial support only to railways designed for Persia's commercial development instead of consenting to a strategical line through the unpeopled deserts of Yezd, Kerman, and Baluchistan. Any line designed to develop Persian or Anglo-Indian commerce would run from the head waters of the Gulf to the centres of population in Persian Irak and join the Russian section at Ispahan. But a trans-continental line for the convenience of travellers to India, and avoiding all the potentially rich parts of Persia, will do little or nothing to regenerate that country or further develop Anglo-Indian trade. In this matter also British and Moslem interests converge. A railway through Eastern Persia into India would be a constant menace on the frontier, and British participation or acquiescence therein would be at variance with the traditional policy pursued with watchful vigilance and at heavy if necessary cost to India for a century past.

The Indian Moslem does not ask for the surrender of any British interests; he simply points out that these interests are in accord with Moslem sentiment and wishes. Yet his incursion into international politics is frowned upon in reactionary Anglo-Indian quarters as if it were in some mysterious and inexplicable way disloyal. People who make these charges might reflect that the Mussulmans of India gain absolutely nothing for themselves, in any material or political sense, from the preservation of the Moslem States; they are simply animated by the sentiments of unity and brotherhood above referred to, which are stronger than these unsympathetic and unimaginative critics can realise.

But with the Turkish reoccupation and retention of Adrianople the tension has been relaxed and the Indian Moslems are once more turning their thoughts to internal affairs. The critics have been perturbed by the appearance on the scene of a new type of Moslem, who, apart from Islamic religion and sentiment, has gone through exactly the same education and training as young Hindus of the same social class. This type did not formerly exist, for in the old days the Hindu and the Mussulman of the same social class were brought up on an entirely different educational basis. The young Mussulman had to make it his chief concern to be well cultured in Persian and Arabic. There were thus few points of contact between Mahommedan and Hindu, and, in the stage of political development India had reached, much less ground for and possibility of unity of effort than now. Take any typical young Mahommedan of the upper middle classes today, and it will be found that, apart from the traditional religion of his family inculcated by his mother, his education has been entirely on the lines of a Hindu of the same class. Even in the case of a student from a Moslem institution like the Aligarh College, the course of studies, the training of the teachers and their outlook, and the probable profession of the student in the future, are the same as in a Government or a Hindu college.

These considerations are even more applicable to the increasing throng of Moslems coming to England and joining Hindu fellow-countrymen at the Universities, the Inns of Court, and the Technical Schools. This potent change, which has attracted much less attention than it has deserved, is not much if any older than the still youthful twentieth century, and it has only begun to make itself felt effectively in actual political life within the last two or three years. The men brought up under the new system are coming to the front, and have influenced the increasing approximation of political views and sentiments among educated men of the different communities. This unity is a measure of the growth of Indian nationhood, and it is the part of wise statesmanship, British and Indian, in the domain of internal affairs, to seek, not so much to satisfy the Mussulmans as Mussulmans or the Hindus as Hindus, as to win the hearty co-operation of all moderate, loyal, and reasonable opinion, wherever it exists. It is the only policy that will succeed, in Lord Morley's phrase, in "rallying the Moderates," and thus forming the most effective instrument in the discomfiture and impotence of the small but active element in Indian life which, as Lord Sydenham has said, must be reckoned as permanently hostile to British rule. While at the one extreme there is a handful of revolutionaries, at the other there is a worthy, substantial but decreasing class of men of the old school who think it right to accept whatever the Government, or even the officials, may decree without exercising any critical faculty thereon. But between these two there is a vast mass of Indian opinion passing through a transition stage, alert, sometimes fault-finding, perhaps suspicious, perhaps not very clearly knowing what it wants, and greatly perplexed and disheartened by such questions as the treatment of Indians in South Africa, greatly anxious and worried about the future of Indians in East Africa and in the island of Zanzibar. With all his weaknesses, this type of man, if rightly handled, is essentially reasonable at bottom, loyal to the King, and fully aware that India's welfare and happiness depend on the continuance of British rule.

The Moslem community may co-operate with the Hindus on a vast number of public questions, but they have their own special needs and outlook, not confined to the international issues to which I have referred. Both the educational and political condition of the Hindus is far in advance in time and also in relative extent, of that of the Mahommedans; and it is not to be forgotten that the difference of religion between them goes to the roots of their social polity.

It has been the work of the All-India Moslem League to give the Mussulmans a political platform and to prevent their disappearance as a national entity on account of the indifference to political issues which formerly characterised them. The League came into existence only some seven or eight years ago, and so far from its work being done, it has reached a stage of evolution in which, if wise counsels prevail, it can do greater service than in the past. The crisis in the affairs of the London League, brought to a head by Mr. Ameer Ali's resignation,* confirms my conviction that the time has fully come for the Indian Mussulmans to realise that the future of the community depends not upon this or that particular leader but upon the people themselves. If there is any danger that excitable younger men may lead the League to an attitude of suspicious impatience, it is for the calmer and more reasonable section to bestir itself and to keep the organisation in its own hands, and meet the opposite party, not with abuse but with argument. The situation is one in which talents hitherto undiscovered may be drawn out for the good of the community in the country as a whole. I am confident that the great mass of educated Moslem opinion is sound and sober, and I believe that in India open discussion on the platform of the League, freed from the restraint of a permanent presidentship, will be the best means of bringing the weight of this opinion to bear on the questions of the day. But the situation of the London League is different, for there the community consists exclusively of two classes – elderly men of weight and standing on the one side, and inexperienced students on the other. It is obviously impossible for the latter to instruct and influence English opinion on Moslem affairs without the guidance from the former. Hence, while I am most anxious to see a reconstruction of the London League I feel it is essential that this should be based upon co-operation with the residents and I, for one, could never join or support an institution run by students only.

To the work of rallying the Moderates of Indian political life, whether Hindu or Mussulman, the British Government can materially contribute by the maintenance of the sympathetic and

* Since the above article was written, the moderate section of the All-India Moslem League has asserted itself, and in response to telegrams from important centres of the League in India Mr. Ameer Ali has consented to resume his presidency of the London League, and H. H. the Aga Khan has consented to become honorary president of that League – EDITOR [of the journal].

progressive policy pursued by Lord Hardinge. Statesmanship should aim at alleviating legitimate discontent, duly recognising the intense national sentiment and pride of educated India, and encouraging it to follow right channels. Articulate Indian opinion has to be allied more and more closely with British rule in a spirit of mutual respect and co-operation. One of the most potent forces in this direction is that of promoting the economic development of the country. We have the lamentable admission that considerable numbers of educated youths in Bengal terrorise remote villages by forming bands of dacoits for purposes of plunder, because they have no other means of livelihood. How this situation arises is shown in a suggestive statement in the decennial "Moral and Material Progress and Condition" Report presented to Parliament a few months ago. The chapter on the condition of the people states (page 377) that in the Bengals:

"The economic development of the country has not kept pace with the educational progress of the people. An ever-growing number of youths are leaving the schools and the University, but fresh avenues of employment are few. Altogether 580,000 persons have a knowledge of English in the two provinces of Bengal and Behar and Orissa, the number having increased by over 200,000 since 1901; but a special census of industrial concerns employing twenty persons or more shows that the total number of Indians engaged in direction, supervision, and clerical work is only 20,000."

Another requirement is to remove the unfortunate impression that Indian students are discouraged from coming to England, and that the facilities formerly open to them at Oxford and Cambridge are restricted for that purpose. Young Indians do not make sufficient allowance for the practical difficulties which arise from the great increase in their numbers since the distant days when an Indian student was given special attention as an interesting novelty in the life of the University. No doubt the system of exotic preparation for professional or official life has grave drawbacks, but until India is much better equipped educationally than at present, ambitious youths will inevitably go abroad in increasing numbers to fit themselves for future success. This being so, nothing can be more foolish than to lead them to direct their gaze to Japan, to the United States, or to Germany, under the apprehension that they may be cold-shouldered in England. Any well-behaved Indian youth coming here should feel and know that he is welcome. Every encouragement should be given to him to mix freely with British contemporaries in study, and to see English life at its best. After all, the great work of the British people in India has been that of broadening and expanding Indian ideals, and it is clearly advantageous that Indians studying outside their own country should come here to absorb English ideas at first hand, rather than spend their most impressionable years elsewhere.

An even more serious matter is the treatment of Indians in South Africa, Canada, and other parts of the King's dominions. This is a source of constant irritation, and is a most powerful weapon in the hands of anti-British extremists. The renewal of passive resistance in South Africa, and the wholesale arrests of Indians for the quiet assertion of rights, taken from them contrary to pledges given, have been most unfortunate from the standpoint of Indian good-will. It is amazing that Colonial statesmen should continue a situation which is utterly inimical to the solidarity of the British Empire; and to the average Indian it is a matter of pained astonishment and doubt that his Majesty's Government – the powerful arbiter of Imperial issues – appeals in vain for justice to be done. And still worse is the grave danger that Zanzibar and Pemba may be handed over to Germany, and that in East Africa a handful of white settlers may repeat some of the injustices that have already made of South Africa a running sore in the relations of England and India. The prosperity of Zanzibar has been made by its Indian merchants and traders . . . Should this island be handed over to Germany for some so-called advantage in the Persian Gulf, a region all Indians are most anxious to see remain in Turkish hands, the shock of this light-hearted way of dealing with an essentially Indian interest would be so great that I, for one, cannot foresee its consequences. Just as disastrous would be a repetition in East Africa generally of the conditions that now exist in South Africa. May the British people realise that the time has come for a decisive cry of "Hands off!" from East Africa, to be addressed to the thoughtless people who wish to repeat the conditions of South Africa there!

Another matter upon which strong feeling prevails is that there should be fuller scope in local affairs for loyal but at the same time free criticism. The widening of the powers and functions of the Legislative Council has done much to give point and force to public sentiment on the larger issues, and this is necessarily reflected in the comments of a Press which, with all its great imperfections, is advancing in ability and is beginning to be really responsive to public needs. The days when not merely the considered will but even the capricious whim of the collector of a district was received without question and obeyed without hesitation have gone by, and in the sphere of every-day administration, no less than in the more conspicuous arena of the Legislatures, Supreme and Provincial, it is necessary for those in authority to give due weight to the general consensus of opinion. The district officer should at least know the direction in which public opinion tends, whether or not he can act upon it with due regard to the wider issues of which he has to take account. Through varying stages of Indian evolution British rule has shown that power of adaptation which is essential to organic vigour. This has been strikingly exemplified in the marked success with which the Morley-Minto reforms have been woven into the administrative fabric. I look to the future with hope and confidence, because I am convinced that British statesmanship will continue to respond to the growth of national consciousness in India, and will thus bring an awakened people into still closer sympathy and co-operation with the aims and ideals of the enlightened rule that has revolutionised the conditions and the ideals of Indian life within living memory.

Source: *The Edinburgh Review,* Edinburgh, January 1914, pp. 1–13.

37

THE STATE OF MUSLIM POLITICS IN INDIA

Reply to the Address of Welcome by the Muslim Community of Burma

Rangoon: 6 February 1914

Work for the "National College" at Aligarh – the generosity of
Muslims of Burma – charter for the University – many universities
needed – the Muslim League – its political programme – co-operation with Hindus and brotherly goodwill towards all communities
– need for regular Hindu-Muslim committees – sufferings of
Muslims in Tripoli, the Balkans and Persia – his resignation from
the Presidency of the All India Muslim League – the London
League – educational work needed in Burma.

Mr. President of the Reception Committee, ladies and gentlemen,
I thank you most sincerely and from the bottom of my heart for
your very kind words of welcome and also for having so very
kindly taken such very great trouble and at so much personal
sacrifice of time given me such a splendid reception. The generous terms in which you refer to me personally have touched
me greatly and I assure you though I do not deserve the naturally
generous terms of reference to me it will be a source of strength,
pleasure and gratitude to feel that I have the affectionate sympathy of beloved co-religionists in my work for the community.
You have very kindly referred to what I have done for the National
College at Aligarh. Well, gentlemen, long ago I realised that it
was my first duty in life to help forward the modern education
of my countrymen and co-religionists and I have never yet come
across an educational institution for Moslems, whether it be large
or small, which has not attracted me. But, alas, gentlemen, I have
not been able always to help. It was always a case of looking out
for the institution that had the greatest claims on me personally,
and thus I have often not been able to do a quarter of what I
should like to have done. You have very kindly referred to my

work with regard to the Moslem University. Gentlemen, long ago, in 1902, I suggested it at Delhi and adumbrated a scheme. Now, thank God, the funds are ready. I cannot tell you how we Moslems of India proper feel grateful to you our brethren of Burma for the kind help and generous assistance you gave us for the university. You have asked me to approach Government and get a charter suitable to the Moslem aspirations. Well, let me assure you that the attitude of the Government of our beloved Viceroy has been most sympathetic not only towards the Moslem but towards the sister university of the great elder sister community of Hindus. Our people must also realise that we should not at the first step expect a free university such as has been gradually evolved at Oxford and Cambridge. In our own interests I think it would be a good thing to accept a compromise on the Government terms and gradually work towards greater freedom of the senate and of wider educational powers over other Moslem institutions. We must, however, remember that ultimately we want many Moslem universities. Our people in India number seventy millions already. We are increasing and such a population must have many universities if it is to reach the standard of Europe and America. Gentlemen, in my humble opinion, if our community met the Government terms in a spirit of good will it would in its interest, be acting most wisely. Now I must thank you for so very kindly referring to and supporting my work for the League. I was the author of the League, for in the spring of 1906 at Aligarh I sketched its plans for my friend the late Nawab Mohsin-ul-Mulk. I am glad to say that the institution has more than justified its existence. We have adopted a wise political programme, the essence of which can be described: first, unconditional and absolute loyalty, devotion and love towards our King-Emperor and his Majesty's Government of India; secondly, good will and co-operation towards our compatriots of all religions, from the great elder sister community of Hindus down to the smallest of races and religions in India; thirdly, the maintenance of our national existence as a separate Moslem nation within the greater Indian nation which is itself but one part in the greatest whole, namely, the British Empire. You refer to the new ideal of the League. Such a loyal and patriotic ideal, true to Emperor and true to fatherland, true to ourselves, was necessary. It is the flag of Islam in India, but let us realise at once that it is a distant ideal that cannot be realised till after generations of effort, and that till then looking up only at the flag in the skies will not carry us forward; it will only retard our progress. We must go on at the plough, work at the solution of the immediate problems before us and help the Government. . .

May we not work hand in hand with the other communities towards a better condition of affairs rather than merely saying "wah, wah," and looking in the skies at our flag? Gentlemen, co-operation with Hindus and brotherly good will towards all communities and all sects of Hinduism is a necessary part of our work if we are to get at salvation. I am glad to see that the relations of the two great communities are better than ever now; but, gentlemen, here too it will not do to rest; we must go ahead, we must have regular committees in every town and hamlet in India of Hindus and Mahomedans to adjust every difficulty as it arises and to nip in the bud every difference before it is born. Gentlemen, I thank you for giving me an opportunity once more for publicly repeating what I have heard from all Moslems in every part of India, our loyalty as a community is unbounded. Our natural and justifiable efforts to relieve the suffering of our religious brethren in Tripoli, the Balkans and Persia and to represent our feelings before the Government has been misrepresented. We must deny all such misrepresentations and caricature of our attitude and prove by our acts that they are wrong. I only resigned the presidency of the central [All India Muslim] League, not because I was dissatisfied but I felt that the political education of the community required a free organisation. I remain an active member as active as ever. I have become an honorary president of the London League and my dear friend, the Right Hon. Syed Amir Ali has, I am happy to say, again become its president so I hope the work, most important work in London, will be carried on as well as ever. Gentlemen, my heart is in your work here in this province. I have watched it from afar. I cannot tell you how grateful I was to see it announced that a generous Memon leader in Bombay had given eight lakhs towards a college in Bombay or Poona. Here we must work and at once towards this end. Gentlemen, let me assure you that I am, with all my experience of Moslems, not only in India but all over the world, at your service. During my ten days stay here I am ready to give you all the advice that you require. It is but for you to command my services during these days. My friend, Mr. Aziz Mirza, visited Burma twice. That example I feel must be followed. Our leaders must come here. I thank you once more most sincerely, and believe me that I am most grateful and touched by your generous kindness.

Source: *The Rangoon, Gazette*, Rangoon, 9 February 1914.

The Aga Khan arrived in Rangoon early on Friday (6 February) morning, along with his personal staff and Mr. Allibhoy Muhammad (who had gone to Calcutta to meet His Highness), on board the *Arankola*. He was received at the port by a Reception Committee consisting of Abdul Karim Jamal (President), Mulla Abdur Rahim (Vice-President), Muhammad Azam (Honorary Secretary), Muhammad Ibrahim Mulla, Haji Ahmad Mulla Daud, V. M. Abdur Rahman, Agha Mahmud, Muhammad Kalameah, Abdul Bari Chowdhury, Ko Ba Oh, A. K. Imamjan, Jivabhoy Bhanji, Ismail Ibrahim Atia and Ismail Ahmad Muhammadi, and the officials, including the Commissioner of Police, Captain Hutcheson, the aid-de-camp to the Lieutenant Governor of Burma, and a number of Muslim elders. Then he was taken by the launch *Industry* to the Lewis Street jetty where a reception was held in his honour, attended by a large gathering representing all the communities of the city. The dais was located at the north end of the *pandal*, where the Aga Khan was seated, with Abdul Karim Jamal sitting on one side of him and Captain Hutcheson on the other.

The proceedings began with a short speech by Abdul Karim Jamal which ran:

"Ladies and gentlemen, on behalf of the reception committee I thank you most heartily for the trouble you have taken to come here this morning and join us in welcoming our distinguished guest. It is hardly necessary for me to say anything by way of introducing to you His Highness Sir Sultan Mahomed Shah; for although this province has not for a long time been honoured with a visit from his Highness, his fame as an ardent worker for the regeneration of his community has long been established here and his name is as much a household word here as everywhere else. To honour such an illustrious nobleman is therefore to do honour to ourselves. With these few words I call upon Mr. Mahomed Auzam to read the address of welcome."

Then Muhammad Azam read out the following address of welcome: "To His Highness Sir Sultan Mahomed Shah Aga Khan, K.C.I.E., G.C.I.E., G.C.S.I., LL.D.. etc, May it please your Highness:- We the undersigned, on behalf of the Musalmans of Rangoon, offer you a hearty welcome on this your second visit to this picturesque land of pagodas and palms. Your Highness is welcomed here not only as the head of one of the Moslem sects, but also as the recognised leader of the whole Moslem community in India, and also as one of the 'empire-builders' in the glorious annals of the British rule. (2) Since your Highness's first visit to this country fourteen years ago the material progress of the Musalmans (all over India) has been marvellous. Your Highness has taken a most prominent part in the development and progress of our community. Ever since your Highness has taken the field, your Highness has been an important factor in the evolution of the Musalmans of India. Your Highness's keen interest in Moslem education and your Highness's generous help to push the educational movements forward are too well-known. Your Highness's liberal annual grant to the great National College at Aligarh and your Highness's permanent scholarships for further studies in Europe are positive proofs of your Highness's keen interest in the amelioration of your co-religionists. Only three years ago your Highness revived the dead and forgotten cause of the Moslem University which is of vital importance to the interest of our community. At your Highness's own expense and at considerable personal inconvenience and sacrifice your Highness travelled throughout the length and breadth of India and begged from door to door to collect the necessary funds for this noble object. Your Highness's own liberal subscription, your Highness's personal efforts and the generous response of the people to your Highness's call have now materialised our dreams. Through your noble efforts the Musalmans have nearly sur- mounted the preliminary difficulties which were sure to hinder the progress of the movement in the beginning. The work would have been in an advanced state by this time had there not been some unpleasant differences of opinion between the community and the Government on some basic principles in the constitution of the university. We are eager to see the differences settled, without losing the Moslem point of view, and the work re-started. Will it be too much to appeal to your Highness's generous heart in the name of those whose welfare is nearest and dearest to your heart, to intervene once more and to request the Government to give a more sympathetic hearing to the wants of the com- munity? We are confident that the liberality of your nature will not refuse a helping hand at this critical juncture. (3) Your Highness's services in the field of politics are as glorious as in that of education. In the year 1906, at the right moment your Highness's political foresight convinced your Highness that the Moslem policy of aloofness from the political arena, if continued, would have been detrimental to our national existence in India. Your Highness rose to the occasion and led the memorable deputation which waited upon His Excellency Lord Minto at Simla, and successfully convinced the Government of the political importance of our community and the desirability of equal treatment in accord- ance with their political importance. Then again, with your Highness's estimable co-operation, the late Nawab Mohsin-ul-Mulk laid the foundation of the All- India Moslem League, to watch and to protect the political interest of our community. This was the dawn of organised Moslem political consciousness in the recent history of India. Your Highness's subsequent efforts in the reform scheme have been very fruitful and gratifying to one and all. More than three years ago your Highness finding that Hindu-Moslem sentiment was becoming estranged and feeling that such a condition was detrimental to the well-being of the country and the Empire, took the initiative and formed a special depu- tation at Nagpore in the year 1910 and went to Allahabad, where the annual sitting of the Indian National Congress was held that year, to meet representative Hindu gentlemen and to devise means to establish cordial relations between the sister communities. This wise and statesmanlike policy of your Highness will ever remain a landmark in the history of Indian nationalism. This effort has not been without a happy and glorious result. We see today that the atmosphere is clearer and the relation more cordial and hopeful than it was some years before. We fervently hope that this noble feeling will grow stronger and stronger every day till it becomes solid and permanent. Last year, at the right psychological moment in our recent history you agreed to the change of the League's constitution which had grown old and effete. The new constitution with its new ideals quite suits the advanced state of our community and has inspired the people with a new spirit of hope and energy. Your Highness, the natural anxiety of Musalmans of India over the Islamic world abroad, the improved relations of the two great communities of India, and the political programme of the League have been made capital of mischievous criticism in India and Great Britain, against our educated and rising young generation. Every sort of calumny founded on imagination and entirely misconstrued stories, were published and directed against us to poison the mind of our benign Government and the British public at large. Your Highness realised the situation and foresaw the consequences which were not free from danger. Your

Highness took the earliest opportunity to contradict and disprove the false charges levelled against us. Your Highness's recent article in the *Edinburgh Review* has proved the hollowness of all these ill-founded and mischievous calumnies, which is a memorable service rendered to the community as well as to the Empire which shall for ever remain vivid and fresh in the minds of generations. Your Highness, we were disappointed to learn that the Moslem League will no longer enjoy the honour and privilege of your Highness's presidentship, but there is great consolation in your assurance to the community that you as one of the members of the League, would continue to take active part with greater freedom than it was possible in the judicial character that attaches to the president. Your beneficent work, your noble example and your name will ever remain in the history of the national politics a source of inspiration for the future generation. Your noble words and wise pronouncements on political questions will be a beacon light to guide the path of Musalmans for many years to come. Your brilliant career and services as the member of the Imperial Legislative Council have been followed up with keen interest by Musalmans and have been no less appreciated and fruitful to the country. Your liberal donations to the Turkish Relief Fund and other causes have also been additional and parallel examples of your generosity and philanthropic nature, which hardly permit you to overlook a deserving cause without extending an ever-ready and voluntary helping hand. (4) Your Highness, a concise statement of the condition of Musalmans in this province will not be without interest to you. This is the youngest province in the Indian Empire. The population of Musulmans is second in numerical strength in this province. It is painful to observe that up to this time no organised effort has been made to raise the masses from the deep depth of ignorance in this province. In the whole province with such a vast Moslem population we have only one Islamia High School, the Mahomedan Randheria School in Rangoon. There are a few middle schools and numerous primary schools. All these schools are maintained by the generosity of private persons and the local aids of the Government. Collegiate education is practically unknown among the Musalmans. Only few Moslem students are at present in the Government College, Rangoon. This deplorable state of Moslem education is due partly to the lack of the united effort of the community and partly to the under-rated value of education. It is, however, satisfactory to note that the recent resolution of the Government of India on Moslem education and the earnest efforts of the Local Government to give the resolution a practical shape have awakened our people to realise their true educational position in this province. On the request of the director of public instruction of Burma the Moslem community has lately submitted a scheme how to encourage and improve the Moslem education in this province on the basis of the said resolution of the Government of India. The Musalmans of this province earnestly hope that their scheme will receive a fair and just treatment at the hands of the authorities of Education Department. The community is now trying to form an organised body for the purpose of watching the educational interest of the Musalmans in this province in future. The whole effort of the community will be directed to raise the present schools up to the standard of high schools and to establish good boarding houses for the students who come for higher standards from the districts. In this province as well as India the lack of funds has been one of the greatest causes in the way of our educational progress. But we earnestly hope that the active sympathy of our rich men and the Local Government will cope with the situation. (5) We are constrained to remark that up to this time this province has been neglected by our Indian leaders; very seldom have they given a thought to the welfare of their co-religionists inhabiting this part of the country. Occasional exchange of views between the Musalman leaders of India and the leaders of this part of the country together with mutual support would go a great way to inspire and up-lift the Musalman population of this province. We hope that your Highness's visit will open a new chapter in our history and will inspire us with new hopes and ambitions. (6) In conclusion your Highness will allow us once more to offer you our hearty welcome on your visit; and we fervently pray that Lord Almighty may grant you long life, health and prosperity so that you may serve your nation, your country and your King with greater energy than you have done before.

"We have the honour to be, Your Highness's most humble servants: (1) A. K. Jamal, (2) Mulla Abdur Rahim, (3) Mohamed Ebrahim Mulla, (4) Haji Ahmed Mulla Dawood, (5) V. M. Abdur Rahman, (6) Aga Mahmood, (7) Mohmed Kalamyah. (8) Abdul Bari Chowdhury, (9) Ko Bo Oh, (10) A. K. Imamjan, (11) Allibhoy Mohamed, (12) Jivabhoy Bahnji, (13) Ismail Ebrahim Atia, (14) Ismail Ahmed Mohamedi, (15) Mahomed Azam."

At the conclusion of his address the Aga Khan was presented with a handsome silver casket by Mr. Jamal and then escorted to a motor car which was in waiting and with Mr. Jamal and friends was driven along Strand Road, to Phayre Street, to Merchant Street, to Messrs. Peer Mahomed's premises which had been decorated with a banner of welcome swung across the street in front of the store. Here a short stop was made while Mr. Peer Mahomed garlanded the Aga Khan and several handsome bouquets were presented. The route then led along Merchant Street, to Mogul Street to the Khoja Mosque where a very handsome *pandal* had been erected and where another short stay was made. At both these places bands of music were in attendance, while the band of the Royal Munster Fusiliers played at the reception *pandal*. On leaving the Khoja Mosque the route lay along Montgomery Street and over the railway bridge, Signal Pagoda Road, King Edward Avenue and along Cemetery Road to Pagoda hill. All the streets were handsomely decorated. It was then decided to visit Mr. Solomon's house in Halpin Road where His Highness was served with tea. Two mounted Indian police of the Rangoon Town police led the way followed by numerous members of the Khoja community on bicycles carrying Union Jacks. The motor car of the Aga Khan was followed by about twenty others and many private horsed conveyances. After tea the party proceeded to 'Brightlands' in Park Road where the Aga Khan will stay during his visit to Rangoon and where the band of the Burma Railways Volunteers was in attendance. He visited the Lieutenant-Governor at Government House about midday and it is understood that Sir Harvey Adamson will return the visit this morning at eleven o'clock. The Lieutenant-Governor has also accepted the Aga Khan's invitation to a garden party to be given by him at 'Brightlands' on Monday, February 17 as he has accepted an invitation from the chairman of the Port Commissioners to be present at the inauguration of the river training works.

On Burma see "Government of Burma", *British Burma Gazetteer*, Rangoon, 1880, 2 vols; J. Chailley-Bert *La colonisation de l'Indo-Chine: l'expérience Anglaise*, Paris, 1892; Charles Crosthwaite, *The Pacification of Burma*, London, 1912; A. Fytche, *Burma: Past and Present*, London, 1878, 2 vols; J. Nisbet, *Burma under British Rule and Before*, London, 1901, 2 vols; and H. H. Dodwell (ed.), *The Cambridge History of India, Vol. VI: The Indian Empire, 1858–1918*, Cambridge, 1932.

38

ADVICE TO THE INDIAN RESIDENTS IN BURMA

Reply to the Address of Welcome Presented by the Indian and Other Communities of Burma

Rangoon: 13 February 1914

National awakening in India – co-operation among different communities and races should be permanent – conditions for political progress – steps towards national development – need for social clubs and associations – the Indian Question in South Africa.

Mr. Chairman and gentlemen, allow me first of all to thank you most sincerely for this splendid address and for the very kind terms in which you have referred to me. The kindness of my countrymen in this province is really boundless. It is impossible for me – words fail me – to express to you my deep sense of gratitude, and how touched I have been by the kindness you have simply showered on me. The fact that my countrymen appreciate to this great extent any services, howsoever humble, that I have or may have rendered towards our beloved motherland is not only a source of great pride and gratitude for me, but will, I am sure, encourage many others to make still greater efforts, for it proves that the nation is waking up and realising what are the broad lines of its future development and progression, and realises also which paths will lead to salvation. (Applause.) The fact of national wakening is proved by many signs, one of which is the fact that all sections and races are joining each other more and more on public occasions for a common cause or a common purpose. (Applause). But, gentlemen, may I make a humble suggestion. Such a spirit of union and co-operation should not be like a mirage, to appear now and disappear tomorrow, or to appear on occasions and disappear shortly after, but we should begin by starting clubs and associations for social, charitable, political, educational and general welfare in which all communities should co-operate. (Cheers.) Gentlemen, our political progress depends in its broadest and widest principles on three essential sound conditions. First and foremost unconditional and absolute loyalty and devotion towards the person and Government of our beloved King-Emperor and his Majesty's dynasty. (Cheers.) Secondly, co-operation of all races and religions on a basis of each respecting the special characteristics of all the others, and also of co-operating for the welfare of each by all. (Applause.) Thirdly, gentlemen, on a thorough standard of efficiency in whatever we are responsible for, so that nobody may ever show the finger towards us and show that we are inefficient in our actions. (Applause.) Gentlemen, these three are the cardinal principles and the cardinal needs, but in order to make these ideals general we have certain immediate and near duties of a humbler nature, but still necessary steps towards our higher ideals. These necessary steps I may describe as co-operation and mutual help in education, in social service, in trade, in economic development. (Applause.) I fully agree with you, [and] have ever since I have thought held the view, that by India and Indian we do not mean men of this race or of that religion, men of one sort or of another, but of all who live in Asia under the dominion or protection of His Majesty our gracious King-Emperor. (Cheers.) As you have been so kind in your references towards me, may I venture to make some practical suggestions for what I consider might be useful steps towards national development? Social clubs for all races, for all communities, I think should be started according to the general importance of the place, not only in capital cities like these splendid cities of Rangoon and Mandalay, but throughout Burma. (Applause.) But in addition to such social clubs I think associations should be started that would constantly meet and regularly meet and encourage regularly courses of lectures by reformers and by experts. They should invite people from various parts of India to come and deliver courses of lectures, courses of public meetings, giving advice on various questions, making suggestions, and requiring discussion after lecture has been delivered, as on similar lines associations in Europe are formed for various purposes and lectures are delivered and discussions then take place, a process that must lead to national awakening and to national education. (Applause.) Such lecturers should be asked to lecture in different languages, but various translations should always be ready so that all present may understand. Such social clubs and associations will not only remove misunderstandings but will prevent them from arising. Gentlemen, the greater the discussion, the greater the occasions on which people meet each other on a common platform, the surer will be the work of the cause and its permanent beneficial results. I thank you again warmly for referring to my work in connection with South Africa, work undertaken I may say in co-operation and in support of the splendid work done by my dear friend the Hon. Mr. Gokhale (applause) and by my lifelong friend, for I have known him since I was a boy, Sir Pherozeshah Mehta (applause.) Gentlemen, I am glad to say that the latest news from South Africa is a little more hopeful, and it is possible that some form, if not entirely satisfactory, still a compromise, may take place. This is not saying much, but the outlook is a little less cloudy than it was a short time ago. Gentlemen, in this relation I think I am but doing my duty, and a pleasant duty for myself, and what I am sure is also the opinion of every one of you who has thought about or studied the question, in stating that the thanks of India are due first and before all to his Excellency the Viceroy who has been a true father and champion of the cause of India in South Africa (cheers.) In this question, as in everything else in this country, the needs are the same. It is the old old story, fairness, co-operation and renunciation of individuals towards the benefits, not the individual benefits but the communal benefits, to further the welfare of the whole of this great nation, which consists of many nations. I thank you again very much, and I assure you that it has been a source not only of pride but of great pleasure to come and see you here and thank you personally. (Loud applause.)

Source: *The Rangoon Gazette*, Rangoon, 16 February 1914.

The leaders of the Indian and other communities residing in Burma hosted a reception welcoming the Aga Khan to Rangoon at the Jubilee Hall at about 5 p.m. The Honourable U. Hpay was voted to the chair, and he started the proceedings with the following words:

"Ladies and gentlemen, I thank you heartily for the trouble you have taken to come here this evening to join us in welcoming our illustrious guest. It is hardly necessary for me to say anything by way of introducing to you His Highness (applause), who has taken a most prominent part in the uplifting of his fellow-beings living side by side in this vast empire of ours, and whose opinion has great weight in the United Kingdom (applause). As His Highness comes to Burma practically on an official visit, he must be welcomed by all the citizens of Rangoon in a manner fitting the occasion (applause). With these few words I call upon U May Oung to read the address of welcome."

The address of welcome was then read out by U. May Oung; it ran as follows:

"To his Highness Sir Sultan Mohammed Shah Aga Khan, G.C.S.I., G.C.I.E., LL.D., etc.

"May it please your Highness – We, on behalf of the Indian and other communities residing in Burma, beg to express our sense of happiness in enjoying the privilege of approaching your Highness on your visit to this province once again. In the first place we ask to be permitted to heartily congratulate the Indian and allied communities in as much as in your Highness India has come to possess a leader of progressive enlightenment and catholic views who had declined to subordinate the general good of a vast continent to the narrow aspirations of any one particular sect or community. Cut off as this province may appear from the mainland of India, Burma is linked to India by more than commercial or even material ties. We watch, albeit at a distance, nevertheless with intense keenness the efforts made by our brethren in India in the direction of political advancement and it is exceedingly gratifying to us to observe that in the grave councils of the dominions not less than in smaller assemblies devoted to communal interests your Highness's voice is raised with that vigour of manliness which sincerity lends to statesmanly sagacity, for the welding of the different communities of the Indian Empire into a united whole. We have not, your Highness, missed to observe the emphasis rightly laid by you on the continuance of benign British paramountcy as an indispensable condition of the fulfilment of those lofty aims for the future of India which your Highness has from time to time foreshadowed. A new spirit of advancement in which we hope humbly to participate is animating the millions of India and it is a fortunate circumstance that the new epoch coincides with the realisation of the beneficence of the British rule as indicated by your Highness and your Highness's political compeers like the Hon. Mr. Gokhale, the Hon. Sir Pherozeshah M. Mehta and others.

"The weighty counsel given to our Moslem brethren from time to time, though it may not have enabled all men of divergent views in the three continents where your Highness has numerous admirers like ourselves, to see eye to eye with your Highness, has left no doubt in our minds that in your Highness's public utterances, and doubtless in private admonitions, the one dominating thought has been the unity and its concomitant the strength of an undivided India. When we speak of India we refer not merely to the Indian communities but to all the communities comprised within the nomenclature Indian as well as allied peoples of Asia who aim at political unity under the British suzerainty and already enjoy amity and concord. For as your Highness is aware, the relationship between the Burmans, the sons of the soil, and the Indians proper is not merely one of cordiality and mutual good-will found on a community of interests; no ethnic or other difference prevent the peoples of the two neighbouring countries, sharing a common civilisation, from forming the closest ties of kinship. From the largest cities to the remotest hamlets, unapproachable by rail or water-way, Burma abounds in neighbourhoods where Burman, Indian and Chinaman, whether official, tradesmen or cultivator, live in harmony unmarred by racial animus. It is in this field, of fusing the sister communities, subjects of one Great King, that your Highness's efforts will have to be especially chronicled by the future historian. Many well-wishers of India have before now endeavoured to remove the great gulf assumed to have been fixed by nature between the various communities in British India. It was given to your Highness to give concrete and solid shape to his happy movement of unification. Of your many and invaluable services to your country and King we take occasion only to allude to one more. Perhaps not the least obligation conferred on us has been your exertion to expose the inhuman treatment of Indians in South Africa, and your Highness's spirited appeal to the powers to ameliorate their condition. We pray to God you be spared long in health to see realised that noble ideal which your benign political prescience has set before a generated Indian nation.

"We have the honour to be, your Highness' most obedient servants, Abdul Karim Jamal, U. Hpay, P. C. Sen, Ahmed Moolla Dawood, Lim Chin Tsong, Moolla Abdur Rahim, U Ba Thein, Yacoob Abdul Ganny, J. R. Das, Mohamed Goolam Hoosein Soorty, W. F. Noyce, B. Cowasjee, Mohamed Hajee Solayman Mall, P. J. Mehta, V. N. Sivaya, S. A. Rahman, U Po Oh, Alibhoy Hakimjee, Mahomed Israel Khan, U May Oung, V. M. Abdur Rahman, S. S. Agabob, Mahomed Ebrahim Moolla, G. K. Nariman, Ahmadulla (alias Ko Ba Oh), K. B. Banerjee, Mohamed Kalamya, Esmail Mohamed Hoosein Patel, Shamjee Gopaljee, Mansukhlal Dawlatchand, Jeewabhoy Bhanjee, A. M. Pillay, V. Madanjit, Premjee Chanda, Ismail Ebrahim Atta, S. Ramnath Reddiar."

The address, enclosed in a beautiful Burmese carved silver casket surmounted by a golden peacock, was then presented to the distinguished guest by Mr. Agha Khan (no relation to the Aga Khan). After this, the Aga Khan was garlanded and presented with a bouquet of flowers by Haji Ahmad Mulla Daud. The Haji also proposed a vote of thanks to the chair, which was seconded by J. B. Das and carried unanimously. Three hearty cheers for the Aga Khan called for by Mr. Madanjit brought the proceedings to a close.

39

VOLUNTARY WORK AND THE WAR EFFORT

Speech at a Meeting of the Indian Volunteers Committee

London: 1 October 1914

Indian Field Ambulance Corps – significance of service to the Empire – mutual co-operation among different communities – rebuke to Lloyd George for comparing the German Kaiser to Prophet Muhammad – Germany's policy and actions – the Cawnpore mosque case.

I am unable to tell you the feelings of pride and joy with which I address my fellow countrymen here whose spontaneous desire to actively serve the King-Emperor in this supreme hour in the destinies of Europe and the Empire has found action in the formation of the Indian Field Ambulance Corps. For weeks past, first under Dr. James Cantlie (cheers) and now under Colonel Baker (cheers) you have been preparing yourselves by diligent training for the task now definitely allotted to you by the War Office and by the Red Cross Society. It will be the proud privilege of most of you to go to the front to minister to the medical and hospital needs of soldiers of our own nationality engaged for the first time in history in fighting on West European soil for the great Empire to which we belong. (Cheers). It is in fact a unique occasion.

You represent a spirit which is universal amongst our countrymen in India and here. Some of them in provincial centres, being fewer in number, have not facilities for combined training equal to yours, but I believe they are no less eager to serve the Empire; and I am glad to know that in some of the University towns young Indians have been attached for training to the Red Cross Section of the Officers Training Corps. A few have quietly offered themselves for Lord Kitchener's New Army, and I believe they have been welcomed, and are welcomed, on passing the same physical tests as are applied to their English comrades. I can only say that I envy them the opportunity of combat, and I envy you the equally necessary, though not equally dangerous, if perhaps not so picturesque, service of which you have taken advantage. I shall be very proud and happy to be one of their number, which I may add is by no means improbable. (Cheers). Do not forget, however, that the services you are about to render are in some ways even more glorious than those of the men in the fighting line. You have to expose yourselves constantly to danger, and you cannot actually take a part in the fighting, so that you will not have the benefit of the excitement that combatant work brings, that helps one to go through. From the very first day when the war commenced our noble and high-souled chairman, Mr. Gandhi, (cheers) whom those who know his work in South Africa cannot help but revere (cheers) urged that there should be no picking and choosing, but that we as Indians must at once go and do any work that came to our hands.

That spirit of patriotism finds expression in the intimation of your Committee to the India Office placing your services unconditionally at the disposal of the authorities, as a proof of India's desire to share the responsibilities, no less than the privileges, of membership of this great Empire. That you should be actuated by these high standards of public duty is in accordance with the confident expectation of those who, like myself, have been closely familiar with the thoughts and the noble aspirations of my educated fellow countrymen. After all, you do but mirror in a different environment the wave of loyal enthusiasm which has swept through our Motherland, and to which I shall make further reference. I feel confident that these patriotic conceptions will actuate all who have undergone training when the time comes for most of you to proceed to the Continent, and for the others to remain behind, for, as you are aware, some are sure to be wounded and many more are sure to come back ill and broken in health. For these reasons I feel sure that many who are remaining behind will be required to go to the front later on. I feel confident that the many wastages that will occur will be easily replaced by further volunteers who will be trained in this country.

In this hour of India's and the Empire's difficulties, happily no differences of race and creed exist in India. They do not count. (Cheers). And the Indian blood that will be shed on the fields of France and Belgium, and, I hope, Germany (loud cheers) will not have been shed in vain if it leads to a permanent disappearance of racial and religious antagonism, or any other suspicion in India. (Cheers). We are absolutely united in the common purpose of taking our full share in the trials and sorrows of the Empire, and in contributing to the sacrifices entailed by the unconquerable determination of the British Empire and her Allies to win through. (Cheers).

I may speak of one matter of special interest to Mussulmans, for it is one in which I am confident we shall have the most cordial sympathy of our Hindu and Parsi brethren. Representations made to me from many quarters, as well as my own reading of the speech, showed that Moslem sensibilities have been deeply wounded by an observation, Mr. Lloyd George let fall in the otherwise inspired and splendid recruiting speech he delivered in London on the 19th September. The just scorn and ridicule that he poured upon the blasphemous claims of the Kaiser to be the weapon and the sword of the Almighty was followed by an unhappy and an unfortunate comparison that there has been nothing like it since the days of Mahomet. (Cries of Shame). It is most unfortunate that, at the time when the Mussulman subjects of the King Emperor, constituting nearly a quarter of the population within His Majesty's Dominions, are eagerly responding to the call of the hour, a leading Minister of the Crown, whom we all respect, should have likened, or should have appeared to liken, the arch enemy of this Empire, who has wantonly plunged Europe and the world into unexampled suffering, with the Prophet of Islam. (Cries of Shame). Gentlemen, the Chancellor of the Exchequer may not be able to reciprocate the veneration for the founder of our faith which we are taught from childhood, to give to the Founder of the Christian faith, but he might at least show towards him the respect and reverence we all accord to the memories of the great sons of Christendom who do not belong, so to speak, to our religion like the Founder of Christianity does.

It is, however, my personal belief and conviction that the observation coming from one who has never lived outside this country, or in contact with Moslem people, was, so to speak, an unconscious sort of passing reference not really meant towards the Prophet of Islam personally . . . I am sure it was not meant to be offensive and was unpremeditated; but I venture to urge that leading statesmen, and also publicists, should be careful not to play thus thoughtlessly and gratuitously into the hands of the enemies of the Empire. (Cheers). You are well aware that though

I have always been convinced that Germany was the most dangerous enemy of Turkey and all other Moslem countries, for she was the one that was most anxious to annex by peaceful penetration Asia Minor and Southern Persia (Laughter). She has been at the same time posing for years past to serve her own needs as a sort of protector of Islam. Heaven forbid that we should have such an immoral protector! (cheers) and is only too eager to turn to mischievous account such unguarded expressions from Englishmen of eminence. Happily, so far as the Moslem and other subjects of the King Emperor are concerned, these efforts of our enemies are absolutely futile. We will never break down, the strong wall of loyalty, based on the certainty and consciousness that not only our truest interests, religious as well as civil, are guaranteed to us by British rule more securely than they could ever be otherwise, but that our ultimate aspirations to rise in everything to the standard of Europe and America can only be obtained through permanent association and union with British rule. (Cheers). We had evidence of this security of even comparatively small religious sentiments only a year ago in Lord Hardinge's wise and courageous recognition of the justice of our complaints in the action of the local authorities in the Cawnpore Mosque case, which had perturbed Moslem feeling throughout the country. In the partnership of Empire to which we are all summoned by the life-and-death struggle of to-day, we Indians, of whatever race or creed, look with confidence to those in high places in the counsels of the Empire to reciprocate the sentiment of respect and goodwill we cherish towards all subjects and sections of His Majesty's Empire. (Cheers) . . .

One small and humble personal explanation. If I do not get anything of a more combatant nature I hope to come with you as your interpreter, if I may. (Cheers). I know English, French, German and Hindustani, and I do not think you will find many interpreters so useful; so that I will earn my bread if I can there. If I do not go it will be because of some *force majeure*, and not through any want of effort on my own part. (Loud cheers).

Source: *The Times of India*, Bombay, 26 October 1914.

The paper's London correspondent reported that the meeting of the Indian Volunteers Committee was held at the Polytechnic, Regent Street. Mr. M. K. Gandhi, the Chairman of the Committee, presided and in opening the proceedings announced that His Highness the Aga Khan had handed him a cheque for £200 to be used to provide extra comforts for the corps at the front. He [Gandhi] said that by offering his services even as a private, His Highness had set a noble example to humbler individuals in readiness for any service for the Empire in such an hour as this.

The correspondent added that the Aga Khan was received with such deafening cheers that it was some time before he could proceed.

40

TURKEY, THE WAR AND MUSLIM INDIA

Message to the Indian Muslims on Turkish Entry into the War

London: 2 November 1914

Turkish entry on the German side a matter of sorrow – Indian Muslims' duty to remain loyal to Britain.

With deep sorrow I find that the Turkish Government has joined hands with Germany, and acting under German orders is madly attempting to wage a most unprovoked war against such mighty sovereigns as the King-Emperor and the Tsar of Russia. This is not the true and free will of the Sultan, but of German officers and other non-Moslems who have forced him to do their bidding.

Germany and Austria have been no disinterested friends of Islam, and while one took Bosnia the other has long been plotting to become the Suzerain of Asia Minor and of Mesopotamia, including Kerbela, Nejef and Baghdad. If Germany succeeds, which Heaven forbid, Turkey will become only a vassal of Germany, and the Kaiser's Resident will be the real ruler of Turkey, and will control the Holy Cities.

No Islamic interest was threatened in this war, and our religion was not in peril. Nor was Turkey in peril, for the British and Russian Empires and the French Republic had offered to solemnly guarantee Turkey all her territories in complete independence if she had remained at peace. Turkey was the trustee of Islam, and the whole world was content to let her hold our Holy Cities in her keeping. Now that Turkey has so disastrously shown herself a tool in German hands, she has not only ruined herself, but has lost her position of trustee of Islam, and evil will overtake her. Turkey has been persuaded to draw the sword in an unholy cause from which she could be but ruined whatever else happened, and she will lose her position as a great

510

nation, for such mighty Sovereigns as the King-Emperor and the Tsar can never be defeated. Thousands of Moslems are fighting for their Sovereigns already, and all men must see that Turkey has not gone to war for the cause of Islam or for defence of her independence. Thus our only duty as Moslems now is to remain loyal, faithful, and obedient to our temporal and secular allegiance.

Source: *The Times*, London, 4 November 1914.

A representative selection of Indian Muslim opinions on the war and Empire and Turkey is reflected in Mir Asad Ali, *The War and Our Duty*, Madras, 1918; J. Parkinson, "The War and the Muslims: From the Standpoint of a British Muslim", *Islamic Review and Muslim India*, October 1914; Syed Hossain, "England, Turkey and the Indian Muhammadans", *Asiatic Review*, February 1915; "Our Muslims and the War", *Candid Quarterly Review of Public Affairs*, November 1915; H. A. Walter, "The War and Islam: India", *Muslim World*, January 1915; "The War Conference and the Empire", *Round Table*, March 1917; and Valentine Chirol, "Islam and the War", *Quarterly Review*, April 1918.

41

THE EXAMPLE OF SIR PHEROZESHAH MEHTA

Speech at a Meeting Held in Memory of Sir Pherozeshah Mehta

London: 8 December 1915

A tribute to Sir Pherozeshah Mehta – his principles – attachment to the British connection for marching to Indian nationhood – his faith in English culture and civilization – his defence of Indian interests and representative institutions – extreme Indian attitudes of violent advocacy or constant flattery – influence of Liberalism on Mehta – ability to take criticism – services to Bombay – inspiring lesson for the Indian youth – local government – tribute to Gokhale and Buddrudin Tayyabji.

It was with pride and mournful satisfaction that I received the invitation to preside at this meeting to do honour to the memory of the greatest citizen of Bombay, my own native city; whose death, following so quickly upon that of his great younger friend and pupil, Mr. Gokhale, we so keenly deplore. It is true that Sir Pherozeshah Mehta had attained to three score years and ten – an age, alas, far too seldom reached by Indian leaders – and that he had spent well nigh half a century in the devoted service of his country; but we could ill afford to lose him at a time when the great principles he so strenuously upheld need to be pursued, for the good of India and of the Empire at large, with more stedfast determination than perhaps ever before. In order to direct attention to those principles by which his valuable career was inspired and guided, I must refrain from dwelling, as I would like to do, upon the many attractive personal characteristics which were disclosed to me by one whom I had the honour of knowing ever since childhood, and with whom I was during the last few years closely united by political and personal friendship.

At this hour of menace to British civilization and liberal institutions, it is fitting to speak first of all of this great patriot's firm hold, amid all mutations, of the need for the maintenance of the British connection with our country as an essential condition of the march to Indian nationhood and ultimate self-government within the Empire. Very shortly after the outbreak of the war he presided at a great meeting of Bombay citizens which proclaimed to the world the devotion of India to the British cause in its day of fierce testing. With an eloquence natural to him, but never more earnest or convincing, he set the tone of an enthusiastic assembly which tendered to the King-Emperor the assurance that "treasuring the prerogative of British citizenship as their dearest possession, the citizens of Bombay are ready cheerfully to submit to all inevitable consequences of the state of war, firmly believing that Great Britain has justly drawn the sword in defence of international rights and obligations." These were no empty assurances on the part of the chairman of the meeting. He was in hearty sympathy with, and by voice and example contributed to, the suspension of political controversy for which the Viceroy asked, in order that attention might be concentrated on the all-important issue of the prosecution of the war to a successful issue.

This attitude of Sir Pherozeshah Mehta conformed to the principles he applied throughout his public life. Amid the storm and stress of years of political activity, he never departed from the spirit of his confession of faith as President of the sixth session of the Indian National Congress at Calcutta in 1890. He then said that he had unbounded faith in the living and fertilizing principles of English culture and English civilization as applied to Indian problems. I can do no better than quote the words in which he declared his political faith in England, which I know was also the lifelong faith of Gokhale, and which is mine also:

"When, in the inscrutable dispensation of Providence, India was assigned to the care of England, one can almost imagine that the choice was offered to her as to Israel of old: 'Behold, I have placed before you a blessing and a curse: a blessing if ye will obey the commandments of the Lord your God: a curse if ye will not obey the commandments of the Lord your God but go after other gods whom ye have not known.' All the greatest forces of English life and society, moral, social, intellectual, political, are, if slowly yet steadily and irresistibly, declaring themselves for the choice which will make the connection of

England and India a blessing to themselves and to the whole world for countless generations."

Time and experience served only to deepen and confirm these convictions; so that many years later, when the voice of the Extremist was heard in the land, he reasserted his declaration of hearty acquiescence in British rule "as a dispensation so wonderful that it would be folly not to accept it as a declaration of God's will." As hundreds of reported debates in the Provincial and Supreme Legislatures, in the Senate of the University of Bombay, and in the Corporation meetings attest, no one could fight more strenuously and powerfully in defence of Indian interests and representative institutions or in advocacy of developments on Western lines than Sir Pherozeshah Mehta. But no one realised more clearly that progress could be best promoted by co-operation with the Government whenever possible, and that mere destructive criticism was harmful. A strong barrier against destructive tendencies, he did great work for India in helping to form and guide a body of moderate opinion which encouraged Lord Morley and Lord Minto to shape their great reform scheme on liberalizing lines.

It is ever so. The sacred cause of Indian progress invariably has been served best by those who have shared with Mehta and Gokhale the attitude of which I have spoken. The ideal of nationhood and the development of free institutions can only be retarded seriously by violent and intemperate advocacy on the one hand; or conversely a senseless and debasing demeanour of constant flattery of every official measure – a cringing attitude that makes superficial observers believe that Indians are incapable of anything except self-humiliation or violent vituperation. It is to the irreconcilable spirit that we owe the Press Act and other measures of prevention and restriction with which Government have found it necessary to arm themselves. By sharp and searching contrast, the career of the great Indian we mourn teaches that the youth who ranges himself on the side of Extremism, under the influence of the ferment of Western ideas he has not assimilated, is doing the greatest disservice to his country, and is contributing to put back the clock of progress.

One influence which greatly contributed to the formation of Sir Pherozeshah's character as a public man, and which has had a beneficient [sic] influence on India, is perhaps not as widely known as it ought to be. In his younger days in this country, he came very deeply under the influence of that sturdy, old fashioned Liberalism which some of my friends say has vanished from among you. I do not know whether it has or not – perhaps it has only been transformed – but I do know that for the remainder of his life Sir Pherozeshah maintained a deep and sincere reverence for the traditions of Gladstone and Bright. That was the secret of much of his outlook on public affairs and the explanation of his invariable moderation and loyalty. I believe it was also the secret of his simple and powerful oratory. He never resented criticism however fierce. "He knew how to stand firm," and I believe he even enjoyed it, like every good fighting man. He learned in this country the valuable lesson never to be restive under criticism.

But there is another and even more important lesson for Young India, so well represented at this meeting, to be gained from the principles which animated our far-sighted and courageous statesman. The lesson of the need for local patriotism is more important, because of more general application than the temptation to Extremism or self-seeking flattery. Sir Pherozeshah will be remembered for generations to come as a devoted son of the city of his birth. He gave to "Bombay the Beautiful" his best thought, his most earnest effort, his most constant and untiring service. It was largely the great local influence he won in advocating municipal reform, in helping Lord Reay's Government to shape the great measure of 1888 and in diligently serving as a member of the Corporation, that contributed to his importance in the wider political sphere. In this respect his career inevitably recalls that of Mr. Joseph Chamberlain, the illustrious father of the Secretary of State for India, who first came into fame as a singularly successful reformer of municipal government in Birmingham. Not only did Sir Pherozeshah, like, the English statesman, remain faithful to the city where he won his spurs to the last day of his life; but when he found that service in the Imperial Legislature took much time and effort from civic affairs, he retired in favour of Mr. Gokhale, and contentedly went back to the nominally smaller stage of provincial and civic polity. If, as is generally acknowledged, Bombay has been more successful than any other Indian city in municipal administration, and this is partly due to the well-devised constitution Sir Pherozeshah assisted Lord Reay to shape, it is also largely due to his stedfast and noble example of devoted citizenship. His dominant power in the counsels of the Corporation was rarely challenged with any chance of success; but this remarkable ascendency would not have been maintained for a generation and more by the mere exercise of his great debating powers and his talent for affairs. It rested on the solid foundation of love for the "Town and Island," and determination in everything to seek its welfare and progress. His "uncrowned kingship" was a status willingly conferred by the representative of the second city of the British Empire under the assurance, confirmed by long experience, that his power would be exercised at all times with a single eye to the public interest.

No more inspiring example could be set for the emulation of Young India. Too often, I fear, Indian youths educated here return to the motherland filled with ambition to shine in the political firmament, to quickly figure in the legislature, to be known the country over as "leaders." But as necessarily only a few can reach the top, a large number gradually lose all connection with public life, and devote themselves entirely to their personal and professional affairs. They wish to begin where the most successful men in public life gained footing after years of apprenticeship in local affairs or other apparently undistinguished service of the people. On the part of the disappointed majority, the opportunities that lie close at hand are despised and neglected. Hence much fine material for the advancement of India runs to waste, and progress in local self-government has been much less marked than would have been the case had it been more generally recognised that local patriotism and seemingly minor service are the seeds of larger opportunities, beside being in themselves worthy objects of ambition for promoting communal good. This is constantly seen by those who look below the surface of English life with its manifold local and unpaid civic activities. The lesson is writ large in the life of Gokhale as well as that of Mehta, for we can never forget the long years of professional drudgery on merely nominal pay the former passed in the Fergusson College, nor the fact that he prized no later office or honour more than his helpful membership of the Poona Municipality. It is by attention to local affairs, by the exercise of local patriotism and effort, in the constructive spirit shown by these two great sons of India, that our country will advance most assuredly and most steadfastly to the realization of her great destiny and that our dreams of progress under the British Crown within the Empire will best be realized.

Such are the lessons which the great and honoured career of Sir Pherozeshah Mehta is calculated to teach. If they are duly learned by India's alert and eager young men, he will still do great things for our beloved country. He being dead will still speak by precept and example, and speak with eloquence and power. I can imagine nothing finer or better for a young Indian patriot than to take heart and carefully study the life-long principles and practice of three men whom I consider three of India's greatest and soundest sons – each an example and an inspiration to all his countrymen and to his own community as well – Mehta, Gokhale, and Buddrudin Tybejee (Loud applause).

Source: *The Times of India*, Bombay, 8 January 1916.

The meeting was held in London, and the report of its proceedings reached India rather late, "no uncommon thing nowadays when the mails are disorganised", as the newspaper put it. "We give it nevertheless because of the interest in the occasion", it added.

After the Aga Khan's speech two main resolutions were passed. The press report continues:

"The main resolution expressed keen sense of the loss suffered by India and her people, and high appreciation of Sir P. M. Mehta's public services extending over half a century, 'during which period, by his sagacious counsel, his unrivalled eloquence, his whole-hearted devotion to the promotion of the public weal, and his fearless advocacy of the rights of his countrymen, he contributed in a conspicuous degree to their political, educational and civic advancement.' It was moved by Lord Harris, whose speech was somewhat lacking in conciseness, owing as he told us, to his having been asked to address the meeting only on entering the hall. He also admitted that he laboured under the disadvantage of being separated by from 20 to 25 years from personal contact with this great Bombay citizen. With more recent experience he could have spoken, he said, with greater accuracy, though certainly not with greater sympathy. But he could speak with accuracy from his recollection of Sir Pherozeshah's political capacity, for while he was Governor probably his mental activities were at their keenest and highest. 'I daresay,' added Lord Harris, to the amusement of his audience, 'that if he had been asked before he passed away which of the Governors of Bombay gave him most trouble he would have said it was me. We were very keen opponents on certain questions, particularly questions in which the Municipal Corporation was largely interested, such questions as education and police charges. I am glad to say this – that while he was a most determined fighter, very keen in pressing his arguments, and very resolute in adhering to the principles which he believed to be right, he was as fair a fighter as I have ever come across, either in India or in England. I should be very sorry to say at this distance of time that in these controversies I was invariably right, and he was invariably wrong. I am certain of this – that at that time I knew I was right. (A laugh). But looking back to those struggles in the softer lights lent by distance, at a maturer age perhaps with less vivid desire to succeed in controversy, I acknowledge that Sir Pherozeshah's arguments were often unquestionably sound, and possibly were sometimes right.'

"Mr. Abbas Ali Baig seconded the resolution.

"After brief speeches from Mr. J. M. Parikh, and Dr. John Pollen, Sir Krishna Gupta moved a resolution of sympathy with Lady Mehta and the family. This was seconded by Mr. T. J. Bennett, who said that Sir Pherozeshah had been spoken of repeatedly as first and foremost a great Bombay citizen. But what did that mean? Bombay had a population almost equal to that of the newest of the Dominions – New Zealand – and therefore anyone who devoted his life

517

mainly to the service of such a city was something more than a local politician. Sir Pherozeshah had his critics, no doubt – but they recognised the high tone of his public life, the high principles for which he fought, and his keen patriotism. Mr. Bennett went on to say that in his recollection of Sir Pherozeshah the first things which stood out were his services to the city under the old Municipal Act. Along with Naoroji Furdonjee, Shapurjee Bengalee, Dosabhoy Framjee, and other great and good citizens of those times, he tried to get as much music as he possibly could out of that somewhat inadequate instrument. And when the instrument was replaced by the Act of 1888, in the shaping of which he had fought hard to secure the fullest possible measure of local self-government for Bombay, he was keen and alert in standing up for the full establishment and preservation of those liberties. People called him a dictator – but to call a man names did not carry us very far. What happened was that, thoroughly understanding the Act, he wanted to make it efficient, and to make the whole administration of the Municipality as efficient as possible. At that time many men who were working the new Act needed a leader, a teacher, a guide. Successive Municipal Commissioners had borne testimony to his most useful service in this respect. He knew of one who acknowledged that he could not have run the Corporation satisfactorily without the assistance of Sir P. M. Mehta. Mr. Bennett closed his speech with one of the most striking things said at the meeting: 'On larger public questions, Sir Pherozeshah took a very cautious view. Whatever his critics may say of him, there is this fact – that for nearly 50 years he had a prominent part in the municipal and political life of Bombay. For a considerable part of that time he was a foremost political leader and teacher. The opinion of Bombay, as largely led and moulded by him, is unquestionably the sanest, the most reasonable, and the most moderate opinion of any part of India.' "

42

THE QUATRAINS OF UMAR KHAYYAM

Foreword to John Pollen's Translation of Umar Khayyam

London: 1915

Middle Eastern poets – reasons for interest in Umar Khayyam in Europe – the appeal of the *Ruba'iat* – translations by Edward Fitzgerald and Dr. Pollen.

In the halcyon days of Persia's intellectual renaissance after the Arab conquest, the Middle East is said to have produced more poets than the whole of medieval Europe, but the works of no Oriental author have aroused the same degree of interest in the European mind as the modest "Ruba'iat" of Omar Khayyām. The secret of this phenomenon may be traced to Omar's thoughts on the inscrutable problems of Life and Death being, to some extent, in harmony with the rational tendencies produced by the collision of modern science with the unquestioning beliefs of a bygone age.

The charm of the "Ruba'iat," which lies in the intensely human spirit pervading them, is enhanced by the poet's inimitable directness of expression, his terse and incisive phrases and a simple grace of style, with that unrivalled and untranslatable music of words to which the sonorous language of Persia peculiarly lends itself. To reproduce these subtle features of the original in a translation is not an easy undertaking. FitzGerald succeeded in a remarkable degree in bringing out the spirit of Omar's quatrains in his famous translation, which in some respects transcends the beauty of the original, but to achieve this end he had to diverge from the letter of the "Ruba'iat" as well as from the sequence of the verses. Dr. John Pollen in his more faithful translation has accomplished a task of greater difficulty, and has done justice both to the letter and to the spirit of the original.

In its simple and attractive garb the version now offered to the public, for the benefit of the Indian soldiers who are now laying down their lives for the Empire on the battlefields of three continents, deserves to find a place on the bookshelves of the numerous admirers of the Poet in the English-speaking world.

Source: John Pollen, *Omar Khayyam, Faithfully and Literally Translated (From the Original Persian)*, East and West, London, 1915, pp. vii-viii.
In his Introduction, Pollen wrote: "I should also like to express my gratitude to His Highness the Aga Khan, who has so kindly favoured me with the graceful foreword to this little volume. Indeed, I do not think I should have made up my mind to publish this version in book-form had it not been for the cordial encouragement of His Highness who, a Persian scholar himself, saw some merit in my Translation" (p. xvii).

The book is made up of 158 quatrains translated "line for line" from Umar Khayyam, and 12 quatrains from Edward Fitzgerald's version along with their translation into Esperanto.

Thanks to Edward Fitzgerald's magnificent rendering of Umar Khayyam's quatrains, the reading public in the West has, for over a hundred years, known Khayyam better than any other Eastern poet. In fact, it is sometimes claimed that, next to the Bible, the *Ruba'iat* has had the largest sale in the Western world in the present century.

Fitzgerald also inspired many others to present the quatrains to European and American readers in their own languages. Thus it came to pass that Khayyam was, and still continues to be, translated in every Western language. For the interest of the reader with a literary taste I give below a list of the notable translations:

English: Edward Fitzgerald (London, 1st. edn 1859, 2nd. 1868, 3rd. 1872), E. H. Whinfield (London, 1st. edn 1883, 2nd. 1901), Edward Heron-Alder (London, 1898), J. H. McCarthy (London, 1889), Richard le Gallienne (London, 1897), J. L. Garner (London, 1898), Mrs M. H. Cadell (London, 1899), Frederick Baron Corvo (from the French of Nicolas, London, 1903), E. F. Thompson, (Worcester, Mass., 1906), G. Roe (Edinburgh, 1907), A. Rogers (Ilford, 1910), C. S. Tute (Exeter, 1926), Friedrich Rosen (London, 1930), J. C. E. Bowen (London, 1961), R. Graves and Omar Ali Shah (London, 1967), P. Mahmoud (Tehran, 1969), Parichehr Kasra (New York, 1975), A. Christenson (Copenhagen, 1927), W. G. Burton (Ryde, Isle of White, 1968), and Edward Fitzgerald, E. H. Whinfield and A. J. Arberry (London, 1949).

French: J. B. Nicolas (Paris, 1867), Fernand Henry (Paris, 1903), J. H. Hallard (London, 1912), Gareiu de Tassy (Paris, 1857), Pierre Pascal (Rome, 1958), E. Désiron (Louvain, 1959) and M. Fouladvand (Paris, 1960).

German: F. Bodenstedt (Breslau, 1881), M. R. Schenek (Halle, 1897), A. F. Grafen (Stuttgart, 1902) and C. H. Rempis (Tuobingen, 1935).

Russian: R. M. Aliyev (Moscow, 1959).

Dutch: J. van Schagen (Amsterdam, 1947) and J. A. Vooren (Amsterdam, 1955).

Italian: F. Gabrieli (Florence, 1944).

Spanish: Enrique Ponce (Santiago, 1927).

Portuguese: Plácido R. Castro (Vigo, 1965).

Swedish: A. E. Hermelin (Lund, 1928).

Polish: Edward Raezyuski (London, 1960).

Welsh: Sir John Morris Jones (Montgomeryshire, 1928).
Hebrew: Joseph Massel (Manchester, 1908).
Latin: H. W. Greene (Boston, Mass., 1898).

On Umar Khayyam and his *Ruba'iat* see Holbrook Jackson, *Edward Fitzgerald and Omar Khayyam*, London, 1899; Arthur Christensen, *Recherches sur les Rubaiyat de Omar Khayyam*, Heidelberg, 1905; J. K. M. Shirazi, *Life of Omar Khayyam*, Edinburgh, 1905; Laurent Tailhads, *Omar Khayyam et les poison de l'intelligence*, Paris, 1905; Otto Rothfeld, *Umah Khayyam and His Age*, London, 1922; Masud Ali Varesi, *Umar Khayyam*, London, 1922; T. H. Weir, *Omar Khayyam the Poet*, London, 1926; A. G. Potter, *A Bibliography of the Rubaiyat of Omar Khayyam*, London, 1929; Swami Govinda Tirtha, *The Nectar of Grace: Omar Khayyam's Life and Works*, Hyderabad Deccan, 1941; Harold Lamb, *Persian Mosaic: An Imaginative Biography of Omar Khayyam Based upon Reality, in the Oriental Manner*, London, 1943; Ahmad Hamid as – Sarraf, *Omar Khayyam . . . His Life, Works and Rubaiyat*, Baghdad, 1949; H. Halbaeh (comp.), *Romance of the Rubaiyat*, Santa Barbara, 1975; and any respectable history of Persian literature.

43

IN DEFENCE OF LORD HARDINGE

Letter to The Times

London (?): 17 July 1917

Indian admiration for Lord Hardinge – attacks on him in the press – Indian soldiers in World War One – the change of policy regarding Mesopotamia – Lord Hardinge's resignation – reforms in the Indian administration.

Nearly a dozen years have gone by since Parliament had the opportunity to hear expressions of Indian opinion at first hand. Unfortunately, there is no Indian now in either House of Parliament – an undoubted loss to the Empire as a whole. If any Indian were now in either House, no matter of what religion, province, or political complexion he might be, he would have been eager to testify in the Mesopotamian debates to the strength and unanimity of Indian admiration for and attachment to Lord Hardinge, and to condemn the ignorant attacks made upon him in some portions of the Press. My countrymen of all shades of thought feel that he has been most unjustly and ungratefully treated, and I am constrained to write on their behalf.

Lord Hardinge's work in India, both in peace and war, should be judged as a whole; and not alone by the temporary breakdown of military arrangements in Mesopotamia. Mr. Montagu himself, a statesman trusted and popular in India, and who knows India better than most people, accurately described him as the most popular Viceroy of modern times, and as showing himself, from first to last, a Viceroy upon whose sympathy and assistance Indians could rely. The hold that Lord Hardinge has upon the affection and gratitude of India has not been diminished by the findings of the Commission, and has been strengthened by the unfair attacks to which he has been exposed. The *Indian Social Reformer*, one of the most thoughtful and important of Nationalist Indian newspapers, and by no means given to flattery, has described the feeling of the people of India for Lord Hardinge as that of veneration – a very true description indeed.

The Mesopotamian breakdown was the inevitable result of the mistaken policy, so long pursued in relation to Indian military resources, actual and potential. Every well-informed man of the world knew, during the last 10 years, the inevitability of a war with Germany, and no attempt was made to adjust the prospective utilization of Indian military strength to such a contingency. The deliberate policy recommended by Lord Nicholson's Commission was to reduce the military expenditure of India to the lowest limits compatible with Indian safety from external landing and from internal commotion. Yet, when the moment of the world-crisis came, Lord Hardinge, rightly trusting India's profound loyalty to the Emperor and her indignant repudiation of German efforts to seduce her to revolt, sent the flower of the Indian Army to France, and it arrived in time to share in the glory of saving Calais. No request from England for help in any of the theatres of war was refused, and in a military sense India had been bled white before the Mesopotamia policy was completely changed by the decision of his Majesty's Government to authorize the advance to Baghdad. Lord Hardinge relied on his military advisers and on the unanimity of expert official opinion, both in London and Simla. His fault was one of too-generous response, considering the means immediately available, to the many calls made upon India. Even the chairman of the Commission has testified in your columns to the force of these considerations.

On the question of the use of private telegrams in relation to matters in which secrecy was essential, it may be remarked that this system was an old inheritance, and was not developed – much less was it established – by Lord Hardinge and Mr. Chamberlain.

Indian opinion heartily endorses the refusal of Mr. Balfour to accept the resignation, twice tendered by Lord Hardinge, of his present appointment. It asks that the malignant persecution of this statesman, who trusted and loved India and who inspired unbounded Indian sacrifices in the first half of the war, should cease; and it shares with Lord George Hamilton the view that time should be utilized not to belittle the great services of the ex-Viceroy, but to effect urgently-needed reforms in Indian administration.

Source: *The Times*, London, 23 July 1917.

The letter was published under the double heading of "Mesopotamia and Lord Hardinge: The Aga Khan's Views."

See also "India under Hardinge and After", *New Statesman*, 29 April 1916; "India under Lord Hardinge", *Quarterly Review*, July 1916; "Lord Hardinge's Return", *The Times*, 24 April 1916; William Wedderburn, "The Viceroyalty of Lord Hardinge", *Contemporary Review*, March 1916; "The New Developments in the Constitution of the Empire", *Round Table*, June 1917; and A. E. Duchesne, "The Mesopotamia Report: and After", *Empire Review*, August 1917.

44

GOKHALE'S LAST POLITICAL TESTAMENT

Letter to The Times

London: 12 August 1917

Tribute to G. K. Gokhale – his political ideas – his "last political will and testament" – his views on financial devolution and the electoral process.

The death of Mr. G. K. Gokhale some six months after the outbreak of war deprived India of the services of an illustrious son, whose constructive statesmanship would have been of the highest value in working out those political readjustments which are universally recognized to be necessary if India is to play an adequate and worthy part in the Imperial developments of the future. From the time of the King-Emperor's Delhi Durbar, when a measure of provincial autonomy was foreshadowed, and especially after Germany drew the sword to bring both West and East under her domination, Mr. Gokhale gave careful consideration to "the next step" on the high road to self-government within the Empire. Though he knew his days were numbered by the insidious disease against which he so bravely struggled, he cherished the general expectation at that time that the war would terminate by the end of 1915, and therefore hoped to live to share in the work of Indian reconstruction.

In the early weeks of 1915 the illness of my honoured friend grew more serious, and I urged him to put on record the ideas he had frequently expressed to me in preceding weeks. Accordingly his last political will and testament, as he termed it, was carefully prepared only a few days before his death, and was entrusted to my care, a duplicate copy being sent, confidentially, for greater safety, to his old political associate, the late Sir P. M. Mehta. In accordance with the author's wishes, immediately after his death I gave a copy confidentially to the Governor of Bombay, and the then Viceroy and Secretary of State for India also received copies. Mr. Gokhale left to my discretion the choice of the right time for any publication, it being understood that in any event this would not be delayed beyond the close of the war. I now fulfil this sacred trust, in the conviction that if the great patriot were alive today he would give his views to the world, now that the proposals of the Government of India for reform are under consideration by his Majesty's Government, and some pronouncement thereon cannot be long delayed. Indeed, my only doubt is whether he would have postponed publication so long. I now communicate his considered opinions, with which I am in hearty agreement, in the assurance that they will have a beneficial effect upon Indian thought and contribute materially to the evolution of a sound progressive policy.

On two points only is any explanation needed. In reference to the plan of financial devolution, Mr. Gokhale recognized that Bengal, with its permanent settlement, might be confronted by difficulties of adjustment; but he looked to the Presidency under autonomous Government to find a solution of the problem by some such expedient as death duties or enhanced income tax. The other and more important point relates to the outline of a plan of indirect elections to the Legislatures through the municipalities and local boards, instead of a direct franchise. His personal preference for direct elections, in so far as they were practicable in Indian conditions, was often expressed to me, and he regretted the fact that in the Morley-Minto reforms very little was done in this direction. But he feared considerable opposition from officials in India to this form of election, and refrained from urging it in the memorandum because he was reluctant to raise controversy by insisting on any point that he did not consider absolutely vital. I am glad to know from many friends that there is now a tendency on the part of the Indian Civil Service to welcome a system of direct elections by the people. Such a system can be applied to the constructive scheme Mr. Gokhale drew up as a final service to his Motherland and the Empire.

Source: *The Times*, London, 15 August 1917

The letter was published under the triple heading of "Mr. Gokhale's Last Testament: Outline of Indian Progress: Provincial Autonomy."

The Times also wrote a 2-column editorial on Gokhale's proposals on the same day. The Aga Khan's letter and Gokhale's memorandum also appeared in the *Manchester Guardian* of 15 August. The letter and its enclosure were commented upon in Shaikh H. M. and Erfan Ali, letter, *Manchester Guardian*, 18 August;

"The Future of India", *New Statesman*, 18 August; and "The Genesis of the Present Situation in India", *Round Table*, December 1917.

Gokhale's memorandum, as printed in *The Times*, ran as follows (full text):

PROVINCIAL AUTONOMY

The grant of provincial autonomy, foreshadowed in the Delhi dispatch, would be a fitting concession to make to the people of India at the close of the war. This will involve the twofold operation of freeing the Provincial Governments on the one side, from the greater part of the control which is at present exercised over them by the Government of India and the Secretary of State, in connexion with the internal administration of the country, and substituting on the other, in place of the control so removed, the control of the representatives of taxpayers through Provincial Legislative Councils. I indicate below in brief outline the form of administration that should be set up in the different provinces to carry out this idea. Each province should have:–

(1) A Governor appointed from England at the head of the administration.
(2) A Cabinet or Executive Council of six members – three of whom should be Englishmen and three Indians – with the following portfolios:–
   (*a*) Home (including Law and Justice);
   (*b*) Finance;
   (*c*) Agriculture, Irrigation, and Public Works;
   (*d*) Education;
   (*e*) Local self-government (including sanitation and medical relief);
   (*f*) Industries and Commerce.

While members of the Indian Civil Service should be eligible for appointment to the Executive Council, no places in the Council should be reserved for them, the best men available being taken – both English and Indian.

(3) A Legislative Council of between 75 and 100 members, of whom not less than four-fifths should be elected by different constituencies and interests. Thus in the Bombay Presidency, roughly speaking, each district should return two members, one representing municipalities and the other district and taluk boards. The City of Bombay should have about 10 members allotted to it. Bodies in the moffussil like the Karachi Chamber, Ahmedabad mill-owners, Deccan Sardars, should have a member each. Then there would be the special representation of Mahomedans, and here and there a member may have to be given to communities like the Lingayats, where they are strong. There should be no nominated non-official members, except as experts. A few official members may be added by the Governor as experts or to assist in representing the Executive Government.

(4) The relations between the Executive Government and the Legislative Council so constituted should be roughly similar to those between the Imperial Government and the Reichstag in Germany. The Council will have to pass all provincial legislation, and its assent will be necessary to additions to or changes in provincial taxation. The Budget, too, will have to come to it for discussion and its resolutions in connexion with it, as also on questions of general adminis-tration, will have to be given effect to unless vetoed by the Governor. More frequent meetings or longer continuous sittings will also have to be provided for. But the members of the Executive Government shall not depend, individually or

collectively, on the support of a majority of the Council, for holding their offices.

(5) The Provincial Government so reconstituted and working under the control of the Legislative Council as outlined above, should have complete charge of the internal administration of the province. And it should have virtually independent financial powers, the present financial relations between it and the Government of India being largely revised, and to some extent even reversed. The revenue under salt, customs, tributes, railways, post, telegraph, and mint should belong exclusively to the Government of India, the services being Imperial, while that under land revenue, including irrigation, excise, forest, assessed taxes, stamps, and registration, should belong to the Provincial Government – the services being provincial. As under this division the revenue falling to the Provincial Government will be in excess of its existing requirements and that assigned to the Government of India will fall short of its present expenditure, the Provincial Government should be required to make an annual contribution to the Government of India, fixed for periods of five years at a time. Subject to this arrangement, the Imperial and the Provincial Governments should develop their separate systems of finance, the Provincial Government being given powers of taxation and borrowing within certain limits.

(6) Such a scheme of provincial autonomy will be incomplete unless it is accompanied by (a) a liberalizing of the present form of district administration; and (b) a great extension of local self-government. For (a) it will be necessary to abolish the Commissionerships of divisions except where special reasons may exist for their being maintained, as in Sind, and to associate small district councils, partly elected and partly nominated, with the collector, to whom most of the present powers of the Commissioners could then be transferred – the functions of the councils being advisory to begin with. For (b) village panchayats, partly elected and partly nominated, should be created for villages or groups of villages, and municipal boards in towns and taluk boards in talukas should be made wholly elected bodies, the Provincial Government reserving to itself and exercising stringent powers of control. A portion of the Excise revenue should be made over to these bodies, so that they may have adequate resources at their disposal for the due performance of their duties. The district being too large an area for efficient local self-government by an honorary agency, the functions of the district boards should be strictly limited, and the collector should continue to be its *ex-officio* president.

THE GOVERNMENT OF INDIA

1. The provinces being thus rendered practically autonomous, the constitution of the Executive Council or the Cabinet of the Viceroy will have to be correspondingly altered. At present there are four members in that Council, with portfolios which concern the internal administration of the country – viz., Home, Agriculture, Education, and Industries and Commerce. As all internal administration will now be made over to the Provincial Governments, and the Government of India will only retain in its hands nominal control, to be exercised on very rare occasions, one member, to be called Member for the Interior, should suffice in place of these four. It will, however, be necessary to create certain other portfolios, and I would have the Council consist of the following six members (at least two of whom shall always be Indian): (a) Interior; (b) Finance; (c) Law; (d) Defence (Navy and Army); (e) Communications (Railways, Post and Telegraphs); and (f) Foreign.

2. The Legislative Council of the Viceroy should be styled the Legislative Assembly of India. Its members should be raised to about 100 to begin with, and its powers enlarged; but the principle of an official majority (for which perhaps it will suffice to constitute a nominated majority) should for the present be continued, until sufficient experience has been gathered of the working of autonomous arrangements for the provinces. This will give the Government of India a reserved power in connexion with provincial administration to be exercised in emergencies. Thus, if a provincial Legislative Council persistently declines to pass legislation which the Government regards to be essential in the vital interests of the province, it could be passed by the Government of India in its Legislative Assembly over the head of the province. Such occasions would be extremely rare, but the reserve power will give a sense of security to the authorities and will induce them to enter on the great experiment of provincial autonomy with greater readiness. Subject to this principle of an official or nominated majority being for the present maintained, the Assembly should have increased opportunities of influencing the policy of the Government by discussion, questions connected with the Army and Navy (to be now created) being placed on a level with other questions. In financial matters the Government of India so constituted should be freed from the control of the Secretary of State, whose control in other matters, too, should be largely reduced, his Council being abolished, and his position being steadily approximated to that of the Secretary of State for the Colonies.

Commissions in the Army and Navy must now be given to Indians, with proper facilities for military and naval instruction.

German East Africa, when conquered from the Germans, should be reserved for Indian colonization and be handed over to the Government of India.

(signed) G. K. Gokhale

On Gokhale see J. S. Hoyland, *Gopal Krishna Gokhale: His Life and Speeches*, Calcutta, 1933; T. V. Parvate, *Gopal Krishna Gokhale: A Narrative and Interpretive Review of His Life and Contemporary Events*, Ahmadabad, 1959; E. Lucia and H. G. D. Turnbull, *Gopal Krishna Gokhale (A Brief Biography)*, Trichur, 1934; Stanley A. Wolpert, *Tilak and Gokhale*, Berkeley and Los Angeles, 1962; D. G. Karve and D. V. Ambedkar (eds), *Speeches and Writings of Gopal Krishna Gokhale, Vol. II: Political*, London, 1966; T. R. Deogirikar, *Gopal Krishna Gokhale*, New Delhi, 1964.

45

INDIA IN TRANSITION
A STUDY IN POLITICAL EVOLUTION

Extracts from a Book

London and Bombay: June 1918

CHAPTER II

THE REASONS FOR REFORM

The likely consequences if changes are not initiated – the examples of Russia and Turkey – the greater association of the people with the government in Japan, Prussia and Britain – Britain's duty in India – allegiance to the British Sovereign and flag cannot last unless changes in the administration are introduced – example of Mesopotamia – the importance of urban dwellers and literate classes in India – changes in the outlook of Muslims throughout the world – the attitude of Muslims in India – the perception of freedom among the Hindus – bring the structure of Indian administration in line with the spirit of the times – forces for the creation of modern administration in South Asia – Britain should not deny India certain forms of constitutionalism – the necessity of sound finances – criticism of British rule in India – the question of taxation – the need to train a modern army in India – a higher standard of citizenship for the people – co-operation between the people and the government – create a modern state.

Soon after undertaking the preparation of this book I was set thinking by a conversation with one of the most distinguished of present-day British publicists, the greatest living authority on Russia and Central and Eastern Europe. His keen intimacy with world politics embraces mankind from China to Peru, but alas! in the course of his long and busy life he has never had occasion to visit India or specially study her affairs. He asked me why India required any marked change of system. Taking into consideration the divisions of the people, the illiteracy of the masses, the rivalries of religions and races, he asked why, confronted by all this clash and backwardness, England could not go on more or less as she had done throughout the nineteenth century, and rule her vast Asiatic dominions with undivided but conscientiously exercised authority.

My friend maintained that divisions being deep and real and political harmony being confined to a small minority of the upper and educated classes, there will be no real need for a change of policy until such time as the masses insist on their rights and take a share in the responsibilities of government. His purpose was, I think, to draw from me a reasoned statement of the case for reform. Coming from the incisive critic alike of the reign and policy of Alexander III and of the ultra-democratic Bolshevists of the hour this view seemed to me singularly unconvincing. If there is one thing which modern history proves, it is this: that unless the government and the governing classes take up the task of raising the masses of the people gradually, but surely, thus founding the fabric of the commonwealth on the widest and deepest basis possible, namely, the whole population, the State renders itself liable to years and years of anarchy and disaster, and perhaps to dissolution.

Look at the Russian portent. Had Alexander II lived a few years longer, had the policy of Loris Milikoff been carried out in 1881, had the last twenty years of the nineteenth century been occupied with construction and education, with uniting the people and the government, and with the evolution of self-government in the various provinces, how different and how happy and healthy Russian history would have been! Taking another instance, the disastrous reign of Abdul Hamid in Turkey might have been one of revivifying forces, had that astute but misguided sovereign devoted the same period to the work of gradual association of the people with the government on the one hand, and to social and cultural development of the masses on the other . . .

Conversely there are examples of countries where a wise and patriotic aristocracy, in association with an intelligent monarchy belonging to the soil, has worked wonders and has so interwoven the interests of every class that even the Socialists are to-day the

531

pillars of the State. Japan is a case in point, and Prussia, whatever its severity and remorselessness towards outside peoples, provides an instance of successful consolidation of all classes through gradual steps of greater association of the people with the government. England herself supplies the outstanding clear-cut example of this healthy development, though she differs from the two other instances quoted by her work having been almost unconscious. Instead of taking place in two centuries, as in Prussia, and in two generations, as in Japan, it has gone on from the dawn of English history.

If the British, on whom historical causes have thrown the ultimate responsibility for the future of India and of surrounding states and nations, were to fail in this their greatest task, Southern Asia would become the theatre of one of the heaviest disasters humanity has faced. Sooner or later, an ignorant and innumerable proletariat, extending over nearly the whole length of Asia from the Red Sea to the Pacific, divided by religion and race and language, would be faced with the problem of self-government and self-development. The course of Russian history in our times provides a tragic warning to those who are responsible for the future of India of the dangers of leaving the apparently well alone, and of not working for the development of the masses in rights and duties alike and in responsibility towards society. It has been well said that the British tenure in India must be one of continuous amelioration.

But apart from these lessons of modern history we have to recognise the existence of internal forces in India proper and in the neighbouring states and principalities that render a policy of standing still or of merely nominal concession a practical impossibility since it would work disaster, in the long run, alike for Britain and for India. These forces may not individually be powerful enough to compel renunciation of existing forms of government; but, taken together and in connection with other world forces which react even in remote portions of Southern Asia, they are so enormous in their effect that a radical change of outlook is necessary. A brief examination of some of the more important of them is desirable.

In the forefront we must place the fact that until the summer of 1914 there was a white and European solidarity *vis-à-vis* Asia and Africa which, though officially unrecognized, was yet the foundation of European policy in the widest sense of the term. A small but suggestive point of nomenclature illustrates my meaning. The British governing classes and the white mercantile community were referred to throughout India as "Europeans," and the general line of differentiation as between the governors and the governed was shown by the terms "European" and "Native," or latterly the more acceptable cognomen "Indian." There were many other signs of the concert of Europe at work, though of course officially unrecognised. The German, French or Italian trader or missionary had social union with the British rulers and business men, carrying inherent privileges that made them members of the same governing European family. But the Great War has broken up that solidarity. The German and Austrian missionary and trader has been interned in India or repatriated, and all and sundry have watched the humiliation of these fallen members of the white race. The most remote villagers have heard of the sepoys who have fought hand to hand with the fairest inhabitants of Europe. The long-maintained racial line of demarcation has been largely replaced by that of allegiance to Sovereign and flag.

For the full establishment of this sound guiding principle the claims of merit and fidelity must become predominant. By universal testimony this war has shown that the loyalty of the people of India to Emperor and Empire is second to none. In no other belligerent country, not even in Great Britain or Germany, have the forces of sedition and anarchy been so minute in proportion to the numbers of law-abiding as in India. The small and insignificant factions which sought to create difficulties at a time of Imperial stress were but as a drop in the ocean, and all classes came forward to help England in her hour of trial. True the numbers of recruits, though vastly in excess of normal requirements, were small compared to the teeming population. But, as will be seen when we discuss the military needs of India, this was due to obvious historical, sociological, and political causes, not to any want of loyalty. Wherever and whenever any help could be given by the people of India it was heartily bestowed. Can the annals of any other country ruled by an essentially foreign governing class responsible to an external Power, show the people coming forward and making equal sacrifices from patriotic motives?

. . . This altogether healthy Indian sentiment cannot last unless changes are introduced in the administration so as to give the people a fuller share and voice in the control of affairs in their own country. Many forces, internal and external, are working to awaken Indians in general, and the urban population in particular, to the reasonableness of their claims to a share in their own government.

And if we turn to neighbouring countries within the orbit of India we find that some have enjoyed to the present time forms of self-government, and others look upon themselves as conquering and independent races. Take the case of Mesopotamia. However bad Turkish rule there may have been, yet, even under Abdul Hamid's absolutist government, there was nominal equality of rights between Turk and Arab. Under the Young Turks, however insubstantial constitutional government may have been, the people of Baghdad and of Basra had the same rights of representation in the Chamber of Deputies as the people of Ismid or Adrianople, though in practice they were reduced to nothing of substantial value.

Yet if Mesopotamia is to become a British or a semi-British province, it is impossible to establish a purely bureaucratic administration among a people who have had at least nominal equality of opportunity with the Turkish rulers. Can it be seriously maintained that Britain can establish a government based in some degree on co-operation of the rulers and the ruled in Mesopotamia, and at the same time continue in India an administration in no sense responsible to the people? Though illiteracy is, alas! still general, though divisions, especially amongst the untaught masses, are deep, there is a general consensus of opinion amongst the upper and middle classes that the establishment of an administrative system more or less responsible to the people, and drawing its forces from their confidence and co-operation, cannot be long delayed.

We all know that the vast Indian majority consists of illiterate peasants and field labourers in the rural districts, but it must not be forgotten that the urban dwellers and the literate classes, though forming but a small proportion of the aggregate total, are still numerous enough to be equal to the population of a secondary European state. In 1911 the urban ratio was 9.5 per cent, and the census recorded more than $18\frac{1}{2}$ million literates. Each year the schools and colleges and factories draw more and more from the great reservoir of the country districts to the towns and cities. No one familiar with modern India will deny that everywhere in the towns and in almost every class, there is a growing desire for a form of government that will allow the Indian to carry his head high as a citizen of a free Empire, and at the same time will provide the means for raising the lower classes of the rural population to a fuller standard of citizenship and life.

Again, a fundamental change has come over the Indian outlook on public affairs. I have often been told by English civilians that the Musulmans need another Sir Syed Ahmed, and that it is a pity that his political policy has disappeared. My answer has always been that Lord Beaconsfield [Benjamin Disraeli] and his Mahomedan policy are as dead as cold mutton. I am not sure if the gentlemen who started the conversation on these lines always realised what this answer conveyed. But here it is necessary to put on record the changed perspective within the last generation.

Twenty-five years ago the average Indian Moslem looked upon himself as a member of a universal religious brotherhood, sojourning in a land in which a neutral Government, with a neutral outlook, kept law and order and justice. His political and communal pride was satisfied by the fact that his co-religionists in Turkey, Persia, Morocco, and (nominally at least) in Egypt enjoyed independence and national sovereignty. While his allegiance was to Queen Victoria, his political self-respect was satisfied by the existence of the Sultans at Constantinople and Fez, and of the Shah and Khedive at Teheran and Cairo. The fact that the British Government was the mainstay and support in the diplomatic arena of the independent Mahomedan States was naturally a source of continued gratification to him. Far be it from me to suggest that all this was actually and consciously thought, and deductions made therefrom. But it is the semi-conscious and the sub-conscious that give atmosphere to national even more than to individual life. It was sub-conscious hostility towards Western Europe that drove Germany into war, and it was sub-conscious sentiment that early in the present century drew the peoples of England and France together, long before they were compelled to draw the sword for the defence of the liberty and civilisation of mankind.

Within this generation, the whole Mahomedan world-outlook has changed. Forces beyond Moslem control led to the disappearance of Mahomedan rule and independence in North Africa. Persia gradually drifted into being merely a name for spheres of influence between Britain and Russia. Turkey herself, the last of the independent Mahomedan dominions, was drawn into the Teutonic orbit, first through economic and semi-political causes, and finally by her participation in the Great War on the German side. I do not suggest that the destruction of the independence of these last Moslem States was conscious and deliberate; but so strong are the world forces of this generation that states and societies which have stood still for centuries have now been overthrown by the strong currents of European and American activity. The net result is that the Indian Mahomedan, instead of holding but the outposts of Islam in the East, sees around him nothing but Moslem societies in a far greater state of decay than his own. The banner of the Prophet is no longer in strong hands in North Africa or Persia, and Turkey has become the political enemy of England and a satrapy of Germany. Under these circumstances, he necessarily looks upon India more and more as the hope of his political freedom and as the centre that may still raise the other Mahomedan countries to a higher standard of civilisation.

Another point to be remembered is that while, under the old conditions, the Mahomedans were doomed to be nothing but a one-fifth minority in an overwhelmingly Brahmanical India, to-day, as the forces of disruption gain strength in Western Asia, it is not improbable that the South Asiatic Federation of to-morrow, of which India must be the centre and the pivot, will contain not only the $66\frac{1}{2}$ millions of Indian Moslems, but the thirty or forty millions more Musulmans inhabiting South Persia, Mesopotamia, Arabia, and Afghanistan. If we turn from numbers to surface of territory, the Islamic provinces of South Asia will be almost as great in extent as the India of yesterday. Hence there is little danger of the Mahomedans of India being nothing but a small minority in the coming federation. No doubt these considerations, again, are sub-conscious and semi-conscious; but they are potent. The Indian Moslem of to-day is no more haunted by the fear of being a powerless minority; nor has he constantly to look for his sentimental satisfaction to the Islamic States outside India.

Turning our gaze from the Moslems to the vast Hindu population, we find among its educated members the feeling that the great conflict announced as a war for liberty and freedom, for the protection of self-development in small countries, such as Belgium and Serbia, carries for the Allies the implication that political freedom is the heritage of every nation, great or small. The principles that render the Allied cause just in Europe are of universal application, *mutatis mutandis*, and lead to the deduction that India, too, must be set on the path of self-government. At this moment India and Egypt are almost the only two stable and advanced great countries where the administration is not in any appreciable degree responsible to the people, and where the foundation of State polity is the theory that the government is superior to the governed. Some fifteen years ago, when, for instance, Lord Curzon and Lord Cromer ruled in India and in Egypt, Russia, Turkey, Persia, and China were all ruled on this principle. But recent transformations in those lands leave the position of India unique. China and the Russias are republics, with nominally the most democratic forms of government, and Persia and Turkey both claim to be considered constitutional monarchies. Thus, in India alone we have a Government that is not only in practice free from internal parliamentary control, but is actually based on the principle that final decisions are in the hands of an administration not responsible to the people, although some opportunities for criticism are given in the Vice-regal and provincial legislatures. The contradictory position of the Government leads to its being open to attack from all quarters, and yet to its being considered anomalous that Indians, alone of the great Eastern peoples, should have no control over their administration. These causes, and many others, have led to general expectation and desire throughout the length and breadth of India that, when the cause of liberty as represented by the Allied armies has led humanity through victory to peace, the structure of Indian administration also may be brought into line with the spirit of the times and a reasonable share of control and supervision be given to the Indian public.

If we turn to the Native States and to the fully or semi-independent countries, such as Afghanistan and Nepal and the Arabian principalities, we find a general recognition on the part of the authorities that the time is coming for sharing their powers with the ruled. The best administered of the Native States and most of the princes desire to establish some form of legislative or other constitutional government. This would serve the two-fold purpose of giving their States the prestige and force of national institutions, and the ruling houses the claim of being united with the people by the ties of co-operation in the work of administration. In Afghanistan some attempt, howsoever nominal, has been made by the present King to lay the foundations of a representative institution. In fact everywhere in South Asia we find local forces striving, if sometimes unconsciously, after forms of administration more or less modern in character and leading to association and co-operation between the sovereign power and the nation. It follows that however excellent the present administration of India may be, however efficient and suited to the conditions of the recent past, it is not for the people of England to deny to their great Eastern Empire those forms of constitutionalism which were first developed in Britain and with the manifestations of which, whether in infancy or vigorous growth, England has always sympathised in the case of other countries on the European, American, and Asiatic continents.

Apart from the general considerations examined hitherto, there are administrative reasons which render imperative a change of system and policy. To begin with, no sounder political theory has been laid down than that maintained by the English economists, namely, good finance is the foundation of good government. It was bad finance that broke up the monarchy in France, and the most disastrous of the present-day examples, Turkey and Russia, point to the same conclusion – that without sound finance ruin overtakes society. In India innumerable Viceroys, Secretaries of State and other competent observers have always held that good finance is fundamental to the moral authority of British rule. If this has been the case in the past, when the work of government was limited, how much more so to-day and to-morrow, when civilised societies expect from their governments the righting of social wrongs, thorough handling of the problems of sanitation and public instruction, and the establishment of a certain level of well-being as the inherent right of every citizen?

Now, British rule in India has been criticised, and rightly criticised, for having allowed the twentieth century to dawn and grow without having grappled fully and successfully with the illiteracy general in India, and with the insanitary environment of the masses so bad that avoidable deaths are counted by the million every year, while the standard of the physique of the masses is deplorably low. The various modern departments of State that lead towards social betterment and social welfare in the West have still to be organised. The Indian public conscience unanimously demands that British rule should come into line with progressive modern ideas and tackle illiteracy and other social problems left far too long unsolved.

We shall be told, rightly, that at bottom, these are questions of bearable taxation. How are we to provide the means for meeting such crying needs of India? There are only two ways: either by co-operation between the Government and the governed and by discussion, proving to the representatives of the people the need, and thus making the Indian public itself the judge of the extent of the necessary sacrifice; or by mere fiat and mandate of the Supreme Government imposing taxation. Lord Cromer always held in conversations which I had with him that a government such as that of Britain in India and Egypt could not maintain itself except by light taxation, and Lord Morley's lately published "Recollections" show him to be of a like opinion. But Lord Cromer's own rule at Cairo laid itself open to the pointed criticism that while the Egyptian peasant grew rich he remained dirty and ignorant, superstitious and slovenly. Does not this go to prove that bureaucratic government, when well-intentioned and paternal, is conscious of some lack of moral right to call for those sacrifices from the people that will raise their condition in the cultural and sociological field *pari passu* with, or in advance of, their economic progress?

In India, however, it is far too late to adopt Lord Cromer's policy of light taxation in preference to modern advancement. The best rulers of Native States have endeavoured in their relatively small way to solve the problems of illiteracy and social betterment. The leaders of India unanimously expect from their Government the steady provision of those agencies which in Europe and America have brought about the fusion of culture between the masses and the classes. It is for the Government to take steps necessary to find the means for carrying out this policy, and this can be done with the co-operation of the representatives of the people and by discussion that will prove to the rulers and the ruled that the resources to be tapped are those that can best bear the burden of greater taxation.

If we turn from the problem of finance to the only other equally important and equally essential principle of government, namely, that of defence, we are forced to the same conclusion: that the sharing of responsibility between the people of India and its government is now necessary. I earnestly cherish the hope of President Wilson that a society of nations may result from the tremendous cost and suffering of these years of conflict, and I am convinced that forms of arbitration and limitation of armaments, through international agencies of control, will arise after the war. Yet no one who looks at the problem of Asia to-day can doubt that India must be prepared and ready to defend herself. Whether Britain keeps Mesopotamia, or whether that rich but neglected land becomes an independent principality or republic under British suzerainty, or whether it goes back to some form of Turkish control, yet its economic relations with India must so grow as to give us in practice a trans-Gulf frontier to defend. The same is true of Persia, and if we look Eastwards, with the growth of Japan and with the problem of our North-East frontier touching China, we cannot afford to neglect India's potentialities.

Now, a small and professional army, such as India had and has to-day, can never possess the reserves and the natural expanding power to meet modern war, with its terrible casualties, with its heavy technical services, with its lines of communication to be conserved and defended. While the Russias will not trouble us for generations, Germany, directly or indirectly, has become an Asiatic Power. Assuming that Turkey loses Mesopotamia and Syria, German military organisation will yet still be supreme on the other side of the Taurus Mountains and in the uplands of Asia Minor. Howsoever friendly modern Japan may be, and howsoever impotent modern China, yet India can never again be left to depend merely on Japanese goodwill and Chinese weakness for her security against attack from the East. Just as Australia, although she has the sea to protect her from sudden attack, has had to organise her defensive forces on modern lines by universal training, so the India of the next decade must develop her internal forces in such a way as to be able to meet any sudden emergency.

In India, with its 315,000,000 inhabitants, universal military service can be hardly feasible and probably will never be necessary; yet some form of fairly distributed national service falling on, say, 10 per cent of the inhabitants of each locality, to be selected by purely physical tests of healthiness and efficiency, can alone meet her problem of defence. No doubt the military training here referred to will not be the two or three years of the German and French Armies, but rather the six months of the Swiss forces. Such is, in fact, the proposal contained in a Territorial scheme submitted to the Indian Government in 1916. Still, this will be such a tax on the energy and life of the people that it is inconceivable that any country should willingly accept it without the imprimatur of her elected spokesmen; nor can such representation be merely nominal as at present. It must comprise men drawn directly from the masses and from every locality.

Thus, from the two essential points of view of finance and defence alike, we come to the conclusion that a higher standard of citizenship, with both greater sacrifices and greater responsibilities, must be imposed on the people if the great work of Britain is not to end in failure. The accomplishment of the task which destiny has placed before England cannot be complete unless India is raised, through social laws and institutions, to the standard of at least a backward European or Spanish-American country. The necessary corollary is that India must be so able to defend herself from foreign aggression as to make her independent of the mere goodwill or the accidental and temporary impotence of her neighbours. Yet neither of these two great conditions can be brought about without the co-operation, through representative institutions, of the people with the Government, and without a thorough change of system that unites the administration with the masses by constant discussion leading to unity of aim between the direct representatives of the people and the highest officers of the Crown.

Thus, from several principal points of view and apart from the many minor lines of argument that lead to the same conclusions, we see that the Government of India needs radical change; that the time has come when it should be no more a mere government of fiat, however excellent the fiat, but an essentially modern State based on the co-operation of every community and of the Government, by giving to the people themselves the right to direct policy. In succeeding chapters I hope to show that this metamorphosis will not only lead to the happiness and contentment of India, but to the strengthening of the British Empire as a whole and to drawing India nearer to England and the Dominions.

CHAPTER III

A FEDERAL BASIS

Preconditions for the Western form of parliamentary government – Bismarck's views – British, French and Swiss experiences – conditions in India not suitable for a centralized form of government – illiteracy in India – Aurangzeb's mistake in the past – federalism the only solution for India – adaptation to local conditions necessary – a future United States of India.

The perusal of the last chapter might lead the man in the street to the facile conclusion that the grant of representative assemblies, such as European States possess, would meet the needs of India, and that a full plan of co-operation between rulers and the ruled could be easily brought about by an edict from the King-Emperor. No such short cut to constitutionalism will do in India. To begin with, parliamentary government so far has been markedly successful only in countries of relatively small area, however populous any such given area may be. England,

France, Germany, Sweden, Italy – you find no country with a greater surface than two or three hundred thousand square miles. We can draw no conclusions from the constitutions of Canada, Australia, and some of the South American republics, because these states are still at the dawn of national life; their populations are but handfuls compared to what they must be when full development is reached. At present society is limited to certain large cities and emporiums of trade, and small, widely scattered rural communities. In the United States, on the other hand, the very name of the country shows that the Republic consists of independent parliamentary communities.

This view of a State, relatively small in area or population, as the best foundation of parliamentary government was held by Bismarck, as I learned from his son, Count Herbert, in Berlin, only two years after the death of the founder of United Germany. In the course of a long conversation about a federation that has been fraught with such momentous consequences to mankind, Herbert Bismarck told me that one of the features which led his father to expect a successful development was that the great majority of administrative affairs would remain in the hands of each of the individual States of the Bundesrat. The Reichstag would deal only with questions relating to the Army, Foreign, and Maritime affairs. Bismarck maintained to the end that organic parliamentary union, such as exists in France and in the United Kingdom, would break down in Germany since the empire, instead of being a compact geographical unit, was a long and scattered dominion. If this could be said of Germany, how much truer it is of far wider empires. And since Russia secured some parliamentary freedom, we have seen inevitable causes leading to her break-up into smaller state organisms. Though the present rush of disruptive forces may be the result of war, ignorance, and the long period of misgovernment, can anyone doubt that, at best, liberty and freedom in Russia would have led to her division into component states?

If, on the other hand, it is maintained that modern science, through vast railways and still more through rapid aerial navigation, has reduced distances, and that probably before the next few years are over aerial travelling will further abridge them, this contention will not remove the condition that only the geographically small parliamentary unit can be free and great. For, as we see, while Science on the one side brings distant places nearer, on the other hand, by giving intensive culture to localities and by highly developing local economic interests, it undoes the results of its first and apparent action. In a large primitive area, while distances are enormous and means of communication few, yet unless great natural obstacles, such as mountains and seas, arise, there is a general similarity of interest and occupation that makes for homogeneity. On the other hand, the higher the development of modern civilisation on a continent, the more heterogeneous and individual its parts become. And if this be true of Europe, with its single type of culture, it is far more applicable to India, where all the four main civilisations of the world are found, and where the problem is still further complicated by relatively minor differences of race, religion, history and development.

Even in a political entity so small in area as the United Kingdom, independently of the embittered controversies caused by Ireland's racial and religious differences, the legislative combination of England and Wales, Scotland and Ireland has presented serious practical drawbacks. The efficiency of the Mother of Parliaments is notoriously hampered by the excessive pressure of detailed work, and the impossibility of more than a few members possessing the requisite local knowledge in reference to private bills, and the other wants of varying districts. Suggestions for the setting up of local parliaments, not only for Ireland and Scotland, but for Wales and homogeneous portions of England, were being made with increasing acceptance before the energies of the Empire had to be concentrated on the mighty task still in hand. France has had a centralised form of government for centuries and, except amongst some of the people of Brittany, and the Basque of the Pyrenees, is as united a nation as can be desired. Yet even in France there are thinkers, in the South at all events, who have yearnings for local parliaments. One of the most successfully governed countries of the world, Switzerland, where you find the ideal combination of liberty and order, is ruled by small, freely elected parliaments over cantons of such compact dimensions that each citizen is a real participant in the affairs of his province. This illustration is specially important because Switzerland, on a small scale, like India on a large one, consists of different nationalities grouped by political union.

Whatever may be said of the general merits of the Indian reform scheme outlined in the joint address of a number of prominent Indians and Europeans submitted to the Viceroy and the Secretary of State in November, 1917, there can be no doubt as to the political soundness of its arguments from history against legislative centralisation in so vast an area:–

"The examples of the United States, Canada, Australia and South Africa, as contrasted with India, China and the dependencies of Spain and France in the eighteenth century, prove that under elective institutions provincial administration cannot be made effective for units of population the size of great nations. Had the United States attempted to develop herself on the basis of five or six provinces, each would, for administrative reasons, have been driven to subdivide itself into minor self-governing provinces commensurate in size with the existing forty-eight States. County councils or district boards cannot take the place of provincial governments, which in nations of a certain magnitude, must be interposed between local authorities on the one hand, and the national government on the other. Hence, the Government of the United Kingdom, with its population of 45,000,000 is increasingly unable to cope with their need for social reform."

In a word, for India, with her vast population, her varied provinces and races, her many sectarian differences (brought to the surface by the present search for the lines of constitutional advance), a unilateral form of free government is impossible. If we include in our survey the far greater grouping of to-morrow, to which we have given the name of the South Asiatic Federation, the idea is still more hopelessly impracticable. It is common knowledge that, even with an administration not responsible to the people and an elaborate bureaucratic system, there have been increasing complaints by the Indian provincial administrations of excessive interference and of being kept in leading strings by the central authority. Masterful Viceroys like Lord Curzon have sought to keep all the threads of administration in their own hands; but when their tenure has expired the provincial officials have renewed their efforts to modify and lessen the control of Simla. Diversified as have been the reform proposals submitted to Mr Montagu during his Indian tour, there has been an extraordinary consensus of opinion that the growth in recent years of the activities of Government render imperative the devolution of some of the powers exercised by the central authority.

An outstanding difficulty in providing a central parliament for India is that the vast majority of the inhabitants are alike illiterate and in such deep poverty as to render impracticable their enfranchisement as electors of an Imperial assembly. Still, this argument should not be used by reactionaries, bureaucrats, and Anglo-Indians generally against the Indian educated classes in their plea for constitutional reform. It must not be forgotten that since the earliest years of the present century Indian leaders, under the inspiration of that lamented patriot G. K. Gokhale, have advocated universal and compulsory free education, in full recognition that its cost will have to be borne in some form or another by the taxpayers of the country. The claim for at least a beginning in this direction has been made by the [Indian] National Congress since 1904. For reasons of a practical kind, which do not seem to me to have been adequate and which are steadily losing their force, officialdom did not see its way to make such a beginning even on a local option basis, until last year, when the Bombay Government supported the Bill of a non-official member which duly passed into law, for giving municipalities power to compel school attendance. It cannot be said that theories of the freedom of the individual and Spencerian ideas of limitation of State activity stood in the way. For, after all, the officials with whom the last word rested have been reared in a country where universal compulsory education has been established for more than forty-five years. The experiment has been tried with substantial success in some of the Native States, under wise and patriotic princes like the rulers of Baroda, Bikaner, Mysore, Kapurthala, Cochin and Bhavanagar. I do not deny the existence of practical difficulties in the application of the principle under the diversified conditions obtaining in the vast territories of British India; but with patient determination these can be steadily surmounted, and it seems to me that there is no strong reason for not giving general local option to confer this great boon on the people, other than the natural reluctance of an overwhelmingly non-indigenous administration to impose new taxation.

Wherever the blame may lie for the illiteracy of the masses, the fact remains that in the face of such ignorance and of the existence of interests so diversified and widely scattered, a central parliament becomes an impossibility. One cannot imagine the Baluch representative in an assembly at Delhi being keen on the needs of Madura, or a Bombay member advocating measures for the development of shipping in Calcutta. The well-known difficulties as to the representation of very small minorities also come in the way. While a mighty minority of many millions, like the Mahomedans, could protect its own interests in a central institution, the smallest and least influential communities, usually to be found in one province, could exert little or no influence at Delhi or Simla.

It should be remembered that the greatest political mistake in

Indian annals was when Aurangzeb overthrew the independent states of the South and tried the impossible task of bringing the whole of India under Delhi. Historically, neither in Buddhist, Hindu, nor Mahomedan times has the entire peninsula been under one single government, and the actual India of to-day contains provinces that were never ruled by either Asoka or Akbar. And to their honour let it be said that, so far, the majority of Indian thinkers have advocated, if not the form, at least the facts of federal government. No doubt, the fear of seeing India again breaking up into component parts has made some Indian thinkers somewhat dubious as to the future under provincial autonomy. As the examples of the United States and Germany on the one hand, and of Russia on the other, have shown, the real danger of a break-up does not come from meeting the wishes of the different component parts, but from over-centralisation and the enforcement of an unnatural uniformity. No, the problem of a free India within the British Empire can only be solved by federalism and by facing this essential fact.

Of course no contemporary federal scheme can be followed in all its details; there must be adaptation to Indian conditions and historical developments. Before going into details it should be observed that we must not be deflected from acceptance of certain broad principles of federalism because they happen to be applied in Germany, any more than we are called upon to adopt them because the United States of America are their earlier home. I yield to no one in the intense horror and detestation I feel in respect to the remorseless barbarity, the disregard of international obligations as to the rules of war, the treachery and trickery, and the enslavement of the inhabitants of conquered areas which have disgraced the German name in the last four years. But the political, like the theological, investigator should "seize the truth where'er 'tis found," whether in the New World or the Old, and must not be blinded to the advantages of certain principles of confederation because they happen to have been applied in a country which has brought so much sorrow and suffering upon mankind.

The bursting of the floodgates of German lust of conquest was due, not to the constitution of her federal system, but to the arrogance and egotism instilled into her people, of set purpose, for a generation past. It is notorious that all classes, and not merely the military and ruling castes, were eager for war. They had grown rich in material things too quickly after the unification of the Empire, and acquired the aggressiveness characteristic of *nouveaux riches.* In the pre-war decade I frequently met middle-class Germans, not of the Junker class, but traders in India and Burma, in the Dutch Colonies, in Siam, China, Japan, America, in various parts of Africa, and on the Continent. They did not conceal their intense longing for war, and usually they blamed the weakness of the Kaiser, derisively calling him "the Pacifist." It is my firm conviction that if Germany had had a Government directly responsible to parliament and removable thereby, the war would have come several years sooner, and probably in 1906 over the question of Morocco.

Wherever we may look for patterns, I now propose to show that for some years to come each Indian province in the initial stages of federalism, must have a constitution that provides, on the one hand, for an independent and strong executive, responsible to the Viceroy and the Secretary of State for tenure of office and appointment; and, on the other hand, for elective assemblies to control finance and legislation. Thus will be built up the future United States of India within the British Empire. This system, leaving the component members of the federation full local autonomy, will best conform to the varied needs of the great peninsula and to the facts of her evolution, and can most readily be adjusted to local conditions.

CHAPTER IV

PROVINCIAL REORGANISATION

The principle of provincial autonomy – his suggestion to Gokhale for reshaping the provinces – separate representation of different interests in the provinces – the ideal size of each province – proposal for provincial re-arrangement – the office of the Governor and the appointment of Indians to it – the appointment of ministers – representation in the legislatures – criteria for the franchise – the establishment of Senates or Upper Houses – powers of the two Houses – self-government in internal affairs.

Anyone acquainted with recent Indian political history is aware that nearly all suggested plans of constitutional reform are based on a greater or less degree of provincial autonomy. Lord Hardinge's Government, which included two warm champions of real devolution in the late Sir John Jenkins and Sir Ali Imam, laid down this principle in unequivocal terms in the famous Delhi despatch of 1911. Most of the outstanding and detailed reform proposals submitted to the Viceroy and Mr Montagu last winter were based on the claim of provincial autonomy, at least over recognised and limited fields. This, too, was the keynote of Mr Gokhale's political testament, which I had the privilege of publishing shortly before the announcement in the House of Commons of the liberalising policy of His Majesty's Government. Though it leaves the Governor-General in Council for the present great powers of intervention in the affairs of the local Governments, the Gokhale scheme was designed to lead, after a few years of practical working, to a form of federalism.

Though my lamented friend wrote out his plan only a few days before his death, he had long pondered deeply thereon, and had discussed the various points both with the late Sir P. M. Mehta and myself. He began expounding his ideas on this head to me in London in the early autumn of 1914. Recognising that the scheme led to federalism, I drew his attention to the consideration that the existing provinces had grown out of the accidents of foreign acquisition and the needs, many of them no longer operative, of bureaucratic administration; in area, population, and still more potent matters of race and language, they were ill adapted to become national states. I proposed that he should found his scheme as far as possible on a plan of reshapement providing a national and linguistic basis. I said that self-government must develop on two lines, one being that of provincial rearrangement with something like the unity of a nationality as far as practicable, and the other the separate representation within each province of religions, castes, and communities, small as well as great. Gokhale agreed with this view, and his skeleton plan recognises the need for separate and direct representation of Mahomedans and other non-majority communities. But he did not feel justified in making provincial regrouping a part of his scheme, because he hoped that the Government would introduce, within a year or two from that date, the provincial autonomy foreshadowed in the Delhi despatch, and that its working, by bringing out the defects of present geographical divisions, would lead to the establishment of ethnic and linguistic groupings.

Now that the war has gone on not only months but years beyond the time Gokhale anticipated, even in his least optimistic hours, the currents of political progress to which men direct their gaze for the future have gained cumulative force, and the foundations to-day must be laid deep and strong. Happily, the task in India, if earnestly faced, does not present insuperable difficulties. I strongly oppose the suggested subdivision of the existing provinces into a considerable number of self-governing states. Such small administrations would unduly narrow down national effort. The unit of provincial self-government must be equal at least to a medium European state. It seems to me that in the Bengal Presidency we have a good example of a suitable and reasonably homogeneous area for federal autonomy. Nor would I divide so ethnically distinct a province as Burma. But in the other major provinces readjustment is necessary. Behar should absorb a few districts from the Central provinces, and the United Provinces should take from what is now the Nagpur Government the Hindi-speaking districts which were formerly under the Agra Administration. On the other hand, two or three of the western districts of the United Provinces belong by affinity to the Punjab.

The Bombay Presidency as now constituted is unduly heterogeneous. With the disappearance of the Central Provinces the Marathi-speaking divisions would naturally fall to Bombay. The great Southern province of Madras would not be greatly changed, excepting that its most north-western districts would fall to Bombay, being nearer the Belgaum and North Kanara districts in character than to the Dravidian south. Bombay would lose Sind, which would substantially help to form what might be called the Indus Province, possibly with Quetta as the capital, and comprising the North-West Frontier Province as well as Baluchistan. Apart from Assam we should thus have eight "major" provinces, roughly equal in area, and each capable of developing a national government. It is true that in Bombay there would be the two main varieties of the original Sanskrit in the Marathi and Gujerati dialects; and in Madras Tamil and Telugu would similarly form the major languages. Everywhere beyond the areas where it is the principal vernacular Urdu would be the recognised home tongue of the Mahomedans. But these and other linguistic variations are inevitable in a sub-continent so diversified as India; and by such a scheme of redistribution there would be much greater approximation than at present to provinces which could honestly be called nationalities, each having an importance and coherence ranking with those of at least some European States.

The Governor of each province should directly represent the Sovereign and hold all official executive responsibility. His powers, while similar to those now vested in the heads of presidencies, would be much larger and far less trammelled by the central authority in India. The appointment would be made, as at present, by the King-Emperor. In one important respect I dissent from most of the systems which have been proposed, for I consider the time has come for including Indians within the field of selection. I grant that there are not many Indians who could fitly hold this exalted office in the reconstituted form; but a beginning could and should be made. The arguments used by Lord Morley a decade ago in wearing down the opposition to appointing Indians to the Government of India and the presidency Executives, may be applied to this claim that, in conformity with the great principles of Queen Victoria's Proclamation of 1858, Indians should now preside over provinces side by side with Englishmen.

The innovation should be made by inviting one of the ruling princes to leave his own territory for five years for the greater field of direction of a provincial administration. To take a concrete case, there is no reason why that patriot-statesman the Maharaja of Bikanir should not succeed Lord Pentland or Lord Willingdon. There are certainly other ruling princes capable of administrating great provinces; but I take His Highness of Bikanir as a shining example, whose qualifications cannot be denied. As to the objection that five years is too long a period for any prince to leave his own territory, it may be answered that a well-run Native State reaches such a degree of automatic good administration that, when its ruler dies, the standard is maintained during long periods of regency. Moreover, nowadays there are usually either heirs-apparent or other relatives of the ruler who could well be trusted to carry on the administration for a quinquennium.

During the period the selected ruling chief would undergo a personal metamorphosis; but I am confident that our best modern princes are quite capable of adapting themselves to such a change of situation. They will be able to play their new part and take up their wider responsibilities, exactly as an Englishman forgets that he is a large landowner in Kent or Surrey when he becomes a governor or ambassador. On a small scale something of the kind occurred when the gallant Maharaja Sir Partab Singh abdicated the Idar *gadi*, and returned to Jodhpur to be regent for his grand-nephew. The English heads of neighbouring provinces would find substantial advantage in the continuity of an Indian ruler of proved administrative ability, dealing with public problems corresponding to his own. Later on ordinary British Indian subjects should be eligible for appointment to governorships; but for some years to come the great responsibility should be limited to Indian princes. It may be undesirable to appoint a ruling chief to the governorship of the province in which his State is situated; but there is no reason why a prince from Rajputana or Central India should not make an excellent head of the Executive in Bengal, Bombay, or Madras.

The Governor should appoint ministers to the various departments of State, for defined periods of, say, four or five years at least, and his choice should be unhampered. Except in the peculiar Helvetian Confederation, no Prime Minister or President in the world has to accept his colleagues at the bidding of an electorate or the legislature. Nor is the exception absolute: for when a federal councillor or minister has been elected, his tenure of office does not depend upon any vote of the Swiss Parliament. The world-wide practice whereby the head of the administration selects his colleagues is based on historical experience, and must be maintained in India. By way of safeguard, however, the legislature might possess the right of removing by a three-fourths majority, an unsuitable or incompetent man at the head of a department. Apart from this minor and negative degree of legislative control, each minister should be entirely responsible to the Crown through the Governor. This would give India the constitution Gokhale and Mehta always advocated, on the basis of the American or the German principle of freedom of the executive from legislative control so far as tenure of office is concerned. An adverse vote would only lead to the dropping of the measure in hand.

The greatest mistake made in the successive reconstitutions of Indian provincial legislatures has been that of limiting the right of representation, in practice if not always in theory, to what may be termed the privileged classes – the best-educated and richest sections of the population. Owing to this serious error the national conservatism necessary to the evolution of a normal modern State, and in India characteristic of the man at the plough, has been artificially prevented from making its voice effectively heard. An exaggerated mid-Victorian form of Liberalism, natural to the classes that now form the narrow electorates, has been dominant. Taxation and representation have not gone together. The provincial legislatures have been far too small to be really representative bodies in such large areas. I am sure an able and popular Governor, such as Lord Willingdon in Bombay, could rule his province much better if he had an assembly of from

180 to 220 almost entirely elected members, instead of about one-fifth of that number nominated and elected, as now, for it could then be representative of every district, community and substantial interest.

Each of the various religions and races, as recorded in the census, would provincially be a *millet*, to use the Turkish term, and each would have a fair share in the assembly directly elected. The franchise might be based on various grounds – a small income or land tax assessment, public service, both civilian and military, education and other tests. Old soldiers of a prescribed period of service, especially all who have participated in the present war, men who in various capacities have travelled far out of India, and those who have served in important posts would have special qualifications for the franchise, but each within his own community. There would still remain large numbers of the less fortunate classes and castes who could not at present be fairly represented, since they do not include any substantial proportion of men with such educational or other qualifications as to pass the reasonable tests applied to other sections. For the present, therefore, it should be the duty of the Governor to nominate a few representatives from these backward communities.

Such an assembly, though falling short of the wide bases of such outstanding types as the House of Commons or the French Chamber, would have the merit of truly reflecting Indian conditions of to-day. I am not advocating an institution for twenty or thirty years hence, but one that could safely and advantageously be introduced without delay, since it would be calculated to strengthen the Executive and promote the contentment of all classes. A natural organic epitome of existing conditions, it would grow, as all healthy political institutions have grown, till it reached a standard similar to that built up stage by stage in the best-governed parts of the world. Since Mahomedans and the land-owning classes received special representation under the Morley reforms, and as a matter of practical politics it is impossible to force the Mahomedan to surrender these rights, this principle must be extended, both on logical and political grounds, to other important communities and interests. This extension would meet the claims, so strongly pressed within the last year or so, of the non-Brahmans of Madras, and of the British and Anglo-Indian communities, as well as of other minority elements, and would stimulate an interest in public affairs on the part of the backward classes.

While the Assembly, apart from the three-fourths vote of

censure by which it could remove individual ministers, would not otherwise control the Executive, it would have full powers within its legitimate sphere of influence. But single Chamber government is to be deprecated, and I strongly advocate the establishment in each province of a Senate or Upper House, of, say, forty or fifty members. Here again, for the present, nomination would be exercised in some instances, while in other cases important bodies or interests, such as the greater municipalities, chambers of commerce, universities, and landlords' associations, would send representatives. Europeans sojourning for long periods in India for commercial or professional purposes would have direct representation in the larger Chamber, and indirect representation in the Upper House. The two Houses, in case of difference of opinion, would vote together as a united assembly, and the point at issue would be decided by a majority. The second Chamber should be constituted *pari passu* with the reconstitution of the existing legislature.

The power of the two Houses over legislation and provincial finance should be subject only to the veto of the Governor. But provincial finance and its sources of revenue will have to be carefully marked out, since the present system whereby the Government of India, or rather the Secretary of State, is the ultimate disposer of these revenues must disappear. At the same time, as a later chapter will show, care must be taken to leave the character of the Government of India sufficiently elastic to provide for ultimate and natural development from a purely British-Indian to a fully South Asiatic federal administration. Once we have the provinces based on nationality, worked out as described, we can well leave them a full measure of self-government for their internal affairs, such as applies to the greater Native States, for example, Hyderabad or Mysore. There would be little for the central Government to interfere with, and that little would be statutorily restricted as time went on.

An objection to be met is that since separate representation may strengthen centrifugal tendencies it is inconsistent with the general language and race bases of provincial readjustment. The answer is that we must legislate to meet actual rather than ideal conditions. The various religions, communities, castes, et cetera, within each great province have very much in common, something national in effort and aspiration, that will meet the difficulty of separate communal representation in practical working and in time. On the other hand, the smaller communities by being assured from the first of their voice in affairs will feel growing confidence in the autonomous system, and the self-respect and self-confidence so necessary to the backward classes in India will steadily grow. There will be awakened in them an enthusiasm for great public interests that now lies dormant, and an increasing fellow-feeling with the leading communities.

A few years' experience of this system would go far to satisfy the crying needs of India. The diversified problems of education, sanitation, public works, commerce and industry would be solved by each State in a natural, healthy way. Each would develop itself sufficiently to become an independent and worthy member of the great South Asiatic Federation destined to take its place by the side of the other dominions within the Empire of the King.

CHAPTER V

THE PROTECTED STATES

The importance of the princely states and their diversity – the devotion of the princes to the British Empire – Queen Victoria's promise regarding the "Native States" – princely states suitable fields for administrative experiments – the achievements of the princes and their sympathy for the aspirations of Indians for self-government – federalism to meet the needs of British India and the "Native States".

No federal scheme for India can be complete or satisfactory if it leaves out of account the Native States, which cover one-third of the area of the Indian Empire and contain some seventy million inhabitants, or two-ninths of the entire population. It is therefore necessary to deal with them before discussing the constitution of the central authority.

It is a familiar though often forgotten fact that these principalities vary in size, climate, density of population, economic, racial, and intellectual conditions to an extraordinary degree. There are great dominions, such as Hyderabad, Mysore, and Kashmir, worthy to rank with kingdoms in Europe. The Nizam of Hyderabad is the equal in power, in dominion, in the number of his subjects, and in the variety of interests to be considered, with the Kings of Belgium or Roumania. Indeed, just as the German Emperor has kings within his dominions, and as we hope some day the independent sovereigns of Persia and Afghanistan will, of their own free will, wish to enter the future South Asiatic Confederation, so, prima facie, there is every reason why the Nizam should, like the former Kings of Oudh, receive the royal title of "Majesty," a concomitant act being the rendition to him of the Berars. A step forward was taken on New Year's Day, 1918, when he was given the special title of "Faithful Ally of the British Government," and the style, new to India, of "His Exalted Highness." This designation is strangely reminiscent of the old Dutch style of "High Mightiness," which was proposed for the President of the United States, but refused by Washington.

Then there are States not so vast in extent where, by intensive culture, commerce and trade have reached such a development as to make them the equals of the richest British districts in India. Some of the principalities go back in tradition and history to the very dawn of civilised society. There are Rajput States, the germs of which must have existed when Alexander encamped on the banks of the Indus, and it is not improbable that orderly governments, under the ancestors or collaterals of some of the present Rajput princes, were carried on in the eras of C,,sar and Augustus. Other principalities, again, date in present form from the early days of British rule, and in some cases were obtained by purchase or by other equally unromantic forms of acquisition from English officials, reluctant to accept further direct responsibility for Indian government. But whether ancient or comparatively new, the individual variations of these autonomous territories are of absorbing interest. Large dominions, like those of Baroda and Gwalior, possess a unity of history and sentiment attaching them to their ruling houses, from which, especially in the case of their present heads, they have received such devoted service as to have established between prince and people a relation almost tribal in the strength of its affection. There are smaller States, such as Kapurthala and Bhavanagar, which are excellent examples of hereditary good government and contentment of the people.

... the princes have proved their devotion to the British Empire, and have made sacrifices such as to win for them the merited title of partners therein. In the last four years they have been enabled, by freewill gifts and sacrifices, to share in the great task of securing a victory for the Allies to an extent which has evoked general admiration and has vastly raised the scale of India's contribution as a whole. Their well-trained Imperial Service contingents, maintained by the Durbars for a generation past, formed an invaluable contribution to the military units in being when war broke out, and the stream of recruitment from the States has enormously helped to meet the pressing need for repair of the heavy wastages of war.

Looking back on the 150 years of British predominance in India, I can see scarcely any other act equal alike in wisdom, justice, and far-sightedness, to Queen Victoria's promise through Canning, on the morrow of the Mutiny, to refrain from the absorption of any Native States into British India. It came to relieve the fears and anxieties aroused, with unhappy results, by the Dalhousian policy of "lapse." Had that policy been vetoed at the time by the Government in Whitehall, I am firmly convinced that Britain's position in India to-day would have been all the stronger, for the existence of Oudh, Nagpur, Satara, and the other sequestered principalities. The aggregate territory from which British Indian revenues are derived would have been less vast, and I do not deny that there would have been some other disadvantages, of a temporary character, but these would have been altogether outweighed. The administrative machinery of British India, now so great and cumbrous, would have been simplified; British rule would have had in those directly concerned sure and honest friends like the princes of to-day, and there would have been a correspondingly larger measure of indigenous government, with all its advantages, side by side with British administration. The builders of United Germany, from Bismarck downwards, have borne witness that the diversified principalities are the mainstay of that Empire, and that destructive anarchy has no more powerful antagonist than a dynasty belonging to the soil, ruling from age to age relatively small areas within a confederation . . .

From the point of view of good administration these areas of indigenous rule, scattered like so many islands of varying size in the sea of British India, are advantageous both to their own inhabitants and to those of surrounding districts. They provide suitable fields for administrative experiments such as could not be applied, without prior test, to the whole of British India. Some States advance the cause of social reform by enactments and orders which English administrators, conscious of their limitations as non-indigenous officials adhering to the principle of strict religious neutrality, have not dared to apply. In some services for the commonweal, such as education and sanitation, there are respects in which the most progressive States are ahead of British India. But it would be unfair to fail to recognise that the stimulus to advancement is reciprocal. The high standard of

British justice, to give but one instance, calls for emulation, as is recognised by almost every State. Here and there are to be found principalities in which the administration of justice and general civil policy leave much to be desired; but happily, with the spread of modern ideals, these have become rare exceptions. Religious liberty prevails in the States as well as in British India. A Moslem ruler, like the Nizam of Hyderabad, is respected and loved by his millions of Hindu subjects, while there are Hindu Princes, such as the Maharajas of Gwalior and Kolahpur (to mention only two names), whose Mahomedan subjects look upon them with almost filial affection and veneration, and who constantly prove that, if Hindus in faith, they are superior as rulers to all sectarian or other narrowing influences.

Again, these indigenous Courts scattered over the great peninsula are the fitting patrons of art in every form. Indian music, architecture, painting and the arts generally, have natural protectors and patrons in the various Durbars. It is not improbable that within the present century some of the dynasties may produce patrons of art as influential as the Medicis, or the princes of Weimar. Some special branches of higher agriculture receive encouragement from the princes, and in many other directions they give a remarkable impetus to the upbuilding of an expanded Indian life, responsive to modern ideas yet distinctive of the country and its peoples.

Increasingly, of late years, some of the best-known princes have been cherishing the ideal of a constitutional and parliamentary basis for their administrations. There can be no doubt that a liberal policy in British India will soon be followed in many of the States by widening applications of the principle of co-operation between the rulers and the ruled. It is most gratifying to Indian patriots to note the sympathy which the princes and nobles have shown with the aspirations of the people of British India toward self-government. After all, these rulers, unlike the small dynasties of the eighteenth and nineteenth centuries in Italy, are children of the soil and have a natural sympathy and fellow-feeling with their countrymen.

There could be no better or more convincing presentation of these aspirations of India, in brief compass, than that given by the Maharaja of Bikanir, in his historic pronouncement at the luncheon of the Empire Parliamentary Association to the Indian delegates to the Imperial War Conference, at the House of Commons, on 24th April, 1917. Those of us who personally know the ruling princes of to-day – so active, hardworking, patriotic,

SELECTED SPEECHES AND WRITINGS

and devoted to the welfare of their people, usually so free from all "side," and, in a word, so different from the legendary maharaja of the imaginative writers of the past – have no reason to doubt that this eloquent plea voiced not only the views of the educated people of India but also those of the average ruling chief. In fact, His Highness of Bikanir spoke on similar lines to his brother princes when they entertained him to dinner in Bombay on the eve of his departure for the Imperial War Conference. It may also be noted that the Maharaja of Alwar's speeches, so full of democratic enthusiasm, have made a considerable impression in India within the last two or three years.

The States cannot be mere spectators of the constitutional changes now impending. The question arises, "What is the part they are to play in the politically free India of to-morrow?" To reduce them gradually to the mere position of great nobles, and to let the power and the individuality attaching to their States pass out of their control would be a crime against history, art, and even nationality. On the other hand, the present standard of relations between the protecting Power and the protected State cannot go on after British India reaches the first stages toward self-government. What is the solution? Happily in federalism we find a system that will meet the need both of British India and of the Native States. It has been maintained in these pages that a successful unilateral form of self-government is impossible even for British India. The great provincial administrations, we have seen, must be autonomous in internal matters. The interference of the central authority, while necessary in the past, must be metamorphosed into that entire non-intervention in State as distinct from Imperial affairs which characterises the Imperial Government of Germany or the United States Government in their dealings with the members of their respective confederations. A similar policy should at once be applied to the Indian principalities. In the succeeding chapter we shall show that the fact that these States are of such varying sizes and importance is not a bar to their incorporation in the proposed federal system.

CHAPTER VI

THE CENTRAL GOVERNMENT

"Imperial and federal powers" for the central authority – foreign affairs, the army, the navy, railway administration and finance – a healthy competition between the provinces in development – the structure of central government – the central legislature – tariffs for the entire federation – federalism would stimulate progress.

As previously indicated, after the grant of autonomy to each newly constituted national State the Government of India would retain temporarily powers of general control over the provincial administrations. But this would be only for the purpose of carrying out with each province individually the various conventions by which authority over the whole series of legislation, finance, and administration comprehended in the term "Home Affairs" would be completely transferred to the constitutional bodies previously described, with the Governor possessing a veto over legislation and finance. If an Assembly rejected the annual budget, the Governor would be entitled to carry on with a repetition of the previous year's financial policy and the existing taxes, as in Japan and Austria.

While, on the one hand, the conventions would assure Home Rule to the States administrations, on the other hand, they would conserve to the central authority those Imperial and federal powers without which the confederacy would go to pieces. We have the historical fact of the existence of major Native States, such as Hyderabad, with treaty rights; and such internal powers as are vested in the Nizam's Government should be exercised by the provincial States. Of the departments retained by the central Government, the first and foremost would be those of close relationship with the Imperial Government in London, through the Secretary of State for India. His position would more and more approximate to that of the Secretary of State for the Colonies, and his Council would be abolished. The right now exercised by the Presidency Governments to correspond with the Secretary of State on certain matters would apply to all the national States; though naturally the interest of the British Cabinet would be much greater in those branches of the administration which would fall to the central Government. Prominent amongst them would be foreign affairs. By this I do not mean

559

relations with the Native States, which are now part of the work of the Foreign department at Delhi, but with external countries, including such future States as may be drawn hereafter within the orbit of the confederation through their own free will and interest.

The Army and Navy would naturally belong to the central Government, and so would maritime affairs generally, including customs. Here some sacrifice on the part of certain Native States will be necessary, for just as the central Government would cede to the provincial authorities all those branches of internal business now administered by the principalities, so the principalities, in conjunction with the provincial States, would have to accept full military and naval and customs control by the Government of India. But this need not interfere with the sentimental connection of each State with its contingent to the Imperial Army. While full control of promotion, brigading, et cetera, would remain in the hands of the central authority, the contingents raised in Native States would carry symbols of their origin, and the princes would be honorary commanders of their respective corps. Apart from customs, the Government of India would receive a settled contribution from each province. In the case of Native States the old and rather humiliating "tribute" paid in some instances, and now amounting to about £617,000, would be abolished and replaced by a uniform percentage of contribution equal to that paid by the provincial States. Public works and sanitation would belong to each province, but railway administration and finance, with uniformity or fair adjustment of rates over the whole extent of the federation, would be a branch of Imperial government.

This system would possess the great advantage of enabling the most progressive provinces to go ahead in their social legislation, without being restricted, as would often be the case under a uniform system, to the pace of the slowest and most backward. In an all-India legislature a project of social reform, such as Mr Bupendranath Basu's Civil Marriage Bill, is almost inevitably judged from the point of view of the provinces least prepared for the advance. Under this scheme of federation education in all its branches, social laws (such as those of succession and marriage), control over the building of tenements and conditions of labour, agricultural improvements, scientific research and medical aid – progress in all these vital interests would become a matter of healthy competition. Each province, while able to adapt its policy to local conditions, would be stirred to do its utmost to lead in the race for political and social development.

No longer cribb'd, cabin'd, and confined by the central secretariats, the advanced parts of the country, such as Bombay or
Bengal, may be expected to reach a standard of social polity that
will be a beacon light for the other provinces to follow.

The headship of the Government of India would naturally
remain with the representative of the King-Emperor, the Viceroy,
to whose position the next chapter is devoted. Then would come
his Cabinet, presided over by the Prime Minister, and containing
members for Defence, Finance and Customs, Railways, External
Commerce, Foreign Affairs, and two Ministers for the Interior.
One of these would have charge of all relations with the federated
authorities, and the other would deal with the judicial, legal,
constitutional, and other branches of federal affairs not otherwise
provided for. Here again the principle of selection for the
Cabinet proposed for the provincial administrations would apply.
The Prime Minister, under the Viceroy's guidance, would choose
his colleagues without restraint as he thought best.

In what is now known as the Imperial Legislature the most
radical change will be inevitable. For the short transitional period
before the Government of India relinquishes detailed control of
the provinces, a strong central legislature, with special representation of the various provinces and races, to help with the
conventions, will be necessary. But after the due establishment
of the federal constitution, the room for Imperial legislation and
as distinct from questions of policy, will be so restricted that my
preference is for a Senate or Council, representing the provinces
and the Native States, instead of needlessly complicating the
federal organisation by the creation of two central chambers,
with little to legislate about.

To this body each of the great provinces should send eight to
ten representatives, some chosen by the Governor and approved
by either one or the other House, and the remainder selected by
each of the Assemblies and approved by the Governor. The great
State like Kashmir, Mysore, or Gwalior would send five representatives, and Hyderabad, as the premier State, seven; and even the
smallest States whose ruler is included in the table of salutes
would have at least one member. As in the German constitution,
where the Federal Council safeguards the interests of every
member of the Bundesrat by giving to the smallest representation
far above its numerical proportion, so here the medium States,
such as Bikanir and Patiala, would have two or three representatives, coming down to at least one member for such principalities
as Janjira or Morvi.

The Senate would legislate for the whole of India when necessary; but the proposed federal constitution will make such
occasions rare or formal. They would ordinarily be confined to
measures such as the Defence of India Act, or dealing with the
protection of the coast, or tariffs, or Army and Navy services. The
Government of India, in exercise of full fiscal autonomy, would
establish for the entire federation the necessary tariffs with scientific schedules. The English Liberal, with his traditional mistrust
of tariffs, too often forgets how totally different is the case of
India from that of his own country. He knows that in England
Protection would mean, in practice, mainly a tax on corn, and
result in raising the cost of various foodstuffs for the poorest
classes. Her dependence on exterior supplies has been most
pointedly demonstrated by the submarine campaign. In India,
on the contrary, the food of the people is home grown, and a very
considerable surplus remains for shipment abroad; the imports
consist to a great extent of articles of luxury or such manufac-
tured articles as can safely be taxed in order to encourage
indigenous industry.

Under the new order of things the atmosphere of Simla or
Delhi should be serene and dispassionate. The Government of
India would be the connecting bond between great national
provinces and principalities, united for common purposes but
varying in organic and natural unity, representing their diversified history, races, religions, and languages. They would be not
like to like, but like in difference:

Not chaos like together crushed and bruised,
But, like the world, harmoniously diffused,
Where order in variety we see,
And where, though all may differ, all agree.

The central federal authority, by promoting happiness, contentment, and development within its vast territories and over
such an immense population, would sooner or later attract its
neighbours in Northern and Western Asia. The benefits of federalism would soon be felt, since it would give a stimulus to progress
which present conditions of centralisation discourage and retard.
At the periodical Imperial Conferences in London, the representatives of Canada, Australia, and the other great Dominions,
would meet those who would voice the claims of an immense
Indian Federation built on the rock of national autonomy in
each of its living members. They would represent an organic

whole which, in very truth, would be a living and vital entity with common interest, looked after by a federal Government and a strong Imperial Executive supervised by the Emperor's representative, the Viceroy, and his Prime Minister and Cabinet, and supported by the Federal Council representing all provinces and principalities.

CHAPTER VII

THE VICEROYALTY

The widening of the franchise – monarchy would form the apex – the consequences of centralization during the Mughal era – subsequent developments – unity brought about by British rule – affection among Indians for the British monarchy – the Viceroy as the representative of the Sovereign – proposal for a non-political royal viceroy – advantages of creating such an office – it must be open to Indians as well as to Englishmen – the functions a non-political royal viceroy would perform.

It is an accepted principle of modern statesmanship that the nation or federation of nations should be as broadly based as circumstances permit upon the opinion of the people, that the larger and more varied the foundations of the national life are made, the stronger will be the body politic. The Reform Act of 1918, enfranchising women and adding millions of men to the British electorate, notwithstanding the probability of mistakes here and there under the influence of these new elements, is yet certain to increase the strength of the realm by giving large numbers a personal and direct interest in the public welfare. Even the governing classes of Prussia and its Court, whose sympathy with democracy is merely opportunist, have come to the conclusion that by the conferment of manhood suffrage the Constitution and the monarchy will gain strength rather than lose it. In India, under the system proposed in these pages, the suffrage will be as wide as is reasonably practicable. Hundreds of thousands of the people will gain a new sense of responsibility in public affairs, and will be stimulated to take an active interest in the internal administration of the country.

While such widening of the base is essential, we must not

overlook the importance of the apex. Without unity of influential guidance national life is inevitably wanting in organic energy. But in searching for the apex of society, as in searching for a reformed Constitution, we must be guided by the history, the character, and the experience of the nation or race. The Presidency of the United States is a fine example of a naturally evolved institution in keeping with the conditions of the soil. But for India, for manifold historical, racial, and even religious reasons, the monarchy can be the only ultimate apex . . .

This is so because from time immemorial, in periods of peace and happiness, India has had in practice its federal sovereigns and its over-lord. It is true that the ancient Hindu monarchy and society had become so weakened a millennium ago and more (probably owing to India's geographical isolation from the then world movements) that in the successive waves of Mahomedan invasion from the North the ancient polity was overthrown. For a long time thereafter Hindu and Moslem political history in India reveals an unconscious attempt on the part of dynasties, principalities, and nations to recreate the common Empire which had been dissolved long before. The men of genius among the Afghan and other dynasties that "had their day and ceased to be" obviously searched for a constitution that would leave local power in the hands of the many rajas, and yet unite their forces for common effort under the central power at Delhi.

Akbar at last, in part by his own military and administrative genius (as carefully shown in Mr. Vincent Smith's lately published critical biography), but infinitely more owing to the working of eight hundred years of historical causes, re-established the position of national emperor. Innumerable national, dynastic, racial, and historical factors culminated in the Great Mogul; but even under his rule seeds were sown that led to a disintegration as widespread as any that took place before his day. It was perhaps inevitable that this ambitious conqueror should over-centralise; but his two much less able successors carried that policy still further. Even the judicious policy of marrying Hindu princesses encouraged the tendency, for many of the rajas whose families had thus become matrimonially linked with the splendid Court of Delhi gradually sunk into the position of nobles instead of retaining that of federal allies.

With Aurangzeb the policy of excessive centralisation culminated. The foolish conquest of the Southern kingdoms, and not religious bigotry, was the real cause of his prolonged conflict with the Hindus of the Deccan. Had he been content to leave the rich kingdoms of Bijapur and Golconda unannexed, it is probable that one of two things would have happened, each equally satisfactory from the point of view of Imperial consolidation. Either the Moslem dynasties of the South would have identified themselves more and more with their Hindu subjects, much as the early Nizams did, and ultimately the Southern kingdoms would have been federated with the empire-nation at Delhi. The other eventuality, that of the Mahrattas under Sivaji wiping away the local dynasties, would still have meant the establishment of a powerful confederacy in the South, but with a natural and inevitable attraction toward the empire of the North. Sooner or later, they would have united for common purposes, while each kept its own internal independence and national character. After careful study of Indian history from the rise of Akbar onwards, I have no hesitation in attributing the break-up of the Mogul Empire and the terrible anarchy of the eighteenth century mainly to the centralising policy of Akbar, Jehangir, Shah Jehan, and Aurangzeb.

I do not suggest that the alternative policy of leaving the principalities independent and bringing about a federal system would have relieved India of internal differences, wars, and complications, any more than it did the Holy Roman Empire of approximately the same period; but I hold that national greatness and freedom would have been maintained. There were not in India, as in Europe, two strong states and dynasties like Prussia and Austria, the Hohenzollerns and the Hapsburgs, to fight a hundred battles till one of them was turned out of the Empire, to return later to the ancient fold, but as an ally. There was no danger that India would see any such drama on her soil as the long-drawn tragedy of which the last act was played at Sadowa. The Moguls were the strongest and best organised of the forces existing in the peninsula, and in the pursuit of a federal policy they would have drawn around them, as planets, the Deccan States and Bengal, the principalities of Rajputna, and the newly born nationality of Afghans.

Fate decreed otherwise . . . For all effective purposes the Mogul Empire had passed away. Hence Nadir Shah or Ahmed Shah Abdali could ravish the beautiful provinces of the North, kill Hindu and Moslem alike, and fritter away wealth and resources they could not but abuse. The tragedy of the triangular rivalry and bloodshed of Sikh, Hindu, and Moslem, so useless and insensate, in the Punjab, has never been painted by a capable historian in the dark colours it deserves. The Kings of Oudh, incompetent and ever looking to foreign alliances for support, destroyed the unity of a province designed by nature to be the right arm of the Empire. Disunited Bengal was the theatre of internecine war until the East India Company, obtaining the Dewani, established absolute and, at that time, by no means too benevolent rule. The southern half of India was degenerating into a vast jungle with the Pindari and the Mahratta ravaging provinces and states in all directions. Amid all this internal unrest the long-drawn contest of various European Powers for supremacy went on, and in particular the English and the French made the South the battleground for the settlement of their European differences.

Still the forces of ordered progress, so dear to the heart of mankind, were triumphant. In spite of a hundred checks and many errors, in spite of individual acts of harshness and injustice that no impartial student can deny, Britain raised India to the status of a great empire. As centuries of disorder and division had led to ultimate union under Akbar, so the generations of disaster and disintegration that followed the decay of the Mogul Empire led by imperceptible degrees to the union of India under Great Britain. That union has grown ever closer till to-day, in a sense more real than Akbar ever reached . . .

The many princes who visited the Court of Windsor during Her Majesty's [Queen Victoria's] reign took back to their territories, both personally and through their entourage, memories of her sincere and maternal affection for her Indian subjects. Her kindness and consideration towards such ordinary Indians as came near the presence, her employment of Indian personal servants, the pains she took to acquire a working knowledge of Hindostani – all this became widely known and appreciated in India. Peasants whom no one would credit with such knowledge often surprised Indians of education by their shrewd remarks on the Good Queen's affection for their country. The many years the Duke of Connaught spent in high military command in India, making friends everywhere, getting known to and learning to understand the people, wove further personal links with the Sovereign. The visits, first of the late King Edward when Prince of Wales, and later the Duke of Clarence, were welcome reminders of the interest of the Royal Family in the country and its peoples.

This sentiment of attachment to the Crown, so consonant with Indian tradition and religious belief, has come to still fuller fruition under our present gracious Sovereign, who is as well known to and as well beloved by his Indian subjects as any emperor could desire. His first visit to India, as Prince of Wales, with its message of Sympathy, and still more his second visit as regnant Emperor, with its message of Hope, are ever near and dear memories to the hearts of the people. The Great War, with its community of sacrifice and suffering, with the ready and unfailing example of patriotic service and self-denial set by the monarch, and the evidences of his deep personal interest in the Indian troops in every theatre of conflict, has deepened and extended this great personal influence of the Royal House. The many Indian princes, gentlemen, soldiers, and others who have had the privilege of coming into contact with His Majesty – and their number has been much increased during the war – have been so many means of communion between the Emperor and his Eastern dominion. The feeling that, after all, India is not governed on the inconceivable theory of her vast conglomerate population being subject to another race, thousands of miles away, but owns allegiance to her own Emperor, is a unifying source of strength . . .

The Viceroy is the only direct representative of the Sovereign in the country. At the same time he is Prime Minister, the head of the executive, the authority to whom the provincial Governors and Lieutenant-Governors appeal for direction and counsel, the president of the Supreme Legislature, the Foreign Minister, and the chief connecting link with His Majesty's Government in Whitehall. He has so many other duties and heavy responsibilities that it is impossible for him, however great his capacities, to provide more than a relatively small proportion of the benefits derivable, either for England or for India, from the position of the Emperor's direct representative. The ordinary newspaper accounts of Viceregal doings and speeches are sufficient to show that the Governor-Generalship, the headship of the Executive, absorbs the major part of the Viceroy's time and thought. While in common parlance he is always known by the latter designation, it is not used in the warrant of appointment issued by the Crown, although in Royal Proclamations both titles are expressed. The standard official authority tells us that the title of Viceroy "appears to be one of ceremony, which may most appropriately be used in connection with the state and social functions of the Sovereign's representative."[1]

With the establishment of any federal constitution, a great change must come over the work of the Viceroy in any case. The

[1] *The Imperial Gazetteer of India*, Vol. IV, p. 16.

time and thought now given to the supervision of provincial administration must be directed more fully to strictly Imperial affairs. Ought not the opportunity to be taken to make a still more radical change, with the object of no longer leaving undeveloped the signal powers for good of the attachment of the people to the Royal House? If the political head of the federal Government at Delhi or Simla is to maintain a united Cabinet and promote a common policy, why should not India accept the experience of every other part of the world that a Prime Minister cannot also successfully play the rôle of viceroyalty?

These considerations, and the natural desire to make permanent the unifying bond of attachment to the Royal House, lead to the conclusion that the time has come to appoint to the viceregency a son or brother of the Sovereign, and to make the tenure non-political. The Royal representative would have his Prime Minister nominated at the same time, and for the same period of five years or so, by the Imperial Government in England; and the Viceroy and the Prime Minister would choose their British and Indian colleagues of the Cabinet. The only argument seriously advanced against appointing a member of the Royal Family as non-political Viceroy when this suggestion was definitely made by myself[1] and others a dozen years ago was that the field for his activities would be insufficient to justify the additional expenditure. This pseudo-reasoning sounds strange from the lips of Britons who have become so familiar for generations with the benevolent activity and unifying influence of a non-political and nation-representing monarch. An examination of only a few of the many advantages of this change will suffice to show that the argument is not only unsound in itself, but starts from a false premise.

In the first place, there would constantly be at the disposal of federal princes and the heads of federal provinces, of the Prime Minister and the members of the Cabinet, as a source of reference and advice, a socially superior, an independent mind, kept informed under the Constitution of all important events and policies, and with the right of advising, warning, and suggesting. These are great and beneficent powers, as is proved by the published *Letters of Queen Victoria*, 1837–1861, and by many biographies of the statesmen of her reign. There would be a second and constant mental influence, detached from direct participation in the controversies of the moment, able to throw a new light on the current problems of politics for the benefit

---

[1] "Some Thoughts on the Indian Discontent," *National Review*, February, 1907.

of the Ministry. Since the control of Whitehall, now extending to small details, would be replaced to a considerable extent by that of the representatives of the States, provincial and indigenous, and, in the domain of Imperial finance, by that of the Federal Senate, there would be still greater need than at present of a permanent representative of the Throne, watching, advising, and, if things went wrong, warning. The position of the prince would raise him above all temptations or suspicion of any such motive as ambition for a great political future in the Parliamentary arena at home, and he would be looked to as the final judge and arbiter of the most important elements in inter-state relations, namely, those of good taste and good behaviour.

Another consideration has to be urged. We have seen that, in accordance with the principle Parliament laid down no less than eighty-five years ago, if a position can be worthily held by an Indian, he should not be debarred therefrom merely on grounds of race. Hence we have urged that appointments to provincial Governorships should not be beyond their reach. Can it honestly be maintained that there are no minds or characters in modern India equal to those of the Viceroys sent out from England? In intellect and character a Bikanir or a Sinha yield to none. If the Viceroyalty is to remain anything less than a constitutional rôle, a position due like the monarchy it represents to the symbolic power of hereditary kingship, then it must be open to Indians as well as Englishmen. No self-respecting Indian will allow for a moment mere racial superiority as an argument for the exclusion of his countrymen.

Then there is the immense and almost untilled field of individual social reform, of charity, and of social effort, which cannot be compassed by our present system of political viceroyalties with their absorbing duties. To take only a few instances: do Indian hospitals secure all the encouragement and supervision they merit? In the widest sense of the term, does not social help – not indeed from race to race or from class to class but from individual to individual – need organisation and encouragement? The seed which the Dowager Lady Dufferin and Lady Hardinge, to name but two Vicereines, steadfastly sowed in India has reached but an infinitesimal growth in comparison both with the need and the possibilities. In all such matters the successive occupants of Vice-regal Lodge, Simla, have done their best; but the conditions render impossible close attention to the social factors which are so important in the up-building of Indian nationality. The

Viceroy, immersed in files, "cases," and interviews with secretaries, is locked up in the summer at Simla, and is still more pressed by administrative duties in the legislative season at Delhi. A non-political Royal Viceroy would be free to travel more frequently, to visit seaside and other resorts, to set the tone of Indian and not merely high official society, and to generally encourage the development of social life in the provinces.

While the princely courts, as previously indicated, would promote art and literature in the widest form, so on an Imperial basis, the Viceroy would be the patron of all that is best in the representation of our emotional life. The two Tagores – the poet and the painter – have shown to Europe what India is capable of, even in these terrible days when everything outside politics is perforce neglected by the State. The Royal Court of Delhi and Simla would be the natural centre for encouragement of the arts. Indian music, both vocal and instrumental, operas, and tragedies appealing to the Indian temperament, would receive the encouragement which, as German history proves, helps to develop national talent and genius in such directions. In a word the Royal Viceroy, as I wrote in the article previously mentioned, "would put himself at the head of all movements, social, literary, economic and artistic, that improved the relations of all sections of society, that destroyed racial and religious particularisms, that helped to amalgamate the parts into a healthy whole."[1]

CHAPTER XVI

ISLAMIC AND TURANIAN MOVEMENTS

Political Pan-Islamism under Sultan Abdul Hamid – an explanation of "right and legitimate" Pan-Islamism – the place of religion in the modern world – the growing Pan-Turanian movement – it will not threaten British influence in Asia if a wise internal and external policy were adopted.

The Great War has disposed, once for all, of a modern international bogey. In the early eighties, when Turkey had just emerged from her disastrous encounter with Russia, her European misfortunes were followed by still greater losses in Africa. Her shadowy protection over Tunis was replaced by French rule;

[1] *National Review,* February, 1907.

and Egypt, through the bungling of its rulers as well as of the late Sultan Abdul Hamid, was metamorphosed in fact if not in name, into a British possession. In Asia, the Arab tribes were increasingly restive. In such circumstances the late Professor Arminius Vambéry, the Hungarian Orientalist, and other Europeans who had the entrée of the Court of Abdul Hamid, let drop words and ideas that led the Sultan into his main political dream of Pan-Islamism. From that day forward, mullahs, fakirs, and other zealous emissaries were all over Asia and Africa preaching the reunion of Islam under Constantinople. The Sultan was encouraged by the astrologer Abdul Huda, as well as by Afghan and Persian readers of portents. Even after the downfall of Hamidism, the Young Turks continued this policy for some years.

Political Pan-Islamism had its foundations on sand, and could not endure. There is a right and legitimate Pan-Islamism to which every sincere and believing Mahomedan belongs – that is, the theory of the spiritual brotherhood and unity of the children of the Prophet. It is a deep, perennial element in that Perso-Arabian culture, that great family of civilisation to which we gave the name Islamic in the first chapter. It connotes charity and goodwill toward fellow-believers everywhere from China to Morocco, from the Volga to Singapore. It means an abiding interest in the literature of Islam, in her beautiful arts, in her lovely architecture, in her entrancing poetry. It also means a true reformation – a return to the early and pure simplicity of the faith, to its preaching by persuasion and argument, to the manifestation of a spiritual power in individual lives, to beneficent activity for mankind. This natural and worthy spiritual movement makes not only the Master and His teaching but also His children of all climes an object of affection to the Turk or the Afghan, to the Indian or the Egyptian. A famine or a desolating fire in the Moslem quarters of Kashgar or Sarajevo would immediately draw the sympathy and material assistance of the Mahomedan of Delhi or Cairo. The real spiritual and cultural unity of Islam must ever grow, for to the follower of the Prophet it is the foundation of the life of the soul.

The spread of this spiritual and cultural Pan-Islamism, this true religion of brotherhood and affection, in our time has been promoted by the facilities of modern civilisation, by the growth of the spirit of liberty, and by the general awakening of the East which began late in the nineteenth century. It had nothing to do with and nothing to receive from the Court of Stamboul. The hopeless theory entertained by Abdul Hamid of reaching political unity among such scattered and different nationalities was as futile as it would be for the Pope of Rome to dream of gathering the Catholics throughout the world under a common temporal sovereignty. This political Pan-Islamism of the late Sultan was finally swept away on the outbreak of the Great War. Religion has more and more become a spiritual force in the modern world, and less and less a temporal one. In this war national and material interests have predominated over religious ties. The sturdy Protestantism of England and America has come to grips with the Lutherism of Germany and the Calvinism of Hungary . . .

The same feature has been observable in Islam. But here new aspirations arose. Whether through personal and dynastic ambition or through deeper racial feelings of antipathy, many of the ruling families of the Arabian Peninsula have broken away from Turkey, notwithstanding all the bonds of religion. An independent Arabian monarchy has arisen in Hedjaz and has helped to clear the Red Sea coast of Turkish troops. Just as the Moslem Albanians were eager to obtain autonomy, so the Moslem Arabs have evinced tendencies toward racial home rule. Whether a united Arabian nationality will once again be reared is a question that no man living can answer.

The one thing clear is that the break-up of the Russian Empire and the disappearance of Hamidian and political Pan-Islamism have revealed a new problem. Like the German and Slav dreams of national unity this political force, though brought into prominence by events, is not a thing of yesterday. The vast majority of the Russian Moslems are of Turko-Tartar origin and language. In the Caucasus and in Persia there is a large Turkish-speaking Turanian element. The eighties saw a literary movement begun both in Constantinople and in Asiatic Russia toward a cultural and linguistic rapprochement of the Anatolians and the other branches of the Turanian family. The preliminary efforts were toward grammatical and linguistic renovation, as well as toward bringing out both prose and poetry on modern European principles, to replace the Persian and Arabic metre but in as pure Turkish as possible.

After the still-born Russian revolution of 1905 and the coming into power of the Young Turk, sources of communication and of sympathy grew. With the outbreak of the world war, and the resulting disappointment of the Porte with the failure of political Pan-Islamism, as shown by the Arab revolt, the governing classes in Turkey turned their hopes eastwards towards their Russo-Persian cousins. Perso-Arabic words were more and more dropped, alike in Turkey and amongst the other branches of the Turanian races, and the names of Mongol heroes were more and more given to children. Such cognomens as Jenghiz, Timur, Baber, Mangu, Ordoghrol, and Hulagu were made fashionable . . .

By way of the Sublime Porte . . . Germany will endeavour to exercise a powerful influence in the Middle East. This serious contingency has to be faced; but I cherish the assurance that if England is true to her traditional principles of liberty, and respect for national aspirations, there will be no danger of her influence in Asia being successfully challenged. A satisfied, autonomous India, an Afghanistan and a Persia whose independence and future are ensured, and receiving from England such economic, commercial, and cultural assistance as an independent country can have from stronger neighbours without humiliation – these will be far too strong, alike in moral and material forces, to fear anything from the Turanian races of Northern Asia.

Though Germano-Turkish influence is reaching Central Asia, in no part of the Middle East will it find the resources either in men or material to give any chance of attacking the foundations of British dominion in Asia, provided the peoples who go to make up, in the widest sense, these spheres of British influence are satisfied and happy. If we carry out the wise internal policy of founding true national self-government through federalism of all the greater races of India; if sincere friendship toward Afghanistan is developed; if toward Persia we follow a genuine policy of helpfulness without any *arrière-pensée* of reducing her right to a national and free government, or making of her a second and impotent Egypt – given these conditions we may be quite sure that the South Asiatic Federation, with England as its friend, protector, and pivot, will be strong enough to meet any aggression, whether from Germanised Turkey or Japan.

The converse proposition may be stated with equal emphasis. The outlook would be most depressing if we took the wrong road of excessive centralisation by an impossible attempt at unilateral instead of federal government in a free India; of reducing Persian independence to a position like that of Egypt or Morocco; or of unjustified humiliation of the Afghan national pride. We should thus travel in the direction of reducing the symbol of Britain to the level of that of the Muscovite Tsar. The body politic would be inoculated with the germs of disease, such as would make India in the long run an easy prey to a combination of attack from without and sedition from within. In modern as well as ancient times great empires not built on the stable foundations of freedom, nationality, and justice, have broken down from the blows of smaller but healthier neighbours. It is for us to follow the moral, genuinely disinterested and nation-conserving policy that will make the free South Asiatic Federation of to-morrow one of the great dominions of that free union of nations of which Britain is the heart and the King-Emperor the beloved head.

CHAPTER XVII

THE PATH TO WIDER CONFEDERATION

Regrets that Edwin Montagu did not use the term "self-government" for India – the concept of responsible government in various countries – the British model not suitable for India – Indian desire for "self-government within the Empire" – criticism of the federal system not well-founded – a tendency for greater aggregations in the international field – India should strengthen ties with neighbouring Muslim states – adopt an attractive policy – the possibility of attracting Afghanistan, the Arab principalities, Persia, Nepal, Bhutan, Tibet and Ceylon to the Confederation.

Our survey of international problems affecting India's neighbours may be followed by tracing in fuller details the intimate connection between satisfactory progress in relations with them and the principles on which Indian constitutional advances, even those of the immediate future, are based. From this and other standpoints, the use of the term "responsible government" instead of "self-government" by Mr. Montagu in the historic announcement to the House of Commons on August 20, 1917, is to be regretted. We know from Lord Curzon (House of Lords, 24th October, 1917) that the terms of the announcement were the subject of "repeated discussion at the Cabinet," and I am convinced that the words "responsible government" were used in order to carry with the Secretary of State and the Prime Minister some more conservative members of the small War Cabinet. It was employed so that the Executive Government hereafter might contain Englishmen, while at the same time the administration became sufficiently liberal to be responsible to the people. The adjective is unfortunate because it carries the technical meaning of a government responsible for its existence to an assembly elected by the people. On the other hand, "self-government" can comprise many and varied forms of expression of the popular will.

Responsible government, in the narrow and technical sense in which Mr. Montagu's announcement is being interpreted in some quarters, has been really successful alone in the United Kingdom, and there only up to a certain point. In England the two-party system, quite inconceivable in India, was held years ago by no less a judge of constitutional history than Bagehot to have been the real cause of the success of this form of government. But in the words of a competent observer to-day 'the breakdown of Parliamentary government, which had become increasingly acute in the years preceding the war, was due to the fact that the British people had persisted in attempting in one Parliament and with one executive to deal with three classes of business," viz. Imperial affairs; questions affecting the United Kingdom as a whole; and the internal affairs of the three countries.[1] Under the stress of war conditions, many of the traditional elements of responsibility of the executive to Parliament are in suspense.

In France, where, for historical reasons, there are many parties, this principle has led to unstable guidance and constant changes in ministries, and has brought to the front in public life a kaleido-scopic crowd of individuals instead of a few outstanding national characters. France is a very great nation, but a sincere admirer who loves her almost as a foster-mother country may be allowed to say that she is great in spite of her governmental system. Sympathetic students of the French Constitution, such as Mr. Bodley, and passionate French patriots, such as M. Déroulède, have regretted that the immediate fear of Caesarism led the founders of the Third Republic to adopt the English model instead of that of the other great Anglo-Saxon State.

In Spain this narrow "responsible" form of constitution has led, as it must in any half-educated country where parliamentary institutions are not a tradition of the people, to Rotativism, which, though nominally responsible to the electorate, is the very negation of good government. At this moment, heroic efforts are being made to do away with the system. So long as Portugal was a constitutional monarchy, the same hopeless plan of Rotativism strangled her development; since her change to republicanism

---

[1] Letter to the *Times*, 5 February, 1918, by Lord Hythe (now Earl Brassey) urging the necessity for a federal form of government in the United Kingdom, both on grounds of efficiency and to provide the one effective solution of the Irish Home Rule problem. This view has gained widespread acceptance since the issue of the Irish Convention report.

constant revolutions and unrest have succeeded the former national inactivity. In Greece, until Venizelos, a man of genius, came to the head of affairs, the reality without the name of Rotativism held sway and nearly ruined that small but gifted people.

On the other hand, who will be so foolish as to say that the United States of America are not composed of self-governing communities? Who will allege that the Federal Government at Washington is not in the truest sense a government of the people, by the people, and for the people? Yet the system by which it exists is diametrically opposed to "responsible government" in the narrow sense. The executive is even more separate and independent of the legislature than in Germany. There the leading ministers are always nominated by the King of Prussia as Prussia's representatives to the Federal Council; and thus, in a roundabout way by belonging to the Upper House, they come into contact with the popular assembly. In America Cabinet Ministers are entirely responsible to the President, and, by the Constitution at least, have no more influence or part in the acts of the legislature than any ordinary private citizen. Nor are they, as in Germany, of practical necessity members of the Senate.

It would be a disaster for India to be forced into the narrow form of constitutionalism that developed with its essential condition of two great rival parties, in England through historical and natural causes, but is now confessedly in need of reform. Mere imitation of features of the British Constitution, we have seen, has had most disillusioning results in the Iberian peninsula and in Greece. It is true that a form of responsibility to parliament has succeeded in the Northern States of Europe; but here it must be remembered that in Sweden, the most important of the three Scandinavian Governments, the system is a half-way house between responsibility as understood in England, and the German practice of separation of powers as between the executive and the legislative bodies. Constitutional government has succeeded only where it has been cast in a form natural to the history and development of the people. In America, with all fidelity to democratic principles, it has taken forms widely different from those of Great Britain. In Japan, also, it is in practice anything but a slavish imitation of the English methods. Indeed, it is nearer to the Swedish than to any other system existing in the West. In Germany and Austria it approaches the American system, though the partition between the executive and the legislature is not so marked.

Why should India be forced to imitate a system of government evolved through many centuries in a geographically small country with two historical parties? Why should India be placed on this Procrustean bed, instead of allowing the more widely elected legislature and an executive with a century and a half of tradition behind it to develop naturally their own inner working, just as they have been evolved in other countries? We want self-government, we want responsible government in the widest sense of the term – that of ultimate responsibility to the people – but we do not want our nascent national institutions to be put into swaddling clothes because one word instead of another was chosen by the British War Cabinet for its public declaration. The Indian peoples, with an instinctive sense of their need, have asked for self-government within the Empire, not for parliamentary institutions on the British model. None of the draft schemes prepared by Indians from that of Gokhale to the joint represen-tation of the National Congress and the Moslem League hypothecate full and immediate responsibility of the executive to the legislature.

It is an unfair and prejudiced criticism of the federal form of government to argue that the free provincial parliaments will be nothing but glorified municipalities. Surely autonomy for our great provinces, with populations of from twenty to fifty millions, with their vast and varied lands, each equal in natural resources to one of the greater European States, is a sufficient field for the ambition and devotion of any patriot. It must be remembered that as true federalists we advocate for the government of each of the great province-states the same measure of ultimate internal independence from the central authorities as is now enjoyed by the Nizam or the Rajput princes over their own territories.

This brings me to the first of two questions I wish to put to the critics of federalism as here advocated. By what other system can the Native States be brought into active union with the rest of India? No scheme of reconstruction can be complete without taking into consideration the 70,000,000 people and the 710,000 square miles comprised within these areas scattered all over India. Can these lands remain permanently out of touch with the great reconstructed India of the future? Or, as an alternative, are we to tear up treaties that assured their princes full autonomy within their respective spheres? Or is it seriously maintained that the central Government, while scrupulously avoiding interference in any question relating to a tiny principality or its court, should at the same time control the great province-states from Simla or Delhi, as if they were nothing but so many territories occupied by superior forces? The history of the past, no less than the justice and symmetry to be sought to-day, leads to the conclusion that we need a federation which can be entered by the greatest provinces and the smallest Native Raj alike without loss of internal freedom, and yet with the assurance that, in all federal matters, they will pull together for a united Empire.

Under the system I have advocated, with its checks, balances, and safeguards, there can be little danger of any province falling into misgovernment. It is common ground with students of Indian affairs that a State like Mysore should have full control of internal policy. If this principle holds good of an essentially non-democratic régime, why should it not apply to our great national states, where legislative and financial control is finally vested in a representative assembly, and where the immovable executive is strong enough to carry out measures of justice and utility?

The second question for the advocate of a unilateral system to ponder is that of the effect on the international future in Asia. An outstanding tendency in the political ferment of to-day is for small nations, while retaining their individuality, to gather to a central, powerful State that carries them along in a common course. In recent years the United States have drawn into their orbit many of the smaller entities of the New World, such as Cuba and the republics of Central America. Germany has Austria, Turkey and Bulgaria ranged with her, and she is ambitious to secure within her sphere of influence the States that have been surrendered through the Bolshevist betrayal of Russia. She dreams of ultimately bringing Holland and Flanders, Denmark, Norway and Sweden, and even Switzerland within her constellation. England and France and Italy have now taken a common route in world politics, carrying with them many wide-flung dominions. Even the three Scandinavian monarchies, free as they ordinarily are from the bewildering entanglements of world-politics, have found that practical independence can only be maintained by greater union and cohesion. We have to-day, in fact, a common North European policy, into which the new Republic of Finland longs to be drawn. It has been ruthlessly invaded because it forms a barrier to Teutonic ambitions in North Western Europe. But the most competent observers are agreed that whatever changes peace may bring, Germany will not turn away her eyes from Middle Asia.

It is for the Indian patriot to recognise that Persia, Afghanistan, and possibly Arabia must sooner or later come within the orbit of some Continental Power – such as Germany, or what may grow out of the break-up of Russia – or must throw in their lot with that of the Indian Empire, with which they have so much more genuine affinity. The world forces that move small states into closer contact with powerful neighbours, though so far most visible in Europe, will inevitably make themselves felt in Asia. Unless she is willing to accept the prospect of having powerful and possibly inimical neighbours to watch, and the heavy military burdens thereby entailed, India cannot afford to neglect to draw her Mahomedan neighbour states to herself by the ties of mutual interest and goodwill.

A lesson of the Great War that even Germany has been reluctantly compelled to recognise is that force, though remorselessly applied by her military leaders, is insufficient to secure the incorporation of weakened nations. In Courland, in Lithuania, in Flanders herself, German policy has wavered between merciless severity and efforts to win the hearts of such elements of the population as the Flemings and the Baltes to her *kultur* and interests. British policy ought to have no such conflict of ideals. Hence it is unthinkable that the British Empire can pursue a course of mere conquest in the Middle East. Such a policy is foreign to her ideals and repugnant to her interests. It would be more disastrous for England and India than almost anything else I can conceive, for it would mean the violation of the principles of humanity and justice, and would provoke continued unrest. On the other hand, a merely negative attitude will not meet the dangers I have indicated. We must have a policy attractive enough to draw toward our centre State the outer nations. A system of federation, just to each member, united by ties of common interest, would serve as a magnet for them. It would be a great harbour light for any weak state of the Middle East.

Once the internal federation was complete and the economic influence northwards and westwards developed, we might expect the Afghans themselves to seek association therein. The fact that Bengal and Bombay, Hyderabad and Kashmir were enjoying full autonomy, would be a guarantee to the Afghans of no risk of loss of independence in entering the federation. Just as the indigenous rulers of Rajputna would have their place, there is no reason why a group of principalities from Arabia and the Southern littoral of the Persian Gulf, should not ultimately become members of the union that will ensure peace and liberty, freedom and order to the south of Asia. Subsequently, Persia herself would be attracted, and just as the natural pride of Bavaria or Saxony has not been diminished by inclusion within the

German Union, so, on a greater and more difficult but happily beneficent basis, the empire of Persia and the kingdom of Afghanistan could honourably enter a federation of which Delhi would be the centre.

Needless to say, no compulsion, direct or indirect, can be employed. The right course is to institute such a type of community of states as to draw the sympathy and practical interest of India's neighbours. The magnet would attract, as time went on, the isolated and remote lands of Nepal, Bhutan, and Tibet. The Crown Colony of Ceylon naturally and historically belongs to India. She is cut off from the mainland by a mere geological accident, and the shallow channels and intermittent rocks that divide her therefrom are already partly, and will soon be completely, bridged by the Indo-Ceylon Railway. A unilateral government of India could have no attraction for the people of the island. They would naturally prefer being governed from Whitehall rather than Delhi, for Whitehall, being so much further away, interferes less, while the Parliamentary institutions of England afford Ceylon guarantees in normal times against injustice and needless mandates from without. The autonomous system would give the *coup de grâce* to the pleas put forward from time to time for the separation of Burma from the Indian Empire, which spring from dissatisfaction with the present centralised control.

In a word, the path of beneficent and growing union must be based on a federal India, with every member exercising her individual rights, her historic peculiarities and natural interests, yet protected by a common defensive system and customs union from external danger and economic exploitation by stronger forces. Such a federal India would promptly bring Ceylon to the bosom of her natural mother, and the further developments we have indicated would follow. We can build a great South Asiatic federation by now laying the foundations wide and deep on justice, on liberty, and on recognition for every race, every religion, and every historical entity.

CHAPTER XXII

EDUCATION FOR THE MASSES

The importance of universal and improved education for India – illiteracy wide-spread in India – its implications – ignorance among

the women – his personal interest in education – Gokhale's bill –
educational movements in the provinces – local legislatures and
compulsory kindergarten and primary education for both sexes –
educational question is one "of life and death for India".

The programme of material development sketched in the three
preceeding chapters will fail of its purpose if the policy of universal and improved education is not adopted and pursued with
persistent earnestness. Even those who have but a slight acquaintance with modern India are well aware that it is, with the possible
exception of China, the most ignorant of civilised countries. The
application of the principles of higher commerce and of scientific
agriculture on any general scale are impossible in an almost
universal state of intellectual darkness under which the daily
labour of life cannot be other than ineffective. The average
peasant can learn little or nothing beyond the most routine forms
of labour, because his illiteracy leaves him devoid of scope for
being taught. A man of genius, though illiterate, such as the
Albanian Mahomed Ali, has now and again been found able to
govern a country by methods far in advance of the standard it
had before reached. But the real tragedy of ignorance is that
while it does not prevent the superior individual from reaching
full development, it so lowers the standard of the people that it
is helpless before superior organisation of any kind.

Most of the ills of India can be ascribed to the general want
of knowledge. Moral and intellectual growth have fallen far
behind the material gifts brought by British rule. Indeed, there
is something inconsistent between the outward equipment of
India, with her roads, railways and irrigation colonies, her armies,
her developing industries, her skilled officials, her courts of
law, her universities, and her scientists, – and yet with an inward
blindness ... The particularly modern facGade of the building
only brings into the stronger relief the intellectual nakedness
of those within. The small proportion of literacy to the whole
uninstructed mass – 59 per thousand at the last census – is
appalling; yet it does not represent the real condition of things,
for the vast majority of so-called literates have had nothing but
the most superficial and fragmentary instruction.[1]

The poverty and disease so general in India is largely attribu-

[1] The Educational Volume of *Statistics of British India* for 1915–16 states that on
the average of the last quinquennium only 11 per cent of the pupils in the
lower primary stage goes to the upper primary stage. "These figures suggest,"
says the official record, "that 89 out of every 100 pupils in the lower primary

table to mass ignorance. Even if a Ross or a Rogers discovers means of preventing the most deadly diseases, the unlettered masses cannot be effectively taught to resist the attacks of the invisible and microscopic enemies of their vitality. There is also the terrible waste of energy arising from the general incapacity of the untaught to recognise the value of time or to distinguish between economy and waste. From higher standpoints this weight of mental destitution is a grievous handicap. It renders the mass of the people incapable of real spiritual culture and of communion with the Unseen, and tends to degrade religion in all its varied forms to the level of an unreasoning superstition. The whole situation is the more saddening owing to the dispro-portion of the distribution of literacy among the two sexes. At the last census only ten females per mille were literate, as com-pared with 106 males. The literacy in English was 95 per 10,000 males, and only one in a thousand females. This means that even in classes and castes where the men have some degree of education, the women are frequently entirely ignorant of the three R's. Since the true culture of the race depends on woman, it follows that the curses of ignorance and superstition are found even in the higher strata of society.

No social duty of the community is more urgent and essential than that of effective educational diffusion. It is sometimes said that the English-educated classes in India have been slow to recognise and press forward the claims of primary instruction. I cannot personally plead guilty to the charge, for throughout my public life I have consistently advocated serious attention to this problem. More than fifteen years have passed since I placed it in the forefront of my humble contribution to the discussion of the Budget in the Imperial Legislature. I expressed regret that year after year went by without serious effort being made from the Imperial Exchequer to raise the standard of intelligence of all classes throughout the country. I asked if it was right in that age of severe economic competition that the vast majority of Indian

stage never go beyond that stage and receive practically no education." Com-menting on this fact in one of its instructive regular Indian articles, the *Times Educational Supplement* (March 14, 1918) says: "It is well known that the scanty instruction received by the great majority of pupils at village schools throughout India does not provide a foundation for subsequent progress. In most cases the children become completely illiterate within ten years of leaving school. It has been calculated that this applies to about 80 per cent of all the village school-children of South India."

children should be brought up without possessing even the rudiments of learning.[1]

Again in 1911, taking advantage of the interest in India aroused by the Coronation of His Majesty, and the presence in England of Indian princes and soldiers, I urged in the *National Review* the taking of immediate steps to overcome mass illiteracy in India; and also to reform and extend secondary and higher education. I dealt with the question from the standpoint of the interests not of India alone, but of those of the Empire as a whole. I claimed that this great problem of educational diffusion should not be attacked piecemeal; that in the long run it would be best and cheapest to face the situation boldly at once and to lay out a sufficient sum to meet the main requirements. I went so far as to say that the salvation of India under British rule rested upon the enlightenment of the masses. Its bearing both on Imperial trade development and on an aspect of defence then destined to be of the most crucial importance within a very few years were discussed.[2]

At the time this was written the issue was before the Viceregal Legislature in concrete form. Earlier in the year Gokhale had introduced a Bill "to make better provision for the extension of elementary education," by giving municipalities and local boards permissive power, under various safeguards, to apply compulsion

---

[1] "My Lord, has not the time come for the commencement of some system of universal primary education, such as has been adopted by almost every responsible Government? The extreme poverty of this country has recently been much discussed both here and in England, and all sorts of causes have been found and given to explain the undoubted fact. But, my Lord, in my humble opinion the fundamental cause of this extreme poverty is the ignorance of the great majority of the people. . . . With the ever-present fact that this country is advancing very slowly as compared with Europe and America, has not the time come for taking a bold and generous step towards some system of universal education suited to the conditions of the various provinces of the country?" – East India, Financial Statement for 1903–4. Parliamentary Bluebook No. 151, 1903.

[2] "It is to this, and from this [educational] development of India as part of an Imperial whole that we must look for the means of strengthening her and the Empire at one and the same time. For India must remain one of the pillars of the British Empire – and a most important pillar, because she is to-day the Empire's largest potential market and the greatest reservoir of manpower within the limits of British heritage. That is why the education of her people is so vital: vital because of the future increase of her commerce, vital because of the almost unlimited areas of cultivation within her boundaries, vital because of her defensive strength and as a half-way house to the great self-governing States of South Africa, Australia, and New Zealand. By edu-

to boys between the ages of six and ten. The opinions of the local Governments were invited, and early in 1912 Gokhale moved that the Bill be referred to a select committee; but this course was officially opposed and the motion was defeated. I think it is now generally recognised that the decision was unfortunate, though it is only fair to say that there was great force in one of the arguments of Sir Harcourt Butler, then Education Member, against the Bill. It was that in a country so vast and so varied in degrees of progress, such legislation ought to be provincial rather than Imperial.

A beginning in this decentralising policy, hitherto rendered difficult by the policy of the Government of India, has now been made. Last year Mr. V. J. Patel obtained sanction for the introduction of a similar, though in important respects a more advanced, measure in the Bombay Legislature. It secured the support of the Government of the liberal and fair-minded Lord Willingdon, and, after careful amendment by a select committee presided over by Sir M. B. Chaubal, was passed into law at the end of last year. The Viceroy subsequently announced that the Government of India have decided not to place obstacles in the way of such provincial legislatures as may decide "on any reasonable measures, whether those are the precise measures which we would ourselves be prepared to initiate or not." Bills after the Bombay pattern have been unofficially introduced in the Bengal and Behar Councils, and in the Punjab the Government have drafted a Bill on comprehensive lines.

These are welcome steps, and it is a matter for keen satisfaction that the principle of compulsion has at last found a place on the Statute-book of British India. But permissive measures, having regard to the slender resources of the local bodies and the

cation there can be trained a people whose past history has proved that they can be fighters and can show a loyalty to their leaders unparalleled in history. Therefore the motto to-day for British and Indian statesmen must be, 'Educate, educate, educate.' Look for a passing moment at the question of man-power. . . . India could put troops into South Africa as quickly as they could be sent from England; she could land soldiers in Australia long before England could do so; and forces from India could reach Western Canada almost as soon as from England. Still more: India from her vast reservoir can supply thousands where England can only send hundreds. . . . If by education the myriads of India can be taught that they are guardians and supporters of the Crown, just as are the white citizens of the Empire, then the realisation that India and the self-governing dominions stand and fall together, bound by a community of interests and a common cause to maintain, will have come. . . . It is imperative to give Indians the education to fit them for their future role in the British Empire." – *National Review*, July, 1911.

present centralisation of State financial control, will not adequately meet the need for a general raising of the standard to be effected within a reasonable period, say the life of the younger members of the present generation. It seems to me that the ideal course is for each local legislature, after autonomous powers have been conferred on the provinces, to make kindergarten and primary instruction compulsory for both sexes, except where want of funds prevents the immediate placing of schools within reach of the population. The advantage of this over the permissive method would be that in every possible place, and to the extent that money was forthcoming, compulsion would take effect. The exceptional and unfortunate districts would be brought within the range of public knowledge and sympathy, and would be in the way of securing the assistance both of public and private funds from without.

If less drastic measures are taken, India will remain handicapped by general ignorance when the economic world position, after the war, provides her with extraordinary opportunities for development. If the problem is played with by leaving the decision to individual localities, largely on the basis of increasing the local rates, we cannot hope to see India attain the wealth and strength we might otherwise reasonably expect by the middle of the present century. The rôle of the local bodies should be that of primary school administration, and the executive work of compulsion should be under the charge of State officials, such as the district officers. Nor must there be compulsion for boys only, which would tend to still further and artificially handicap the position of Indian women. It is a matter for satisfaction that the first compulsion Act, that of Bombay, makes no differentiation. I cannot too strongly emphasise the importance of *pari passu* application of the compulsory principle to both sexes. In those instances where there are practical difficulties so great as to make a general application of compulsion impossible for the time being, there should be a fair basis for apportionment between schools for boys and for girls. The facilities for the latter should be equalised with those for the former, and the progress toward general education should everywhere be based on the equitable principle of not permitting the enormous disparity between the literacy of the two sexes to continue.

There is no running away from this need for educational diffusion, since it is a question of life and death for India. No compromise as to providing this essential groundwork of national development can be tolerated. I am well aware that the problem is largely one of finance; but care must be taken not to allow an undue proportion of the funds made available to be swallowed up in bricks and mortar. Indian opinion is strong in the view that, having regard to the urgency of the need for educational diffusion, we must not, in these early stages, allow the construction of school houses to delay the more vital work of teaching. There are evidences that this view is also held by thoughtful English educationalists in India.[1] Teaching, as the Buddha and other great lights in the religious evolution of India personally demonstrated, can be carried on by men with a sense of vocation in the humblest places and under apparently untoward conditions. The greatest teachers of ancient India were forest dwellers and gathered their students round them in the open air. A slowing of the pace in order to wait for good buildings and other conditions of an ideal state of things would be a crime against the young life of India and her future generations.

CHAPTER XXIII

HIGHER EDUCATION

Secondary and technical schools – educational facilities for girls – local needs and means – in addition to traditional universities thirty or forty residential teaching universities needed – a few institutions on the Swiss model – explore other models – the responsibility of the community – duties of the present generation of Indians – the media of instruction – a broad linguistic base necessary – English as the medium of instruction in the main universities – university education for women – scientific and research institutions.

The legitimate boundaries of primary instruction have to be determined in laying down any sound programme of secondary teaching. This important point should be settled by each province state according to its conditions, needs, and means. The secondary and technical schools should be of the nature of a

---

[1] "The modern tendency in India to extravagance in bricks and mortar for schools and colleges should be checked. Many experienced observers believe that far less expensive buildings than those at present erected are adequate for Indian educational purposes. . . . It is for the State to put money into the making of men far more than into ornate buildings. In particular the national [primary] schools should be of the simplest construction." – The *Times* Educational Supplement, Indian article, 29th November, 1917.

voluntary superstructure on the foundations of the primary and obligatory courses. The question of early technical and scientific instruction for those who do not contemplate the advanced teaching that can only be obtained from university work should be considered when the average secondary "gymnasia" are formed. An indirect but clear aim of the teachers should be to give the boys and girls such interest in their work as to make it an individual ambition and desire to become undergraduates for the purpose of pursuing the higher branches of special training. Thus economical reasons would operate as to the extent of individual study, and promising students who could possibly afford it would continue their training as undergraduates for their own benefit and that of the nation.

Under a system of general elementary compulsion we shall soon be faced with the question whether there is to be what is known as co-education in all the secondary institutions. The ideal solution will be for parents to have the option of sending their daughters to the secondary institutions open to all, but at the same time to provide sufficient special institutions for girls to develop and meet the national requirements for the education of women on lines which take account of Indian traditions and standards. Each province state would be required to make provision, according to the standard of local needs and means, for sufficient secondary education both to provide workers of every kind in the middle walks of life, and to make the road to higher knowledge broad enough for everyone with the means and aptitudes to reach the university. These are the ideals of the secondary institutions of the United Kingdom, where only a very small proportion of pupils proceed to the university or even attempt to matriculate.

In the realms of higher education, the system initiated sixty years ago and only now being modified by new foundations, of setting up a very few central examining universities, affiliating colleges over immense areas, has proved unwieldy and mechanical. It is unknown in other parts of the world, and is too soulless to be a living, energising method of building up the intellectual and moral life of the nation. Since these great universities have grown with the modern history of India, I do not favour their abolition. They should remain and be given a reasonable extent of federal jurisdiction and power. But, side by side with them, we need not one or two merely, but thirty or forty residential teaching universities, as well as examples of the continental type of lecturing and free universities. We must have no rigid, cast-iron system of universal application. As Lord Hardinge's Government declared five years ago, only by experiment will it be found out what types of universities are best suited to the different parts of India.

It is for her to profit by the accumulated experience of more-advanced countries, bringing into her service, side by side and in many places, the varying methods by which society has so far endeavoured to provide the higher culture. For instance, in a country like India, where many men after reaching a mature age and winning a reasonable degree of financial independence show a commendable thirst for knowledge, there is much to be said for the provision of a few universities on the model of the excellent institutions of Switzerland, providing for every age and class, at moderate fees, regular lectures and courses in different fields of study, and granting degrees according to the creative work of the individual. It is not for so vast a country to take one European or American example for slavish imitation, but to bring into her service all the best-known forms and types, in order to provide scope for developing particular capacity.

Here, again, as in all other branches of the educational problem, the financial issue is important. One advantage of universities open to all ages, as in Switzerland and France, is that many well-to-do people will attend the courses, and that some at least of those who benefit by its teaching will be moved to render substantial financial help. More and more, as time goes on, will wealthy citizens be impelled by the earnest educational spirit abroad to give of their abundance, and those of moderate means of their sufficiency, to the cause of education in all the variety of its needs. But private munificence cannot take the place in educational provision which rightly falls to the community as a whole. It is for each province state to shoulder the main responsibility for the attainment of the ideal set forth in the gracious words of the King-Emperor, in replying to the address of the Calcutta University in January, 1912. The ideal is that of a network of schools and colleges so that, in the words of His Majesty, "the homes of my Indian subjects may be brightened and their labour sweetened by the spread of knowledge with all that follows in its train, a higher level of thought, of comfort, and of health." Just as certain generations in Europe, namely, those of 1790 to 1815, and of the present day, have been called upon to bear the immense sacrifice of guarding the future of their countries from foreign aggression and military subjection, so the present generation in India must make greater sacrifices than would have been requisite but for past neglect, to deliver her from the grip of ignorance, poverty, and disease.

Closely associated with this beneficent campaign is the difficult and passion-raising question of media of instruction. In many quarters English is regarded as the fitting all-prevailing *lingua franca* of higher education. This feeling found strong expression in the Imperial Legislature some three years ago, when an unsuccessful motion in favour of greater resort to the vernacular media in secondary schools drew from Mr. Surendranath Bannerjee the declaration that any proposal involving a curtailment – even a possible curtailment – of the area of English instruction would be viewed in Bengal with misgiving, and even with alarm. Yet there are vast numbers, especially in Northern India, who would like Hindi to become not only the *lingua franca* of higher instruction, but the national language and tongue of the whole country. Others, especially among the Mahomedans, have similar dreams respecting Urdu, the other great branch of Hindostani. But I believe the great majority of instructed Indians regard with considerable apprehension these passionate disputes about the vernaculars, an unhappy feature of modern life borrowed from European racial and linguistic quarrels in "ramshackle empires" (to use Mr. Lloyd George's phrase), such as Austria-Hungary, Russia, and Turkey.

Patriotic instincts should lead Indian thinkers and statesmen to resist the desire of one part of Upper India to impose its language, Hindi, on the rest of the peninsula. We saw in an earlier chapter that it was the centralising policy of the North that broke up the Mogul Empire. It is curious that even now, in the provinces where that Empire set up its successive capitals, there is a marked tendency to claim to be "the real India," and to look upon the great provinces of the South and East as mere addenda. The carrying out of any such spirit in the linguistic field would strike a fatal blow at the successful establishment of the great, federated, vital, unmechanical India of to-morrow.

If it be maintained that differences of languages will weaken the national unity, we may adduce by way of disproof the example of the Swiss Confederation. This well-knit political unity, as strong and real as any to be found, and covering a tiny area in comparison with India, has three essentially different languages, French, German, and Italian, and innumerable patois of each of them are spoken. The United States of America have been frequently quoted as an ideal for Indian federation, and yet more newspapers and books in different languages are produced in the vast Republic than in the whole of Europe put together. To force the beautiful Bengali language, with its rich and growing literature, the mother tongue of Rabrindranath [*sic*] Tagore, to give up its national position in this day of its development would be a crime against culture and civilisation. Mahrati, Gujarati, Tamil, and Telugu have still to develop their literary possibilities. But philological history gives us many examples of a language, after centuries of oral use by large numbers, taking on a literary character and breaking out like water cutting a channel down the rocks. Thus Italian lived a subterranean life for centuries until the imaginative genius of Dante forced recognition from the world. We may confidently anticipate that the great languages of Southern India, under the quickening impulse of the Renaissance, will reach literary maturity, and each make its characteristic contribution to the wealth of human culture and civilisation.

Again, it would be an act of cruel vandalism to deprive the Indian Mahomedan of Urdu. Nor would the deprivation be merely sectional, for it is spoken and written by large numbers of people of other faiths, and in origin it is very much more the work of cultured Hindus, well versed in Persian and Arabic, than of Mahomedans. Gifted Hindu writers of Urdu have contributed from the first to this day to its poetic and prose literature, as is clearly shown in Sir George Grierson's monumental *Linguistic Survey*,[1] and it would be a calamity, through a narrow and short-sighted particularism, to deprive large numbers of Hindus from the pleasure and instruction they derive from a language that has intimate relations with the classical tongues of Western Asia. For the humanistic culture of India, as for her political development, we must have as broad a basis as possible: ordered variety instead of a mere mechanical similarity.

Let all the main Indian languages and their literary potentialities receive the fullest encouragement, with universities devoted to them when possible. The fact that the differences between the main groups, if we except the Dravidian South, are not cardinal, such as between, say, Finnish or Magyar, or French and Dutch, should in the long run lead to each gaining strength from the development of the other. Philological science long ago taught us that languages are the natural expression of a people's inner life and mentality. To artificially force some to adopt the idioms of others is nothing but a cruel injustice only appropriate to the ideals of Prussian kultur. Pragmatism and vital character

[1] Vol. IX: Indo-Aryan Family, Central Group; Part I: Western Hindi and Panjabi. Calcutta. Govt. Press. 1916.

and quality are the essential needs – not imitation of some external ideal of unity which, when artificially propped up, say by the Tsars from Peter the Great to Nicholas II, leads to the greatest disasters and divisions. The India hoped for in this book is one in which the love of a common Motherland will be expressed and exercised in every form and language. It seems to me a wise decision on the part of His Exalted Highness the Nizam to make Urdu the language of the Osmania University he is establishing, but with English a compulsory subject.

Still, as I have sought to define, not a Utopian and perfect India of the far-off future, but an India that can and ought to be shaped for the morrow of peace, it has to be regretfully recognised that as things are it is not practicable, except in the singular situation of the premier State, to set up the main universities with any other language than English as the medium of instruction. To translate the wide range of text-books and other literature necessary for an adequately equipped university must be a costly and in many respects difficult task, and unless backed up by the power of a mighty prince such as the Nizam, is liable to break down in the present stage of literary development of the Indian vernaculars.[1] The task of the day is to concentrate on the creation of varied universities teaching in English, some based on the residential system; others open to matriculated students from affiliated colleges and examining for degrees; and others, on the Swiss model, open to all and bestowing their honours according to the creative work brought before the university authorities, without investigation of the general qualifications of the writers.

Under such varied systems, the problem of the higher education of women would be less difficult than that of primary and secondary instruction. In the case of the non-residential examining colleges, the women can be enrolled at affiliated institutions. Where the Oxford and Cambridge model is followed, it will be necessary to start special residential colleges for them. Universities of the third category on the Swiss model, as in Paris and Lausanne, will be equally open, regardless of sex, for lecture courses, a small payment being made for each course.

Science and natural philosophy must play a leading part in the curriculum of each kind of university that has been advocated. There must also be higher scientific and research institutions all over the country. The Indian Institute of Science at Bangalore,

---

[1] I do not forget that after modern universities were established in Russia and Japan, they had to depend upon translations for decades, and the native language developed naturally with time.

initiated by Jamsetjee Tata, and Sir Jagadis Chunder Bose's Research Institute in Calcutta – inspired by a noble ideal of pure scholarship – these are models which should be followed on a large scale both in the provinces and principalities. Special institutions are also needed for the study of higher geology and mineralogy, and also for medical and pathological research, with which I deal in the following chapter. The broad aim must be to make India sufficiently well equipped educationally to give her sons the general and special culture they seek, so that the ambitious should no longer be under the virtual compulsion to spend years of their normal student life abroad.

CHAPTER XXVI

THE STATUS OF WOMEN

The position of women in Islam and Hinduism – female mortality in India – the importance of women in society – women in the West – the relationship between the status of women and social advancement – the position of women in India – movements for female emancipation – happiness and welfare of women must be an end – women under Islam and Hinduism – the need for legislation – women's franchise – the pace of reform can be faster in India – the status of women and general political reforms – women's potential for sacrifice – women and national regeneration.

The social reformation considered in the last four chapters depends in large measure on the recognition afforded to the rights and status of the female half of the population. The Prophet of Islam (who has been so cruelly libelled in the Western world, by ignorance or malice) was wont to say that men can but follow in the footsteps of their mothers towards Paradise. And it was not for nothing, according to Moslem belief, that his first convert was a woman. The word "harem," often held by the uninformed to signify a prison, or something worse, means in reality "the sacred presence," and is derived from the same root as the word used for the Holy Places of Mecca and Medina. In the ancient epics and thought of the Hindus, too, there are to be found correspondences with the veneration enjoined by Islam toward women. The Hindu ideal of womanhood has been that of a necessary counterpart without whom a man himself cannot obtain salvation.

When we consider the scientific and natural importance of woman to society, we find that numerically they fall somewhat below the male population. In India as a whole at the last census the proportion of females per thousand males in the actual population was 954. In Western Europe, on the other hand, the number of females per thousand males varied from 1093 in Portugal and 1068 in England and Wales, to 1013 in Belgium and 1003 in Ireland. Sir Edward Gait, the Census Commissioner, while admitting that the Western Europe proportions are exceptional attributes this marked difference to the relatively high mortality amongst females in India. In natural conditions there is always a slightly greater birth of boys than of girls; but infantile mortality being higher amongst boys, the preponderance tends to disappear. Sir Edward holds that the advantage which nature normally gives to girls in this way is neutralised by the social conditions of Indian life, and particularly by premature marriage and child-bearing, and the laborious toil in the fields of the women of the working classes.[1]

Biologically the female is more important to the race than the male. While average women are capable of earning their own livelihood like men, they are the guardians of the life of the race, and only through their natural constitution are they able to bear the double burden. Experience shows the strong probability that the active influence of women on society, under free and equal conditions, is calculated not only to bring about practical improvement in the domestic realm, but also a higher and nobler idealism into the life of the State. Those who know Moslem society from within readily admit that its higher spiritual life owes a great debt to the example and influence of women. To-day, as in the lifetime of the Prophet, probably the majority of devout and reverent followers of His teaching are women. In Christendom too the enthusiasm, idealism, and steadfast faith of the weaker sex are of the highest value, notably in the Catholic Church. The surrender in the West of the lives of many women to piety and good works is a great antidote to the evils of general and habitual selfishness.

In relatively young countries, such as Australia, New Zealand, and some of the American States where votes have long been given to women, beneficial results have followed, and at least some of the curses of modern civilisation have been greatly mitigated. Notably the drinking saloons have been reduced in numbers and hours of trade, and have been subjected to closer

[1] Census of India, 1911. General Report, chapter vi.

supervision, while in many of the federated States they have been abolished. Even in England, where women have secured political enfranchisement only within the present year, some of the out-standing social scandals have been removed, or at least greatly mitigated, by their determined and self-sacrificing labour. In the Great War the women of the United Kingdom, France, Italy, and there is reason to believe of Germany, have eagerly devoted themselves to manifold forms of toil, at office, munition factory, and farm, and near the "front" for war purposes. They have proved themselves in patriotism and selflessness the equals of men. Refining ideas and, probably, the subconscious instinct to preserve the bearers of the race, have prevented women from actually taking the field, except in Russia, where women by their steadfastness often put to shame deserting and mutinous soldiery. But many thousands of English and French women have served the Army behind the lines, well within the danger zone; and one has only to be in London or Paris on a raid night to see the calm, heroic work performed by nurses, and the fortitude of their sisters, generally speaking.

No progressive thinker of to-day will challenge the claim that the social advancement and general well-being of communities are greatest where women are least debarred, by artificial barriers and narrow prejudice, from taking their full position as citizens. Hence it is with deep sorrow that the admission must be made that the position of Indian women is unsatisfactory, that artificial obstacles to their full service of the commonwealth are every-where found, and that, from the point of view of health and happiness alike, women suffer needlessly through chains forged by prejudice and folly . . . These and other social evils have so handicapped India that it is impossible to conceive of her taking a proper place in the midst of free nations until the broad principle of equality between the sexes has been generally accepted by her people.

The present abrogation of this principle is the more to be deplored since the natural intelligence and ability of Indian womanhood are by no means inferior to those of their emanci-pated sisters. There are abundant indications that the Indian woman, given the same chances as her more fortunate Western sisters, could contribute no less fully to the general advancement. The Dowager Lady Dufferin wrote in her descriptions of Vice-regal life: "I have never seen women more sympathetic, more full of grace and dignity, more courteous, or more successful in the art of giving a really cordial reception to a stranger than those I met behind the purdah." We all know Indian *grandes dames*, Oriental types of such famous leaders of English society as Lady Palmerston, Sarah Lady Jersey, and Lady Waldegrave. Many of the princes owe a very great deal to the wise counsel of their mothers and wives. Amongst the commercial and trading classes, so great is the natural intelligence of many women that, in spite of the handicap of seclusion, they become real companions, helpmeets and advisers of their husbands. In a word, the natural material for feminist progress in India is good, but it is artificially kept in swaddling clothes.

The best mind and thought of the country has long seen the need for improvement in the position of women. Their emancipation has figured, from the first, in the teaching and practice of the Brahmo Samaj, and was long since effected by the small but progressive Parsee community. Social reform movements have carried on tireless crusades against the disabilities of the gentler sex, in the earlier years against vehement opposition as the late Byramji Malabari found when he was instrumental in securing legislation (1891) for raising the age of consent from ten years to twelve. To-day there is ever growing recognition of the need for educational facilities for women. Aspirations in this respect which have been stirring throughout the world are making themselves felt in India. "Thoughts have gone forth whose power can sleep no more."

Yet the change in the feminine standpoint has been coming very gradually, largely owing to a very serious mistake made by mere man at the starting-point of reform. The constant argument has been that of the necessity for providing educated and intelligent wives and daughters, sisters and mothers, for the men. This well-meaning but insolent assumption that it is for some relation, however advanced from present standards, to the other sex that women need intellectual cultivation, has inevitably tended to direct the movement into narrow and deforming channels. The time has come for a full recognition that the happiness and welfare of the women themselves, must be the end and purpose of all efforts toward improvement.

Happily, one of the great religions of the country, Islam, assures women economic independence, giving them regular and settled rights of succession to property. Under Islamic law they are not, as in England till the passing of the most far-reaching of the Married Woman's Property Acts (1882), as still in France, Italy and other parts of Catholic Europe, reduced to being after marriage and in the absence of deeds of settlement, nothing but the dependents of their husbands and to the latter having control of their pre-nuptial property. Amongst the Hindus the economic position of women is often contradictory, under interpretations of personal law governing their social customs, and differing from province to province and also as between various divisions and castes. Generally speaking the Hindu joint family system, as petrified by case-made law, operates to turn widows and married women into either domestic tyrants or slaves. It is often a question of luck in legal argument and evidence, whether or not an assertive lady of the family obtains control of the common purse, and so reduces the independence of others in the household as to render impossible a full, rich, and responsible individual life. It is to be hoped that the province states of to-morrow will be able, through their popular assemblies, to enact measures to ensure economic freedom and a reasonable uniformity of independence to Hindu women generally.

Having regard to the present constitution of Indian Government, with the absence of responsibility to the people, the reluctance of the British authorities to undertake legislation affecting the social customs of the people can be well understood. One cause of the "leave it alone" tendency is that conditions vary so greatly in different parts of the peninsula, and the work of the central Government is so absorbing that thorough consideration cannot be given to the conflicting issues which social legislation is calculated to raise. The province state, in close touch with representatives of all schools of thought, will not be so hampered. It will be in a position to further raise the age of consent, to legislate for the economic independence of women by ensuring to them the use of their own property, for giving widows and daughters the right to claim their shares and leave the joint family if so disposed. By civil marriage bills it should be made possible for natural choice in mating on both sides to extend over the whole of society. Such legal measures are essential as corollaries of voluntary social reform. Human nature being what it is, if the laws of a country are prejudicial to women, the good intentions and earnest efforts of philanthropists and reformers will not suffice to rectify the injustice done by society at large. It would be as reasonable to expect voluntary effort and goodwill to prevent robbery and theft, as to imagine that the same agencies will change for the better the condition of society, so long as the laws of the State inflict injustice on the classes to be benefited.

It is now an accepted principle of progressive rule in the West that general impartation of elementary education cannot be left entirely or even mainly to philanthropic or voluntary effort, but to be thorough and complete must be provided by the State, which is, after all, the executive arm of society as a whole. Such provision in India, as elsewhere, must be based on the principle of sex equality. This will do more good than all the speeches and crusades so long carried on for the improvement of the condition of women. In addition the various legislatures must rectify the hampering burdens imposed on Indian life by judge-made laws which have hardened what were formerly but fluid states of social economy, answering to changing conditions. The purdah system would automatically disappear if society as a whole, represented by the State, gave women education and economic freedom in their conditions of life. The reform of the laws of property should extend to women of other faiths the rights in the economic sphere which Islam bestows. It is an unfortunate fact that, through ignorance, Mahomedan ladies are not always able to assert their full rights; but this defect will be remedied by means of education.

Throughout these pages certain well-defined and by no means rare qualifications have been suggested as giving the individual the right to a direct vote for the provincial state assembly, such as a low minimum income or land tax, and moderate literacy in the vernacular. Now it is essential that the tests for enfranchise-ment applied to men should be extended to the other sex. If this measure of justice is not made an integral part of the widened franchise system, we may admit without further discussion that comparatively little can be expected from voluntary reform of the social position of women. If the extraneous fact that in Great Britain women suffrage has come some eighty-five years after the first great Reform Act is to be regarded as setting the pace for India, the proposed franchise measure will largely fail, for they will be founded on bad statesmanship and fundamental injustice toward one half of society. The argument that Indian reform should be on a time scale more or less corresponding with Great Britain's constitutional developments "slowly broadening down from precedent to precedent" is singularly inept, for it fails to take into account India's responsiveness to the spirit of the age. She can profit from the experience of other countries by firmly treading the roads they have made after generations of painful effort.

I have shown that Indian women are by no means wanting in natural intelligence, and with the confidence that comes of long observation, I assert that the Indian woman who has property or education manages the one and can use the other certainly as well as any man of the same social position. It would be a signal advantage to the State to have both the intuition and the naturally conservative influence of women operating in political life. Socially unjust laws would then have much shorter shrift than at present. No scheme of political reform based on the co-operation of the people with the rulers can or will succeed, if it is vitiated by the radical defect of closing the door to women on the irrational ground of sex, and not accepting equal qualifications as conferring equal rights. It may be pointed out that in India any "danger" of a substantial majority of women voters will not exist, as it would in England if absolutely equal rights had been bestowed, instead of the age of qualification for women being fixed as high as thirty. For a long time to come universal suffrage in India is out of the question, and while property and educational qualifications provide the standards the number of women enjoying the franchise will certainly be much smaller than that of men. This relative disproportion would be considerably enhanced under the proposal to enfranchise men who have rendered military service, *ipso facto.*

We must not build up the fabric of the autonomous State on weak and one-sided foundations. I am confident that an assembly to the election of which Indian women had contributed would keep nearer to the facts and needs of life, to the real and actual in the country, than one selected by men alone. I have urged that the basis of the State should be broadened in order to give the people as a whole occasion for understanding and responding to the call of sacrifice for the commonwealth. Is it to be maintained that the women of India are less capable than the men of realising the need for sacrifice? Or are we to impose on them the acceptation of responsibility to society at large without participation in the political shaping of the State? The progressive modernisation which depends on co-operation and understanding between the rulers and the ruled will be impossible in India unless women are permitted to play their legitimate part in the great work of national regeneration on a basis of political equality.

CHAPTER XXVII

BRITISH AND INDIAN SOCIAL RELATIONS

Abhorrence of claims of superiority on grounds of race or colour
– lack of good social relations between the rulers and the ruled –
the tendency to exaggerate the issue – discrimination on the railways – the need for flexibility in social relations – how sports
promotes good relations between Englishmen and Indians – the
influence of social clubs – the disappearance of the *purdah* system
among the upper classes – the potential role of legislative
assemblies and the Royal Viceroy – the cultivation of real affinities
between the races.

Since the status of Indian women has been a considerable factor
in discussions of the question of social relations between Britons
and Indians, its consideration may fitly follow the previous
chapter. It is with some reluctance, however, that I take up the
subject, for I have always felt that the tendency in many quarters
has been to exaggerate its importance, and to overlook certain
obvious considerations. I yield to no one in abhorrence of claims
to superiority based on grounds of race or colour alone. I have
often heard distinguished officials maintain that one of the outstanding causes of political discontent in India is the lack of good
social relations between rulers and ruled. The evils of arrogant
pretension in the diversified social structure of India are great;
but I must confess that this aspect of the matter has been presented in exaggerated forms on both sides, and its influence for
good or evil has been greatly over-rated.

The fact is that the political desires and economic necessities
and ambitions of India derive their momentum from within; so
that even if the social relations between "Europeans" (as they
were classed before the war) and Indians had been ideally good,
these political and economic aspirations still would have the same
forces behind them calling for change. There is something very
fanciful in the idea that mere social reunion would suffice to
create a good understanding between officials and people, when
we remember that the number of Indians who could come into
friendly contact with higher officials on the basis of the equality
which intellectual culture and other standards of life bring would
be but a drop in the ocean of the Indian population. Lord
Morley's repeated observation when at the India Office that bad

manners, reprehensible in any part of the world, are a crime in India, is true so far as it applies to the conduct of officials in their business character and quality as administrators, in other words as public servants. But we must not go to the extreme of imagining, as some have done, that each Englishman and woman in India is an unofficial ambassador of that race to peoples of another civilisation, and that his or her manners, or want of them, constitute a burning question.

When complaint is made that certain institutions are closed to Indians on racial grounds, we must be careful not to lump together things having no real resemblance. We must distinguish between services of public utility and the action of private bodies or institutions. Nothing can be more objectionable than that the railways, now mainly State-owned, though often worked by companies, should differentiate to the extent that they do between accommodation for European and Indian intermediate and third-class passengers, or that there should be cases of gross incivility and even of ill treatment by European travellers of Indians who are seeking or have obtained accommodation in the higher classes for which they have purchased tickets. On the other hand, there is something at best childish, and at worst nauseating, in the longing shown by a few snobs to force their way into purely British clubs.

The true solution of the social problem is to leave Indians and Englishmen to form close friendships, as they have done in the past and will do in the future, when there is mutual esteem and appreciation, and to allow them to develop expressions of their sentiment according to the circumstances of the case. A Brahman, to whom the admission of beef to the cook-house would occasion intense horror, can only be expected to receive his English friends in afternoon calls, or over a chess-board, or at a bridge table. On the other hand, the Parsee naturally carries on his intercourse by an invitation to dinner or lunch. Amongst Indians themselves there are clearly marked groups accustomed to regular social intercourse, and there is nothing extraordinary or unnatural in English exiles from their own land often preferring, in brief hours of relaxation, to meet each other rather than Indians.[1]

---

[1] "We must take human nature as it is, and not harshly blame the instinct which makes Englishmen, who are day by day immersed to the eyes in Indian interests and affairs, hunger for one little spot where they can, for an hour or two, entirely shut out the obsession of the Orient." – Mr. William Archer's article "Manners in India," *Fortnightly Review*, July, 1914.

Where tastes are common, such as the love of sports, ranging from public and popular recreations like racing and cricket, to the select and expensive sports of polo and big game shooting, the natural interests of Englishmen and Indians have long brought them together on the healthy basis of equality and emulation of sporting skill. In December last some 150,000 spectators witnessed the progress of the Bombay quadrangular cricket tournament, extending over eight days, between British, Hindu, Mahomedan, and Parsee teams. Mr. E. W. Ballantine tells us that in all his travels in pursuit of cricket, during which he has seen tremendous crowds and extraordinary enthusiasm, he has never watched so impressive a sight. Lord Harris, a quarter of a century ago, when he encouraged the game so much as Governor of Bombay, "sowed seeds which have brought forth wonderful fruit," including the "narrowing of prejudices which existed between one community and another."[1] Lord Willingdon, as Mr. Ballantine points out, has followed the example of Lord Harris in encouraging cricket both by example and precept. He has started a sports club which bears his name, and there is good ground to share the hopes of the founders that it may become to Western India what Ranelagh and Hurlingham are to London, what Saint-Cloud and La Boulie are to Paris.

Even social clubs on an expressly non-racial basis, such as the Calcutta Club and the Orient Club in Bombay, have done good work within the few years of their existence. Such situations will have a great future when wealth and culture have made the average standard of comfort and rational recreation amongst Indians in society as high as amongst the Europeans there. Clubs will then arise to meet the felt want, and both races will be glad to belong to them. Something of this kind is taking place in Cairo. For many years there was social aloofness between the Egyptians and the Europeans. Then the former instituted the well-known Mohammed Ali Club. The cuisine and other amenities were so excellent that the most cultured members of the European colony were readily enrolled on its books and are among the frequenters. In the regenerated India of to-morrow, it is to be hoped that not only the present great institutions for Europeans and the present smaller clubs for Indians may co-exist, but that still finer clubs open to all generally eligible without distinction of race, will add to the amenities of life in the East.

As was hinted at the beginning of this chapter, an important

[1] Article in *Evening News*, 25th March, 1918.

phase of the social question in the quite recent past was that practically all Indian ladies, excepting among the Parsees and one or two reformed Hindu bodies, such as the Brahmo Samaj, held to the purdah system. To-day amongst the upper classes that system is fast disappearing, faster than many in England or even Englishmen in India realise . . .

The large legislative assemblies proposed in these pages will have the great incidental advantage of bringing the leading officials as a class into touch with representatives of India drawn from every section of society. Hitherto, not the least of the misfortunes of India's narrow political life has been that only a handful of men in each province have been associated with the administration by this channel. Thus the field of acquaintanceship has been narrowed out of all relation to the varied interests and condition of the people. For many men quite as acceptable, worthy and able as those on Government House lists, no way of access has existed. The large legislative assemblies of to-morrow will open to many worthy citizens, not only opportunities for usefulness, but also social vistas now generally limited to lawyers or rich men. Again, a Royal Viceroy, holding his court not only at Imperial Delhi, but during his tours of the country at Bombay or Calcutta, Baroda or Mysore and giving the entreĸe to merit irrespective of race or colour, will be a potent factor in bringing about social fusion and mutual understanding.

After all, however, the keynote to improved relations is the cultivation of real affinities. In no part of the world can we expect thorough understanding and intimacy between men of different race, unless they are drawn together by some common bond of interest such as service of the public weal, sport, literature, or art. Social union as a hot-house plant is doomed to failure; but I cherish the conviction that in the India of the near future men of both races will have occasion for strengthening their natural mutual goodwill by the means I have suggested.

CHAPTER XXIX

THE LIMITS OF BRITISH TRUSTEESHIP

The contention that the British people are the real rulers and owners of India – the Indian peoples' appeal for justice and self-determination – a broad-based Indian deputation to England – the wisdom of granting self-government to South Africa – the power to rule India centralized in a few hands – inadequate attention in the House of Commons to Indian problems – neglect of trusteeship – the aspirations and demands of well-informed Indians – only a small minority in favour of severing the British connection – the present framework of Indian rule and administration must be altered – his faith in British democracy.

There are still many English writers, Imperialists of high ability, who argue that the people of the United Kingdom will be untrue to their trust if they permit their responsibility for the good government of India to be substantially encroached upon by the people of that country. It is claimed that since the Government of India, through the Secretary of State, is responsible to Parliament, and the House of Commons and the Ministry are responsible to the British electorate, the latter are the real rulers and owners of India. This contention does correspond to the facts of the case during the last sixty years, namely, since the transfer of the administration to the Crown.

These six decades, however, have been years of preparation and political awakening, gradual at first, but cumulative and receiving a great impetus from the changed outlook the war has brought to mankind throughout the civilised world. The people of India, through their educated leaders, are addressing a serious and reasoned appeal to their fortunate British fellow-subjects, who, in addition to control of their own political affairs, in a very real sense own the soil of India. This appeal to British democracy is based both on principles of justice and rights of self-determination for nations, and on the practical necessity for meeting the actual conditions of the country. The various schools of thought as to the details of the advances required have been seeking to influence opinion in England. If the Indian people have the political sense of which there are growing signs, they will not be content with merely sectional presentations of the case to the British electorate, should the reforms proposed by the War Cabinet prove manifestly inadequate. We should then probably see a thoroughly representative deputation, not only of well-known Congress and Moslem League politicians, but of men of distinction from every class and community, men who have held the highest appointments open to Indians, landlords and nobles who have proved their loyalty to the Emperor and to their own country and race, and representatives also of the depressed classes. Such a deputation, made up of every school of progressive political thought, would address itself directly to the great British democracy.

An important consideration is that, under the Reform Act of the present year, England has become, in fact as much as in theory, a real democracy. The ultimate power is now in the hands of many millions of men and women whose free-born outlook never has been and will not be in sympathy with arbitrary power. When the eyes of the British public are opened to the fact that it is seriously argued on its behalf that a form of political ownership is at the foundation of England's rule in India, it will recoil from responsibility for the continuance of such political subordination in a vast country of which the great bulk of the British electorate, in the nature of the case, can have little or no knowledge. The great political principle for which the British Empire, and particularly the United Kingdom, have made sacrifices in life and treasure without parallel in history for four years is, in the words of the Prime Minister, "to make the world safe for democracy." This principle carries the corollary, as Mr. Lloyd George has freely recognised, that the civilised nations should have powers of self-determination and self-development. It is such powers that the voice of India, by an overwhelming majority, will demand after the war.

I rejoice in the thought that this claim to the right of self-determination has not to be pleaded and justified before a Kaiser and Imperial Chancellor in their closet, but before the great British public – all the greater now that something like universal suffrage exists. We appeal to the nation which, through Sir Henry Campbell-Bannerman and the most democratic House of Commons hitherto elected, carried out the wisest constitutional measure so far recorded in the history of the twentieth century – the conferment of self-government on the then lately conquered Dutch of South Africa and their British former enemies of the two Boer Republics. This sagacious act, rendered possible the federation of South Africa, and a real union of both races. It provided the Empire in the hour of supreme need with a Botha and a Smuts, and rendered impotent the long-continued and secret machinations of Germany in that part of the Empire. One trembles to think what might have happened in South Africa after the outbreak of war in 1914 but for the courageous and far-sighted statesmanship of Sir Henry Campbell-Bannerman's Cabinet and the Parliament of 1906.

India's want of confidence in the working of the theory that the people of England are her ultimate owners is not based on merely national pride or purely idealistic reasons. The responsibility such proprietorship connotes has been so vicariously exercised as to devolve normally upon a small circle of men, and more particularly upon a Secretary of State whose continuance in office has been dependent far less on the relative merit and advantage of his services to India than on the exigencies of party convenience, or on the verdict of the electors on subjects having no relation to India. His salary has not been placed on the British estimates, and the control of Parliament over Indian affairs has been more nominal than real.

This unreality has been evidenced by the inadequacy of the attention the House of Commons has paid, during two generations of recognised responsibility to the many misfortunes of its distant ward. How many debates, how many critical divisions, how many proposals to share the sacrifice in the battles against cholera and malaria, plague and poverty, do the pages of Hansard record? How often, with what voices, and with what power, has the House of Commons discussed the need for overcoming mass illiteracy in India? In what general elections of Parliament have votes been affected in any appreciable degree by the terrible poverty-famines or poverty-plagues of that distant country? It is true there have been animated debates, sometimes critical for the Cabinet of the day, on Indian affairs. But for the most part they have had their significance, as in the case of the repeated controversies on the cotton duties, in the voting strength of powerful home interests antagonistic to the just claims of India, such as having her tariffs shaped in her own interests rather than those of Lancashire manufacturers. Again, while some Indian grievances, for instance the "melancholy meanness" of exacting from her in whole or part the cost of using her troops in wars not directly affecting her security, have been challenged by votes of censure from the front Opposition bench, too often such debates have been marked by the desire to secure a party triumph more than by the prickings of conscience in respect of the trusteeship. In normal conditions, particularly since the burden of Parliamentary work accumulated and the time of private members' motions had been more and more curtailed, the only Indian debate of the year of any consequence has been that connected with the nominal submission of the Indian Budget, usually many months after its proposals have taken effect. In spite of frequent protests from the few members interested in India, the discussion has been relegated to the fag end of the session, often on the last effective day when members have been hurrying out of town. The smallness of attendance on these occasions has been notorious, and in the words of the present Secretary of State, shortly before he was called to the India Office, the tone of the debates "was unreal, unsubstantial, and ineffective."[1] Even this annual review has been abandoned during the war, the last debate of the kind taking place as long ago as 1913.

The fact is that since the transfer to the Crown in 1858 there has been a decided, and in some respects a progressive, deterioration of the influence exerted by the British Parliament over Indian administration. Before that time, when the Charter of the East India Company was to be renewed, select committees of investigation were set up and recorded evidence in which abuses were brought to light and remedies were demanded. On the basis of the reports made the successive Charter Acts ordained reforms and modified the powers of the Company in the direction of increased Parliamentary control. An outstanding example is the great Act of 1833, the Magna Charta of India, which to a great extent, unhappily, has remained a dead letter. Thus under the old reкgime a distinct and direct responsibility was exercised by Parliament.

The transfer to the Crown, while bringing great advantages to India, had the unfortunate effect of whittling away this responsibility, on the one hand by centralising control in the Secretary of State and his Council, without their salaries being placed on the Parliamentary supply estimates, and, on the other hand, by bestowing a vague and general responsibility on the electorate. As was inevitable, the system has worked out in practice to neglect by the British people of their trusteeship for a vast unknown conglomeration of races of a different civilisation thousands of miles distant. Such impartial writers as the late Sir William Hunter have estimated, on the basis of statistical and other material, that at least 60,000,000 Indians, a number equal to all the white races of the Empire, can afford but a single meal a day, and suffer the pangs of inadequate nourishment from birth to death. Has this mass of poverty ever been an outstanding problem at any British general election? Has it been so much as touched upon in the electoral manifestos of party leaders, or even in the address of Ministers from the India Office appealing to their constituents?

No doubt till such time as India obtains the full measure of self-governing responsibility now exercised by Canada, Australia, New Zealand, and South Africa, her fate must depend, to a

[1] Parliamentary Debates, House of Commons, 12th July, 1917.

certain extent, on the will of the British democracy. To his honour let it be said that the average well-informed man in India is not claiming that this goal can be reached in the near future. He knows that it can only come in strength and durability as the fruit of practice and experience – possibly painful experience – in intermediary stages of political advancement and self-determination. But this is no excuse for a policy of mere negation. He is quite definite in the demand that the present system under which India remains one of the poorest and most backward countries of the world, should be replaced. He is prepared to see the vast political experience of Britain still leading the destinies of India in foreign and military affairs, in the adjustment of Imperial taxation, in the development of India's foreign trade, in her relations with the other parts of the Empire, and in assuring all classes and castes a fair share of electoral power. On the other hand, in respect to internal provincial administration, to taxation for the spread of education and the provision of sanitation, to the removal of the economic and other causes which have brought about the impoverishment both of the soil and the people – in these matters he is convinced that the best judges would be the representatives of the people themselves, and those executive officers, British and Indian, whose position is now far too aloof to make them strong national influences, but who, in hearty co-operation with the elected assemblies, will lead India along the path toward a happier future. Further, he maintains that the only sure preventative of the transferred powers falling into the hands of a caste oligarchy or a minority of the rich and educated, is to frankly accept the diversity of Indian conditions by giving all classes direct representation. The assemblies for the creation of which he pleads must be so constituted that the nation as a whole, including the women, will exert its natural and legitimate influence.

In respect to the practical results of such devolution of authority from the British electorate to the representatives of all the communities of India, there is a tragic non-comprehension on the part of some conservative elements in England. They believe that such rights would be exercised in the direction of breaking away from the British connection. It is true that (largely owing to a system which, like a load on the chest, checks or prevents even small self-willed movement) there are foolish and mad individuals who may be styled anarchists, since they regard separation from the Empire as the legitimate aim and ambition of their country. For the British electorate and Parliament to

allow their generosity and sense of justice toward the vast peninsula to be consciously influenced and deflected to the smallest
extent by the existence of this small body of freaks would be at
once so inequitable and so wanting in the sense of proportion
as to be wholly inconsistent with British political traditions. It is
difficult to believe that some of those who most magnify the
importance of such passing and insignificant manifestations of a
perverted spirit of anarchy could challenge this view with any
strength of conviction. It is not surprising that the belief is entertained by India that they use this horrible fact simply as a handy
argument and weapon to beat back her legitimate aspirations
toward a worthy place within the Empire. By way of reassurance,
not of exculpation, it may be recalled that every great country,
except Great Britain herself and United Germany, has passed
through epochs in which anarchism has shown its teeth. This was
the case in France a quarter of a century or so ago, when President Carnot, perhaps the most estimable politician of the Third
Republic, was assassinated at Lyons. Italy too has had her bad
times, as well as Ireland and the United States. In unhealthy
political conditions, like those of Russia under the Tsardom, the
disease finds fertile soil and becomes endemic. But in a healthy
State, where the process of amelioration is continuous, the fever
is thrown off in the course of a few years.

To maintain that the system of the last sixty years must be
continued in the interests of law and order is to wholly misunderstand the spirit and aspirations of enlightened Indian opinion.
If such counsels are listened to and no substantial instalment of
reform is proposed to Parliament, the conclusion of the war
would be the signal for strenuous efforts to place the situation
prominently before the British electorate, in whose sense of
justice and fair play India will have staunch faith and confidence
until it has been proved to her that this faith has been misplaced.
Counter agitation on the part of conservative elements in
England, leading to contentious argument at the hustings, is to
be deprecated. Whatever the result, whichever side was vanquished, such agitation would leave bitter memories behind. The
illogical framework of Indian rule and administration cannot in
any case go on unaltered, having regard to the pledges of August
10, 1917. I am convinced that if a large measure of initiative is
not given to India by those in authority, the British democracy,
with its inherent sense of right and wrong, will see to this being
done.

Source: *India in Transition: A Study in Political Evolution*, Philip Lee Warner,

London, 1918. It was simultaneously published in Bombay by Bennett, Coleman and Co., The Times of India Office.

See its reviews in *The Times Literary Supplement,* 27 June 1918; the *Spectator,* 29 June 1918, pp. 670–1; Valentine Chirol, "India in Travail", *Edinburgh Review,* July 1918, pp. 147–66; William Johnson, "Review of the Aga Khan's *India in Transition*", *Asiatic Review,* October 1918, pp. 524–6; and *The Dial* (New York), vol. 67 (1919), p. 315. The book was quoted in its leading article by *The Times* on 24 August 1918. It was also noticed by *The Times Educational Supplement* of 27 June 1918.

In order to enable the reader to know why and under what circumstances the Aga Khan wrote the book and what was its scope I reproduce below his foreword and the complete table of contents.

On the page preceding the Foreword are two lines of poetry:

For, always roaming with a hungry heart,
Much have I seen and known.

"ULYSSES," TENNYSON.

The book is dedicated to his mother.

FOREWORD

Mr. Montagu's historic announcement last August that he was to proceed to India to discuss the extent and form of the "substantial steps" to be taken in the direction of self-governing institutions, and to receive with Lord Chelmsford the suggestions of representative bodies and others, confirmed me in the intention I had formed on finding I was debarred on medical grounds from Army service in the Allied cause to return to India last winter. I cherished the hope that I might be of some small service to my country in helping to shape some of the representations which might be made, and contributing to the success of so momentous a mission by a British statesman whose zeal and devotion in promoting the welfare of India had greatly impressed the Indian people during the time of his Under-Secretaryship at the India Office.

My plans and hopes were thwarted, however, by a painful and tedious malady requiring surgical treatment in Europe, and fully six months of rest and retirement in a prescribed climate. The eminent specialists consulted were peremptory in refusing my appeal to be permitted to carry out my plans. They were confident that within two or three weeks of my landing in Bombay I should be laid aside by severe illness, making it quite impossible for me to render the public service I had in view. Their assurances that acceptance of their advice and the regimen prescribed would most probably restore me to vigorous health are being confirmed as time goes on.

The bitterness of my disappointment was considerably mitigated when, acting on the suggestion of valued friends, I obtained the assent of the specialists to my spending two or three hours daily during my enforced retirement and rest in consecutive literary work, for the purpose of presenting a detailed exposition of my views on Indian reconstruction. I have been approached frequently in the past dozen years or so by publishing houses with requests to write a book on current topics. Though the idea was not without attraction, I did not consider that the time was ripe to bring it to fruition; and I continued to limit my public utterances to speeches in India and in England, and to occasional review and newspaper articles. I now felt it a duty, as well as a privilege, to give a detailed exposition of my thoughts on India, and my hopes and aspirations for the future, as a contribution to the many-sided problem Mr. Montagu has been investigating.

The reader will pardon, I trust, these personal details since they are required for an understanding of the conditions in which my views have been formulated and presented. They may be pleaded in mitigation of shortcomings in execution, of which I am only too conscious. In my retirement the verification of references has not been easy, nor have I had the opportunities of consultation on questions of fact or policy which might otherwise have been available. The revision of proofs, in the later stages, I have been compelled to leave to others, in order to obviate any greater delay than present difficulties of book production in England imposes.

My limitations, however, have not been without their compensations. Enforced exclusion from the arena of day by day discussion in India, however disappointing, may have contributed at least to the dispassionateness with which I have sought to temper the ardour of my Indian patriotism and my belief in the inherent possibilities of my countrymen under the more favourable political conditions I advocate. Though outside the current, I have been able to watch its course with the help of many kind correspondents and occasional visitors, and by careful study of the organs of opinion in India.

Moreover, writing and thinking almost within hearing of the thunder of battle in Europe, I have been in a better position to apply to the Indian problem the widened outlook derived from a close and frequent contact with political systems and affairs outside, as well as within, my own country. Further, thrown so fully on my own resources, I can at least claim that the work, whatever its demerits, is an original and strictly personal contribution to the Indian problem. Many of the opinions I express will not be new to leaders of political and social thought in many lands with whom for years past I have discussed the future of India. Such views can also be traced in my occasional writings, though they have undergone development in the last four fateful years. We none of us stand where we did before the events of July and August, 1914, brought us to the watershed of contemporary history. The war has enormously changed the political and social outlook throughout the world in the direction of strengthening those forces of democracy and national self-determination, of liberty and progress, for which the Allies have made so many sacrifices.

One further word of explanation is desirable. I have studiously avoided any attempt to penetrate the plans which may have been formulated by the Secretary of State and the Viceroy as a result of their consultations, and which have still to be disclosed at the time I write. I make no claim to any inspiration in the guise of "intelligent anticipation". The proposals of His Majesty's Government are to be issued for public discussion, and will be embodied in a Bill to be submitted to Parliament in due course. I cherish the hope that this contribution to the subject may be of some service in helping to mould the moderate yet earnestly progressive ideas, both in Great Britain and India, on which, when all is said, the satisfactory and continuous solution of the complex Indian problem depends.

AGA KHAN.

18 *May*, 1918.

CONTENTS

CHAPTER PAGE
FOREWORD vii
I. SOCIAL ORGANISATION 1
II. THE REASONS FOR REFORM 15
III. A FEDERAL BASIS 33
IV. PROVINCIAL REORGANISATION 43
V. THE PROTECTED STATES 54
VI. THE CENTRAL GOVERNMENT 62
VII. THE VICEROYALTY 69
VIII. LOCAL SELF-GOVERNMENT 82
IX. THE CIVIL SERVICE 89
X. THE POLICE 98
XI. THE JUDICIARY 104
XII. OVERSEAS SETTLEMENTS 113
XIII. INDIA'S CLAIM TO EAST AFRICA 123
XIV. FOREIGN POLICY 133
XV. GERMANY'S ASIATIC AMBITIONS 142
XVI. ISLAMIC AND TURANIAN MOVEMENTS 156
XVII. THE PATH TO WIDER CONFEDERATION 162
XVIII. ARMY AND NAVY 173
XIX. INDUSTRIES AND TARIFFS 186
XX. CREDIT AND COMMERCE 193
XXI. AGRICULTURE 201
XXII. EDUCATION FOR THE MASSES 215
XXIII. HIGHER EDUCATION 224
XXIV. PUBLIC HEALTH 233
XXV. THE DEPRESSED CLASSES 244
XXVI. THE STATUS OF WOMEN 253
XXVII. BRITISH AND INDIAN SOCIAL RELATIONS 264
XXVIII. EFFICIENCY AND STABILITY 270
XXIX. THE LIMITS OF BRITISH TRUSTEESHIP 276
XXX. INDIA'S SHARE IN THE WAR 286
XXXI. CO-ORDINATED PROGRESS 295
INDEX 303

611

46

TRIBUTE TO E. S. MONTAGU AND LORD SINHA

Speech at a Banquet Hosted in Honour of Lord Sinha

London: 7 March 1919

Tribute to Edwin Samuel Montagu – reform proposals should be finalized soon – India's desire to be a Dominion under the British Crown – Muslim sacrifices during the First World War – Wilsonian principles of peacetime reconstruction should be applied to Muslim countries – tribute to Lord Sinha and the Maharaja of Bikaner for taking up the Muslim case – cause of Hindu–Muslim friction – remedy – reasons for representation of Muslims on a communal basis.

Your Highness, my Lords and Gentlemen, it gives me great pleasure to be entrusted with the toast of "The Guests." I have no time to speak of them individually, and can only say that we are gratified that so many distinguished men, including representatives of the Dominions and members of both Houses of the Legislature, are with us to-night. It is especially gratifying that the ex-Viceroy to whom India owes so much, Lord Hardinge (cheers), is able to be with us on a flying visit from his important duties in Paris. I couple with the toast the name of the Secretary of State for India (cheers), and most cordially associate myself with the tributes paid to him here this evening. I have had the privilege of his acquaintance for many years, and therefore have long had reason to greatly admire his breadth of view and statesmanship. He has an absorbing and, indeed, a passionate affection for India. We have the fullest confidence that while he is Secretary of State, no effort will be wanting to secure a great advance by placing India on the high road of the destiny proclaimed for her in the announcement of 20th August 1917, which was in itself a

612

moral justification for British rule in India. It is to be hoped that the committee work connected with the reform proposals will soon be completed, so that the Secretary of State may be in the position to submit his Bill to the judgment of Parliament and of the people of India as well as of this country. There is need of promptitude, for India has already waited long, and this is assuredly a case in which a stitch in time saves nine. India's absorbing desire is to be a Dominion under the British Crown. Loyalty to our King-Emperor is the keynote of our aspirations. (Cheers.)

In those aspirations the Mahomedans of India fully participate. (Cheers.) No one can say that during the war they did not play the game in the most determined and self-sacrificing spirit. (Cheers.) So long as there was the slightest danger to the Empire, we Moslems shed our blood in the struggle which, for obvious reasons, demanded from us exceptional sacrifices. All we ask, now that the cause for which we, too, fought, has prevailed, is that the Wilsonian principles of the Peace reconstruction, in which we honestly believe, should be applied to Islamic countries also. (Cheers.) Where the Moslems have been long established, where they are a majority, or even a large minority, they should not be exposed to proscription in, or the monstrous idea of expatriation from, the countries where they have been settled for centuries. Now that at last the terrible nightmare of Tsardom, with its bear-like grip, has been removed, the Wilsonian principles should be applied to the liberated Mahomedan countries of Central Asia and the Caucasus, and to that ancient empire and home of culture, Persia. Moral ideas know no boundaries of race or faith, and we ask for justice for Islamic no less than for other communities. (Applause.)

Having been much in Paris of late, I have had opportunities of seeing for myself with what devotion and singleness of purpose the Maharajah of Bikaner and Lord Sinha, in association with Mr. Montagu, have put the Moslem case. I have been told by many friends that though neither of the Indian delegates are Moslems, they have fully realized that on these external questions, Indian interests are Mahomedan interests alone. (Cheers.) On one occasion I found them at midnight deep in preparation of a memorandum concerning the Islamic case.

As was indicated in a short debate in the House of Lords on Tuesday, much is made by the opponents of Indian reform of occasional manifestations of friction between the Moslems and their Indian fellow-countrymen. The remedy for such occurrences, as Lord Sinha so wisely indicated, is the spread of education and steadfast industrial development, for their root causes are not religion and race but ignorance and poverty. For generations, and in the ordinary course, Mahomedans and Hindus have lived together in amity both in British India and Native States. I will mention as a ready example appropriate to the occasion that our esteemed Chairman has ruled the State of Bikaner for thirty years, and that twenty have passed since he attained his majority. In that long time, throughout the 23,000 square miles of his territory, there has been only one occasion of a Hindu-Moslem disturbance in a district town, and that, too, not of a serious nature. Some eleven years ago there was a threatened disturbance in another town, but it was averted by the prompt measures taken by the Durbar. (Cheers.) With these small exceptions the two communities have lived for generations side by side on terms of the greatest amity and goodwill. Again, take the case of the Nizam. The great majority of his subjects are Hindus, but their devotion to him is as great as that of the Mahomedans who share his faith. The two communities are welded together in Hyderabad because he and his ancestors are shining examples of Islamic toleration. (Cheers.)

Why, then, it will be asked, do you wish to retain communal representation for the Mahomedans? Well, the best answer is that some of the most brilliant and far-sighted Hindu leaders have recognized this need. The ever-lamented Gokhale in his late years was an ardent believer in communal representation for Mahomedans. He felt that the attitude of confidence and trust toward the younger sister of India on the part of the eldest child, who naturally had enjoyed the best opportunities, so far from weakening the case for united Indian nationality, was one of the surest ways to promote both the happiness and unity of the whole Indian family.

My Lords and Gentlemen, I give you the toast of the guests, coupled with the name of Mr. Montagu. (Loud applause.)

Source: *The Insistent Claims of Indian Reforms: Speeches at a Banquet in London on 7 March 1919*, Philip Lee Warner, London, 1919, pp. 34–7.

A report of the speeches delivered at the dinner appeared in *The Times* of 8 March 1919.

"The relevance of other speeches, made by Major-General His Highness the Maharaja of Bikaner, G.C.S.I., G.C.I.E., G.C.V.O., K.C.B., A.D.C. to His Majesty, the Right Honourable Edwin S. Montagu, M.P., Secretary of State for India, and the Right Honourable Lord Sinha of Raipur, K.C., Parliamentary Under-Secretary of State for India, warrants their verbatim reproduction here. Their text is preceded by an account of the banquet and of the persons attending it.

In celebration of the appointment of the Right Hon. Baron Sinha of Raipur as Parliamentary Under-Secretary of State for India and his elevation to the peerage, a dinner was given in his honour at the Savoy Hotel, London, on 7 March 1919.

"Major-General His Highness the Maharajah of Bikaner presided, and had on his right hand the guest of the evening, and on his left hand the Secretary of State for India, the Right Hon. E. S. Montagu. The large and distinguished company included His Highness the Aga Khan, the Marquess of Sligo, the Right Hon. H. A. L. Fisher, M.P. (Minister of Education), the Right Hon. the Earl of Donoughmore, Lord Carmichael, the Right Hon. G. Barnes, M.P. (Member of the War Cabinet), the Right Hon. Lord Hardinge of Penshurst, H. H. the Maharajah of Mayurbhanj, Lord Leigh, the Maharaj Kumar of Bikaner, the Right Hon. Lord Islington, Lord Willingdon, Lord Elphinstone, Lord Lamington, the Earl of Cromer, the Right Hon. Lord Gainford, Earl Brassey, the Right Hon. Sir George E. Foster, the Right Hon. Herbert Samuel, the Hon. Sir Arthur Lawley, Lord H. Cavendish-Bentinck, M.P., Sir Walter R. Lawrence, Major Sir Philip Grey Egerton, Sir Thomas Berridge; Sir William Duke, Sir Charles Bayley, Sir Murray Hammick, Sir Marshal Reid, Mr. B. N. Basu, and Mr. W. D. Sheppard (members of the India Council); Colonel Sir James Dunlop Smith, Sir John Stanley, Sir J. D. Rees, M.P., the Right Hon. Sir Henry Craik, M.P., Surgeon-General Sir Havelock Charles, Mr. T. J. Bennett, M.P., Lieutenant-General Sir H. V. Cox, Colonel L. M. S. Amery, M.P. (Under-Secretary of State for the Colonies), Sir M. M. Bhownaggree, Colonel C. E. Yate, M.P., Mr. W. R. Gourlay, Sir Abbas Ali Baig, Mr. P. C. Lyon, Sir Robert Fulton, Mr. Charles Roberts (formerly Under-Secretary of State for India), Mr. William Archer, the Hon. S. K. Sinha, Mr. A. Yusuf Ali, Mr. S. R. Bomanji, Mr. M. H. Ispahani, Sir Treverdyn Wynne, Mr. A. Ezra, Mr. T. Lall, and many others, including the officers of the Maharajah of Bikaner's suite.

"After the toast of His Majesty the King-Emperor had been honoured,

"LORD CARMICHAEL said that in the absence through illness of Mr. Ameer Ali, his co-signator of the dinner circular, it fell to him to mention the large number of letters received expressing regret at inability to be present. The Prime Minister was kept away by his duties in Paris. Lord Curzon, detained by the pressure of public business, wrote that Lord Sinha "well deserves this compliment." The messages from Lord Sinha's colleagues at the Peace Conference in Paris were especially cordial. The Right Hon. Sir Robert Borden wrote that it would have given him the greatest possible pleasure to be present, and to express his profound appreciation of the great service which Lord Sinha has given to the Empire. The Right Hon. W. M. Hughes, and the Right Hon. H. J. Massey wrote similarly. The Right Hon. A. J. Balfour wrote that it was a great disappointment to him that he should perforce be absent on so interesting and important an occasion. Telegraphing later, Mr. Balfour asked to be allowed to join in the warm congratulations Lord Sinha would receive. The Right Hon. Sir Joseph Cook wrote that it would have given him the greatest pleasure to testify by his presence "to my feelings of personal esteem for Lord Sinha and my great gratification at his personal and official success." The Right Hon. Sir Joseph Ward telegraphed that if not detained in Paris he "would have been delighted to have assisted in doing honour to the distinguished representative of India who by his ability, loyalty, and devotion to duty has won distinction both for himself and for the great country he represents." General Smuts was kept away by influenza.

"Letters of regret were also received from the Right Honourables Bonar Law,

W. S. Churchill, Walter Long, the Marquess of Crewe, Sir Eric Geddes, A. Chamberlain, Viscount Sandhurst, Lord Parmoor, Viscount Haldane, Sir John Simon, Earl Crawford, Lord Ribblesdale, Lord Stamfordham, Lord Reay, and Viscount Bryce; also from Lord Chesterfield, the Earl of Portsmouth, Lord Colebrooke, Lord Glenconner, Lord Inchcape, Lord Ampthill, the Earl of Sandwich, Sir Herbert Roberts, Colonel Clive Wigram and many others.

"HIS HIGHNESS THE MAHARAJAH OF BIKANER, who was received with loud applause, said:

'Your Highness, My Lords and Gentlemen – I consider it a privilege to preside here in response to the invitation of the Committee, and to propose the toast of the Right Honourable Baron Sinha of Raipur. (Cheers.) I have the greatest pleasure in thus associating myself wholeheartedly with his other friends – and their name is legion – to offer our warmest congratulations upon the honour which His Imperial Majesty the King-Emperor has been graciously pleased to bestow upon Lord Sinha by his call to the Privy Council, his elevation to the peerage, and his appointment as Parliamentary Under-Secretary of State for India. (Cheers.)

'Another object of this function is to enable his fellow-countrymen to give expression to their grateful appreciation of the true statesmanship and the rare stroke of imagination which prompted the Secretary of State to suggest, and the Prime Minister to accept, the appointment. (Hear, hear.) India welcomes this step as clearly emphasizing the determination of His Majesty's Government to carry through, without unnecessary delay, a substantial measure of constitutional reform. We perceive in this appointment a striking reassertion of the purpose of the British Government to continue, and extend, in spirit and in letter, the fulfilment of the solemn pledges given in the Charter Act of 1833, and renewed in what all Indians treasure as their Magna Charta – Queen Victoria's gracious Proclamation of 1858, that race or creed are no disqualification for admission to offices under the British Crown. (Hear, hear.) Further, we rejoice to see in this selection yet another practical illustration of the welcome change in the angle of vision regarding Indian affairs, and of the better understanding and increased mutual confidence and respect between Englishmen and Indians, induced by a closer association and prolonged comradeship in arms in every theatre of the War. This longed-for consummation has been rendered further practicable by the complete victory of the forces of our King-Emperor and his Allies – to which, we are proud to feel, India has contributed her full share (cheers) – and the ultimate vindication of justice, right, and liberty, over might and brute force.

'My friendship with Lord Sinha, dating back many years, has been strongly cemented by our close contact as colleagues at the Paris Conference, and previously at the first Imperial War Cabinet and Conference. I can, therefore, speak with intimate knowledge of the guest of the evening. I do not propose to give a detailed catalogue of his many gifts and virtues, for to do so in his presence would put a strain upon one of the most conspicuous of his gifts – his unassuming, yet dignified, modesty. (Cheers.)

'Lord Sinha combines a profound patriotism for his mother country with the utmost loyalty to the British Crown, and a grateful appreciation of all that India's connection with Great Britain has meant for his native land. (Hear, hear.) His high sense of public duty, his political insight, and his strength of character, have been demonstrated in many ways – and not least by his never having attempted to court cheap popularity by playing to the gallery. (Cheers.)

616

He has always unhesitatingly spoken and acted according to the dictates of his conscience in support of what appeared to him to be the best for India, as also for the British Empire. Law, order, and good government have been as dear to him as the continued political advancement of his countrymen.

'These characteristics have distinguished Lord Sinha, alike in exerting, in his private capacity as an Indian gentleman, that personal influence for the common good which his honourable record and untarnished reputation have won for him; in presiding over a session of the Indian National Congress; or in occupying the chair of Macaulay, and Maine. From that farsighted Viceroy, Lord Minto, downwards, it was universally admitted that he maintained the highest traditions of the Law Membership. And the same qualities have been shown on the three consecutive occasions of his representation of British India at the counsels of the Empire. His sterling worth has won for him both East and West of the Suez Canal the respect of Englishmen and Indians alike. (Hear, hear.) Lord Sinha holds the wonderful record of being the first Indian appointed Standing Counsel, and afterwards Advocate-General, in Bengal; the first Indian to be a member of the Viceroy's Executive Council; the first Indian to be made King's Counsel; the first Indian statesman to be a Privy Councillor and to be a member of His Majesty's Government and, of course, the first Indian peer. (Cheers.) His country is justly proud of this great Indian who has led the way in so many spheres with such conspicuous merit and success.

'It is, therefore, not too much to say that if there was one Indian whose appointment as Under-Secretary was certain to evoke widespread approbation it was Lord Sinha. The cordial reception which, with the innate sense of justice and fair play characteristic of the British people, has been extended to Lord Sinha's appointment with virtual unanimity by the responsible press and informed public opinion of this country have been noted with lively gratification in India.

'But there have been a few – we are glad to feel, only a very few – exceptions which have been wounding to the self-respect of Indians, and which have shown how acute a form political and party differences and racial prejudices can take. In the short time at our disposal it is possible to deal only with a few of the insinuations and misrepresentations of those who, posing as experts on India, have been assiduously carrying on an anti-reform – I do not hesitate to say an anti-Indian – campaign.

'It is an open secret – and I hear that that popular Governor, Lord Willingdon (cheers), told the story in a sympathetic speech at the dinner recently given in his honour – that for some years the highest authorities in India had been urging upon His Majesty's Government the pressing necessity for a declaration of British policy in relation to Indian aspirations. I think I can add without impropriety that it subsequently fell to the lot of those of us who had the honour of representing India here two years ago further to press this consideration. This view was accepted by that high-minded statesman, Mr. Austen Chamberlain. His successor, within a few weeks of receiving the seals of office, made the most welcome and historic announcement of the 20th August, 1917 (cheers), with the full authority of His Majesty's Government and the concurrence of the Government of India. Two months later, in the Upper House, Lord Curzon showed the necessity for this action in the following eloquent terms:

You cannot unchain the forces which are now loosened and at work in every part of the world without having a repercussion which extends over every hemisphere and every ocean; and believe me, the events happening in Russia, in Ireland, in almost every country in Europe, the speeches being made about little nations and the spirit of nationality, have their echo in India itself. If the noble Viscount [Lord Midleton] had been at the India Office in the past summer he would have been the first to bring to us those serious representations continually coming from the Government of India and its head, and to have called upon us to take action and make some pronouncement. That is exactly what happened, and this statement of policy, not at all challenging, couched, I think, in most moderate and certainly in well thought-out terms, was the subject of repeated discussion at the Cabinet.

'The Declaration and the official visit to India of Mr. Montagu, at the express invitation of the Viceroy, were productive of immense good (cheers) – a view which is widely shared by both the Princes and people of India.

'We knew some of our old Anglo-Indian friends too well to expect them to be in real sympathy with such a Declaration. And no reasonable person will for a moment cavil at honest differences of opinion. But what do we find? On the 30th of October, 1917 – several days before Mr. Montagu had reached India on the mission with which His Majesty's Government had specially entrusted him – the Indo-British Association held its inaugural meeting in London. The minutes of its proceedings were published under the surprising title of "The Interests of India." (Laughter.) Perhaps it was chosen because one of the professed objects of the Association is, we are told, "to promote and foster the unity and advancement of the Indian peoples." (Laughter.) The methods, arguments, and manifold activities of the Association have, however, singularly disguised this avowed aim; and all that we can say is – save us from such friends. (Cheers.)

'The Association does not expressly oppose the Declaration. But its real hostility to the policy of His Majesty's Government is revealed in almost every phase of its activity. From the first it has been developing a ceaseless pamphlet-eering and press propaganda. The booklets and leaflets it issues so freely are intended to alarm the ordinary man as to the condition of India, to belittle in every possible way the educated classes of that country – and indeed everyone who has the temerity to disagree with its views – and to appeal to the personal and class interests at one time of the working man, at another – and more frequently – of business firms participating in Indian trade. Such firms were asked by circular, intended to be private, but which found a publicity unwelcome to the authors, for subscriptions to the Association of any sums from £1,000 downwards. The suggestion was made in this begging letter that such subventions should be regarded as "an insurance premium for business interests in India." Now, we believe in an industrial as well as a political future for our country, but we have yet to learn that the Indian Empire exists for exploitation by any particular commercial interests. As my right honourable friend, Mr. Chamberlain, publicly said when Secretary of State, India refuses to be regarded any longer in the economic sphere as a mere hewer of wood and drawer of water. But industrial development means increased purchasing power, and British trade stands to gain and not to lose thereby.

'My Lords and Gentlemen, unless I have been greatly misinformed, I think that the word "reaction" has not been entirely unknown in connection with your domestic policy. (Laughter.) And one section of your extremists in this country – for India has no monopoly of this class of people (laughter) – is sounding shrill notes of alarm about India. Without going back to earlier occasions, we recollect that similar cries were raised some twelve years ago,

when the Morley-Minto Reforms were under consideration; but with this difference, that as there is now an Indo-British Association, the anti-reform agitation
is more noisy and persistent. Uneasily conscious that they are fighting a bad
case, the Association – and in my remarks to-night I include generally the
writers and speakers who have been co-operating in the campaign – freely
resort to vituperation and personal abuse. Indians – including the dangerous
and scheming Bengali peer on my right (laughter) – have been indiscriminately
branded as agitators, and India represented as seething with sedition and crime.

'The policies of four consecutive Secretaries of State – Lord Morley, Lord
Crewe, Mr. Austen Chamberlain, and Mr. Montagu – and of three consecutive
Viceroys – Lords Minto, Hardinge, and Chelmsford (cheers) – have been
criticised in the most unjust terms. In fact, the "non-contents" would have you
believe that they are right and that the Prime Minister, His Majesty's Government, the Secretary of State, the Viceroy, and the Government of India are all
wrong. (Laughter.) We are even asked to believe that Mr. Montagu and Lord
Chelmsford are out to weaken British authority in India, and that they are
courting a grave political disaster. The burden of their jeremiad comes to this:
Carry the reforms through, aim at responsible government in India, and you
strike a blow at the rule of the King-Emperor in India. But they have deliberately
suppressed the fact that the Indian leaders fully recognize and have repeatedly
stated that their ideal of self-government can only be realized by India
remaining an integral part of the British Empire. This recognition is prompted,
not only by that deep and universal loyalty of the Indian people to their beloved
Sovereign which their religion and traditions enjoin, but also by what has been
termed "reasoned attachment."

'The mendacity and unfairness of such a campaign is nowhere more conspicuous – and that is saying a great deal – than in a pamphlet of the Association,
under the title of "Danger in India: Sedition and Murder," an annotated
epitome of the findings of the Rowlatt Committee. You can imagine how eagerly
anti-reform capital is made therein of these findings. Lamentable and serious
as are the outrages dealt with in the Report, they relate to the nefarious activities
of an infinitely small number out of a loyal Indian population of 315 millions,
constituting one-fifth of the inhabitants of the globe. (Cheers.) The "Times of
India," an English-owned and edited journal, which merits as fully to-day, as
when uttered, Lord Curzon's description as the greatest newspaper in Asia – in
an article headed "The danger in England" – has characterized the comments
of the pamphlet as "conspicuous for their deliberate admixture of lies and bad
logic." (Cheers.) After giving chapter and verse in support of this statement,
the "Times of India" concludes:

We confess to a feeling of shame when we find Englishmen banding together,
as they are doing in London, to oppose the Reform scheme by every method,
fair or foul, that they can think of. It is the final stage surely on the slippery
path of dishonest politics when the Indo-British Association joins hands with
the Extremists not only in opposing the Reform scheme, but in an attack
on the Moderate Party.

'It has even been stated that Lord Sinha's peerage and appointment will be
resented by the Indian Army. Now, I claim some acquaintance with that Army.
I have, in participation with it, had the honour of fighting under the British
flag in Asia, Africa, and Europe – (loud applause) – my first campaign dating
back nineteen years. My own subjects freely enlist in the Indian Army. I have

no hesitation in contradicting this absurd allegation, and I only wish our critics had been present in Paris the other day when, on our visiting together a club for Indian troops, three very lusty cheers were given in honour of Lord Sinha. (Hear, hear.)

'It cannot too often be emphasized that India, especially in the last decade or so, has been progressing at such a rapid rate that the people who left the country even five years ago are not entitled to speak as experts. And it is all very well to refer to isolated incidents and opinions of individuals – usually anonymous – claiming to represent this or the other class in India. What India asks is that her affairs should be judged as a whole and by the public declarations of her responsible leaders.

'We also take our stand upon the far-sighted declarations and policies of a succession of English statesmen who have been associated with the Indian administration. The Indians are nothing if they are not loyal to their friends, and gratefully responsive to fairness, sympathy, and understanding. And let me say frankly that Indians, Princes and people, indignantly resent the abuse to which Lord Hardinge, Mr. Montagu, and Lord Chelmsford have been subjected. (Loud cheers.) We in India often wonder whether it is realized fully in this country how inestimable was the value of Lord Hardinge's services during his Viceroyalty. (Applause.) At the luncheon given to the Indian representatives last year, Lord Sinha rightly interpreted the general feeling in India when he assured Mr. Montagu of India's trust in him and of the warmest gratitude and approbation of her people for his courage, devotion, and statesmanship. (Cheers.) May I take this opportunity of assuring Mr. Montagu of the high regard and friendship of the Princes of India and of the warmth of their feelings towards him? When the heat and strife of political controversy have passed, the names of Mr. Montagu and Lord Chelmsford will go down to posterity as of two great Englishmen who helped in the upbuilding of a stronger imperial fabric in the post-war reconstruction. (Applause.)

'Finally, I must deal with an issue on which I claim a first-hand knowledge, at least not inferior to that of the Indo-British Association or even of vehement leader-writers in organs echoing its views. (Laughter and cheers.) The impression has been very freely conveyed that the Princes of India are hostile not only to Lord Sinha's appointment, but also to the reforms under contemplation. As one who has the honour to represent in England, for the second time, the Princes of India, I feel it my bounded duty to give to this gross misrepresentation the most authoritative and emphatic denial.

'May I preface what I have to say with a word of explanation? As is well known, the Indian Princes belong to no political parties, whether here or in India. Their territories, representing an area of about one-third of the vast Indian Empire, are outside the limits of British India proper, and British jurisdiction is inapplicable therein. The interests of the Princes and their subjects – who constitute more than one-fifth of the entire Indian population – are thus already safe-guarded in many ways by treaties of friendship and alliance concluded, almost invariably at least a century ago, and sometimes longer, between the Rulers and the East India Company. When the administration of British India was transferred to the Crown more than sixty years ago, these treaties were accepted as permanently binding both by Queen Victoria and the British Parliament. Such assurances have been graciously reiterated by each successive British Sovereign, in regard to the pledges and rights secured by the Princes through such treaties.

'It follows that in matters relating to administrative reform in British India, the Ruling Princes are, in the direct sense, disinterested parties, actuated by no selfish considerations or personal motives, and that they have no axe to grind. I hope that their loyal and deep devotion to the King-Emperor and their attachment to the Empire need no words from me. (Cheers.) Their only concern is to see such measures adopted as will further popularize, strengthen, and preserve the ties that bind England and India together. They have amply demonstrated time and again that in any matter endangering the Empire they can always be relied upon unhesitatingly to fight for the British Throne, and to range themselves in a solid phalanx on the side of constituted authority. (Hear, hear.) Nothing is more true than what has been repeatedly stated by the high officers of the Crown and the Princes themselves that there is a very great and real identity of interests between the British Government and the Princes.

'Is it conceivable, therefore, that the Princes would be in sympathy with, much less advocate, any measure of a revolutionary nature, or prejudicial to the stability of the King-Emperor's rule in India?

'Nearly two years ago, speaking publicly in London for the Princes, I stated that the Rulers of the Indian States, far from being alarmed at or resenting any political advance in British India, would rejoice at such progress. Nevertheless, persistent allegations to the contrary have continued to be made by Lord Sydenham and others. It has even been stated in a recent book, described in Mr. Garvin's paper, by one speaking with authoritative knowledge of India, as "a harmful and spiteful contribution to the study of Indian reform," that some of us – and the reference to myself is obvious – do not represent the views of our brother Princes; whilst in another page it is definitely asserted that the Maharajah of Patiala and myself were merely re-echoing the "gentle words" of Lord Sinha! (Laughter.)

'I propose, therefore, to show categorically and conclusively the clear and unmistakable views held by the Princes of India generally in this connection. This is what the late Nizam of Hyderabad, the most senior of the Ruling Princes of India, wrote officially in 1909 to Lord Minto regarding the Morley-Minto Reforms and Lord Sinha's appointment as the first Indian Member of Council:

> ... Your Excellency will ... quite understand how gratified I was to learn of the wise, generous, and liberal policy pursued by Your Excellency and the Secretary of State for India in giving effect to the principles announced in the Queen's Proclamation of 1858 ... by appointing an Indian as a member of your Executive Council and two Indians as members of the Council of the Secretary of State. This liberal policy, as also the enlargement of the Legislative Councils, will, I earnestly trust, serve to allay the present unrest and to remove altogether the seditious movement which is happily confined to a very small minority.

'Without any disrespect, it can be said that His late Highness belonged to the old school, so that his observations are all the more significant.

'The following is to be found in the Princes' speech in reply to the Viceroy's address at the Conference of Ruling Princes, held in Delhi in November 1917, which I was charged by a large and representative gathering of Princes to read:

> In your speech Your Excellency has referred to the recent pronouncement made by the Secretary of State. The loyal attachment of the Ruling Princes to the King-Emperor is proverbial, and we consequently rejoice at the further

accession of strength that this pronouncement and the impending political changes will bring to His Imperial Majesty's Empire by the enhanced loyalty, happiness, and contentment of His Indian subjects. As Indians again we rejoice at the aspirations of our fellow-countrymen in British India being thus further met by this sagacious act of British statesmanship. Might we ask your Excellency kindly to convey to Mr. Montagu on his arrival here assurances of our warm welcome and our good wishes for the success of his mission?

'I might explain that the Princes' speech does not represent the views of any individual Ruler, but that the draft is adopted only after the most careful scrutiny and previous discussion at a general meeting of the Princes.

'In a note by Sir John Hewett, criticizing the Indian Reform proposals, which was issued by the Indo-British Association, he said:

It is easier to ascertain who will be opposed to the scheme than who will support it,

'and included the Ruling Princes amongst the various "interests" who, he added:

it is certain . . . will be opposed to it,

'and wrote:

If the Maharajah of Patiala correctly interprets the feeling of the Ruling Princes, they will assuredly not be found to be enthusiastic supporters of the Scheme.

'This imputation brought forth an immediate and clear public denial from His Highness.

'Again, at the Conference held only in January last, the Maharajah Scindia of Gwalior, one of the most important Princes of India, in reading the reply of the Princes to the Viceroy's address, said:

It inspires us with the brightest hopes for the good of humanity and the peace of the world to find the British Throne, to which we are bound by very close ties, more secure than ever before. . . . This security, which is broad-based upon the affection and good will of the people is, we firmly believe, going shortly to find its counterpart in the adoption of liberal measures calculated to improve the machinery of the governance of India. These measures, which are irrevocably promised, will bring in their train enhanced loyalty and contentment in India, and the ampler they can be made, with a due regard for the conditions that are, and the quicker they can be enforced, the greater will be their certain result. . . . Both the amplitude and the expedition are assured by the combination which we all regard to be of happy augury, viz., the continuation of Your Excellency's Viceroyalty and the re-appointment to the Secretaryship of State for India of the Right Hon. E. S. Montagu. The recent elevation of our distinguished countryman, Sir Satyendra Sinha, to the peerage, and his appointment to an office in the British Government, is an example of true insight, great political imagination, and what is even more important, of genuine honesty of purpose, and we refuse to credit the libel, from wherever it emanates, that in this measure of simple justice to a people there is even the slightest taint of party or other questionable tactics.

'Further comment is surely unnecessary, but, if the Indo-British Association is still unconvinced, I shall be happy to publish several more speeches in the same strain made by Princes representing the various Provinces of India in the last few years. (Laughter and cheers.)

'My Lords and Gentlemen, we are now face to face with one of the most critical periods in the political regeneration of India under the aegis of the British Crown. The decisions regarding Indian constitutional reform ultimately reached in this country must irrevocably affect, for good or ill, India's future political progress. (Cheers.) Thus a very grave responsibility lies on His Majesty's Government, and the British Parliament and people. It rests with them, by seizing the golden opportunity now offered of handling the Indian problem in a sympathetic and liberal spirit, with imagination, breadth of view and boldness, to bring about the greater happiness and the enhanced loyalty and contentment of the people of India. Thereby they will be doing a great service, not only to India, but also to the Empire as a whole, and will be acting in accord with the best traditions of Great Britain, the nursing mother of representative institutions and free nations. She has taught us to appreciate fully the rights and liberties of citizenship, which, now more than at any previous time, have become the natural aim and desire of every civilized people all the world over. Not only will India be placed well on the road to the goal of responsible government; as an integral part of the Empire she will be enabled to bear a still greater share in Imperial burdens and responsibilities. A great deal of what has come to be known as "legitimate unrest" will further subside, and the anxiety and uncertainty in men's minds will be replaced by an ever increasing confidence in the fulfilment of Britain's glorious mission in India. Instead of being discredited and disheartened, the ranks of sobriety, moderation, and restraint will receive constant accessions of strength. A loyal, developing, and contented India will be an asset of immense value to the Empire. (Cheers.)

'On the other hand, should reactionary tendencies prevail in wrecking or whittling down the reforms, or leading to inadequate or half-hearted measures, inconsistent with the spirit and letter of the Declaration, a situation of extreme gravity will be created. Speaking under a strong sense of duty to the King-Emperor and the vast Empire under his sway, I wish to sound this solemn note of warning. Should the counsels of the opponents of genuine reform be followed, feelings of bitter disappointment and grievous wrong will be dominant throughout the length and breadth of India. (Loud cheers.) The full force of that dissatisfaction no man can gauge; but it must be obvious that in comparison with it the unrest and discontent of recent years would seem small. Should such a situation ensue, it is a matter for earnest consideration, whether the Indian people would be held solely responsible at the bar of history for results which would be as deplorable as they would be unfair both for Great Britain and for India. Let me assure you as an Indian, that India's Princes and people ardently desire progress without disorder, reform without revolution. (Cheers.)

'We are persuaded to expect better things than that the British Government and Parliament should accept the guidance of reactionaries whose activities and constant libels on the Indian peoples are responsible in no small degree for the unrest, and which constitute a barrier to better feelings and closer understanding between Indians and Englishmen, and have so baneful an influence upon impressionable youths. Let us not forget Edmund Burke's striking axiom that "a great empire and little minds go ill together." As Lord Carmichael, another popular Governor, pointed out in the House of Lords last August, we cannot stand still; we must either go back or go forward. To go back, he said, is a policy the people of the Empire will not tolerate. Liberality, sympathy, and bold statesmanship have invariably answered well and advanced the greatness of the Empire in the past – notably in the case of the South African Union – and they will certainly not be misplaced in the India of to-day. (Cheers.) Some two and a half years before the outbreak of war, His gracious Majesty said in his ever-memorable speech at Calcutta:

> Six years ago I sent from England to India a message of sympathy. To-day, in India, I give to India the watchword of hope. On every side I trace the signs and stirrings of new life.

'India has amply proved her right to share in the fairer and better world which we have all been promised on every hand, at the victorious termination of the mighty struggle. If the British Government will but seize occasion by the hand to shape the promised reforms on bold and generous lines at the earliest possible opportunity, they will confirm the solidarity of the widely varied dominions of His Imperial Majesty George V by strengthening the most enduring ties between England and India – those of mutual trust and helpfulness. (Loud applause.)

'My Lords and Gentlemen, I give you the toast of Lord Sinha."

"THE RIGHT HONOURABLE LORD SINHA, who was received with great enthusiasm, said:

'Your Highnesses, my Lords and Gentlemen – I can hardly express my sense of gratefulness to your Highness for the very kind, much too kind, and cordial terms in which you have proposed the toast of my health, and to you, my Lords and Gentlemen, for your very generous response. I should be more than human, less than human if I may say so, if I failed to be touched to the innermost recesses of my heart by this warm expression of your goodwill towards me, and I say without exaggeration that it will leave an abiding impression on my mind. But I am sure you will not think me vain enough to take this generous appreciation on your part of the position to which I have been called by the King-Emperor as in any sense personal to myself. My appointment as Under-Secretary of State for India is a striking illustration of the principle which Great Britain has adopted in the government of our commonwealth as applied to India. We, the loyal Indian subjects of His Majesty, have been holding fast for now more than sixty years to the gracious proclamation of Queen Victoria, emphasizing the abolition of all distinctions of race and religion in the administration of India as the great Charter of our rights; but slowly, steadily, almost imperceptibly, the march of events has taken us far beyond the position which that great proclamation gave us. India has been given a recognized and honoured place in the central councils of the Empire in war and peace, her Princes and her people have been treated as the equal custodians of our joint heritage, and Indian aspirations are measured to-day not in terms of our country, great as she is, but in terms of a greater fatherland of which India forms an integral part. (Cheers.) Indian representatives have participated on equal terms with the rest of the Empire in the anxious deliberations of war and peace; and though I frankly confess (not in any spirit of assumed humility, but in all seriousness) that I am all too unworthy of the great honour done to me, England has shown to the world that in her Imperial family she recognizes the claims of all its members and disregards the prejudices which have prevailed for centuries.

'I have no doubt that you are here to-night, not so much to do honour to me as to put the seal of your approbation to this policy, to let all whom it may concern know that England is not going to retrace her steps, because the danger with which she was threatened is over, but that she holds fast to that great principle of freedom and equality in vindication of which she staked her very existence. (Loud cheers.) It is that aspect of my appointment which has given such universal gratification to my countrymen. I have had the honour of receiving congratulatory telegrams which have come pouring in from all parts of India, and indeed from all parts of the world wherever there are Indians, from our great ruling Princes, from heads of ancient religious foundations, from our territorial aristocracy, from the leaders of Indian thought of all shades of opinion, and resolutions of approval and gratitude have been passed by different provincial councils, municipal corporations, district boards, public associations, and at public meetings in towns and villages. What can be the meaning and the significance of this universal acclamation from India? It is not because of me, for I only occupy the position of an illustration of a great principle; it is because that great principle to which I have referred has been so strikingly upheld and vindicated, and more especially because such vindication has largely dispelled, as I firmly believe, the doubts and misgivings which were everywhere arising in India owing to indiscriminate and ill-informed attacks against the educated classes of India, not merely by irresponsible critics in the Press, but even by some who have held high and responsible office in India.

'And, sir, I should like to take this opportunity to enter a solemn protest, not so much against scornful sneers or offensive epithets, for these may be left to be their own answer, but against the idea that appears still to prevail in certain quarters that the educated classes of India are unfriendly to British rule. If by British rule is meant autocracy and domination in the name and under the garb of efficiency, we are opposed to it. (Loud applause.) We should not be worthy of our long connection with Great Britain and of our education if we were not. It is this critical attitude of mind which has in the past brought down upon our devoted heads invectives of reactionary politicians and officials. And I cannot do better than quote one sentence from an article published as long ago as 1895 by the late Sir Richard Garth, K.C., a Tory Member of Parliament and a former Chief Justice of Calcutta, nobly defending the classes whom he knew so well against similar attacks which were then being made:

What have they done to deserve this choice invective? I will tell you what they have done. They have dared to think for themselves, and not only for themselves, but for the millions of poor ignorant people who compose our Indian Empire. They have been content to sacrifice their own interests and to brave the Government in order to lend a helping hand to these poor people.

'I do not deny that there have been occasional aberrations on the part of a very small number, but I venture to think that, when not due to enemy intrigues, these have been almost solely due to the doubts and misgivings I have already referred to – often unreasonable, often unfounded, but still there. I can only express a hope that in the future no act or speech of responsible journalists and statesmen will foment or add to these suspicions. (Cheers.)

'Sir, I venture to assert that the educated classes, without exception, ardently desire to remain within the fold of the British Empire with the status of equal British citizens. They desire equality within the Empire and not severance therefrom. (Cheers.) How otherwise is it possible to understand the thrill of pleasure which was felt by all India when Lord Morley referred to me as "one of the King's equal subjects"? How otherwise can we explain the wave of enthusiasm that has passed over India with regard to my recent preferment? This is how one of the best organs of Indian public opinion – "The Leader" of Allahabad – expressed it: "An Indian, and a member of His Majesty's Government! We confess that the historic event powerfully stirs our imagination and fills us with a new gratitude towards England. Truly is that silver-girt isle the home of liberty and justice! Long may she live and prosper." (Loud applause.)

'Sir, I must also take this opportunity to say what a source of peculiar pride and pleasure it is to me that hosts of my Anglo-Indian and British friends, officials as well as non-officials, have sent me their congratulations in terms no less appreciative so far as I am personally concerned, and what is more precious to me – recognizing equally with my own countrymen the political value of the unprecedented step that has been so boldly taken by those who are responsible for the future destiny of this far-flung Empire. To all and each of these friends of mine, I have tried to reply either by cable or by letter, but I take this opportunity of thanking them again, singly and collectively.

'The Press, too, both in this country and in India have accorded almost without exception their sanction and approval to my appointment and elevation, and I should like to express grateful thanks, both for myself and my country, for their generous attitude. I hope I may be pardoned for referring to another personal aspect of the matter. I know that there are many countrymen of mine far more deserving than myself of the honours which have been bestowed upon me. ("No, no.") I can honestly say, I wish that these honours had gone to one of them. But uppermost in my mind to-day, and indeed ever since the date of my appointment, has been the thought that there was one man who would and could have done far the greatest service to India if my position to-day were his – Gopal Krishna Gokhale (loud applause) – whom India shall ever mourn as one of her most patriotic sons and whose untimely death was one of the greatest of our misfortunes. Nor can I help giving expression to a poignant sense of regret that that true friend of Indian aspirations, than whom no man worked more hard or more unselfishly for our advancement – Sir William Wedderburn (cheers) – should not have lived to see what I am sure he would have hailed as a token of the new spirit which to-day animates Great Britain in her relations with India. A high British official and friend of mine has written to me that India has taken my appointment as "clearly showing that His Majesty's Government mean business when they declare that it is their intention to raise India to the position of an equal partner in the Empire." (Cheers.)

'I have no doubt they mean business, and I am confident that a liberal and a generous scheme of reforms will be passed by the Parliament of this country – and that the pre-occupations of the coming peace and the necessity for full consideration of the Reports of the different Committees will not cause any great delay. I am confident that a reform scheme will be in operation within the next twelve months. (Cheers.)

'There is at present, at any rate, one well considered scheme before the public – the Montagu-Chelmsford scheme. I agree with so much of what is said in a leading article of yesterday's "Times" that I make no apology for quoting one sentence from it:

> The great need of the Montagu-Chelmsford scheme at this juncture is neither laudation nor abuse, of both of which it has had far too much, but constructive criticism of which there has been far too little.

'I am not going, therefore, to discuss the merits or the demerits of that scheme. But may I state shortly what I understand to be the position?

'There is complete unanimity as to the wisdom and necessity of the policy declared by His Majesty's Government on the 20th August 1917. The only proposal yet before the public as a well-considered attempt to give effect to that policy is the Montagu-Chelmsford scheme. Large parts of that scheme are accepted by all shades of opinion, viz.: (1) A close connection between the Indian States and British India; (2) the necessity of as complete decentralization as possible as between (a) the Secretary of State in Council, (b) the Government of India, and (c) the provincial Governments; (3) the necessity of complete freedom in matters of local self-government; (4) a much larger infusion of the Indian element in the superior services, civil and military; (5) full industrial development; (6) a broadening of the franchise for all Legislative Councils, so as to make them more truly representative; and (7) a transfer of so much control as is consistent with the interests of law and order broadly speaking from the bureaucracy to the representatives of the people. Controversy centres principally round the extent of such control and the method of such transfer. When there is so much agreement I trust it is not too much to hope that means may be found to arrive at some solution satisfactory to all parties concerned in the matters upon which there is a difference of opinion. (Cheers.)

'I hope, Your Highnesses, my Lords and Gentlemen, I may not be charged with presumption if I venture to utter a few words with a view to the adjustment of these differences. These words are not my own, but those of the Rev. W. E. S. Holland, a well-known and universally respected missionary educationist, who has lived many years in India. They were published in the Indian number of the "Overseas Journal":

> Yet the alternative is our own continued domination: not self-determination in India, but a foreign rule: beneficent, no doubt, as heretofore: but that is the very claim the Germans advance as their right to dominate the world. Or is our championship of the right of nations to free self-determination only political camouflage for war propaganda against Germany? No, as Sir Henry Campbell-Bannerman once so well said: "Good government is no substitute for self-government." If we have to choose between the loaves and fishes of fat and soft security under domination, and all the ennobling pains and risks that make us men, we will choose the arduous path to freedom every time. And because we know it is the highest good, we must choose that for others as well as for ourselves, so far as they are in our hands. Of course it means taking risks. But that way men are made. What makes us pause is this: that the risks have to be run by India, not by us. Political experience cannot be bought second-hand. Nor will India any longer be content with the offer of security and comfort in place of freedom. It is too late to go back upon the world's pronouncement in favour of popular government; and the thought-nerves of the world, that have so decided, now run through

India from end to end. This is the exhilarating task that now confronts British statesmanship: the training for freedom of one-fifth of the entire world's population, of peoples besides whose hoary civilization, millenniums old, we seem to be but a mushroom growth of yesterday. And we shall not shirk it. (Cheers.)

'Thus speaks a free-born Englishman and, may I add with all respect, a faithful follower of Christ's teaching. In the editorial notes of the same journal we read as follows:

Our task ... must be to render every assistance in our power towards the development of an autonomous India within the Empire, while that of the educated Indian must be to exercise wise patience and restraint, and realizing that the pace must be set for the average rather than the exceptional man, he must work for the unifying and educating of his fellow-citizens.

'These are wise words which both Englishmen and Indians may well keep in mind. We have trusted England in the past. I appeal to my countrymen not to lose this trust in the future. Though probably I should not say so, England has given conspicuous proof, if proofs were needed, that she deserves all our trust (applause) in the responsible duties that His Majesty has been graciously pleased to entrust to me.

'Your Highness, this is perhaps not the occasion when I should give expression to my personal obligations to you for all the kindness and consideration I have received from you for many years past. But I feel I cannot let this opportunity pass without thanking you publicly for the wise advice and ungrudging co-operation which I have received from you during the time it has been my privilege to be associated with your Highness in our high Imperial duties. And India will thank you for having exploded so many myths which are used by the opponents of Indian aspirations. I trust it will be no longer possible to suggest with any truth that constitutional reforms are not favoured by the Indian princes and the Indian Army, or that they look with disfavour on the appointment of Indians to high office under the Crown.

'Your Highness, my Lords and Gentlemen, I once again express my grateful thanks to you for the great honour you have done me. (Loud cheers.)'

"THE SECRETARY OF STATE FOR INDIA, who received a great ovation, said:
'After this substantial feast, gastronomic and intellectual, I am reluctant to detain you many minutes. But I do want to take this opportunity for a little plain speaking. (A Voice: "That's what we want.") The politician who regards it as the prime function and duty of his life to promote the welfare and advancement of the Indian Empire, labours under the disadvantage of the rareness of occasions on which he can speak to audiences in England on this subject. If, therefore, I abuse your hospitality to-night, it is because I have got the chance of saying just one or two things that are uppermost in my mind.

'It is now a little more than eighteen months since I accepted the responsible and high office I now hold, and my experience in that time gathered in India, in England, and in Paris, has amplified and magnified the conviction with which I became Secretary of State, that the reform of the Government machine in India is vital and urgent and ought not to be delayed. (Loud Cheers.) The whole spirit of our deliberations across the Channel to-day is that Empire can alone be justified by the freedom and liberty which it guarantees, and the motive of the world's statesmanship at this moment is a hatred and detestation of ascendancy and domination. (Loud Cheers.) Therefore I say, my Lords and Gentlemen, that those who would stand in the way of Indian reform in this direction are not only in my opinion enemies of the British Empire, but are setting themselves athwart of worldwide influences. (Cheers.)

'I am part author of a scheme of Indian reform published for criticism. Never has anything been asked for, to which a more generous response has been given. (Laughter.) In pamphlets and in books, in streams and in deluge, criticism has poured forth, much of it helpful and constructive but also much of it prejudiced and ill-willed. His Highness, the Maharajah, and Lord Sinha have said something about the unfortunate effect of such strictures. As I listened to their speeches, I felt that they conveyed a lesson for those who write about India, of the harm that can be done by ill-considered words, and the mischief that can be wrought by forgetting the sensitiveness of people who are striving for progress. For the British politician abuse and criticism, however ill founded and imaginative, are the bread and butter upon which he lives. (Laughter.) Sometimes it is a matter of astonishment to those who do not live in England that we hardly take the trouble to answer those who make abuse their stock-in-trade. People who write and speak on India, however, often forget that their words are for more than domestic consumption.

'The one thing proposed by the Viceroy and myself which seems to meet with universal satisfaction is the great project of decentralization. (Cheers.) In a speech I once made, and which I have not since been allowed to forget, before I was appointed to my present office, I dragged into a discussion in the House of Commons on Mesopotamia, by the kindness and toleration of the Speaker, a picture of an India for which we should strive, consisting of a group of self-governing provinces or dominions, masters in their own houses, joined together for the common purposes of the country as a whole by the Government of India, and joined by a never-ending bond to the Empire which made them and gave them their liberty. (Cheers.) Now, nothing on the administrative side seems to me so obvious in the present administration than the irritation which is felt by those who constitute the Government of India with the horrible institution called the India Office. (Laughter.) It is only equalled by the irritation that is felt by those who constitute the provincial Governments with the horrible institution which is known as the Government of India. (Laughter.) My Lords and Gentlemen, this phenomenon, which is so shocking when you meet it in a partnership arrangement, seems to me inevitable when one authority sits on the head of another. I well remember looking at an excellent picture in "Punch," drawn, I think, by Du Maurier, of the inside of an episcopal palace, when a letter was opened from a rector asking permission to do something or other in his parish. The bishop was warming himself in front of the fire, his wife was knitting in the armchair, and their small son in a sailor suit was laboriously writing a letter: "Dear Mr. So-and-so, Daddy says you mustn't." (Laughter.) That is the irritating part. Some inscrutable decree is passed many hundreds of miles away, from Delhi or London, often unintelligible to those who receive it, preventing the man on the spot from doing what he wants. Harmony cannot be obtained, a quick solution of present difficulties cannot be achieved unless the Government of India is allowed to run its own affairs, and the Governments of the provinces are similarly given a free hand. (Applause.)

'Yes; but where does that take us? There can be only one substitute for authority from above. There can be only one substitute for the ultimate control of the British Parliament – and that is the control of the people of India. (Loud and long-continued cheering.) If I stopped at decentralization, I should have the unanimous support of the Indo-British Association. (Laughter.) The Governor would no longer be hampered by tedious and irritating despatches from London; he would be ruler of his own country without the necessity of bothering about the opinions of his Legislative Council. The purpose of the Viceroy and myself, however, is by no means to increase the bureaucratic character of governments in the provinces. Decentralization can only be effective, and autonomy can only be brought about, by the substitution of responsible government for government by the India Office. (Cheers.)

'But where does this lead us? It means that the substitute of government by despatch is government by vote. It has often been said that the reforms we propose have the unfortunate feature that they presume that Indians are unfit to govern themselves. That is not so. To-night I am surrounded by Indians who hold, or have held, high places. We are convinced of the fitness of many. It is a question not of Indians but of India. What we want to see is how India learns to use the vote on which the whole machinery will depend. (Cheers.) Can Indians grudge a few years in which to see how the franchise works? How many people vote in India to-day? Only a few handfuls. The work of Lord Southborough's committee will enfranchise millions of Indians. Will they vote? Will they know what a vote means, and what can be achieved by it? Will the constituencies which the Committee will devise be representative of the Indian Empire? If the British Parliament is the custodian of the growth of self-government in India we must have a few years in which to study the stages of that growth; and Indians have no right to tell us that in providing for this we are acting too cautiously or with too much hesitation.

'The first thing to do is to devise a representative electorate. That brings me to the subject of communal representation. I repeat, that to my mind this is an unfortunate expedient, fraught with many risks. (Hear, hear.) However, everything else, theoretical and practical, must be sacrificed to obtaining representative legislative councils. If communal electorates are the only means to this end – provided that they are designed to give the representation demanded by the necessity of the case – well, then, there must be communal representation. (Hear, hear.) But if such electorates are advocated simply, as I fear they are sometimes advocated, because there are still in the world believers in the old theory that if you split a country up you can govern it more easily, then communal representation is to be rejected. (Cheers.)

'I hasten to add that I make an exception for the Mahomedans, to whom we are bound by pledges as solemn as any Government ever gave to any people. To those pledges I am convinced that we shall remain faithful (cheers) until the day comes when the Mahomedans themselves tell us that there is no necessity for separate electorates.

'May I say one more thing, prompted by the remarks of His Highness the Aga Khan? I for one do not believe that there is any essential antagonism between the interests of one section of the Indian people and any other. (Loud cheers.) If in the Peace Conference it is unfortunate that India is represented by three men, none of whom is a Mahomedan, I can assure the Mahomedans of India that their peculiar interests and aspirations are as zealously voiced and as sympathetically considered by my two colleagues and myself, as the opinions, desires, and wishes of any other section of the Indian people. (Hear, hear.)

'I want to say one word about the Indian Civil Service. There is no doubt in the minds of all thinking men that any unprejudiced and well-informed observer of Indian history and conditions will agree that the services rendered to the country by the Indian Civil Service will stand for ever conspicuous as the greatest work ever accomplished in the history of the world by the men of one country for the people of another. But it is sometimes said that the result of the reforms proposed will be to alter and prejudice the position of the Indian Services. Yes, it will alter the position. This is a time for plain speaking. The announcement of 20th August 1917 promised the transfer of responsibility. From whom, to whom? To the people of India from the Civil Service of India. (Cheers.) If we said to the Civil Service to-day that their political position will be the same in the future as it has been in the past, the announcement of His Majesty's Government becomes meaningless. (Hear, hear.) For the past ten years I have been in close association with the Home Civil Service. Is their position unendurable? Is there any doubt about the great imperial services they render because they are subordinate to the policy laid down by Parliament? There is, believe me, for the Indian Civil Service an indispensable and honourable part in the future of India. The pronouncement of eighteen months ago meant nothing unless it meant that the political destinies of India are to be gradually reposed in the people of India, and gradually taken from those who have gloriously built up India as we know it today. (Loud cheers.) Although any talk of reform in any country brings out of retirement those who walk, dangerously as it seems to me, with their heads over their shoulders, gazing admiringly on the past, I do not believe that there is any Civil Servant in India who thinks (though it is sometimes claimed on their behalf) that the appointed destiny of the country can be delayed or altered in the interests of the Services. (Loud cheers.)

'I turn from the position of the Civil Service to that of Indian workers. It is for Parliament to decide what the Act will be. What I do know is, that the reforms that are wanted for India to-day are not concessions flung to the hungry politician, but the opening of the clearly marked road which will lead the people surely to their appointed destiny. (Loud cheers.) Nothing matters to me – the irritation, the peculiar anomalies, the novelties, the friction which are prophesied – so much as to be sure of seeing before us the road we are going to take. (Cheers.) Suppose, as I claim for the reform scheme which the Viceroy and I have published for criticism, that the future stages of progress depend, not upon agitation, but on the principles that constitute the essential ingredients of future stages, what have Indians to do? I tell you that there is only one way of ensuring rapid progress along that road, and that way does not lie in making political speeches abusing a race or class, or abusing your partners in the great experiment. Is there nothing definite that Indians can do during the transitional stages? No tongue can exaggerate the benefits of British rule in India. But education is still confined to a very small minority. Industrial development is in its infancy. Does anybody in this audience realize that last year in the great influenza epidemic no less than six million people died in India? In the State ruled by our Chairman, I believe that one out of seven died. The horrors of war are nothing to the influenza epidemic which has visited the whole earth. But has not the exceptional mortality in India something to do with poverty and the consequent lack of resisting power? (Cheers.) I say, supposing the questions of public health, education, and industrial development were in the power of Indians to work out for themselves, would these be dishonourable tasks? Would they not be the tasks for laying the foundation of a great Empire in the future?

'The basis of this dinner is the honour we desire to do to our guest, Lord

Sinha. He and I are called upon to work together as colleagues in the India Office. It was a proud moment of my life when I learned that the recommendation of Lord Sinha as my comrade had been accepted by His Majesty, though at the time I felt a sorrow which you will all understand at the loss of Lord Islington (cheers), to whom I owe very much for his friendship and assistance, and to whom India owes very much. (Cheers.) Lord Sinha's association with me has only been a short one; but we are associated together with the single purpose of benefiting the Indian Empire. It seems to me that if you forget personalities and just think of an Englishman and an Indian thus working together in the control of Indian administration, you will have an excellent example of the co-operation and unison between the two races which has been and, believe me, will continue to be a creative force of all the best work to be done for India. I do not believe that, as has been said, the experiment upon which the Government has embarked is a leap in the dark. I believe that the growth of Parliamentary and self-governing institutions is an inevitable consequence and result of British rule. Whether I consider the aspirations of India, or the interests of the British Empire, or the work which has been done by my fellow countrymen in India, I feel confident that the result of their labour in association with Indians, the only vision that they ought to desire to see achieved is a peaceful and prosperous India, in which Indians will walk the highways of their own country conscious that they are the controllers of its destinies. (Loud and long-continued cheers.)'

"LORD CARMICHAEL briefly proposed the health of the Chairman in a humorous speech, and His Highness expressed his acknowledgements."

47

THE POST-WAR FUTURE OF TURKEY

Letter (with Sayyid Ameer Ali) to The Times

London: 3 June 1919

Plea for the Muslim case on behalf of Turkey – the British Prime Minister's pledge regarding the maintenance of Turkish Empire in the homelands of the Turkish race – anxiety of Indian Muslims – possible consequences of non-observance of the pledge – British Government should not be deterred by developments elsewhere.

At this critical moment we regard our duty, as citizens of the British Empire, to plead once more for a considerate hearing at the Peace Conference of the Mussalman case on behalf of Turkey.

The tranquil development of Asia, and especially of India, closely concerns England. We venture to submit that in the light of the anguish and pain which the threatened dismemberment of Turkey has created among Muhammadans it is for England to stand by the Prime Minister's solemn pledge which will always remain memorable in the annals of the world as the statement of a farsighted and just policy, which had the desired effect of calming the anxiety of Muslims and enlisting their co-operation in the war against German ambitions. His words, already quoted by prominent public men with a knowledge of the Muhammadan mind, will not lose force by repetition. After stating some of the objects of the burden of war that we had undertaken he said as follows: "Nor are we fighting to deprive Turkey of its capital or of the rich and renowned lands of Asia Minor and Thrace, which are predominantly Turkish in race." And he proceeded to clinch his assurance in the following words: "While we do not challenge the maintenance of the Turkish Empire in the homelands of the Turkish race *with its capital at Constantinople* (the italics are ours), the passage between the Mediterranean and the Black Sea being internationalised and neutralised, Arabia, Armenia, Mesopotamia, Syria, and Palestine are in our judgement entitled to a recognition of their separate national condition."

Nothing could be more explicit nor more emphatic than the Prime Minister's pronouncement made in the name of England. It remains, therefore, for England to satisfy the Associated Powers that the wholesale destruction of Turkey is not compatible with the interests of her Empire or her good faith towards the vast millions of her Mussalman subjects. The Minister for India, responsible for her peace and good government, did not overrate by one word the extreme gravity of the situation, or the dissatisfaction and resentment to which the attempt to throw over the Prime Minister's pledge has given rise in India and elsewhere.

At this moment a great scheme of constitutional reform in India is on foot: its complete success must, to a great extent, depend on the whole-hearted and loyal co-operation of all his Majesty's Indian subjects. It would, in our opinion, prove a real calamity if the Mussalman community, numbering over 72 millions, were to stand aloof in sullen bitterness.

We believe that no statesman is more alive to the dangers of the situation than the Secretary of State for India. What do the Mussalmans want: what do we plead for? Neither they nor we ask for any new status for Turkey. We consider it, however, our duty to urge, for the fair name of England, nay of the British Empire, that the pledge our Prime Minister in the name of England gave to the world, and in particular to the world of Islam, should be maintained; and that the Turkish Sovereign, as the Caliph of the vast Sunni congregation, should be left in absolute possession of Constantinople, Thrace and Asia Minor stretching from the north of Syria proper along the Aegean coast to the Black Sea – a region "predominantly Turkish in race". It would, in our opinion, be a cruel act of injustice to wrench any portion of this tract from Turkish sovereignty to satisfy the ambitions of any other people. Instead of bringing peace to Western Asia, such a settlement will sow the seeds of constant wars, the effect of which cannot be expected to remain confined to the country where they happen to be waged.

For the defection of the unscrupulous adventurers who dragged their stricken people, who had already undergone great misery, into the world war, Turkey has been sufficiently punished by the secular expropriation of some of her richest provinces. But we submit that the maintenance of the Ottoman sovereign's spiritual suzerainty in those countries, whilst maintaining his prestige and thus conciliating Mussalman feeling, would be the means of making the position of the Mussalman rulers or governors of those countries unimpugnable. But so far as Thrace, Constantinople, and the homelands of the Turkish race are concerned Mussalman feeling from top to bottom is absolutely opposed to any interference under any shape with the Sultan's sovereignty.

We ask your permission to add one more remark. The Afghan outbreak, which we deplore, should not be used, as seems to be suggested in some quarters, for the purpose of avoiding the fulfilment of the Prime Minister's pledge or the due consideration of the feelings and sentiments of the Mussalman people. The outbreak in India did not deter Mr. Montagu from carrying out his promise to his Majesty's Indian subjects: nor should outbreaks like those of the Afghans or Kurds deter the fulfilment of the Prime Minister's assurance or from doing what is an act of simple justice dictated by both policy and humanity.

Source: *The Times*, London, 6 June 1919.

The letter was written from 41 Sloane Street, London, the home of Sayyid Ameer Ali.

As this and several other writings of the Aga Khan in the following pages deal with the status of Turkey in the post-war world and the Khilafat Movement in India, it is proper that the history and background of the Turkish issue be narrated here in some detail. The following treatment is drawn from my *The Indian Khilafat Movement, 1915–1933: A Documentary Record* (Pak Publishers, Karachi, 1972, Introduction, pp. xvii–xxv); which also contains a comprehensive bibliography on the subject on pp. 379–94.

When the Holy Prophet died he nominated no successor. As soon as the news reached the leaders of the Muslim community of Medina they, led by Umar and Abu Obaidah, took action to get Abu Bakr elected to the vacancy. Abu Bakr's election was carried by oral acclamation at a private meeting of his supporters. On the following morning all the Muslims assembled in the mosque and swore allegiance to the new Khalifa. Muslim historians have recorded that before his death Abu Bakr nominated Umar as his successor. Whether this was true or not, the fact was that Umar was acceptable to the Muslims and no objection was raised against his succession to the venerable Abu Bakr. When Umar lay dying of a fatal wound received at an assassin's hand he is said to have named six persons as electors to choose his successor. They chose Uthman. When Uthman was assassinated by a group of people who were unreconciled to his infirm rule the Khilafat passed to Ali.

There seems to be no doubt that some form of election was employed in the choice of the first four Khalifas. They reached the office because they were agreeable to the community, not because of any hereditary principle or of any consideration of relationship to the Prophet.

With the coming of the Umayyads in 661 the Khilafat passed to Muawiah, who hastened, in 676, to nominate his son Yazid as his successor. The hereditary principle was, for the first time, established in Islam. This precedent was generally followed by the Abbasids also.

The Prophet had been Head of State and Head of Church at the same time. He formulated and controlled the political policy of the community. He was the supreme authority in all military matters. He was the final law-maker and law-giver. He was the ultimate court of law from whom there was no appeal. He was the inspired Apostle of God whose religious opinions brooked neither doubt nor dispute. He also led the prayers as Imam of the congregation. The prophetic function ceased with him, and his successors therefore could not exercise this function. But all other authority passed on to the first four Khalifas, the Khulafa-i-Rashadeen.

The Prophet had been Rasul Allah, Apostle of God. When Abu Bakr succeeded him, an official designation was needed to describe his status. He ordered that he should be addressed by the modest title of Khalifa Rasul Allah, successor of the Apostle of God. On Uthman's coming to office the title was automatically expanded to cover the succession and he became Khalifa of the Khalifa of the Apostle of God. Soon, however, the length and clumsiness of the description led to the adoption of the simple word Khalifa. This is the origin of the Khilafat.

Another title which usually went with the Khilafat was that of Amirul-Mumineen, Commander of the Faithful. Umar was the first to adopt it and soon it became an integral part of the Khalifa's titles. It emphasized the military and secular aspect of his function.

Still another title enjoyed and used by the Khalifas was that of Imam. The Prophet had always led the prayers in the mosque at Medina and after his demise his successors continued to perform this duty. Leadership in public worship was regarded as a symbol of leadership in general.

These three titles describe the different aspects of the Khalifa's authority. As Khalifa he was the successor of the Apostle of God. As Amir-ul-Mumineen he was the highest secular authority in the community. As Imam he was the leader of the faithful in public worship.

In pre-Islamic Arabia the orator of the tribe was called the Khateeb. He also acted as judge in primitive society, and his pronouncement from the seat of authority was known as Khutbah. When the Prophet made an announcement from the *minbar* of the mosque it was called a Khutbah. His successors continued to do likewise, but with the expansion of Muslim power and the appearance of delegated authority the original importance of the Khutbah was lost. Gradually it became, and it remains so to our time, an address given by the Imam to the congregation just before the Friday or Eid prayers, consisting of praise and glory to God, blessings upon the Prophet, his descendants and companions, and a prayer for the reigning sovereign. The name of the monarch or ruler is mentioned, and a change in name means either the accession of a new ruler or the transfer of authority from one government to another.

After many vicissitudes the Khilafat passed, in 1517, from the last Abbasid Khalifa at Cairo, Mutawakkil, to Sultan Salim, the Ottoman conqueror of Egypt. There it stayed till March 1924 when the Turks abolished the institution and expelled the Khalifa.

The Ottoman Empire has figured prominently in British foreign policy. On what has gone down in European history as the Eastern Question, English sympathies were first given to Turkey for two politico-strategic reasons. Russia posed a threat to British imperial interests in Asia, and therefore a friendly

Turkish Empire was a British asset. The need for safeguarding the Indian Empire became another element in the formation of British attitude towards Turkey. Palmerston was notoriously pro-Turkish and anti-Russian, and the Crimean War was fought to protect the integrity of Turkey and to put a stop to the expansion of Russia in the East. With Disraeli this policy did not change, for he too thought it to be in the British imperial interest that Turkey should be strong.

With the coming of Gladstone this policy was forsaken. Britain was now more interested in the future of Armenia. Turkey was no longer a country to be wooed and won, but an Asiatic intruder in Europe to be kept in its place and an Islamic Empire on the fringe of Christendom to be liquidated. How could a Muslim power maintain itself in Europe? The Ottoman Empire was an out-dated theocracy which had no further use for British world interests. The earlier it was wiped off the face of the earth the better it would be for the West.

Here it is relevant to recall that this anti-Turkish sentiment coincided with – and was aggravated by – the then current belief that the Indian Mutiny was the handiwork of the Muslims. This added a bitter edge to British opinion. Had Britain come to the defence of the Turks and saved them from the Russian bear so that their co-religionists in India could rise against the British in revolt? Was this the reward of the traditional pro-Turkish policy?

Another complication appeared in this tangled web of political prejudice, religious sentiment and historical enmity. The Sultan of Turkey was not only the head of the Ottoman Empire but also, since the days of Salim, the Khalifa of the world community of Islam. It is true that Khilafat was a purely Sunni institution and that the Shias did not acknowledge the supreme religious and spiritual status of the Khalifa. But he was also the head of the only surviving Muslim empire, and this aspect of his position appealed in equal measure to Sunnis and Shias. On the Khilafat question, therefore, Muslim India was united against the British. The Khalifa's powers must be maintained. The Ottoman Empire must stand as it was before the war. European (and particularly British) designs aimed at the dismemberment of Turkish territories were resented in India and gave birth to the Khilafat movement.

This movement had obvious religious basis. The Muslim concern for the future of the Khalifa was apparently an Islamic sentiment. To this was added the general feeling that European powers were fastening upon Muslim states in North Africa and the Middle East. Russian advance in Turkestan, French control of northern Africa, British interference in Persian and Afghan affairs, Italian occupation of Tripoli – all this was in Muslim eyes an unmistakable and deliberate plan to destroy Islam in the world. Then came the Turco-Italian conflict and the Balkan wars in which Britain did not come to the rescue of Turkey as Muslim India had expected it to do.

With the coming of the Great War matters were made infinitely worse by Turkey joining the Central Powers against Britain and her allies. When Turkey fought against Britain, the Indian army fought for Britain and therefore against Turkey. As the Indian army counted a great number of Muslims in its ranks, the situation was indeed grave. But the old habit of loyalty asserted itself. Confidence in the British sense of fairness overcame Muslim suspicions and misgivings. In consequence Muslim India took her full share in the war effort. The explosion came at the end of the hostilities when a peace treaty with the vanquished Ottoman Empire was going to be signed.

Muslims were beginning to take a rose-coloured view of the future of Turkey. They had a close affinity with Turkey on religious grounds. They were also, in their minds, not far removed from Britain. They looked forward to an amicable settlement of the problem with matters turning out in favour of Turkey. Mr. Lloyd George's declaration that Britain was not fighting to deprive Turkey of her territorial integrity held out a hopeful chance.

But the Treaty of Sèvres, which the Allies signed with Turkey on 10 August, 1920, dashed the hopes of Muslim India. It took away large slices of Ottoman territory – Eastern Thrace, Gallipoli, Smyrna, the Straits and the Dardanelles, the Aegean Islands – and distributed them among the victors of war. Muslims reminded Mr. Lloyd George of his promises and of Muslim loyalty, but to little avail. They were rapidly losing their patience as well as their trust in British pledges. They believed that the Peace Conference was bent on the destruction of Islam. Much excitement prevailed and a seething restlessness took hold of Muslim politics.

It is against this background that the documents collected here should be viewed.

The arguments advanced by the Khilafat leaders in support of their claims on behalf of Turkey may be summarized as follows:

1. Turkey is the sole surviving Muslim political power in the world. If it disappears or is reduced to the position of a small, weak, third-class state, it will be an irreparable loss to Islam.

2. Muslims of all races and nationalities must come to the aid of Turkey for she has been in the past the shield of Islam. For centuries she has shed her blood for the glory of the faith and has striven for the victory and greatness of Islam. It will be an act of unforgivable ingratitude not to help her in her hour of peril.

3. So far Turkey, and Turkey alone, has stood in the way of Russian ambitions in the East. In the nineteenth century she prevented the expansion of Russia and this was instrumental in saving the British Empire in India. The British should acknowledge this debt to Turkey, and they should also realise that a weakened Turkey will mean the disappearance of an effective barrier between Russia and the British possessions in Asia. (This argument was addressed to the British imperial conscience.)

4. Turkey joined the Central Powers and declared war on the Allies, not because she was an enemy of Britain and her friends, but simply because she was mortally afraid of her ancient enemy, Russia, and when she found Russia on the side of the Allies it was a foregone conclusion that she would cast in her lot with Germany and against Russia. (Maulana Muhammad Ali gave this argument in reply to Mr. Lloyd George's remark that Turkey had no quarrel with Britain and therefore should not have joined Germany.)

5. In January 1918, Mr. Lloyd George had publicly declared that Britain was not fighting to deprive Turkey of her ancient and renowned lands. The British Prime Minister must fulfil this pledge and maintain the integrity of the areas which are Turkish in race.

6. India's contribution to Allied war effort must be appreciated. Without Indian manpower British arms would not have triumphed, particularly in the Near and Middle East. Now that victory has been won this precious help should be acknowledged by deferring to Indian wishes.

7. The British Empire is the biggest "Muslim empire" in the world. Sheer imperial interests demand that the government of this Empire should not alienate the sympathies or offend the sentiments of its vast Muslim subjects.

8. India is united in her concern for the future of Turkey. Hindus and

Muslims equally share the feeling that the British Government is not dealing with the Turkish issue with an open mind and the desire that the Allies should meet all reasonable demands of the Turks and their Indian sympathisers.

9. The powers of the Khalifa should be maintained intact. The temporal authority of the Khalifa and the means to exercise it are matters of religious belief which brook no abridgement. To weaken this authority will be a deliberate and calculated offence to Islam.

10. It is an integral part of Muslim belief that the holy places of Islam must always remain under Muslim control. This overrules not only the laying of direct non-Muslim control over Arabia and other places but also the imposition of mandates and trusteeships over them.

11. It is also an essential tenet of Islam that the Khalifa must be the supreme over-lord of the holy places. Therefore, even if Hedjaz is made politically independent of Turkish control, the King of Hedjaz should receive his investiture from the Sultan-Khalifa.

12. The Muslims believe that the Jazirat-ul-Arab should never come under non-Muslim control. The Jazirat-ul-Arab, according to Muslim history, tradition and belief, does not mean the Arabian peninsula alone, but also includes Syria, Mesopotamia and Palestine. As the name indicates, Arabia is an island with the waters of the Euphrates and the Tigris marking its fourth boundary.

13. The principle of self-determination, on which the peace treaties are claimed to be founded, must be applied to the component parts of the Turkish Empire in the same way as it has been applied to other peoples like the Poles and the Yugoslavs.

14. The constitutional development of India towards the status of a self-governing member of the British Empire is rendered meaningless if on such a vital matter the British Government is not prepared to lend a sympathetic ear to a demand which is made by the whole of India and is backed by the Government of India.

Some of these arguments were based on facts which even the British Government could not and did not deny. But then the claim was made that Indian wishes were taken into consideration in the making of the peace treaty with Turkey. When the Treaty of Sèvres was concluded Mr. Lloyd George declared in the House of Commons, and it was repeated by the Viceroy in his message to the people of India, that the terms of peace were influenced and determined by Indian, and particularly Indian Muslim, wishes. This was an untruth which even the Prime Minister must have uttered without conviction. The Treaty did not reflect the acceptance of a single demand of the Khilafatists, and Mr. Lloyd George must have known this.

All the arguments based on religion were not acceptable to the British, nor, in the sequel, to the Turks. The Khilafatists did not go into the merits of the Osmanli title to the Khilafat. The means by which the Khilafat was transferred to Sultan Salim could bear more than one interpretation. But there was no theological discussion on this point, either in India during the Khilafat movement, or in Turkey at the time of the abolition of the institution. The Khilafatists' silence on this matter is understandable. They were not concerned with the manner by which the Ottomans had succeeded to the Khilafat. There was a Khalifa in Constantinople. He had been there for four centuries. He was the spiritual and temporal head of Islam. He was accepted as such by the world of Islam. Now his power, his status, his future as an independent ruler, were in jeopardy. He must be supported against his enemies. Were he deprived of his authority or made subservient to a non-Muslim power, the Muslims of the world would, for the first time in their history, be without an ordained head. It is true that there had been in the past occasions when the Khalifa's writ did not run throughout the Islamic world. There had also been times when the Khalifa was defeated in battle and his court and family were humiliated. But never, never in fourteen hundred years, had there been a Khalifa who owed his authority to the sanction of a Christian power or was indebted for his existence to the pleasure of a non-Muslim state. That is how the Khilafatists thought and argued, and for them it was irrelevant to talk about the validity of the Ottoman title to the Khilafat. It was not the title that was in dispute, but the freedom to exercise the authority it carried.

It is impossible to doubt the deep sincerity of the Khilafat movement. Its leaders were men of invincible conviction and unshakeable faith who were glad to go to prison and even to accept the hangman's noose for what they believed to be true and right. It was a matter in which to compromise was to be an apostate. There could be give and take in politics; there could be no bargaining in religion. It was an article of belief that the Khilafat must stand sure and complete, and that was that. It was futile to compare the Khilafat with Papacy and to draw relevant or irrelevant conclusions. It was purposeless to argue that Turkey was beaten in fair battle and that the victor must dictate to the vanquished.

This deep religious feeling explains the distress caused to Indian Muslims by the abolition of the Khilafat. The decision of the Turkish Grand National Assembly was a bitter shock, not only because it betrayed an ignorance of Indian Muslim sentiment on the point, not only because it showed how little was Turkish gratitude for what India had done for them, but, above all, because it did not lay in Turkish hands to take such a decision. Khilafat belonged to the world of Islam, not to any individual Muslim country, and no one state or people could sit in judgment on its existence or its future.

Was the Khilafat movement a mere interlude, brief and pointless, in the history of Muslim India? Or, was it an important, memorable, new chapter in the national struggle? Each historian will exercise his privilege of giving an answer. For one who has no claim to that title it sufficeth to conclude with some observations of a general character.

On the credit side several things can be mentioned. It trained the Muslims in the art of political action and agitation. For the first time a definite and precise plan of action was drawn up and executed. It also brought the extermists [*sic*] and the moderates on one platform, or at least gave unity of their outlook. There was little in common between the Aga Khan and Maulana Muhammad Ali or between Sayyid Ameer Ali and Dr. M. A. Ansari. But the "loyalists" and the "agitators" worked to the same end. Whether the "rebels" were creating a furore in India or the "constitutionalists" were writing to *The Times* in England, the aim was identical. Never again was this synchronisation of political action in India with publicity in Britain to be achieved.

The Khilafat movement also destroyed the myth of Muslim loyalty. The spectacle of the agitating Muslims was such a break with the past that at first the British rubbed their eyes and refused to believe what they saw. The friends of yesterday had become the enemies of today. Whether this metamorphosis was caused by the exigencies and follies of British foreign policy or by an inherent British enmity of Islam is irrelevant. The net result was that the mutual trust, carefully nurtured by the efforts of forty years, was gone and with it the old method of conducting politics. This change was also due to the Hindu-Muslim unity which lasted just as long as the Khilafat issue was in the forefront.

Gandhi had thrown himself wholeheartedly into the fray because, as he confessed, it was an opportunity of uniting the two people which might never recur. The Muslims welcomed this reinforcement, for it swelled the ranks of the agitators and brightened the chances of success. This alliance was a new phenomenon in Indian history and created false hopes in countless breasts.

However, this unity did not last long. Even before the final battle was won cracks had begun to appear in the entente. For a careful observer there were signs of the things to come in this rift. Many Muslims learnt one important lesson: that Hindu-Muslim differences were too deep to be bridged over by passionate professions of friendship and even by united action in the political field. The movement, in effect, underlined the basic Hindu-Muslim schism which nothing could heal. Never again were the two communities to combine forces against the British.

The movement also threw up some effective leaders among the Muslims. Effective, but not really first class. As the movement was highly emotional it was easier for the fire-eating demagogue to get himself lionised than for the cautious constitutionalist to catch the public eye. There was no Jinnah or Fazl-i-Husain among its leaders. By definition the movement was religious and anti-British. Therefore, by definition it excluded the westernised and co-operative public men from its ranks. The need of the moment was to rouse popular emotions to snapping point, to make fighting speeches to scare the British, to preach sedition even to the soldiers, to issue threatening statements promising dire consequences, and, if necessary, to go to jail to prove one's love for Islam. Only a special kind of leadership was capable of this, and it ruled the roost.

Within these limitations and in their own province of activity, the Khilafat leaders were good tacticians and effective politicians. They rarely looked beyond the movement and had no vision of the future. But they were all sincere men, passionately attached to their religion and fanatically devoted to the welfare of Turkey. As long as the campaign lasted they rode on the crest of the wave of popular acclaim. There was no end to which the masses were not ready to go at their bidding. But when the emergency passed away a calm resembling death settled upon Muslim India. New problems arose which the old leadership had not anticipated and for which they had no solution. For a time, in fact for the next eight years, politics were static and the masses confounded. It is in this sense that the Khilafat leadership was a failure and the movement itself a pointless interlude.

One would have thought that the success of the Khilafat movement would teach the Muslims one elementary lesson: that in unity lies strength. A joint effort had led them to victory, and in future too they should seek their appointed goal in unity. But no sooner had the movement come to an end than the Muslims were once again divided into "nationalists" and Leaguers, extremists and moderates, pro-separate electorate and anti-separate electorate. It seems that it is only in moments of dire danger that Muslims can stand shoulder to shoulder and defy the common enemy. This has been proved again and again in Muslim political history all over the world.

Religion was the *raison d'être* of the Khilafat movement, and this had one important result for the later growth of Muslim nationalism. By emphasizing Islam the movement made the Muslims conscious of their being Muslims. Of course, the feeling of being a separate religious group was at least as old as the time of Sayyid Ahmad Khan. Later the demand for separate representation was also based on the claim that their religion set them apart from other Indians. But it was only now that they felt, with unprecedented intensity, that they were

641

Muslims first and Indians afterwards. This was a triumph for Muslim nationalism, for it provided a base on which other unities could be built. And this, as far as we can see, was the only permanent contribution of the Khilafat movement to the larger problem of nationalism. It was a contribution, however, which no historian can afford to under-estimate or ignore.

The All India Khilafat Conference had the following presidents from 1921 to 1933:

July 1921	Karachi	Muhammad Ali
December 1921	Ahmedabad	Hakim Ajmal Khan
December 1922	Gaya	M. A. Ansari
December 1923	Cocanada	Shaukat Ali
December 1924	Belgaum	Saifuddin Kitchlew
December 1925	Cawnpore	Abul Kalam Azad
May 1926	Delhi	Sayyid Sulaiman Nadvi
February 1927	Lucknow	Haji Abdullah Haroon
December 1927	Madras	Maulvi Muhammad Shafi
December 1928	Calcutta	Muhammad Ali
May 1931	Bombay	Abdul Majid Badayuni
September 1932	Ajmere	Shaikh Abdul Majid
December 1933	Lucknow	Sayyid Murtaza Bahadur

Information on the years 1920, 1929, and 1930 is not available. Newspapers and the *Indian Annual Register* stopped publishing news of Khilafat Conference meetings after 1933. It has not been possible to establish the exact date on which the Conference ceased to exist.

48

INDIAN MUSLIM SENTIMENT AND TURKEY

Letter (with Sayyid Ameer Ali) to The Times

London: 2 August 1919

A fresh memorial on the Turkish question by Muslims, Hindus and Englishmen – possible consequences of punitive measures against Turkey – the sentiments of Muslims in India regarding Turkey and the Ottoman sovereign.

A fresh memorial to which we also are signatories, extensively signed by Muslims, Hindus and Englishmen, has just been submitted to the Prime Minister, strongly protesting against the new design attributed to the Peace Conference for the dismemberment of Turkey and the disintegration of the Turkish nation. It is a reasoned document, and we trust it will receive due consideration from Mr. Lloyd George and his colleagues who have the settlement of this momentous matter in their hands.

But we beg leave to trespass on the hospitality of your columns to call the attention of the British public, who are deeply concerned in winding up the war business, to the fact that the design of despoiling Turkey of Constantinople and Thrace, of giving her seaports to other nations, of shutting her off from all access to the sea and to the markets of the world, and penning up 6 or 7 millions Muslims on the Plateau of Anatolia, placing the rest under subjection to alien races, will be no "settlement" at all; it will, in our opinion, be a real tragedy and the gravest of blunder. The British public, we hope, will realize what this design, if carried into effect, would in truth mean. It would shut off the "penned up" nation from all communication with their co-religionists in other parts of the globe: it would debar them from intercourse with other nations: it would deprive them of all chances of progress and development; it would sow the seeds of discontent and cruel racial wars and feuds, and would be the cause of perpetual unrest in the whole of Asia, not to speak of the unquenchable bitterness it would create in the hearts of the Mussalmans all over the world.

Ever since the grant of the Dewanny in 1765 to the East India Company by the Emperor of Delhi and Lord Lake's Treaty in 1802, the Mussalman element has been among the most steadfast to the British Crown. And now, to appease the ambitions and "earth-hunger" of certain nationalities whose help in this war can hardly be compared with the sacrifices the Mussalman soldiers brought to the cause of England, we have turned their devotion, to put it mildly, to something akin to embitterment. Whether the feeling of the Mussalmans of India in regard to Turkey and the Ottoman Sovereign is old or new is immaterial. It is a living and universal sentiment and must be counted as a factor in practical politics. Is it wise, is it statesmanlike, to treat this living sentiment in the way, we are told, the Peace Conference proposes to do?

Source: *The Times*, London, 2 August, 1919.
The letter was written from 41 Sloane Street, London, which was Sayyid Ameer Ali's residence. It bears no date.

49

SUFFRAGE FOR THE INDIAN WOMEN

Letter to The Times

London: 8 August 1919

Attitude of the Southborough Report on the question of women's suffrage – disagrees with Lord Southborough's opinion – the great majority of Indian women of the well-to-do classes not in seclusion – many British officials in India not in touch with the life or aspirations of the people – women should share the sacred right of enfranchisement – a question of justice – women should protest against these obsolete views.

The summaries given in *The Times* of the proceedings of the Joint Select Committee on the India Bill go to show that the attitude of casual negation on the question of women suffrage adopted in the Southborough Report, and endorsed by the Government of India, is without substantial foundation. Lord Southborough himself admitted that he was very much astonished at the volume of evidence in favour of female enfranchisement; but he brushes it aside as so much political idealism. It seems he has forgotten that the world is governed by ideas, and that true progress is rooted in idealism.

One member of the Franchise Committee, Mr. Malcolm Hogg, was in favour of the removal of sex disqualification, but not of making special arrangements for recording women's votes. I entirely dissent from Lord Southborough's opinion that the reservation "robbed the gift of all its merit." We are not setting up the public hustings and open voting of a past age of England nor is the number of male electors – some five million for the whole of British India – large enough for the jostle of the ballot station to be so serious as Lord Southborough and Sir James Meston suggested. The great majority of Indian women of the well-to-do classes, *e.g.*, the better class of cultivators, are not in real seclusion. The official witnesses who hold that very few women will go to the polling booth forget that purdah ladies go into the law and registration courts all over the country, and give evidence in relation to the transfer of property, &c. As owners of land and other property, purdah women play parts in the affairs of the countryside day by day which make ludicrous the suggestion that there would be anything revolutionary in recording a vote once in three years or less.

Sir James Meston's statement that female enfranchisement would present many difficulties, practical and social, is an instance of the regrettable fact that while many conscientious British officials spend their working lives in administrative duties in India, they never enter into a real understanding of the life or aspirations of the people – national, social, or religious. Only one man in a hundred, a Woodroffe in Calcutta, a Pollen or a Beaman in Bombay, gains such real understanding of the people he serves. It is painful to Indian readers that men who have attained high distinction in the Civil Service should have to be seriously asked if they would be shocked at the inclusion of women in the electorates. No Indian, not even the most conservative, will be shocked by the proposal that now that the sacred right of enfranchisement is to be given on a substantial scale to men, women should share it, just as they share the sacred rights of property.

I do not believe that Sir James Meston and Lord Southborough are right in the opinion that very few women would exercise the franchise; but the point is not pertinent to the issue. The question is one of justice, and not of the degree to which the right would be used. The logical deduction of the assertions of Sir James Meston and Lord Southborough about Indian womanhood would be to take away from them the rights of property and of equality before the civil law they have enjoyed for centuries. My general views on this question can be seen in some detail in my book, "India in Transition", published before the issue of the Montagu-Chelmsford Report. But I feel it my duty to the hundreds of venerable and sensible purdah ladies of position I know in India to register this protest against the obsolete views of men who have attained to place and power in India, but who have never taken the trouble to know the people among whom they do office work.

Source: *The Times*, London, 11 August 1919.

The journal published the letter under the double headline "Indian Women and the Vote: The Aga Khan on Obsolete Views." The place from where the Aga Khan wrote it is not given in the text, nor the date on which it was written or posted.

The report whose specific recommendation on female franchise drew these strictures from the Aga Khan was *East India (Constitutional Reforms): Lord Southborough's Committee: Report of the Franchise Committee,* London, 1919, Cmd. 103. The committee had been appointed by the Secretary of State for India to inquire into questions connected with the franchise and other matters relating to constitutional reforms, with Lord Southborough as its chairman.

See also the Aga Khan, et. al., "Indian Reforms: A Symposium", *Indian Review,* October 1919.

50

THE MAKING OF THE 1919 REFORMS

Evidence Before the Joint Select Committee on the Government of India Bill

London: 10 October 1919

His concept of responsible government – the powers of non-official members of the Provincial Legislatures – Provincial Executives – dual form of government – the tenure of the offices of Ministers – powers of the Governor – suggestion for the provision of referendum – limitations on the powers of the Legislatures – the scope of the Legislative Assembly – the bicameral system – the Governor General's Executive Council – modification of the powers of the Secretary of State and the Governor General – periodic reviews – the need for a clear framework for rules – views on the report of the Southborough Franchise Committee – the system of diarchy – utility of an Upper House in the Legislature – communal representation – India Office – women's franchise – federalism – the Council of State – the Initiative and the Recall – the Secretary of State's Council – Indian representation in the Executive Council – the representation of the "depressed" and other classes – a wider Confederation – Great Britain's prestige and influence in India – widening of the franchise – make the Bill more precise.

MEMBERS PRESENT:
LORD BRODRICK (Viscount MIDLETON).
Lord SYDENHAM.
Lord SINHA.
Mr. BENNETT.
Sir HENRY CRAIK.
Mr. MONTAGU.
Major ORMSBY-GORE.
Sir J. D. REES.
Mr. SPOOR.

The Right Honourable the Lord BRODRICK (Viscount MIDLETON) in the Chair.

His Highness AGA SULTAN Sir MAHOMED SHAH, AGA KHAN, g.c.s.i., g.c.i.e., is called in; and examined, as follows:–

Lord *Brodrick* (Viscount *Midleton*).
8644. Your Highness had been good enough to answer certain questions submitted to you, and the Committee have the advantage of knowing your views in respect of those questions? – Yes.

The following are the questions and answers: –

1, 2. Do you accept the proposition that it is desirable to bring about the progressive realisation of responsible government in India? and, if so, how do you define the expression "responsible government"? And do you generally accept the proposition contained in the preamble? 2. Do you think that the realisation of responsible government in the Provinces involves the establishment in provincial legislatures of a substantial elected majority (Clause 6)? – The preamble to the Bill is in my judgment appropriate and satisfactory. I accept the term "responsible government," though as an ideal my preference is for self-government either on the American federal plan or on Swiss lines, leaving ultimate power through the initiative, the referendum, and perhaps the recall. But the facts of the situation have to be recognised. Our future is linked with Great Britain and not with the United States, or Switzerland – and still less with an abstract perfect State conceived by the mind of a Plato. For a century and a half English institutions and sentiments have been moulding Indian political ideas. The very fact that this Bill is before the British Parliament shows that we must seek progress at this transitional stage in conformity with English views and English institutions. Under these circumstances "responsible government" must be our way towards evolving in the future some plan more suited to a congeries of great States, such as India will become, and I believe the way will be found in something akin to the American federal plan, plus the initiative and the referendum and possibly even the recall. Meanwhile acceptance of the formula "responsible government" postulates the necessity for making the electorate as wide as possible, as well as the establishment in the Provincial Legislatures of a substantial elected majority.

3. Do you think that the non-official members of the Provincial Legislatures should possess power to control the actions and policy of the Executive? Do you think they possess such power at present? – The non-official members of the Provincial Legislatures certainly influence, but do not control, the actions and policy of the Executive. Such control should now be given in the transferred spheres; and I look forward to the day when, through the referendum and the initiative, the electors will fully supervise their representatives.

4. Do you think that there are certain matters or functions of Government in the Provinces in which at present the Provincial Executive must remain responsible to the Secretary of State and Parliament, and must therefore be in a position to enforce its wishes? – As the Joint Report points out, there are great differences in the measure of advancement in the various provinces. Of Bombay I should say that all distinctly Provincial work could be safely left to the control of the electorate; and probably to the same can be said of the two other Presidencies. But in the inland Provinces a varying measure of reservation may be necessary.

5. If you accept the propositions stated under Questions 1 to 4, do you think that the dual form of government embodied in the Bill is the best means of securing them? If not, what are your objections to that feature of the Bill, and by what other means would you attempt to secure the objects in view? – From its nature dualism cannot be a permanent solution. But all our work is spadework at present, and it is difficult to imagine any other coherent scheme for the transitional period. Dualism will prepare the ground and make full responsible government inevitable in time.

7, 8. If you consider a dual form of government, acceptable in principle, are there any points of detail the modification of which you regard as necessary? If so, what are those points, and what modifications would you suggest? 8. In particular, do you think (i) that Ministers should hold office "during pleasure"? – i.e., should be liable to removal if they are unable to support the action decided upon in their department by the Governor or if they fail to retain the confidence of the Legislature (Clause 3 (1))? (ii) that the Governor should have power to disregard the opinion of his Ministers if he considers that action in accordance with that opinion is inconsistent with the due discharge of his responsibilities (Clause 3 (3))? (iii) that the Executive Council should in all Provinces normally consist of one official European and one non-official Indian (Clause 4)? (iv) that the Governor should have power to dissolve his Legislative Council (Clause 7 (4))? – When dyarchy is established modifications must grow out of experience; but it is important to remove, on initiation, any unnecessary ground for friction and difficulty. For instance, I cannot imagine any self-respecting Minister remaining in office if he is over-ruled in his department on important issues. He should not be subject to dismissal by the Governor, for I believe that reliance can be placed on the honourable traditions which will grow up round the appointment. An adverse vote of the Legislature on the proposals of a Minister should not automatically bring about his retirement; a vote for his removal carried by a two-thirds majority should be needed. The power of the Governor to disregard the opinion of his Ministers if he considers that the proposed action would be inconsistent with the discharge of his responsibilities is desirable at present as a safeguard from the British point of view. The practical utility of such power, however, may be doubted. In my judgment the best guarantee that hasty, unfair or partial legislation will not be carried out, and also the best protection for the Governor himself, will be for a method of referendum to be added to the constitutional framework even at this initial stage. When in perplexity between the advice of his officials and the secret reports of the police on the one hand, and the behests of the Legislature on the other, the Governor could then avoid the anxieties and doubtful results of dissolution by submitting the measure in dispute to the people by referendum. This plan would politically educate the electors, keep their interest in public affairs keen and vigilant, and ultimately lead to the initiative and the regular use of the referendum in all cases of importance. This alternative method is free from the objection of complete novelty. It is successfully worked in the Swiss Confederation of free Cantons. I support the clauses which provide that the Executive Council in all Provinces should normally consist of one official European and one non-official Indian, and that the Governor should have power to dissolve the Legislature.

9. Referring back to Questions 2, 3 and 4, if your answers to the first and third of these are in the affirmative, and if you think that the Legislatures should be given greater powers of

control and influence than they possess at present, do you regard the limitations imposed generally by Clause 9 of the Bill upon their financial and legislative powers as (i) suitable, or as (ii) unnecessarily severe, or as (iii) inadequate to safeguard the responsibilities which the Government owes in the last resort to Parliament (Clause 9)? – The restrictions upon the financial and legislative powers of the Legislatures embodied in Clause 9 are unnecessarily severe so far as Bombay and Bengal are concerned, however requisite they may be in some provinces. They are, on the whole, more than adequate to safeguard the responsibilities which the Government owes in the last resort to Parliament.

10. In particular, (i) do you think that the Legislature should have power with whatever limitations to vote supplies (Clause 9 (2))? (ii) Do you accept the plan of Grand Committees as the means of giving to the Government the power to secure essential legislation in the event of their failure to carry their propositions in the Council? If so, have you any modifications of detail to suggest? If not, what other method would you suggest to secure the object in view? – The Legislature should certainly have power to vote supplies. I am not enamoured of the elaborate machinery of the Grand Committee for securing essential legislation refused by the Legislature. It may be necessary for the first few years; but after five or six years I would resort to the natural and constitutional solution of dissolving the House on important occasions when the whole policy of the Administration is under successful challenge. In cases where only one measure is the cause of friction I would use the referendum. Thus the people would be trained in responsibility through a general election or the referendum.

11. Do you accept the position adopted in the Bill (Part II.) that the time has not yet come to give the Legislative Assembly a similar measure of control over the Central Government as that given to Provincial Legislative Councils over Provincial Governments? – I do not entirely accept the position of the Bill that the time has not come to give the Legislative Assembly a similar measure of control over the Central Government as that given to Provincial Legislatures over the Provincial Governments. Powerful arguments have been addressed to the Joint Committee in favour of making at least a beginning of responsible government in the central sphere. I would instance two important departments, Public Works and Education, as capable of being handed over to a responsible Minister at

headquarters without unduly fettering the Government of India in the discharge of its responsibilities to Parliament and the Empire.

12, 13. Do you agree that it is advisable none the less to provide for a substantial elective majority in the Indian Legislature (Clause 16)? 13. Do you accept the plan of a dicameral [*sic*] Legislature as arising out of this, as constituting both a satisfactory machine for the ordinary purposes of legislation and as affording the means to the Governor-General in Council to secure legislation which he regards as essential (Clauses 14, 15 and 16)? – There should be a substantial majority of elected members in the Indian Legislative Assembly. I do not favour, in principle, the bicameral plan for the Central Government, since it may retard true federalism. But at present I see no prospect of applying the federal principle, nor of the British Parliament accepting single-chamber machinery for All-India legislation. Hence I accept a bicameral system as a *pis aller*, but the composition proposed for the second chamber is too official and inadequately representative. Though here, too, my ideal is self-government through the referendum, initiative and recall, I do not at this stage urge the establishment in the central sphere of these ultimate solutions.

14. Do you accept the provisions of the Bill as to the course of legislation in the Indian Legislature (Clause 20 (3) and (4))? Or do you regard them as unnecessarily restrictive on the popular will, or as an inadequate means of ensuring to the Governor-General in Council the discharge of his responsibilities? – The clauses relating to the course of legislation in the Indian Legislature are unnecessarily restrictive, and seem based on distrust of the common sense of the people.

15. Do you accept the changes made by the Bill (Clause 21) in the constitution of the Governor-General's Executive Council? If not, what are your reasons, and what modifications would you suggest? – I welcome the modification of the existing statutory restrictions on appointments to the Governor-General's Executive Council. I would suggest that the two departments previously mentioned – Public Works and Education – should be made into memberships whose holders would be responsible to the Legislative Assembly and that the remaining places should be filled in equal proportions by Europeans and Indians.

16. Do you think that the development of Provincial

autonomy, on the one hand, and of self-government in the Provinces on the other, involves any modification of the provisions of Sections 2, 33 and 45 of the Government of India Act (Clause 23)? – Modifications of the powers of superintendence, direction and control possessed by the Secretary of State over the Indian administration and by the Governor-General in Council over the Provincial Governments are essential to the working of this legislation. The modifications required seem to me as a layman to be but vaguely implied in the Bill as it stands, and I think that in broad outline they should be given definite statutory expression. As time goes on and Indians learn in the school of responsibility I look for great advances on the present implied modifications, advances which will in due time lead to true federalism.

17. Do you agree that the gradual realisation of responsible government involves periodical examination of progress by independent authority, and that the provisions of Clause 28 of the Bill are well designed to afford such examinations? – Unquestionably the gradual realisation of responsible government involves periodical examination of progress by independent authority. India is changing so rapidly, and the war has so keenly stimulated her material development and the political consciousness of her people, that I think ten years is too long a period between the investigations to be made by statutory commissions. I should prefer seven years, and would remind the Committee that the India of 1919 is entirely different in outlook from the India of 1912.

18. Are there any matters which it is proposed in the Bill to deal with by rule which you would suggest should be provided for in the Bill? – The Bill leaves far too much to rules to be made hereafter. I recognise the force of the arguments of the memorandum of the Secretary of State (Cd. 175; 1919) for leaving changes to be worked out in detail in the form of rules, especially for a measure so transitional in character. But in my humble judgment the framework should be more clearly visible in the Bill and less scope should be left for the exercise of the mere personal inclination or the prejudices of party outlook by successive Secretaries of State or Governors-General. Sober progressive opinion in India has strong confidence in Mr. Montagu and his reforming purposes; but it knows that political changes in England (wholly unconnected with Indian affairs) may occur at any time, leaving the personality of the head of the India Office in the critical days of inaugurating the new

order an uncertain and disturbing factor. The skeleton character of the present Bill may be contrasted with the care and detailed exactitude of the measure which, in 1858, transferred the administration from a trading company to the Crown.

19. Have you any observations to offer on the Reports of Lord Southborough's Committees and of the Committee on the Home Administration of Indian Affairs? – The report of the Southborough Franchise Committee is seriously defective in two respects. The first is the non-admission of women to the franchise. I need not recapitulate the arguments on this subject in my book, "India in Transition." I will only say that Indian women, even though in purdah, are neither slaves nor fools. Property, often to a large amount, is found in their hands, and frequently the working of the joint family system makes a woman the practical head of the family or house. The rudiments of English Parliamentary government are being bestowed upon India; and no substantial ground has been shown for confining them to a moiety of the people. The second great defect of the Southborough scheme is that the question of Referendum is totally ignored, though there are many reasons for accepting it as a constitutional instrument specially suited to Indian conditions. In India the elected members are liable to be charged by officials and conservative observers with failing to reflect the real mind of the electors they represent. It is a country, too, where the educated leaders show an eagerness and haste for legislation bringing the social laws, touching the lives of the people at large at many points, more into conformity with Western opinion than the masses may understand or appreciate. This being so, the best safeguard of the Governor in the exercise of his discretion and of British opinion, which is still the final court of appeal, is that when doubt arises on important matters the opinion of the people should be known, not only on general policy, which can best be shown by a general election, but on the particular measure under consideration. For these reasons and to bring home to the electorate a sense of responsibility, as well as to keep their representatives in touch with the opinion of all classes of voters, a modified form of referendum is necessary even at this stage. I suggest that it should be applied not at the unrestricted discretion of the Governor, but only when he carries with him a high proportionate minority – say 40 per cent. – of members of the Legislature voting on the question.

But with the development of responsibility time will bring the referendum and the initiative can be made the constitutional method, as in Switzerland, of settling all first-class questions on which opinion in the Legislature is sharply divided, arising between one general election and another, alike in the Provinces and in the Central Government. With these important reservations, I accept generally the proposals of the Southborough Committees as, on the whole, not unsuited to the period of transition, though there may be details capable of amendment with much advantage.

8645. I would venture to ask you in the first instance one or two points to elucidate your answers. You say that dualism cannot be a permanent solution. Now with regard to diarchy, we have had two views put before us: One is that the electorate, or the Legislative Council, should have a partial control of all matters, and the other is that they should have a complete control of certain matters. Which, in your opinion, is more desirable? – I think, given the declaration of the 20th August, that a responsible government is the final objective in view, that the second solution can be the only first step. I do not see how the first solution can possibly be a first step towards responsible government ultimately by stages. They must have complete control of some; then only will they begin to have responsibility in the full sense.

8646. Consider this point. If you give Ministers a complete control of certain subjects you would know where the responsibility lay, would you not? – Yes.

8647. Would it not be more desirable that whatever was a subject for the Legislative Council, it should be clearly understood with whom the responsibility lay? – That is the solution of giving complete responsibility on certain subjects, and then, it is clearly understood where the responsibility lies.

8648. It rather depends. If you have a Cabinet, so to speak, in which we will say there are four members, two Ministers and two appointed by the Governor-General, it is possible, is it not, that the Ministers might be outvoted in the Cabinet, and the policy of the vote in regard to such subjects as the Ministers have to deal with might not be that of which the Ministers approve? Which is most desirable, that Ministers should be the arbiters, so to speak, of the policy they introduce, subject, of course, to a possible veto by the Governor at a later stage, or that they should be the spokesmen of the Government in which they might not be in the majority? – I say with the objective of responsible government in view they must have a free hand in those departments vis-a-vis the electorate and vis-a-vis the elected body; that means vis-a-vis the Legislature.

8649. You realise that would hardly be so under the Bill as it stands; you cannot have that with collective responsibility? – As you know better than I do, in politics theory and practice rarely agree after a few months of practice. We cannot foresee how it will exactly work. Nobody who tries now can see how it will exactly work in these questions of details. There will be a good deal of give and take in the Governor's own room. I rely a great deal on the good sense of the people who are made to work any scheme. I do not care what scheme you put forward, you cannot so safeguard it as to be absolutely sure that it will never work crookedly.

8650. In connection with your wish to secure real responsibility, you think the power of the Governor to disregard the opinion of his Ministers ought to be modified by a referendum? – Yes, I am a great believer in the referendum.

8651. The referendum has been usually adopted has it not, in the case of a well educated electorate? Would you consider that in its initial stage, at all events, an Indian electorate was sufficiently advanced for a referendum? – Well, I think it is a much simpler question to put to an electorate. "Will you have this particular measure or not?" It is a much simpler question to put to an ordinary man than the many different questions which will be on each plank, and out of which he will have to work out in his own mind so much in favour of one and so much in favour of the other. I think the referendum is more fit for an early stage. Because, historically, in England it did not happen to work in that way does not prove that the other is a more advanced way.

8652. We are not allowed to try it in this country, but you think it might be given in India? – Yes, and even in this country, as you know better than anybody else Lord Salisbury, Mr. Chamberlain and a lot of people have wanted it in the past. They have said many measures would never have got through except for the sake of other measures which people wanted. You know that as well as I do.

8653. You recognise that a great deal in this measure will be experimental? – Yes.

8654. Does not that affect your view at all with regard to

beginning by touching the position of the Central Government? – Well, I think in those particular subjects it will be very much better that it should be touched. I think it will have a vitalising effect on it.

8655. If you had Clauses 14 to 17, which affect the Central Government, would you prefer to have one Assembly or to have two – to have an Upper House, a Senate, or whatever it may be called – a Council of State? – I am an out-and-out Federalist for India. I am not very much taken up with the idea of the Government of India having two Houses. On the other hand, I realise that at this stage immediately real Federalism we are not prepared for. I will not say we are not prepared for it in India, but the people with whom the government of India ultimately lies are not ready to go in for that big scheme. Given those circumstances I would accept a Second House for the Government of India. Of course it is in the nature of a compromise between a hesitating policy on one side and an advanced policy on the other; there is no getting away from that.

8656. Which, in your opinion, would be best understood in India? It is obvious there must be cases in which both in the Provinces and in the Central Government the supreme authority will have to exercise its power. Is it best that where the supreme authority differs from the Legislative Council it should exercise its power directly or after consideration by a second body such as is proposed – a Grand Committee, or some other body? Which would you rather have? Which would be better understood in India? – I think it would be a protection for the Government to have an Upper House. I realise fully that it is a protection. They take the responsibility to a great extent. It is a shield really in a way. Personally, I think it depends very much on the measure. If it is a measure of foreign policy, or something like that, the Executive Authority could come in far more, but if it is a measure of home policy, my personal liking is entirely for the referendum. If you do not know which policy is really liked by the people, who will be the ultimate sufferers or gainers, go to them directly, and, even if they make mistakes, through those mistakes they will learn.

8657. Supposing the referendum were not adopted, do you think a direct veto by the official responsible, or a further consideration by interim bodies, would be an advantage? – Then, I think, the second House would be advantageous. I think it would be more constitutional, and more in keeping with the principles for which we are sitting here.

8658. I should like to ask you a general question about franchise: Do you think that the views of the Indian people generally will be best obtained by imitating our European system of franchise as far as it can be, or by a large use of communal representation? – I am a strong believer in communal representation. I think I was one of the active authors of getting it admitted long ago. I believe where the community is large enough, and where it wants it, it ought to get it. But that applies to minorities. If you want to protect a majority you must do it through the referendum. That is the only protection for a majority not to be misled by their representatives.

8659. I think your interests are not so much in Madras as in other parts. Therefore I will not carry you into that controversy; but, generally speaking, you think we shall get a better representation throughout India of the opinion of the people by communal representation? – I am convinced of it, and I am convinced that Indian nationality will come quicker and better and in a more wholesome way.

8660. You make a remarkable statement here in regard to the Bill being, in your opinion, too much in skeleton, and you say too much is left to rules to be made hereafter. The great object that I understand you have in view is that there should be certainty and stability? – Yes. I would not have every detail marked out, but I would go a little further than at present. The present one is very skeleton, as you see.

8661. Would you wish the powers in the Bill to be so far set out that there may be no suspicion in India that they may be modified or changed according to the feelings of any individual Secretary of State? – Yes; or I should say of any very small body of men, that it should not be possible for a handful out there, or two or three men here, practically to change it till it has no resemblance to any of the original ideas on which it was built.

8662. I think you have seen, unofficially, a good deal at the India Office, have you not? You have a good many communications with various Secretaries of State? – Yes; but my experience has not been in the general administration of the India Office.

8663. Have you noticed any want of touch with Indian opinion in the India Office? – It depends very much on the Secretary of State. I was myself a member of a Committee, as perhaps you know, that went into the question of the India

Office and I unhesitatingly signed the Majority Report. By that I stand, as far as the India Office is concerned.

8664. You say it depends very much on the Secretary of State? – Yes.

8665. You find some Secretaries of State more autocratic than others. Is that what you mean? – As to the autocratic part, of course, it is very difficult for a man who is not actually inside to know what their relations are with their Council. Even if he is not autocratic in his Council Chamber, when he comes out and speaks to a man who deals with him he is the Secretary of State. We do not know what circumstances brought about his opinions.

8666. At all events you signed the Majority Report? – I did.

8667. You fully recognise that whatever form Indian opinion takes it must be represented at the India Office for the benefit of Secretaries of State in some very definite form. If you dispense with the Council of India you cannot dispense with some similar body for advising. Is that your view? – Even that Majority Report is in the nature of a compromise. We had many discussions. The whole Bill from beginning to end is a tentative attempt. It is the first step. As a temporary measure the majority came to the conclusion that our proposals were the best way out. One of your Committee was a colleague of mine there.

8668. But you recognise, do you not, that the Secretary of State, as the representative of Parliament here, must retain a paramount power with regard to Indian affairs? – Well, I say always till responsible government is complete – till that time – till this reaches its logical end.

Mr. *Bennett.*

8669. You are. [*sic*] I see, a very convinced believer in the referendum? – Yes.

8670. May I say that it seems rather a hobby with you: would you admit that? – No. I have seen its working in Switzerland.

8671. Is it not one condition under which a referendum can be satisfactorily applied that the issue should be very definite and clear, and sharply cut? – Just now there is a very big question of the pay and conditions of labour in Switzerland. It is to be decided by the referendum in the next few weeks. That is a sufficiently diffuse question to be solved in that way.

8672. But if the referendum is to take the place of that second consideration which the Grand Committee or the

Council of State would give, is it not a procedure that would be a little too complicated for frequent use? – Of course it would be, for frequent use. I do not say that side by side with the referendum you cannot have a secondary body for the minor things.

8673. But you would not regard it, therefore, as a complete substitute for that second consideration? – No. In none of the countries where it has been tried has it been made complete; it has only been made a final decision.

8674. You do not suggest it as a substitute? – No, I suggest it as the final arbiter.

8675. Not to be frequently resorted to? – The initiative depends on the number of people who ask for it, and the referendum depends on the number by which it has been defeated, or the importance of the question. Those have been the lines on which it has been tried, and I believe it has been tried in some of the American states – in South America certainly.

8676. I need not say that you are a very convinced believer in communal representation? – That is so.

8677. As applied to cases in which it is clearly necessary? – Yes.

8678. But you do not put it forward as a good thing in itself? – Good in itself, for where? In India it is good in itself.

8679. But other things being equal, you would avoid it if you possibly could, would you not? – Of course I dare say in an ideal state I would avoid it, and I would avoid it, if I were German, in Germany.

8680. Having in view the necessity of creating a national feeling in India, you would avoid it, would you not? – No, I would bring it along, because I think it is through that that people will get confidence in order to take further steps toward national union.

8681. But the more you rely on communal representation the more you will be dependent upon it, will you not? – I do not think so. Look at the case of the Mohammedans. Mr. Gokhale, who was at first very doubtful about communal representation, ended his days by being a convinced believer in it, as far as Mohammedans were concerned. Why? Because he saw what happened in practice. He often told me that what led to it was Lord Lansdowne's first Bill. I often brought to his notice that with Lord Lansdowne's first Bill so complete was the separation of the Mohammedans from the Council that it left a feeling of grievance that led to opposition and to a certain amount of suspicion, and it was that, as he himself admitted, that led to the agitation of 1906–7–8. Since then things have worked much better.

8682. You do not agree, then, with the authors of the report, in looking forward to a time when the whole of the communities of India will be merged into one? – I think it is a pious wish. If the authors really thought that was the best they would have suggested it now.

8683. You are in favour of removing the disqualification which it is suggested should be placed upon women voting? – Yes.

8684. You are warmly in favour of that? – Yes; I would give women who have the same conditions the same advantages as men.

8685. Have you seen figures detailing the extent to which women in the Bombay Presidency have exercised the municipal vote? – I do not think, to begin with, the municipal vote is a thing to go by.

8686. No; but it is helpful so far as it goes, is it not? – Even in this country a lot of people do not use the municipal vote. You do not expect, in the first stage in India, that they should use the municipal vote on the same lines as the political vote. It is a great problem here, as you know.

8687. Take such a fact as this, for instance, that out of 1,598 women voters on the register in Bombay City 649 voted: You would regard that as an answer, so far as it goes, to the complaint that women would not exercise the vote – that the vote would be no use to women because they have not exercised it sufficiently? The percentage is 41 per cent.? – I think that is very good.

8688. Do you regard it as satisfactory? – Yes. I know European countries where, in a general election, you do not get that.

8689. It does not differ very much from the percentage of the whole of the voting in a general election in this country? – No. I had no idea it was so big as that.

8690. What do you mean by Federalism in India? Does that mean a Federation of Native States as well as British India? – Ultimately, yes. Ultimately I hope we shall take in many of the neighbouring States and bring them in as a sort of Zollverein working with the British Empire throughout the world; but, of course, these are dreams.

8691. There is no practical step in the direction of Federalism which you wish to take? – Yes. I say the more independence you give to these Provinces, to their Chambers, and to their electorates, and the more you can make each of them self-supporting, except in those wider military and economic questions, the sooner you will bring about Federalism.

8692. Do you think the present proposals go far enough in relaxing the control, more particularly financial, of the Government of India over the Provinces? – Personally, I do not. Personally I would like to see it as far as possible, but on the other hand I can understand the hesitation of the Government of India at this moment at the first step letting the reins get still looser.

8693. With regard to the Council of State, we have had a good deal of evidence pointing out the very unsatisfactory proposals at present before us, whereby the Council of State derives its origin from the same sources and the same electorate as the Legislative Assembly. Have you any definite proposal that you could put before us for an alternative method of selecting the Council of State? – The only way which I have suggested in a book which I wrote is, that the Council of State should more and more represent the Provinces directly. That is a step towards Federalism. That is what was tried in Germany, and is being now tried, I believe, in the new German constitution, and on a big scale in America and South America.

8694. Do you think there would be any serious objection in Indian opinion if, in the first period, the Council of State were nominated by the Provincial Governors, so many from each of the eight Provinces? – That is the system which prevailed in Germany up to its new constitution, as you know; each of the Federal Governments sent them as plenipotentiaries; they went really as Ministers of those Governments.

8695. Do you think there would be serious objection? Admittedly they would be nominated, and not have any electoral sanction behind them. If they were nominated by the Provincial Governors, what would you say to that? – That is very much the scheme I have sketched out in my own book. Of course, as an author one has a freedom which one has not when working with other people.

8696. In addition to the referendum you add the Initiative and the Recall? – Yes, the Initiative especially. I think it is very important.

8697. The Recall is what I want to ask you about? – I am not ready at this moment for that. I say ultimately the Recall. To begin with by "Recall" is understood one thing in America and different things in France and Switzerland and Italy, but the Initiative, I say, ought to go with the referendum; the two ought to go together.

8698. Has any education about the referendum taken place in the Indian Press – is it before the Indian public in any way? – No; but it is such a simple idea that I think it appeals to the looser Indian minds. From my own experience of Indians, my own countrymen with whom I have lived, I think, it is a thing which any class will understand.

8699. I have heard it suggested, turning to another question which you have been asked, the question of women franchise, that while both Mohammedan and Hindoo women would undoubtedly exercise the franchise in Bombay and Madras, in Northern India there would be far greater difficulties. Would you admit that it might be desirable to make a distinction between different Provinces of India with regard to women's franchise? – Certainly not, on the contrary, I say the only objection in regard to Northern India would be that they would not use the power. Well, let us see whether they would or they would no [*sic*]. Let us give them a chance. Why should we assume that they will not before it has been tried?

8700. I have heard it stated that a greater proportion of Hindoo women would exercise the franchise than Moham-medan women. Do you think that is true? – According to communal representation that would not affect it very much. The principle of communal representation is a protection for them.

8701. That would be an answer? – That is obvious, is it not? I see in England other causes stop women's suffrage from developing in the early stages. Into those causes I need not go.

8702. With regard to the report of the Crewe Committee, where you and I were colleagues, supposing we cannot get our proposals for an advisory Committee in lieu of a Council, would you rather have the Council kept, or would you rather abolish it altogether as Professor Keith says? – In our discussions I was one of those who were for absolute abolition, as you know. I accepted that as a compromise.

8703. And if we fail to get the compromise you would rather have the Council abolished? – Yes. I signed that Report, and I stand by that. But if it is left out it is quite a different question.

8704. I merely wanted to get your view on that particular point. Your reason is, that you think the existence of the Council tends to bring to Whitehall a large number of subjects which ought to be dealt with in India? – To a certain extent; and it gives the Secretary of State a sort of false security. He thinks he is in touch with direct opinion, when he may be only in touch with the indirect opinion. It is a bad atmosphere for him.

8705. Supposing we fail to get our advisory committee as we suggest in the Majority Report, and the Council is abolished, how would the Secretary of State get his Indian opinion in England? – I have great faith in the human element. I hope the Secretary of State will be generally a man of considerable ability and experience of various affairs. He may have been out in India, he may have seen people, and the means of communication in the future will be quicker necessarily, and you do not want him to be an expert. You want him to be a judge rather than an expert.

8706. You rather agree that during the first period of ten years the Secretary of State ought to have at his elbow almost a certain number of Indians who are in touch with Indian feeling and Indian thought independent of official communications? – That is, of course, our Joint Report. That is the scheme we bring forward, because he will have both sides. But if one side is to go I do not see how he can have the other. If the Secretary of State's Council goes I do not see how he can have Indian members on his Council.

Lord *Sinha.*

8707. On the question of Franchise, would your Highness consider that it is desirable to adhere to what is called the Lucknow Compact? – I do, on the question of Hindoo and Mohammedan, certainly.

8708. And it would be unwise to disturb that? – I would not touch it, and if the Mohammedans took anything else I would strongly advise them to stick to that.

8709. On the question of transferred subjects, would your Highness be in favour of education on the whole being transferred, or only a part being transferred to the Ministry? – I want education everywhere, including the Government of India, transferred, as you see.

8710. Yes, I have seen that. With regard to the Central Government, apart from the introduction of responsibility in the form that your Highness suggests, would you consider that it would go some way towards that object if we have an increase in the addition of Indian members in the Executive Council? The Report recommends two. If we have an increase in the Indian members, and especially the means of selection from amongst the members of the Legislative Council, would that go some way towards the scheme which your Highness recommends? – If we do not get responsibility in the Government of India, then certainly I would like to see half and half, and I think half and half is the minimum. Anything else would be a perpetuation of the present state of affairs.

8711. In your Highness's opinion would that give some amount of satisfaction to both Hindoo and Mohammedan public opinion in India if we fail to get any element of responsibility in the Central Government? – Yes; if you fail to get that, that is the next best.

8712. In your very interesting book "India in Transition" you wrote: "Responsible government in the narrow and technical sense in which Mr. Montagu's announcement has been interpreted in some quarters has really been successful alone in the United Kingdom, and there only up to a certain point," and then you went on to show how badly it has worked elsewhere, and you say "It would be a disaster to India to be forced into the narrow form of constitutionalism that has developed with its essential condition of two rival parties"? – Yes.

8713. Do you realise fully that it is responsible government, in that narrow technical sense, which you so strongly condemn, that has brought us into the dual system with all the many attendant evils which we all feel? – The answer to that is the preamble here. We are dealing with English people. It is they who have got the future of India in their hands. Our destiny is not our own to say: "This is the plebiscite," or "This is the system and we will take it." Given the fact that the English historical development took this line, and that we have been 150 years with them, we will have on the one hand to work that system, and on the other hand right it as it goes along.

666

That is how constitutions have developed in other countries, too. As to the evils, for instance, in some countries, like Spain and France, to which I have referred, at this moment there are great movements in both countries to right them. I think that will come through the people as it goes along.

8714. Your general view is that India must seek progress in conformity with English views and English institutions. Now do you not agree that neither in this, nor in any civilised country in the world, would anyone dream of setting up a divided Cabinet? – There is no other country of three hundred millions governed by forty millions 5,000 miles away. You must take facts as they are. The whole thing goes together. We are here. There is no getting out of it. It is a purely problematical development. There it is. There are the facts before one. We cannot be logical and illogical.

8715. Do you think it is wise to introduce into the preamble of the Bill the term "Responsible government" in its narrow technical sense, which you have stigmatised? – Of course, if I had had the making of the declaration I would have put "self-government," but it was not I who did that. It was not my job.

8716. Would you prefer that the Bill should be amended, and point to the better government of India or something of that sort? – Well, "Better government" is a term which has been associated with so many Irish Home Rule Bills. I have seen so many of them go in and out that I would not touch that point. I have seen three of them in my own short life – "Better Government of Ireland" Bills.

8717. You have pointed out that we have made the very great mistake in the past of limiting the right of representation to the "richest and most educated" of the population, and you say it is owing to that most serious error that "national conservatism, which is necessary to the evolution of the modern state, has been artificially prevented from making its voice effectively heard." To remove that, you propose that each of the various religions and races as recorded in the census would provincially be a *milit*, to use the Turkish term, and each would have a fair share in the Assembly directly elected? – Yes.

8718. That is your view as to communal representation, with which you are heartily in sympathy? – Yes.

8719. Now, taking the case of Bombay, where there are five million Mahrattas, who have supplied us with fine fighting men during the war, and who have sent in a powerful plea for special representation, would you give it to them? – Personally, I would give it to anybody who wants it, and who are numerous enough to ask for it. If they are a majority that protection would be by the referendum as I foresee it. That is the real protection for the majority from being misled by a small handful, who might get in on a wave of enthusiasm, and misrepresent their electorate.

8720. The Government of India has pointed out that the representation of the depressed classes under the Southborough Committee's Report is inadequate. There are 60,000,000 of these people, as you know, and they do some of the most essential work of India. Do you think they should have it? – Certainly. I would make the franchise as wide as possible.

8721. Do you consider it vital that the agriculturists and working classes should be liberally represented, having regard to the fact that they provide nearly the whole of the revenue? – Certainly. I have advocated that throughout in my books and writings.

8722. Do you think that if we are to obtain real Indian opinion those classes, and those special classes to which you have referred, should be represented as far as possible by their own people? – Yes. Of course in the case of labour people guilds and so on could be made. A great deal of that must develop as we go along.

8723. You have strongly advocated the enfranchisement of women. My information is that that would be resented by large numbers of high caste Hindoos and by orthodox Moslems. Is that wrong? – How could they resent it? The Moslems have not resented them having the right to property for 1,300 years. In Moslem countries they have the rights of citizenship.

8724. Is not that rather a different matter? – Why should they resent it? I cannot imagine that it should be an insult to a woman to give her the right to vote. It gives her that human dignity which goes with it.

8725. I do not think it is a question of an insult; but your opinion is strongly that it would not be resented? – I am certain of that. I think the other way round would be resented, and the resentment would come on England and not on anybody else. It would make a cause of dissatisfaction in the home, as far as I can see.

8726. Do you not think it is rather a delicate matter for a Government to deal with, because it really might look like an interference with the social and religious customs of India? –

Then you would have to do away with all the legal system; you would have to do away with all sorts of things.

8727. You know that a very strong feeling has been aroused about the Inter-caste Marriages Bill, and the Government has been attacked merely for publishing and circulating that Bill. Do you not think it would be better, therefore, that the Government should stand aside from this Women's Franchise question and leave it entirely in the hands of the new Council? – No, I do not. The two things are not on all fours at all – the Inter-caste Marriage Bill and the other question. The difference is enormous. One is giving a woman a right to protect her property. I have heard any number of purdah women say in the past that expenses were run up by men in the municipalities, and they, the women, had to pay the taxes.

8728. You would not be satisfied to leave that question to be decided by the representatives of the people themselves? – If you immediately make a referendum in India I would not mind it, but there is no likelihood of that, so you ought to take the responsibility, if you take the responsibility of all the rest.

8729. You have spoken very strongly about the referendum. Do you know any country in approximately similar conditions to India in which the referendum has been adopted? – In Switzerland there are four different languages, and no religions hate each other so much as those which are very near to each other, like the Calvinists and some other Protestants out there. There are the Catholic French and the Protestant French. It is the most divided country in Europe. My own experience has been that the referendum is one of the things which has kept them together.

8730. But there are not 80 per cent. of uneducated people in Switzerland? – But you are not giving the vote to 80 per cent., are you?

8731. Not at first? – You do not give the referendum to them either.

8732. Have you considered the machinery and expenditure which will be required to take the referendum from 5,200,000 people scattered about all over India? – I do not know; you could do it through the Post Office, like the Savings Bank, you know.

8733. Do you think that a referendum worked through the

Post Office would be free from fraud on a huge scale? – The Savings Bank system has not been full of fraud, has it?

8734. There are not 5,200,000 people who are dealing with the Savings Bank, and surely there is no analogy between those two cases? – People bring letters in. I do not see the difference between putting them in and putting the other in.

8735. Now you know so well what false rumours can do in India: all the troubles in the Punjab and the very sad loss of life which accompanied them were really due to falsehoods circulated about the Rowlatt Bill –

Mr. *Montagu.*] I do not want to interrupt Lord Sydenham, but a Commission has been appointed to inquire what the causes of the Punjab troubles were, and I should very much prefer that the form of the question should be altered – if Lord Sydenham will say "it was alleged."

Lord *Sydenham.*

8736. I will say it is alleged. (To the *Witness.*) Would it not be possible by those means to vitiate what might seem to be a simple issue on a referendum? – No; I think the simpler it is the less people are liable to be led away by rumours – the simpler the question put. And as to the Punjab, I have not been there, and I want to see what the causes were.

8737. In your book I think you deprecate two Chambers in the Central Government after the short transitional period? – Yes.

8738. Have you modified that view at all? – In my book I have advocated Federalism, after which their duties will be reduced enormously. When their duties are reduced enormously, I modify my views. When it is a Federal Assembly, including Afghanistan, Persia, Thibet and Siam, I would modify my views.

8739. Do you not think that setting up two Chambers now might prejudice your ultimate Federal scheme of a single Chamber? – I think as time goes on, as the Provincial things develop, the second Chamber will gradually have less and less work to do.

8740. It will ultimately disappear of inanition? – Yes; and become a sort of Foreign Affairs Committee.

8741. What you contemplate after the transition period is federation, in which all the major States join? – Yes; the Indian States.

8742. Do you really think the chiefs of those great States would ever abandon the powers they now possess in order to enter the federation? – The powers put forward in my book they do not possess now, except in a very minor way. The Post Office, for instance, they do not possess now.

8743. You realise nobody can enter the federation without abandoning powers? – Yes; but they do not possess those.

8744. There are particular powers they do not possess now? – Yes; so I do not see where they would lose.

Lord *Brodrick* (Viscount Midleton).
8745. Are you speaking of the powers as to Foreign policy? – Yes; and the Post Office.

Lord *Sydenham.*
8746. In the future you are looking forward to a very great Eastern Federation, including Afghanistan, Persia, and a few other places? – Yes.

8747. I am sure you realise that a Federal constitution is the most difficult of all to work, and that it is only possible when the component parts are on the same level of advancement? – I do not see that.

8748. You do not think so? – No. I have known the United States. It is not on the same level all over.

Mr. *Montagu.*
8749. Have you discussed the referendum idea with any other Indians? – No.

8750. Have you ever heard it mooted from Indian sources? – I have suggested it to the late Mr. Gokhale and others, and I have told Lord Sinha about it. I have often suggested it to them.

8751. Is it really a very simple question – I mean that which the voter has to decide? – It is in Switzerland and some of the American States, and in Australia. It is the sort of thing the Indian mind, as I know it or as I imagine I know it, would understand.

8752. Do you think it is really a simpler problem to the man who receives a referendum paper to vote for a Bill rather than to vote for a man? – I think so.

8753. Do you think the electors in this country would have

found, for instance, the issues of the late strike a simple question to decide? – Would that have ever gone to a referendum?

8754. I was only asking you whether it is always a simple question which has to be decided in a referendum; that is all. The second question I wanted to put to you was this. Supposing your idea of Federalism in India were to come about, the Central Government would gradually have fewer and fewer powers: Would it ever disappear altogether? – No, because for foreign affairs, military, postal, possibly aerial communications, and so on, it would have to go on.

8755. Meanwhile, the Provinces would have more and more to do? – Exactly.

8756. And the scheme which is known as diarchy is only applicable, is it not, to a Government which has a considerable number of powers left to it? – Naturally, yes.

8757. Therefore, is it not true to say that diarchy may never be necessary or expedient in the Central Government? – At present the Central Government keeps so many powers at this first stage.

8758. What sort of power have you in your mind that the Central Government has still to keep that it will not keep eventually? – For instance, education: They have still a finger in that pie.

8759. Under the scheme of the Bill, and Mr. Feetham's Committee's Report, it is a very little finger, is it not? – There is a certain amount in irrigation, and so on. If that finger were abolished, my hesitation would also be diminished to that extent.

8760. With regard to women's suffrage, is it your idea that arrangements should be made for women in purdah to vote? – Special arrangements?

8761. Yes? – I do not know what in normal cases is done in the Law Courts, but I would not go further than that. I would not give them more protection than they have now in insisting on their property rights.

8762. What sort of matter which it is proposed to deal with by rule would you like to deal with in the Bill? – I meant more enfranchising powers.

8763. Supposing that on questions of that kind this Committee were to report upon the policy that ought to be embodied in the rule, and their report was accepted by both

Houses of Parliament, would not that remove the vagueness of the Bill? – That would, and that is what I have put that in for as urging the very measure you suggest.

Sir *Henry Craik.*

8764. Would you apply this referendum to all-India matters as well as to Provincial matters? – At the first initial stage I would keep it to the Provinces.

8765. Perhaps the difficulties of a referendum over three millions of people might appal one? – No; it is not that, when we see how well public utility services go on over vast areas.

8766. You must recognise that the proportion of voters in the referendum in Switzerland is much larger than it would be in India? – Yes.

8767. You have only something like 1 or 2 per cent. of the population voting, and a large number even of those who vote are not literate in India? – Yes; and many perhaps would not vote.

8768. So that you would only have about 1 or 2 per cent. of the population voting in this referendum, and of that 1 per cent., about four-fifths would be illiterate? – Those are the facts of Indian life to-day.

8769. That makes a certain distinction between it and Switzerland, you admit? – If a man is intelligent enough to see all for which a candidate stands –

8770. Still, the mere fact that he is illiterate, and it would have to be explained to him, means it must go through some other person's hands? – They only put a cross in any country, either for or against.

8771. You think a question could be put so plainly that a cross would give a vote? – Well, the plank on which a man elects to stand.

8772. I understand you do not contemplate the application of it to all questions? – No. The whole Bill is tentative.

8773. Now about communal representation. While you are in favour of it, you admit the difficulties and evils which are pointed out so strongly in the Joint Report, paragraph 231? – Certainly, I would not have put those evils in that strong way.

8774. But you admit it is contrary to the general principles of popular representation? However desirable in this case it may be, it is inconsistent with that? – No; I do not think so. I cannot see the inconsistency.

8775. Then you rather differ from the Report? – On that particular point.

8776. What is your opinion as to the form which communal representation should take? Would you be disposed to accept the nomination as suggested in paragraph 232 of the Joint Report as a means of getting communal representation? – No.

8777. You are against that? – Yes; I am against nomination.

8778. Are you in favour of the principle of having a certain number of seats allotted, earmarked as it were, for each community? – For each community, yes.

8779. That they should have a number of seats, the occupants of which must belong to that community? – That is the practice of communal representation.

8780. But, of course, there is another, that instead of reserving a certain number of seats you should have special voting lists? – No; I want the seats.

8781. You want the seats; you do not want special voting lists? – No; the system of the Lucknow understanding.

8782. The form of communal representation your Highness would like is not nomination and not special electoral lists, but the reserving of a certain number of seats? – Yes. I am not in a position to say there may not be one or two small communities here and there which at first may need nomination; but it would be on such a small scale.

8783. And in every case reserved seats; in no case special lists? – That is so.

Sir J. D. Rees.

8784. Does the referendum which you recommend connote an increased electorate, or do you recommend it for the Southborough electorates, which you accept? – I accept the Southborough electorate, as I accept the whole Bill, as a practical compromise out of the difficulties of the present time.

8785. But in that case? – In that case I accept it for the electorate.

8786. The referendum is designed to avoid the necessity for frequent elections? – Yes; for general elections; and also people saying that a man has got in on certain planks and then used his powers for quite different and other objects. That is the great argument for it.

8787. Are the Mahrattas of Bombay generally Hindoo cultivators? – I have known Mahrattas of that class.

8788. What is the majority of them? – They would be cultivators – they must be.

8789. Are they widely different from the cultivators elsewhere. Is there any special difference attached to Mahrattas, economic, or religious? – No; but the language is different, as you know.

8790. Is there any distinguishing characteristic, economic or religious? – I do not know much about the inner religious differences of Hindoos. I am not in a position to say.

8791. From your knowledge of Bombay, do you see anything distinctive about Mahrattas which would call for particular special representation? – Well, as a matter of fact, where I have lived all my life everybody is a Mahratta who is not a non-Mahratta.

8792. You do not see any particular reason? – No.

8793. Are they a particularly depressed class? – No; I should not have said so.

8794. Are they oppressed? – No; they are like all the other peasants.

8795. May I ask if, amongst the Mohammedans in India, it is at all a usual feature for the higher classes to ill-treat or oppress or treat with contempt the lower classes? – No.

8796. Are the Hindoos less kindly people than the Mohammedans? – No.

8797. Do you accept the picture, which has often been placed before the Committee, of Hindoo society being of such a character that the upper classes and castes – of course, there is that distinction – oppress the lower classes and castes? – No; not oppress.

8798. You do not accept it? – Personally, I do not like the idea of classes and castes; but that is a different thing.

8799. You are in favour of communal representation. Do you approve of the reservation of a large proportion of the general seats for non-Brahmins, Brahmins being a mere small fraction of the population? – You say "non-Brahmins"; I do not know what people mean by that, because it means Mohammedans, it means Parsees, it means native Christians.

8800. I will say non-Brahmin Hindoos? – There again, as far as I can see, that would include all kinds of Hindoos. Do you mean the depressed classes or the trading people?

Lord *Sinha*] There are 155 different classes, we are told.

Sir *J. D. Rees.*

8801. I gather you would answer my question in the negative. Do you approve of the special reservation of a large proportion of the general seats provided for non-Brahmin Hindoos? – No.

8802. With regard to the enfranchisement of women, without raising the question of principle at all, I know your opinions from your book and evidence. Have you explored Mohammedan opinion? Is your opinion as representative on this point as one would be inclined to think? – I will tell you one of the things which brought me early in life to think that the municipal suffrage should be given, namely, the complaints of purdah women and other Moslem ladies about the fact that they have no way of protecting their rights with regard to taxation.

8803. I was not on the principle. I wanted to ask you how far you had explored Mohammedan and Hindoo opinion. I specially excluded the merits of it? – I thought that was an answer, because if they were not in favour of it they would not have complained.

8804. Did you receive complaints from Mohammedans and Hindoos to any great extent? – No; but such people as I have seen in the course of my life have constantly complained.

8805. An objection has been raised to female suffrage on the ground of the purdah, that it would be difficult for purdah women to record their vote. I would like to ask you whether a widespread misapprehension does not exist in this country as to the extent to which the purdah prevails in India? – Yes, I think so.

8806. Is it not the case that purdah is a Mohammedan institution which has only been adopted out of imitation, or because the Mohammedans were the ruling race, by the rich amongst the Hindoos? – I do not admit the first part that purdah is a Mohammedan institution. It is a very old and ancient one in the East generally – in China. That is why I would not answer that without putting that reservation.

8807. Subject to that? – Subject to that I say it is by no means common amongst Hindoos except in certain parts of India.

8808. Is it not exceedingly uncommon? – Yes.

8809. Most rare? – Yes, except in Rajputana I have never seen it.

Lord *Brodrick* (Viscount *Midleton*).] The Secretary of State wanted to ask one question with regard to the answers which you gave Sir Henry Craik.

Mr. *Montagu.*

8810. Perhaps I am wrong, but I am a little afraid there was some confusion between you and Sir Henry Craik. He put to you this question: Do you prefer communal representation by separate electorates or by the reservation of seats, and you replied, by the reservation of seats as in the Lucknow Compact? – Yes, by separate electorates, reserving the seats for them – the two together.

8811. Then let me repeat the question which I think Sir Henry Craik had in mind in order to get it clear. There are two proposals for insuring minority representation; one is by maintaining the general electorate, and reserving seats in a plural constituency? – Oh, no, the other way round. I beg your pardon; I am very much obliged to you.

8812. I thought some of your Mohammedan friends in India might object? – That is my conviction. I am very sorry I misunderstood.

Mr. *Spoor.*

8813. You state here in the first paragraph of your Memorandum, "Our future is linked with Great Britain," and you refer to the fact that for the last century and a half our English institutions have been moulding Indian political ideas? – Yes.

8814. Now it has been suggested – in fact I believe it has been stated by one witness – that it is regarded as an object of the Bill that British influence and British control should be in the course of time entirely eliminated from India, or that as a matter of fact that would be the tendency if this Bill is passed, that more and more British control and British influence and British prestige, I suppose, would decline. Do you share that opinion? – Not at all. I think it would improve the prestige as I understand it for righteousness and honour and justice, and that is the only prestige I would accept.

8815. But so far as British control is concerned, I take it you would admit it is inevitable that that would lessen as time went on? – Yes. That is the Preamble of the Bill, is it not?

8816. And that in consequence of that the tendency will be for India to develop her own political institutions rather than to continue to copy ours – that is necessarily copy ours? – Yes. As they saw where your institutions did not fit in in practice they would be modified.

8817. You seem also to be of opinion that even at the start the electorates should be made as wide as possible. Are you of opinion that the proposed electorate is in any degree satisfactory, even at the beginning? – As you know, a Commission was sent out; they studied things on the spot; they suggested this as a compromise. It is very difficult for one man who has not seen all the facts and so on, to say: "Well, I do not approve of this; go so much further," or "so much less."

8818. But in your opinion it is apparently desirable that the electorates should be extended? – As wide as possible.

8819. We have had it suggested in the course of the Committee's sittings that it might be possible to include a larger number of industrial workers? – Yes.

8820. From your experience of India, do you think that this is practicable? – I should welcome it if it were practicable.

8821. What is your opinion of that proposed method by which it could be done? One method proposed was that the basis of qualification for the franchise might be the earning capacity of workers. Do you think that is a practicable and desirable scheme? – I do not know enough about how it would work. I do not know how you could do it, in order to be able to reply, "Yes" or "No," but if it can be worked it would be a very good thing.

8822. You agree as to the desirability of including as many of the workmen as possible? – Yes; and as wide a franchise as possible in the interests of all concerned.

8823. In your fourth paragraph you speak of Bombay and the other two Presidencies, and you express the opinion that all distinctively provincial work could be safely left to the control of the electorate? – Yes.

8824. Would you recommend what has already been proposed here, that complete provincial autonomy might be tried in certain cases and diarchy in others so that the two experiments could run side by side? – In Bombay I would welcome it. In Bombay, my own Province, I would say we are perfectly fit to run our own show, but that might raise opposition in other Provinces.

8825. Do you think that as far as Bombay is concerned, and probably the other two Presidencies, it would be practicable? – In provincial matters, yes, in Bombay.

8826. With reference to Budget control, you are of opinion that the restrictions embodied in Clause 9 are unnecessarily severe so far as Bombay and Bengal are concerned? – Yes.

8827. Do you not think that complete Budget control throughout the Provinces is desirable if you are to have any really effective measure of self-government? – I am certain about Bombay that complete Budgetary liberty is necessary.

8828. I take it that what would apply to Bombay would apply with equal force to other Provinces that may have reached a similar standard? – Yes.

8829. With regard to the question which Lord Midleton referred to, and Mr. Montagu also, in paragraph 18 of your Memorandum, as to the lack of definiteness in the Bill, do you think that there is any degree of danger in that lack of definiteness? I mean so far as it is unsatisfying to Indian public opinion? – Mr. Montagu corrected it in suggesting that this Committee might make certain proposals to remove that lack of definiteness, and make it a little less skeleton, and if that came in the body of the Bill, that would, of course, remove that trouble.

8830. In the event of the suggestion which Mr. Montagu has made, and which some of us hope will be adopted, not being adopted, do you think there is any degree of danger in the fact that the Bill is merely a skeleton? – Yes; I think so. I think it would very much take off the advantages of the Bill.

8831. It would contribute to continued agitation in India? – Yes; it would be the cause of legitimate disapproval.

8832. There is only one last question; I hope Lord Midleton will allow it: It is with reference to your proposal for progress towards Federalism in India. You have great faith in the Federal system. In this scheme of yours would you agree to the inclusion of Burma in the present Bill? The Committee has been asked by Burma's delegates if Burma could not be included in the Bill. Having regard to your idea that in the course of time the tendency will be towards Federalism over the whole of

India, do you think that at the present juncture it would be desirable that Burma should be included? – Well, of course, I am a strong believer that Burma ought to have been included from the first. Apart from Federalism, from the few occasions I have been in Burma that is the conclusion I came to long ago, that any attempt to separate Burma from India is a wrong step.

Lord *Brodrick* (Viscount Midleton.] We are very much obliged to your Highness for your evidence.

(The Witness is directed to withdraw.)

Source: *Joint Select Committee on the Government of India Bill, Vol. II: Minutes of Evidence,* ordered by the House of Commons to be printed, 17 November 1919, His Majesty's Stationery Office, London, 1919, pp. 487–96.

The Committee consisted of the Earl of Selborne, Duke of Northumberland, Marquess of Crewe, Lord Brodrick (Viscount Midleton), Lord Islington, Lord Sydenham, Lord Sinha, F. D. Acland, Bennett (initials not given), Sir Henry Craik, E. S. Montagu, Sir J. D. Rees, Spoor (initials not given) and Major Ormsby-Gore. On 10 October, when the Aga Khan appeared before the Committee, only the following members were present: Lord Brodrick (in the Chair), Lord Sydenham, Lord Sinha, Bennett, Sir Henry Craik, E. S. Montagu, Major Ormsby-Gore, Sir J. D. Rees, and Spoor.

The Committee met 29 times between 16 July and 15 October and heard 69 witnesses. The report of the Joint Select Committee was published in November 1919 by His Majesty's Stationery Office, London.

On the making of the 1919 reforms see the command papers bearing the numbers Cd. 9109 and 9178, and Cmd. 103, 123, 141, 175, 176, 187, 207, 228, 234, 433, 610, 724, 757, 764, 765, 768, 812, 813, 814 and 974; E. S. Montagu, *An Indian Diary,* ed. by Venetia Montagu, London, 1930; "Constitutional Reform in India", *Round Table,* September 1919; H. E. A. Cotton, "Constitutional Reform in India", *Contemporary Review,* July 1919; A. H. L. Fraser, "Indian Constitutional Reforms", *Contemporary Review,* January 1919; Bernard Houghton, "The Federation of India", *Political Science Quarterly,* June 1919; "National Mismanagement, IV: The New Indian Constitution", *Spectator,* 6 December 1919; H. L. Stephen, "The Proposed Indian Reforms", *Empire Review,* March 1919; Harold Stuart, "Constitutional Changes in India: Views of Mr. Montagu and Lord Chelmsford Examined", *Empire Review,* April 1919; "The India Bill", *New Statesman,* 7 June 1919; "The Indian Legislative Council", *Round Table,* December 1919; "The Indian Reform Bill", *Spectator,* 14 June 1919.

The Times of 11 October 1919 carried a fairly detailed report of the Aga Khan's evidence before the Joint Select Committee under the headlines: "Indian Reform: Aga Khan's Criticisms of the Bill: Qualified Support."

51

THE DIMENSIONS OF THE TURKISH PROBLEM

*A Memorial to the Prime Minister of England
on Behalf of His Majesty's Muslim Subjects*

London: 12 December 1919

Imperative necessity of appeasing Turkey – a united Indian demand – causes of apprehension – the future of Asia Minor – the solidarity of Islam – dismemberment of Turkey will be an outrage – mandate on Turkey rejected – Turkish suzerainty over Hejaz – a strong Turkey in British imperial interest.

Sir,

1. In view of the ferment and general unrest prevailing among the Muslim nations all over the world, we, the undersigned British and British-Indian subjects of His Majesty, feel it our duty to urge respectfully on His Majesty's Government the imperative necessity of a policy towards Turkey that would lead to appeasement. This ferment, which in some parts has taken a violent form of expression, is mainly due to the universal apprehension that it is proposed to further dismember the Turkish Empire and to completely destroy the free life and political power of the few remaining Muslim states.

2. Although we are not afraid at present of any untoward consequences, we are convinced that the perpetuation of the existing bitterness among our Muslim fellow-subjects in India would seriously retard the peaceful progress and development of the country. And it is for this reason that the efforts of the Indian Muhammadans to urge upon His Majesty's Government the fulfilment, Sir, of your memorable pledge (of January 1918) have met with so much sympathy among the Hindu community.

3. The three causes which have primarily created the apprehen-

sion and ferment referred to in the preceding paragraph are, firstly, the belief that in violation of the pledges which secured the adhesion of Islamic peoples to the Allies in the World War, it is proposed to sever from Turkey provinces and districts predominantly inhabited by the Turkish people; secondly, that it is intended to impose a suzerainty (by whatever name it may be called) over the Turkish sovereign which would fundamentally affect his status and prestige as the religious and spiritual head of the largest portion of the Islamic world; and thirdly that it is designed as is suggested in the press to retain the protectorate of the Sacred Cities of Islam in non-Muslim hands, which would be in absolute conflict with the religious laws of the Muslims.

4. In our opinion, it is perfectly possible for His Majesty's Government to meet on all these points the wishes, and to remove the apprehensions, of the King's Muslim subjects, and thus bring about appeasement and create afresh the old steadfastness without distracting in the smallest degree from its power, prestige or authority, or militating against the main objects of the Allies.

5. With regard to the first ground of complaint, we beg to make the following remarks: Mesopotamia, Syria and Palestine are proposed to be detached from the Turkish Empire on the ground that they are predominantly inhabited by non-Turkish Muslims intermixed with other communities. This expropriation is proposed with the avowed object of giving the people of these provinces autonomous Governments of their own choosing. The same principle has been applied to Hedjaz, and the Sherif of Mecca has been made the King of that part of Arabia which acknowledged allegiance to the Turkish state.

6. But none of these considerations apply to Asia Minor (Turkey proper), extending from the Aegean Sea to the confines of Persian Kurdistan, or to Thrace (the *Vilayet* of Adrianople), or to Constantinople. The question under reference has, it is respectfully submitted, been confused by fallacious arguments and still more fallacious figures. An impartial inquiry by an Allied Commission would incontestably prove the correctness of our assertions, which are based on the official statistics for the year 1914, anterior to the War and long before there could be any reason to manufacture or manipulate figures. In that year the population of Constantinople, leaving out odd numbers, stood, according to nationality and faith, as follows:

Muslims, 560,000; Greeks, 205,000; Armenians, 82,000. We

believe no appreciable variation has taken place since. In the *Vilayet* of Adrianople the population stood as follows:

Muslims, 560,000; Greeks, 224,000; Armenians, 19,000. In the Sandjak of the Dardanells [*sic*]:

Muslims, 149,000; Greeks, 8,000; Armenians, 2,000. Asia Minor, speaking subject to correction, consists of 29 *vilayets* of which Smyrna or Aidin, with the support of Smyrna on the Aegean, is the most important. In this *vilayet* the population numbered as follows:

Muslims, 1,249,000; Greeks, 299,000; Armenians, 20,000. We have learnt with horror from credible sources that since the Greek invasion nearly 10,000 Muslims have been killed, large numbers are missing, and over 100,000 are homeless refugees.

7. In the face of the above facts we can hardly bring ourselves to believe that His Majesty's Government or the Supreme Council would be disposed to tear any part of these territories away from the Turkish nation, to whom they belong, not merely by ties of race and religion but also from the fact that Muslims form the preponderant element in the population. Even in the Eastern Districts the unifying effects of a common faith, common ideals, and common religious traditions have produced between Muslims of different stocks a solidarity the strength of which it would be rash to under-estimate.

8. We beg respectfully to submit that the attempt to sever these districts from Turkey would conflict with all the basic principles on which the Allies and Associated Powers have rested the righteousness of their cause, and it would be an outrage on humanity and every principle of justice. The utmost the minority is entitled to ask is equal treatment and equal rights and protection against injustice and wrong and that object, in our opinion, can be more fully assured by other and wiser methods. A violent disruption of the existing status, or the forcible expatriation of the vast majority of Muslims, would inevitably lead to trouble, the end of which cannot be foreseen, and would intensify the present ferment and keep it alive for generations.

9. With regard to the idea of imposing a "mandate" on Turkey, in plainer words, placing her under the suzerainty of some foreign Power, the signatories to this memorial consider that it would be a deliberate and gratuitous insult to Muslim religious feeling, the result of which could be disastrously mischievous to the interests of our Empire, as it would permanently alienate from us our Muslim fellow-subjects. The object in view, in our

opinion, can be fully obtained by adopting a magnanimous policy towards Turkey. If the policy towards her on the present occasion is magnanimous and untinged by any suspicion of vindictiveness, we believe that Turkey would renew her application for the service of competent Englishmen, which England refused before in deference to the wishes of the late Czar's Government. The influence of the British Ambassador in Constantinople, combined with that of European and American specialists whose services we believe would, after a just and equitable peace be freely invoked by the Turkish Government in the world of resuscitation and the re-organization of their country, would be a sure guarantee for peaceful consolidation.

10. Regarding Mecca and Medina, we consider that it would be most unwise and highly detrimental to the interests of our world-wide Empire to claim or to exercise, directly or indirectly, a protectorate over them. We venture to suggest that while the administration of these Sacred Cities might be left in the charge of the autonomous Government of Hedjaz, in order to legitimise the position of its ruler in the eyes of the vast Sunni population of the world, he should receive, as the representative of their spiritual head, his investiture from the Caliph-Sultan.

11. Finally, we desire to express our conviction that in view of the fact that England holds in her hands the destinies of vast millions of people in Asia, and, since the War ended, has taken charge of many more millions, it behoves her not to overlook the dangers that threaten and have always threatened her dominancy from the north. Whether Russia and the great territories she claims in Asia are Bolshevist or Czarist, we consider that the danger will always be the same. We believe that the existence of a strong Turkey would form a barrier against this ever-present danger, the value of which it would be the greatest mistake to overlook.

We have the honour to be, Sir,

your most obedient servants,

The Rt. Hon. the Earl of Abingdon.

H. H. the Aga Khan, G.C.S.I.

The Rt. Hon. Lord Ampthill, G.C.S.I., G.C.I.E.

The Rt. Hon. Sayyid Ameer Ali, P.C., C.I.E.

A. S. M. Anik, Esq.

Sir Mancherjee M. Bhovanagree, K.C.I.E.

Lt.-Col. E. J. Bridges.

Captain F. N. Bennett, J.P.

The Hon. S. M. Bhurgari.

K. N. Bahl, Esq., Oxford.
Lady Evelyn Cobbold.
John D. Cobbold, Esq., J.P.
Major-General J. B. B. Dikson, C.B., C.M.G.
Captain C. F. Dixon-Johnson.
Col. W. Bromley Davenport, J.P., D.L., D.S.O.
Jamnadas Dwarkadas, Esq.
Admiral the Rt. Hon. Sir Edmund R. Fremantle, G.C.B., C.M.G.
Major-General Lord Edward Gleichen, K.C.V.O., C.M.G., D.S.O.
Captain E. H. Griffin, D.S.O.
Jafferbhoy Ghulamhussain, Esq.
Muhammadbhoy Ghulamhussain, Esq.
The Hon. Mr. Yacoob Husain.
Shaikh Abdul Hamid (of Sialkot), Esq.
John J. Hogg, Esq., O.B.E.
Sir J. G. Harbottle, Milburn.
T. W. Harries, Esq.
The Rt. Hon. Lord Parmoor, P.C.
M. H. Ispahani, Esq.
Lt.-Col. D. C. Phillott, M.A., Ph.D.
The Hon. Philip C. T. Ritchie.
Dr. D. Kalyanwala, M.R.C.I.
W. O'Sullivan Molony, Esq.
Sir Theodore Morison, K.C.I.E.
Julian A. B. Palmer, Esq.
George Palmer, Esq.
Marmaduke Pickthall, Esq.
R. V. Reynolds, Esq.
Gordon Roy, Esq.
A. W. Stanton, Esq.
H. Seppings Wright, Esq.
Maulvi Sadruddin.
Captain E. F. H. Smith.
K. P. Kotwal, Esq.
Percy Stephens, Esq.
O. Sunthralingam, Esq.
Rev. McDougall, Esq. [*sic*.]
Nanak Chand, Esq.
Abdul Hamid, Esq.
M. H. Kidwai, Esq.
M. Seth, Esq.

Source: *The Indian Annual Register 1921*, Calcutta, n.d., Part I, pp. 145–8.
    This memorial is to be read as a precursor of the Khilafat Conference. It

contains nearly every argument which the Indian Muslims later used in support of their demands.

It speaks volumes for the Aga Khan's concern for Turkey and his influence in Britain that he could persuade so many distinguished Britons to sign the memorial.

52

THE FUTURE OF INDIA

Speech at a Dinner in Honour of E. S. Montagu

London: 19 December 1919

The Montagu-Chelmsford reforms "a leap out of the dark" – tribute to the Secretary of State for India – public opinion has been stirred by the events in Amritsar – the future of Turkey and other Muslim states of concern to Muslims in India – Hindus join Muslims in asking for a generous peace settlement with Turkey – the British Prime Minister's assurance regarding Turkey two years ago – a community of interest in making the reforms successful – the Indian desire for a legitimate place ultimately as an equal partner in a confederation of nations.

The reforms with responsibility definitely fixed between the various elements in the administration, are not a leap in the dark, but a leap out of the dark. There are many Indians – and I am one of them – who would gladly have gone farther in some respects, but patriotism and wisdom call us to accept the Act as it stands as a vindication of Centre opinion and reasonable compromise. We acclaim the chief author in the Secretary of State whom we know and trust as a passionate lover and clear-sighted friend of India, and we rejoice in the triumph he has won by making the compromise so excellent.

While we hail the rising sun of India's new day, we cannot be blind to certain lowering clouds on the morning sky. It is to be deeply regretted that the week which has seen the passing of the Bill in the House of Lords has also seen public opinion deeply stirred by the revelations from Amritsar. The matter is *sub judice*, and all I need say is that, with Mr. Montagu at the India Office, we have the fullest confidence that the issue can safely be left to the British sense of fair play, justice, and honour. Further,

687

it is impossible in a gathering which includes many Indian Moslems not to refer to the anxious thought which is uppermost in our hearts. The fate of Turkey, as well as that of the Moslem States which have arisen from the welter of confusion following on the disappearance of Tsarist Russia, still hangs in the balance. There could be no greater mistake than to regard these questions as remote from Indian interests. To the 70 million Moslems they are vital, as real and as near as, for instance, was the treatment of the Uitlantiers in the Transvaal by Kruger 20 years ago.

The day has passed, and will never return, when Indians were content to shut their eyes to, and have no influence upon, Asiatic foreign policy. To Moslems the problems I have named, touching as they do religious and social sentiments, are so near that they cannot be called in reality foreign questions. In a multitude of ways our Hindu fellow-countrymen have shown that they so deeply sympathize with us and so join us in asking for a generous peace with Turkey that will not punish the unborn members of that remarkable and historic race for the errors of a handful of men who allowed themselves to be dominated by the cajolery and threats of Germany, that we can honestly call this a national Indian question. The prayer is the more insistent because it is based on grounds so reasonable that they could not be better stated than in the famous speech of the Prime Minister two years ago, which did so much to calm the Moslems of the British Empire and to encourage their continued cooperation in the war against Prussian militarist ambitions. I need not remind you of his unqualified assurance that Britain was not fighting "to deprive Turkey of its capital or of the rich and renowned lands of Asia Minor and Thrace, which are predominantly Turkish in race." We may reasonably claim that the policy of freedom and self-determination of nationalities which was then placed in the forefront of Allied aims should be applied to Moslem as well as to Christian lands – to Daghestan and Azerbaijan born out of Russian chaos, as fully as to Finland and Georgia.

In the changed relations between England and India we celebrate tonight, there is a community of interest in making the reforms an unquestionable success. The clear call alike to civilian services and to Indians, as well as to the champions of both in England, is to accept the *fait accompli* and to labour for its vindication in the eyes of contemporary history. The Anglo-Indian official who has retired or is nearing the limit of his service may be likened to a weary woodcutter in the jungle who has contributed to making a way through. If, after long battle with dense undergrowth his eyes are dazzled by the light of these reforms, we should thankfully recognize that he also has had a share in making them possible. The general acquiescence given to this legislation by Parliament and the country shows that the great English people is entirely sympathetic with Indian claims. If we turn from opinion here to the man on the spot we find that the Viceroy, the man at the helm in India *par excellence,* has been fully associated with our guest in the long and toilsome journey which has brought us to this goal. Distinguished members of the Indian Civil Service, such as Lord Meston, Sir William Duke, Sir Claude Hill and Sir Archdale Earle, and many others, have been enthusiastic and convinced, if discriminating, supporters of reform. It is by no means certain that if a *plebiscite* of the I.C.S. was taken on this subject a majority would be against us.

In the light of the history of the past five years English public opinion recognizes that India is loyal and asks only for her legitimate place ultimately as an equal partner in the confederation of nations united by the rule of a beloved Emperor and his dynasty . . .

Source: *The Times,* London, 20 December 1919.

"On 19 December the Indian residents in London met at a dinner at the Savoy Hotel to celebrate the passing of the Government of India Bill and to honour E. S. Montagu in appreciation of his services to India. The Aga Khan was in the chair, and among the company were Raja Sir Hari Singh, Lord and Lady Islington, Lord and Lady Carmichael, Sir J. D. and Lady Rees, Major and Lady Ormsby Gore, Sir M. Bhownaggree, Lady Lawrence Jenkins, Sayyid and Mrs Ameer Ali, Sir E. and Lady Boyle, Mr and Mrs Ispahani, H. G. Wells, B. N. Basu, Mr. and Mrs. N. C. Seth, Sir Michael Sadler, Sir M. Visresvarays, Sir J. C. and Lady Bose, Sir J. and Lady Brunyate, Commissioner Booth Tucker, Mrs Naidu, Sir Sankeran Nair, and Commander and Mrs Wedgwood. Letters regretting inability to be present and expressing great appreciation of Montagu's efforts on behalf of India were read out from Lord Sinha, Lord Morley, Lord Southborough and Lord Meston.

"After the Aga Khan's speech, Montagu, in responding, said that he agreed with every word the chairman had said with regard to Turkey. Ever since he had assumed office he had voiced those views, and he proposed to go on voicing those same views. He believed that, whatever the fate of Turkey, at the moment nothing could possibly destroy the vigour and the principle behind the common purpose of the Moslem States of the world. Referring to the Punjab, he said they could easily understand that the occurrences there during his term of office had, from their very beginning, caused him the deepest perturbation and anxiety. There were many lessons to be learned from them. Whatever the cause, riot set free retaliatory machinery which ought to be a warning to those who, under whatever provocation, transgressed the law and endangered order. That gathering that night would be conspicuous among all gatherings to suspend judgment on allegations, and even on newspaper-reported evidence, until the full facts of the case were before them. That audience, numbering among it so many young men, would be the first to put themselves in the shoes of a soldier called upon to fulfil to the best of his capacity and to the best of his sense of duty the terrible responsibility that lay upon him. Let the young Indian think of himself as a general asked to restore or to preserve order. Let him think that there was no time for consultation and discussion; that upon him depended the safety of India and of Europe; and that he might be wrong in acting too quickly, and he might be wrong in acting too slowly! Let them know first the facts, and then it would be for the Government of the Empire and the Government of India, acting upon the recommendations of the Viceroy and of himself, to do two things – to fulfil their proud task of giving to the officers of his Majesty all the support to which they were entitled; and, secondly, to vindicate in the eyes of the world the justice and honour of British rule. (Cheers.)

"He did not understand the complaints that had been made about the information that had reached this country. When the incidents occurred in the Punjab it was their united determination that there should be an impartial and an authoritative inquiry. When that inquiry was completed the results would be published, and when the results were published they would take that action which the reports rendered necessary.

"With regard to the celebration of the passing of the India Bill, Mr. Montagu said the Bill certainly presented a compromise, but, looking back upon its history and upon his share in it, he conscientiously believed that he had compromised upon no principle, and that when the Act came to be worked the path of India to full self-government was a matter merely of time, and depended entirely upon Indians themselves. They could transform and perfect the system of local government in India from the village right away up, and he was certain that when they came back to the Mother of Parliaments to claim their right in virtue of the experience of their conduct under that Bill they would come to open doors and a wide welcome, and history would show that India had won for itself the status of a self-governing country among the nations of the world. (Cheers.)"

On Montagu, who is unique in British Indian history for having won the approval of both Hindus and Muslims, see *E. S. Montagu: A Study in Indian Polity*, Madras, May 1925; Asiaticus, "India: Mr. Montagu and His Mission", *National Review*, November 1917; "The Outlook in India", *New Statesman*, 29 December 1917; Harold Stuart, "Constitutional Changes in India: Views of Mr. Montagu and Lord Chelmsford Examined", *Empire Review*, April 1919; E. S. Montagu, "Letter to the Prime Minister Resigning his Post", *The Times*, 10 March 1922, and "Speech on his Resignation", *The Times*, 13 March 1922; M. F. O'Dwyer, "India without Mr. Montagu and Gandhi", *Fortnightly Review*, August 1922; "The India Office Crisis", *The Civil and Military Gazette*, Lahore, 5 April 1922; and, of course, E. S. Montagu, *An Indian Diary*, ed. by Venetia Montagu, London, 1930. He still awaits a biographer.

53

BRITISH POLICY IN THE EAST – I

An Article

London: 5 November 1920

The British should leave Mesopotamia alone – reservations about recommendations of the Esher Committee – vision of India as a self-governing and free dominion tied to Britain and other dominions – regret that the Indian viewpoint about British policy in the Near East is disregarded – results of this – the example of pre-war Germany – Great Britain's relations with the Oriental world and the League of Nations – implications of the Esher Committee Report – the garrisoning of Indian troops in Mesopotamia and elsewhere in the Middle East repugnant to India – maintenance of order and good government in Mesopotamia and Persia not the business of Britain and India – British policy may prove disastrous to British relations with India.

I wish to state to the British public my views upon the policy at present directing British actions in Mesopotamia and other Eastern regions. I further wish to point out the reflex effect of this policy upon Indian opinion, and to set forth reasons why, as I hold, it is advisable for Great Britain to terminate as soon as may be convenient her entanglements in the areas occupied during and since the war by British and Indian troops.

The conclusions I desire to submit are not materially modified by the announcement of the steps now being taken to form Arab administrative and legislative organizations in Mesopotamia. My contention is that Mesopotamia should be left alone, and that the British and Indian military occupation should cease. There is no present indication of withdrawal, the troops have recently been greatly increased in numbers, and, in any case, Mesopotamia must evidently continue to be garrisoned and held so long as there are British troops in North Persia. Consequently, the new messages from Baghdad leave my views for the most part unchanged.

The report of the Esher Committee on the Army in India has caused very deep anxiety to me, and, I am sure, to all Indians. Our anxiety has been deepened by the prevalent rumour that many of the larger recommendations of the report, as well as the new principles it seeks to lay down regarding permanent Indian military participation in operations in the Near and Middle East, are to be accepted and adopted forthwith.

All my life I have been a convinced and serious believer in the importance, not only to Great Britain and to India, but also to mankind and to civilization at large, of strengthening the true links which unite India to the British Empire. I believe in the development and growth of India into a vast self-governing and free Asiatic Dominion, attached to Great Britain and the other Dominions by the ties of a common Sovereignty and flag, and by a community of political, economic, and intellectual interests. I know that similar views are cherished by very large numbers of thoughtful Indians.

But it would be idle to conceal the fact that ever since the Armistice most Indians who think as I do have had their faith and their hopes constantly and increasingly shocked. We have watched with growing apprehension the vague policy of Asiatic adventure pursued, apparently without coherence and without clear direction, by the Central [British] Government to which we have been proud to render obedience. Our misgivings have been deepened by the discovery that the views of the Government of India, still less Indian public opinion, count for little or nothing in the settlement of Imperial policy in the East. The Indian point of view, whether official or otherwise, appears to be almost entirely disregarded.

The immediate results of the new habit of ignoring the Indian attitude towards external Imperial questions is unhappily plain today. While the British Empire has drifted into difficulties and entanglements in the Near and Middle East, the political situation in India is causing natural alarm. For that situation the Imperial policy of the Home Government is, in my view, partly responsible. It is true that the national consciousness of India has been steered, and perhaps excessively moved, by that violent wave of moral and intellectual unrest which the war produced in nearly every nation; but in the case of India the actions of Great Britain in the Near and Middle East have been a potent contributory cause of unrest. The success of the great [Montagu-Chelmsford] Reform Scheme, which imperatively required to be launched in a period of calmness, has therefore been jeopardised.

No one, I hope, will accuse me of belittling or of seeking to diminish British influence in Eastern countries. I have always advocated the use of British aid, without pressure or political sovereignty, in stimulating economic growth among the free and independent peoples of Central and Western Asia.

But we are now confronted with profoundly different conceptions officially expressed by Great Britain. Between the convictions I have personally felt and the wild and reckless ventures undertaken in the name of Great Britain in the Near and Middle East since the armistice, there is a great gulf. That gulf is widened by the general policy underlying the recommendations of the Esher Committee, which seems to contemplate some sort of active British hegemony of the Middle East, with the Indian Army, rather than the British Army, as its sword and buckler.

I heartily agree with many of the technical recommendations of the Esher Committee for improving the efficiency of the Indian Army, and for bettering the conditions of the officers and men. With their suggestion that the Indian Army should henceforth be scattered about and used at will outside India at the bidding of the Imperial General Staff, in pursuit of objects regarding which India will never be consulted, I most profoundly disagree. It is a wrong and a risky policy, and it makes the Indian Army a possible danger to the Empire instead of a bastion of strength.

Let me explain what I mean by these last words. I cannot do better than quote in illustration the case of Germany.

Before the war Germany's army was undoubtedly as efficient as any in Europe: her officers and men were contented; and yet that vast military machine not only brought disaster to the world, but led to Germany's own undoing and caused her to sink lower than after Jena. Why? Because, as Lord Haldane and others, including Ludendorff and Tirpitz, have shown, there was no clear and conscious policy behind the German army. It was neither an instrument of offence or defence, but was rather an organization the existence of which induced those who controlled it to embark upon adventures without either clearly perceiving their goals or counting their probable gains. The German army was, in fact, a source of temptation, and its presumed perfection drugged clear thought. I may also say that those who know the history of the Second Empire in France will agree that it had to end in disaster. In spite of the material qualities of the French, and their brilliant political ability, the fact that there was no definite and coherent policy behind the glamour of Napoleon III led the statesmen of the Second Empire into unnecessary and deplorable adventures.

If we now turn to the present attitude of those who control British Imperial policy in Asia, we find in certain respects an extraordinary resemblance to the mental principles which swayed pre-war Germany and the French Second Empire. The parallel can be traced in the vague and cloudy ideas which prevail among British statesmen regarding the supposed value and necessity of the measures they undertake in the Near and Middle East. For the sake of imaginary British interests, they are frittering away real and immediate advantages. I am sure that they are also setting in motion tendencies which must produce grave dangers in the future.

The Esher Report proves this contention. The Esher Committee has gone far beyond its terms of reference. It has sought to deal, not simply with the improvement of the Indian Army, which was its allotted task, but rather with the general military policy of the Empire as a whole, and it has done so upon lines which may prove fatal.

Ever since the war ended grave contradictions of outlook and action, of debate and policy, have blurred Great Britain's relations with the Oriental world. Look at the question of the League of Nations. India and Persia are already members of the League. Egypt expects to enter into membership very soon, and I hear from direct sources that one of the main ambitions of Afghanistan is to join the League on an equal footing with other nations. The moral influence of the League is bound to depend very largely upon Great Britain's relations with it. Yet, how can we believe that British advocacy of the League is sincere, when we are confronted by such a document as the Esher Committee's Report, with its open and naked suggestion of preparations for military enterprises and activities in the Near and Middle East? Are we not compelled to think that British praise of the League may be mere lip-service?

Let me submit another instance of the uncertainty of British policy. Mr. Montagu distinctly told the Esher Committee that it should recommend nothing which would prevent India from arriving at the *status* of a Dominion in the British Empire. I may add that the famous Declaration of the British Cabinet in 1917 is interpreted by every Indian as a solemn pledge that India shall eventually have all the advantages and liberties enjoyed by Canada and Australia and South Africa, although the Declaration does not state this in so many words. Yet, if the principles underlying the Esher Committee's report are put into practice, the military forces of India will not even be under the control of the Government of India. The War Office and the Imperial General Staff will have the last word, not only as to organization, but also as to utilization. This means that India will remain a Dependency for ever.

I know we are told that the organization suggested by the Esher Committee will be common to all the Dominions, including India. The statement is an insult to Indian intelligence, for we are well aware of the jealous manner in which the other great Dominions insist on retaining control of their own forces. If there is a real need for centralizing in London the control of the Empire's military forces, why should not Canada and Australia be invited to lead the way in accepting this new principle? We know they will never do so. Is it surprising, therefore, that British sincerity is doubted by India?

People in Great Britain do not seem to understand how widely the British promise of ultimate Dominion *status* is mistrusted by Indians. They do not seem to know that even Mr. Montagu, who was the mouthpiece of the Declaration, is often attacked in India on the ground that he never really meant what he said. Personally, I have complete faith both in Mr. Montagu and in the sincerity of Great Britain, but when I look at the Esher Report I can well understand the suspicions of some of my countrymen.

I have said that British policy in the East is full of contradictions. I ask the public to compare the cases of Egypt, of India, and of Mesopotamia. The British Government are about to concede self-government and relative freedom from control to Egypt. Yet while you do this for Egypt, while you even propose to withdraw your troops to the Suez Canal, you inflict upon India, to whom you are promising evolution to a Dominion, the greater part of the burden involved in the difficult, expensive, and ruinous task of occupying Mesopotamia. It is true that you find the money for Mesopotamia, but India is forced to provide the bulk of the troops required for the garrison; and let me say that while India joined with the utmost alacrity in the Great War, she regards this Mesopotamian undertaking in its present form with repugnance. All these expeditions and garrisons in Palestine, in Mesopotamia, and elsewhere, for which India is furnishing most of the troops, are in direct conflict with the old and sensible principles upon which the plans for the defence of India, which is the chief task of the Indian Army, were based. When the Tsardom was at the fullness of its power, and long before the Anglo-Russian Convention of 1907, it was always understood that if occasion arose, India would be defended immediately outside her own borders, in Afghanistan or in Seistan. Now, at a period when Russia is probably reduced to impotence for many years to come, we actually have troops in Northern Persia, near the Caspian, and until recently we had them in Central Asia also! In saner times the absurdity of these distant enterprises, as well as their futility and great cost, would have made them impossible.

I urge that the British public should now recognize clearly that the maintenance of order and good government in such countries as Mesopotamia and Persia is no part of their business any more than it is the business of India. Great Britain is penetrating into areas outside her legitimate Asiatic sphere. I deplore her policy, for I know it to be dangerous.

In any case, it is not right and proper that India should be called upon to bear heavy financial and military burdens, and to maintain an army in excess of her own requirements, in order that her forces may be used without her consent and outside her own shores, to further the vain and grandiose dreams (or rather nightmares!) of a few statesmen and soldiers six thousand miles away. I warn my British friends that a high taxation of India for military purposes, and for an Army to be chiefly used elsewhere in the manner suggested by the Esher Committee and the Imperial General Staff, implies a policy which may eventually prove disastrous to British relations with India.

Source: *The Times*, London, 5 November 1920.

This was a special article written by the Aga Khan for the journal. In the introductory lines, *The Times* called him "one of the foremost of the Mahomedan princes in India". The headlines to the article were: "British Policy in the East: The Aga Khan's Protest: What Indians are Thinking: A Reasoned Warning."

The report which the Aga Khan criticised so strongly contained the findings and recommendations of the Army in India Committee, commonly known as the Esher Committee after its chairman. It was appointed in 1919 with the following membership:

Lord Esher(chairman)
Sir Michael O'Dwyer
Lieut.-Gen. H. V. Cox
Lieut.-Gen. Sir Havelock Hudson
Lieut.-Gen. Sir Claud W. Jacob
Lieut.-Gen. J. P. du Cane

Sir Godfrey Fell
Major-Gen. Sir Webb Gillman
Malik Sir Umar Hayat Khan Tiwana
Sir K. G. Gupta.
The report of the committee was issued in two parts: the first on 3 November 1919, the second on 19 May 1920.

54

BRITISH POLICY IN THE EAST – II

An Article

London: 6 November 1920

Conditions under which Bolshevism will flourish in India – restore
to the Indian army the primary task of defending India – comparisons between Egypt and Mesopotamia misleading – the folly of
imposing British imperialism on Mesopotamia – contradictions
of British policy – the oil deposits of Mesopotamia – British forces
in Persia should be withdrawn – recent British intervention in
Persia a mistake – allow Indian troops to return to India.

In the first part of these observations, I endeavoured to suggest
some of the principles which should guide British policy in the
Near and Middle East. I deprecated the present contradictory
character of that policy; urged that the wild adventures in which
Great Britain is involved should be abandoned; pointed out the
danger of dragging India and her troops into these enterprises;
and traversed with frankness the principles set forth in the Esher
Committee's Report, which contemplate the continuous employment of large portions of the Indian Army in other countries of
the East. In this second part I propose to address myself more
closely to the problems presented by Mesopotamia and Persia,
two countries of which I may claim to possess intimate knowledge.
But before entering upon these topics I should like to say a word
about the Bolshevist menace to India, one of the few Indian
questions which seem to interest the British public.

If Bolshevism ever becomes dangerous to India, it will be partly
due to the mistakes of British policy. To fritter away men and
money in other Eastern lands is to create in India the discontent
in which Bolshevist propaganda flourishes. There will be danger
if India comes to the conclusion that those of her sons who went

to defend liberty in France and Belgium in 1914 have merely established a precedent for the use of Indian troops to destroy such liberties as may be left in Central and Western Asia. A discontented India, mistrustful of British promises, is Bolshevism's only chance.

But if British policy is rightly conceived, the spread of Bolshevist doctrines in India is highly improbable; and in any case the threat of an invasion of India by Bolshevist troops is fantastic. Trotsky's badly fed, badly trained, and often insubordinate soldiers could never cross the deserts and the mountains which separate them from India. The transport difficulties are insuperable. There are no roads and no railways, and even the communications established in Central Asia by the Tsardom are decaying.

No, there will be no risk from Bolshevism if Great Britain sticks to her old policy, and restores the Indian Army to its primary task of defending India. But if the ideals of the Esher Committee and the Imperial General Staff are to prevail, and if the Indian Army is marched about in other Asiatic countries in a manner which may lead it to suppose that it is an instrument for external aggression, then anything may happen. It must be remembered that the Indian soldiers are not automata, but are endowed with minds like other human beings. They are not so unthinking as in former days. Even the Sikhs are changing, and in time the Gurkhas also may alter their outlook upon life.

Turning now to Mesopotamia, I would say that where British opinion goes astray is in the comparisons constantly made in the London press, and in public speeches, between Mesopotamia and Egypt. The basis of comparison is almost wholly wrong. The British public are being misled when they are told that they can easily repeat in Mesopotamia the episode of their control of Egypt. The true analogy is not with the Egypt of 1882 but with the Afghanistan of 1878.

When the rebellion of Arabi made British intervention inevitable, Egypt had been for sixty years the most settled and pacific nation in the East. From the time of Muhammad Ali down to the appearance of Lord Cromer the country had been practically free from anarchy and serious lawlessness. The people were obedient and docile, and there was nothing resembling the tribal dissensions traceable elsewhere. The whole population was packed into accessible areas in the Delta and on the narrow cultivated strips beside the Nile. Lord Cromer had only to step into the seat of Ismail, and all obeyed him.

In Mesopotamia the exact reverse prevails. The Turks never really established their rule in that region, and were satisfied if things looked reasonably smooth on the surface. Before the advent of the Turks, who came less than three hundred years ago, we must go back to the time dealt with by the "Arabian Nights" to discover any system of orderly government in Mesopotamia. The thin population is scattered over an enormous area, and is therefore doubly difficult to control. The dominating factor is jealousy. The people are split up into tribes and sects which are mostly jealous of each other, but all united in jealousy of the foreigner. The atmosphere is that of perpetual strife.

The real parallel for present British policy in Mesopotamia is Lord Beaconsfield's unwise policy towards Afghanistan. The mistakes of Lord Beaconsfield were rectified by the British nation in 1880 through Lord Ripon, who acted with the full knowledge and approval of Mr. Gladstone's Government. Lord Ripon shattered the vague dreams about Afghanistan, and recognized that the Afghans were free to do wrong in their own country if they chose; but he protected India from any danger through Afghanistan by establishing a firm grip upon Quetta and Chaman. We should apply this lesson to Mesopotamia. There is one clear strategic point beyond which there should be no interference. That point is the port of Basra, or, if it be preferred, Kurna, where the tidal waters cease. Above that point Great Britain should seek to exercise influence, but not domination. Her one necessity is to hold the entrance to the Gulf, but in these far places she should not go out of reach of her ships.

It must be obvious that with aeroplanes and armoured cars and machine-guns Great Britain can establish some sort of permanent rule in Mesopotamia if she so desires; but she will do it only by exterminating a large proportion of the population. I should regard such a proceeding as the most senseless form of Imperialism which Great Britain has ever visited upon the East.

It may be objected that unless British rule is imposed in some form, actual or virtual, the Arabs of Mesopotamia will continue to quarrel among themselves. It is, indeed, more than likely that there will be no real subsidence of the present unrest for a year or two, yet if it is made clear that there will be no further interference from without, I am convinced that stronger internal movements will begin, and that they will make for an autonomous, if loosely knit, Mesopotamia in the near future. The one thing certain is that the people of Mesopotamia will never find their own salvation while their country is full of British and

Indian soldiers. Whether they settle down or not, it is not the duty of either Great Britain or of India to impose strange systems upon a people whom they have professed to rescue, who have shown them that they now wish to be left alone, and who are fighting for what they believe to be their freedom.

It has been eloquently urged that if the Mesopotamian Arabs are to learn the arts of self-government they must be placed under an elaborate service of British military and civil officials, backed by a powerful army of occupation. But is not this another example of the confused and contradictory political thought which at present clouds Great Britain's Oriental policy? I beg my readers to look at the Montagu-Chelmsford Report on Indian Reforms, where the people of India are told that the only way to learn self-government is to be released from official control and British leading-strings. You have one story for India, and now for Egypt also, and quite a different story for Mesopotamia.

Next, there is the theory of collapse. British statesmen persuade themselves that if the strong arm of their nation is withdrawn, both Mesopotamia and Persia will collapse. In this matter I am of the same way of thinking as the late Lord Salisbury, who once stoutly said that he refused to believe that China would break up. These ancient lands are not likely to collapse, and Britons need not impoverish themselves and wear themselves out in trying to hold them together. Very much the same sort of thing was said in 1879 and 1880 about the consequences of retirement from Afghanistan; but the Afghan nation, instead of collapsing, found new strength when the British retired from Kabul and Kandahar.

Then we are told that Mesopotamia is a wonderful derelict granary. Even if the suggestion is true, it will take many years of work and expenditure to make the country profitably productive. Why do we not first enter upon the work of reclamation in British India and in the Native States, where there is still so much to be done? In any case, I am sceptical about Mesopotamia as a granary. The soil of that region has been deteriorating for hundreds of years, and it was being impregnated with saline deposits for two centuries or more before the Turks arrived. My view is that the task of reclaiming Mesopotamia as a granary is very problematical.

As to the oil deposits, I may mention that I am a considerable shareholder in companies which hope to exploit the oil of Mesopotamia; but personally I do not expect either the British or the Indian taxpayer to put his hand into his pocket, in order that my income may be slightly increased, and I think it wrong that Mesopotamia should be a burden on the taxes. Expert opinion seems to be divided as to the quantity and quality of Mesopotamian oil; but in any case the right solution is not Government action or protection.

The oil industry should be developed upon normal economic lines. There is nothing to prevent the oil companies from subsidizing the Arab tribes to a moderate extent in return for the protection of their works and pipe-lines. In Mexico, when lawlessness was rife, when the Government was constantly changing, when both life and property were insecure, the great oil companies succeeded in protecting the oil-fields. They did it by judicious expenditure, by the skilful diplomacy of their representatives, and by the employment of a certain number of the inhabitants of the country. The same may be done in Mesopotamia. I know that Arab character well. If properly approached by Englishmen and such Orientals as know their business, the Arabs will fully co-operate in the protection of the oil properties. It will be to their interest to do so, and they are not blind to their interests. Such a method could be adopted for a small fraction of the present huge cost of the military occupation of Mesopotamia.

I am equally convinced that all the British forces now in Persia should be at once withdrawn, and that British relations with Persia should be placed upon a friendly diplomatic and commercial basis. This could be done far more easily than the British public are given to suppose. No one who knows the Persians, as I have every reason to do, will believe that Bolshevism can spread among them, provided the exploitation of the masses of the people by a small minority of prominent persons, who are bolstered up by British arms, is terminated. Certain vested interests in Persia will clamour for the retention of British forces near Teheran, because they fear the day of reckoning with those whom they have wronged. Yet it is not to the interest of either Great Britain or India to support this or that clique in Persia. Our object should be to enter into frank and honest relations with the whole Persian people, and this is not being done today. Instead of encouraging the Persians to lead upon British strength, we should tell them to organize upon national lines, and to depend upon their own resources to protect themselves against the Bolshevists. From every point of view, including that of Persia herself, the more recent active intervention of Great Britain in Persian affairs has been a mistake. I write of what I know.

In conclusion, I would again urge that the troops of India should be permitted to return without delay to their own shores. India will always be proud that her soldiers played an important part in the overthrow of Germany and her confederates; but there is a world of difference between India's share in the Great War and her present compulsory participation in a new policy which she dislikes. Great Britain should be very careful how she uses Indian troops for these purposes, because India has no voice in the disposal of her Army. My recollection is that by the Act of 1858, and I think at Mr. Gladstone's instance, Indian troops must be kept in India unless the House of Commons decides otherwise. If this salutary provision remains valid, it seems to have been strangely neglected.

Great Britain is still the moral trustee for India. She will be violating her trusteeship if she refuses to allow those portions of the Indian Army which are overseas to return home within a reasonable time. Should another danger like that of 1914 reappear, Great Britain will assuredly find that India, in common with the other great Dominions, will joyously and willingly spring to arms and give her all for the defence of the Empire.

Source: *The Times*, London, 6 November 1920.
This second part of the article appeared with the headlines "Our Mistakes in Mesopotamia: Withdrawal Urged: How to Protect the Oil Industry: British Policy in Persia."

55

INDIA'S CONNECTION WITH BRITAIN

Interview with the Press

Bombay: 22 January 1921

Lord Reading's appointment as Viceroy – disorder in Persia – revise the peace treaty with Turkey – dominion status for India – amend the Esher Committee Report – the Punjab affairs – advice to the Indians.

H. H. the Aga Khan, in the course of an interview with [the] representatives of the local press, stated that he attached great importance to Lord Reading's appointment as Viceroy. Once he was convinced of the pressing needs of India, his opinion and views would carry weight with the Government in England. The Aga Khan believed that the disorder in Persia was an echo of the unjust Turkish peace and that the suspicions of Persians would not be allayed until the treaty were revised and the revision should be undertaken under England's initiative. If England so acted her moral prestige would not only be restored but it would bring peace and prosperity to the Near East and India. He felt sure France and Italy would join England if she came forward to revise the Treaty. He did not believe that the Greek offensive would be successful without the backing of the Allies and if it failed one part of the Treaty which affected the Turkish territory assigned to Greece would disappear. He was, therefore, of opinion that taking advantage of the Greek King's return the Allied Governments should revise the treaty with good grace.

With regard to India's connection with Britain, the Aga Khan said if India has a dominion Government within the British Empire it will have all the advantages of independence and of belonging to the Empire and will get all that any country can desire. A dominion, he repeated, is never held by force. "I have

every hope, now that India is awaking to her national responsibilities, she will herself take up the question of Indians in the
Colonies in a way befitting her place in the world ... Those who
are co-operating with [the] Government, it is for them to show
to India that co-operation can and will cure her national ills from
which we all suffer. If the Co-operationists succeed in having the
report of the Esher Committee thoroughly revised and secure an
army that will suit the needs of India, well, that will go a long
way to show that Co-operation is indeed a vital and living force
and not bankrupt."

With regard to Punjab affairs the Aga Khan said:– If the
offenders are properly punished and if the victims are, as far as
possible, recompensed, and if care is taken that in future martial
law of this kind will be rendered impossible, then the Punjab
question is settled.

The Aga Khan gave the following message to the people:–
"There must be, as Mr. Gandhi also has often insisted, no bloodshed and non-violence. Second, national self-respect must be
kept. All Indians whether they do not approve of Non-co-operation, or whether they do approve, must as much as possible –
the more the better – continue to meet in round table conferences and hear each other's views. We must remember that to
the outside world we are yet a unit and though the spectacle of
political differences of opinion and internal divisions are healthy
signs, yet we must, like the monarchists and royalists on the one
hand and the anarchists and socialists of France on the other,
for the outer world remember that above all and beyond all India
lives. For the outside world India is one. To my countrymen I
must say that they must not at this moment forget that India has
her finance and her army, her foreign policy and other interests
to care for and that if they do not take interest in all these public
affairs their grasp of India's national questions and interests will
be lost."

Source: *The Civil and Military Gazette,* Lahore, 25 January 1921.
The text of the interview was circulated by the Associated Press of India.

56

INDIA DESIRES

Speech at the Farewell Luncheon to Lord and Lady Reading

London: 13 March 1921

Tribute to Lord and Lady Reading – the Duke of Cannaught's advice regarding events in the Punjab – India's desire for equal citizenship in the British Empire – the goal of self-government – Hindus and Muslims in agreement on the Turkish Question – contribution of Indian Muslims to the Allied cause – Indian desire to see the Treaty of Sèvres revised.

I rejoice in this opportunity to participate in this gathering of Indians in London in honour of the Viceroy-designate and to wish him God-speed in the great mission he goes out to discharge (Cheers). It would be no kindness to our eminent guest to seek to blink the fact that the call he is answering is one of the most difficult that can possibly be entrusted to any subject of the Crown at present. He can be under no illusion on the subject. The difficulty of the task is abundantly attested by the fact that it has been placed on one who has reached the topmost heights of his profession and is in the place of chief authority in the administration of justice, and one, moreover, who has proved himself a great ambassador and diplomatist, and whose financial work at the Treasury in the crisis of the early days of the war showed what an admirable Chancellor of the Exchequer he would make. On Thursday evening Lord Reading discountenanced the suggestion of my friend, Sir Ali Imam, that acceptance of this position was an act of self-sacrifice; but we may at least be certain that, having regard to the state of health of the gracious lady who goes to India with him, he would not have left the great judicial post he has adorned save under the constraining sense of public duty. We rejoice in the courage and patriotism which has led him to accept the call of the King-Emperor, based as it is on the desire to give India of the very best that English public life can offer. (Cheers).

In his moving appeal at the inauguration of the Indian Legislature at Delhi the Duke of Cannaught urged that the unhappy events in the Punjab and the controversies to which they gave rise should be forgotten and forgiven. Would it become any of us to discount in the slightest degree the earnest appeal of such an old and tried friend of India as His Royal Highness (Cheers); but it is at least permissible to say that the necessary accompaniment of forgetfulness and forgiveness is the sense of equal citizenship in the British Empire – (cheers) – and that in India – post-war India – there is no room for arbitrary divisions into first-class and second-class categories of friendship. This recognition is the more essential since the goal of policy in India is not in dispute. Lord Reading begins his Viceroyalty with the great asset which has fallen to none of his predecessors, that "swaraj" (self-government to translate the word literally) is the avowed aim both of the British Government and of the Indian people. (Cheers). The word has been used by the Duke of Cannaught on behalf of the King-Emperor, and whatever differences there are upon it relate only to the time and methods by which it will be attained. Indians and Englishmen are swimming together in the same stream toward this goal. (Hear, hear).

But India has not the same self-centredness as in the pre-war days. She has come into the community of nations, and her vision, enlarged by war experience, is no longer confined to her own affairs. The last few years have happily witnessed a wonderful unity between Hindus and Mahomedans, and they now see most political issues in common. (Cheers). There can be no greater mistake than to suppose that the Hindus are not in the fullest sympathy with their Mahomedan brethren in reference to the Turkish question. The Prime Minister told the House of Commons in February, 1920, that we could not have won the war against Turkey without the aid of Indian troops. They, indeed, bore the chief brunt of the warfare in the Near and Middle East. Obviously, to the large proportion of the Indian soldiery belonging to the Islamic faith this service in Eastern lands imposed a far greater sacrifice than can be realized by Western peoples of other faiths. There is an essential unity of belief and a basis of common civilization in Mahomedan countries. But inheritors of this possession from India and other lands linked with Allied countries fought in the war against brother Moslems in the assurance that the high moral principles which the Allies proclaimed from the very beginning of the struggle would be scrupulously upheld, that the liberty and self-determination of nations, whether weak or strong in the military sense, would be respected in the East as well as in the West, and that there would be no element of violence in the terms of peace.

Indian feeling being what it is, and Indian idealism being so strong, can you wonder that the question of the treatment of Turkey should be regarded as providing a test whether or not India is in the full sense of the term a partner in the Empire? This is a case in which, with due regard to general Imperial obligations, India's desires should be no secondary consideration. One of the greatest assets of the British Empire throughout the world is that of faith in the pledges and undertakings of those in authority, and its conservation is of incalculable importance. The people of India are one with the people of Great Britain in looking on the King-Emperor as their own national Sovereign. It ought not to be possible for them to feel that, while they are praised in war, their sentiments are disregarded in peace. If the majority of the British people regard those sentiments with impatience and as negligible, they would seem to lack those ideas of the meaning of Imperial unity which we Indians have been brought up to believe. We ask unitedly for a full revision of the Treaty of Sèvres. (Cheers).

I believe that if this great act of justice and recognition of India's *locus standi* is given, a new and helpful spirit will arise in my country, not so much through changes in men or in parties as by the inherent weight of the act itself. (Cheers). I am confident that its influence for good will reach much farther than the most elaborate efforts apart therefrom could achieve. There could be no better augury for the success of the application of Lord Reading's great qualities of mind and heart to India than the revision of the Turkish Peace Treaty, on lines acceptable to Indian sentiment. (Cheers). Not only would this step auspiciously inaugurate the new Viceroyalty, but it would constitute the first united attempt of England and India to apply to a great Imperial problem the principle of Swaraj, which is now universally acknowledged to be the Indian goal. (Cheers).

Source: *The Times*, London, 14 March 1921.

On Lord Reading see Sayyid Sirdar Ali Khan, *The Earl of Reading: A Sketch of a Late Career at the Bar, on the Bench, in Diplomacy, in India, Together with an Authorized Report of His Speeches Delivered in India*, London, 1924; Lord Mersey, *The Viceroys and Governors General of India, 1757–1947*, London, 1949; Marquess of Reading, *Rufus Isaacs, First Marquess of Reading*, London, 1945, 2 vols; A

Barrister, "The New Viceroy: Some Personal Impressions", *The Civil and Military Gazette*, 20 January 1921; "Lord Reading and the Indian Viceroyalty", *Spectator*, 8 January 1921; Cecil Kaye, "Lord Reading's Viceroyalty: Then and Now", *Asiatic Review*, April 1927; "Lord Reading: Success Against Difficulties", *The Times*, 3 April 1927; George Pilcher, "Lord Reading's Indian Viceroyalty", *Edinburgh Review*, April 1927.

57

INDIAN MUSLIM CONCERN FOR TURKEY

Telegram to Lord Reading

London: 8 July 1921

Urge the British Government to make peace with Turkey – sentiments of Indian Muslims on the Turkish question.

Now that Greece has twice refused mediation by the Powers, and has decided to enforce the Sèvres instrument of injustice by war, we respectfully beg your Excellency to press upon his Majesty's Government to leave Greece alone and make such early peace with the Turkish nation as would satisfy Mohammedans and create a calm atmosphere in India for political reconciliation. As delegated by the Government of India, it is our duty to make it clear that Mohammedans can never consider Constantinople or the Caliphate safe unless Eastern Thrace and Smyrna remain under Turkish sovereignty, and unless that sovereignty is real and complete. We beg your Excellency to press the same upon your own and India's behalf. We are convinced that both France and Italy are willing to give full satisfaction on these points.

Source: *The Morning Post*, London, 9 July 1921.
   This telegram was sent jointly by the Aga Khan and Seth Chotani (who was referred to by the paper as "of the Indian Moslem Delegation").

58

PEACE WITH TURKEY

Letter to The Times

Paris: 8 November 1921

Peace with Turkey on a just and equitable basis needed – views of *The Times* on Greek occupation – Turkish question a danger to the peace of the British Empire – exasperation among Muslims – how it can be removed – contribution of Indian Muslims to Britain's war effort against Turkey – Indian views deserve attention – steps Britain should take – the position of the Sultan-Caliph – consequences of not settling the Turkish question – Entente Cordiale between Britain and France.

The leading articles in *The Times* of November 2 and 5 upon the Near Eastern problem impel me to write urging that Great Britain should now make every effort in conjunction with France to terminate the strife in the Near East and to conclude peace with Turkey upon a just and equitable basis.

The Times of November 2 said that the Treaty of Sèvres is obsolete, and that "the Greeks have failed in their attempt to maintain by force their claims in Asia Minor against the Kemalists". It observed that the Greeks should be persuaded "to moderate their claims even to the point of evacuating Asia Minor, in no part of which can they in their own strength remain secure"; and it pointed out that "the rich commercial possibilities of Constantinople are stifled by the Allied occupation, and the city has become an intolerable problem to those who are responsible for its protection and administration". On November 5 *The Times* said that "the speedy evacuation of Anatolia by the Greeks is desirable" and it declared that the Greek advance in Asia Minor has made of the Kemalist movement "a powerful force, that is now the only force to be reckoned with in Turkish national life, and has provoked reverberations far beyond Turkish territory". With the observations I have quoted I profoundly agree.

The failure of the Entente to conclude peace with Turkey and to restore to the Turks their capital and their historic homeland has created a situation which has long been poisoning the atmosphere of the Near and Middle East. I am well aware of the preoccupations of the Entente statesmen in Central Europe and elsewhere, but nothing can justify the attitude of passive neglect which has permitted the Turkish question to drift until it has become a definite danger to the peace of the British Empire. The treatment meted out to the Turks has aroused the most intense exasperation throughout the whole of Islam. It is responsible for most of the difficulties which now perplex Great Britain in Asia. It has driven some of the more extreme Turks to enter into relations with the Bolshevists of Russia, with whom the majority of Muhammadans have very little in common. The future of Mesopotamia can never be peaceful until Asia Minor settles down to a prosperous peace. The policy adopted towards the Turks is a direct cause of the growing misunderstanding with Persia, for, though the Persians are Shias, the inner unity of Islam is a fact which non-Muslims can hardly realize. How can we expect the Muhammadan nation of Persia to maintain intimate relations with Great Britain when the Persians see the Greeks permitted, and in the past encouraged, to wrest from their co-religionists, the Turks, some of their oldest and most famous provinces? I am convinced that the Turkish question is at the root of the failure to come to a satisfactory agreement with Afghanistan. Settle the Turkish problem, give the Turks fair play, convince the Muhammadan world that Great Britain and her Allies do not intend to stifle the national existence of Turkey, and I am certain the difficulties at Kabul would quickly disappear. Above all, the healing of the Turkish sore would instantly remove the only cause of unrest among the Muhammadans of India, which has recently had such unhappy consequences.

I feel that the nature of Indian Muhammadan opinion upon the Turkish question is still grievously misunderstood in Great Britain. It is of no use for Englishmen whose memories of India relate to the distant past to contend that Indian Muhammadans have only a factitious interest in Turkey and the Sultan-Caliph. We have to deal with the position as it exists today. Islam in India is deeply interested in the welfare of the most important independent Muhammadan State in the world. The Muslims of India do not want to see Turkey blotted out, and they fear that such is the aim of Turkey's enemies. The problem has been largely transformed by the war. The British Empire overthrew the Turks, but the Indian Army was the Empire's spear-point in the Turkish campaigns. The Indian troops, Muslim and Hindu alike, loyally answered the King Emperor's call and went forth to war against the Turks in an obedient and unquestioning spirit. Many among them may not have liked the task, but they did their duty bravely and fearlessly. It was mainly through the help of India that the Turks were brought to their downfall, and India feels that her views should receive attention in the subsequent settlement. Indian anxieties about the fate of Turkey were to some extent allayed by the Prime Minister's famous pronouncement, in which he said in effect that Turkey would be spared. It was afterwards contended that this memorable pledge was conditional upon the instant surrender of Turkey, which was not forthcoming. I can only speak of things as they are, and I say that India believed in the Prime Minister's promise and still desires to see it fulfilled. It is so easy to do reasonable justice to Turkey, so dangerous for the well-being of India to let the misunderstanding grow and grow until it hangs like a dark cloud over all the countries between the Maritza and Ganges. Will not Great Britain, for whom the problem contains such peril, now do her utmost to set these matters at rest?

What should be done? I urge that the least possible basis of a permanent settlement is to restore to Turkey immediately and fully her sovereign rights in Anatolia and Asia Minor. There will never be any peace in the Near and Middle East while the Greeks remain in military occupation of any part of the Asiatic mainland. Greece has disregarded the advice of her best friends in Europe. I have great admiration for the national spirit and enterprise of the Greeks, but Greece has been persuaded against her true interests to appeal to the sword, and she has signally failed. She should realize all the facts of the situation and withdraw from Asia altogether, leaving the Turks in undisputed possession of the territories which they have held for many centuries. This is the first condition of a just settlement.

The next imperative necessity is that the Turks should receive back their capital of Constantinople, a course of which *The Times* has already approved. They should be allowed to resuscitate their civil and financial administration, and if this were done it would soon be found that the finances of Turkey would improve. At present the economic condition of Turkey is chaotic, and it is bound to remain so until her sovereign rights over her capital and her Asiatic provinces are restored. A matter of even greater importance and interest to all Muhammadans of all sects is that the Sultan-Caliph should be freed from the scarcely veiled bondage in which he is detained. The humiliating position of the Sultan-Caliph causes the most intense grief and anger in all Muhammadan communities. He is far worse off than the Pope in the Vatican, for at least the Pope is the "prisoner" of his own people and of Catholics and has freedom in international intercourse, and is not surrounded by foreign troops and their staffs.

If the Entente followed the right course of action, I am assured that the unity of aim could soon be established between the Sultan of Turkey and his advisers, and Mustafa Kemal Pasha and those associated with him. This anomaly of two Governments in Turkey is the outcome of unwise foreign intervention. Released from external pressure and left free to act together for a single object, Constantinople and Angora would at once join in establishing a strong National Government in Turkey. The Turks must be given the opportunity of developing a free national State. This is the only possible solution of the problem, but the restoration of Constantinople and the return of the Greeks to their own country are essential preliminaries. The Turks cannot be extinguished, and if they are left as they are today they will struggle for years until they have recovered their rights.

The dangers in the East will not be removed until the Turkish question is settled on the lines I have indicated, and I would add that the unrest among the Mussalmans of India is likely to continue until justice is done. Lord Chelmsford, as Viceroy, fully realized and advocated the necessity of a just peace, though unfortunately, owing to his innate modesty, his action did not receive in India the public recognition that it merited. Both Lord Reading and Mr. Montagu are plainly aware of the truth. Lord Reading, in a recent speech, has said that he has steadily pressed the claims of the Turks. The efforts of Mr. Montagu in the same direction are known to us all, and have won for him personally the gratitude of the Islamic world.

Upon the recent separate negotiations of representatives of France with the Kemalists at Angora I do not offer any comment. I would say this, however; I firmly believe that the maintenance of not merely the Entente but the Entente Cordiale between Great Britain and France is essential not only for the peace of Europe and Asia and the safety of both countries but for the future of human civilization itself. The Entente is in peril through the course of events in the Near East, partly owing to the past reluctance of the British Government to intervene, as should have been done long ago, and as France has finally done. I hold that the Near Eastern question can only be settled by the joint action of Great Britain and France, working cordially together, and I am certain it is not too late for both Governments to achieve this happy result, assuring Turkey a free national existence and the Islamic world peace and contentment.

Source: *The Times*, London, 12 November 1921.
  The address in Paris from where the letter was written is not given.

59

REMEMBERING SIR PHEROZESHAH MEHTA

Foreword to H. P. Mody's Biography of Sir Pherozeshah Mehta

Bombay: 1921

Long acquaintance with Sir Pherozeshah – his political convictions and activities – his influence – he was not understood by the officialdom – the consequences of this – a moral for the youth of India – Sir Pherozeshah's charity for the Indians – a synthesis of patriotism and particularism – committed to dominion self-government for India – aware of the difficulties – personal meetings in 1910 and 1915.

It is with great reluctance that I have accepted the author's kind invitation to write this Foreword, for I am well aware of my shortcomings for the task. Unlike many others happily still alive, I did not get to know Sir Pherozeshah till the very evening of his life. Thus I had little direct knowledge of that great period when he helped to mould Indian political aspirations. Nor had I the advantage of co-operation with him in his great work of making Bombay a self-governing city. Under these circumstances a great deal that could have been rightly said must be passed in silence. However I can claim one advantage over his contemporaries, and that is that I see the giant in truer perspective. While I was still a boy, Sir Pherozeshah, with his well-known generosity, would often spend half an hour or so explaining to my youthful curiosity the governing principle underlying his political convictions and activities. Later, from the time when he last visited London onwards, I saw him more often, and came more and more to understand the grandeur and simplicity of his character and to appreciate the qualities that had won for him, I must say, the discipleship of men so different and yet so powerful and strong as Gokhale and Ranade, Budrudin [Tayyabji] and Wacha. Nay, it was characteristic of Sir Pherozeshah that his influence guided men older than himself who had been in the political field much longer, and it also spurred the young patriots to further aspirations. Such was the case with Dadabhai Naoroji himself, and with many others whose names are dear to India.

It is one of the tragedies of Indian history since British Rule that Sir Pherozeshah was never understood or appreciated by officialdom and Anglo-India. Had his doctrines been followed earlier, we might not have such a dark and cloudy atmosphere as overhangs the land to-day . . .

Had the principles and the hopes with which in the Eighties he took his stand on Indian aspirations been even gradually realized, had they even received fair and unprejudiced consideration, the later and final estrangement of Tilak and Gandhi would probably never have taken place. Not only the Montagu-Chelmsford Reforms, but even the more elementary rights, came far too late, for those vital years of the Eighties and Nineties had left such an atmosphere of distrust that it has weighed down the final work of reconciliation foreshadowed in the famous declaration of August, 1917. A moral that no Englishman in India should forget can be drawn from the fact that for forty-five out of his seventy years of life Sir Pherozeshah was for the average Anglo-Indian the personification of a dangerous demagogue. . . . Had any of the administrative and financial reforms suggested by the Mehta of the Eighties and Nineties received fair and just consideration, would the present day patriotism and incredulity separate the thinking youth of India from England?

But for young India too there is a moral. Sir Pherozeshah never despaired, and till the very end believed in the conscience of England. All the rebuffs and disappointments of four decades and more did not sour his large and generous nature. One other and a still more necessary moral can be drawn by the India of the future from this, perhaps, her greatest nineteenth century son. It was the breadth and depth of his true charity for his countrymen; for he never judged harshly or unkindly even the meanest of his own worldly antagonists. Personal ambition, the desire for wealth and fame never interfered with his great work in life. I have known in my time many leading statesmen, men of letters, men to whom fame has come in many lands. Some like Gokhale had avowedly renounced the world. Not one can I recall whose real indifference to personal advancement or success was so great as Sir Pherozeshah's. Not only in old age would he open his arms to welcome a Gokhale as his successor, but before he had himself reached the meridian of life, he was

717

never jealous but ever ready to advance a possible rival such as Telang or Budrudin, Ranade or Chandavarkar. All he insisted on, all he demanded, was that the Motherland should receive a recruit sincere and devoted to her cause. In a land of divisions of caste and religion, of race and occupation, of provincial interests and religious differences, Sir Pherozeshah in his very life perhaps unconsciously showed the greatest synthesis of patriotism and particularism. A Parsi of Parsis, who could never be mistaken for any other race, who was proud of every quality which has gone to distinguish that ancient people, he was yet an Indian of Indians ever looking forward to a future worthy of India's population and resources and not handicapped by her past misfortunes. A Bombayite passionately devoted to his city and to his Presidency, yet he was the standard bearer of the cause of United India. His simple nature was so free from hypocrisy and conceit that while he could admire the renunciation of Gokhale and the sacrifices of B. G. Tilak, he never realized that while he had not taken any such vows or made any such declaration, he had made in his own life perhaps the greatest sacrifice of all. I have heard of him in his last years as being regarded as a dead weight to the cause of Indian progress. Nothing could be more false. His was not a nature to be satisfied with half measures. The full goal of Dominion self-government within the Empire was as clear to him as to any other patriotic son of India, but again the strength of his practical nature gave him such patience that without forgetting the beacon in the distance, he could see the thorns that made the path difficult and dangerous.

These were the great outstanding qualities that impressed themselves more and more on me from my last meeting with him in London in 1910 until my final interview in Bombay in 1915. With age, his political wisdom and sagacity seemed to gain direction and strength, and had he been spared but a few years longer, he would have become the leader of the constitutional opposition, a party of criticism and power that would, with the awakened India of to-day, have made her advance to full self-government, if not easier, surer and more certain.

Source: H. P. Mody, *Sir Pherozeshah Mehta: A Political Biography*, The Times of India Press, Bombay, 1921, pp. vii-ix.
  The book was reprinted by the Asia Publishing House of Bombay and London in 1963 with the Aga Khan's foreword intact, though the title page of the reprint carried the words "with corrections".

In the Preface Mody wrote: "My principal obligations are to the Aga Khan for his great kindness in contributing a very thoughtful and admirable little Foreword . . ." (p. xii).

60

ISSUES IN INDIAN POLITICS

Interview with The Bombay Chronicle

Bombay: 3 February 1922

Edwin Montagu's and Lord Chelmsford's contributions to the Khilafat issue – his own involvement with the Turkish question – how
Indians should view it – attitudes in England and France – aspirations of the Turks – potential strength of Turkey – Non-Co-
operators and Co-operators must work together on the Turkish
Question – position of Indians in East Africa open to many dangers.

Interviewed by a representative of "The Chronicle" His Highness
informed him that his time had been employed, almost exclusively, in furthering the objects the Turkish Nationalists had in
view. On the burning Indian questions the Aga Khan refused to
give any opinion as he thought that they changed every moment
– and he had been absent from India nearly eleven months, as
he said. He paid a tribute to Mr. Montagu's services in regard to
the Khilafat question and said nobody could have done better.
Even the ex-Viceroy Lord Chelmsford was exerting his influence
on the right side. As for Lord Northcliffe's opinions, His Highness
thought that nobody was more difficult to be convinced than his
friend the "newspaper Napoleon" but once he was convinced
there could be no stauncher friend. He asked Indians never to
despair of a proper solution of the Turkish question, and never
to accept anything as a finality. He warned Indians to beware of
their position in East Africa.

His Highness said: It is not easy my giving any opinion as to
Indian questions, because I have been away for nearly eleven
months and the whole of this time my public activity was concentrated on the Turkish question. Indian affairs, internally, have
moved so fast that even coming in a few hours since my arrival I

see considerable difference, such as the wearing of Gandhi caps and use of Khaddar in the streets. In these circumstances, any expression of opinion about Indian subjects would be presumptuous on my part. My present concentration, which I hope will continue until the Turkish question is settled, on this one subject, does not indicate less patriotism or less fervour about India's own progress than that of any other of my countryman [sic], but, according to my lights, sincerely believe that the Turkish question, which is most urgent and in which the future welfare of the whole Moslem world and the sentiment and affection of 70 millions of Indian citizens are bound up needs my entire services. The one reason I can claim for this rather, apparently, egotistical interpretation is that I have studied the Turkish question and been in touch with the Turks of all thoughts for the last twenty years and more.

Well, we will discuss the Turkish question. I feel exactly like a man who is swimming across the stormy lake, who has reached a good long way, but who is still, in no sense, near the shore of safety, on the opposite side. At this moment, and with all the knowledge I have, it would be disloyal to my countrymen either to advise despondency or elation. The Turkish question is in midstream. I cannot, at present, even foretell whether there will be success or failure. To my Mussalman and my Hindu countrymen I may say: "Don't let go; keep on at it. Persist, but please don't bring into your persistence passion and racial hatred, but confidence in your good cause and in your inherent strength."

It is my duty, and it is a very simple truth and justice, to say that Mr. Montagu has been not only a hearty champion of our cause, but he is the very guardian, and no man not even Mr. Gandhi, even if he had been the Secretary of State for India, could have done more. I have come to know, since he retired, that Lord Chelmsford had advanced our cause with great vigour and strength. But the fact is they have not succeeded finally. On the other hand, we are a long way off from utter failure too.

In England, public opinion is divided, but it would be unfair to say that there are not large and powerful sections, in all political parties and among all classes, who must fully sympathise with our cause. In France, the Turkish cause has won a complete victory in public opinion and estimation and, of course, in France there are sections of society who are still opposed to this idea, yet they do not count amongst the bulk of the nation. It was not without hesitation, that I came out at this time, but I believe that there will be time enough to get back before the proceedings really get much further. What the solution will be, whether it is going to be favourable or unfavourable, I am at least quite determined, at any cost to myself, to be there, even if I have to be quite alone in the struggle.

You are asking me about the letter of Lord Northcliffe. Nobody who has the honour and privilege of knowing him, as well as I do, can doubt for one moment that he could be the last man to think of such a thing as "divide and rule," for I know well how difficult it is to convince him of the right and wrong of anything, but once convinced what a straightforward and stalwart champion he is!

With a little luck, perhaps, by the end of 1922, we may see a healthy, strong national Turkey, such as the Turks themselves have dreamed of, as an idea, starting in a new career of prosperity and peace. The Turkish patriots have a clear and simple and honourable idea. It is not imperialism, or Pan this or Pan that, but based on their legitimate rights to national independence, development and progress as an absolutely free country. At no price will they accept old "servitudes." On the other hand, they do not want to have subject races. The ideal they have put before themselves is a progressive national state like Spain or Sweden. The last thing that Mustapha Kemal Pasha and his associates wish to bring into their country is a position of political superiority for Moslems over all other religions. All faiths must be equal in the Turkish State and the minorities must have the same protection and privileges as those enjoyed by the majority. I am convinced that the Turks, if given a fair chance and twenty years of peace, will become a great source of strength for the world's civilisation, and not only for Asia, but even for Europe. They will become a bridge and bring about good-will amongst men, which is badly needed to-day in this world. Their example of progressive development, such as Spain and Sweden and other national States have carried, – and they are fit for it, – will have a good effect on Persia, on Afghanistan and many other Eastern countries.

I think, I may claim at this moment, I am working hard to bring about a favourable settlement, although I cannot go into the details, either after success or after failure. That is all.

On the Turkish question Non-Co-operators and Co-operators must work together. And we should not divide our forces even if there be a dim chance of success and I think it is little more than a dim chance. Should I ever be able honestly to say that the Turkish question is now solved with success, for defeat we must never accept whatever happens, then there is one question, I think, that needs a very serious consideration of some Indians who are not up to their neck in Indian internal politics, that is the question of the position of Indians in East Africa. It is open to many dangers.

Source: *The Bombay Chronicle*, Bombay, 4 February 1922.
The Aga Khan arrived in Bombay in the morning of 3 February from England after an absence of nearly one year. On landing at the Mole station he was given a reception and address by the Ismaili community.

61

CANCER MORTALITY

Letter to The Times

London (?): 7 June 1922

The question of whether or not cancer is more common in the West – its prevalence in India and other Eastern countries – the effects of tea and coffee.

The question whether or not cancer is more particularly a disease of Western civilization is of the utmost importance, and if, as a layman, I venture to participate in the discussion I do so as a warning against investigation being side-tracked without adequate consideration of facts which do not bear out such a conclusion. I have had opportunities of inquiry and personal observation in many Eastern lands, as well as in the West, and I gave the matter some special study when preparing my book "India in Transition."

It is generally thought that cancer is a disease of middle life and of old age. If, then, the incidence of this scourge is less noticeable in such countries as India and East and Central Africa than in those of the West, the natural explanation is that in those tropic lands the attainment of advanced middle life and of old age is rare. The "simple life" in the case of the vast majority in India means hard, almost unending toil, on coarse, innutritious, and often inadequate food. The man with all the appearance of a patriarch may be still in the forties. The Indian Census figures show a remarkably small percentage of people advanced in life, although the tendency, both from ignorance and from a desire for the respect of neighbours, is greatly to overstate the actual age. But cancer is by no means unknown in India amongst the few who reach middle life. It is, however, much more noticeable in the hardier races of the Frontier and Afghanistan, as well as among the Arabs and the Persians. I think that one explanation is that, while infant mortality with them is very heavy, when the years of childhood are past men and women do survive to ages more comparable to those attained in Western lands, this being probably due to their more generous diet, their hardy habits, and their outdoor life.

If tea-drinking has any effect in increasing liability to cancer, as Lord Rayleigh has suggested, the disease should long have been prevalent in Japan, where that beverage has been generally consumed for generations, and if coffee is also a contributory cause the Beduin Arabs should be specially liable, for they have drunk coffee for centuries.

Source: *The Times*, London, 8 June 1922.
The letter was probably written from France where the Aga Khan used to spend his summers.

62

A ROYAL VICEROY

An Article

London: 21 June 1922

Some misconceptions about the East prevalent among the English people – traditionally Eastern kings were in contact with their people – Englishmen must be realistic – the example of the Prince of Wales's visit to India – the King's message to the Indians – proposal for a non-political Royal Viceroy and a Prime Minister.

It was my privilege to witness some of the episodes of the tour of H.R.H. the Prince of Wales in India, and I was present at the closing enthusiastic scenes at Karachi. From my friends in various parts of India I have learned something of the effect his visit produced in provinces to which I did not go.

Most people in this country, and perhaps not a few Englishmen in India, have quite a wrong idea of the things which most impress Indians when associated with Royalty, or with persons of princely rank. They fancy that the King-Emperor, or the Prince, or the maharajahs must always be seen by the public seated upon elephants or rhinoceroses, or other beasts. They suppose that the ruler or the princely visitor must never appear except as the central figure of a pageant or procession, and that if he moves about in a more simple way the people will be disappointed. These conceptions of the East are almost wholly misleading. It is quite true that on great solemn occasions a pageant or an elaborate ceremony is expected in India, just as it is in this country. Probably the culminating pageant in the long history of India was the great Imperial Durbar held at Delhi by the present King-Emperor upon his accession. I doubt whether a more marvellous and inspiring spectacle had ever been seen in India, and I do not think we shall look upon its like again. But the average

726

Indian, whether peasant or landowner or man of business, does not expect to see a pageant frequently, and maharajahs are more accustomed to move about in motor-cars or on horseback than upon an elephant – a very uncomfortable animal to ride.

My point is that when people over here picture Indian princes as only appearing on elephants surrounded by a crowd of retainers, they are assuming that the ruler carefully holds himself aloof from his subjects. Nothing is more false. All the traditions of the greatest Kings of the East show that they constantly came into contact with the very humblest of their people. When our august King-Emperor rode through the streets of Calcutta attended by only an equerry, when our gracious Queen-Empress turned aside from formal gatherings and visited ancient Indian cities and fortresses in the utmost simplicity and talked to the people she met there, their Majesties were only carrying out the old Asiatic custom that Monarchs must mix with their subjects, lest they remain unknown to the masses.

I hope Englishmen, when they think about India, will get away from the elephants and try to get down to the plain earth. It was perhaps the greatest merit of the Prince of Wales while in India, and certainly the thing the public appreciate most, that he always tried to lessen the ceremonial gatherings and to mix with the people. The opportunities were too few, but the Prince sought them whenever he could, even though sometimes he had to break rigid regulations. One such occasion was at the Poona races, where he mingled with the crowd on the racecourse like any ordinary visitor. Another occasion, I am told, was on the night of his departure from Bombay, when escorts were swept aside and his car slowly passed to the railway station surrounded by overwhelming and enthusiastic crowds. In England these may seem little things, but in India they mean much. India does not always want to see its rulers clad in robes of State. One of the greatest poets the East ever produced, Roumi, once wrote:- "We want eyes that will recognize the King, whatever dress he may wear."

The unaffected simplicity of the Prince's bearing upon all occasions, and his efforts to abstain from pomp and formality, set an example which has not been lost upon the younger princes of India. Sometimes I fear that our Indian princes may forget the ancient traditions and surround themselves with ceremonious practices not in keeping with this democratic age. Perhaps I am wrong, but in any case the methods of his Royal Highness taught a wholesome lesson which will have a great influence and will not soon be forgotten. Under modern conditions those who hold great hereditary positions will not succeed in retaining public confidence unless they abandon all tendencies to remoteness and seek knowledge of those below them in rank. In Europe these considerations are well understood. Apart from our gracious King and Queen, I may instance the King of Italy, and that Monarch who is very deeply beloved by her people because of her traditional intimacy with them, the Queen of Holland.

Another thing which endeared the Prince of Wales to the people of India was his intense love of all forms of sport. They deeply admired his courage, his daring, and his coolness. They expect their rulers to be courageous, and in the Prince of Wales they were not disappointed. I have met Englishmen who honestly supposed that the spirit of sport was introduced into India only under British rule. Nothing could be farther from the truth. The very game of polo, in which the Prince is so proficient, had its origin in Persia. Sporting records go back to the very beginning of Indian history. Chandragupta, with whose name the authentic story of Indian history begins, was a mighty hunter until quite late in life, and so was the Emperor Asoka. The Moguls were sportsmen before everything else, and so were Shivaji and the Maharrata princes. The long association of the Rajputs with sport is familiar knowledge. Indians love a good sportsman, and they found one in the Prince.

I talked to a great many so-called Extremists while I was in India at the time of the Prince's visit. Even those who had abstained from joining in the welcome to his Royal Highness on account of their differences with the Government told me that they liked the Prince, and admired and respected him as a man more than they could say. In spite of political clouds, I believe that if the vast majority of Indians could express a verdict they would be warm in their personal devotion to the Prince and to the Crown. It may sound a paradox, but it is true.

The Message which the King-Emperor sent to India through the Prince of Wales contains the following noble passage:–

"In the spirit of sympathy my Son has followed from afar your fortunes. It is now his ambition by his coming among you to ripen good will into a yet fuller understanding. I trust and believe that when he leaves your shores your hearts will follow him and he will stay with you, and that one link the more will be added to the golden chain of sympathy which for these many years has held my Throne to India. And it is my warmest prayer that wisdom and contentment, growing hand-in-hand, will lead India into ever-increasing national greatness within a free Empire – the Empire for which I labour and for which, if it be the Divine will, my Son shall labour after me."

We all trust it may be many decades before the Prince of Wales enters upon the exalted task described in these memorable words, but meanwhile I would plead that the lesson taught by the good results which have flowed from the Prince's visit to India should not be ignored. It is now fifteen years since I developed, in an article in the *National Review*, the proposal for a Royal Viceroy of India which I had already long meditated. After more than a decade, I again put forward the suggestion in an expanded form in my book "India in Transition", published in 1918.

The ties which unite India to the Royal House should be strengthened by the appointment of a permanent non-political Royal Viceroy, one of the sons of the King-Emperor. Such a Viceroy would have to be prepared to give the best years of his life to India. The customary five years' appointment would not suffice. The Royal Viceroy would have to live in India and for India. My proposal presumes that the Viceroy would be associated with a Prime Minister, chosen for a term of five years by the Home Government, who would discharge the political duties now devolving on the Viceroy. A non-political Royal Viceroy would, at his Court, be the natural head of the princes and of the public men of India. He would travel much, would encourage the main-fold [*sic*] arts of the country, and would be the centre of the social life of the Indian Empire.

From time to time I have discussed this suggestion with many hundreds of people in India, and I have always found it received with warm approval, and even with enthusiasms. The recent changes in the polity of India add greatly to the desirability of putting the scheme into effect on completion of the term of Lord Reading, who has shown such wisdom and foresight in adminis-tration. The return of the Prince of Wales, whose visit has been attended with such good results, induces me to bring forward this scheme once more. I am sure that India would welcome it, and its greatest advantage would be that it would instantly lift the King's representative, upon whom more depends than England is aware, out of the arena of political controversy.

The Prince's tour has produced some important lessons con-cerning the future of British rule in India, of which I am and have always been an ardent supporter, and we should profit by these lessons while there is yet time, for there is not too much time.

Source: *The Times*, London, 21 June 1922.

63

BONAR LAW AND THE TURKISH QUESTION

Letter to The Times

London: 9 October 1922

Bonar Law is wrong in assuming Muslims would interpret British withdrawal from Turkey as a defeat – Muslims believe otherwise – Muslims are neither backward nor ignorant.

I beg you to allow me, as a Muslim, to take exception to a passage in Mr. Bonar Law's letter, published by you on Saturday.

Mr. Bonar Law says that a British "withdrawal" would have been "regarded throughout the whole Mussalman world as the defeat of the British Empire". He further makes a remarkable allusion to the danger which he supposes "would arise as a consequence of what would have been regarded as British impotence in the face of a victorious Turkish army".

I have, perhaps, a better knowledge of the "Mussalman world" than most people, and, without in the least wishing to engage in controversy with so distinguished a statesman, I feel compelled to traverse these particular suggestions most emphatically.

It is a slur on the intelligence of Muhammadans, and an assumption that they are absurdly ignorant, to imply that they do not know the relative strength and resources of the mighty British Empire and of this new and unpretentious Turkish National State, shorn of all its outlying provinces. Far from regarding withdrawal as an act of weakness, Muslims in all countries would have instantly said that Great Britain had shown a strong man's generosity in ceasing to bar the way to the return of the Turks to their national home. Mr. Bonar Law shows a distressing misconception of Mussalman feeling if he supposes that withdrawal would have been contemptuously described as "impotence" by Muslims. They would have hailed such an act of

731

joy, and would have held it to be a proof of new and better relations between Britain and Islam.

I cannot tell you how great will be the shock to Muhammadans to find that a universally respected statesman like Mr. Bonar Law, who has been the leader of a great political party, and who may fill the highest office, so completely misunderstands Muhammadan psychology, and, in particular, holds in such low esteem the intelligence of His Majesty's loyal Muhammadan subjects throughout the Empire.

May I point out that the French and the Italians withdrew from Chanak without suffering any loss of prestige among Muhammadans? The prestige of France in the world of Islam never stood higher than it does today. In all my life I have never known any Western Power so highly honoured among Muhammadans as is now the case with France. It is no secret that Marshal Lyautey has declared that his Government's policy in Turkey has helped him very much in his great work for civilization in North Africa. Would not the Viceroy's task in India have been greatly facilitated if British policy in the Near East had been more closely on the lines followed by France?

People must not think that Muhammadans are living in a very backward condition. I have even found an aged Mullah, who did not know a word of English, studying a translation of the "Statesman's Year Book", which had been specially prepared so that he might know the resources of the various countries of the world. In the last decade the Muhammadans, who are not ignorant savages, have learned the difference between the logical and sincere friendship of a great nation like France and the theatrical and false advances of the ex-Kaiser, ever ready to stab his "friends" in the back.

While I felt that Mr. Bonar Law's statements could not pass unchallenged, I prefer, at this stage, to make no further comment on the Near Eastern situation, which I – like the King's loyal Muslim subjects – rejoice to see is improving.

Source: *The Times*, London, 10 October 1922.
It was written from the Ritz Hotel, Piccadilly, London, where the Aga Khan normally stayed on his short or long visits to London.
Bonar Law wrote the following letter, which was published on 7 October (written from 24 Onslow Gardens), entitled by the journal "The Near East: Pronouncement by Mr. Bonar Law: 'We Cannot Act Alone': The Choice Before France":
Sir, – I have followed with the greatest anxiety recent events in the Near East, and the position at this moment seems to me very alarming. It would serve no

useful purpose to criticize or even to consider the circumstances which have led up to the present situation; what is alone important is to find the right course of action to be taken now.

When the Greek forces were annihilated in Asia Minor and driven into the sea at Smyrna, it seems to me certain that, unless a decisive warning had at once been issued, the Turkish forces, flushed with victory, would have attempted to enter Constantinople and cross into Thrace. If they had been allowed to do so, what would have been the result?

In the first place, our withdrawal in such circumstances would have been regarded throughout the whole Musulman world as the defeat of the British Empire, and, although it may be true that the supposed pro-Greek sympathies of the British Government have alienated Musulman feeling in India, the danger of trouble in India from that cause would be as nothing in comparison with the danger which would arise as a consequence of what could have been regarded as British impotence in the face of a victorious Turkish army.

Further, such an advance of the Turkish forces would probably have meant a repetition in Constantinople of the recent events in Smyrna; it would certainly have involved Thrace in horrors similar to those which have occurred in Anatolia, and the probability – indeed, I think it a certainty – of the renewal of war throughout the Balkans.

It was, therefore, undoubtedly right that the British Government should endeavour to prevent these misfortunes. It is not, however, right that the burden of taking necessary action should fall on the British Empire alone. The prevention of war and massacre in Constantinople and the Balkans is not socially a British interest; it is the interest of humanity. The retention also of the freedom of the Straits is not specially a British interest; it is the interest of the world. We are at the Straits and in Constantinople not by our own action alone, but by the will of the Allied Powers which won the war, and America is one of these Powers.

What, then, in such circumstances ought we to do? Clearly the British Empire, which includes the largest body of Mahomedans in any State, ought not to show any hostility or unfairness to the Turks. In the agreement arranged with the Allies in Paris by Lord Curzon, proposals were made to the Turks which are certainly fair to them, and beyond these terms in my opinion, the Allies ought not to go.

I see rumours in different newspapers, which I do not credit, that the French representative with the Kemalist forces has encouraged them to make impossible demands. The course of action for our Government seems to me clear. We cannot alone act as the policemen of the world. The financial and social condition of this country makes that impossible. It seems to me, therefore, that our duty is to say plainly to our French Allies that the position in Constantinople and the Straits is as essential a part of the Peace settlement as the arrangements with Germany, and that if they are not prepared to support us there, we shall not be able to bear the burden alone, but shall have no alternative except to imitate the Government of the United States and to restrict our attention to the guarding of the more immediate interests of the Empire.

64

POSSIBILITY OF A TURKISH SETTLEMENT

Interview with The Times of India

Bombay: 15 December 1922

Turkish question not resolved – support from British newspapers
– question of the holy places not understood – a powerful Turkey
will be a source of strength for Britain.

In the course of a brief interview, the Aga Khan told the representative of the *Times of India* on Friday night that his mind was still preoccupied with the difficult question that confronted the Turkish Empire and he had determined to serve the best interests of Islam. They were yet a long way off from a final solution, but if they kept their spirits and applied the lessons of history to the present question, they would yet live to see a satisfactory solution of the most intricate and delicate position.

After emphasising the need of exercising wise statesmanship on the part of Turkish statesmen, the Aga Khan said: I want to impress one thing upon my co-religionists; it is the help that several powerful organs of English public opinion have rendered to the cause of peace. I must at once say that we owe a deep debt of gratitude to the *Daily Mail,* the *Evening News* and the *Mirror.* Their firm, constant and logical advocacy and counsel of moderation had produced a tremendous effect on the man in the street in England, and it is after all the opinion of the man in the street that counts for anything in the Government of England. If it were not for these powerful papers in educating the opinion of the man in the street and rousing them to a sense of justice and fairplay to Turkey, I do not know what would have happened in those critical days of September and October last. It is fair and necessary to state that for months and months past and from different angles of vision the *Morning Post* and *Daily Express* have constantly urged peace and good-will towards the Mahomedan countries, and I am convinced that the majority of Englishmen and those who form the backbone of the British Empire – I mean the man in the street – desire a fair and final settlement of the difficulties that have gradually grown up during the last thirty or forty years; and they realise the inequity of the dead Treaty of Sèvres.

The difficulty was that the question of the holy places was not properly understood by the man in the street in England and Englishmen cannot, therefore, make up their minds rapidly on the subject, but there are enough signs on all hands in England that the number of people desiring a fair and final settlement of the Turkish question is daily growing. To this day our whole case about the holy places has not been properly understood by Englishmen, and we must continue to enlighten them about their special treatment.

I believe great efforts will be needed yet before a just appreciation of the real issues is secured, but I have every reason to hope that once public opinion realises how little the Moslems' real desires and ambitions are in opposition to Great Britain and the Empire, then there will be every possibility of a satisfactory settlement which when once effected will relieve Indian Moslems from the burden of preoccupation of non-Indian questions for many years to come. International difficulties, especially after bitter memories of a disastrous war will take long to settle, and I entreat Moslems to remember that fact and not become impatient at delays. I have always spoken my mind plainly and emphatically because I believe that every well-wisher of Islam and the British Empire will be only doing a great service to the cause of justice and peace by indicating where the danger lies. I am a strong believer that a powerful Turkey will be a source of great strength to the British Government and the alliance between the two nations will be the effective means of securing the peace of the world in the future.

In conclusion the Aga Khan said that a lasting peace will be secured between Great Britain and Turkey and that the alliance will prove of mutual benefit to both and the world at large.

Source: *The Times of India*, Bombay, 16 December 1922.
   The Civil and Military Gazette of the same date also carried the interview.
   The Times of India reported:
"His Highness the Aga Khan arrived in Bombay on Friday by the mail steamer MACEDONIA and was accorded an ovation by the Moslem community on his landing at the Baliard Pier. A large shamiana was erected on the north-west

side of the Baliard Pier station where a reception was held and His Highness was hailed as a pillar of Islam, and as a saviour who had striven his utmost to preserve the integrity of Turkey. Besides the members of the Moslem community, a large number of Hindus and Parsis were also present to accord a cordial welcome to the Aga Khan, who is regarded as the great Indian patriot. His Excellency the Governor was represented by Major Vaux, Military Secretary, who had arrived at the Pier long before the arrival of the mail steamer. After receiving the homage of the Moslem community in the shamiana, the Aga Khan drove to the Khoja Jamatkhana and there he met the members of his Jamat and then proceeded to his bungalow at Land's End Road, Malabar Hill, where hundreds of telegrams of welcome from different parts of India were awaiting his arrival.

"When His Highness the Aga Khan left India for England in April last he declared to a representative of the *Times of India* that he had made a study of the Turkish question his own to the exclusion of every other subject, and he had concentrated his attention and energy on the satisfactory solution of the Turkish question and the bringing about a modification of the Treaty of Sèvres, and he entreated the Moslems of India to continue to support the Angora Government and to do their utmost by deeds and words to bring about a lasting peace between England and Turkey and secure justice for the latter. During his stay in Europe he dedicated his services to the cause of Turkey and Islam and threw in his great weight and influence to secure a satisfactory solution of the Turkish question. At the present critical juncture in the history of Islam his presence and advice will no doubt be beneficial to Indian Moslems and to the Empire."

65

COUNSEL TO THE MUSLIMS OF INDIA

Speech at the Anjuman-i-Islamia High School, Bombay

Bombay: 15 January 1923

The problem of Turkey and the Muslim feeling – comparison with the movement in Russia to free the southern Slavs – the settlement of Turkish Question in sight – attitude of the English people and the English press – problems of Muslims in Bombay – government service and liberal professions open to a few – trade, commerce and agriculture for the majority – prepare Muslim youth to adjust to new conditions – training in commercial matters vital – importance of English and other subjects – social implications – education of girls – renaissance of India – depressed classes – work of Christian missionaries – help for fellow Indians.

I must thank you for your courtesy in inviting me to distribute prizes this afternoon and I assure you that I feel honoured for this mark of esteem. It is many years since I was in this hall presiding at a similar ceremony and great events have taken place in the world, the effects of which were bound to be felt in every corner of the world of Islam.

Since the armistice, one might say that one thought has been supreme throughout the world of Islam, namely, the problem of Turkey. In India we instinctively felt what was at the time the common soul movement throughout the length and breadth of Islam. Nor was this phenomenon unique or a special manifestation of the common civilisation and temperament of Islamic peoples. Russia had gone through a similar movement stronger than the Czar or the Government, when in the seventies in spite of the will of the autocrat and the responsible Government, in spite of the passionate advocacy of Tolstoy, the nation insisted that the southern Slavs must be freed.

737

But there are many signs that not only the worst is over but that a final solution for the settlement of the Turkish question is within sight. It is true that the problems affecting the holy places and Jezirul-al-Arab have not been yet approached, leave alone solved, but here again once the great problem of Turkey is peacefully settled, adjustments satisfactory to Islamic sentiment should follow if there be still any statesmanship left. So at this moment we can rightly once more begin concentrating on our own great problems here and now, in this country and in this Presidency and in this City.

Before I leave the Turkish question it is my duty to bear witness that the overwhelming majority of the English people were sincerely anxious that good and friendly relations should grow up once more between their great Empire and the Turkish nation. No one who lived through the critical days of last autumn in London can ever forget the real goodwill and earnest desire to be fair with the Turk which prevailed amongst the overwhelming majority of the English people. I would indeed be wanting in honesty if I should fail to tell you that I consider it essential that the Moslems of this country should realise that whatever a few noisy party men may have said or may still say, the backbone of England, the man in the street, and his organs such as the *Daily Mail,* the *Daily Express,* the *Evening News* and a great many provincial papers have sincerely and earnestly desired that after these years of strain and stress a healthy national Turkey should arise and should enjoy peace and prosperity amongst the nations of the world.

Any man who knows John Bull knows perfectly well that it was his inherent sense of fair-dealing and fair-play that brought him round to see through the fog of exaggeration and prejudice that had been raised before his eyes and that the present goodwill towards the Turks as a nation is not due to the influence of this or that extraneous body but to the sterling commonsense and clear vision of the average Englishman himself. This being the position to-day, even a rupture of one or two conferences will not take us far from a new era of goodwill and friendship.

We must look at our own immense difficulties, economic, social, educational, etc., here and now. Unfortunately, one cannot separate these activities in daily life. They overlay. Now in this great city, the economic, the educational and the social welfare of the Mussalmans stand, or fall together and in order to meet our needs before taking any further steps we must carefully consider what ought to be our legitimate objective. Is it for the best that we should turn out the largest possible number of Moslems with a high literary or scientific education – the largest possible number of graduates seeking entrance into the narrow paths of the liberal professions or Government Service?

I, for one, cannot but look upon the final selection of such an objective as anything short of disastrous for the Moslems of this City and by the secondary effects disastrous for the Moslems of Western and Southern India. Government service, the liberal professions, high scientific specialism are necessary in every civilised society but they are in the nature of protective coverings for the central stream of national and social life and the moment they try to usurp the functions of the real body they degenerate and even their own vitality and energy are replaced by a mere formalism. For the overwhelming majority in a healthy society the objective must be trade and commerce, agriculture and livestock farming. But it is infinitely more necessary to remember this central truth when one happens to be a citizen of a great city with unbounded commercial possibilities. The present ruler of this Presidency has truly and well laid in New Bombay the foundations of a city that may well some day be second to none in the world and admitting that Karachi in the north or other ports in the East and the South may tap areas that Bombay regards as its own hinterland, even admitting a full development of similar ports in India, the natural and inevitable country of which Bombay must remain the commercial metropolis will be at least equal to Germany in population and natural resources.

We all sincerely hope and trust that the splendid ideal placed before the nation in the Minority Report of the Fiscal Commission in brilliant words that India may hold a commanding position as one of the industrial countries may come true: but supposing for the sake of argument that India is condemned to remain an essentially agricultural country, yet the ordinary agricultural world of the natural hinterland of Bombay will be great enough to assure a future of great prosperity to this beautiful city. This being the case what is the right objective for the Mahomedans of this City? What is the educational, social and economic ideal for the future? In my opinion it can only be that the three great commercial communities, Memons, Khojahs and Borahs, should bring up their youth in a way that they may adjust themselves to the new conditions which will lead to economic success in the Bombay of the future.

In Great Britain, as you are aware, there has been a tendency of recent years to employ more and more university men with brilliant academic careers behind them in commercial affairs. Such men, however, can naturally enter the field comparatively late in life, rarely much before 23, but there are reasons for seriously doubting that what prevails to-day in England would succeed in India or would have succeeded in England when her development was still in its embryonic stage as India's is to-day. The same was true of economic Germany. After she had got over the first twenty or thirty years of her great commercial epoch, the need for highly cultured minds at the head of economic activities was felt, but we are still far away from that period and the reason why in the first decade of development we need men with a less advanced culture is simply and solely that if we can judge by the experience of other countries young men, men well under 20, alone can acquire the commercial mentality without which success is impossible.

To-day the graduate, the brilliant scholar of 22 or 23, has gone too far to be able to come back to the elementary commercial activity which alone is in keeping with our elementary state. Yet the old-fashioned gentleman, splendid as he was in trade in the fifties and sixties or even twenty years ago, is undoubtedly handicapped. I am not in a position to quote examples because I would touch on personal matters which have come to my knowledge through the confidence of friends, but I could quote you many cases of Indians and Moslems in particular all over the country who, having only an old-fashioned education, thrived in trade and commerce, but who, entirely due to the very handicap of not knowing modern conditions, were forced to have the work of a life-time undermined during the last few years. It was not merely bad trade conditions. It was absence of working knowledge of modern affairs that ruined many a millionaire.

The budding commercial apprentice of to-morrow must have a thorough working colloquial knowledge of one foreign language and that foreign language must be English because apart from any other considerations it is the language of commerce throughout the world. He must know arithmetic: he must know geography: he must know the elements of science. He must be under 20 in any case. How are we to get innumerable boys under 20 with a good working knowledge of the three R's and of their own local conditions. This is the problem for the Mahomedans of this City and this Presidency. The instruction must have gone beyond the matriculation but need not lead to being a graduate but whatever has to be learned must be learned thoroughly; mastery is needed.

In this city, two of the most distinguished Moslem millionaires of the younger generation, both of them holding high honours from the State, have, I believe, suggested giving large sums for the advance of education. May I appeal to them not to forget the commercial activity which alone will assure to their communities a future more brilliant than the past? There are other large benefactions and benefactors. To all of these gentlemen I appeal and to you the leaders of the community also to find ways and means by which the rising generation may meet the great commercial struggle which is sure to come.

As I said just now, the economic, social and educational welfare of a nation go hand in hand and I cannot leave off without referring to the social implications of our problem. I was told only yesterday by a friend that it was seriously proposed to introduce universal compulsory education in this great City for all of both sexes with one single exception, Mahomedan girls. Can it be possible? I can only say that if such a thing came to pass its results would be a Treaty of Sèvres this time not for Turkey but for the Mussalmans of this City. The very essential for producing the wide-awake, alert young man of under 20 to go into commercial life is to keep abreast of the intellectual movements of the day with our daughters. Without this cooperation of both sexes you may produce learned and wise students, scholars and scientists, great doctors and lawyers but you will never produce that stream of alert, active men going into commerce and holding their own with the average Englishman and American, the German and the Japanese. I implore you not to forget the education of girls and if for reasons which I for one fail to see, in spite of the usual excuses the City cannot educate its Mahomedan girls, well then let the Mahomedan communities do so, especially the three commercial ones.

One last word and I have done. We hear a great deal of the renaissance of India, another risorgimento, compared with that of Italy and Japan, taking place in India. But the sure way by which the reality of this movement can be proved is the solution which the people of this country as a whole and amongst them by their number and status the Moslems of India should bring to the immense problem of the 60 million depressed classes and untouchables. I hear the cynic whispering "blind leaders of the blind." Yes, in every great city of India you see scores of unfortunates who have lost their sight leading others who have still further misfortunes added to the infirmity of blindness. By all means to the extent we find our path let us carry our still more unfortunate brother along with us. Whether we be blind or far-seeing we should try and carry our neighbours with us.

In the days of my youth it was the fashion amongst certain classes of all communities to look with amused indifference on the work that was being done by the missions of all European denominations and countries. To-day is there a single honest man who will refuse to honour and respect the great heroic and magnificent work at the cost of enormous wealth and labour, which Christian missions of all denominations and some of the most important coming from foreign countries like America, France and Germany, carry on in this country amongst the depressed classes? I am glad that some of the leaders of the Hindus are starting to pay the Christian missions the greatest of all compliments – imitation. Are we Mussulmans alone to follow the sure and easy path of selfishment [*sic*]? No, just as rightly you forgot your own problems during the last few years in the face of the disaster that then threatened your fellow Moslems in the Near East – men who were drawn to you by the ties of a common civilisation and of not unsimilar manners and habits. So, do not be entirely absorbed with your own problems and forget those of not fellow-Moslems but fellow-Indians: men of not unsimilar races and certainly of the same country amongst whom we live and thrive? If the renaissance, if the revival, is real and genuine this great work of service towards those who are by our side and in still greater trouble through no fault of their own will not be entirely left undone by the Moslems of this City, of this Presidency, and of India.

Source: *The Times of India*, Bombay, 16 January 1923.
The Civil and Military Gazette of Lahore carried a shorter report (circulated by the Associated Press) on 18 January. *The Times of India* gave this report of the function:
"The prize distribution ceremony of the Anjuman-i-Islam High School was performed by His Highness the Aga Khan in the Anjuman Hall, Hornby Road, Bombay on Monday afternoon. There was a large and distinguished gathering. Among those present, being the Hon. Mr. H. S. Lawrence, the Hon. Mr. C. V. Mehta, the Hon. Khan Bahadur Sheikh Ghulam Husein Hidayatallah, Haji Sulem Abdul Wahed, the Hon. Mr Justice Kajiji, Hon. Sir Ibrahim Rahimtoola, Aga Shah Rookshah Mr. Kaji Kabriuddin, Mr Mahomedbhai Hajibhai, Mr. Husenali Mahomedbhoy, Mr Rahim Chinoy, Mr. S. I. Haji, and Khan Bahadur Hakim Dayam.
"The procedure opened with the reading of the report by Mr G. V. Panandikar, the head master, after a programme of recitations in Persian, Urdu, Gujerati, and English was gone through the boys who participated in the same acquitting themselves creditably. H. H. the Aga Khan then made an important speech. Referring to the Turkish problem, he said there were signs that the

worst was over and that a final solution for its settlement was within sight. He bore testimony to the fact that the overwhelming majority of Englishmen were sincerely anxious that good and friendly relations should grow up once more between their great Empire and the Turkish nation and he foresaw a new era of goodwill and friendship.

"The headmaster's report stated that the past year had been one of unprecedented anxiety and trouble. In the first place, their work had been considerably interrupted by the prevalent fever in the city. Secondly, three of the Mahomedan graduate teachers left the school abruptly on account of the non-co-operation movement. Their greatest trouble, however, arose from the stir and commotion that had unsettled the minds of the students, several of whom joined the newly started national schools. On the other hand, there were also commendable instances of students who were so attached to the institution that they refused to join the N.-C.-O. movement, although for this they were actually turned out of the orphanages which fed, clothed and sheltered them. These students would have had to go without further education had it not been for the timely help of Khan Bahadur Hakim Mahomed Davam, the Secretary, who rendered monetary assistance to such students from the trust funds of the late Haji Ismail Haji Allana, which were at his disposal. The number of students have dwindled this year from 235 to 204. This decline is chiefly due to the N.-C.-O. movement, which has also considerably retarded the admissions. There was no wonder, therefore, that the receipts from fees were very poor and the financial position very unsatisfactory. However, through the untiring efforts of the present office-bearers, a princely donation of Rs. 2,00,000 was secured from the charities created under the will of the late Haji Ahmed Hasham.

"A vote of thanks to His Highness the Aga Khan was proposed by Mr. Justice Kajiji and was carried with acclamation."

66

THE INDIAN QUESTION IN KENYA

Letter to The Times of India

Bombay: 23(?) January 1923

Relations between Indians and the white settlers in Kenya – danger
to the interests of the British Empire – immediate threat in East
Africa – Indian respect for law and order – consequences of "lynch
law" – racial outbreak in Kenya will weaken the Empire – a deputation to Kenya – British Empire an association of people of all
races – European non-officials in India should use their influence
and convince the white settlers.

Though it is possible to exaggerate the immediate consequences
of the present situation in Kenya, I feel that unless steps are
taken to put the relations of the settlers and the Indians on a
sound footing, great and indeed incalculable injury may be done
to the interests of the Empire as a whole. We saw only three years
ago how the Turkish question affected this country and it would
be a misfortune if now that the main lines of settlement are
within sight and that there is every reasonable hope that sooner
or later the question of the Jezira and the Holy places will be
settled, another problem directly affecting Indian sentiment
should arise outside this country and compete in the public
mind and conscience with the great and growing problems of
economic, financial and political reconstruction which are facing
this country, just as they are all states. The immediate danger in
East Africa is that a few hot heads may commit acts that will affect
the mind and imagination of Indians not only there and now
but here and in the future.

Great Britain's connection with India has brought this country
many benefits, but one of the greatest is undoubtedly the fact that
the Indian has gradually absorbed the Anglo-Saxon sentiment of

respect for law and that private vengeance and political and religious acts of violence have grown rarer than in many countries.

Nothing shows better the civilisation of a state than the comparison between the frequency of violence from purely sordid motives or from motives that in themselves are not expressions of low passion. In countries where crime is entirely due to the former, such as Great Britain, it means that the degenerates alone break the law, while in countries where men take the law into their own hands from better motives the people have not yet learnt the essential and elementary fact that such actions, even if right and legitimate, should be brought about by the general consensus of opinion rather than by individuals or parties. If at such a period in India's history when crimes due to political, racial and religious motives are being more and more condemned by opinion of all schools of thought – if at such a period in a colony where respectable and law abiding and some most loyal Indians have made a home for generations – "lynch law" is, once started, the great work, for civilisation in this country will be immediately thrown back for decades.

In the years before the Great War it was not uncommon to hear German publicists refer in private conversations to the British and French Empires as the two *Piebald* Empires of the West but they learnt in Flanders and in France that great empires can appeal to men of all races when their ultimate foundation is sound. I fear that a racial outbreak between Europeans and Indians with race as the dividing line may weaken those very roots that led to the success of the Empire in the Great War. The Government of India as such will no doubt do what is within its power provided the matter is brought to its notice but there are two lines of action by the public of this country that might lead to an improvement of the situation and help the case of the Indian Government. The first is that my countrymen of all schools of thought should select two or three universally respected individuals, men like Mr. Sastri who knows the colonial better than anyone I can think of, and send them as bearers of a message of expostulation and reconciliation to the settlers in East Africa from one public of British Empire to another, and make a direct attempt at improvement of feeling. The other is to the European non-officials of this country and their organisations. If they really realise that the British Empire of the future should be an association of co-operation between men of all races and creeds and customs, then indeed in the case of East

Africa above all portions of the Empire, they should use their full influence and power to bring about a better general feeling and to convince the colonials that whatever the short view, in the long run their own interests make it necessary to have a large and prosperous and happy Indian colony in Kenya.

Source: *The Times of India*, Bombay, 26 January 1923.

There is no date on the letter, and one may presume that it was written on some date between 22 and 24 January.

Apparently the Aga Khan passed on a copy of his letter to the Bombay correspondent of *The Times* before its publication in *The Times of India*, because the London journal carried in its issue of 27 January the following dispatch from its Bombay man dated Bombay, 25 January, headlined "The Aga Khan's Warning":

"Writing in *The Times of India*, the Aga Khan says: 'Unwise steps in Kenya would do incalculable harm to the Empire. If on the eve of a settlement with Turkey another external problem directly affecting Indian sentiment arose, reconstruction in India would be thrown back. One of the greatest blessings that Great Britain has brought to India is respect for the law. It at a time when crimes in India due to political, racial and religious motives are increasingly condemned by all schools of thought, lynch law were started in a colony where respectable and law-abiding Indians have made their home for generations, the great work for civilization in this country would be thrown back for decades. A racial outbreak in Kenya may weaken those very roots which conduced to the success of the Empire in the war."

For the question of the Asian settlers in East Africa see Robert G. Gregory, *India and East Africa*, Oxford, 1971.

As a sizeable Ismaili community lives in East Africa and the Aga Khan wrote and spoke about the area on several occasions the reader might find it useful to know the literature available to him on the region. Hence the following select bibliography:

East Africa (as a whole): R. L. Moreau, *Africans musulmans: des communautés en mouvement*, Paris, 1882; J. S. Trimingham, *Islam in East Africa*, Oxford, 1964; E. A. Brett, *Colonialism and Underdevelopment in East Africa: The Politics of Economic Change, 1919–1939*, London, 1973; O. W. Furley and T. Watson, *A History of Education in East Africa*, New York, 1978; R. G. Gregory, *India and East Africa: A History of Race Relations Within the British Empire, 1890–1939*, Oxford, 1971; V. Harlow and E. M. Chilver (eds), *History of East Africa, Vol. II*, Oxford, 1965; D. A. Low and Alison Smith (eds), *History of East Africa, Vol. III*, Oxford, 1976; J. S. Mangat, *A History of the Asians in East Africa, c. 1886–1945*, Oxford, 1969; K. Rai, *Indians and British Colonialism in East Africa, 1883–1939*, Patna, 1979; A. D. Roberts (ed.), *The Cambridge History of Africa, Vol. 7, from 1905 to 1940*, Cambridge, 1986; Michael Crowder (ed.), *The Cambridge History of Africa, Vol. 8, from c. 1940 to c. 1975*, Cambridge, 1984; "The Indian Problem in East Africa", *Round Table*, March 1922; Robert G. Gregory, "Churchill's Administration of East Africa: A Period of Disillusionment", *Journal of Indian History*, August 1966; Aziz Esmail, "Towards a History of Islam in East Africa", *Kenya Historical Review*, Vol. 3 (1975), pp. 147–58; and D. P. and Y. P. Ghai (eds), *Portrait of a Minority: Asians in East Africa* (2nd edition), Nairobi, 1970.

Kenya: N. Leys, *Kenya*, London, 1924; G. H. Mungeam, *British Rule in Kenya, 1895–1912*, Oxford, 1966; Margaret Strobel, *Muslim Women in Mombasa,*

1890–1975, New Haven, 1979; J. B. Webster et. al., *A Bibliography on Kenya*, Syracuse, 1967; and Bethwell A. Ogot, *Historical Dictionary of Kenya*, Metuchen, New Jersey, and London, 1981.

Tanganyika: R. Heussler, *British Tanganyika: An Essay and Documents on District Administration*, Durham, N.C., 1972; J. Iliffe, *A Modern History of Tanganyika*, Cambridge, 1979; and S. R. Walji, "A History of the Ismaili Community in Tanzania", unpublished Ph.D. thesis, University of Wisconsin, 1974.

Tanzania: Laura S. Kurtz, *Historical Dictionary of Tanzania*, Metuchen, New Jersey, and London, 1978; and A. H. Nimtz, "Islam in Tanzania: A Bibliography, *Tanzania Notes and Records*, Vol. 72 (1973), pp. 51–74.

Zanzibar: N. R. Bennett, *A History of the Arab State of Zanzibar*, London, 1978, and *The Arab State of Zanzibar: A Bibliography*, Boston, Mass., 1984.

67

REFORMS IN INDIA AND KENYA

Interview with the Associated Press of India

Bombay: 14 March 1923

Possible review of the Indian Constitution – attitude of Europeans in Kenya – forthcoming Muslim meeting in Bombay.

Interviewed by the Associated Press, His Highness the Aga Khan replying to the question as to whether the British Government considered the revision of the Indian Constitution possible or necessary before the expiry of the statutory period, said that the British were practical people not impressed by tall talk or big words. They would be impressed by the use Indians made of the Reforms. If the best men in India went to the Councils and worked them up, improving conditions, the British public were far more likely to be impressed, otherwise they would regard Indians as mere talkers.

With regard to His Highness' protest against the European attitude in Kenya, he said that he still protested against the European attitude in Kenya. He was sure the India Office would do its best, but Indians should not let the matter slide. He hoped the deputation headed by Mr. Sastri would get full support from all Indians. Many thoughtful people in England realized the damage done to British prestige and the Empire by the behaviour of the whites in Kenya; but again the matter depended upon themselves. If they could not carry on vigorous propaganda in England then the position would become clearer.

In regard to the objects of the Muslim meeting in Bombay, His Highness emphatically denied that the programme published by his conference means the creation of a new Muslem [*sic*] party in India. It meant merely that as soon as Turkey's peace was signed Moslems should concentrate on united efforts towards the improvement of Moslem conditions where such were within their powers.

Source: *The Civil and Military Gazette*, Lahore, 17 March 1923.

No background to the interview is furnished by the newspaper or the Associated Press of India.

68

HOPES OF TURKISH PEACE

Reply to the Address of Welcome Presented by the Muslims of Madras

Madras: 15 March 1923

Plea for co-operation among the people of different creeds – hopes for a just and lasting peace with Turkey – tribute to the British newspapers.

His Highness the Aga Khan expressed heartfelt thanks to his fellow Moslems of Madras for the great kindness they had shown during his visit and for the generous terms in which they had referred to his services. When Their Excellencies the Governor and Lady Willingdon asked him to come and see them His Highness felt sure that during his stay he would have the chance of meeting the leading Moslems of Madras City, and he was happy to say that he had made here many friends, who, he hoped, would all some day regard him as an old friend. They had referred to his work as not entirely sectional and he regarded it as their chief civil duty to co-operate with all their fellow subjects, irrespective of creed or race. The educational institutions created by Moslems effort [*sic*], such as the Aligarh University and numerous minor institutions all over India, helped not only their community but by encouraging Moslem education the whole of the Empire's advance. India could not afford to have backward millions.

Referring to the mention of his services towards the maintenance of the independence of Turkey and the improvement of her relations with the West, His Highness said: Though I fully realise the immediate dangers ahead and though peace is not yet an accomplished fact, I have great hopes that not only we will soon have peace but that this time it will be a just and lasting one. The relations between Great Britain and the new national

Turkish State will not only be correct but cordial. I do not think that the Moslems generally realise how sincerely friendly are the sentiments of the average Englishman towards the Turks. Now that he has at last begun to understand the real bearings of this problem, unless through our negligence and indifference we let him be again misled by interested and prejudiced parties, he will assist in his quiet but sure and irresistable [*sic*] way with fair play towards the Turks. We must not forget the famous despatch of Lord Reading's Government which put on record the views of the Government of India last year and we Moslems owe a real and deep debt of gratitude to the great organs of public opinions [*sic*] in England, especially to the *Daily Mail*, the *Evening News* and the *Daily Express* for opening the eyes of Englishmen and indeed for preventing a senseless and disastrous war from taking place. The Moslems who worked in Europe during these years of change and unrest will agree with me that the most valuable, active, and ever ready help came from a friend who I am delighted to see amongst us to-day, Mr. Isphani. It would be difficult for me to repay all I owe him for the help and assistance in furthering various public causes, Indian and Islamic, with which I was associated.

Looking to the future His Highness said Moslems could not for the second time in their history again go to sleep. He hoped when the Turkish peace was concluded the live forces which made such a deep impression on not only their countrymen but also on the Empire and the world would not be allowed to dissipate their strength and vitality in mere verbal discussions or indifference. The educational, economic, political, social and cultural fields of activity alike needed their combined attention. This immense work would need organisation, propaganda, preparation and sincere goodwill and consideration for others. Concluding, His Highness said: "And be sure if we succeed in improving Moslem conditions we will have done a great service for India as a whole for all its other great races and creeds and for the worldwide commonwealth of nations of which I believe we are destined to be honoured as an integral part."

Source: *The Times of India*, Bombay, 17 March 1923.

The Civil and Military Gazette of 18 March also published a report, but without giving the exact date of the reception.

According to *The Times of India*,

"The Moslem citizens of Madras entertained H. H. the Aga Khan this evening at the Khalellabad residence of Khaleel Shirzi. There was an imposing gathering, representative of all communities and different political opinion, European and Indian, with a good sprinkling of ladies.

"An address on behalf of the Moslem community, welcoming His Highness to Madras, appreciating his valuable services to the cause of the Muslims and expressing sincere thanks to His Highness, was read by Sir Haji Ismail Sait and presented to His Highness by Abdul Hakim enclosed in a silver casket. Mr. Isphani read an address on behalf of the Persian community."

The Aga Khan left Madras for Bombay on 15 March soon after the reception.

69

THE POLITICAL SITUATION IN INDIA

Interview with The Times of India

Bombay: 7 April 1923

The second conference at Lausanne and Turkey – regret at the dissolution of the Muslim League – Britain should aim at Turkey's friendship – Turkish aspirations – deplorable relations between Indians and Europeans in Kenya – justice for Indians in Kenya – Hindu-Muslim unity – best Muslim men should enter the legislatures – constitutional methods and our goal – appeal to save the Muslim League – safeguard and develop Islamic ideas and civilization in the country.

His Highness the Aga Khan expressed the hope that the second conference at Lausanne would lead not only to peace but to strong friendship with England and he was led to this hope by the changed attitude and understanding of the majority of Englishmen towards Turkish questions. His Highness regretted to find that the Moslem League, which he had been instrumental in creating and consolidating as a powerful body of Moslem political thought, had been practically dissolved. While he spoke with a tinge of regret about the inevitable dissolution of the League under the present circumstances he looked forward to the formation of a new and powerful organisation which might profoundly influence Moslem ideas and civilisation and which might safeguard and develop national ideals and national progress.

In the course of the interview His Highness, speaking about the prospect of peace with Turkey, said: "It is to be hoped that the British Government will follow the healthy wholesome and manly attitude of the British public as expressed in practically all the independent organs of influential public opinion in England. If the British Government keeps in touch with up to date English ideas and makes the necessary endeavour to obtain not only peace but friendship with Turkey it will usher in a new era of peace and goodwill in the East. The Turkish case is simple. They have lost their non-Turkish territory but they have won back and seriously mean to keep at any price – even to the last drop of their blood – their full independence and liberty within their national frontiers. Most Englishmen accept this position and indeed have defended it. The Foreign Office unfortunately does not realise that Turkey must be treated as an independent Power, just as Mexico or Brazil, Bulgaria or Portugal, and that no concession that does not admit of this full independence and sovereign rights, which Afghanistan herself enjoys, can ever be accepted by the Turkish or the Moslem world. I hope and I believe that the second attempt at Lausanne will lead to a successful result and will bring about the desired peace in the East and real friendship between England and Turkey. Turkey wants her national independence for her own national salvation – and she wants nothing but justice. Fortunately the British Government and British people had their eyes opened and the Moslem case fully and fairly placed before them in the historic document sent by our present most sympathetic and liberal-minded Viceroy and his cabinet.

Speaking of the deplorable relations now existing between Englishmen and Indians in Kenya His Highness said:- "I do not think there can be any two opinions amongst any people – Hindus, Mahomedans, Parsis, Indian Christians, extremist or moderate – about the rights of Indians in that colony. Indian traders were established along those coasts for centuries. Men like Sir Tharia Topan and other enterprising Indian merchants, who settled down there for years for peaceful mercantile pursuits, materially helped to consolidate British influence in the Colony and Indians are now asked to consent to become second-class citizens in such a country and to accept a subordinate and humiliating position. I consider this very unfair and derogatory to the self-respect of Indians and we must fight this matter to a finish till justice has been done to our cause. I was asked by Mr. Sastri to go with the delegation. I am willing and ready to co-operate as a free lance with Mr. Sastri and the Mission which it is proposed to send but I realise that it should be led by a leader of public opinion like Mr. Sastri who has recently been in close touch with colonial affairs while during recent years I for my part have concentrated my energy and attention upon the right solution of the Turkish question. Indians have an inherent right to live in Kenya on equal terms with the British people and they will not accept a subordinate position in that colony especially as they have contributed a good deal to its peaceful progress and prosperity."

Turning to the problem of Hindu-Mahomedan unity, His Highness said: "I have for years and years worked to bring about goodwill between Hindus and Mahomedans. I am convinced that there is absolutely no cause for ill-will. When there is something tangible to quarrel about you can make peace by compromise or concession. Unless there is any particular or tangible cause of quarrel, neither concession nor compromise is of any use. All I can say is that I implore Hindu leaders of thought and influence to approach Moslem problems in the spirit of Gokhale and Gandhi. In the same way I entreat my Mahomedan brethren to view Hindu problems in the spirit of Badruddin Tyabji. Each must help to solve the special problems affecting their respective communities. If that spirit of mutual help and toleration were to guide Hindus and Moslems it is obvious that there would never occur a tangible cause for any quarrel. The Hindu extremists will join hands with Moslem extremists whilst Hindu Liberals will join hands with the Moslem Liberal party; in the same way the Moslem extremists will work with Hindu extremists and the Moderates with the Liberal party. But if they all pursue the common cause of advancing national interests there will be no quarrel between any of them and they will be able to work in unity for the advancement of their respective communities and of their country."

Asked as to whether His Highness could suggest a legislative programme for the Mahomedan members of the Central and Provincial legislatures His Highness said: "It is necessary in the best interests of the community that the best men should enter the Councils. We must send our best men with a definite mandate to work for national progress and advancement so that the pace of the reforms may be accelerated and India may advance to her legitimate position as a predominant partner in the councils of the Empire. I repeat that, in spite of the salt tax, we must determine to keep our best men in the Councils. It must be realised that a great Viceroy like Lord Reading is a great national asset in the sense that apart from the exceptional crisis, which has unfortunately now arisen, the daily business of government must not be hampered but carried on by one who has been a life-long believer in liberal principles. It would be fatal for them if they shirked responsibility and ran away from the Legislature. They must face the situation and do their best to pass legislation which may promote nation-building activities in the country. We want in the Councils all the best men that India can produce. Quick and rapid results cannot be expected by constitutional methods, but these constitutional methods lead surely and steadily to our goal. The ultimate goal will not be attained in a year or two. It will take years to accomplish our aim and object, but our efforts will be attended with success provided we make earnest endeavours to advance the cause of the people and be prepared for service and sacrifice in the right spirit."

"I am sorry", His Highness concluded, "to say that the Moslem League has been practically dissolved. As a political body it is perhaps inevitable that the League should be dissolved as extremists and liberals are working hand in hand with other organisations and associations possessing or advocating their respective views and opinions. I think, however, that a separate organisation is necessary for dealing with important questions such as the Haj or pilgrimage and also with other questions relating to Arabia and so forth. I believe that a special organisation may be able to accomplish a good deal towards attaining progressive union in the community and so might have a great influence on Moslem life and thought. I implore my fellow religionists not to allow the League to become a half-dead institution; if necessary they should enlarge and broaden its constitution from a purely political into a general body for safeguarding and developing Islamic ideas and civilisation in this country."

Source: *The Times of India*, Bombay, 7 April 1923.

The interview was given to the newspaper on the day the Aga Khan left Bombay for England. It was also reproduced in *The Civil and Military Gazette* of 10 April as circulated by the Associated Press of India.

70

ON THE LAUSANNE TREATY WITH TURKEY

Message to the Muslims

Lausanne: 27 July 1923

The new treaty between Turkey and the Great Powers – its contents
– its significance – how Indian Muslims could help Turkey now –
the Arabs in an unsatisfactory position – Turkey on the threshold
of a new era.

I am sending this message from Lausanne, where for the first
time in history a Treaty has been signed on behalf of a Muhammadan nation upon absolutely equal terms with the Great Powers
of the West. The Treaty reflects the greatest credit upon the
steadfast leadership of Ghazi Mustafa and the patient diplomacy
of Ismet Pasha, while it also reveals the earnest desire of Great
Britain and France and the other Western Powers to be good
friends with Turkey and with all Islam.

Under this great Treaty Turkey will become an independent
and compact national State. The fetters which so long held her
enchained have been struck off. Turkish sovereign powers will
no longer be impaired by the excessive and anamolous privileges
enjoyed in the past on Turkish territory by the subjects of other
countries. No foreign troops will remain on Turkish soil. The
freedom obtained by the Turkish national State is complete.
The historic Caliphate of Constantinople is maintained. The
Turks receive their capital back without any restrictions, and they
also recover the sacred city of Adrianople and their territories in
Thrace.

The Turks owe this highly satisfactory settlement to their own
sacrifices and their own courage and fortitude, but they also owe
it to the good will of the peoples of Great Britain and France,
whose influence has always been directed towards the conclusion

of a just peace with Turkey and the restoration of close ties with the Muslim world. It signifies that past quarrels are at an end. It ought to mean that the Turkish national State, which is as independent as Sweden, should be able to make new and lasting friendships with the Western Powers. It puts an end to a hundred years of strife largely due to the inferior position imposed in the past upon the Turks.

To Muslims dwelling in India and in other parts of the British Empire or in mandated territories I would say that in my belief the leading statesmen of Turkey now sincerely wish to be on good terms with Great Britain as well as with France. I feel sure they will welcome eagerly the renewal of trade and commerce, and that under the Treaty business intercourse will flourish as it could never have done in the old days.

I would say to my friends in India that nothing should be done to embitter the new relations now beginning between Turkey and Great Britain. On the contrary, every effort should be made to remove old causes of differences and to make a fresh start. Instead of the Caliphate movement, which is out of date and can serve no useful purpose, the Muhammadans of India ought to try to help Turkey to bind her wounds and to recover her lost property. Indian Muhammadans should remember that this treaty has the warm support of the King-Emperor and his advisers.

The best advice I can give to all Muslims, both in India and elsewhere, is to do their utmost to assist this new national Muhammadan State in its hour of need. This can best be done, not by talking politics, but by taking practical steps. Turkey has suffered grievous losses, and her people require direct aid. We ought to send from India special missions to restore sanitation, to bring back health, and to encourage movements for child welfare. It is to the youth of Turkey that we must look for the salvation of the country, and how can we do it better than by helping the children? I have myself handed £1,000 to the Turkish delegates at Lausanne for the succour of Turkish orphans.

I recognise that the Treaty still leaves the Arab peoples who are outside its scope in an unsatisfactory position, but I think that time will heal the Arab problem, which is not insoluble. Meanwhile the sanctity and security of the Holy Places are assured.

I earnestly commend to all Muslims this historic Treaty, which gives the Turks a new place in history of which they will undoubtedly prove worthy. Turkey is on the threshold of a new era. Her leaders do not want us to make more bad blood between her and the Western Powers. Let us therefore leave politics alone, and turn ourselves to the task of offering such help as we can to the new State, which will assuredly become the brightest star in Islam.

Source: *The Times*, London, 28 July 1923.

For the text of the Treaty of Peace with Turkey and the Accompanying Straits Convention of 24 July 1923 see *Parliamentary Papers, 1923*, Treaty Series no. 16, Cmd. 1929, London, 1923. The full text of the treaty is reproduced in K. K. Aziz, *The Indian Khilafat Movement, 1915–1933: A Documentary Record*, Karachi, 1972 pp. 246–56. On the treaty see *Lausanne Conference on Near Eastern Affairs, 1922–1923 (Proceedings)*, Parliamentary Papers, 1923, Turkey No. 1, Cmd. 1814; R. H. Davison, "Middle East Nationalism: Lausanne Thirty Years Later", *Middle East Journal*, Vol. 7 (1953), pp. 324–48; A. P. Thornton, *The Imperial Idea and Its Enemies: A Study in British Power*, London, 1959; Ahmed Amin, *Turkey in the World War*, New Haven, 1930; George Lenczowski, *The Middle East in World Affairs*, Ithaca, 1962; Elizabeth Monroe, *Britain's Moment in the Middle East, 1914–1956*, London, 1963; Anne Williams, *Britain and France in the Middle East and North Africa, 1914–1967*, New York, 1968; M. S. Anderson, *The Eastern Question, 1774–1923: A Study in International Relations*, New York, 1966; and A. J. Toynbee, *Survey of International Affairs, 1925, Vol. 1: The Islamic World Since the Peace Settlement*, London, 1927. For contemporary views see Abdullah Yusuf Ali, "The New Turkish Peace", *Indian Review*, March 1923; Abbas Ali Baig, "Peace with Turkey in its Relation to Anglo-Muslim Goodwill and the Khilafat", *Asiatic Review*, October 1923; S. Kesava Iyengar, "The Lausanne Conference", *Hindustan Review*, July 1923; Ben Kendim, "New Turkey", *Edinburgh Review*, July 1923; "Lausanne Conference", *Round Table*, March 1923; "The Peace Treaty: Summary of Original Articles", *The Civil and Military Gazette*, 9 February 1923; "Lausanne Conference Breakdown: Lord Curzon's Responsibility", *Islamic Review*, March 1923.

On the Treaty of Sèvres see A Special Correspondent, "The Turkish Treaty: A Critical Survey", *The Civil and Military Gazette*, 20 May 1920; "The Turkish Treaty", *Indian Review*, May 1920; Valentine Chirol, "The Outlook in India", *Quarterly Review*, July 1922; "Europe and the Turks", *New Statesman*, 16 September 1922; Valentine Chirol, "The End of the Ottoman Empire", *Edinburgh Review*, October 1920; "Problems of Europe: The Adriatic, Thrace and Constantinople", *Round Table*, March 1920; "The Changing East", *Round Table*, September 1920; K. D. Umarigar, "The Turkish Peace Terms", *New Review*, July–August 1920.

By October 1922 the Greeks had been beaten decisively by the Turks, the last of the foreign troops had been expelled from Anatolia, and an armistice had been signed on 11 October. The Allied powers now realized the futility of the use of force and the obsoleteness of the Treaty of Sèvres. On 27 October they invited the Imperial Ottoman Government at Istanbul and the Provisional National Government at Ankara to attend a peace conference at Lausanne. On 1 November the Grand National Assembly (the parliamentary arm of the Provisional National Government) abolished the Sultanate and three days later declared the Ottoman Government to be no longer in existence. It was thus the National Government alone which represented Turkey at the peace talks which were held on 20 November 1922 to 4 February 1923, and from 23 April 1923 to 24 July 1923. Turkey was prepared to accept the separation of the Arab provinces, but insisted on the maintenance of the integrity of Anatolia proper and the security of Istanbul, on an assurance of Turkish participation in any regime for the Straits, and on the abolition of the capitulations. The final treaty was signed on 24 July 1923 between Turkey and Britain, France, Italy, Japan, Greece, Bulgaria and Rumania. It was the only negotiated peace treaty of the First World War. All the basic principles laid down in the Turkish conditions of peace found their way into the treaty.

The Convention of the Straits was one of the instruments of the Treaty of Lausanne. Russia signed the Convention on 14 August 1923, but later failed to ratify it.

71

THE NEW MUSLIM WORLD

An Article

London: October 1923

Positive response to the Treaty of Lausanne in the Muslim world –
historical perspective on relations between Muslim countries and
Europe during the last 150 years – Turkey and the First World War
– the Treaty of Sèvres – the average Englishman's attitude to Turkey
– task before Mustafa Kamal Pasha – other Muslim states not likely
to be hostile towards Europe – aspirations of modern Islam –
statesmen of Europe should encourage the emergence of truly
independent Muslim states – the Arab states – proposal for an Arab
federation – independence for the Arabs – prospects for peaceful
relations.

1. Treaty of Peace with Turkey and other Instruments, signed
    at Lausanne on July 24, 1923, Treaty series No. 16, Cmd.
    1929. H.M. Stationery Office.
2. An Englishwoman in Angora. By GRACE ELLISON. Hutch-
    inson. 1923.
3. Report of 'Iraq Administration, October, 1920 – March, 1922.
    By Sir PERCY COX. H.M. Stationery Office. 1923.

Observers in Europe, not excluding those ordinarily well
informed, may have been somewhat surprised at the manifestations of joy with which the Peace of Lausanne was received not
only in Turkey, but throughout the Islamic world, and particularly
in those portions of the King's dominions and in independent
countries like Egypt, closely related to Great Britain by various
intimate ties, where there is a large Moslem population. The
immense satisfaction with which the outstanding features of the
treaty have been received by the Moslem peoples is based on
reasons which can be properly appreciated only when viewed in

761

the perspective of the relations of Moslem countries to Europe during the last hundred and fifty years.

Till the early years of the nineteenth century the Turkish capitulations and the various privileges and exemptions demanded by the European Powers for the Christian subjects of the Porte did not matter greatly in their actual, as distinct from their theoretical, derogation of the sovereignty of the Sultan. Turkey was a powerful State isolated from Western Europe, and the means of communication then at the disposal of the Western world were altogether insufficient for using in a way markedly antagonistic to Turkish interests the powers which the capitulations and other limitations of the authority of the Porte conferred upon the foreigner. The change came before and during the Victorian era; stage by stage science placed at the disposal of the West and of Russia, with her constant menace to Turkey from the north, immense material advantages, such as steamships, railways and modern armaments. The position of the Porte became less and less tolerable, and Turkey was able to survive only because during the greater part of the nineteenth century England and Austria, and later Germany and Austria, were vitally interested in preventing Russia or any other individual Power from absorbing the Turkish provinces of the Ottoman Empire.

In our own day, under the ambitious and unscrupulous scheming of Wilhelm II, Germany supplanted Great Britain as the powerful friend and ally of Turkey, with disastrous consequences not only for the Porte, but for Europe and the world. The ultimate result of Prussian ascendancy in Constantinople was to bring Turkey into the war on the side of Germany, in spite of the fact that the overwhelming majority of the people, and even of the governing classes, were convinced of the folly of such participation, and desired nothing better than to maintain neutrality throughout the great conflict.

With the coming of the Armistice it was recognised throughout the world that a new chapter had been opened in the history of mankind, and that for better, for worse, great readjustments were essential. Throughout the later stages of the war, and especially after the participation of the United States, Allied and American statesmen claimed to be fighting for certain fundamental principles of justice, nationalism and freedom. Their formulation profoundly affected the thought of Asia, no less than that of Europe and the two Americas. The direct result was that the Turkish people, and with them the Mahomedan world, expected

762

a peace that would leave Turkish Turkey intact and free, and would provide for the various populations of Arabia at least the possibility of a united Arab Federation. These anticipations were encouraged by definite statements of policy in regard to Turkey authoritatively made in the last few months of the war.

Nothing could be more inevitable and natural than the keen disappointment and indignation of the Moslem world when, in disregard of the excellent principles laid down while the issue of the war had still to be decided, the so-called Sèvres Treaty was forced upon the reluctant representatives of Constantinople. It was a treaty only in name, for it made Turkey and Arabia no more than vassal States and colonies. Placing the former under a virtual over-lordship of the Allies, and taking from her every shred of real independence, it gave Smyrna to the Greeks and thereby provided the opportunity to despoil and devastate a large part of Anatolia. The short-sighted men who insisted on imposing the Sèvres Treaty had forgotten the inherent fidelity of the Moslem races. The Turkish population, with the moral support of the whole of Islam, rose as one man, and after immense sacrifices and suffering, for which history scarcely affords a parallel, the way to full freedom and independence was at last secured. Much light is thrown upon these heroic exertions of a people worn by a dozen years of almost continuous warfare, and upon the strength and persistence of the national ideals inspiring them, in the graphic pages of Miss Grace Ellison's record of her experiences, "An Englishwoman in Angora." As I wrote on the morrow of the signature of the Lausanne Treaty, the Turks were determined either to perish as a conquered nation, or to be absolutely free.

Now that, under Ghazi Mustapha Kemal, freedom has been won by persistent and costly effort, some people read with surprise the testimony of Miss Ellison and other observers that, of all foreign countries, England stands first in the regard and confidence of the Turkish people. Yet this is the natural, almost the inevitable, result of permanent mutual interests and sympathies which have shown themselves stronger, happily, than all the outpourings of old prejudice and fanaticism. Last autumn, when the Coalition recklessly contemplated intervention in support of the defeated and routed Greek army, its own fate was sealed and Mr. Lloyd George was soon thrust from power. The particular and recognised organs of the Englishman-in-the-street, such as the *Daily Mail*, the *Daily Express*, the *Evening News*, and many others all over the country, had advocated ever since the

Armistice the cause of a just peace with Turkey; and it was now shown that the average Englishman would not be moved by the passions and prejudices of men with antiquated views into a needless and disastrous war with a people with whom he had no quarrel.

This attitude was recognised and cordially appreciated in Turkey, together with the fact that during the last stages of the protracted Lausanne Conference the representatives of Great Britain did not oppose that complete freedom which the Turks rightly postulated as the only condition that could lead to enduring peace. If Turkey has won her way in the field and in the international council chamber to a position in the world which she had not held for generations, she has done so by the self-sacrificing devotion of her sons to national ideals which the ordinary Englishman respects and understands. He will watch with sympathetic interest the discharge of the heavy task now before Ghazi Kemal Pasha and his colleagues of upbuilding in peace a people impoverished by many years of war, with all the dislocation of commerce and enterprise it has brought. Such sympathy will be greatly appreciated by the Turkish people, and will strengthen the ties of new friendship between the two countries, one expression of which will be the welcoming of British goods to the Turkish markets.

While Turkey is by far the most important single factor in Anglo-Moslem relations, she is still only part of a greater whole. The most cursory observer cannot fail to recognise, in the light of recent history, how important it is that the five more or less independent Islamic States should establish satisfactory relations with one another, with the Moslem peoples under Great Britain, France and Russia, and with Europe and America. A survey of the problem will be facilitated by an indication of the present status of each of these countries.

Turkey and Afghanistan are now free to manage their own affairs, and have a status not different in essentials to that of other Sovereign States, whether large or small, such as Great Britain, Sweden or Peru. The relations of Turkey and Afghanistan with all other States are governed by international law and international usage. The ancient Empire of Persia is independent at least in theory, but foreigners retain the advantages of the capitulations, with consular jurisdiction and all its implications. Egypt has at last reached the goal of her ambitions – the recognition of her national sovereignty. In Egypt, however, not only are the capitulations still maintained, but Egypt has special relations with Great Britain that to a certain extent modify her real independence. The fifth Moslem Power, Arabia, is the danger spot; and in all probability if any serious problem arises in our day to strain Anglo-Moslem relations, and revive old perils, it will have its origin among the sands and mountain ranges of Arabia.

The five States mentioned are united by the ties of a common civilisation and religion, and by that general similarity of ideas and manners which, though modified by local conditions, prevails throughout Islam. But one conclusion may be drawn with confidence: unless Europe – or some particular European State – unduly interferes with these Moslem States in a manner inconsistent with international usage, no responsible organs of Mohammedan thought or opinion would consider it to be their interest to bring about any coalition or alliance between the five Moslem States with a hostile intention toward any other nation.

The reasons for this conclusion are plain. The Moslems in the British Empire are everywhere a minority of the inhabitants of the countries in which they are found, except in far-away West Africa and in the scarcely less remote Malay Peninsula. The Arabs of South-Western Africa and the Sahara under French rule are like some vast island, separated from the rest of Islam. Geographical and political considerations make it more expedient for Turkey, Persia, Afghanistan or Egypt, to be on intimate and friendly terms with a Great Power such as England or France or Russia, than to draw on themselves the suspicion of Europe by an over-intimate confederation. It is not merely improbable, it is well-nigh impossible, as being antagonistic to the interests of any of the free Moslem Powers, that they should seek active intervention in Western affairs, or should go beyond ordinary cultural and fraternal intercourse between themselves.

European observers, handicapped as they are by not being actually within the great Islamic movements of the present day, do not understand fully the great sympathy of one Moslem people or nation for another. The persistent aspirations of the modern world of Islam are toward the upbuilding of independent national States, not dangerous to other peoples from a military or naval point of view, but free from foreign tutelage, and working toward that cultural and intellectual improvement necessary to bring Islam into line with the great progressive countries of the world to-day. The leaders of serious thought in Turkey or in Persia, in Afghanistan or in Egypt, are not aspiring to curtail, under the banner of pan-Islamism, the independence or individuality of any non-Moslem State. They seek only to develop their own independence and individuality to the utmost on national and State foundations. The nearest parallel in Europe to their projected relations is that of the three Scandinavian States. Among these there exists great similarity of manners, customs and aspirations. But in our own lifetime Norway was separated from Sweden, and those two States, together with Denmark, are each as jealous of their independence and individuality as any Power, whether great or small, can be.

If the statesmen of Europe, and especially the guides and teachers of the British Empire, recognise their own permanent interests, they will encourage to the utmost this wholesome and desirable Islamic movement. They will give their moral support to the upbuilding of a truly independent Turkey, Persia, Egypt and Afghanistan, each working out its own national salvation by peaceful and cultural methods, and improving not only its own civilisation, but ultimately that of the world in general by contributing to the common stock those virtues which have been associated through the centuries with Islamic culture.

The one great cloud in this horizon, as already indicated, is the case of Arabia, and other portions of the former Turkish Empire. Mandates have been accepted under the Peace treaties in Syria and Mesopotamia by France and Great Britain, and the Palestinian question is one of great perplexity. Apart from these extraneous difficulties, the Arab race is divided into minor sovereignties and principalities. The history of Arabia for at least five hundred years, and even during the Turkish occupation of the main centres, demonstrates the enormous influence in the Arabian life of tribal pride and polity. It is in these regions of our survey of Islamic States that we find those vague and uncertain conditions, those inner divisions, and those possibilities of sudden upheavals that encourage European domination and European occupation. On the other hand, we must bear in mind this important factor in the problem: that the Arabs have never forgotten their racial unity, nor lost their active desire to achieve it politically.

In my humble judgment the right solution of the Arab question will call for a greater application of statesmanship and breadth of outlook from the leaders of Great Britain and France than is required for any other international problem of the East. Unfortunately, both these great Powers are entangled with Arab mandates and responsibilities, which the United States has taken care to avoid. I have no doubt as to what the solution should be. In spite of passing and temporary difficulties, the public opinion of Western Europe, and especially of England, should insist on working for a real and free Arabia, a federation of small States with Mecca or Medina as its cultural centre, and including Syria and Palestine. Thereby a great act of international justice would be achieved, and a dangerous focus of infection and trouble in the East would be transformed into another healthy and thriving Moslem State, to take its place by the side of the four others – not indeed as an ally of any one of them, but as a member of the League of Nations.

Will the man-in-the-street, who insisted a year ago on justice and fair dealing with Turkey, insist before it is too late that the Arabs, who rendered such immense service to the cause of the Allies throughout the war, should also attain the national independence from intervention and control which Turkey and Afghanistan have secured? In this case, of course, a quality will be needed for which the French have an excellent expression – *doigté*. That quality is rare, but it is not beyond the best statesmanship of Great Britain.

It must be recognised that there can be no dominant central Power in the Arab countries, and that dynasties, and in fact thrones and constitutions, will have to be of an elastic nature. For though the Arabs, unlike the Turks and the Afghans, are of one race and religion, they are rooted deeply in local and tribal patriotisms ... But these difficulties should not be insoluble, at any rate if Western Powers are not continually intervening to impose their will in these matters.

If the public opinion of England insisted that its governing classes should seek to bring about, by whatever means at their disposal, a truly free Arabia from the frontiers of Turkey to the Indian Ocean, and from the Mediterranean to the Persian Gulf, I am convinced that agents could be found in Great Britain with such intimate knowledge of the conditions in the countries concerned as to render possible the discharge of this difficult task. Such a solution of the Arab question would, once for all, remove all likelihood of friction in the Near East between Great Britain and France on the one side, and on the other side between the British people and the five independent Moslem nations, as also between them and their Moslem fellow-subjects and fellow-citizens of the British Empire.

Source: *The Edinburgh Review*, Edinburgh, October 1923, pp. 230–6.

72

APPEAL TO TURKEY TO RETAIN THE KHILAFAT

Letter (with Sayyid Ameer Ali) to the Turkish Prime Minister

London: 24 November 1923

Concern about the diminishing status of the Caliph – why Indian Muslims supported Turkey's struggle – possible consequences of diminution of the Caliph's prestige.

As consistent friends of new Turkey and in full sympathy with her aspirations as an independent member in the comity of the free nations of the world, we desire, with your permission, to invite the attention of the Grand National Assembly to the very disturbing effects the present uncertain position of the Caliph-Sultan is exercising among the vast populations who belong to the Sunni communion. We have noticed with the greatest regret that Islam, as a great moral and cohesive force, is losing among large sections of the Sunni population, owing to the dimunition in the Caliph's dignity and prestige, its weight and influence. For obvious reasons we do not wish to particularize the facts, but its [*sic*] absolute accuracy cannot be gainsaid.

2. In the Sunni communion, we need not point out, the spiritual headship forms the link which binds the followers of Islam as a vast congregation. When the Caliphate was in peril from outside attacks, Musalman feeling all over the world was violently agitated, and the Muslims of India gave their sympathy and support to the Turkish nation in the belief that in fighting for their independence they were fighting also for the preservation intact of the institution which symbolized Muslim solidarity.

Throughout those critical times we strenuously pleaded for the Turkish cause. And a British Muslim Organization has, ever since the Turco-Italian War in Tripoli and Cyrenaica, devoted its energies in endeavouring to alleviate the untold suffering and distress among the Turkish people. Our observations and suggestions, therefore, we trust, will receive a courteous hearing from Your Excellency's Government regarding a question in which we, in common with all Muslims, take the deepest interest.

3. It must not be supposed for a moment from our remarks that we wish to suggest that the powers of the people's representatives should be in any degree curtailed. What we respectfully urge is that the religious headship of the Sunni world should be maintained intact in accordance with the *Shariyyet*. In our opinion, any dimunition in the prestige of the Caliph or the elimination of the Caliphate as a religious factor from the Turkish body politic would mean the disintegration of Islam and its practical disappearance as a moral force in the world – a contingency which, we are sure, neither the Grand National Assembly nor His Excellency the President Ghazi Mustafa Kemal Pasha can view with equanimity.

4. In our opinion the Caliph-Imam symbolizes the unity of the Sunni Communion: and the fact that he is a member of the Turkish people and is a descendant of the founder of the Turkish nation gives to Turkey a position pre-eminent among Islamic nations.

5. For fourteen centuries it has been the cardinal principle of the *Ahl-i-Sunnat*, and on this, we believe, is the *Ijmaa-i-Ummat*, that the Caliph, the Vice-gerent of the Prophet, is the Imam of the Sunni congregations, and that between him and the general body of worshippers, there is a nexus which knits together the *Ahl-i-Sunnat*. This mystical element cannot be eradicated from the Muslim mind without creating discord in the world of Islam.

6. We need not remind Your Excellency that even when the Caliph-Imam lost his temporal power the great Kings and Chieftains sought and obtained from him investiture in order to validate their title to rule and to lead at prayers, the usual concomitant of secular authority. If Islam is to maintain its place in the world as a great moral force, the Caliph's position and dignity should not, in any event, be less than that of the Pontiff of the Church of Rome.

7. For these reasons, among others equally cogent, we, as the two friends of Turkey, respectfully urge upon the Grand National

Assembly and its great and far-sighted leaders the imminent necessity for maintaining the religious and moral solidarity of Islam by placing the Caliph-Imamate on a basis which would command the confidence and esteem of the Muslim nations and thus impart to the Turkish State unique strength and dignity.

Source: *The Times*, London, 14 December 1923.

This letter created considerable stir in Turkey and caused an unfortunate sequence. According to Professor Toynbee, copies of it were sent simultaneously to leading Turkish newspapers of Constantinople without any indication that it was not an open letter. The letter made excellent news, and several newspapers immediately published it, with the result that the Turkish Prime Minister read it in the press before the original communication was put before him officially. Contemporary reports said that the original letter had reached the Ministry of Foreign Affairs at the same time as the editors of the newspapers had received their copies. But the letter was written in English and had to be sent to the translation department of the Foreign Office. Bureaucracy is always slower and more inefficient than the press; the government translator took longer on his job than did his counterpart in the newspaper office. Thus it came to pass that the letter appeared in the press before it was presented to the authorities.

However, Toynbee does not produce any evidence in support of his version of events. Unfortunately, most historians of this period have accepted his account, though his open bias against Turkey and his unconcealed sympathies for the Greek cause should have warned them against taking his report for granted. Toynbee and his supporters have overlooked Sayyid Ameer Ali's letter to *The Times* of 15 December 1923 (published in the issue of 17 December), in which he stated clearly that "our letter to Ismet Pasha was dispatched registered to Angora nearly a week before copies were sent to the Constantinople paper".

The Angora Government lost no time in reacting to the letter. On 8 December, on a motion by Ismet Pasha, the Grand National Assembly decided in a secret sitting to establish a special "Tribunal of Independence", before which were brought the editors of the three offending newspapers which had had the temerity to publish the letter. They were Husain Jahyad Bey of the *Taneem*, Velid Bey Ebuz-Ziya of the *Tevhid-i-Efkyar*, and Ahmed Jevdet Bey of the *Iqdam*. They were, however, acquitted on 2 January of the following year.

Ismet Pasha did not even try to conceal his anger at the letter. In a harshly worded statement, given to a special correspondent of *The Times* in Angora, he said that the Aga Khan and Ameer Ali were foreigners and therefore incompetent to discuss the constitution of Turkey. Besides, they were Shias, and, therefore, without any qualification to pontify on a Sunni institution. *The Times* of 29 December 1923 carried the full text of this statement.

I reproduce here what I wrote about this incident in my *Ameer Ali: His Life and Work* (Publishers United, Lahore, 1968, pp. 96–7): "One can understand Ismet Pasha's outburst without justifying it. The Turks were not yet fully out of the wood. There was danger of internal strife. On some points the liberal-*cum*-military leadership and the old-fashioned masses did not agree. In these conditions it was easy to construe any extraneous counsel, however well intentioned, as an act of unwarranted impudence and to exaggerate its supposed dangers. But what is difficult is to appreciate the unmeasured tone of the Prime Minister's public criticism, which took no notice of Ameer Ali's and the Aga Khan's strenuous and passionate defence of Turkish interests over the last five years. Ismet Pasha was not unaware of the sacrifices which the Indian Khilafat leaders and their followers had cheerfully made for the sake of his country. He knew that they had courted arrest, had languished in prison for long years, and had suffered much in the anti-British campaign which had swept India when the future of Turkey was in jeopardy. To attack the motives of men like Ameer Ali and the Aga Khan was not only an act of folly but also of discourtesy. It was reported that at that time there was a general impression in Turkey that the authors of the letter were instigated by the British Government which was anxious to see the Republican Government overthrown and the old Ottoman dynasty restored to power. No evidence in support of this has yet turned up, and for a man of Ismet Pasha's intelligence and experience to give credence to such rumours, and to base his denunciation on them, means that blind passion had superceded prudence. For the Indian leaders it was not unnatural to be appalled at Turkish ingratitude."

For this episode see the references cited in the above paragraphs and also A. J. Toynbee, *Survey of International Affairs 1925, Vol. 1: The Islamic World Since the Peace Settlement*, London, 1927, pp. 56–9.

73

REASONS FOR THE APPEAL TO TURKEY

Letter to The Times

London: 16 December 1923

Explanation of motives behind the letter to the Prime Minister of Turkey on the Caliphate issue – past record of his views on Muslim nations – respect for Mustafa Kamal Pasha.

You published on Friday the joint letter of Mr. Ameer Ali and myself to General Ismet Pasha, on the status of the Caliph-Imam, with a covering communication from Mr. Ameer Ali repudiating for us both the least desire to interfere in the politics of Turkey. I feel it my duty, however, to explain more fully my personal position, in view of certain allegations and insinuations made by defenders of the action of the Angora authorities in arresting for treason the editors of three Constantinople newspapers which published our letter.

The first of the two allegations with which I wish to deal is that I wrote to the Prime Minister of Turkey at British instigation and with the object of forwarding British intrigues in that country. So far from my action being suggested by any British authority, I can state that I did not discuss the question directly or indirectly with any Englishman, official or non-official. The only person with whom I had any consultation on the subject was my old friend Mr. Ameer Ali, the veteran champion of the cause of Islam.

My activities in respect to post-war Anglo-Turkish relations are on record to a large extent. Whether public or private, they have had but one motive, viz., the development and maintenance of friendly relations on terms of equality of sovereignty, between Great Britain and the most prominent of Muslim nations. In season and out of season I have urged on such Englishmen as cared to listen to me the importance of sincere friendship with Turkey, and thus with the Islamic world, and the need to renounce once for all any ideas of intervention or interference in the development of sovereignty or independence of Muslim nations, including not only Turkey, but Persia and Afghanistan. These views have been attacked with asperity from some British sources: but I am happy to know that a great, and steadily increasing, number of Englishmen have come to see that, not in attempts to uphold what are known as "prestige politics", but along the lines of cordial relations in spirit and in letter, as established by international law and usage, the true interests of Britain will best be conserved.

The second allegation against me, no less amazing and absurd than the first, is that I signed the joint letter in order to help certain reactionary and Monarchist intrigues of Turkish parties ill-disposed towards the newly established Republic. My answer is that since the Armistice I have had no relation of any sort or kind with any Turkish party or individual that has been in opposition to the Angora Government. Since the establishment of the National Assembly I have made it a strict rule to meet only such Turks as I believed to have the confidence of the Angora authorities, for I recognised that they alone represented the views of the majority of the Turkish people.

Nothing could be further from the fact than the suggestion that I desire a return to the monarchical form of government or the re-establishment of the political Sultan-Caliphate. On the contrary, I have always held that Republican institutions are particularly well suited to purely Islamic societies. The democratic brotherhood of the first century of Islam has always been cherished by pious Muslims as an ideal towards which their efforts for social and political reconstruction in their own lands should turn. With these ideals I have sympathised from early youth. So far from wishing ill to the newly established Republic, I yield to none in the desire to see it consolidated so as to be beyond menace from any quarter, internal or external.

This desire is in no sense inconsistent with another life-long belief as one who, while belonging to the Ismailiah school of Islam, yet follows the tradition of Ali and Hassan, his eldest son – viz., that the essential unity of Islam is of far greater importance than any sectarian differences. For this reason I have advocated the establishment of a strong Caliphate above parties and politics. Like the overwhelming majority of the Muslims of the world, I hold that the honour of providing the occupant of the throne of the Caliph should, in Islamic interests generally, be a privilege of the Turkish nation; and, further, that it should be retained in the family which has held it for so many centuries, thus avoiding the raising of issues which would lead to eager aspirations and jealousies in ambitious quarters.

Given this admission, it is clearly essential in the interests of the Turkish Republic itself, and of securing the real moral contentment which Islam, like the rest of the world, so greatly needs today, that the Caliph should enjoy in Turkey, and should receive from all Muslim States headed by that nation, at least general homage and veneration equal to that which Catholic States voluntarily offer to the Pope. So far from this solution being in any sense revolutionary, it is no more than a reversion to the traditions prevailing in Baghdad during the later Abbassid period. A similar custom prevailed when the Egyptian Abbassid Caliphs resided in great honour as leaders of Islam at Cairo, without interfering in any way with the political destinies of Egypt.

My object, Sir, in collaborating with Mr. Ameer Ali in the appeal to General Ismet Pasha bears no relation to the motives so falsely attributed to me. It was none other than to prevent any decay of the immense respect which Islam generally (and no one more than myself) has for the Ghazi and his fellow soldier-statesmen who successfully delivered Turkey from the shame of the servitude that was prepared for her at Sèvres. Such decay is inevitable as the result of the natural resentment the great body of Muslims will feel if the Caliph is permanently reduced to a position out of harmony with his unique dignity and spiritual office.

Source: *The Times*, London, 17 December 1923.
    The letter is undated, but the urgent circumstances attendant upon the issue to which it is addressed make it a reasonable assumption that it was written and dispatched immediately before its publication in the newspaper.

74

DANGERS OF A FRESH WAR

Interview with the Press

Bombay: 13 January 1924

Prevention of another war at all costs – pretenders to the Caliphate.

The Aga Khan declared that the most serious question confronting India was the possibility of the outbreak of a fresh war.

In His Highness's opinion, war must be prevented at all costs, and this should not be very difficult, as neither the financial nor the industrial resources of India could stand the strain of a new war with a neighbour, while such a war would put back the clock of material, moral, and political progress.

The Aga Khan had little to say regarding the Caliphate question. He explained that he had written a letter to *The Times* for the purpose of warning the Turkish Government against the possibility of the appearance of numerous pretenders to the Caliphate.

Source: *The Times of India*, Bombay, 14 January 1924.
The interview was given soon after the Aga Khan had landed at Bombay on his arrival from Europe.

75

OPTIMISM AND GOOD WILL

An Article

London: 13 April 1924

Forthcoming debate in the House of Commons on India – very little hostility in India against the Europeans as persons – main obstacle to good relations between India and Britain – Indian views on race relations in Kenya and the Turkish Question – burden on the Indian army – internal security – Indian Muslims and the independence of Muslim states – rejection of the Finance Bill by the Central Legislature – existing taxation heavy and obnoxious – expenditure for economic development – trust men on the spot – Lord Crewe's Committee – unsatisfactory constitutional position of the provinces – scrutiny of the working of the reforms – goal of responsible government.

On Tuesday evening the House of Commons will devote a scanty three hours or less to a motion promoted by the Conservative Opposition, viewing with anxiety recent events in India and regretting the lack of a clear statement of policy with regard thereto by his Majesty's Government.

No thoughtful man familiar with present-day India can fail to share this anxiety, however much he may differ from the grounds which may be advanced for it in the debate. The old easy conditions have passed away and relations with British authority are strained.

From contact with people of the most varied condition and outlook in my recent tour in India, I can make one reassuring statement: There is very little hostility, in spite of what may be said to the contrary, to the Englishman as an Englishman or to the European as such.

Such race hostility has been condemned, not only by Mahatma

Gandhi, but by many other leaders of thought. Much has been said of boycott and suggested embargoes on British goods. But there is every willingness to do business with this country – as Englishmen travelling for their firms or engaged in commerce in India find – given the right political equation.

The main obstacle to better relations is the widespread impression that India has a step-motherly Government, from which her interests get full play only when there are no other interests nearer home for the authorities in Whitehall to conserve. It is a widespread belief that when such interests arise India's wishes go to the wall. One illustration of which I was constantly reminded in India is that of the treatment of Indians in Kenya. Another example often talked of is the disregard of Indian sentiment on the question of the preservation of effective Turkish sovereignty after the armistice, until the Turks defeated Greece in Asia Minor and once more proved themselves formidable.

The outstanding example talked of, and one that does incalculable harm, is the fact that in regard to the military provision for India and to frontier policy the final word rests not with the people of India, not with the Government of India, not even with the Secretary of State, but with the War Council and the General Staff in Whitehall. There is loud complaint that, at the cost of the Indian taxpayer the strength of the Indian garrison and its composition are related to the requirements of the Empire as a whole, rather than to India's own needs.

In regard to internal security, those needs could be met much more appropriately and economically by efficient flying corps, armoured cars, and light cavalry than by the present composition of the Army in India. Of a really formidable external enemy there has been no danger from the date of the Anglo-Russian Agreement to this day. The invasion of the rocky fastnesses of Afghanistan by our troops is a difficult proposition, as the experience of the first and second wars with that country showed; but on the other hand any attempt by the Afghans to gain conquests on the soil of India would present a military problem so negligible that they could soon be defeated and turned back.

India asks that there should be as few scares of war with adjacent countries as possible. This is essential, because these neighbours, in so far as they are of military consequence are Moslem States, and their independence is a question of very great importance to the Indian Mohammedan. His Turkish sympathies of recent years are applicable also to these Asiatic Moslem States.

It has been felt in this country, where political aptitude has been developed through the centuries, that the rejection of the Finance Bill by the Legislative Assembly at Delhi was a foolish and gratuitous piece of obstruction. I do not write in its defence, but I would point out that the core of the Indian case is this: The greater part of the expenditure of the central authority being for military purposes, and the Legislature having no control over that expenditure, it was felt that the whole budgetary provision should be rejected, in the spirit of the man who says: "You have taken the cream; and we do not want the skim milk."

The Indian argument is that excessive defensive insurance is imposed upon her, willy nilly, in time of peace, and that she is required to make her preparations on a much wider scale, proportionate to her resources, than is made in Great Britain. She can ill afford preparations on so great a scale on the ground that something may turn up to justify them. The existing heavy taxation is obnoxious largely because it represents so much unproductive expenditure, and the real authority for its outlay lies with the War Office in Whitehall.

If the money spent on this excessive insurance could be diverted in these years of peace to internal economic development, the wealth of the country would so increase that in a few years the Army Budget could be adequate to the most exacting of reasonable standards without straining the public patience.

India also asks that England, under the new system of British and Indian administrative partnership, should trust her agents on the spot. She sends out a Viceroy and other Englishmen of high calibre, but their hands are tied. At present, save in regard to tariff policy, little or no progress has been made in establishing the convention so wisely suggested by the Parliamentary Joint Select Committee of 1919 that, as far as possible, where the Government of India and its legislature are agreed, the Viceroy should be virtually freed from the interference of the Secretary of State. The reforms scheme depended for success upon the strength of each link in the chain; but, unhappily, this link remains unforged.

The need for it was set forth most clearly at the time in the report of Lord Crewe's Committee on the work of the India Office under the new dispensation; but that important State paper has been quietly pigeonholed and overlooked.

An obstacle to success of the reforms is the fact that some of the provinces under dyarchy are miniature Indias, in the sense that they lack the characteristics of being linguistic and economic units. This means costly administration and unnecessary friction. There should be earnest effort to make each unit of provincial dyarchy as homogeneous as conditions will permit. The Joint Parliamentary Committee had not time to work out a scheme, but clearly recognised that it would be a requirement of the future.

The time has come for an examination of the working of the reforms. Every one who has had experience of them in the last three and a half years knows that there are many features which call for reconsideration and adjustment, without in any way changing the fundamental conceptions set forth in the preamble of the Act, and particularly the declaration of the goal of progressive realisation of responsible government within the Empire. It is not a question, in my judgment, of a premature asking for further advance, but one of securing the necessary conditions for advance. Dyarchy can succeed only in a healthy and wholesome atmosphere and this will not be secured until the issues I have presented for public consideration have been faced with sincerity and courage.

Source: *The Sunday Express*, London, 13 April 1924.

A summary of this article was circulated by the Reuter's agency from London and was published by *The Civil and Military Gazette* of 14 April.

The Sunday Express introduced the article in these words:

"H. H. the Aga Khan, one of the greatest of India's princes, and the spiritual head of Indian Moslems, delivers through the columns of the 'Sunday Express' a message and a warning to the whole Empire.

"His warning is against the perils of a policy of drift in India, of refusal to satisfy the claims of India to more complete consideration. His message is one of optimism and good will.

"Such a statement from such a source has outstanding importance in view of an important debate on Indian affairs in the House of Commons on Tuesday. It comes at a time when the attention of the Empire is focussed on Indian problems. It will compel world-wide interest."

76

INDIA'S STEEL INDUSTRY

Letter to The Times

London: 28 April 1924

The proposals of the Indian Tariff Board on India's steel industry – the best interests of India are linked to her industrial development – benefits for the British engineering industry – adaptation the right course for the British manufacturer.

Your valuable digest of the Indian Tariff Board regarding the steel industry shows that the Board has been making, not a bludgeon to strike indiscriminately at the import trade, but a rampart behind which the Indian steel industry can be firmly established within the next few years.

British engineering firms cannot be expected to welcome these proposals; but it is to be hoped in the interests of both countries – and above all of their own trade – that they will not organize any agitation or exercise political influence against the scientific tariff now proposed. Indian public opinion would regard such activities as in the nature of an attempt to force a maturing ward to sacrifice her own good for that of her trustee. That the best interests of India's development are linked with her new industrial activities is incontrovertible. It was most fortunate for the Empire that a beginning had been made when the war came. Jamsetjee Tata and his successors were among the real artisans of victory.

The British share of the iron and steel trade with India is not so great as in pre-war days, owing to the severity of Belgian and other competition, which is likely to become more intense in view of an industrial and economic entente between French and German interests in Lorraine and the Ruhr. It may be hoped that the British manufacturer will meet the changed situation with his usual enterprise and resource. The extension of steel production in India will mean an increasing demand for machinery, plant, and other products of the highly organized British engineering industry. Your digest shows that a large range of steel goods and railway material and almost all classes of machinery and hardware escape the proposed protective taxation, on the ground that they are not produced in India. It follows that abundant scope is left for the efforts of British firms to hold their own and develop their trade against non-Indian competition.

The prosperity of India must inevitably mean a larger demand for the more valuable products of English industry. For this class of British manufacturers India cannot become a competitor for generations to come. The highly educated and scientifically trained British workmen of tomorrow will find an unlimited market for finished articles in a prosperous and contented India. The encouragement of the infant industries of India will ultimately do more to solve the problem of unemployment and overproduction in this country than any other single cause that I can find. Remonstrance and regret in regard to the new Indian fiscal policy lead nowhere; and political pressure in opposition thereto would be most harmful. The right part for the British manufacturer is that of adaptation to the growing and varied requirements of Britain's best market.

Source: *The Times*, London, 29 April 1924.
The letter, written from the Ritz Hotel, Piccadilly, London, was published under the headlines: "Indian Tariff Proposals: Protection for Steel Industry: The Aga Khan's Views."

77

THE MOROCCAN WAR SUFFERERS

Letter (with Lord Lamington and Sayyid Ameer Ali) to The Times

London: 17 October 1924

Sufferings among the people of the Riff in Morocco – need for a medical mission – appeal for funds.

The British Red Crescent Society has received an appeal for medical help to relieve the suffering among the people of the Riff country, which is especially severe and pathetic among the women and children, who are the chief sufferers in the struggle going on in their midst. In the bombing operations carried on by the Spanish aeroplanes they appear invariably to suffer most.

It would be an act of humanity to send a medical mission to these unfortunate people. Besides helping the noncombatant population and the sick and wounded, it would be able to mitigate the hardships of the Spanish prisoners. We regret, however, that the funds of the society are not adequate for the purpose. The committee, therefore, venture to appeal to the generosity of the public, which, in the relief of human suffering and distress makes no discrimination of race or religion, for help to send out a properly equipped mission. We feel confident that both the French and Spanish authorities will afford every facility to such a mission of mercy. Contributions are requested to be sent to the bankers of the society, Messrs. Coutts and Co., 440, Strand, W.C., marked for "Riff Medical Mission."

Source: *The Times*, London, 18 October 1924.
   In fact, the letter was sent to the journal on behalf of the British Red Crescent Society, 18 Sloane Street, London SW1, by Lord Lamington, the Aga Khan and Sayyid Ameer Ali.

78

LORD MILNER'S "CREDO"

Letter to The Times

Aix les Bains: 3 August 1925

Views on Lord Milner – Lord Milner's view of the British Empire
– India's position – Indians proud of their culture – development
of international peace and arbitration – the League of Nations –
organized labour and peace – British Empire on a broad basis.

Lord Milner's powerful and brilliant intellect, his steadiness and
strength of purpose, and his self-effacing patriotism give to the
extracts from his papers, posthumously published in your
columns, a value and significance which challenge close attention. I have been pondering over his "Credo" in the last few days
and with great diffidence I offer the criticism that his attitude of
mind was in some respects inadequate to the many-sided needs
of the British Empire as we know it today.

Taking the racial or cultural view of Imperialism, Lord Milner
wrote himself down "a British race patriot". Now if the dominions
of his Majesty consisted only of the British Isles and the colonies
founded and mainly peopled by the British race this view might
or might not be best. But long before what are now known as
the "sister nations" across the seas attained their present status
and importance the issue was settled by the acquisition of India,
the home of three-fourths of the subjects of the British Crown.
In the modern post-war world it is impossible to rule permanently
so vast and populous a land as India as a second-class portion of
the Empire, because it is outside the charmed circle of those
portions which are dominantly British in administration, colonization, and outlook. It is equally impossible, on such a basis, for
India to be content with junior partnership in a world of cultural
and racial jealousies and exclusive sympathies. To call India a

Dominion in an Empire based on British race patriotism alone would be an absurdity.

In the sixteenth century the Portuguese sought a solution of the problem of a permanent hold on India by colonization, inter-marriage, and conversion to the Roman Catholic faith. In his day Macaulay was influenced by a similar purpose of Anglicization, though by different means and more particularly by the spread of Western teaching and ideas. Today attempts at assimilation are unacceptable to either side. While ready to follow England in such realms as science, industry, hygiene, and sport, we take our stand on our own culture in the realm of the spirit. Indians, whether Hindu or Moslem, are no less proud than Englishmen of their own traditions and teachings in religion, philosophy, poetry, romance and art. Nor are the interests and aspirations of the African races under the British flag to be overlooked in this connection.

In my humble judgement the ultimate solution of the problem of England's piebald Empire lies in consistent leadership along the paths of international peace and culture, in conformity with the traditional magnanimity and forbearance of the British race. The proudest and in the long run the best use of the unequalled political genius of that race is to take the lead in the development of international peace and arbitration. The inspiration of this high purpose will appeal to Indian idealism; my countrymen can co-operate heartily and willingly in such a world policy. Further, it will open the door to the solution of the difficult racial problem with which the Empire is confronted.

The League of Nations has noble aims, but it is now generally admitted that it was founded in a time of passion and bitter resentment, and sought to assure future right by present wrongs. The League is the child of an aged mother – namely, the Old-World Imperialism that led to the conflict begun 11 years ago. In consequence the infant is sickly and weak; but it lives and may grow. Behind the ideas in which the League was conceived there is the moral momentum for far greater leadership by the British race in world politics than can come from the exclusiveness derived from a natural aptitude being dominantly turned to race interests alone.

Nothing is more significant in world affairs in our time than the eagerness with which, in every free land, organized labour has thrown its influence on the side of peace and international good-will as the sure means of human prosperity and happiness. The manual workers recognise that these blessings are dependent on peaceful solution in an age of wonderful scientific developments which in war may bring destruction on multitudes in a single hour. One of the vital factors in securing peace is to broad-base the Empire on mutual and equal service, irrespective of race limitations. If this standard is applied we may see the fulfilment of the dream of the Socialist poet:–

There shall come from out the noise of strife and groaning:
A broader day, juster brotherhood,
A deep equality of aim, postponing
All selfish seeking to the general good.
There shall come a time when each shall to the other
Be as God would have him, brother to brother.

Source: *The Times*, London, 5 August 1925.
On Lord Milner see W. B. Luke, *Lord Milner*, London, 1901; J. E. L. Wrench, *Alfred, Lord Milner: The Man of No Illusions, 1854–1925*, London, 1958; J. Marlowe, *Milner: Apostle of Empire: A Life of Alfred George the Right Honourable Viscount Milner of St. James's and Cape Town, K.G., G.C.M.G., 1854–1925*, London, 1976; E. B. Iwan-Mueller, *Lord Milner and South Africa*, London, 1902; Lionel Curtis, *With Milner in South Africa*, Oxford, 1951; Vladimir Halpérin, *Lord Milner and the Empire: The Evolution of British Imperialism*, London, 1952; Edward Crankshaw, *The Forsaken Idea: A Study of Viscount Milner*, London, 1952; W. Nimocks, *Milner's Young Men*, London, 1970; K. K. Aziz, *The British in India: A Study in Imperialism*, Islamabad, 1976; and any good history of British Imperial theory and practice.

79

HOW TO LIVE LONG

An Article

London: 8 December 1925

Physique during childhood – Eugen Sandow's advice – boxing – running and walking – the spiritual value of physical beauty – weight reduction – colour in clothing – sleep – diet – physiques of different people – the cult of physical training in India.

All my life I have been keenly interested in the kindred subjects of exercise and diet, and their influence on the general health and fitness of the human body. As a child I did far too little exercise. I was brought up to ride well from the time I was about five years old, and rode regularly until I was about sixteen or seventeen. It was then I wanted to take a short walk of about $1^1/_2$ miles and found to my chagrin that at the end of it I was completely exhausted. And I had been in the habit of riding about 20 miles some three or four times a week. Riding had left me soft in all muscles with the exception of those actually exercised.

It was then I decided to improve my physique. I came in touch with the late Eugen Sandow, who gave me some excellent advice which I have never forgotten. Later I took up boxing. I know of no exercise so physically beneficial as a combination of the French and British boxing methods – the French for the digestive and internal muscles and the legs, and the British for the arms, back and shoulders.

Although I am now forty-nine, I never miss a day without exercising, preferably boxing or kicking. At one time I used to have a sparring partner sent over to my rooms at the Ritz from the National Sporting Club. In the summer months I often rise very early, put on a sweater, and go for a run through Green

Park, up Constitution Hill, and back again before breakfast. If I am in France, I usually go to Aix-les-Bains, not for the waters, but to enjoy long walks in the mountains, which is a splendid exercise.

Never a day goes by but I spend at least fifteen to twenty minutes in some form of physical exercise. Even when I am in India or in Africa, where I have to work very hard – sometimes eighteen hours a day – I always make time for that necessary physical exertion which is so essential for bodily fitness.

For years I played golf and tennis, but I find that neither of these games is adequate; nor is hunting. The majority are only able to indulge these sports once or twice a week, which is contrary to the body's requirements. The average English gentleman does practically nothing in the way of sport for five days a week, and then indulges himself over the week-end.

He is unquestionably wrong. He should, at least once a day, and oftener if he can, take some pleasurable and vigorous exercise. Unless he does so his whole body becomes ungainly and horrible, which is the most ungrateful way of returning thanks to "God Who made us in His own image," for, although I do not believe that we are actually made in the image of God, I believe that physical beauty has a spiritual value.

Walking is a good exercise if it is not allowed to be merely a saunter through the streets. A good swinging pace of between four and five miles an hour is ideal. I do a good deal of walking, and usually cover about ten miles in two and a half hours. I think it is a very bad thing for one who is heavy to try to reduce his weight by any form of exercise or diet. Rather should he try to get hard and remain big instead of being merely soft and large. Softness is the enemy, not size.

I have a very strong aversion from colours when exercising. Coloured socks, coloured trousers, or underclothes are, I think, unhealthy, and I am against the wearing of tweeds for the same reason. White cotton, white drill, white shoes seem cooler; flannels or serges or woollens that are porous are to be preferred most. Too much sleep dulls the brain and also precludes taking full advantage of many of the beauties of nature. In my many crossings over to the Continent and world travels I usually try to journey by night so that I may enjoy the dawn as it breaks on the sea or on different landscapes. Unfortunately in summer-time it is not practical politics to be up before sunrise every morning, though in winter I always see the dawn, usually from some spot in the East or on the high seas, and sometimes on the Riviera.

Five or six hours of regular sleep and a ten-minute nap either before dinner or immediately after lunch or in a motorcar when being driven are quite enough for most of us. If one allows himself only that he is likely to sleep the whole time and not to lie awake with insomnia. It is the same as getting full value out of a twenty-minute walk which might have taken two hours.

In regard to diet, I believe that we eat too much, and for this reason I think we should all drop one or two meals a week, which is my own practice. That means that on three days a week I take only one solid meal. I think that is more natural and simpler, and much less boring than some of the elaborate regimes that have been worked out by others. On ordinary days I have fruit and coffee for breakfast, and later take a big lunch. At tea-time I take tea only, and no solids. It is my custom at dinner to take a meal that is much smaller than my lunch.

I have no fads and few special fancies. I accept what is put before me, and the better the food the more I enjoy it. What a person enjoys is, in my opinion, good for him. Colour, which is to be avoided in clothing for exercise, is a stimulant in food. A beautiful apple or peach becomes tempting because of its colouring, and seems more enjoyable. Fruits are adequate for breakfast; I will not even admit a piece of bread to my table for this meal.

Travelling about the world I have always been interested in observing the physique of different peoples. I have noticed that the French seem to have improved enormously during the past thirty years. That cannot be due to the army, because military service was already in existence, but must have come from the practice of sport before and after military service. Football may have helped considerably. I know of no class of men in the world so magnificent as the officers of the British Army, especially those of the old army, which, I am sorry to say, has almost disappeared.

I think that physically English women look healthier and fitter than all other women. Here in England women shop assistants conform to the Shop Hours Act and do not work so long as in other countries, where women manage the businesses and the men spend so much time in the cafés, bazaars, theatres, etc.

In India the cult of physical training, which was very popular some forty years ago, has unfortunately receded, a retrogression I regard with great misgiving. The old and generally popular sport of wrestling is dying out. The people of India are going in for cricket, hockey, tennis. This means that after playing these games in their youth the great Indian public will grow up to exercise one or two days a week as the majority do in England and for the rest of the time will only watch semi-professionals playing.

Source: *The Evening Standard*, London, 8 December 1925.

    This article breaks the monotony of the long string of political statements and is a pleasant and welcome reminder that the Aga Khan was a human being, leading a normal physical existence, before he was a politician and a leader. The article was the fifth in a series of the same title in which various public figures told the readers of the popular and widely circulated London evening paper about their lifestyle, diet and care aimed at good health and a reasonably long span of life. The two-column article was signed by the Aga Khan and carried his photograph.

80

FELICITATIONS TO THE SHAH OF PERSIA

A Message

London (?): 21 December 1925

Congratulations from himself and his followers – prayer for a glorious future for Iran.

On the occasion of your Imperial Majesty's election by the will of the nation to the historic throne of the Persian Empire, I pray your Majesty to accept the most respectful and sincere congratulations of myself and my followers. I pray that under the guidance of your Majesty the great Persian nation may regain the glorious civilization of the era of Shah Abbas, and that your Majesty may live in history no less renowned for justice and humanity than Karim Khan Zand.

Source: *The Times*, London, 22 December 1925.

The message was sent in French and published in *The Times* in English translation.

Raza Shah Pahlavi, the recipient of the message, was originally the leader of an Army Cossack Brigade who declared himself king and founded the Pahlavi dynasty in 1925. Like Mustafa Kamal Atatürk in Turkey, he sought to modernize Persia, curbed the power and authority of the conservative religious leaders, and set the tone for a nationalistic policy. In 1934 he changed the name of the country to Iran. At the beginning of the Second World War, Iranian territory was occupied by Allied troops and the Shah was obliged to abdicate. He died in exile in South Africa in 1941.

The Aga Khan's ancestors had lived in Iran for several centuries before his grandfather migrated to India. Iran contains a large number of Ismailis.

Raza Shah's rise to power and career have been treated in some detail in Ali Akbar Siassi, *La Perse au contact de l'occident*, Paris, 1931; Vincent Sheean, *The New Persia*, New York, 1927; Angelo Pollaco, *L'Iran di Rezá Sciá Pahlavi*, Venice, 1937; Herbert Melzig, *Resa Schah: die Aufsteig Irans und die Grossmächte*, Stuttgart, 1936; Essad Bey, *Reza Schah: Fiedherr, Kaiser, Reformator*, Vienna, 1936 (English tr. by Paul Maerken and Elsa Branden, *Raza Shah*, London, 1938); Émile Lesueur, *Les Anglais en Perse*, Paris, 1922; J. M. Balfour, *Recent Happenings in*

Persia, Edinburgh and London, 1922; Hasan Arfa, *Under Five Shahs*, London, 1964; and A. H. Hamzavi, *Persia and the Powers*, London, 1946. Besides these contemporary or first-hand accounts, there are later scholarly or general works dealing with his period: Amir Banani, *The Modernization of Iran, 1921–1941*, Stanford, 1961; Werner Zurrer, *Persien zwischen England und Russland, 1918–1925*, Bern and Frankfurt, 1978; Ahmad Mahrad, *Iran auf dem Weg zur Diktatur: Militarisierung und Widerstand, 1919–1925*, Hanover, 1972 (repr. 1976); Donald N. Wilber, *Riza Shah Pahlavi: The Resurrection and Reconstruction of Iran, 1878–1914*, Hicksville, 1975; J. M. Upton, *The History of Modern Iran*, Cambridge, Mass., 1960; G. Lenczowski, *Russia and the West in Iran, 1918–1949*, Ithaca, N.Y., 1949; R. W. Cottam, *Nationalism in Iran*, Pittsburgh, 1964; Leonard Binder, *Iran: Political Development in a Changing Society*, Berkeley and Los Angeles, 1962; P. W. Avery, *Modern Iran*, London, 1965; P. M. Holt, Anna K. S. Lambton and Bernard Lewis (eds), *The Cambridge History of Islam, Vol. I: The Central Islamic Lands*, Cambridge, 1970; and his son's version of events in Muhammad Riza Shah Pahlavi, *Mission for my Country*, London, 1961.

81

THE FUTURE OF INDIAN INDUSTRY

Interview with The Times of India

Bombay: 8 January 1926

Anxiety about the economic situation in India – unsatisfactory state of Indian industries – textile industry in Bombay on the point of breaking up – danger of India becoming a purely agricultural country – Japanese competition – need for a policy.

In an interview to a representative of the *Times of India*, the Aga Khan said that Indians should concentrate more and more on economic questions. He proceeded to say:

"I am anxious about the economic situation in India. His Highness the Maharaja Gaekwar at the Industrial Conference held at Ahmedabad some twenty-two years ago remarked that our political salvation depended upon our economic prosperity and position. I am grieved to see that our economic situation has gone from bad to worse. The steel industry has been made to exist by large doses of bounties, the cement industry is going, the smaller ones like glass and so on are struggling for existence – the main industries just exist; the jute industry of Bengal is not really an industry but a monopoly given by Nature – a present from Nature to Bengal. The only national industry is the textile which – Heaven forbid – is on the point of breaking up in Bombay. This will naturally bring ruin not only to Bombay City but practically to the future in industrialism in this country and the country will become a purely agricultural continent producing raw material and rebuying at an enormous loss and a heavy sacrifice, leaving the lion's share to go to other countries and enrich the foreigner. The Japanese are from their point of view quite right in trying to dump our markets but it is ruinous to our country. Every civilised country has tried protection the moment it found itself face to face with ruin and on the verge of extinction. I would implore our public men to concentrate their attention on protection against Japanese competition and save their crores in industries not only in Bombay but throughout the country and thus protect industrialism in the country. That is the issue at stake – the life and death struggle for industrialism. What we really need is a good and healthy policy of protection with a well-considered schedule and an automatic rising and falling tariff. If we want this and if we need give imperial prefer- ence to Manchester let us give it at least to free ourselves from the competition of countries where as in Japan the conditions are quite different from ours."

Source: *The Times of India,* Bombay, 9 January 1926.
  The paper does not give the date at which the interview took place. In normal circumstances it would have been conducted on the day previous to its publication. Hence the date of 8 January that I have given it. But there is no conclusive evidence to confirm it or, alternatively, to deny it.

82

THE TREATMENT OF THE INDIANS IN SOUTH AFRICA

Speech at a Public Meeting Held to Protest Against the Treatment of Indians in South Africa

Bombay: 15 January 1926

Recalls the first meeting in 1896 over which he presided – forty years of humiliation for the Indians in South Africa – concessions made by the Indians – Mahatma Gandhi's heroic struggle – fund to help the struggle in South Africa – another meeting twenty years ago – final appeal to the leaders of South Africa – the Smuts-Gandhi Agreement – the whites need not fear Indians who are law-abiding and hard-working – final appeal to the conscience of the white man to drop the anti-Asiatic bill.

It is thirty years since I first had the honour of presiding at a meeting of my countrymen to protest against the treatment of Indians in South Africa. I should be sorry indeed if I had to try and remember how many public meetings in this town and in other places in India, in the Caxton Hall, how many committee meetings of the Indian Overseas Association in England, how many private consultations with Sir Phirozeshah Mehta, Bowna-gree, H. Wadia, [Tej Bahadur] Sapru and Messrs. Gokhale and [H. L.] Polak and others, I have attended during these last thirty years. Looking back it seems to me the long and unending series. Nor can I forget that when in 1896 I first attended a meeting of this description, this was already an old grievance and that for already more than a decade it had been agitating the minds of our settlers in Africa and thinkers in this country. Ladies and gentlemen, these simple and dull statements of biographical facts are to my mind more eloquent than any words at my command to describe what our people have gone through in that part of the world. It means forty years of humiliations inflicted upon them of harassing legislation and ordinances, of offensive rules and regulations of constant pin-pricks and of many bludgeon blows borne with characteristic patience, with forebearance, with fortitude, and these forty years have seen also on the part of the leaders of the Indians in South Africa and of the leading Indians in this country the succession of concessions of the so-called compromisers to give up the inherent rights for the sake of peace and in order to save the small number of our people out there from total ruin and the final destruction of their self-respect. Not only the claims of a common Imperial Citizenship, not only the respect which their willing services to the cause of the development of South Africa but many promises have been forgotten. I need not now remind you of the heroic struggle carried by Mahatma Gandhi in 1906 which lasted till 1914, of the Borough-ordinances and township franchise, of the licensing ordinances, of the social and political humiliations which have been heaped on our people. Gentlemen, you will soon hear from the representatives of our countrymen out there the disastrous effects of the now proposed legislation.

I hope I am not giving away a secret, but I understand that Mr. Petit is moving the Imperial Indian Citizenship Association, of which he is Honorary Secretary, to contribute Rs. 50,000 to the fund which the South African Deputation proposes to raise in this country to help them in the struggle for the elementary rights of citizenship in South Africa.

Some twenty years ago I had the honour of presiding at a meeting of the citizens of this city in the Town Hall and of those who then addressed that meeting I think there are but two now alive who will address you to-day, namely, Mr. Baptista and myself. I then urged immediate steps towards retaliation and reciprocity. But now today and on this occasion and speaking as man to man I want to make one final and I hope not unfriendly appeal to the leaders of South Africa. Before it is too late they should not finally close the doors of understanding and conciliation in our face. I appeal to them first of all that the great concessions made by Indians in the well-known Smuts-Gandhi Agreement should be accepted as final in the letter and in the spirit and that nothing should be done to go back on that agreement. I appeal to the many right-thinking men in South Africa to whom Mr. [C. F.] Andrews has referred in his despatches to use all their influence that the spirit of that agreement should be for ever kept alive. The overwhelming majority of the Indians in South Africa are African born or natives of that country or descendants of those who worked for Africa, and they themselves work for the common welfare and development of that vast dominion. Many were brought to labour on a mere pittance so that the capitalist Whites should prosper. I appeal to them to remember that the Smuts-Gandhi Agreement and the many present laws and restrictions make White domination in South Africa a certainty and that there is no real danger to their narrow ideas from our competition, which is in fact co-operation, towards the economic development of that country. I appeal to the conscience of the White races out there and I should like to put a few definite questions to them.

Do the statistics prove that the Indian is a law-breaker, a criminal? Certainly not. Is he an anarchist, a revolutionary, a bomb-thrower? No.

Is the Indian the owner of the dram-shop, of the house of ill-fame, of the gambling-hole? No. . . .

Has the Indian taken his unseemly Hindu-Muslim squabbles, his caste and sectarian bickerings to South Africa? Certainly not. Out there and beyond the seas the instinctive common-sense of the Indian has asserted itself, and in the smaller India outside we do find United India. Well then, gentlemen, let us take another series of accusations. We are accused of sanitary dangers from our customs and habits. Has the Indian been the champion of conscientious objection to vaccination in South Africa? Has he objected to inoculation against plague or has he by his careless use of water helped malaria? Certainly not.

Is he a debauche or drunkard? Most certainly not. Throughout that continent he has shown his qualities, patience, hard work, simple and innocent domestic enjoyment, and if in some way his standard has not been that of the European, it is because as labourer he was not protected and was forced for the welfare of his master to accept wages which reduced him below the White Standard.

Ladies and gentlemen, once more I make this final appeal to the conscience of the white men out there not to forget our common Empire, our membership of the League of Nations, our common humanity, the earnest pleadings of Sapru during the last Imperial Conference, the many friendly concessions of Gokhale and Gandhi, and above all the loyal co-operation in the daily business of life for more than fifty years of the Indians of

South Africa and to voluntarily and graciously drop this needless, obnoxious and humiliating Bill.

Source: *The Times of India*, Bombay, 16 January 1926.

The important parts of the proceedings of the meeting were reported thus by the newspaper:

"Bombay recorded its unanimous and emphatic protest against the impending anti-Asiatic legislation of the South African Government at a very largely attended public meeting held in the Excelsior Theatre on Friday evening under the presidentship of His Highness the Aga Khan. It was one of the most influential and representative gatherings seen in Bombay in recent times and was sponsored by all the important public bodies of the city. Those who participated in the proceedings were representatives of all nationalities and all shades of opinion. A note of intense resentment ran through all the speeches against what was characterised as the 'most inhuman treatment' meted out to Indians in South Africa. All the speakers voiced a strong determination to carry on the struggle to the bitter end while one speaker, while confessing that he was warned to be careful about what he said, could not forbear advocating retaliation against the South African Government, in favour of which step he claimed there was a strong body of opinion in this country. H. H. the Aga Khan, speaking as man to man, appealed to the South African leaders to accept as final, in the letter and the spirit, the great concessions made by Indians in the well-known Smuts-Gandhi agreement and to do nothing to go back on it, though at one time he had urged the adoption of immediate steps towards retaliation and reciprocity. The utterance next in importance to that of the President was made by Dr. Abdul Rahman, the leader of the South African deputation to India, who in an eloquent and spirited address explained the whole situation and declared that they in South Africa would die in the last ditch rather than surrender their elementary rights.

"Mr. Ratansi D. Morarji proposed and Mr. Byramji Jejeebhoy seconded that H. H. the Aga Khan should take the chair and the proposition was carried with acclammation.

"Mr. J. B. Petit, Honorary Secretary of the Imperial Indian Citizenship Association, read messages of sympathy received from Mr. Jamnadas Dwarkadas, the South African Indian Congress and the Cape British Indian Council.

"Sir Chimanlal Setalvad moved the following resolution:–

"(a) 'That this meeting of the Citizens of Bombay, held under the joint auspices of the Imperial Indian Citizenship Association, the Indian Merchants' Chamber and Bureau, the Bombay Provincial Congress Committee, the Central Khilafat Committee, the Bombay Swaraj Party, the Bombay Muslim League, the National Municipal Party, the Rashtriya Stree Sabha, the Home Rule League, Parsi Rajkiya Sabha, National Home Rule League, British Indian Colonial Merchants' Association, the Bombay Progressive Association, the Bombay Presidency Association, and other Associations, views with the gravest apprehension, and enters its emphatic protest against the Areas Reservation and Immigration and Registration (Further Provision) Bill, which is in violation of the 1914 Gandhi-Smuts Agreement, and has for its object the compulsory Segregation of Indians, the deprivation of their trading and proprietary rights, and the ultimate elimination of the Indian community, as openly declared by Dr. Malan, Minister of the Interior.'

"(b) 'This meeting earnestly requests the Government of India to urge upon the Union Government the necessity of a round table Conference before any further action is taken by the Union Government in respect of the proposed Bill; and should their reasonable proposal be declined and the Bill forced through the Union Parliament, this meeting appeals to His Excellency the Viceroy to advise the Imperial Government to disallow the measure under Section 65 of the South African Act.'

"The mover said that the treatment of Indians in South Africa had been a shameful history of broken pledges and studied insult and humiliation with the avowed object of squeezing out the Indians from South Africa. Even President Kruger had attempted no more than residential segregation and not the commercial segregation contemplated by the present South African Government. On the eve of the Boer War, Lord Lansdowne mentioned the treatment of Indians as one of the causes of going to war with the South Africans. How impotent the Imperial Government had now become, exclaimed Sir Chimanlal. Was this the treatment that the Imperial Government was going to give to India, which went to the rescue of the Empire in 1914? If the Imperial Government was going to sit with folded hands without trying to prevent pledges from being broken, the speaker did not know what was going to become of the Empire: it might cut the very foundations of the British Empire.

"Seconding the proposition, Mr. M. A. Jinnah questioned whether the case of the Indians in South Africa was such as could be subjected to any pros and cons. He held it was not debatable nor arguable. The Bill on the anvil contemplated the extermination of Indians settled there.

"Sir Stanley Reed supported the motion. He said his interest in the effort to secure for their fellow-citizens justice wherever they might be living was unabated. Whatever differences might exist in India on other political questions, there was unanimity of opinion in regard to the position of Indians in South Africa. He supported the resolution because the threatened action of the South African Government was a breach of an honourable instrument, namely, the Agreement of 1914, because every citizen of the Empire had the right to attain in every part of the Empire his full social and economic stature, and because the policy on which the South African Government had embarked must be fatal to civilisation itself, whatever its effects on the Indian community. In associating himself with the broad policy expressed in the resolution, Sir Stanley declared: 'All history goes to prove that no Government can thrive on injustice, and that the oppression of any minority shatters the principle of justice, which is the bed-rock of society.'

"Mr. H. P. Mody further supporting the proposition said that although opinion had been unanimous in India, the position had steadily grown worse till at last a peaceful industrious and frugal population was being hounded out of the country regardless of all considerations of ethics and political morality. Unless backed up by force, such a question had a very poor chance of success at present and, although he had been warned to be careful about what he said, he made bold to state that if the last attempt at settlement by negotiations failed, nothing was left but retaliation. Though deemed by some as ineffectual he thought its moral force would be considerable, and at any rate it was better than standing still.

"Put to the vote, the resolution was unanimously carried.

"Mr. J. B. Petit then moved a resolution urging the Government of India, after consulting the legislature, to send to England a strong deputation including representatives of the South African Indian Congress to place before the British Cabinet, Parliament and public the grave consequences of the South African Government's policy as illustrated by the Asiatic Bill. He wanted the deputation to declare that the patience of Indians was exhausted. The policy of the South African Government was offering a wanton and inexcusable insult to India and to Asia and even to the man who gave them their religion, namely, Christ – that would be its logical conclusion. He warned the authorities that this was the beginning of a great war, mightier than that of 1914, which was going to sweep the world – a war between the white races and the entire coloured population. The question was not, however, incapable of settlement, given a strong Government of India.

"Seconding the motion, Mr. Balubhai J. Desai called the Bill a 'lawless law' and said that by their act of injustice the South Africans had already banished Christ. The mills of God ground slowly, but they ground with exact repayment for every insult, every injustice, done by one man to another. There might be an answer to 'internal autonomy,' to legal conundrum, but there was no answer to the law of God.

"The resolution was carried.

"Mr. Joseph Baptista, proposing that the above resolutions be forwarded to the Government of India, complained that the reward for India's blood spilt on the fields of Flanders was that the Britons and the Boers were conspiring to drive the Indians bag and baggage out of South Africa.

"Mr. Lalji Naranji seconded the motion stating that the Government of India had no right to that title if they would not espouse the cause of Indians.

"Mr. M. R. Jayakar proposed a resolution pledging the meeting to support the Indians in South Africa morally and financially. So often had they been told by Britain that if India were united she would win, that he was tempted to say: 'Here is an opportunity to the British Government to show the truth of their dictum.' Personally he was doubtful of success, because the history of the past 40 years was one of successive humiliations and ever stronger worded resolutions. He wanted the deputation suggested in a previous resolution to tell the Englishmen that the present was the acid test on which the doctrine of the British Empire was going to be judged by India. The Britishers must be told that England would lose India if the present South African policy was allowed to be continued.

"Mr. B. G. Horniman seconding the resolution said it made his blood boil to think that Englishmen should be capable of such degrading oppression as Dr. Abdul Rahman had described. It was only so long as India was disunited and did not co-operate to achieve self-government that her sons would continue to receive the treatment that they were getting at the hands of the white self-governing colonies of the Empire.

"Mr. Mirza Ali Mahomed Khan and Mr. Meyer Nissim also spoke on the resolution and it was carried unanimously.

"Mrs. Sarojini Naidu in proposing a vote of thanks to the President said that 161,000 Indians were looking eagerly to that meeting. India was no longer the appealing India with folded hands, but an angry India declaring "within the Empire if possible, outside the Empire if necessary." Words were for her poetry; for her national work the words should be translated into action. The only remedy for the suffering of Indians abroad was Swaraj at home, for slavery, being the disease of the mother-country, was inherited by her children abroad. Mrs. Naidu appealed for unity in India and reminded His Highness that he should lead his countrymen on in the struggle of Indians abroad.

"Mr. K. Natarajan seconded the motion, which elicited a rousing response, and the meeting came to an end after it had lasted for over two hours."

83

APPEAL ON BEHALF OF A MOSQUE

Speech at the Stone-laying Ceremony of a Mosque

Nairobi: 24 March 1926

Attendance of non-Muslims at the ceremony – the finances of
the mosque and an appeal to all Muslims – congratulations to the
Engineer-in-Chief.

The Aga Khan ... thanked the non-Muslim gentlemen who by
their attendance had shown sympathy to their cause. It demonstrated that all religions were sacred, and entitled to sympathy
and respect.

It was with great pleasure that he had accepted their invitation
to lay the stone. The finances of the mosque were not very strong,
and he thought an appeal to India must be made. In a floating
and big population such as they had in Kenya, there was a pressing need for a mosque and he hoped that all Muslims in
East Africa, Uganda and the Sudan would contribute towards so
deserving an object.

The design, which pleased him greatly would add to the beauty
of the city.

Source: *The East African Standard*, Nairobi, weekly edition, 27 March 1926.
   The ceremony was held at 5 p.m. and was attended by a large number of
people. Besides the leaders of the Indian community in the town, there was a
fair sprinkling of Europeans, including the Mayor, Field Jones and Captain
Thom.
   Mr Malik (the newspaper does not give his full name or the initials), speaking
on behalf of the Indian community, extended "the heartiest welcome" to the
distinguished visitor and informed the audience that the construction of
the mosque had begun the previous year and had now reached the arches
stage. He thanked the Aga Khan for having agreed to lay the skewback stone
to the main arch. The cost of the building, he said, was estimated at £20,000,
and the Aga Khan had donated Shs. 30,000 to this fund.

After delivering his short speech, the Aga Khan proceeded up the stone spiral staircase to a platform over the main arch and with a silver trowel applied the first cement to the stone which was then lowered and fixed in its place. He then conversed for a while with those present and congratulated Major Brown, the Engineer-in-Chief, on his work.

84

PATRIOTISM AND SOCIAL REFORM AMONG KENYA'S INDIANS

Summary of Two Addresses Given Before the Ismaili Community

Mombasa: 1–7 April 1926

Progress in worldly and spiritual matters – female education – loyalty of Indian immigrants to Kenya.

The substance of his advice contained in two addresses concerned the welfare of his followers in worldly and spiritual matters. He dealt more particularly with the need of living economically, attending to child welfare, maternity and cleanliness. He also strongly urged the necessity for proper female education.

In the course of his addresses the Aga Khan upheld the cause of true patriotism. He maintained that Indians who had come to Kenya and were making their livelihood in Kenya must also make their home in the new country. He severely disapproved any tendency on the part of Indians to make money in the new country with the intention of eventually taking the gains to India. He said in effect this country is now your home and you must make friends with all around you.

Source: *The Mombasa Times*, Mombasa, 15 April 1926, and *The East African Standard*, Nairobi, 17 April 1926.
  The Aga Khan arrived in Mombasa on 31 March 1926 from the Highlands and left for France on 8 April. During this week he visited the Ismaili schools for boys and girls, expressed his satisfaction with the progress in the educational field, contributed a large amount of money to these schools, and also gave handsome donations to the Social Service League and to a number of mosques.
  It is not clear from the newspapers' reports where the two addresses mentioned in them were given.

85

ON INDIAN UNITY

Statement to the Press

Bombay: 9 December 1927

Desire to unite the Muslims – misgivings regarding the boycott movement – the future of separate electorates – overall unity of India.

... The Aga Khan ... expressed a strong desire to do all in his power to unite the community and to lead it along the path of sobriety and prudence. Though he is anxious not to commit himself to any statement before he has acquainted himself fully with the political situation in India, the Aga Khan did not disguise the fact that he entertained the gravest misgivings as to the consequences of the boycott movement.

Referring to the non-cooperation movement of 1921, the Aga Khan said: "The last time a boycott came in the Liberals got their chance. If the Liberals stand out now a handful of reactionaries will have their say before the Commission, excluding both the Liberals and the extremists, whose case will fail by default." His sole object, he said, was to try to unite all the conflicting elements in the community. "I cannot possibly join any faction. My object is not to join a faction but to try to bring about union of the various schools of thought."

After saying that the future of the separate electorates was a matter for those electorates themselves to decide, the Aga Khan said that he did not mean that he was interested only in Moslems. He said: "I am moved only by love for India. The whole country is divided, and while these divisions last progress is impossible."

Source: *The Times*, London, 10 December 1927.
  The statement was given by the Aga Khan on his arrival in Bombay from Europe by mail-boat. The newspaper's correspondent in Bombay, while sending

the report of the statement, opened his dispatch with the words: "Many of the leading Moslems have been silent about the Statutory Commission, and the general explanation is that they have been waiting for the Aga Khan's opinion."

86

AN APPEAL FOR A PERMANENT MUSLIM ORGANIZATION IN INDIA

A Manifesto

Bombay: 29 December 1927

Relations between Hindus and Muslims – reform of Muslim political organization – the need for a permanent Muslim governing body – relations with the British – the question of a national army.

The Aga Khan has issued a manifesto addressed to all Indian Moslems in the course of which, after referring to the importance of settling the question of their relations towards Hindus and of reforming their political organization in order to meet the change in political conditions, he makes an appeal to the elected Moslem representatives in the Legislatures as having all real political power in their hands. He suggests that they should constitute a permanent Moslem governing body, which shall direct the political activity of the community and be in a position to speak with authority and enter into binding compacts both with Hindus and with the British Government.

His Highness is of opinion that the absence of such an organized body, with binding authority with the masses, is the "reason for the failure of all efforts of the Viceroy and others to lay a solid foundation for mutual understanding and confidence and intercommunal peace."

The Aga Khan adds that he mentions the British Government as well as the Hindus because "the British will be in India as long as we can see, and cannot be spirited away merely by being ignored."

The Aga Khan urges the need for establishing such a body when the Constitution is in the melting-pot and when such questions as a truly national army are in the front rank of problems associated with constitutional growth. Before real home rule is possible India must be in a position to undertake her own defence through her own sons.

Source: *The Times*, London, 30 December 1927.

The manifesto, transmitted from Bombay by the Reuters agency, was issued at a time when leaders of the All India Muslim League were quarrelling among themselves about the venue of the coming annual session of the party. The League itself was split into a Jinnah faction and a Shafi faction (led by Sir Muhammad Shafi) on the issue of whether to co-operate or not with the newly appointed Indian Statutory (Simon) Commission, and there were a host of smaller parties contending for Muslim loyalty.